OUT OF MANY

VOLUME I

OUT OF MANY
A HISTORY OF THE AMERICAN PEOPLE

BRIEF SECOND EDITION

JOHN MACK FARAGHER
YALE UNIVERSITY

MARI JO BUHLE
BROWN UNIVERSITY

DANIEL CZITROM
MOUNT HOLYOKE COLLEGE

SUSAN H. ARMITAGE
WASHINGTON STATE UNIVERSITY

 PRENTICE HALL, UPPER SADDLE RIVER, NJ 07458

Library of Congress Cataloging-in-Publication Data

Out of many : a history of the American people / John Mack Faragher
  . . . [et al.]. —Combined 2nd ed., brief ed.
    p.   cm.
  Includes bibliographical references and index.
  ISBN 0-13-841495-5
  1. United States—History.   I. Faragher, John Mack
  [E178.1.0935   1999]
  973—dc21   98-5458
                                                       CIP

Editorial Director: *Charlyce Jones Owen*
Executive Editor: *Todd R. Armstrong*
Assistant Vice President of Production & Manufacturing: *Barbara Kittle*
Editorial/Production Supervision: *Harriet Tellem*
Development Editor: *Leslie Carr*
Manufacturing Manager: *Nick Sklitsis*
Prepress and Manufacturing Buyer: *Lynn Pearlman*
Creative Design Director: *Leslie Osher*
Art Direction, Interior Design, Cover Design: *Ximena Tamvakopoulos*
Line Art Coordinator: *Guy Ruggiero*
Cartographers: *Carto-Graphics*
Cover Photo Research: *Karen Sanatar*
Cover Photograph: *James G. Clonney (1812–1867), Militia Training/*
      Pennsylvania Academy of the Fine Arts

This book was set in 10/12 Galliard by The Clarinda Company and was printed
and bound by Courier Company Inc. (Kendallville). The cover was printed by The
Lehigh Press Inc.

© 1999, 1995 by Prentice-Hall, Inc.
Simon & Schuster /A Viacom Company
Upper Saddle River, New Jersey 07458

Printed in the United States of America
10 9 8 7 6 5 4 3 2

ISBN 0-13-841479-3

Prentice-Hall International (UK) Limited, *London*
Prentice-Hall of Australia Pty. Limited, *Sydney*
Prentice-Hall Canada Inc., *Toronto*
Prentice-Hall Hispanoamericana, S.A., *Mexico*
Prentice-Hall of India Private Limited, *New Delhi*
Prentice-Hall of Japan, Inc., *Tokyo*
Simon & Schuster Asia Pte. Ltd., *Singapore*
Editora Prentice-Hall do Brasil, Ltda., *Rio de Janeiro*

TO OUR STUDENTS, OUR SISTERS, AND OUR BROTHERS

BRIEF CONTENTS

CONTENTS

MAPS

GRAPHS AND SUMMARY TABLES

PREFACE

Out of Many, A History of the American People, Brief Second Edition, offers a distinctive and timely approach to American history, recounting the story of our country by focusing on the experiences of diverse communities of Americans. The idea of community provides a lens through which to examine the complex historical forces shaping people's lives at any given moment in our past. The debates and conflicts surrounding the most momentous issues in our national life—independence, emerging democracy, slavery, westward settlement, imperial expansion, depression, war, technological change—were largely worked out in the context of local communities. A community focus encourages the exploration of the persistent tensions between life lived locally and those larger decisions and events that continually reshape the circumstances of local life. Each chapter opens with a description of a representative community. Some of these community portraits feature American communities struggling with one another: African slaves and English masters on the rice plantations of colonial Georgia, or Tejanos and Americans during the Texas war of independence. Other chapters open with portraits of communities facing social change: the feminists of Seneca Falls, New York, in 1848, the sitdown strikers of Flint, Michigan, in 1934, and the African Americans of Montgomery, Alabama, in 1955. As the story unfolds we find communities growing to include ever larger groups of Americans: during the Revolution Continental soldiers from every colony forging a national patriotic army at Valley Forge, and in the 1920s the creation of a national movie-going community that dreamed a collective dream of material prosperity and upward mobility.

We prepared this brief edition to serve the needs of one-semester courses, teachers who assign supplemental readings, or anyone interested in a more condensed narrative of American history. While this volume is about two-thirds the length of the full-length version, it retains the distinct point of view that makes it unique among all college-level American history texts. The community focus remains fully in place as the integrating perspective that allows us to combine political, social, and cultural history.

Out of Many is also continental in its approach. Selecting examples from all regions of the country, we encourage students to see America as the enormous nation it is. The founding of the first European settlements in the New World, for example, we illustrate with a vignette of seventeenth-century Santa Fé, New Mexico. We present territorial expansion into the American West from the point of view of the Mandan villagers of the upper Missouri River of North Dakota. The policies of the Reconstruction era we introduce through the experience of African Americans in the Sea Islands of South Carolina. With community introductions from New England to the South, the Midwest to the far West, *Out of Many* is the only American history text that adopts a truly continental perspective.

In these ways *Out of Many* breaks new ground. We continue to believe, however, that the traditional turning points of the American past remain critically important. The Revolution and the struggle over the Constitution, the Civil War and Reconstruction, the Great Depression and World War II are watershed periods for us. In *Out of Many* we seek to *integrate* the narrative of national history with the story of our many communities. The Revolutionary and Constitutional period tried the ability of local communities to forge a new unity, and success depended upon the ability to build a nation without compromising local identity. The Civil War and Reconstruction formed a second great test of the balance between the national ideas of the revolution and the power of local and sectional communities. The Depression and the New Deal demonstrated the impotence of local communities and the growing power of national institutions during the greatest economic challenge in our history. Rather than telling two stories—one of the people, the other of the nation—the community focus of *Out of Many* weaves them into a single compelling narrative.

Special Features

Out of Many, Brief Second Edition, combines the best of the traditional American history textbooks with a new approach. We have strengthened that approach in this new edition. Each chapter includes features that aid student use and offer an exciting new look.

◆   Outlines at the opening of each chapter summarize all the important topics and at a glance tell students what they can expect from the chapter.

- New in this edition, Key Topics highlight for students the important concepts of each chapter.

- Abundant illustrations and photographs include many never before used in an American history text. There are *no* anachronistic graphics—each one dates from the historical period under discussion. The extensive captions treat the graphics as visual evidence of the American past, providing full documentation and an explanation of their significance.

- Maps—more than in any competing American history text. New to this edition is an emphasis on the topography of the country. Also new to this edition are special "map pages" that focus attention on the geographic dimensions of historical change.

- Review Questions, new to this edition, help students to summarize and reinforce the material of each chapter.

- Chronologies at the conclusion of each chapter provide students with a quick review of the main points and dates.

- A short list of Recommended Reading at end of chapter is designed to be accessible to the interested introductory student.

Changes in the Brief Second Edition

The success of *Out of Many* has been gratifying, and in this brief second edition we have tried to strengthen its unique approach. But there are also some important revisions.

- Strengthened coverage of political history, especially of national politics.

- Several completely new community introductions that broaden coverage of all parts of the continent. The community theme has been strengthened throughout all the chapters.

- Increased treatment of racial and ethnic diversity as an essential part of the book's basic narrative.

- Expanded treatment of the West in American political and social history.

- Increased coverage of America's immediate neighbors, Mexico and Canada.

These and other changes have resulted in the substantial revision and rewriting of many chapters:

- A new introduction, "Community and Diversity," helps students understand the major themes of the book.

- Chapter 5 has been rewritten to compare and contrast the North American Empires of the Spanish, French, and British. Expanded coverage of the Enlightenment in America and the Great Awakening emphasizes the growing divergence between the British colonies and other colonial settlements.

- Chapter 7 has been substantially revised to emphasize the contrasting character of the Patriot and Loyalist forces during the Revolution. New material focuses on the reaction of the Spanish and French in North America to the Revolution.

- Chapter 9 includes greatly expanded coverage of the War of 1812 and new material on the struggle against Spanish colonial authorities in Texas before 1821.

- Chapter 15, substantially revised to focus on the political divisions of the 1850s, includes a new introduction on the Lincoln-Douglas debates as community events.

- Chapter 18 has been substantially revised and rewritten to include the new scholarship on the American West, particularly the new Indian history.

- Chapter 22 includes new material on Mexican migration during World War I, and on vigilante justice in the mining camps of the border region.

- Chapter 25 has been substantially rewritten to incorporate the newest scholarship on World War II.

- Chapter 31 incorporates developments since 1992 and includes substantial new material on the importance of the personal computer in contemporary America.

Classroom Assistance Package

In classrooms across the country, many instructors encounter students who perceive history as merely a jumble of names, dates, and events. The key to bringing dimension to our dynamic past for students is a scholarship-laden, pedagogically rich text accompanied with a multimedia classroom assistance package that brings the 1600s through the 1990s alive. The package that accompanies *Out of Many* includes print and multimedia supplements that are designed to reinforce and enliven the richness of our past and inspire students with the excitement of studying the field of history.

Print Supplements

Instructor's Resource Manual

Prepared by William D. Young, Johnson County Community College, and Elizabeth Neumeyer, Kellogg Community College

A true time-saver in developing and preparing lecture presentations, the *Instructor's Resource Manual* section of this indispensable guide contains chapter outlines, detailed chapter overviews, activities, discussion questions, readings, and information on audio-visual resources.

Test Item File

The *Test Item File* offers a menu of more than 1,500 multiple-choice, identification, matching, true-false, and essay test questions and 10–15 questions per chapter on maps found in each chapter. The guide includes a collection of blank maps that can be photocopied and used for map testing purposes or for other class exercises.

Prentice Hall Custom Test

This commercial-quality computerized test management program, available for IBM DOS, Windows, and Macintosh environments, allows instructors to select items from the *Test Item File* and design their own exams.

Transparency Pack

Prepared by Robert Tomes, St. John's University

This collection of more than 160 full-color transparency acetates provides instructors with all of the maps, charts, and graphs in the text for use in the classroom. Each transparency is accompanied by a page of descriptive material and discussion questions.

Study Guide, Volumes I and II

Prepared by Elizabeth Neumeyer, Kellogg Community College

The Study Guides are designed according to a SQ3R (Survey-Question-Read-Recite-Review) methodology. Each chapter includes a brief overview, a list of chapter objectives, an extensive questioning technique applied to chapter topics, study skills exercises, identification of terms, multiple choice, fill-in-the-blank, matching, short answer, and essay questions. In addi-

tion, each chapter includes two to three pages of specific map questions and exercises.

Understanding and Answering Essay Questions

Prepared by Mary L. Kelley, San Antonio College

This brief guide suggests helpful study techniques as well as specific analytical tools for understanding different types of essay questions and provides precise guidelines for preparing well-crafted essay answers. This guide is available free to students upon adoption by the instructor.

Reading Critically about History: A Guide to Active Reading

Prepared by Rose Wassman and Lee Ann Rinsky

This guide focuses on the skills needed to learn the essential information presented in college history textbooks. Material covered includes vocabulary skills, recognizing organizational patterns, critical thinking skills, understanding visual aids, and practice sections. This guide is available free to students upon adaption by the instructor.

Documents Set, Volumes I and II

Prepared by John Mack Faragher, Yale University, and Daniel Czitrom, Mount Holyoke College

The authors have selected and carefully edited more than 300 documents that relate directly to the theme and content present in the text and organized them into five general categories: community, social history, government, culture, and politics. Each document (approximately two pages in length) includes a brief introduction as well as a number of questions to encourage critical analysis of the reading and to relate it to the content of the text. The documents are available free to the instructor and for a nominal fee to the student with the purchase of the textbook.

Themes of the Times

The New York Times and Prentice Hall are sponsoring *Themes of the Times,* a program designed to enhance student access to current information of relevance in the classroom. Through this program, the core subject matter provided in the text is supplemented by a collection of current articles from one of the world's most distinguished news-

papers, *The New York Times*. These articles demonstrate the vital, ongoing connection between what is learned in the classroom and what is happening in the world around us. To enjoy the wealth of information of *The New York Times* daily, a reduced subscription rate is available. For information call toll-free:1-800-631-1222.

Prentice Hall and *The New York Times* are proud to co-sponsor *Themes of the Times*. We hope it will make the reading of both textbooks and newspapers a more dynamic, involving process.

Retrieving the American Past: A Customized U.S. History Reader

Written and developed by leading historians and educators, this reader is an on-demand history database that offers 52 compelling modules on topics in American History, such as: *Women on the Frontier, The Salem Witchcraft Scare, The Age of Industrial Violence,* and *Native American Societies, 1870–1995.* Approximately 35 pages in length, each module includes an introduction, several primary documents and secondary sources, follow-up questions, and recommendations for further reading. By deciding which modules to include and the order in which they will appear, instructors can compile the reader they want to use. Instructor-originated material—other readings, exercises—can be included. Contact your local Prentice Hall Representative for more information about this exciting custom publishing option.

Multimedia Supplements

History on the Internet

Adapted by David A. Meier, Dickinson State University

This brief guide introduces students to the origin and innovations behind the Internet and provides clear strategies for navigating the complexity of the Internet and World Wide Web. Exercises within and at the end of the chapters allow students to practice searching for the myriad of resources available to the student of History. This 48-page supplementary book is free to students using *Out of Many*.

Out of Many Interactive Edition

This exciting new electronic version of the Comprehensive version of the text on CD ROM (for IBM PC and Macintosh) utilizes the technology of *Power*CD®, exclusively developed by Zane Publishing, leaders in the field of multimedia technology. The Interactive Edition features more than 120 minutes of self-playing multimedia presentations, historical photographs with captions, more than 600 interactive study questions to strengthen the student's understanding of U.S. History, additional interactive essay review questions, the complete *Webster's New World College Dictionary*, Third Edition, and the complete text of *Out of Many*. With *Out of Many Interactive Edition* the past has never been so vibrant, so accessible, and so interesting.

Out of Many Website

Address: *http://www.prenhall.com/faragher*

In tandem with the text, students can now take full advantage of the World Wide Web to enrich their study of American history through the *Out of Many* website. This study resource will correlate the text with related material available on the Internet. Features of the website will include chapter objectives, study questions, news updates, labeling exercises, and much more.

Acknowledgments

In the several years it has taken to bring *Out of Many,* Brief Second Edition from idea to reality, we have often been reminded that although writing history sometimes feels like isolated work, it actually involves a collective effort. We want to thank the many people whose efforts have made the publication of this book possible.

At Prentice Hall, Todd Armstrong, Executive Editor of History, has supported us and seen us through the entire publication process. Leslie Carr performed the important task of developing the Brief manuscript, supervised by Susanna Lesan, Editor in Chief of Development. Harriet Tellem, Production Editor, with her usual high standards discovered and resolved any and all problems in the production process. And Ximena Tamvakopoulos created the handsome design of this edition.

Among our many other friends at Prentice Hall we also want to thank: Phil Miller, President; Charlyce Jones Owen, Editorial Director; Sheryl Adams, Marketing Manager; Leslie Osher, Creative Design Director; and Holly Jo Brown, Editorial Assistant.

Although we share joint responsibility for the entire book, the chapters were individually authored: John Mack Faragher wrote Chapters 1–8; Mari Jo Buhle wrote Chapters 18–20, 25–26, 29–30; Daniel Czitrom wrote Chapters 17, 21–24, 27–28, 31; and Susan H. Armitage wrote Chapters 9–16.

Historians around the country greatly assisted us by reading and commenting on our chapters. For the commitment of their valuable time, we want to thank those who aided us in preparing the first edition:

Donald Abbe, Texas Tech University
William L. Barney, University of North Carolina
Alwyn Barr, Texas Tech University
Peter V. Bergstrom, Illinois State University
William C. Billingsley, South Plains College
Bill Cecil-Fronsman, Washburn University of Topeka
Victor W. Chen, Chabot College
Matthew Coulter, Collin Country Community College
Kenneth Goings, Florida Atlantic University
Fred R. van Hartesveldt, Fort Valley State College
Raymond M. Hyser, James Madison University
John Inscoe, University of Georgia
John C. Kesler, Lakeland Community College
Frank Lambert, Purdue University
Susan Rimby Leighow, Millersville University
Janice M. Leone, Middle Tennessee University
George Lipsitz, University of California, San Diego
Judy Barrett Litoff, Bryand College
Jesus Luna, California State University
M. Delores McBroome, Humboldt State University
Dr. Larry Madaras, Howard Community College
Robert L. Matheny, Eastern New Mexico University
Warren Metcalf, Arizona State University
M. Catherine Miller, Texas State University
Gregory H. Nobles, Georgia Institute of Technology
Dale Odom, University of Texas at Denton
Christie Farnham Pope, Iowa State University
Susan Porter-Benson, University of Missouri
Marilyn D. Rhinehart, North Harris College
Neal Salisbury, Smith College
Steven Schuster, Brookhaven Community College
John David Smith, North Carolina State University
Mark W. Summers, University of Kentucky
John D. Tanner Jr., Palomar College
Robert R. Tomes, St. John's University
John Trickel, Richland Community College
Robert C. Vitz, Northern Kentucky University
Charles Reagan Wilson, University of Mississippi
William Woodward, Seattle Pacific University
Loretta E. Zimmerman, University of Florida

Over the past several years, the following were of great help to us in developing the second edition:

Richard H. Abbott, Eastern Michigan University
Guy Alchon, University of Delaware

Don Barlow, Prestonsburg Community College
Debra E. Barth, San Jose City College (CA)
Peter H. Buckingham, Linfield College
Virginia Crane, University of Wisconsin, Oshkosh
Jim Cullen, Harvard University
Thomas J. Curran, St. John's University
Richard V. Damms, Ohio State University
Emmett M. Essin, East Tennessee State University
Mark F. Fernandez, Loyola University
Leon Fink, University of North Carolina, Chapel Hill
Michael James Foret, University of Wisconsin, Stevens Point
Joshua B. Freeman, Columbia University
Glenda E. Gilmore, Yale University
Don C. Glenn, Diablo Valley College
Lawrence Glickman, University of South Carolina
Mark Goldman, Tallahassee Community College
Gretchen Green, University of Missouri, Kansas City
Mark W. T. Harvey, North Dakota State University
James A. Hijiya, University of Massachusetts at Dartmouth
Peter N. Kirstein, Saint Xavier University
Glenn Linden, Southern Methodist University, Dallas, TX
Judy Barrett Litoff, Bryant College
Larry Madaras, Howard Community College
John F. Marszalek, Mississippi State University
Scott C. Martin, Bowling Green State University
Thomas Matijasic, Prestonsburg Community College
Gerald McFarland, University of Massachusetts, Amherst
Sam McSeveney, Vanderbilt University
Norman H. Murdoch, University of Cincinnati
Edward Opper, Greenville Technical College, Greenville, SC
Charles K. Piehl, Mankato State University
Carolyn Garrett Pool, University of Central Oklahoma
Russell Posner, City College of San Francisco
John Powell, Pennsylvania State University, Erie, PA
Megan Seaholm, University of Texas, Austin
Nigel Sellars, University of Oklahoma, Norman
Patrick Smith, Broward Community College
Michael Miller Topp, University of Texas at El Paso
Phillip H. Vaughan, Rose State College
F. Michael Williams, Brevard Community College
Harold Wilson, Old Dominion University

Each of us depended upon a great deal of support and assistance with the research and writing that went into this book. We want to thank: Kathryn Abbott, Nan Boyd, Krista Comer, Crista DeLuzio, Keith Edgerton, Carol Frost, Jesse Hoffnung Garskof, Jane Gerhard, Todd Gernes, Melani McAlister, Cristiane Mitchell, J. C. Mutchler, Tricia Rose, and Jessica Shubow.

Our families and close friends were supportive and ever so patient as this project slowly made its way to completion. But we want especially to thank Paul Buhle, Meryl Fingrutd, Bob Greene, and Michele Hoffnung.

ABOUT THE AUTHORS

Chris Freitag

John Mack Faragher

John Mack Faragher is the Arthur Unobskey Professor of American History at Yale University. Born in Arizona and raised in southern California, he received his B.A. at the University of California, Riverside, and his Ph.D at Yale University. He is the author of *Women and Men on the Overland Trail* (1979), which won the Frederick Jackson Turner Award of the Organization of American Historians, *Sugar Creek: Life on the Illinois Prairie* (1986) and *Daniel Boone: The Life and Legend of an American Pioneer* (1992), winner of *The Los Angeles Times* prize as best biography of the year. He serves on the editorial board of the *Western Historical Quarterly*.

Mari Jo Buhle

Mari Jo Buhle is Professor of American Civilization and History at Brown University, specializing in American women's history. She is the author of *Women and American Socialism, 1820–1920* (1981) and coeditor of *The Concise History of Woman Suffrage* (1978) and *Encyclopedia of the American Left* (1990). She currently serves as an editor of a series of books on women and American history for the University of Illinois Press. Professor Buhle holds a fellowship (1991–1996) from the John D. and Catherine T. MacArthur Foundation.

Daniel Czitrom

Daniel Czitrom is Professor and Chair of the Department of History, Mount Holyoke College. He received his B.A. from the State University of New York at Binghamton and his M.A. and Ph.D. from the University of Wisconsin, Madison. He is the author of *Media and the American Mind: From Morse to McLuhan* (1982), which won the First Books Award of the American Historical Association. His scholarly articles and essays have appeared in the *Journal of American History, American Quarterly, The Massachusetts Review,* and *The Atlantic.* He is currently completing *Mysteries of the City: Culture, Politics, and the Underworld in New York, 1870–1920.*

Susan H. Armitage

Susan H. Armitage is Professor of History at Washington State University. She earned her Ph.D. from the London School of Economics and Political Science. Among her many publications on western women's history are three coedited books: *The Women's West* (1987); *So Much to Be Done: Women on the Mining and Ranching Frontier* (1991); and *Writing the Range: Race, Class, and Culture in the Women's West* (1997). She is an editor of *Frontiers: A Journal of Women's Studies.*

OUT OF MANY

COMMUNITY AND DIVERSITY

One of the most characteristic features of our country has always been its astounding variety. The American people include the descendants of native Indians, colonial Europeans, Africans, and migrants from virtually every country and continent. Indeed, as we approach a new century, a tide of immigrants from Latin America and Asia rivals the great migration from eastern and southern Europe a hundred years ago. The struggle to make a nation out of our many communities is what much of American history is all about. That is the story told in this book.

Every human society is made up of communities. A community is a set of relationships that link men, women, and their families into a coherent social whole, more than the sum of its parts. In a community people develop the capacity for unified action. In a community they learn, often through trial and error, how to adapt to their environment. The sentiment that binds the members of a community together is the origin of group identity and ethnic pride.

In the making of history, communities are far more important than even the greatest of leaders, for the community is the institution most capable of passing a distinctive historical tradition to future generations. Communities of people—whose lives are bound together in multiple ways—range in size from local neighborhoods to nations. This book examines American history from the perspective of community life, an ever-widening frame that has included larger and larger groups of Americans.

The title of our book was suggested by the Latin phrase selected by John Adams, Benjamin Franklin, and Thomas Jefferson for the Great Seal of the United States: *E Pluribus Unum,* "Out of Many Comes Unity." National unity could not be imposed by a powerful central authority but had to develop out of mutual respect for Americans of different backgrounds.

Out of Many is the promise of America and the premise of this book. The underlying dialectic of American history, we believe, is that as a people we need to locate our national unity in the celebration of the differences that exist among us; these differences can be our strength, as long as we affirm the promise of equality in the Declaration of Independence. Protecting the "right to be different," in other words, is absolutely fundamental to the continued existence of democracy, and that right is best protected by the existence of strong and vital communities.

Today, with the many social and cultural conflicts that abound in the United States, some Americans have lost faith in that vision. But our history shows that the promise of American unity always has been problematic. Centrifugal forces have been powerful in the American past, and at times the country has seemed about to fracture into its component parts. Our transformation from a collection of groups and regions into a nation has been marked by painful and often violent struggles. Our past is filled with conflicts between Indians and colonists, masters and slaves, Patriots and Loyalists, northerners and southerners, easterners and westerners, capitalists and workers, and sometimes the government and the people. Americans often appear to be little more than a contentious collection of peoples with conflicting interests, divided by region and background, race and class.

We have not always lived up to the American promise, and there is a dark side to our history. It took the bloodiest war in American history to secure the human rights of African Americans, and the struggle for full equality continues nearly a century and a half later. During the great influx of immigrants in the early twentieth century, fears led to movements to "Americanize" the foreign born by forcing them, in the words of one leader, "to give up the languages, customs, and methods of life which they have brought with them across the ocean, and adopt instead the language, habits, and customs of this country, and the general standards and ways of American living." Similar thinking motivated Congress to bar the immigration of Asians and other ethnic groups into the country, and to force assimilation on American Indians by denying them the freedom to practice their religion or even speak their own language. Such calls for restrictive unity resound in our own day.

The process through which diverse communities have come to share a set of common American values is one of the most fundamental aspects of our history. However, it did not occur because of compulsory "Americanization" programs, but rather because of the influence of free public education, the appeal of popular participation in democratic politics, and the impact of popular culture.

American educator John Dewey recognized early in this century that "the genuine American, the typical American is himself a hyphenated character, international and interracial in his make-up." The point, Dewey believed, "is to see to it that the hyphen connects instead of separates." We the authors of *Out of Many* share Dewey's perspective on American history. "Creation comes from the impact of diversity," wrote American philosopher Horace Kallen. We also endorse Kallen's vision of the American promise: "A democracy of nationalities, cooperating voluntarily and autonomously through common institutions, . . . a multiplicity in a unity, an orchestration of mankind." And now, let the music begin.

1

A CONTINENT OF VILLAGES, TO 1500

AMERICAN COMMUNITIES

CAHOKIA: THIRTEENTH-CENTURY LIFE ON THE MISSISSIPPI

As the sun rose over the river bottom, people walked down the narrow city streets to their places of work. Some hurried to shops, where they manufactured tools, crafted pottery, worked metal, or fashioned ornamental jewelry—goods destined to be exchanged in the distant corners of the continent. Others left their densely populated neighborhoods for the outlying countryside, where in the humid summer heat they worked the seemingly endless fields that fed the city. From almost anywhere, people could see, rising from the city center, the great temple where priests in splendid costumes acted out public rituals of death and renewal.

This scene describes life not in preindustrial Europe but in thirteenth-century North America. These people lived and worked on the alluvial soil of the Mississippi River, across from present-day St. Louis, at a place archaeologists have named Cahokia. In the mid-1200s, Cahokia was an urban cluster of perhaps 30,000 people. Its farm fields were thick with corn, beans, and pumpkins, crops no European had ever seen. The temple, a huge earthwork pyramid, covered fifteen acres at its base and rose as high as a ten-story building. On top were the sacred residences of chiefs and priests, who dressed in elaborate headdresses made from the plumage of tropical New World birds.

Cahokia thrived, then withered and died in the fourteenth century, as did dozens of other urban clusters along the banks of North America's vast inland river system. Cahokia's people left us no written records. Instead, the central mound and dozens of smaller ones in the surrounding area, as well as hundreds more throughout the Mississippi Valley, remained to puzzle the European immigrants who resettled the valley in the eighteenth and nineteenth centuries. Treasure seekers plundered them, and later the mounds were dynamited and plowed under for farmland. Cahokia's central mound survived because its summit became the site of a monastery.

Thanks to modern archaeology, we now know that the vast urban complex of Cahokia, stretching six miles along the Mississippi from the tenth to the fourteenth centuries, was constructed by the ancestors of contemporary Indian people. We know its residents were not nomadic hunters but farmers. These agricultural people, whom archaeologists call the Mississippians, developed a highly intensive system of farming that supported densely settled urban centers. At Cahokia, hundreds of acres of crops fed the most populated urban community north of the Valley of Mexico. We also know that the city of Cahokia included large numbers of specialized artisans, and that it was renowned for the manufacture of high-quality flint hoes, exported throughout the Mississippi Valley. Cahokia was at the center of a long-distance trading system that linked together hundreds of the Indian towns of the continent. Copper came from Lake Superior, mica from the southern Appalachians, and conch shells from the Atlantic coast.

We know that the temple mounds and other monumental public works at Cahokia were aspects of a society dominated by an elite class of priests and rulers. The great Cahokia mound was a human-constructed acropolis from which the elite could look down on their subjects from their adobe palaces. These structures must have inspired awe in the people of the city. In Cahokia, then, we see the beginnings of the modern state, supported by tribute. There is no indication, however, that the Mississippians had developed a system of writing. We know that the Cahokians lived in a sophisticated community, the product of thousands of years of history, but without written documents we cannot know their own version of that history.

Every human society is made up of communities. A community is a set of relationships that link men, women, and their families into a coherent social whole, more than the sum of its parts. In a community people develop the capacity for unified action. They learn, often through trial and error, how to adapt to their environment. The term *community* is often used to convey a sense of harmony and social peace, but the social process through which communities are defined, governed, and directed often includes a great deal of conflict. In the making of history, communities are far more important than even the greatest leaders, for the community is the institution most capable of passing a distinctive historical tradition to future generations. Communities of people—whose lives are bound together in multiple ways—range in size from local neighborhoods to nations. This book examines American history from the perspective of community life—an ever-widening frame that has included larger and larger groups of Americans.

Over many centuries the Indian peoples of North America developed a variety of community types, each with its own system of family and social organization, each

having a unique relationship to the environment. The wonders of Cahokia were but one aspect of the little-understood history of the Indians of the Americas.

KEY TOPICS

◆ **The peopling of the Americas by migrants from Asia**

◆ **The adaptation of native cultures to the distinctive regions of North America**

◆ **The increase in complexity of many native societies following the development of farming**

◆ **The nature of Indian cultures in the three major regions of European invasion and settlement**

Settling the Continent

"Why do you call us Indians?" a Massachusetts native complained to Puritan missionary John Eliot in 1646. Christopher Columbus, who mistook the Arawaks of the Caribbean for the people of the East Indies, called them *Indios.* By the middle of the sixteenth century this Spanish word had passed into English as *Indians,* and was commonly used to refer to all the native peoples of the Americas. Today anthropologists often use the term *Amerindians,* and many people prefer *Native American.* But most indigenous Americans call themselves Indian people.

Who Are the Indian People?

At the time of the first European contacts at the beginning of the sixteenth century, the native inhabitants of the Western Hemisphere represented over 2,000 cultures, spoke hundreds of different languages, and made their livings in scores of fundamentally different environments. Just as the term *European* includes the English, French, and Spanish, so *Indian* covers an enormous diversity among the peoples of the Americas. A number of Spanish observers thought through the problem of Indian origins. In 1590 Joseph de Acosta reasoned that because Old World animals were present in the Americas, they must have crossed over by a land bridge, which could have been used by humans as well. A few years later, Enrico Martin speculated that because no such land passage had been found between the Americas and Europe, it must exist in the unexplored far northwest of the continent, and the people using it must thus have been Asians. In the 1650s Bernabe Cobo, who had lived most of his life in the Caribbean, argued that Indian people had to have been in America for centuries because of the great variety of native languages. Here were the principal elements of the migration hypothesis: Indian people were descended from a common stock of Asian migrants, had arrived by way of a northwestern land passage, and had experienced a long and independent history in the Americas.

Certainly no single physical type characterizes all the native peoples of the Americas. Despite being called "yellow men" or "redskins" by colonists and frontiersmen of the eighteenth and nineteenth centuries, few fit those descriptions. The color of their skin ranged from mahogany to light brown, and most had straight, black hair, and dark, almond-shaped eyes. But only when Europeans compared them with other continental groups, such as Africans, did they seem similar enough to be classified as a group. Modern laboratory analysis of

blood samples reveals that the most distinctive marker of Native American populations is blood type: the vast majority have type O blood, and a few type A, but unlike Old World peoples, almost none have type B.

Migration from Asia

The most ancient human fossils in the Americas share a common dental pattern with fossils found in northeastern Asia. Because modern Asian populations include all three blood groups, however, migrations to the New World must have occurred before the evolution of the modern Asian type, which scientists date at about 30,000 years ago. The evidence from geneticists and linguists points to a move to the Americas from Asia 25,000 to 30,000 years ago—about the time that Scandinavia and Japan were being settled.

At the time of the migrations from Asia to the Americas the Northern Hemisphere was experiencing

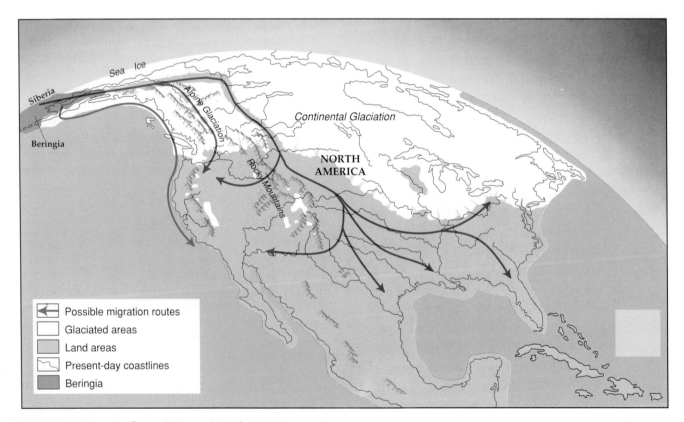

Migration Routes from Asia to America

During the Ice Age, Asia and North America were joined where the Bering Straits are today, forming a migration route for hunting peoples. Either by boat along the coast, or through a narrow corridor between the huge northern glaciers, these migrants made their way to the heartland of the continent as much as 30,000 years ago.

the final Ice Age, which characterized the geological epoch known as the Pleistocene. Huge glaciers locked up massive volumes of water, and sea levels were as much as 300 feet lower than they are today. Asia and North America were joined by a huge subcontinent of ice-free, treeless grassland, 750 miles wide from north to south. Geologists have named this area Beringia, from the Bering Straits. Summers there were warm, winters cold, dry, and almost snow-free. This was a perfect environment for the large mammals known as *megafauna*—mammoth and mastadon, bison, horse, reindeer, camel, and saiga (a goatlike antelope).

Beringia also attracted Stone Age hunter–gatherers who lived in small, nomadic bands and subsisted almost entirely on these megafauna. The animals provided them not only with food but also with hides for clothing and shelter, dung for fuel, and bones for tools and weapons. Hunting bands were driven to expand by the powerful force of their own population growth and the pressure it placed on local resources. Following the big game, and accompanied by a husky-like species of dog, hunting bands gradually expanded through Beringia, moving as far east as the Yukon River basin of northern Canada.

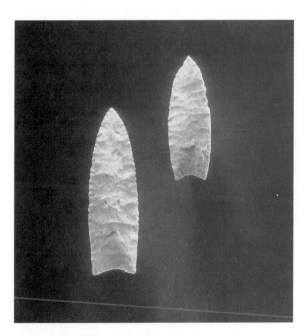

These Clovis points are typical of thousands that archaeologists have found at sites all over the continent, dating from a period about 12,000 years ago. When inserted in a spear shaft, these three- to six-inch fluted points made effective weapons for hunting mammoth and other big game.

Archaeologists disagree about the dating of these earliest migrations. Some estimate the migrations occurred 27,000 to 30,000 years ago; others believe they took place much later, perhaps around 15,000 B.C.E. Because much of Beringia was later submerged beneath rising seas, definitive archaeological evidence of migration from Asia may be difficult to find. No specimens of human fossils have yet been uncovered there.

Huge glaciers blocked southern movement during most of the last Ice Age, but occasionally a narrow land corridor opened up along the eastern base of the Rocky Mountains. Hunting bands following this corridor south could have emerged on the northern Great Plains—a hunter's paradise teeming with megafauna of great variety—as early as 25,000 years ago. Migrants may also have moved south in boats, following the Pacific coastline. Rapid population growth would have enabled these groups to populate the entire Western Hemisphere in only a few thousand years. Remarkably, the oral traditions of many Indian peoples depict a long journey from a distant place of origin to a new homeland. Europeans have recorded the Pima people of the Southwest singing this song:

> This is the White Land; we arrive singing,
> Headdresses waving in the breeze.
> We have come! We have come!
> The land trembles with our dancing and singing.

Clovis: The First American Technology

The tools found at the earliest North American archaeological sites consist of crude stone or bone choppers and scrapers, similar to artifacts from the same period found in Europe or Asia. About 12,000 years ago, however, there seems to have developed a much more sophisticated style of toolmaking, named after the site of its discovery near Clovis, New Mexico.

Clovis bands were mobile communities numbering perhaps thirty to fifty individuals from several interrelated families. They returned to the same hunting camps year after year, pursuing seasonal migration within territories of several hundred square miles. Near Delbert, Nova Scotia, archaeologists discovered the floors of ten tents arranged in a semicircle, their doors opening south to avoid the prevailing northerly winds. Both this camp and others found throughout the continent overlooked watering places that would attract game. Hunters apparently drove animals into shallow bogs, killed them with spears, and butchered them.

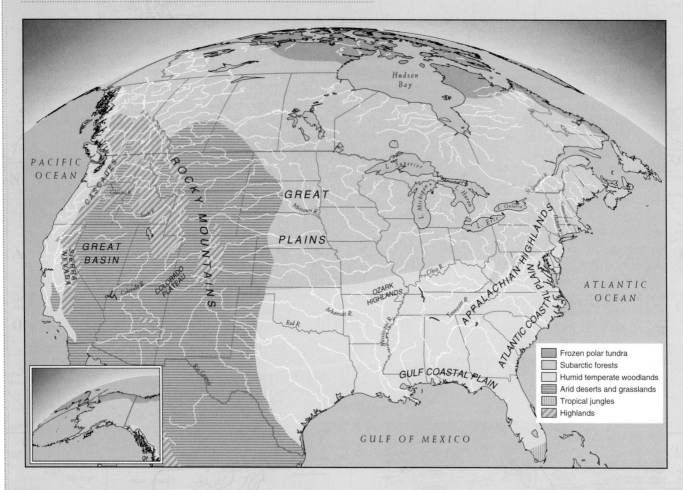

■	Frozen polar tundra
	Subarctic forests
	Humid temperate woodlands
	Arid deserts and grasslands
	Tropical jungles
	Highlands

THE REGIONS OF NATIVE NORTH AMERICA

Occupying more than a third of the continent, the United States is alone among the world's nations in encompassing all five general classes of global climate: tropical jungles, arid deserts and grasslands, temperate woodlands, subarctic forests, and frozen polar tundra.

The country also contains some of the world's largest lakes, most extensive grasslands, and mightiest rivers.

All peoples must adjust their diet, shelter, and other material aspects of their lives to the physical conditions of the world around them; thus a knowledge of the way in

The Beginning of Regional Cultures

About 15,000 years ago a global warming trend began to alter the North American climate. The giant continental glaciers began to melt, a shift so pronounced by 8000 B.C.E. that it marks the passing of the Pleistocene epoch. As the glaciers retreated, the northern latitudes were colonized by plants, animals, and hu-

mans. Meltwater created the lake and river systems of today and raised the level of the surrounding seas, flooding Beringia as well as vast stretches of the Atlantic and Gulf coasts and creating fertile tidal pools and offshore fishing banks. These monumental transformations produced new patterns of wind, rainfall, and temperature, reshaping the ecology of the entire continent. The result was the distinct North American regions of today. The great integrating force of a single continental climate faded, and with its passing a

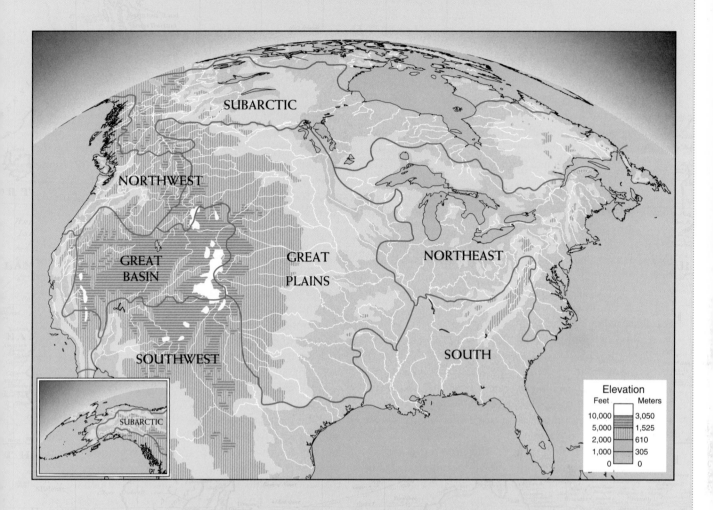

SUBARCTIC

NORTHWEST

GREAT
BASIN

GREAT
PLAINS

NORTHEAST

SOUTHWEST

SOUTH

SUBARCTIC

Elevation

Feet		Meters
10,000		3,050
5,000		1,525
2,000		610
1,000		305
0		0

which geography and climate combine to form regions is a prerequisite to understanding the cultures of the peoples of America. Using the concept of culture areas, anthropologists divide the continent into several fundamental regions that have played an important role in the history of the continent for the past 10,000 years.

The Indian peoples of North America were first to develop distinct cultures suited to the regions in which they lived. Just as regions shaped the lifeways and history of Indian peoples, after the coming of the Europeans they nurtured the development of regional American cultures.

continental Clovis culture fragmented into many different regional patterns.

Regions have always played an important role in American history. Occupying more than a third of the continent, the United States is alone among the world's nations in encompassing all five general classes of global climate: tropical jungles, arid deserts and grasslands, temperate woodlands, subarctic forests, and frozen polar tundra. It also contains some of the world's largest lakes, most extensive grasslands, and

mightiest rivers. These variations in climate and geography combine to form the distinct regions of America: Northeast, South, Great Plains, Great Basin, Southwest, Northwest, and California. Within these regions, human communities have had to adapt to nature, developing their own ways of life. Indian peoples were the first in North America to embark on the long journey toward regionally distinct cultures, developing a wide variety of food sources to support their growing populations.

Hunting Traditions of the Plains and Forests

One of the most important effects of this massive climatological shift was the stress it placed on the megafauna, whose lowered reproduction and survival rates forced hunting bands to intensify their efforts. The combined effects of warmer climate and greater hunting eventually led to what some archaeologists have called the Pleistocene Overkill.

As the megafauna declined, hunters on the Great Plains turned to the herds of American bison, more commonly called buffalo. In archaeological sites dating to about 10,000 years ago, a new style of tools is found in association with animal remains. This technology, a refinement of the Clovis tradition, features more delicate but deadlier points. Archaeologists have given this new tradition the name Folsom, after the site of the first major excavation in New Mexico. In one dramatic find, a Folsom point was discovered embedded between the fossilized ribs of an ancient species of bison. Somewhat later, this technology evolved into a tradition that archaeologists call Plano; the points are found with grinding tools for vegetable foods, demonstrating the development of a varied diet on the Great Plains.

Archaeological finds suggest the growing complexity of early Indian communities. Folsom and Plano hunters must have been among the first to make jerky, or dried strips of meat, and pemmican, a mixture of dried meat, animal fat, and berries that can keep into the winter when stored in hide containers. These characteristic products of the Great Plains would become the staple food items of the European fur traders in the West.

The passing of the Pleistocene was followed by a final wave of Beringia migrants: the Athapascans, or Na-Dene people. After entering North America, they moved southeast from Alaska, following the wake of the melting western glacier. From 7,000 to 4,000 years ago, they settled the boreal forests in the northwest of the continent. Although they eventually adopted a technology similar to that of neighboring peoples, the Na-Dene maintained a separate cultural and linguistic identity. Athapascan speakers later migrated from their northern homeland, journeying across the Great Plains to the Southwest.

In a final migration from Asia that took place about 5,000 years ago, the Eskimos (or Inupiat) and Aleuts, other hunting peoples, crossed the flooded Bering Straits by boat. The Eskimos colonized the polar coasts of the Arctic, the Aleuts the Aleutian Islands (which are named for them) and the southern coast of Alaska.

Desert and Forest Communities

The retreat of the glaciers led to new subsistence traditions in other regions: desert foraging in the arid Great Basin, fishing along the northwest coast of the Pacific, and hunting and gathering in the forests of the humid eastern half of the continent. These developments took place roughly 10,000 to 2,500 years ago, during the Archaic period.

In the Great Basin of present-day Utah and Nevada, the warming trend associated with the end of the Ice Age created a desert where once there had been enormous inland seas. Here Indian people developed Desert Culture, a way of life based on the pursuit of small game and the intensified foraging of plant foods. Small mobile communities or bands of desert foragers migrated within rather small territories. They lived in caves and rock shelters, where archaeologists today find their artifacts. In addition to stone tools, there are objects of wood, hide, and fiber, wonderfully preserved for thousands of years in the dry climate.

The innovative practices of the Desert Culture gradually spread from the Great Basin to the Great Plains and the Southwest, where foraging techniques began to supplement intensive hunting. Archaeologists estimate that about 6,000 years ago Indians developed an economy capable of supporting some of the densest populations and the first permanently settled communities in North America. Another dynamic center in the West developed along the northwest Pacific coast, where Indian communities developed a way of life based on the use of abundant fish and sea mammals.

There were similar trends east of the Mississippi. Before the eighteenth and nineteenth centuries, the whole of eastern North America was a vast forest. Archaic forest communities achieved a comfortable and secure life based on their sophisticated knowledge of the rich and diverse available resources, a principle that archaeologists call *forest efficiency*.

Indian communities of the forest hunted small game and gathered seeds, nuts, roots, and other wild plant foods. They also developed the practice of burning the woodlands and prairies to produce a *climax growth* of berries, fruits, and edible roots. These burns provided both harvestable food and an attractive environment for grazing animals, which were hunted for their meat and hides. Another important resource was the abundant fish of the rivers.

The Development of Farming

The exploitation of a wide variety of food sources during the Archaic period eventually led many Indian people to develop and adopt the practice of farming. The dynamic center of this development in North America was the highlands of Mexico, from which the new technology spread north and east.

Mexico

Archaeological evidence suggests that plant cultivation in the highlands of central Mexico began about 9,000 years ago. Ancient Mexicans developed crops that responded well to human care and produced larger quantities of food in a limited space than plants growing naturally. Maize was particularly productive; over time it was adapted to a wide range of American climates, and farming spread throughout the temperate regions of North America.

As farming became increasingly important, it radically reshaped social life. Greater productivity spurred population growth to even higher levels. Farming systems could support large and densely settled communities such as Cahokia on the banks of the Mississippi.

Archaeological evidence suggests that by 1000 B.C.E., urban communities governed by permanent bureaucracies had begun to form in Mexico. By C.E. 650, a highly productive form of irrigation farming was supporting an urban civilization of more than 200,000 people in the high valley where Mexico City stands today. This was the capital of the Toltec people. An elite class of leaders controlled an elaborate trading system that stretched from present-day Arizona south to Central America. This network may have included coastal shipping connections with the Inca civilization of Peru, which developed at about the same time. Urban communities had a highly specialized division of labor. Artisans manufactured tools and produced clothing, stoneware, pottery, obsidian blades, and more. The bureaucratic elite collected taxes and tribute to maintain this vast urban structure. They had armies of workers construct monumental edifices such as the Pyramids of the Sun and Moon, the ruins of which remind us today of the marvels of that ancient world.

City-states developed throughout Mexico and Central America, dominating the farmers of the countryside and waging war against one another. The rulers displayed their power through terrifying public rituals of human sacrifice and even cannibalism atop their grand pyramids. With fabulous art and architecture, highly developed math and science, and several systems of glyphic writing, the Indians of Mexico and Central America had developed a civilization with all the traits of the classic European varieties. Eventually, the Toltecs were overthrown by invaders from northern Mexico known as the Aztecs. (For a discussion of the Aztecs, see Chapter 2.)

The Resisted Revolution

Historians once described the development of farming as the Neolithic Revolution. They believed that agricultural communities offered such obvious advantages that their neighbors must have rushed to adopt this way of life. Societies that remained without a farming tradition must simply have been too "primitive" to achieve this breakthrough; vulnerability to fickle nature was the penalty for their ignorance. This interpretation was part of a scheme of social evolution whose proponents viewed human history as the story of technological progress, with hunters gradually developing into civilized farmers.

But there is very little evidence to support this notion of a "revolution" occurring during a short, critical period. The adoption of farming was a gradual process, one that required hundreds, even thousands, of years. Moreover, ignorance of cultivation was never the reason that cultures failed to take up farming, for all hunter–gatherer peoples understand a great deal about plant reproduction. The Menomini Indians of the northern forests of Wisconsin, for example, when gathering wild rice, purposely allowed some of it to fall back into the water to ensure a crop for the next season.

Rather than freeing men and women from the tyranny of nature, farming tied people to a work discipline unlike anything previously known in human history. Like the development of more sophisticated traditions of tool manufacture, farming represented another stage in the economic intensifications that kept populations and available resources in balance. As this new technology became available, cultures in different regions assessed its advantages and limitations. In regions such as California and the Pacific Northwest, acorn gathering or salmon fishing made cultivation seem a waste of time. In the Great Basin, several peoples attempted to implement a farming system, but ultimately failed. Before the invention of modern irrigation systems, which require sophisticated engineering, only Archaic Desert Culture could prevail in this harsh environment. In the neighboring Southwest, however, farming resolved certain ecological dilemmas and transformed the way of life. It seems that where climate favored cultivation, people tended to adopt farming as a prominent or supplemental form of production, thus continuing the Archaic tradition of diversity in food production. In a few areas, repeated increases in cultivation pushed in the direction of an urban civilization like that of central Mexico.

Increasing Social Complexity

Farming created the basis for much greater social complexity within Indian communities. Most important were significantly more elaborate systems of kinship. Greater population density prompted families to group themselves into clans. Often different clans became responsible for different social, political, or ritual functions. Clans became an important mechanism for binding together the people of several communities into a tribe. Tribes, based on ethnic, linguistic, and territorial unity, were led by leaders or chiefs from honored clans, who were often advised by councils of elders. This council sometimes arbitrated disputes between individuals or families, but most crimes—theft, adultery, rape, murder—were avenged by the aggrieved kinship group itself.

The primary function of chiefs was the supervision of the economy, the collection and storage of the harvest, and the distribution of food to the clans. Differences in wealth, though small by the standards of modern societies, might develop between the families of a farming tribe. These inequalities were kept in check by redistribution according to principles of sharing similar to those operating in foraging communities. Nowhere in North America did Indian cultures develop a concept of private ownership of land or other resources, which were usually considered the common property of the people and were worked collectively.

Indian communities practiced a rather strict sexual division of labor that in its details varied tremendously from culture to culture. Among foraging peoples, hunting was generally assigned to men, while the gathering of food and the maintenance of home-base camps was the responsibility of women. This pattern probably originated during the long Paleolithic era. But the development of farming called these patterns into question. In Mexico, where communities became almost totally dependent on their crops, both men and women worked in the fields. Where hunting remained important, the older division of labor remained, with women responsible for field work. Later, English colonists viewed Indian women working in the cornfields as oppressed, whereas Indians viewed colonial men working in the fields as doing "women's work."

In most North American Indian farming communities, women and men belonged to separate social groupings with their own rituals and lore. Membership in these societies was one of the most important elements of a person's identity. Marriage ties, on the other hand, were weak, and in most Indian communities divorce was usually simple: The couple separated without a great deal of ceremony, the children almost always remaining with the mother. All Indian women controlled their own bodies, were free to determine the timing of reproduction, free to use secret herbs to prevent pregnancy, induce abortion, and ease the pains of childbirth. All this was strikingly different from European patterns, in which the rule of men over women and fathers over households was thought to be the social ideal.

Farming communities were thus far more complex than foraging communities. But they were also less stable, for growing populations demanded increasingly large surpluses of food, and this need often led to social conflict and warfare. Moreover, farming systems were especially vulnerable to climatological disruptions such as drought, as well as ecological crises of their own creation, such as soil depletion or erosion.

Farmers of the Southwest

During the late Archaic period, from 5,000 to 3,000 years ago, the southwest region of the continent experienced increased levels of rainfall and more abundant local resources. As a result, human populations proliferated. Mexican cultivated plants first appeared in the area during this period, and their casual cultivation became a supplement to gathering and hunting.

But about 3,000 years ago, in one of the periodic shifts that punctuate the history of climate, drier conditions suddenly threatened the balance between population and resources. It seems to have been in this context that systematic farming was first adopted by the Mogollon. This group, named for the area along the southern Arizona–New Mexico border where they thrived, cultivated maize, beans, and squash with digging sticks until the thirteenth century C.E. Living in permanent villages near mountain streams and along ridges, these people devised ingenious pit houses, well suited to the temperature extremes common to the region. Called *kivas* by their Pueblo descendants, these subterranean rooms also served as storehouses for crops and as the centers for religious ceremony.

Sometime after the establishment of these Mogollon villages, a colony was established along the floodplain of the Salt and Gila rivers in southern Arizona by an emigrant group from Mexico called the Hohokam ("those who are gone" in the language of the modern Pimas and Papagos of the area). The Hohokam built and maintained the first irrigation system in America, channeling river water many miles to desert fields of maize, beans, squash, tobacco, and cotton. The number and variety of Mexican goods uncovered at a site near present-day Phoenix called Snaketown—rubber balls, mirrors of pyrite mosaics, copper bells, and fashionable ear ornaments—suggest that this was a community of Mexican merchants where locally mined turquoise was traded for manufactured goods. The Hohokam even developed a process for etching shells with animal designs. With platform mounds for religious ceremonies and large courts for ball-playing, theirs was a sophisticated desert outpost of classic Mexican civilization.

The Anasazi

The best-known farming culture of the Southwest developed several hundred miles to the north in the Four Corners area, where Arizona, New Mexico, Utah, and Colorado meet on the plateau of the Colorado River. Called the Anasazi ("ancient outsiders" in the Navajo language), this culture first took shape when growing populations made a transition from nomadic gathering to village cultivation during the first century C.E. In the eighth century a pronounced shift to a drier climate presented the Anasazi with the choice of reverting to nomadism or finding ways of adapting and improving their farming systems. Like most cultures confronted with such a dilemma, they chose to intensify their productive system.

The classic period of Anasazi culture followed. In terraced fields irrigated by canals flowing from mountain catchment basins, they grew high-yield varieties of maize. They supplemented this with the meat of animals hunted with the highly effective bow and arrow. The Anasazi are admired for their fine basketry and exquisite painted pottery, but it is their urban architecture that most awes visitors to the region today. Anasazi communities lived in multistoried apartments—later called pueblos by Spanish invaders—clustered about central plazas; kivas were used for storage and religious ceremonies. Among the most spectacular of their ruins are those at Chaco Canyon, where Pueblo Bonito, completed in the twelfth century, contains over 650 interconnected rooms. It memorializes the Golden Age of the Anasazi.

A devastating drought from 1276 to 1293 (precisely dated with the aid of tree-ring analysis) resulted in repeated crop failures and eventual famine. The Anasazi were confronted with an additional difficulty: the arrival of bands of Athapascan migrants who for a thousand years or more had been gradually moving south from subarctic regions. These people were the immediate ancestors of the Navajos and the Apaches, and judging by their descendants, they must have been fierce fighters. By the fourteenth and fifteenth centuries, the Athapascans were raiding Anasazi farming communities, taking food, goods, and possibly slaves. The dramatic Anasazi cliff dwellings at Mesa Verde, Colorado, constructed at about this time, may have been built as a defense against these raiders. Gradually the Anasazi abandoned the Four Corners altogether. Their movements have not yet been fully traced, but most of the migrants seem to have resettled in communities along the Rio Grande, joining with local residents to form the Pueblo people of modern times.

Earliest Farmers of the Eastern Woodlands

Archaeologists date the beginning of the farming culture of eastern North America, known as Woodland, from the first appearances of pottery about 3,000 years ago. Woodland was based on a sophisticated way of life that combined gathering and hunting with the cultivation of a few crops such as tobacco and sunflowers. Pipes, which appear at about the same time in archaeological digs, suggest the early local production of tobacco, whose cultivation spread north from the Caribbean region, where it had first been domesticated. Sunflowers were one of a variety of locally domesticated plants. These eastern peoples lived most of the year at permanent community sites, but moved seasonally to take advantage of the resources at different locations.

Even before maize was adapted to these colder northern latitudes, there were movements toward an increasingly settled existence and more complex social organization. The first of these, beginning about 3,000 years ago and extending through the first two centuries C.E., is called the Adena tradition, after an archaeological site near the center of Adena influence on the upper Ohio River. The Adena people lived in permanent villages and built elaborate burial mounds, the most famous of which is the Great Serpent Mound of southern Ohio, the largest effigy earthwork in the world.

Then, in the first to seventh centuries C.E., the Hopewell peoples settled in the Mississippi–Ohio Valley region. The Hopewell people were devoted to *mortuary cults*. Local communities honored the dead through

The Great Serpent Mound in southern Ohio, the shape of an uncoiling snake more than 1,300 feet long, is the largest effigy earthwork in the world. Monumental public works like these suggest the high degree of social organization of the Adena people, one of the first cultures of eastern North America to settle in permanent villages. They were primarily gatherers and hunters, but had begun to farm native crops such as sunflowers, pumpkins, and tobacco.

ceremony, display, and the construction of elaborate burial mounds. Chiefs mobilized an elaborate trade network that included obsidian from the Rocky Mountains, copper from the Great Lakes, mica from the Appalachians, and shells from the Gulf Coast. These materials were used in the production of grave goods that represent a high point of artistic expression.

Both the Adena and the Hopewell traditions flourished and then collapsed, victims perhaps of shifting patterns of climate. Local communities continued to practice their late Archaic subsistence strategies, but lowered productivity made it impossible for them to continue the expensive cultural displays demanded by their mortuary cults. Following the collapse of Hopewell, however, several important innovations appeared in the East. The bow and arrow, developed on the Great Plains, appeared east of the Mississippi about the seventh century, greatly increasing the efficiency of hunting. About the same time, Indian farmers developed a new variety of maize called Northern Flint; it had larger cobs and more kernels, yet matured in a shorter time, and so was perfect for northern temperate latitudes. Also about this time a shift from digging sticks to flint hoes took place, further increasing the productive potential of maize farming. On the basis of these innovations, a powerful new culture known as Mississippian arose, because its influence was greatest in the river valley.

The Mississippians were master maize farmers who lived in permanent villages along the river bottoms. At key sites, clusters of villages grew into dense urban centers with residential neighborhoods and central plazas marked by huge platform mounds. A sophisticated division of labor included artisans, priests, and an elite class of rulers. The most important of these cities was Cahokia on the Mississippi, the urban heart of Mississippian America. Other regional centers with thousands of residents were located on the Arkansas River near Spiro, Oklahoma, on the Black Warrior River at Moundville, Alabama, at Hiwassee Island on the Tennessee, and along the Etowah and Ocmulgee rivers in Georgia.

These centers, linked by a vast water transportation system, became the earliest city-states in North America, hierarchical chiefdoms that extended their control over the farmers of the surrounding countryside. With continued population growth, these cities engaged in vigorous and probably violent competition for the limited space along the river bottoms. It may have been the need for more orderly ways of allocating territories that stimulated the evolution of political hierarchies. The tasks of preventing local conflict, storing large food surpluses, and redistributing foodstuffs from farmers to artisans and elites required a leadership class with the power to command. Mound building and the use of tribute labor in the construction of other public works testified to the power of chiefs, who lived in sumptuous quarters atop the mounds.

Mississippian culture reached its height between the eleventh and thirteenth centuries C.E., the same period in which the Anasazi constructed their desert cities. Both groups adapted to their own environment the technology spreading northward from Mexico. Both developed impressive artistic traditions, and their feats of engineering reflect the beginnings of science. They were complex societies characterized by urbanism, social stratification, craft specialization, and regional trade—except for the absence of a writing system, all the traits of European civilization.

Warfare and Violence

The late thirteenth century marked the end of several hundred years of weather very favorable to maize farming and the beginning of a century and a half of cool, dry conditions. Although the changes in climate in the Mississippi Valley were not as severe as those that devastated the Anasazi of the Southwest, over the long term they significantly lowered the potential of farming to support growing urban populations. Some archaeologists have suggested that one consequence of this extended drought may have been greatly increased violence and social disorder.

Warfare among Indian peoples certainly predated the colonial era. Organized violence was probably rare among hunting bands, who seldom could manage more than a small raid against an enemy. Certain hunting peoples, though, such as the southward-moving Athapascans, must have engaged in systematic raiding of settled farming communities. Warfare was common among farming confederacies fighting to gain additional lands for cultivation. The first Europeans to enter the South described highly organized combat among large tribal armies. The bow and arrow was a deadly weapon of war, and the practice of scalping seems to have originated among warring tribes, who believed one could capture a warrior's spirit by taking his scalp lock. (During the colonial period, Europeans warring with Indians placed bounties on scalps, encouraging an increase in the practice, and it spread widely among the tribes of other regions.) Sculpted images of human sacrifice found at Mississippian sites suggest that the inhabitants practiced a war–sacrifice–cannibalism complex similar to that of Mexico.

The archaeological remains of Cahokia reveal that during the thirteenth and fourteenth centuries the people surrounded the central sections of their city with a heavy log stockade. There must have been a great deal of violent warfare with other nearby communities. Also during this period, numerous towns formed throughout the river valleys of the Mississippi, each based on the domination of farming countrysides by metropolitan centers. Eventually conditions in the upper Mississippi Valley deteriorated so badly that Cahokia and many other sites were abandoned altogether, and as the cities collapsed, people relocated in smaller, decentralized

communities. Among the peoples of the South, however, Mississippian patterns continued into the period of colonization.

North America on the Eve of Colonization

The Indian Population of America

The first Europeans to arrive in North America found a continent populated by more than 350 native societies speaking nearly as many distinct languages.

Most historians believe that the population of America north of Mexico in the early sixteenth century numbered between 7 and 12 million, with another 25 million in the complex societies of the Mexican highlands. At that time the population of the Western Hemisphere as a whole was 60 to 70 million, about the same as Europe's population.

Population density in North America varied widely according to ways of life. Scattered bands populated the Great Basin, the Great Plains, and subarctic regions, while the foraging peoples of the Northwest and California were densely settled because of the high productivity of their fishing and gathering economies. The Southwest, South, and Northeast contained the largest populations, and these were the areas where European explorers, conquerors, and colonists first concentrated their efforts.

The Southwest

The single overwhelming fact of life in the Southwest is aridity. Summer rains average only ten to twenty inches annually, and on much of the dry desert cultivation is impossible. However, a number of rivers flow out of the pine-covered mountain plateaus. Flowing south to the Gulf of Mexico or the Gulf of California—narrow bands of green winding through parched browns and reds—they have made possible irrigation farming along their course.

On the eve of colonization, Indian farmers had been cultivating their southwestern fields for nearly 2,000 years. In the floodplain of the Gila and Salt rivers lived the Pimas and Papagos, descendants of the ancient Hohokam. Working small irrigated fields along the Colorado River, even on the floor of the Grand Canyon, were the Yuman peoples. In their oasis communities, desert farmers cultivated corn, beans, squash, sunflowers, and cotton, which they traded

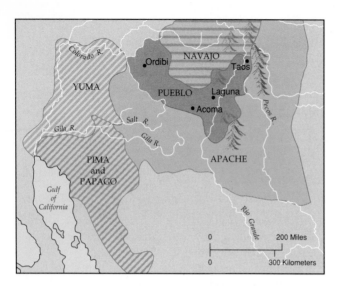

Southwestern Indian Groups on the Eve of Colonization

The Southwest was populated by desert farmers such as the Pimas, Papagos, Yumans, and Pueblos, as well as by nomadic hunters and raiders such as the Apaches and Navajos.

throughout the Southwest. Often described as individualists, desert farmers lived in dispersed settlements that the Spanish called *rancherias,* their dwellings separated by as much as a mile. That way, say the Pimas, people avoid getting on each other's nerves. Rancherias were governed by councils of adult men whose decisions required unanimous consent, although a headman was chosen to manage the irrigation works. Ceremonialism focused appropriately on rainmaking; one ritual required everyone to drink cactus wine until thoroughly drunk, a state of purification that was thought to bring rain.

East of the Grand Canyon lived the Pueblo peoples, named by the Spanish for their unique dwellings of stacked, interconnected apartments. As we have seen, this building style originated with the Anasazi, who during the great population relocations of the fourteenth century joined with other indigenous groups to form the numerous Pueblo villages. (Today the Pueblos occupy the oldest continuously occupied towns in the United States.) Although speaking several languages, the Pueblos had a great deal in common, most notably their commitment to communal village life. A strict communal code of behavior that regulated personal conduct was enforced by a maze of matrilineal clans and secret religious societies; unique combinations of these clans and societies formed the governing systems of different Pueblo villages. Seasonal public ceremonies in the

village squares included singing and chanting, dancing, colorful impersonations of the ancestral spirits called *kachinas,* and the comic antics of clowns who mimicked in slapstick style those who did not conform to the communal ideal.

The Athapascans, more recent immigrants, also lived in the arid deserts and mountains. They hunted and foraged, traded meat and medicinal herbs with farmers, and often raided and plundered these same villages and rancherias. Gradually, some of the Athapascan people surrounding the Pueblo villages adopted their neighbors' farming and handicraft skills; these people became known as the Navajos. Others, more heavily influenced by the hunting and gathering traditions of the Great Basin and Great Plains, continued their hunting and raiding ways, and were given the name Apaches.

The South

The South enjoys a mild, moist climate with short winters and long summers, ideal for farming. From the Atlantic and Gulf coasts, a broad fertile plain extends inland to the Piedmont, a plateau separating the coastal plains from the Appalachian Mountains. The transition between plateau and coastal plain is marked by the Fall Line, an area of rapids and waterfalls on the descending rivers. The upper courses of the waterways originating in the Appalachian highlands offered ample rich bottom land for farming. The extensive forests, mostly of yellow pine, offered abundant animal resources. In the sixteenth century, large populations of Indian peoples farmed this rich land, fishing or hunting local fauna to supplement their diets. They lived in communities ranging from villages of twenty or so dwellings to large towns of a thousand or more inhabitants.

Mississippian cultural patterns continued among the peoples of the South. They were organized into confederacies of farming towns, the most powerful living along the Gulf coast and the river bottoms. Because most of these groups were quickly decimated in the first years of colonization, they are poorly documented. We know the most about the Natchez, farmers of the rich floodplains of the lower Mississippi delta who survived into the eighteenth century before being destroyed in a war with the French. Overseeing the Natchez was a ruler known as the Great Sun, who lived in royal splendor on a ceremonial mound in his village capital. When out among his subjects he was carried on a litter, the path before him swept by his retinue of servants and wives. Natchez society was class-based. Noble families were represented on the Great Sun's council of advisers and

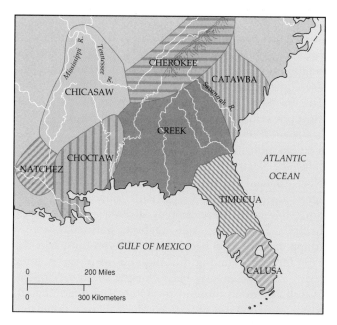

Southern Indian Groups on the Eve of Colonization

On the eve of colonization the Indian societies of the South shared many traits of the complex Mississippian farming culture.

appointed village peace and war chiefs. Persistent territorial conflict with other confederacies elevated warfare to an honored status among the Natchez, and public torture and human sacrifice of enemies were common. The Natchez give us our best glimpse at what life would have been like in the community of Cahokia.

Tribes in Florida formed central towns that proved highly vulnerable to conquest. The looser confederacies of the interior were considerably more resilient. Among the most prominent of these were the Choctaws in present-day Mississippi and Alabama, the Chickasaws in western Tennessee, and the Creeks in Georgia, each confederacy having several dozen towns. On the mountain plateaus lived the Cherokees, the single largest confederacy, which included more than sixty towns. Farming was somewhat less important in the highlands than along the coast, hunting somewhat more so. There were no ruling classes or kings, and leaders included women as well as men. Most peoples reckoned their descent matrilineally (back through generations of mothers), and after marriage husbands left the homes of their mothers to reside with the families of their wives. Women controlled household and village life, and were influential in the matrilineal clans that linked communities together. Councils of elderly men governed the confederacies, but were joined by

clan matrons for annual meetings at the central council house. These gatherings could last days or even weeks because everyone, male or female, was given the opportunity to speak.

The peoples of the South farmed the same crops, hunted in the same kind of piney woods, and lived in similar villages. They celebrated a common round of agricultural festivals that brought clans together from surrounding communities. At the harvest festival, for example, people thoroughly cleaned their homes and villages. They fasted and purified themselves by consuming the "black drink," a libation that induced visions. They extinguished the old fires and lit new ones, then celebrated the new crop of sweet corn with dancing and other festivities. During the following days, villages, clans, and groups of men and women competed against each other in the ancient stick-and-ball game that the French named lacrosse; in the evenings men and women played chunkey, a gambling game. The peoples of the South had much in common, but their tribal confederacies were often at war with one another.

The Northeast

The Northeast, the colder sector of the eastern woodlands, has a varied geography of coastal plains and mountain highlands, great rivers, lakes, and valleys. After C.E. 500, cultivation became the main support of the Indian economy in those places where the growing season was long enough to bring a crop of corn to maturity. In such areas of the Northeast—along the coasts and in the river valleys—the populations of Indian peoples were large and dense.

The Iroquois of present-day Ontario and upstate New York have lived in the region for at least 4,500 years. They were among the first northeastern peoples to adopt cultivation. The archaeological evidence suggests that as they shifted from primary reliance on fishing and hunting to maize farming, they relocated their villages from river bottoms to hilltops. There Iroquois women produced crops of corn, beans, squash, and sunflowers sufficient to support fifty *longhouses,* each occupied by a large matrilineal extended family. Some of those houses were truly long; archaeologists have excavated the foundations of some that extended 400 feet and would have housed dozens of families. Typically, these villages were surrounded by substantial palisades, clear evidence of intergroup conflict and warfare.

Population growth and the resulting intensification of farming in Iroquoia stimulated the development of chiefdoms there as elsewhere. By the fifteenth century

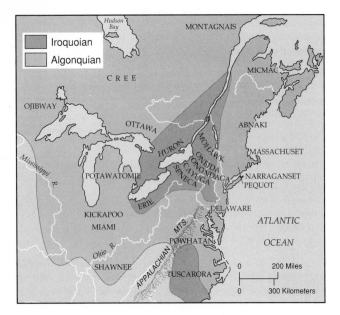

Northeastern Indian Groups on the Eve of Colonization

The Indians of the Northeast were mostly village peoples. In the fifteenth century five Iroquois groups—the Mohawks, Oneidas, Onondagas, Cayugas, and Senecas—joined togehter to form the Iroquois Five Nation Confederacy.

several centers of population, each in a separate watershed, had coalesced from east to west across upstate New York. These were the five Iroquois chiefdoms or nations: the Mohawks, Oneidas, Onondagas, Cayugas, and Senecas. Iroquois oral histories collected during the nineteenth century recall this as a period of persistent violence, possibly the consequence of conflicts over territory.

Historians believe that the Iroquois founded a confederacy to control this violence. The confederacy outlawed warfare among the member nations and established regulated forms of gift exchange and payment to replace revenge. Iroquois oral history refers to the founder of the confederacy, Chief Deganawida the lawgiver, as "blocking out the sun" as a demonstration of his powers, suggesting that these events might have taken place during the full solar eclipse that was visible in the Northeast in 1451. As a model, the confederacy used the powerful metaphor of the longhouse; each nation, it was said, occupied a separate hearth but acknowledged descent from a common mother. As in the longhouse, women played important roles in choosing male leaders who would represent their lineages and

chiefdom on the Iroquois council. The confederacy suppressed violence among its members, but did not hesitate to encourage war against outside groups such as the neighboring Huron or the Erie, who constructed defensive confederacies of their own at about the same time. The Iroquois Confederacy would become one of the most powerful forces during the colonial period.

The other major language group of the Northeast was Algonquian, which included at least fifty distinct cultures. North of the Great Lakes and in northern New England the Algonquians were hunters and foragers, organized into bands with loose ethnic affiliations. Several of these peoples, including the Micmacs, Crees, Montagnais, and Ojibwas (also known as Chippewas), would become the first producers in the early fur trade. Among the Algonquians of the Atlantic coast, from present-day Massachusetts south to Virginia, as well as among those in the Ohio Valley, farming led to the development of settlements as densely populated as those of the Iroquois. In contrast with the Iroquois, most of the Algonquians were patrilineal. They lived in less extensive dwellings in smaller villages, often lacking palisade fortifications. Local communities were fairly autonomous, but central confederacies nevertheless took shape during the fifteenth and sixteenth centuries. Among these groupings were the tribes or nations of the early colonial era, including the Massachusets, Narragansets, and Pequots of New England, the Delawares and the peoples of Powhatan's confederacy on the mid-Atlantic coast, and the Shawnees, Miamis, Kickapoos, and Potawatomis of the Ohio Valley.

Conclusion

The history of the Indian peoples of North America was linked to the physical development of the continent, and in response to their various regional environments they created ways of life that continued to shape North America during the colonial era. Exaggerated tales of fabulous wealth in the Pueblo towns lured the Spanish conquistadors northward. Colonists remained to farm the land, something they could not have done without learning much from the Pueblos, the Pimas, and the Papagos about the arid Southwest. The first European colonists in the South depended on the Indians to supply them with rich harvests from their extensive fields, the legacy of the Mississippian period of North American history. This mild and fertile region became the prime location for the first productive plantation economy of the English colonies, which grew Indian tobacco for export. Along the northeast coast, English colonists settled the former village sites of Algonquians, planting Indian corn in the same fields and fishing in the same waters. In short, it is impossible to imagine European colonial societies without the prior existence of Indian communities.

"Columbus did not discover a new world," wrote historian J. H. Perry. "He established contact between two worlds, both already old." Likewise, the world of North America did not suddenly change with the arrival of Europeans in the sixteenth century. In the first encounters, Indian peoples were generally wary, but curious and ready to trade. The European colonists who came to settle faced thousands of Indian communities with deep roots and vibrant traditions. It would be more than two centuries before colonists outnumbered Indians. Indian communities viewed these colonists as invaders, and called on their traditions and their gods in defending their communal homelands.

CHRONOLOGY

25,000 B.C.E.	Oldest fossil evidence of humans in the Americas
13,000 B.C.E.	Global warming trend begins
10,000 B.C.E.	Clovis technology
9000 B.C.E.	Extinction of big-game animals
8000 B.C.E.	Beginning of the Archaic period
7000 B.C.E.	First cultivation of plants in the Mexican highlands
5000 B.C.E.	Athapascan migrations to America begin
4000 B.C.E.	First settled communities along the Pacific coast
3000 B.C.E.	Inupiat and Aleut migrations begin
2000 B.C.E.	Mexican crops introduced into the Southwest
1000 B.C.E.	Beginning of Mogollon and Adena cultures
	First urban communities in Mexico

250 B.C.E.	Hohokams found the village of Snaketown
500 C.E.	High point of Hopewell culture
650	Bow and arrow, flint hoes, and corn in the Northeast
1000	Tobacco in use throughout North America
1150	Founding of Hopi village of Oraibi, oldest continuously occupied town in the United States
1200	High point of Mississippian and Anasazi cultures
1276	Severe drought begins in the Southwest
1300	Arrival of Athapascans in the Southwest
1451	Founding of Iroquois Confederacy

Review Questions

1. List the evidence for the hypothesis that the Americas were settled by migrants from Asia.
2. Discuss the impact of environmental change and human hunting on the big-game populations of North America.
3. Review the principal regions of the North American continent and the human adaptations that made social life possible in each of them.
4. Define the concept of forest efficiency. How does it help to illuminate the major development of the Archaic period?
5. Why did the development of farming lead to in-

creasing social complexity? Discuss the reasons why organized political activity began in farming societies.

6. What were the hunting and agrarian traditions? In what ways did the religious beliefs of Indian peoples reflect their environmental adaptations?

7. What factors led to the organization of the Iroquois Confederacy?

Recommended Reading

BRIAN M. FAGAN, *The Great Journey: The Peopling of Ancient America* (1987). An account of the Asian migration to the Americas, told through the study of archaeology. For new discoveries, which keep pushing the dating further back, see recent issues of *National Geographic* and *Scientific American*.

STUART J. FIEDEL, *Prehistory of the Americas* (1987). The best introduction for the nonspecialist, covering the first migrations, the development of technologies, and the spread of farming.

ALVIN M. JOSEPHY JR., editor, *America in 1492* (1992). Important essays by the leading scholars of the North American Indian experience. Includes a beautiful collection of illustrations and maps as well as an excellent bibliography.

ALVIN M. JOSEPHY JR., *500 Nations: An Illustrated History of North American Indians* (1995). Published to accompany a popular television series, this magnificent volume includes historic illustrations as well as facinating computer re-creations of the pre-European human landscape of America.

ALICE B. KEHOE, *North American Indians: A Comprehensive Account* (1992). The best general anthropological survey of the history and culture of the Indians of North America. Organized by culture areas, the new edition covers all the peoples of the continent and includes the most recent scholarship.

ROBERT SILVERBERG, *Mound Builders of Ancient America: The Archaeology of a Myth* (1968). A brilliant history of opinion and theory about the mound builders, combined with a review of the best archaeological evidence available at the time.

WILLIAM C. STURTEVANT, general editor, *Handbook of North American Indians,* 20 vols. (1978–). The most comprehensive collection of the best current scholarship. When complete, there will be a volume for each of the culture regions of North America; volumes on origins, Indian–white relations, languages, and art; a biographical dictionary; and a general index.

RUSSELL THORNTON, *American Indian Holocaust and Survival: A Population History Since 1492* (1987). The best introduction to the historical demography of North America. In a field of great controversy, it provides a judicious review of all the evidence.

CARL WALDMAN, *Atlas of the North American Indian* (1985). A collection of essential maps, from the first migrations to the present. More than simply an atlas, however, it is a comprehensive introduction to the Indian history of North America. Contains an excellent bibliography.

2 WHEN WORLDS COLLIDE, 1492–1590

AMERICAN COMMUNITIES

THE ENGLISH AND THE ALGONQUIANS AT ROANOKE

It was late August 1590 when English ships sailed through Hatteras Inlet into Pamlico Sound, off the coast of present-day North Carolina, and made their way north through rough seas to Roanoke Island. Governor John White had returned to relieve the first English community transplanted to the shores of North America. That group included some sixty-five single men and twenty families, including White's daughter, son-in-law, and granddaughter. The last of these, Virginia Dare, was the first English baby born in America.

Anxiously he went ashore to the little fortified settlement, but "we found the houses taken down" with many possessions "spoiled and scattered about." Suddenly he spied near the entrance to the fort some writing on a tree trunk: "in fair capital letters was graven CROATOAN." White had instructed the colonists to leave such a message if they had to move, and, if there was trouble, to mark it with a cross. White noted with relief that this carving was "without any cross or sign of distress." Croatoan was a friendly Indian village fifty miles south. Sure that his people awaited him there, White left the island for his ship.

The Roanoke settlement was sponsored by Walter Raleigh, a wealthy adventurer who sought profit and prestige by planting an English colony in the New World. His first expedition to the area, in 1584, reported that the coastal region was densely populated by a "very handsome and goodly people." These Indians, the most southerly of the Algonquian coastal peoples, enjoyed a prosperous livelihood farming, fishing, and hunting from their small villages of one or two dozen longhouses. At "an island which they called Roanoke," the English were "entertained with all love and kindness" by a chief named Wingina. Wingina was the "big man" of several surrounding villages, and he viewed these visitors as potential allies in his struggle to extend his authority over still others. So when the English asked his permission to establish a settlement on the island, he readily granted it. Wingina sent two of his own men back with them to England, to make preparations for the colonizing expedition.

Raleigh's first colony in this land, which he established in 1585 and christened Virginia in honor of Elizabeth I, the virgin queen, was a dismal failure. Manteo and Wanchese, the Indian emissaries, were extremely helpful in preparing the "scientific" component of the mission, led by Thomas Harriot, a scholar from Oxford University, and John White, a trained artist. These four men worked at learning one another's language, and there seems to have been a good deal of mutual respect among them. But when the two Indians returned with the English to Roanoke late in the summer of 1585, they had very different messages for their people. Manteo, from the village of Croatoan, was fascinated by the English, and argued that their technology and weaponry would make them powerful allies. Wanchese of Roanoke, however, offered disturbing reports of the savage inequalities of English society, and warned of the brutality of the soldiers who composed the majority of the colonists. Indeed, Raleigh hoped to establish a lucrative trade in furs and a flourishing plantation agriculture, but most of all, he and the other investors in the expedition hoped to discover gold or silver. In any case, subjecting the Indians was essential, for they were to become the serfs of the English masters.

A colony such as this one—some 100 soldiers and adventurers with plunder foremost in their minds—was incapable of supporting itself. After building a rough fort on the island, the English went to Wingina for supplies of food. With the harvest in the storage pits, with fish running in the streams and game flocking the woods, Wingina did the hospitable thing. After all, it was, the duty of a chief to distribute presents and incur obligations. But as fall turned to winter and the stores declined, the constant English demands began to tax the resources of the Indians. Rather than hunt or fish, the colonists were out exploring for precious metals. They attacked several outlying villages, burned longhouses and cornfields, and kidnapped women. By the spring—traditionally the "starving season" for the Indians, before the crops were up and the game fat—Wingina and his people had had enough. But the English caught wind of the Indians' rising hostility, and in May 1586 they surprised the Roanoke villagers, killing several of the leading men and beheading Wingina. Soon thereafter the colonists returned to England, leaving a legacy of violence and hatred in their wake.

John White and Thomas Harriot, who had spent their time exploring the physical and human world of the coast and recording their findings in notes and sketches, were appalled by this turn of events. To Raleigh, Harriot

argued that the attack came "upon causes that on our part might easily enough have been borne." White put forth a new plan for a colony of real settlers, a group of English families who could form a community that could live in association with the Indians. "There is good hope," wrote Harriot, that "through discreet dealing" the Indians may "honor, obey, fear and love us." Harriot and White clearly thought English civilization was superior to the civilization of the Indians, but their vision differed from that of the plunderers.

In 1587 Raleigh arranged for White to return as governor of a new family colony to be planted on the Chesapeake, north of Roanoke. When White and the other settlers arrived at Roanoke to pick up some heavy equipment left there, however, the ship's captain abandoned them so that he might be free to attack rich Spanish ships in the Caribbean. Despite their good intentions, these colonists had to live with the reputation left by the former expedition. Within a month one of their number was shot full of arrows as he fished for crabs. The attackers were led by Wanchese, who after Wingina's death became the most militant opponent of the English among the Roanoke Indians. Manteo, baptized a Christian, remained White's friend and supporter.

White retaliated by attacking Wanchese's village, but the Indians fled into the forest with few casualties. Knowing that their entire mission hung in the balance, but without a ship large enough to carry them all back to England, the colonists begged White to sail home in the one small seaworthy ship they had, to press Raleigh for support. With great reluctance he left, arriving to find war threatening between England and Spain. Three years of frustrating delay passed before White was able to return to Roanoke for the third time with supplies and additional men in August of 1590.

Anxious to speed southward to Croatoan, White and his men reboarded their ship. But heavy seas prevented them from reaching the village. Eventually tossed home on a stormy sea, White never returned to America. The English settlers of Roanoke became known as the Lost Colony, their disappearance and ultimate fate one of the enduring mysteries of colonial history.

Today many historians believe that those English men and women probably went with Manteo to Croatoan, and lived out the rest of their lives beside the Algonquian villagers. When Virginia Dare and the other children grew up, they must have married into Indian families—an ironic end to Raleigh's vision of conquest.

A French peasant labors in the field before a spectacular Catholic cathedral in a page taken from the illuminated manuscript Tres Riches Heures, *made in the fifteenth century for the Duc de Berry. In 1580 essayist Montaigne talked with several American Indians at the French court who "noticed among us some men gorged to the full with things of every sort while their other halves were beggars at their doors, emaciated with hunger and poverty," and "found it strange that these poverty-striken halves should suffer such injustice, and that they did not take the others by the throat or set fire to their houses."*

KEY TOPICS

♦ **The European background of American colonization**

♦ **Creation of the Spanish New World empire and its first extensions to North America**

♦ **The large-scale intercontinental exchange of peoples, crops, animals, and diseases**

♦ **The French role in the beginnings of the North American fur trade**

♦ **England's first overseas colonies in America**

The Expansion of Europe

There may have been many unrecorded contacts between the peoples of America and the Old World before the fifteenth century. Archaeological excavations at L'Anse aux Meadows on the fogbound Newfoundland coast provide evidence for a Norse landing in North America in the tenth or eleventh century. But the contact with the Americas established in 1492 by Christopher Columbus had earthshaking consequences. Within a generation of Columbus's voyage, continental exchanges of peoples, crops, animals, and germs had reshaped the Atlantic world. The key to understanding these remarkable events is the transformation of Europe during the several centuries preceding the voyage of Columbus.

European Communities

Western Europe was an agricultural society, the majority of its people peasant farmers. Farming and livestock raising had been practiced in Europe for thousands of years, but great advances in farming technology took place during the late Middle Ages. The increased supply of food helped the population of western Europe nearly triple between the eleventh and fourteenth centuries.

Most Europeans were village people, living in family households. Men performed the basic field work; women were responsible for child care, livestock, and food preparation. In the European pattern, daughters usually left the home and village of their families to live among their husband's people. Women were furnished with dowries, but generally excluded from inheritance. Divorce was almost unknown.

Europe was a world of social contrasts. Most land was owned by a powerful group of landlords who claimed a disproportionate share of wealth and power. These feudal lords commanded labor service from peasants and tribute in the form of crops. The landlords were the main beneficiaries of medieval economic expansion, accumulating great estates and building castles. A small class of freehold farmers also benefited from the rebuilding of Europe, but the majority of peasants experienced little improvement in their standard of living.

Europeans were Christians, united under the authority of the Roman Catholic Church, whose complex organization spanned thousands of local communities with a hierarchy that extended from parish priests all the way to the pope in Rome. At the core of Christian belief was a set of communal values: love of God the father, loving treatment of neighbors, and the fellowship of all believers. Yet the Catholic Church itself was one of the most powerful landowners in Europe, and it devoted its considerable resources to awe-inspiring display rather than the amelioration of poverty and suffering. It insisted on its dogmas and actively persecuted heretics, nonbelievers, and believers in older, "pagan" religions, who were branded "witches." The church legitimized the power relationships of Europe and counseled the poor and downtrodden to place their hopes in heavenly rewards.

For the great majority of Europeans, living conditions were harsh. Most rural people survived on bread and porridge, supplemented with seasonal vegetables and an occasional piece of meat or fish. Infectious diseases abounded; perhaps a third of all children died before their fifth birthday, and only half the population reached adulthood. Famines periodically ravaged the countryside. A widespread epidemic of bubonic plague, known as the "Black Death," swept in from Asia and wiped out a third of Europe's population between 1347 and 1353.

By 1500 Europe's agricultural economy, strengthened by the technological breakthroughs of the Middle Ages, had recovered, and its population had nearly returned to its former peak of about 30 million. Although Europe's social structure was hierarchical and authoritarian, its agricultural systems had the capacity for far greater growth than the farming economy of the Americas.

Western Europe in the Fifteenth Century

By the middle of the century, the monarchs of western Europe had unified their realms and begun to build royal bureaucracies and standing armies and navies. These states sponsored the voyages that inaugurated the era of European colonization.

The Merchant Class and the Renaissance

The economic growth of the late Middle Ages was accompanied by the expansion of commerce, especially trade in basic goods such as cereals and timber, minerals and salt, wine, fish, and wool. Commercial expansion stimulated the growth of markets and towns. The heart of this dynamic European commercialism lay in the city-states of Italy.

During the late Middle Ages, the cities of Venice, Genoa, and Pisa launched armed, commercial fleets that seized control of trade in the Mediterranean. Their merchants became the principal outfitters of the Crusades, a series of great military expeditions promoted by the Catholic Church to recover Palestine from the Muslims. The conquest of the Holy Land by Crusaders at the end of the eleventh century delivered into the hands of the Italian merchants the silk and spice trades of Asia. Tropical spices—cloves, cinnamon, nutmeg, and pepper—were in great demand, for they made the European diet far less monotonous for the lords who could afford them. Asian civilization also supplied a number of technical innovations that further propelled European economic growth, including the compass, gunpowder, and the art of printing with movable type—"the three greatest inventions known to man," in the opinion of sixteenth-century English philosopher Francis Bacon.

Contact with Muslim civilization allowed access to the most important ancient texts lost in Europe but preserved in the great Muslim libraries of Alexandria (Egypt) and Baghdad (in what is now Iraq). A revival of interest in classical antiquity sparked the period of intellectual and artistic flowering during the fourteenth and fifteenth centuries known as the Renaissance. The revolution in publishing (made possible by the perfection of the printing press and movable type) helped to spread this movement throughout the elite circles of Europe.

In art, as in literature and philosophy, the Renaissance celebrated human possibility. The Gothic style of medieval cathedrals, whose soaring forms were intended to take human thoughts heavenward, gradually gave way to the use of measured classical styles, encouraging rational reflection. In painting and sculpture there was a new focus on the human body. Artists modeled muscles with light and shadow to produce heroic images of men and women. These were aspects of what became known as *humanism,* a revolt against religious authority in which the secular took precedence over the purely religious. The Renaissance outlook was a critical component of the spirit that motivated the exploration of the Americas.

The New Monarchies

The Renaissance flowered amid the ruins of the plague-ridden fourteenth century. Famine and disease led to violence, as groups fought for shares of a shrinking economy. In Flanders during the 1320s, peasants rose against both nobility and church, beginning a series of rebellions that culminated in the great English Peasants' Revolt of 1381. Meanwhile, civil and international warfare among the nobility decimated the landed classes and greatly reduced their power, and the Catholic Church was seriously weakened by an internal struggle between French and Italian factions.

During this period of social and political chaos, the monarchs of Western Europe emerged as the new centers of power, building their legitimacy by promising internal order as they unified their realms. They began the construction of royal bureaucracies and standing armies and navies. In many cases, these new monarchs found support among the merchant class, which in return sought lucrative royal contracts and trading monopolies.

The alliance between commercial interests and the new states was another important development that prepared the way for European expansion.

Portuguese Explorations

Portugal, a narrow land along the western coast of the Iberian Peninsula with a long tradition of seafaring, became the first of these new kingdoms to explore distant lands. Lisbon, the principal port on the sea route between the Mediterranean and northwestern Europe, was a bustling, cosmopolitan city with large enclaves of Italian merchants. By 1385 local merchants had grown powerful enough to place their own favorite, Joao I, on the throne, and he laid ambitious plans to establish a Portugese trading empire.

This ship, thought to be similar to Columbus's Niña, *is a caravel, a type of vessel developed by the naval experts at Henry the Navigator's institute at Sagres Point, in Portugal. To the traditional square-rigged Mediterranean ship, they added the "lanteen" sail of the Arabs, which permitted much greater maneuverability. Other Asian improvements, such as the stern-post rudder and multiple masting, allowed caravels to travel farther and faster than any earlier ships, and made possible the invasion of America.*

A central figure in this development was the son of the king, Prince Henry, known to later generations as the Navigator. In the spirit of Renaissance learning, he established an academy of eminent geographers, instrument makers, shipbuilders, and seamen at his institute on the southwestern tip of Portugal. By the mid-fifteenth century, as a result of their efforts, all educated Europeans knew that the earth was round.

Using faster and better-handling ships called caravels, the Portuguese plied the Atlantic coast of northwestern Africa for direct access to the lucrative gold and slave trades of that continent. By the time of Prince Henry's death in 1460, they had colonized the Atlantic islands of the Azores and the Madeiras and founded bases along the west African Gold Coast. In 1488 Portuguese captain Bartholomew Diaz rounded the southern tip of the continent, and ten years later Vasco da Gama, with the aid of Arab pilots, reached India. The Portuguese eventually erected strategic trading forts along the coasts of Africa, India, and China, the first and longest-lasting outposts of European world colonization, and gained control of much of the Asian spice trade. Most important for the history of the Americas, they established the Atlantic slave trade. (For a full discussion of slavery, see Chapter 4.)

Columbus Reaches the Americas

While working as a seafaring merchant, Christopher Columbus, a young Genoan, developed the idea of opening a new route to Asia by sailing west across the ocean. Such a venture would require royal backing, but when he approached the various monarchs of Europe with his idea, their advisers laughed at his geographic ignorance, pointing out that his calculation of the distance to Asia was much too short. They were right, Columbus was wrong, but it turned out to be an error of monumental good fortune.

Columbus finally sold his idea to the monarchs of Castile and Aragon, Isabella and Ferdinand. These two had just completed the *Reconquista,* a centuries-long struggle between Catholics and Muslims that finally ended Muslim rule in Iberia. Now they became interested in opening lucrative trade routes with Asia. Columbus's expedition symbolized the Spanish monarchs' hopes for trade and conquest.

His ships left Spain in August of 1492, pushed west across the Atlantic by the prevailing trade winds. They arrived at a site somewhere in the Bahamas, now thought by many to be Samana Cay. However, Columbus believed he was somewhere near the Asian main-

land. He explored the northern coasts of Cuba and Hispaniola before heading home, fortuitously catching the westerly winds that blow from the American coast toward Europe north of the tropics. One of Columbus's most important contributions was the discovery of the clockwise circulation of the Atlantic winds and currents that would carry thousands of European ships back and forth to the Americas.

Leading Columbus's triumphal procession to the royal court were a number of kidnapped Taino Indians from the Bahamas, dressed in bright feathers with ornaments of gold. The natives, Columbus noted, were "of a very acute intelligence," but had "no iron or steel weapons." A conflict between the Tainos and several armed Spaniards had ended quickly with the deaths of two natives. "Should your majesties command it," Columbus announced, "all the inhabitants could be made slaves." Moreover, he reported that "there are many spices and great mines of gold and of other metals." In fact, none of the spices familiar to Europeans grew in the Caribbean and there were only small quantities of precious metals in the riverbeds of the islands. But the sight of the little gold ornaments worn by the Indians had infected Columbus with gold fever. On his return, he left a small force behind in a rough fort on Hispaniola—the first European foothold in the Americas.

The monarchs, enthusiastic about Columbus's report, financed a convoy of ships in late 1493 to begin the colonization of the islands. On his return to Hispaniola, Columbus found his fort in ruins and his men killed by Indians who had lost patience with continuing Spanish outrages. Columbus destroyed the nearby native villages, enslaving the Tainos and demanding tribute in gold. He sent boatloads of slaves back to Spain, but most soon sickened and died, and the supply of gold quickly ran out. By the time of Columbus's third voyage in 1500, the Spanish monarchs had become so dissatisfied with these results that they ordered Columbus home in leg irons.

Columbus made two additional trips to the Caribbean, both characterized by the same violent slave raiding and obsessive searching for gold. He died in Spain in 1506, still convinced that he had opened the way to Asia. This belief persisted among many Europeans well into the sixteenth century. But others had already begun to see the discoveries from a different perspective. Amerigo Vespucci of Florence, who voyaged to the Caribbean in 1499, was the first European to describe the lands as *Mundus Novus,* a New World. When European geographers finally named these continents in the sixteenth century, they called them America, after Vespucci.

The Spanish in the Americas

A century after Columbus's death, before the English had planted a single New World colony of their own, the Spanish had created a huge and wealthy empire in the Americas. In theory, all law and policy for the empire came from Spain; in practice, the isolation of the settlements led to a good deal of local autonomy. The Spanish created a caste system, in which a small minority of settlers and their offspring controlled the lives and labor of millions of Indian and African workers. But it was also a society in which colonists, Indians, and Africans mixed to form a new people.

The Invasion of America

The first stages of the Spanish invasion of America included frightful violence. Armies marched across the Caribbean islands, plundering villages, slaughtering men, and capturing women. Columbus and his successors established an institution known as the *encomienda*, in which Indians were compelled to labor in the service of Spanish lords. Rather than work, one conquistador noted, many Indians took poison, "and others hanged themselves." Faced with labor shortages, slavers raided the Bahamas, and soon had entirely depopulated them. The depletion of gold on Hispaniola led to the invasion of the islands of Puerto Rico and Jamaica in 1508, then Cuba in 1511. Meanwhile, rumors of wealthy societies to the west led to scores of probing expeditions. The Spanish invasion of Central America began in 1511, and two years later Vasco Núñez de Balboa crossed the Isthmus of Panama to the "South Sea," the Pacific Ocean. In 1517 Spaniards landed on the coast of Mexico, and within a year they had made contact with the Aztec empire.

The Aztecs had migrated to the Valley of Mexico from the deserts of the American Southwest in the thirteenth century, just as the Toltec empire was in the last stage of collapse. (For a discussion of the development of Mexico, see Chapter 1.) The warlike Aztecs settled the marshy lake district of the valley and built the city of Tenochtitlán. By the early fifteenth century they had come to dominate the peoples of the highlands, in the process building a powerful state. Tribute flowed into Tenochtitlán from all over Mexico and Central America. In public rituals designed to appease their gods, Aztec priests brutally sacrificed captives atop the grand pyramids. By 1519 the population of the Aztec capital numbered approximately 300,000; the city was five times the size of the largest city in Spain.

Hernán Cortés, a veteran of the conquest of Cuba, landed on the Mexican coast with armed troops in 1519. Within two years he overthrew the Aztec empire, a spectacular military accomplishment that has no parallel in the annals of conquest. The Spanish had superior arms and horses. The Indians found the latter terrifying, mistaking mounted men for four-legged monsters. But these were not the principal causes of the Spanish success. Aztec resistance was impeded by a rigid bureaucracy that was fatally late in responding to the crisis, and the resentments of the many native peoples who lived under Aztec oppression, forging Spanish–Indian alliances that would become a model for the subsequent European colonization of the Americas. In the aftermath of conquest, the Spanish unmercifully plundered Aztec society, providing the Catholic monarchs with wealth beyond their wildest imagining. Later, the discovery of rich silver mines and the exploitation of Mexican labor through the encomienda system turned Spain into the mightiest state in Europe.

The Destruction of the Indies

The Indian peoples of the Americas resisted Spanish conquest, but most proved a poor match for mounted warriors with steel swords and vicious bloodhounds. However, the record of the conquest includes many brave Indian leaders and thousands of martyrs. The Carib people (from whom the Caribbean takes its name) successfully defended the outermost islands until the end of the sixteenth century, and in the arid lands of northern Mexico the nomadic tribes known collectively as the Chichimecs proved equally difficult to subdue.

Some Europeans protested the horrors of the conquest. Principal among them was Bartolomé de las Casas, a Spanish Catholic priest who had participated in the plunder of Cuba in 1511, but who several years later suffered a crisis of conscience and began to denounce the conquest. Long before the world recognized the concept of universal human rights, Las Casas was proclaiming that "the entire human race is one," which earned him a reputation as one of the towering moral figures in the early history of the Americas. Las Casas had powerful supporters at court who made repeated but unsuccessful attempts to reform the treatment of Indians.

In his brilliant history of the conquest, *The Destruction of the Indies* (1552), Las Casas blamed the Spanish

"The Cruelties used by the Spaniards on the Indians," from a 1599 English edition of The Destruction of the Indies *by Bartolomé de las Casas. Las Casas passionately denounced the Spanish conquest and defended the rights of the Indians. These images were copied from a series of engravings produced by Theodore de Bry that accompanied Las Casas's original edition.*

for the use of cruelties on the Indians that resulted in millions of deaths—in effect, genocide. Translated into several languages and widely circulated throughout Europe, Las Casas's book was used by other European powers to condemn Spain as a means of covering up their own dismal colonial records. Although later scholars disputed Las Casas's estimates of huge population losses, recent demographic studies suggest that the native people of Hispaniola numbered in the hundreds of thousands when Columbus arrived, and fifty years later they were reduced to a few hundred. In Mexico the 1519 population of 25 million plummeted to only a million a century later.

Las Casas was incorrect, however, in attributing most of these losses to warfare. To be sure, thousands of lives were lost in battle, but these deaths were but a small proportion of the overall population decline. Thousands more starved because their economies were destroyed or their food stores taken by conquering armies. Even more important, native birth rates fell drastically after the conquest. Indian women were so "worn out with work," one Spaniard wrote, that they avoided conception, induced abortion, and even "killed their children with their own hands so that they shall not have to endure the same hardships."

Epidemic disease was the primary factor in the drastic reduction of the native population. Pre-Columbian America seems to have had no virulent epidemic diseases, so Indian peoples lacked the antibodies necessary to protect them from European germs and viruses. A shipload of colonists carried smallpox to Hispaniola in 1516, causing an epidemic in the Caribbean that crossed into Mexico by 1520, eventually spreading along the trading network through both continents. In 1524 smallpox devastated Peru, strategically weakening the Inca empire eight years before it was conquered by Spanish conquistador Francisco Pizarro. Spanish chroniclers wrote that this single epidemic killed half the native Americans it touched. Disease was the secret weapon of the Spanish, and it helps explain their extraordinary success in the conquest.

It is possible that the New World sent one disease—syphilis—back across the Atlantic. The first recorded epidemic of syphilis in Europe took place in Spain in 1493, and many historians think it may have been carried home by the sailors on Columbus's ships. By 1495 the disease was spreading rapidly among Europe's armies, and by the sixteenth century it had found its way to Asia and Africa. The passage of diseases between the Old and New Worlds was one part of the large-scale continental exchange that marks the beginning of the modern era of world history.

Intercontinental Exchange

The most obvious exchange was the vast influx into Europe of the precious metals plundered from the Aztec and Incan empires of the New World. Most of the gold

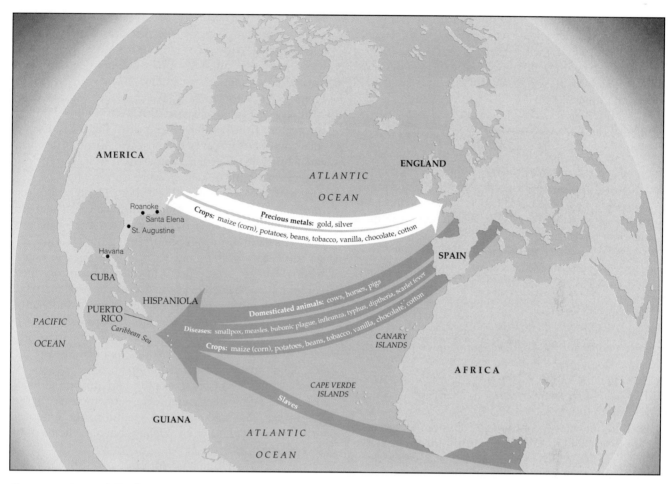

AMERICA

ATLANTIC

OCEAN

ENGLAND

Roanoke
Santa Elena
St. Augustine

Havana

CUBA

HISPANIOLA

PUERTO
RICO

Caribbean Sea

PACIFIC

OCEAN

Crops: maize (corn), potatoes, beans, tobacco, vanilla, chocolate, cotton

Precious metals: gold, silver

SPAIN

Domesticated animals: cows, horses, pigs

Diseases: smallpox, measles, bubonic plague, influenza, typhus, diptheria, scarlet fever

Crops: maize (corn), potatoes, beans, tobacco, vanilla, chocolate, cotton

CANARY
ISLANDS

AFRICA

CAPE VERDE
ISLANDS

Slaves

GUIANA

ATLANTIC

OCEAN

Intercontinental Exchange

The exchange between continents of crops and animals, microbes and men, marks the beginning of the modern era of world history.

booty was melted down, destroying forever thousands of priceless Indian artifacts. Silver from mines the Spanish discovered and operated in Mexico and Peru tripled the amount of silver coin circulating in Europe between 1500 and 1550, then tripled it again before 1600. The result was runaway inflation, which stimulated commerce and raised profits but lowered the standard of living for the majority.

But of even greater long-term importance were the New World crops brought to Europe. Maize (Indian corn) from Mexico—the staff of life for most North Americans—became a staple crop in Mediterranean countries, the dominant feed for livestock elsewhere in Europe, and the primary provision for the slave ships of Africa. Over the next few centuries, potatoes from Peru provided the margin between famine and subsistence for the peasant peoples of northern Europe and Ireland.

These "miracle crops" provided abundant food sources that went a long way toward ending the persistent problem of famine in Europe.

The new tropical crop tobacco was first introduced to Europe about 1550 as an antidote against disease, but was soon in wide use as an intoxicant. American vanilla and chocolate both became highly valued. American cotton proved superior to Asian varieties for the production of cheap textiles. Each of these native plants, along with tropical transplants from the Old World to the New—sugar, rice, and coffee were among the most important—supplied the basis for important new industries and markets that altered the course of world history.

Columbus introduced domesticated animals into Hispaniola and Cuba, and livestock were later transported to Mexico. The movement of Spanish settlement into northern Mexico was greatly aided by an advancing wave of livestock, for grazing animals seriously disrupted native fields and forests. Horses, used by Spanish stockmen to tend their cattle, also spread northward. Eventually they reached the Great Plains of North America, where they transformed the lives of the nomadic hunting Indians.

The First Europeans in North America

Ponce de León, governor of Puerto Rico, was the first conquistador to attempt to extend the Spanish conquest to North America. In 1513 he landed on the southern Atlantic coast, which he named in honor of the Easter season—*pascua florida*. *Florida* thus became the oldest European place name in the United States. But the first attempt to penetrate the mystery of North America was mounted by Hernando de Soto, a veteran of the conquest of Peru. After landing in Florida in 1539 with a Cuban army of over 700 men, he pushed hundreds of miles through the heavily populated South until he was repulsed by Choctaw and Chickasaw warriors. Thus the native peoples of the South remained in control of their country for another 250 years.

In the year of the de Soto expedition, 1539, Spanish officials in Mexico launched a second attempt to conquer North America, this one aimed at the Southwest. Francisco Vásquez de Coronado led 300 mounted men and infantry and 800 Indian porters north along well-marked Indian trading paths, passing through the settlements of Piman Indians near the present border of the United States and Mexico and finally reaching the Pueblo villages along the Rio Grande. The initial resistance of the Pueblo people was quickly quashed. But Coronado was deeply disappointed by these towns "of stone and mud, rudely fashioned," and sent out expeditions in all directions in search of legendary cities of gold in an empire imaginatively described by an earlier Spanish adventurer. He led his army as far north as the Great Plains, where they observed great herds of "shaggy cows" (buffalo) and made contact with nomadic hunting peoples, but returned without gold. For the next fifty years Spain lost all interest in the Southwest.

The Spanish New World Empire

By the late sixteenth century the Spanish had control of a powerful empire in the Americas. A century after Columbus, some 200,000 European immigrants, most of them Spaniards, had settled in the Americas. Another 125,000 Africans had been forcibly resettled on the Spanish plantations of the Caribbean, as well as on the plantations of Brazil (see Chapter 4). The Portuguese had colonized Brazil under the terms of the Treaty of Tordesillas, a 1494 agreement dividing the Americas between Spain and Portugal. Most of the Spanish settlers lived in the more than two hundred urban communities founded during the conquest, including cities such as Santo Domingo in Hispaniola; Havana, Cuba; Mexico City, built atop the ruins of Tenochtitlán; and Quito, Peru, at the center of the conquered empire of the Incas. Only a small number of Spaniards and their offspring lived in the countryside. There they supervised Indian or African workers in mining, ranching, or agriculture. Because European women constituted only about 10 percent of the immigrants, from the beginning male colonists married or lived with African or Indian women. The result was the growth of large mixed-ancestry groups known respectively as *mulattoes* and *mestizos*. The Spanish established what has been called a frontier of inclusion, their communities characterized by a great deal of marriage and sexual mixing between male colonists and native women. Hundreds of thousands of Indians died, but Indian genes were passed on to generations of mestizo peoples, who became the majority population in the mainland Spanish American empire. Descendants of those peoples of mixed European and African ancestry have been a consistent and integral subcommunity in the Caribbean. The coming of the Spanish to the Americas marked the death of many peoples, but also the birth of several new ones.

Populated by Indians, Africans, Spanish colonists, and their mixed offspring, the New World colonies of Spain made up one of the largest empires in the history of the world. The empire operated, in theory, as a highly centralized and bureaucratic system. But the Council of the Indies, composed of advisers of the Spanish king who made all the laws and regulations for the empire, was separated by a tremendous distance from local colonial affairs; what looked in the abstract like a centrally administered empire often tolerated significant local autonomy. Passive resistance and sometimes outright defiance of central authority were common in this system. This was reflected in the well-known phrase of local officials: "I obey but I do not execute."

Northern Explorations and Encounters

When the Spanish empire was at the height of its power in the sixteenth century, the merchants and monarchs of other important European seafaring states looked across

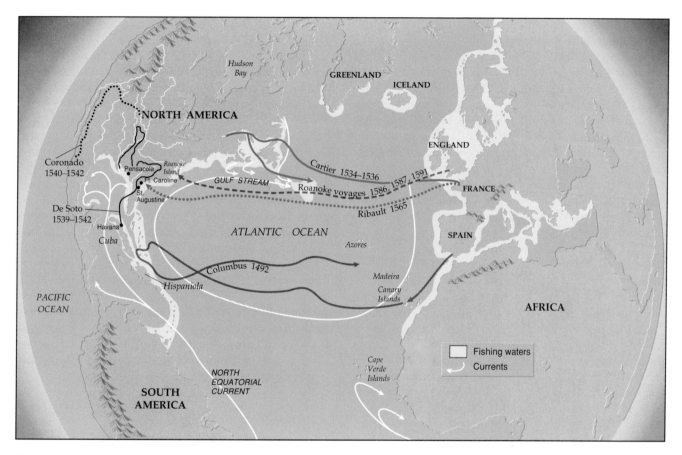

European Exploration, 1492–1587

By the mid-sixteenth century Europeans had explored most of the Atlantic coast of North America and penetrated into the interior in the disastrous expeditions of De Soto and Coronado.

the Atlantic for opportunities of their own. France was first to sponsor expeditions to the New World in the early sixteenth century. At first the French attempted to plant settlements on the coasts of Brazil and Florida, but Spanish opposition ultimately persuaded them to concentrate on the North Atlantic. Not until the second half of the sixteenth century did England develop its own plans to colonize North America. With the Spanish in Florida and the French establishing close ties with coastal tribes as far south as present-day Maine, the English focused on the middle latitudes.

The Reformation

The religious revolt against Catholicism known as the Reformation began when German priest Martin Luther publicized his differences with Rome in 1517. Luther declared that eternal salvation was a gift from God not related to works or service to the Roman Catholic

Church. His protests—*Protestantism*—fit into a climate of widespread dissatisfaction with the power and prosperity of the church and were taken up by John Calvin, a more radical theologian. In his doctrine of predestination, Calvin declared that God had chosen a small number of men and women for "election," or salvation, while condemning the vast majority to eternal damnation. Calvinists were encouraged to demonstrate thrift, industry, sobriety, and personal responsibility, which Calvin argued were signs of election and essential to the Christian life.

Sixteenth-century England became deeply involved in these struggles to reform the Catholic Church. At first King Henry VIII of England (reigned 1509–47) supported the church against the Protestants. But in England too there was great public resentment of the ostentatious display of the church and the drain of tax money to Rome. When the pope refused to grant Henry an annulment of his marriage to Catherine of

Aragon, daughter of Ferdinand and Isabella of Spain, the king exploited this popular mood. Taking up the cause of reform in 1534, he declared himself head of a separate Church of England. He later took over the English estates of the Catholic Church—about a quarter of the country's land—and used their revenues to begin constructing a powerful English state system, including a standing army and navy. Working through Parliament, Henry carefully enlisted the support of the merchants and landed gentry for his program, parceling out a measure of royal prosperity in the form of titles, offices, lands, and commercial favors. By the mid-sixteenth century he had forged a solid alliance with the wealthy merchant class.

The Protestant movement also took root in France, but with a very different outcome. Calvin's French followers, known as the Huguenots, were concentrated among merchants and the middle class, but also included many of the nobility. In 1560 an attempt by a group of Huguenot nobles to seize power in the French state was defeated, and this began nearly forty years of religious struggle in France. In 1572 the French crown directed the murder of more than 3,000 Huguenots in Paris, and many more throughout the country. This bloodshed, known as the St. Bartholomew's Day Massacre, made France infamous as the enemy of Protestantism, which was growing in popularity in England. In 1589 the Huguenot Henry IV became king of France, but found it impossible to govern until he converted to Catholicism four years later. His Edict of Nantes of 1598 established the rights of Huguenots to their views but made Roman Catholicism the official religion of France. Thus England and France moved in very different directions during the Reformation.

The First French Colonies

The first French attempt to establish colonies in North America culminated efforts by Huguenot leaders who dreamed of a Protestant refuge in the New World. In 1562 Jean Ribault and 150 Protestants from Normandy landed on Parris Island, near present-day Beaufort, South Carolina. The party began constructing a fort and crude mud huts. Ribault soon returned to France for supplies, where he was caught up in the religious wars. Meanwhile, the colonists nearly starved, finally resorting to cannibalism before being rescued by a passing British ship. In 1564 another French expedition under Ribault established the Huguenot colony of Fort Caro-

line on the St. Johns River of Florida, south of present-day Jacksonville.

By this time the Spanish had established a foothold along the Atlantic coast of Florida. They were not interested in settlement, but wished rather to protect their fleets riding the offshore Gulf Stream home to Spain. Seeing Fort Caroline manned not only by Frenchmen but by French Protestants—deadly enemies of the Catholic monarchs of Spain—the Spanish crown sent Don Pedro Menéndez de Avilés, captain general of the Indies, to crush the Huguenots in 1565. He established the Spanish fort of St. Augustine on the coast, south of the French, then marched overland through the swamps to surprise them with an attack from the rear. "I put Jean Ribaut and all the rest of them to the knife," Menéndez wrote triumphantly to the king, "judging it to be necessary to the service of the Lord Our God and of Your Majesty." More than five hundred Frenchmen lay dead on the beaches of Florida; the French attempt to plant a colony along the South Atlantic coast had ended in disaster. But St. Augustine remained to become the oldest continuously occupied European city in North America.

Fish and Furs

Of far more lasting significance for the French overseas empire was the entrance of French fishermen into the waters of the North Atlantic. It is possible that fishing ships from England, France, Spain, and Portugal had discovered the great northern fishing grounds long before Columbus's voyages. Certainly by 1500, hundreds of ships and thousands of sailors were regularly fishing the coastal waters of the North Atlantic.

The first official voyages of exploration in the North Atlantic used the talents of experienced European sailors and fishermen. With a crew from Bristol, England, Genovese captain John Cabot reached Labrador in 1497, and in 1524 Tuscan captain Giovanni da Verrazano sailed with a crew from France, exploring the North American coast from Cape Fear (in today's North Carolina) to the Penobscot River (Maine). Anxious to locate empires to conquer or a passage to the spice trade of Asia, the French king commissioned experienced captain Jacques Cartier. In 1534, 1535, and 1541, Cartier reconnoitered the St. Lawrence River, which led deep into the continental interior, and established France's imperial claim to the lands of Canada.

Northern Europeans thus discovered the northern Indians, and the Indians in turn discovered them. Na-

In his sketch of this "Capitaine" of the Illinois nation (drawn about 1701), French artist Charles Becard de Granville carefully noted the tattooing of the warrior's face and body, his distinctive costume and feather headdress, his spear and tobacco pipe.
National Archives of Canada/The Thomas Gilcrease Institute of American History and Art, Tulsa, OK.

tive tales told of seeing the approach of floating islands (ships) with many tall trees (masts) and hairy bears (sailors) running about in the branches.

The contacts between Europeans and natives took a different form along the North Atlantic coast than in the tropics: relationships were based on trade rather than conquest. The Indians immediately appreciated the usefulness of textiles, glass, copper, and ironware. Seeing Cartier's approach, the Micmacs waved him ashore. "The savages showed marvelous great pleasure in possessing and obtaining iron wares and other commodities," he noted in his report. For his part, Cartier was interested in the fur coats of the Indians. Europeans, like Indians, used

furs for winter clothing. But the growing population of the late Middle Ages had so depleted the wild game of Europe that the price of furs had risen beyond the reach of most people. The North American fur trade thus filled an important demand and produced high profits.

By the end of the sixteenth century, over a thousand ships per year were trading for furs along the northern coast. Among these European traders, the French were probably the most numerous, and in the early seventeenth century began to consolidate their hold by planting colonies along the St. Lawrence.

Sixteenth-Century England

Like the first colonial efforts of the French, the English movement across the Atlantic was tied to social change at home. Perhaps most important were changes in the economy. As the prices of goods rose steeply—the result of New World inflation—English landlords, their rents fixed by custom, sought ways to increase their incomes. Seeking profits in the woolen trade, many converted the common pasturage used by tenants into grazing land for sheep, with the result that large numbers of farmers were dislocated. Between 1500 and 1650 a third of all the common lands in England were "enclosed" in this way. Deprived of their traditional livelihoods, thousands of families sought employment in the cities. The population of London grew from 60,000 to 200,000 over the sixteenth century, and other urban areas expanded similarly. It was a time of great disruption and poverty for common folk, but increasing prosperity for landlords and merchants.

Henry VIII of England died in 1547. He was succeeded by his young and sickly son Edward VI, who soon died, then by his Catholic daughter Mary, who attempted to reverse her father's Reformation from the top. She added her own chapter to the century's many religious wars, martyring hundreds of English Protestants and gaining the title Bloody Mary. But upon Mary's death in 1558, her half-sister Elizabeth I (reigned 1558–1603) came to the throne. Elizabeth sought to end the religious turmoil by tolerating a variety of views within the English church. Criticized by radical Protestants for not going far enough, and condemned by Catholics for her "pretended title to the kingdom," Elizabeth nevertheless gained popularity among the English people with her moderate approach. The Spanish monarchy, the head of the most powerful empire in the world, declared itself the defender of the Catholic faith, and vowed to overthrow her. England

and Spain now became the two principal rivals in the Catholic–Protestant confrontation.

Early English Efforts in the Americas

It was during Elizabeth's reign that England first turned toward the New World. Its first ventures were aimed at breaking the Spanish trading monopoly with tropical America. In 1562 John Hawkins inaugurated English participation in the slave trade, violating Spanish regulations by transporting African slaves to the Caribbean and bringing back valuable tropical goods. In 1567 the Spanish attacked Hawkins, an event English privateers such as Francis Drake used as an excuse for launching a series of devastating and lucrative raids against Spanish New World ports and fleets. The voyages of these English "Sea Dogs" greatly enriched their investors, including Elizabeth herself. The English thus began their American adventures by slaving and plundering.

A consensus soon developed among Elizabeth's closest advisers that the time had come to enter the competition for America. In a state paper written for the queen, Richard Hakluyt summarized the advantages that would come from colonies: they could provide bases from which to raid the Spanish in the Caribbean, outposts for an Indian market for English goods, and plantations for growing tropical products, freeing the nation from a reliance on the long-distance trade with Asia. These colonies could be populated by the "multitudes of loiterers and idle vagabonds" of England, who could support the enterprise by farming the American soil. He urged Elizabeth to establish such colonies "upon the mouths of the great navigable rivers" from Florida to the St. Lawrence.

Although Elizabeth refused to commit the state to Hakluyt's plan, she authorized several private attempts at exploration and colonization, and even invested in these ventures herself. In the late 1570s Martin Frobisher conducted three voyages of exploration. Walter Raleigh and his half-brother Humphrey Gilbert, soldiers and adventurers, planned the first colonizing venture in 1578, but it was never launched. Then in 1583 Gilbert sailed with a flotilla of ships from Plymouth; he landed at St. John's Bay, Newfoundland, where he encountered fishermen from several other nations but nevertheless claimed the territory for his queen. Gilbert's ship was lost on the return voyage.

Raleigh followed up his brother's efforts with plans to establish a colony southward, in the more hospitable climate of the mid-Atlantic coast. Although the Roanoke enterprise of 1584–87 seemed far more likely to succeed than Gilbert's, it too eventually failed. The greatest legacy of the expedition was the work of Thomas Harriot and John White, who mapped the area, surveyed its commercial potential, and studied the Indian residents. Harriot's *A Briefe and True Report of the Newfound Land of Virginia* (1588) was addressed mainly to the problem of identifying the "merchantable commodities" that would support the settlement, for without products a colonial system was impossible. He and White provided the most accurate and sensitive description of North American Indians made at the moment of their contact with Europeans.

King Philip II of Spain was outraged at the English incursions into territory reserved by the pope for Catholics. He had authorized the destruction of the French colony in Florida, and now he committed himself to smashing England. In 1588 he sent a fleet of 130 ships carrying 30,000 men to invade the British Isles. Countered by captains such as Drake and Hawkins, who commanded smaller and more maneuverable ships, and frustrated by an ill-timed storm that the English chose to interpret as an act of divine intervention, the Spanish Armada foundered. Half the ships were destroyed, their crews killed or captured. The war continued until 1604, but the Spanish monopoly of the New World had been broken in the English Channel.

Conclusion

The Spanish opened the era of European colonization in the Americas with Columbus's voyage in 1492. The consequences for the Indian peoples of the Americas were disastrous. The Spanish succeeded in constructing the world's most powerful empire on the backs of Indian and African labor. The New World colonies of Spain were characterized by a great deal of mixing between the mostly male colonists and native women; in this sense they were communities of inclusion. Inspired by the Spanish success, both the French and the English began to make feeble attempts to colonize the coast of North America. By the end of the sixteenth century, however, they had not succeeded in establishing any colonial communities of their own. The colonists of Roanoke had become part of an Indian community. In the next century, the English adopted another model of colonization, the transplantation of complete communities of families across the Atlantic.

CHRONOLOGY

1000	Norse settlement at L'Anse aux Meadows	1534	Jacques Cartier first explores the St. Lawrence River
1347–53	Black Death in Europe	1539–40	Hernando de Soto and Francisco Vásquez de Coronado expeditions
1381	English Peasants' Revolt		
1488	Bartholomeu Días sails around the African continent	1550	Tobacco introduced to Europe
1492	Christopher Columbus first arrives in the Caribbean	1552	Bartolomé de las Casas's *Destruction of the Indies* published
1494	Treaty of Tordesillas	1558	Elizabeth I of England begins her reign
1497	John Cabot explores Newfoundland	1562	Huguenot colony planted along the mid-Atlantic coast
1500	High point of the Renaissance	1565	St. Augustine founded
1508	Spanish invade Puerto Rico	1572	St. Bartholomew's Day Massacre in France
1513	Juan Ponce de León lands in Florida	1583	Humphrey Gilbert attempts to plant a colony in Newfoundland
1514	Bartolomé de las Casas begins preaching against the conquest	1584–87	Walter Raleigh's colony on Roanoke Island
1516	Smallpox introduced to the New World	1588	English defeat the Spanish Armada
1517	Martin Luther breaks with the Roman Catholic Church	1590	John White returns to find Roanoke colony abandoned
1519	Hernán Cortés lands in Mexico		

Review Questions

1. Discuss the roles played by the rising merchant class, the new monarchies, Renaissance humanism, and the Reformation in the development of European colonialism.
2. Define a frontier of inclusion. In what ways does this description apply to the Spanish empire in the Americas?
3. Make a list of the major exchanges that took place between the Old World and the New World in the centuries following the European invasion of America. Discuss some of the effects these exchanges had on the course of modern history.
4. In what ways did colonial contact in the Northeast differ from contacts in the Caribbean and Mexico?
5. In what ways might the English experience in Ireland have shaped expectations about American colonization?

Recommended Reading

CYCLONE COVEY, TRANSLATOR AND EDITOR, *Cabeza de Vaca's Adventures in the Unknown Interior of America* (1983). The captivity narrative that lured the Spanish into North America. An eye-opening story of the peoples and places of the pre-Conquest Southwest.

ALFRED W. CROSBY, JR., *The Columbian Exchange: Biological and Cultural Consequences of 1492* (1972). The pathbreaking account of the intersection of the biospheres of the Old and New Worlds.

CHARLES GIBSON, *Spain in America* (1966). The best introductory history of the Spanish American empire.

LEWIS HANKE, *The Spanish Struggle for Justice in the Conquest of America* (1949; reprint, 1965). The classic account of Las Casas's attempts to rectify the wrongs against the Indians.

IVOR NOËL HUME, *The Virginia Adventure, Roanoke to James Towne: An Archaeological and Historical Odyssey* (1994). The chief archaeologist of colonial Williamsburg tells the story of early Virginia through artifacts and tracings on the land.

MIGUEL LEON-PORTILLA, *The Broken Spears: The Aztec Account of the Conquest of Mexico* (1962). The history of the Spanish conquest as told by the Aztecs, drawn from manuscripts dating as early as 1528, only seven years after the fall of Tenochtitlán.

SAMUEL ELIOT MORISON, *The European Discovery of America: The Northern Voyages, A.D. 500–1600* (1971) and *The Southern Voyages, A.D. 1492–1616* (1974). The most detailed treatment of all the important European explorations of the Americas.

J. H. PARRY, *The Age of Reconnaissance* (1963). This readable book illuminates the background of European expansion.

DAVID BEERS QUINN, *Set Fair for Roanoke: Voyages and Colonies, 1584–1606* (1985). The story of Roanoke—the Indian village, the English settlement, and the Lost Colony. It includes the latest ethnographic and archaeological findings.

KIRKPATRICK SALE, *The Conquest of Paradise: Christopher Columbus and the Columbian Legacy* (1990). Despite its harsh view of Columbus, this biography provides important information on the world of the Caribbean and the disastrous effects of the encounter with Europeans.

CARL ORTWIN SAUER, *Sixteenth-Century North America: The Land and the People as Seen by the Europeans* (1971). An excellent source for the explorations of the continent, providing abundant descriptions of the Indians.

DAVID E. STANNARD, *American Holocaust: Columbus and the Conquest of the New World* (1992). Argues that the Spanish inaugurated a genocidal policy that continued into the twentieth century.

3

PLANTING COLONIES IN NORTH AMERICA, 1588–1701

AMERICAN COMMUNITIES

COMMUNITIES STRUGGLE WITH DIVERSITY IN SEVENTEENTH-CENTURY SANTA FÉ

It was a hot August day in 1680 when the frantic messengers rode into the small mission outpost of El Paso with the news: the Pueblo Indians to the north had risen in revolt; the corpses of more than 400 colonists lay bleeding in the dust. Two thousand Spanish survivors huddled inside the Palace of Governors in Santa Fé, surrounded by 3,000 angry warriors. The Pueblo leaders had sent two crosses into the palace—white for surrender, red for death. Which would the Spaniards choose?

Spanish colonists had been in New Mexico for nearly a century. Franciscan priests came first, followed by a military expedition from Mexico in search of precious metals. In 1609, high in the picturesque foothills of the Sangre de Cristo Mountains, the colonial authorities founded "the royal town of the holy faith of St. Francis," soon known simply as Santa Fé. Colonization efforts included the conversion of the Pueblo Indians to Christianity, making them subjects of the king of Spain and forcing them to work for the colonial elite who lived in the town.

In the face of overwhelming Spanish power, the Pueblos adopted a flexible attitude. Twenty thousand of them converted to Christianity, but most of these thought of the new religion as simply an appendage to their complex culture. The Christian God was but a minor addition to their numerous deities; church holidays were included in their own religious calendar and celebrated with native dances and rituals.

Most ethnographers agree that the Pueblos were a sexually spirited people. Many of their public dances included erotic displays and sometimes ended in spectacles of public intercourse, symbolizing the powerful force that brought the separate worlds of men and women together, and also community. The celibacy of the Franciscan priests not only astounded the Pueblos but horrified them, for it marked the priests as only half-persons. They also found the Franciscan practice of subjecting themselves to prolonged fasts and tortures such as self-flagellation inexplicable. The missionaries, on the other hand, outraged by what they considered Pueblo sacrileges, invaded underground kivas and destroyed sacred Indian artifacts, publicly humiliated holy men, and compelled whole villages to perform penance by working in irrigation ditches and fields.

Such violations of the deepest traditions of Pueblo community life eventually led to the revolt of 1680. In New Mexico, several years before, the Spanish governor had executed three Pueblo priests and publicly whipped dozens more for secretly practicing their religion. One of those priests, Popé of San Juan Pueblo, vowed to overthrow the regime, and during the next several years he carefully organized a conspiracy among more than twenty Indian towns. The revolt came off with remarkable precision throughout the colony.

From within Santa Fé's Palace of Governors, when the Indians demanded their surrender, the Spanish sent back the red cross, signaling defiance. But after a siege lasting five days the Pueblos agreed to allow most of them to flee south to El Paso, "the poor women and children on foot and unshod," in the words of one Spaniard's account, and "of such a hue that they looked like dead people." The Indians then ransacked the missions and churches, desecrating the holy furnishings with human excrement and leaving the mutilated bodies of priests lying on their altars. They transformed the governor's chapel into a traditional kiva, his palace into a communal dwelling. On the elegant inlaid stone floors where the governor had held court, Pueblo women now ground their corn.

Santa Fé became the capital of a Pueblo confederacy led by Popé. He forced Christian Indians to the river to scrub away the taint of baptism. Then he ordered the destruction of everything Spanish. But this the Pueblos could not do. The colonists had introduced horses and sheep, fruit trees and wheat, new tools and new crafts, all of which the Indians found useful. Moreover, the Pueblos sorely missed the support of the Spanish in their struggle against their traditional enemies, the nomadic Navajos and Apaches. Equipped with stolen horses and weapons, these nomadic tribespeople had become considerably more dangerous, and their raids on the unprotected Pueblo villages became much more destructive after the colonists fled. With chaos mounting, Popé was deposed in 1690, and many of the Indians found themselves thinking the unthinkable: if only the Spanish would come back!

Come back they did, beginning in 1692, and after six years of fighting succeeded in reestablishing Spanish authority. But both sides had learned a lesson, and over the next generation the colonists and the Indians reached an implicit understanding. Pueblos dutifully observed Catholicism in the missionary chapels, while missionaries tolerated the practice of traditional religion in the Indians' underground kivas. Royal officials guaranteed the inviolability of Indian lands, and Pueblos pledged loyalty to the Spanish monarch. Pueblos turned out for service on colonial lands, and colonists abandoned the system of forced labor. Together the Spanish and the Pueblos held off the nomadic tribes for the next 150 years. Colonist and Indian communities remained autonomous, but they learned to live with one another.

KEY TOPICS

- ◆ **A comparison of the European colonies established in North America in the seventeenth century**
- ◆ **The English and Algonquian colonial encounter in the Chesapeake**
- ◆ **The role of religious dissent in the planting of the New England colonies**
- ◆ **The restoration of the Stuart monarchy and the creation of new proprietary colonies**
- ◆ **Indian warfare and internal conflict at the end of the seventeenth century**

The Spanish and French in North America

At the end of the sixteenth century the Spanish and the French were the only European powers directly involved in North America. The Spanish had built a series of forts along the Florida coast to protect the Gulf Stream sea lanes used by the convoys carrying wealth from their New World colonies. The French were deeply involved in the fur trade of the St. Lawrence River. Early in the seventeenth century both were drawn into planting far more substantial colonies—New Mexico and New France—in North America. Because neither France nor Spain was willing or able to transport large numbers of people to populate these colonies, both relied on a policy of converting Indians into subjects, and in both New Mexico and New France there was a good deal of cultural and sexual mixing between colonists and natives. These areas became frontiers of inclusion, where native peoples were included in colonial society, and they contrasted dramatically with the frontiers of exclusion established later by the English.

New Mexico

After the 1539 expedition of Francisco Vásquez de Coronado failed to turn up vast Indian empires to conquer in the northern Mexican deserts, the Spanish interest in the Southwest faded. Although the densely settled farming communities of the Pueblos may not have offered wealth to plunder, they did offer a harvest of souls, and by the 1580s Franciscan missionaries had entered the area. Soon, however, rumors drifted back to Mexico City of rich mines along the Rio Grande. The hopes of Spanish officials that they might find another Aztec empire were rekindled. In 1598 Juan de Oñate, a member of a wealthy mining family, financed a colonizing expedition with the dual purpose of mining gold and souls.

Moving north into the upper Rio Grande Valley, Oñate encountered varying degrees of resistance by Pueblos. At Acoma, Oñate lay seige. Indian warriors killed dozens of Spaniards with their arrows, and women and children bombarded the attackers with stones. But in the end, the Spanish succeeded in climbing the rock walls and laying waste to the town, killing eight hundred men, women, and children. All surviving warriors had one of their feet severed, and more than five hundred people were carried off into slavery. "If you who are Christians cause so much harm and violence," a Pueblo asked one of the priests, "why should we become Christians?" In 1606 Spanish authorities in Mexico recalled Oñate for his failure to locate the fabled gold mines.

The Spanish were about to abandon the colony, but after publicizing a surge in Christian conversions among the Indians, the church convinced the monarchy to subsidize New Mexico as a special missionary colony. In 1609 the new governor, Don Pedro de Peralta, founded the capital of Santa Fé, and from this base the Franciscans penetrated all the surrounding Indian villages.

The colonial economy of New Mexico—based on small-scale agriculture and sheep raising—was never very prosperous. The Indians were forced to labor for colonists and priests. As one Spanish official put it,

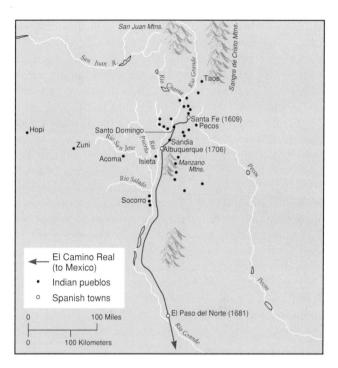

New Mexico in the Seventeenth Century

By the end of the seventeenth century, New Mexico contained 3,000 mostly mestizo settlers in several towns, surrounded by an estimated 50,000 Pueblo Indians living in some fifty farming villages. The isolation and sense of danger among the Hispanic settlers are evident in their name for the road linking the colony with New Spain, Jornada del Muerto, "the Road of Death."

"One comes to the Indies not to plow and sow, but only to eat and loaf." After the initial conquest, few new colonists came up the dusty road from Mexico. Population growth was almost entirely the result of unions between colonial men and Indian women.

The First Communities of New France

In the early seventeenth century the French devised a strategy to monopolize the northern fur trade that had developed in the sixteenth century. In 1605 Samuel de Champlain, an agent of the Royal Canadian Company, helped establish the outpost of Port Royal on the Bay of Fundy. Three years later he founded the town of Quebec at a site where he could intercept the traffic in furs to the Atlantic. He forged an alliance with the Huron Indians, who controlled access to the rich fur grounds of the Great Lakes, and joined them in making war on their traditional enemies, the Five Nation Iroquois Confederacy. In his diplomacy, Champlain relied on the tradition of commercial relations that had developed between Europeans and Indians during the sixteenth century. He sent agents and traders to live among native peoples, where they learned native languages and customs, and directed the flow of furs to Quebec.

France encouraged families to settle the colony of Acadia, the tidal shores of the Bay of Fundy, and the colony of Canada. It was the second of these that became the heart of New France. Small clusters of riverbank farmers known as *habitants* lived on the lands of *seigneurs,* or landlords. These communities, with their manor houses, Catholic churches, and perhaps a public building or two, resembled the towns of northern France. By using Indian farming techniques, habitants were able to produce subsistence crops, and eventually they developed a modest export economy. But the communities of Canada looked west toward the continental interior rather than east across the Atlantic. It was typical for the sons of habitants to take to the woods in

their youth, working as agents for the fur companies or as independent traders. Most returned to take up farming, but others remained in Indian villages, where they married Indian women and raised families. Such French traders were living on the Great Lakes as early as the 1620s, and from the late 1660s to the 1680s the French established outposts at each of the strategic points on the lakes. By the 1670s French fur traders and missionaries were exploring the reaches of the upper Mississippi River. In 1681 fur trade commandant Robert Sieur de La Salle navigated the mighty river to its mouth on the Gulf of Mexico and claimed its entire watershed—a great inland empire—for France. The strength of New France lay in its extensive trading system.

England in the Chesapeake

England first attempted to plant colonies in North America during the 1580s, in Newfoundland and at Roanoke Island in present-day North Carolina. Both attempts were failures. England's war with Spain lasting from 1588 to 1604, suspended colonization efforts, but thereafter the English once again turned to the Americas. In contrast to the inclusive Spanish and French colonies, the English adopted an exclusionary approach. They pushed Indians to the periphery rather than incorporating them into colonial communities.

Jamestown and the Powhatan Confederacy

Early in his reign, King James I (reigned 1603–25) issued royal charters for the colonization of the mid-Atlantic region by then known as Virginia to English joint-stock companies, which raised capital by selling shares. In 1607 a London group of investors known as the Virginia Company sent ships to the Chesapeake Bay, where a hundred men built a fort they named Jamestown, in honor of the king. It was destined to become the first permanent English settlement in North America.

The Chesapeake was already home to an estimated 20,000 Algonquian people. The English colonists were immediately confronted by Powhatan, the powerful *werowance,* or leader, of a confederacy of Algonquin tribes. Powhatan had mixed feelings about the English. The Spanish had already attempted to plant a base nearby, bringing conflict and disease to the region. But he looked forward to valuable trade with the English, as well as their support for his struggle to extend his confederacy over outlying tribes. As was the case in Mexico and along the St. Lawrence, Indians tried to use Europeans to pursue ends of their own.

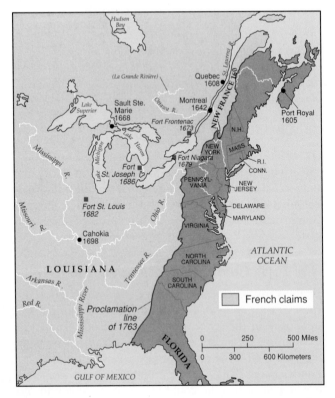

New France in the Seventeenth Century

The heart of New France was the communities stretching along the St. Lawrence River between the towns of Quebec and Montreal.

A scene from John Smith's memoirs (1624) engraved by artist Robert Vaughan. Pocahontas, the daughter of Chief Powhatan, intervenes to save Smith from execution.

The English saw themselves as conquistadors. Abhorring the idea of physical labor, they survived the first year only with Powhatan's material assistance. Like the first Roanoke colonists (see Chapter 2), they were unable to support themselves. "In our extremity the Indians brought us corn," wrote John Smith, the colony's military leader, "when we rather expected they would destroy us." Jamestown grew so dependent on Algonquian stores that in 1609 Smith and his men began to plunder food from surrounding tribes. In retaliation, Powhatan decided to starve the colonists out. He now realized that the English had come "not for trade, but to invade my people and possess my country." During the terrible winter of 1609–10 scores of colonists starved and a number resorted to cannibalism. By spring only 60 remained of the more than 900 colonists sent to Virginia.

Determined to prevail, the Virginia Company sent out a large additional force of men, women, and livestock, committing themselves to a protracted war against the Indians. By 1613 the colonists firmly controlled the territory between the James and York rivers.

Worn down by warfare and disease, Powhatan accepted a treaty of peace in 1614.

Tobacco, Expansion, and Warfare

Tobacco provided the Virginia colonists with the "merchantable commodity" for which Thomas Harriot, the scientist who accompanied the Roanoke expedition, had searched (see Chapter 2). In 1613 John Rolfe developed a hybrid, and soon the first commercial shipments of cured Virginia leaf reached England. Tobacco had been introduced to English consumers by Francis Drake in the 1580s, and the smoking craze had created strong consumer demand by the 1610s. Tobacco provided the Virginia Company with the first returns on its investment. However, its cultivation quickly exhausted the soil, creating pressures for further expansion into Indian territory. Because tobacco also required a great deal of hand labor, the company instituted what were called—headright grants—awards of large plantations to men on the condition that they transport workers from England at their own cost. Between 1619 and 1624 more than 4,500 English settlers arrived, many with families, but high mortality rates, probably the result of epidemics of typhoid fever, kept the total population at just over a thousand.

As the English pressed for additional lands, Opechancanough, Powhatan's brother and successor, prepared the Chesapeake Algonquians for a final assault on the invaders. He encouraged a cultural revival under the guidance of the shaman Nemattanew, who instructed his followers to reject the English and their ways but to learn the use of firearms. This was the first of many Indian resistance movements led jointly by strong political and religious figures. The uprising, which began on Good Friday, March 22, 1622, completely surprised the English. Nearly 350 people, a quarter of the settlers, were killed. Yet the colony managed to hang on. In fact, during this time the neighboring colony of Maryland was established. But the attack stretched into a ten-year war of attrition in which horrors were committed by both sides.

Lasting until 1632, the war bankrupted the Virginia Company. In 1624 the king converted Virginia into a royal colony. Although disease, famine, and warfare had taken a heavy toll, the booming economy led to a doubling of the English colonial population every five years from 1625 to 1640, by which time it numbered approximately 10,000. Opechancanough emerged as undisputed leader of the still independent Chesapeake Algonquian confederacy, but smaller tribes, decimated by casualties and disease, were forced to accept English domination. By 1640 the native population of the Chesapeake had declined to about 10,000.

Numerical strength thus shifted in favor of the English. In 1644 Opechancanough organized a final desperate revolt in which over 500 colonists were killed. But the Virginians crushed the Algonquians in 1645, capturing and executing Opechancanough. Today some 1,500 people who trace their roots to Powhatan's confederacy live in Chesapeake Indian communities. They attend their own churches and schools, and some work at fishing, hunting, and farming while others commute to work in metropolitan Richmond or Washington, D.C.

Indentured Servants

At least three-quarters of the English migrants to the Chesapeake came as indentured servants. In exchange for the cost of their transportation to the New World, men and women contracted to labor for a master for a fixed term. Most indentured servants were young, unskilled males who served for two to seven years, but some were skilled craftsmen, women, or even children (the latter were expected to serve until they reached the age of twenty-one).

Work in the tobacco fields was so backbreaking that many servants tried to escape, although capture could mean a doubling of their terms of service. On reaching the end of their service, servants were eligible for "freedom dues": clothing, tools, a gun, a spinning wheel, or perhaps food to help them get started on their own. Most former servants headed west in the hope of starting a farm in the backcountry.

Reliance on indentured labor was unique to the English colonies. New France had little need for systematic servitude because French colonists generally did their own labor, and the Spanish in places such as Santa Fé depended on the labor of Indians. African slaves were first introduced to the Chesapeake in 1619, but slaves were more expensive than servants, and as late as 1680 they made up less than 7 percent of the Chesapeake population. For many servants, however, the distinction between slavery and servitude may have seemed academic. In the hard-driving economy of the Chesapeake, many masters treated servants cruelly, and women especially were vulnerable to sexual exploitation. The harsh system of indentured labor prepared the tobacco masters of the Chesapeake for the transition to slavery that occurred during the second half of the seventeenth century. (Chapter 4 discusses the slave system and its implications for the

American economy and society as well as for slaves and masters themselves.)

Community Life in the Chesapeake

Because most migrants were men, whether free or indentured, free unmarried women often married as soon as they arrived in the Chesapeake. English men seemed to suffer a higher rate of mortality than women in the disease-ridden environment of the early Chesapeake, and widows remarried quickly, sometimes within days.

Visitors from England often remarked on the crude conditions of community life. Prosperous planters, investing everything in tobacco production, lived in rough wooden dwellings. On the western edge of the settlements, freed servants lived with their families in shacks, huts, or even caves. Colonists spread across the countryside in search of new tobacco lands, creating dispersed settlements and few towns. Before 1650 there were few community institutions such as schools and churches. Meanwhile, the Spanish in the Caribbean and Mexico were building communities that would grow into great cities with permanent institutions.

In contrast to the colonists of New France, who were developing a distinctive American identity because of their close commercial connections with Native Americans, the colonial population of the Chesapeake maintained close emotional ties to England. Colonial politics were shaped less by local developments than by a continuing relationship with the mother country. There was little movement toward a distinctively American point of view in the seventeenth-century Chesapeake.

New England

Both in climate and in geography, the northern coast of North America was far different from the Chesapeake. Merchantable commodities such as tobacco could not be produced there, and thus it was a far less favored region for investment and settlement. Instead, the region became a haven for Protestant dissenters from England, who gave the colonies of the north a distinctive character.

Puritanism

Most English men and women continued to practice a Christianity little different from traditional Catholicism. But the English followers of John Calvin (see Chapter 2), known as Puritans because they wished to purify and reform the English church from within, grew increasingly influential during the last years of Elizabeth's reign. Their emphasis on enterprise meant that the Puritans appealed to merchants, entrepreneurs, and commercial farmers, those most responsible for the rapid economic and social transformation of England. They argued for reviving communities by placing reformed Christian congregations at their core to monitor the behavior of individuals. Puritanism was as much a set of social and political values as of religious ones, a way of managing change in troubling times. By the early seventeenth century Puritans controlled many congregations, and had become an influential force at the universities in Oxford and Cambridge, training centers for the future political and religious leaders of England.

King James I, who assumed the throne after Elizabeth's death, abandoned her policy of religious tolerance. However, his persecution of the Puritans merely stiffened their resolve and turned them toward overt political opposition. An increasingly vocal Puritan minority in Parliament criticized King Charles I (reigned 1625–49), James's son and successor, for supporting High Church policies—which emphasized the authority of the church and its traditional forms of worship—as well as for marrying a Catholic princess. In 1629, determined to rule without these troublesome opponents, Charles adjourned Parliament and launched a campaign of repression against the Puritans. This political turmoil provided the context for the migration of thousands of English Protestants to New England.

Early Contacts in New England

The northern Atlantic coast seemed an unlikely spot for English colonies, for the region was dominated by French and Dutch traders. In 1613 the English, desperate to keep their colonial options open, dispatched a fleet from Jamestown that destroyed the French post at Port Royal on the Bay of Fundy and harassed the Dutch on the Hudson. The following year John Smith explored the northern coastline and christened the region New England. But Smith's plans for a New England colony were aborted when he was captured and held prisoner by the French.

Then a twist of fate transformed English fortunes. From 1616 to 1618 a plague ravaged the native peoples of the northern coast. Modern estimates confirm the testimony of a surviving Indian that nine-tenths of his people had died. The native population of New England as a whole dropped from an estimated 120,000 to less than 70,000. So crippled were the surviving coastal societies that they could not provide effective resistance to the planting of English colonies.

Plymouth Colony and the Mayflower Compact

The first English colony in New England was founded by a group of religious dissenters known to later generations as the Pilgrims. They were called Separatists because they believed the Anglican establishment was so corrupt that they must establish their own independent congregations. Backed by the Virginia Company of London and led by Pilgrim William Bradford, 102 people sailed from Plymouth, England, on the *Mayflower* in September 1620.

The little group, mostly families but also a substantial number of single men hired by the investors, landed in Massachusetts Bay. To preserve order, the Pilgrim leader, William Bradford, drafted the Mayflower Compact, and in November the men did "covenant and combine [themselves] together into a civil body politic." It was the first document of self-government in North America.

Weakened by scurvy and malnutrition the first winter, the Pilgrims were rescued by Indians. Massasoit, the *sachem* (leader) of the Pokanokets, offered the newcomers food and advice in return for an alliance with them against his enemies, the Narraganset tribe.

The Pilgrims succeeded during the first two or three decades in establishing the self-sufficient community they desired. By midcentury, however, the Plymouth population had dispersed into eleven separate communities, and diversity had begun to disrupt this separatist retreat.

The Massachusetts Bay Colony

In England the political climate of the late 1620s convinced a number of influential Puritans that the only way to protect their congregations was emigration. In 1629 a royal charter was granted to a group of wealthy Puritans who called their enterprise the Massachusetts Bay Company, and an advance force of 200 settlers left for the fishing settlement of Naumkeag on Massachusetts Bay, which they renamed Salem.

The Puritan emigration to Massachusetts became known as the Great Migration, a phrase that would be repeated many times in American history. Between 1629 and 1643 some 20,000 people relocated to New England. Most arrived in groups from long-established communities in the east of England and were often led by men with extensive experience in local English government.

Indians and Puritans

The Algonquian Indians of southern New England found the English very different from the French and Dutch traders who had preceded them. The principal concern of the English was not commerce—although the fur trade remained an important part of their economy—but the acquisition of Indian land for their growing settlements.

Ravaged by disease, the Wampanoags' northern neighbors, the Massachusetts, were ill-prepared for the Puritan landings that took place after 1629. The English believed they had the right to take "unused" lands, and depopulated Massachusetts villages became prime targets. However, conflicts between settlers over title made it necessary to obtain deeds from Indians, and the English used a variety of tactics to pressure them into signing quitclaims. Disorganized and demoralized, many coastal Algonquians soon placed themselves under the protection of the English.

By the late 1630s the most powerful tribes in the vicinity of the Puritans were the Narragansets of present-day Rhode Island and their traditional enemies, the Pequots, principal trading partners of the Dutch. In 1637 the Narragansets, in alliance with the English, who were looking for an excuse to smash the Dutch, went to war against the Pequots. Narraganset warriors and English troops attacked the main Pequot village, killing most of its slumbering residents, including women and children. Unaccustomed to such tactics, the shocked Narragansets cried out to the English: "It is too furious, it slays too many."

New England Communities

Back in England, the conflict between King Charles and the Puritans in Parliament broke into armed conflict in 1642. Several years of violent confrontation led to the execution of the king in 1649 and the proclamation of an English Commonwealth, headed by the Puritan leader Oliver Cromwell. Because the Puritans were on the victorious side in the English Civil War, they no longer had the same incentive to leave the country.

New England's economy had depended on the sale of supplies and land to arriving immigrants, but in the 1640s the importance of this "newcomer market" declined with slackening migration. Lacking a single exportable commodity, New Englanders were forced to diversify into a variety of enterprises, including farming, fishing, and lumbering. Merchants began constructing what would become, by the end of the century, the most sizable shipping fleet in the colonies. The development of a diversified economy would provide New England with considerable long-term strength.

The communities of New England were distinct from those of the Chesapeake because the vast majority of the Puritans had come in family groups with few servants. The monarchy provided the Puritans with a model for the family. Like kings or governors, parents were expected to control their children.

However, it is a mistake to regard the Puritans as "puritanical." Although adultery was a capital crime in New England, Puritans celebrated sexual expression

Mrs. Freake and Baby Mary, *by an unknown Boston artist in 1674. The mother wears the standard Puritan costume for women, although her decorative banding, lacework, and jewelry mark her taste as rather sumptuous by New England standards. One young Puritan woman who wore lace garments to the meetinghouse wrote that "the elders with others entreated me to leave them off, for they gave great offense." The baby is clothed like her mother, reflecting the view that children were simply miniature adults.*

Unknown artist. *Mrs. Elizabeth Freake and Baby Mary.* 1671–74. Oil on canvas. 108 × 93.4 cm. Worcester Art Museum, Worcester, MA. Gift of Mr. and Mrs. Albert W. Rice.

within marriage. Couples were expected to be in love when they married. Courting couples were even allowed to lie in bed together, with their lower bodies wrapped in an apron and separated by a board—a practice called bundling.

The family economy operated through the combined efforts of husband and wife. Men were generally responsible for field work, women for the work of the household, which included gardening, tending to the dairy and henhouse, and providing fuel and water. Women managed a rich array of tasks, and some independently traded garden products, milk, and eggs. Still, the cultural ideal was the subordination of women to men. Married women could not make contracts, own property, vote, or hold office. A typical woman, marrying in her early twenties and surviving through her forties, could expect to bear eight children and devote herself to husband and family.

The Puritans stressed the importance of well-ordered communities as well as families. Colonists often emigrated in kin groups that made up the core of the new towns. The Massachusetts General Court, the governing body of the colony, granted townships to proprietors representing a congregation. These men then distributed fields, pasture, and woodlands in quantities proportional to the recipient's social status, so that wealthy families received more than others. Settlers clustered their dwellings at the town center, near the meetinghouse that served as both church and civic center. Some towns, particularly those along the coast such as Boston, soon became centers of shipping. These clustered settlements and strong, vital communities made seventeenth-century New England quite different from Chesapeake society.

The Puritans also built an impressive system to educate their young. In 1647 Massachusetts required that towns with 50 families or more support a public school; those with 100 families were to establish a grammar school that taught Latin, knowledge of which was required for admission to Harvard College, founded in 1636.

Dissent and New Communities

The Puritans emigrated in order to practice their variety of Christianity, but they had little tolerance for other religious points of view. Religious disagreement among the colonists soon provoked the founding of three new colonies. Thomas Hooker, minister of the congregation at Cambridge, disagreed with the policy of restricting suffrage to male church members. In 1636 he led his followers west to the Connecticut River, where they founded the town of Hartford. In 1637 a group of London Puritans holding even stricter beliefs than the colonists of Massachusetts established the colony of New Haven on Long Island Sound. Connecticut absorbed New Haven upon receiving a royal charter in 1662.

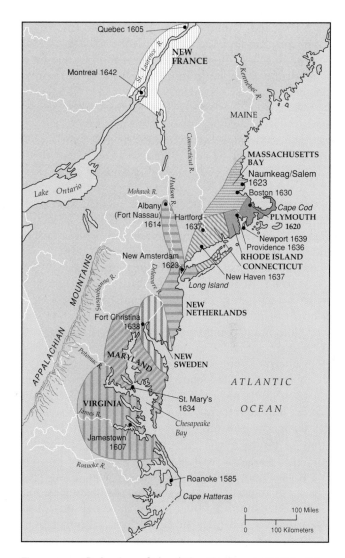

European Colonies of the Atlantic Coast, 1607–39

Virginia on Chesapeake Bay was the first English colony in North America, but by the mid-seventeenth century Virginia was joined by settlements of Scandinavians on the Delaware River and Dutch on the Hudson River, as well as English religious dissenters in New England. The territories indicated here reflect the vague boundaries of the early colonies.

Another dissenter was the minister Roger Williams, who came to New England in 1631 to take up duties for the congregation in Salem. Williams believed in religious tolerance and the separation of church and state (discussed in Chapter 5). He also preached that the colonists had no absolute right to Indian land, but must bargain for it in good faith. These were dangerous ideas, and Williams was banished from the colony in 1636. With a group of his followers, he emigrated to the Narraganset country, where he purchased land from the Indians and founded the town of Providence.

The next year Boston shook with another religious controversy. Anne Hutchinson, the wife of a Puritan merchant who had arrived in New England in 1634, was a brilliant woman who led religious discussion groups that criticized various Boston ministers for a lack of piety. The concentration of attention on good works, she argued, led people to believe that they could earn their way to heaven, a "popish" or Catholic heresy in the eyes of Calvinists. Hutchinson was called before the General Court, where the Puritan leaders made it clear that they would not tolerate a woman who publicly criticized men, and she was excommunicated and banished. She and her followers moved to Roger Williams's settlement, where they established another community in 1638.

In 1644 Roger Williams received a royal charter creating the colony of Rhode Island, named for the principal island in Narraganset Bay, as a protection for these dissenting communities. A new royal charter of 1663 guaranteed self-government and complete religious liberty.

By the 1670s Massachusetts's population had grown to over 40,000, most of it concentrated in and around Boston, although there were communities as far west as the Connecticut River valley and in the northern regions known as Maine (not separated from Massachusetts until 1820), as well as in New Hampshire, set off as a royal colony in 1680. Next in size after Massachusetts was Connecticut, its population numbering about 17,000. Plymouth's 6,000 inhabitants were absorbed by Massachusetts in 1691. The British colonial population grew steadily through the century, then increased sharply in the closing decade as a result of the new settlements of the Restoration Colonies.

The Restoration Colonies

The Puritan Commonwealth established in England after the execution of King Charles attempted to provide a measure of central control over the colonies with the passage in 1651 of an Act of Trade and Navigation intended to keep Dutch ships out of England's overseas possessions. But the regime was preoccupied with English domestic affairs and left the colonies largely to their own devices. Cromwell ruled as Lord Protector of the Commonwealth, but the new order failed to survive his death in 1658. Desperate for political stability after nearly two decades of civil war, Parliament restored the Stuart monarchy in 1660, placing Charles II, son of the former king, on the throne. At the same time, Parliament retained for itself certain significant powers of state. One of Charles's most important acts was the establishment of several new proprietary colonies based on the model of Maryland, known as the Restoration Colonies.

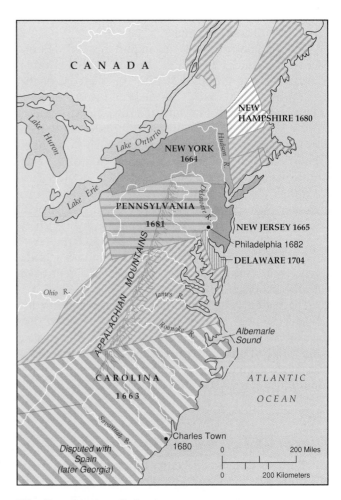

The Restoration Colonies

After the restoration of the Stuart monarchy in 1660, King Charles II of England created several new proprietary colonies along the Atlantic coast.

Early Carolina

In 1663 the king issued the first of the Restoration charters, which called for the establishment of a new colony called Carolina that stretched from Virginia south to Spanish Florida. Virginians had already begun moving into the northern parts of this territory, and in 1664 the Carolina proprietors appointed a governor for the settlements in the area of Albermarle Sound and created a popularly elected assembly. By 1675 North Carolina, as it became known, was home to 5,000 small farmers and large tobacco planters.

Settlement farther south began in 1670 with the founding of coastal Charles Town (Charleston today). Most South Carolina settlers came from Barbados, a Caribbean colony the English had founded in 1627, which had grown rich from the production of sugar. By the 1670s the island had become overpopulated with English settlers and Africans. The latter, imported as slaves to work the plantations, made up a majority of the population. Hundreds of Barbadians, both masters and their slaves, relocated to South Carolina, lending a distinctly West Indian character to the colony. By the end of the seventeenth century South Carolina's population included 6,000 settlers, some 2,500 of them enslaved Africans.

From New Netherland to New York

In 1664 Charles created another new colony by granting to his brother James, the duke of York, a vast territory from Maine south to the Delaware River. Its boundaries conflicted with the lucrative Dutch colony of New Netherland on the Hudson River, which Charles wanted.

The Dutch controlled trading posts in India, Indonesia, and China and sugar plantations in Brazil, as well as the fur trading and farming colony of New Netherland, which extended from Manhattan (established 1623) upriver to Albany (established 1614). They had succeeded in overwhelming the small colony of Swedes on the lower Delaware River, incorporating that region into their sphere of influence in the 1640s.

The Dutch forged a commercial alliance with the Iroquois Confederacy, who began a series of military expeditions known as the Beaver Wars. In the late 1640s the Iroquois attacked and dispersed the Hurons, who had long controlled the flow of furs from the Great Lakes to the French in Montreal. As a result of these wars, the Dutch trading system was extended deep into the continent. Meanwhile, persistent conflict with coastal Algonquians erupted in a series of brutal wars. By the 1660s most of these Indians had withdrawn into the interior.

Long a center of European commerce, the Netherlands had risen to become the greatest merchant and naval power of the Atlantic world in the seventeenth century. Then, in the middle of that century, the English began to challenge the Dutch. The two powers fought an inconclusive naval war in the English Channel during the early 1650s, and a decade later clashed along the West African coast. In 1664 an English fleet sailed into Manhattan harbor and forced the surrender of New Amsterdam without firing a shot.

New Netherland was renamed New York in honor of the duke of York. Otherwise little was done to disturb the existing order, the English preferring to reap the benefits of this profitable and dynamic colony. Ethnically and linguistically diversified, accommodating a wide range of religious sects, New York was the most heterogeneous colony in North America. The Dutch communities of the Delaware Valley became the English proprietary colony of New Jersey in 1665, but continued to be governed by New York until the 1680s. By the 1670s the combined population of these settlements numbered over 10,000, with more than 1,500 people clustered in the governmental and commercial center of New York City.

The Founding of Pennsylvania

In 1676 proprietary rights to the western portion of New Jersey were sold to a group of English Quakers that included William Penn, who intended to make the area a religious haven for members of the Society of Friends, or Quakers. A dissenting sect, the Quakers were committed to religious toleration and pacifism. In 1681 King Charles granted Penn a huge territory west of the Delaware River. The next year Penn supervised the laying out of his capital of Philadelphia.

Penn wanted this colony to be a "holy experiment." In his first Frame of Government, drafted in 1682, he included guarantees of religious freedom, civil liberties, and elected representation. He also attempted to deal fairly with the Algonquian Indians, not permitting colonization until settlement rights were negotiated and lands purchased. In 1682 and 1683 he made an agreement with the sachem Tammany of the Delaware tribe. Although Pennsylvania's relations with the Indians later soured, during Penn's lifetime his reputation for fair dealing led a number of Indian groups to resettle in the Quaker colony.

During the first decade of Pennsylvania's settlement, over 10,000 colonists arrived from England, and agricultural communities were soon spreading from the Delaware into the fertile interior valleys. In 1704 Penn approved the creation of a separate government for the area formerly controlled by the Scandinavians and Dutch, which became the colony of Delaware. In the eighteenth century Pennsylvania became known as America's breadbasket, and Philadelphia became the most important colonial port in North America.

Conflict and War

Pennsylvania's ability to maintain peaceful relations with the Indians proved the great exception, for the last quarter of the seventeenth century was a time of great violence throughout the colonial regions of the continent. Much of this warfare was between colonists and Indians, but intertribal warfare and intercolonial rivalry greatly contributed to the violence. It extended from Santa Fé—where the revolt of the Pueblos was the single most effective instance of Indian resistance to colonization—to the shores of Hudson's Bay, where French and English traders fought for access to the rich fur region of the north.

King Philip's War

During the nearly forty years of peace that followed the Pequot War of 1637, the Algonquian and English peoples of New England lived in close, if tense, contact. Several Puritan ministers, including John Eliot and Thomas Mayhew, began to preach to the Indians, and several hundred Algonquian converts eventually relocated in Christian Indian communities called praying towns. Outside the colonial boundaries, however, there remained a number of independent Indian tribes, including the Wampanoags and the Narragansets of Rhode Island and the Abenakis of northern New England. The extraordinary expansion of the Puritan population, and their hunger for land, created pressures for further expansion into those territories.

In 1671 the Wampanoags were forced by their Pilgrim allies to concede authority over their home territory. This humiliation convinced the Wampanoag sachem Metacomet (called King Philip by his English teachers), son of Massasoit, that his people must break their half-century alliance with Plymouth and take up armed resistance. Meanwhile, the Puritan colonies prepared for a war of conquest.

In the spring of 1675 Plymouth magistrates arrested and executed three Wampanoag men for the murder of a Christian Indian. Fearing the moment of confrontation had arrived, Metacomet appealed to the Narragansets for a defensive alliance. The United Colonies (the New England colonies led by Massachusetts Bay) and New York—each hoping for territorial gain—took this as the moment to send armed forces into Narraganset country, attacking and burning a number of villages. What became known as King Philip's War soon engulfed New England.

Metacomet, or King Philip, in a mid–eighteenth-century engraving by Paul Revere of Boston. Like his father, Massasoit, Metacomet tried to cooperate with English colonists but finally had to fight to maintain his authority. For many years after the war, the leaders at Plymouth kept his severed head on display. Because his remains never received an honored burial, say the descendants of the Wampanoags, Metacomet's ghost still rises and walks about his homeland.

At first things went well for the Indians. By the beginning of 1676, however, their campaign was collapsing. A combined colonial army invaded Narraganset country, burning villages, killing women and children, and defeating a large Indian force in a battle known as the Great Swamp Fight. In western New England Metacomet appealed to the Iroquois for supplies and support, but instead they attacked and defeated his forces. Metacomet retreated back to his homeland, where the colonists annihilated his army in August 1676.

In their attack on Metacomet's army, the Iroquois were motivated by interests of their own. Casting themselves in the role of powerful intermediaries between other tribes and the English colonies, the Iroquois wanted to subjugate all rival trading systems. In a series of negotiations conducted at Albany in 1677, the Iroquois Confederacy and the colony of New York created an alliance known as the Covenant Chain, which sought to establish Iroquois dominance over all other tribes as well as New York dominance over all other colonies. During the 1680s the Iroquois pressed their claims as far west as the Illinois country, fighting the western Algonquians allied with the French trading system.

At the end of King Philip's War, some 4,000 Algonquians and 2,000 English colonists were dead, and dozens of native and colonial towns lay in smoking ruins. Measured against the size of the population, it was one of the most destructive wars in American history. Fearing attack from Indians close at hand, colonists attacked and killed the Christian Indians of the praying towns. The war marked the end of organized Indian resistance in New England. Yet a number of the praying towns, such as Mashpee on Cape Cod, as well as communities of Narragansets, Pequots, and other tribal groups, survived into the twentieth century. Their several thousand residents have an alternative perspective on the history of New England.

Bacon's Rebellion

At the same time as King Philip's War, another English–Indian confrontation took place in the Chesapeake. In the 1670s the Susquehannock people of the upper Potomac River came into conflict with the tobacco planters expanding from Virginia. Violent raids in 1675, led by wealthy backcountry settler Nathaniel Bacon, included the indiscriminate murder of Indians. The efforts of Virginia governor William Berkeley to suppress these unauthorized military expeditions so infuriated Bacon and his followers that in the spring of 1676 they turned their fury against the colonial capital of Jamestown itself. Berkeley fled across the Chesapeake while Bacon pillaged and burned the capital. Soon thereafter Bacon died of dysentery, a common fate of the day, and his rebellion collapsed. The next year Virginia signed a treaty ending hostilities with the Indians, but most of the Susquehannocks had already returned to New York, where they joined the Covenant Chain of the Iroquois.

This brief but violent clash marked an important change of direction for Virginia. During his tenure as "General of Virginia," Bacon had issued a manifesto demanding not only the death or removal of all Indians from the colony, but also an end to the rule of aristo-

SUMMARY TABLE	*Conflict and War*	
King Philip's War	1675–76	Armed conflict between the Indian peoples of southern New England and the Puritan colonies for the control of land.
Bacon's Rebellion	1675–76	Backcountry settlers attack Indians and colonial authorities try to suppress these attacks.
Wars in the South	1670s–1720s	British colonists in the Carolinas incite Creeks, Cherokees, and other Indian tribes to attack and enslave the mission Indians of Spanish Florida.
The Glorious Revolution in America	1689	Colonists in Massachusetts, New York, and Maryland rise up against the colonial governments of King James II.
King William's War	1689–97	The first of a series of colonial struggles between England and France, fought principally on the frontiers of northern New England and New York.

cratic "grandees" and "parasites." The rebellion thus signaled a developing conflict between frontier districts such as Bacon's and the established tidewater region where the "Indian problem" had long since been settled. Colonial authorities in Virginia and North Carolina began to favor armed expansion into Indian territory, hoping to gain the support of backcountry men by enlarging the stock of available colonial land. Moreover, planters' fears of disorder among former servants encouraged them to accelerate the transition to slave labor.

Wars in the South

There was also massive violence in South Carolina during the 1670s, as colonists there began the operation of a large-scale Indian slave trade. Charleston merchants encouraged Yamasees, Creeks, Cherokees, and Chickasaws to wage war on Indian tribes allied to rival colonial powers: the mission Indians of Spanish Florida, the Choctaw allies of the French, and the Tuscaroras, trading partners of the Virginians.

This vicious slave trade extended well into the eighteenth century, and thousands of southern Indians were sold into captivity. Most of the Indian men were shipped from Charleston to West Indian or northern colonies; the Indian women remained in South Carolina, where many eventually formed relationships and had children with male African slaves, forming a racial–ethnic group known as the *mustees.*

The Glorious Revolution in America

Upon Charles II's death in 1685, his brother and successor, James II, began to strengthen royal control over the colonies. In his most dramatic action, the king abolished the charter governments of the New England, New York, and New Jersey colonies because they had grown too independent. In England the same imperious style on the part of the king alienated Parliament, and in a bloodless transition, afterward known as the Glorious Revolution, Parliament deposed King James in 1688 and replaced him with his daughter and Dutch son-in-law, Mary and William of Orange.

In the colonies the Glorious Revolution resulted in a series of rebellions against the authorities set in place by King James II. The government of England did not fully reestablish its authority in these colonies until 1691–92, when Massachusetts, New York, and Maryland all were declared royal colonies.

King William's War

The year 1689 also marked the beginning of nearly seventy-five years of armed conflict between English and French forces for control of the North American interior. The Iroquois–English Covenant Chain challenged New France to press even harder in search of commercial opportunities in the interior. In the far north the English countered French dominance with the establishment of Hudson's Bay Company, a royal fur trade monopoly.

Hostilities began with English–Iroquois attacks on Montreal and violence between rival French and English traders on Hudson's Bay. These skirmishes were part of a larger conflict between England and France called the War of the League of Augsburg in Europe and King William's War in the North American colonies. This inconclusive war was ended by the Treaty of Ryswick of 1697, which established an equally inconclusive peace. War between England and France resumed only five years later. The result of this quarter-century of violence was the tightening of the imperial reins.

Conclusion

At the beginning of the seventeenth century the European presence north of Mexico was extremely limited: two Spanish bases in Florida, a few Franciscan missionaries among the Pueblos, and fishermen along the North Atlantic coast. By 1700 the human landscape of the Southwest, the South, and the Northeast had been transformed. More than a quarter million Europeans and Africans had moved into these three regions, the vast majority to the British colonies. Indian societies had been disrupted, depopulated, and in some cases destroyed. The Spanish and French colonies were characterized by the inclusion of Indians in the social and economic life of the community. But along the Atlantic coast the English had established communities of exclusion, whose implications for the future of colonist–Indian relations were ominous.

CHRONOLOGY

1598	Juan de Oñate leads Spanish into New Mexico	1660	Stuart monarchy restored, Charles II becomes king
1607	English found Jamestown	1675–76	King Philip's War
1608	French found Quebec	1675–76	Bacon's Rebellion
1609	Spanish found Santa Fé	1680	The Pueblo Revolt
1620	Pilgrim emigration	1681	La Salle explores the Mississippi
1622	Indian uprising in Virginia	1688	The Glorious Revolution
1625	Jesuit missionaries arrive in New France	1689–97	King William's War
1629	Puritans begin settlement of Massachusetts Bay	1698	Reconquest of the Pueblos completed
1649	Charles I executed	1701	English impose royal governments on all their colonies

Review Questions

1. Using examples drawn from this chapter, discuss the differences between colonizing frontiers of inclusion and exclusion.
2. What factors turned England's Chesapeake colony of Virginia from stark failure to brilliant success?
3. Discuss the role of religious dissent in the founding of the first New England colonies and in stimulating the creation of others.
4. Compare William Penn's policy with respect to Indian tribes with the policies of other English settlers, in the Chesapeake and New England, and with the policies of the Spanish, the French, and the Dutch.
5. What were the principal causes of colonial violence and warfare of the late seventeenth century?

Recommended Reading

JAMES AXTELL, *The European and the Indian: Essays in the Ethnohistory of Colonial America* (1981). A readable introduction to the dynamics of mutual discovery between natives and colonizers.

CARL BRIDENBAUGH, *Vexed and Troubled Englishmen, 1590–1642* (1968). A social history of the English people on the eve of colonization, emphasizing their religious and economic problems.

W. J. ECCLES, *France in America* (1972). The most comprehensive introduction to the history of New France.

RAMÓN A. GUTIÉRREZ, *When Jesus Came, the Corn Mothers Went Away: Marriage, Sexuality, and Power in New Mexico, 1500–1846* (1991). A brilliant new interpretation of colonial New Mexico.

EDMUND S. MORGAN, *American Slavery, American Freedom* (1975). A classic interpretation of early Virginia. Morgan argues that early American ideas of freedom for some were based on slavery for others.

NEAL SALISBURY, *Manitou and Providence: Indians, Europeans, and the Making of New England* (1982). One of the best examples of the new ethnohistory of Indians; a provocative intercultural approach to the history of the Northeast.

DAVID J. WEBER, *The Spanish Frontier in North America* (1992). A powerful new overview that includes the history of New Mexico and Florida.

PETER H. WOOD ETAL., EDS., *Powhatan's Mantle: Indians in the Colonial Southeast* (1989). Essays detailing the conflict and consort between colonists and natives in the South.

4

SLAVERY AND EMPIRE, 1441–1770

AMERICAN COMMUNITIES

African Slaves Build Their Own Community in Coastal Georgia

Africans labored in the steamy heat of the coastal Georgia rice fields, the breeches of the men rolled up over their knees, the sack skirts of the women gathered and tied about their hips, leaving them, in the words of one shocked observer, "two thirds naked." Standing on the banks of canals that channeled water to the fields, African slave drivers, whips at the ready, supervised the work. Upriver, groups cut away cypress and gum trees and cleared the swampland's jungle maze of undergrowth; others constructed levees, preparing to bring more land under cultivation. An English overseer or plantation master could be seen here and there, but overwhelmingly it was a country populated by Africans.

These plantations were southern extensions of the South Carolina rice belt. Although slavery had been prohibited by Georgia's original charter of 1732, the restriction was lifted when Georgia became a royal colony two decades later. By 1770, 15,000 African Americans (80 percent of the region's population) lived on several hundred coastal rice plantations owned by a small elite of whites.

Rice was one of the most valuable commodities produced in mainland North America, surpassed in value only by tobacco and wheat. The growth of rice production in the lower South was matched by an enormous expansion in the Atlantic slave trade. Having no experience in rice cultivation, planters pressed slave traders to supply them with Africans from rice-growing regions such as the Windward Coast of West Africa. In its work force, its methods, and even its tools, southern rice culture was patterned on an African model.

Although in the eighteenth century the number of North American blacks who were "country born" (native to America, and thus born into slavery) grew steadily in the eighteenth century, the majority on the rice plantations continued to be what were known as "saltwater" Africans. These people had endured the shock of enslavement. Ripped from their homeland communities in West Africa by slave raiders, they were brutally marched to coastal forts. There they were imprisoned, subjected to humiliating inspections of their bodies, and branded on the buttocks like animals. Packed into the holds of stinking ships, they were forced into a nightmarish passage across the Atlantic Ocean. When finally unloaded on a strange continent, they were sold at dockside auctions, then once again marched overland to their destinations on

New World plantations. On the rice plantations of isolated coastal Georgia, enslaved Africans suffered from overwork and numerous physical ailments that resulted from poor diet, minimal and inappropriate clothing, and inadequate housing. Mortality rates were exceptionally high, especially for infants. Colonial laws permitted masters to discipline and punish slaves indiscriminately. They were whipped, confined in irons, castrated, or sold away, with little regard for their relations with family or friends.

Africans struggled to make a place for themselves in this inhospitable world. Because many of the slaves of the rice coast had a knowledge of rice cultivation, they had enough bargaining power with their masters to win an acceptance of the familiar work routines and rhythms of West Africa. Thus low-country plantations operated according to the *task system:* once slaves finished their specific jobs, they could use their remaining time to hunt, fish, or cultivate family gardens. Masters often complained that "tasking" did not produce the same level of profit as the gang labor system of the sugar plantations, but African rice hands refused to work any other way.

Many still ran away, like slaves everywhere in the Americas. Some fled in groups, heading for the Creek Indian settlements in northern Florida, or toward St. Augustine, where the Spanish promised them safe haven. Some struck out violently at their masters: a group of nine Africans from a Savannah plantation killed their master and stole a boat, planning to head upriver, but were apprehended as they lay in wait to murder their hated overseers.

So slaves resisted. But like slaves throughout the New World, the majority of enslaved Africans and African Americans of the Georgia coast remained and built communities of their own within the heartless world of slavery. Plantation slaves married, raised children, and over time constructed African American kinship networks. They passed on African names and traditions and created new ones. These links between individuals and families formed the basis for reestablished communities. African American slave communities combined elements of African languages and English to form dialects that allowed newly arrived people from many different African ethnic groups as well as American-born slaves to communicate with one another. Neither individuals nor families alone can make a language; that is something only a community can do. The common African heritage and a common status as slaves supplied the basis for the African American community and culture, in which dance, song, and story were refitted to New World circumstances and traditional African arts, such as woodworking, iron making, and weaving, were reestablished. Through their culture, the slaves shared a powerful awareness of their common oppression. They told or sang dialect tales of mistreatment, as in this song of *Quow*, the punished slave:

> Was matter Buddy Quow?
> I ble Obesha bang you. . . .
> Dah Backrow Man go wrong you, Buddy Quow,
> Dah Backrow Man go wrong you, Buddy Quow.
>
> [What's the matter Brother Quow?
> I believe the overseer's beat you. . . .
> The white man's wronged you, Brother Quow,
> The white man's wronged you, Brother Quow.]

Just as European settlers planted colonial communities, so Africans, who made up the largest group of people to come to North America during the colonial era, constructed distinctive communities of their own. The history of African Americans includes the story of the Atlantic slave trade, the plunder of Africa, and the profits of the empire. But it is also a story of achievement under the most difficult circumstances, and of the making of families, kin networks, and communities. They "labor together and converse almost wholly among themselves," a minister wrote of low-country slaves. "They are, as 'twere, a nation within a nation."

The Beginnings of African Slavery

Household slaves had long been a part of the world of Mediterranean Europe. However, many Europeans were disturbed by the moral implications of enslaving Christians, and in the early fifteenth century the pope excommunicated a number of merchants engaged in selling such captives. However, Africans and Muslims were sufficiently different in culture and appearance to quiet those concerns.

One of the goals of Portuguese expansion in the fifteenth century was access to the lucrative West African trade in gold, wrought iron, ivory, tortoiseshell, textiles, and slaves that had been dominated by the Moors of northern Africa. The pope awarded the Portuguese a monopoly on African coastal trade. Portuguese traders found it efficient to leave the kidnapping of men and women for slavery to Africans, who were willing to sell the captured slaves in exchange for European commodities. By the 1450s a small but regular slave trade between Africa and Europe was in place.

The greatest market for these slaves was the large sugar plantations the Portuguese established on their island colony of Madeira, off the coast of northern Africa.

Sugar and Slavery

Sugar and slaves had gone together since Italian merchants of the fourteenth century imported the first cane sugar from the Middle East and set up the first modern sugar plantations on the islands of the Mediterranean. Thus the use of Africans as slaves came to the Americas along with the spread of sugar production. One of the first products Columbus introduced to the New World was sugar cane. Sugar plantations were soon operating on the island of Hispaniola. At first the Spanish tried to use the native Indian people as a slave labor force, but

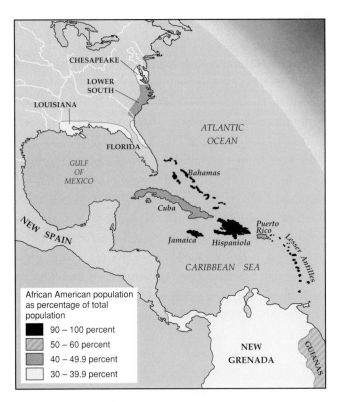

Slave Colonies of the Seventeenth and Eighteenth Centuries

By the eighteenth century the system of slavery had created societies with large African populations throughout the Caribbean and along the southern coast of North America.

because disease and warfare had so reduced the indigenous population, colonists soon turned to African slaves who were already working in Spain. Meanwhile, the Portuguese, aided by Dutch financiers, created a center of sugar production in Northeast Brazil that became a model of the efficient and brutal exploitation of African labor. By 1600 some 25,000 enslaved Africans labored on the plantations of Hispaniola and Brazil.

The Dutch, using their experience in Brazil, became responsible for the next extension of slavery in the Americas. In 1630 they seized Brazil and for over twenty years they controlled this lucrative colony. Skilled at finance and commerce, they greatly expanded the European market for sugar, converting it from a luxury item for the rich to a staple for European workers. It was the Dutch who introduced sugar cultivation in the tropics. As a result, Barbados became the most valuable of England's colonies. Once the profitability of sugar had been demonstrated, the English sought to expand their Caribbean holdings by seizing the island of

Jamaica from the Spanish in 1655 and making it over in the image of Barbados.

The French repeated the process. They first developed sugar plantations on the small island of Martinique, then seized the eastern half of Hispaniola from the Spanish and created a sugar colony called St. Domingue (today's Haiti). Caribbean sugar and slaves had become the centerpiece of the European colonial system.

West Africans

The men and women whose labor made these tropical colonies so profitable came from the long-established societies and local communities of West Africa. In the sixteenth century more than a hundred different peoples lived along the coast of West Africa, from Cape Verde south to Angola. In the north were groups such as the Wolof, Mandingo, Hausa, Ashanti, and Yoruba; to the south the Ibo, Seke, Bakongo, and Mbundu.

In all these societies the most important institution was the local community, which was organized by kinship. Decisions about production, storage, and distribution were generally made by clan leaders and village chiefs; local courts arbitrated disputes. Men often took a second or third wife. This marriage system, known as *polygyny,* produced very large composite families with complex internal relationships.

West African societies were based on sophisticated farming systems many thousands of years old. Africans practiced shifting cultivation: they cleared land by burning, used hoes or digging sticks to cultivate fields, and after several years moved on to other plots while the cleared land lay fallow. Men worked at clearing the land, women at cultivation and the sale of surpluses in the lively West African markets.

Farming sustained large populations and thriving networks of commerce, and in some areas kingdoms and states developed. Along the upper Niger River, where the grassland gradually turns to desert, towns such as Timbuktu developed into trading centers. There were a number of lesser states and kingdoms along the coast, and it was with these that the Portuguese first bargained for Africans who could be sold as slaves.

West Africans were accustomed to regular agricultural labor. This was important, because it proved to be practically impossible to convert large numbers of foraging or nomadic peoples into efficient plantation workers. Moreover, varieties of household slavery were common in West African societies, although slaves there were often treated more as members of the family than as mere possessions. The West African familiarity with "unfree" labor made it possible for African and European traders to begin the trade in human merchandise.

The African Slave Trade

The movement of Africans across the Atlantic to the Americas was the largest forced migration in world history. The Atlantic slave trade, which began with the Portuguese in the fifteenth century and did not end in the United States until 1807 (and continued elsewhere in the Americas until the 1870s), is a brutal chapter in the making of America.

The Demography of the Slave Trade

Scholars today estimate that slavers transported 10 to 11 million Africans to the Americas during the four-century history of the trade. Seventy-six percent arrived from 1701 to 1810—the peak period of colonial demand for labor, when tens of thousands of people were shipped from Africa each year. Of this vast multitude, about half were delivered to Dutch, French, or British sugar plantations in the Caribbean, a third to Portuguese Brazil, and 10 percent to Spanish America. A much smaller proportion—about one in twenty, or an estimated 600,000 men, women, and children—were transported to the British colonies of North America. With the exception of the 1750s, when the British colonies were engulfed by the Seven Years' War, the slave trade continued to rise in importance in the decades before the Revolution.

Among the Africans brought to the Americas, men generally outnumbered women two to one. Because most Africans were destined for field work, this ratio probably reflected the preferences of plantation owners. The majority of captured and transported Africans were young people, between the ages of fifteen and thirty. Nearly every ethnic group in West Africa was represented.

Slavers of All Nations

All the nations of Western Europe participated in the slave trade. Dutch slavers began challenging Portuguese control at the end of the sixteenth century and during the sugar boom of the seventeenth century the Dutch became the most prominent slave-trading nation. The English also entered the trade in the sixteenth century.

For the most part the European presence in Africa was confined to outposts, although the Portuguese

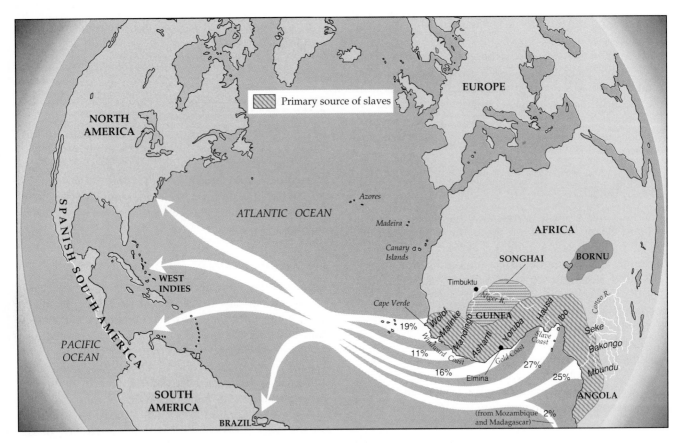

The African Slave Trade

The enslaved men, women, and children transported to the Americas came from West Africa, the majority from the lower Niger River (called the Slave Coast) and the region of the Congo and Angola.

established a colony in Angola. By the early eighteenth century, more than two dozen trading forts dotted the 220 miles of the Gold Coast alone. As the slave trade peaked in the middle of the century, however, the forts of trading companies gave way to independent traders who set up operations with the cooperation of local headmen or chiefs. This informal manner of trading offered opportunities for small operators, such as the New England slavers who entered the trade in the early eighteenth century. Many great New England fortunes were built from profits in the slave trade.

The Shock of Enslavement

The slave trade was a collaboration between European or American and African traders. Dependent on the favor of local rulers, many colonial slave traders lived permanently in coastal forts and married African women, reinforcing their commercial ties with family relations. In many areas a mixed-ancestry group became prominent in the coastal slave trade. Continuing the practice of the Portuguese, the grim business of slave raiding was left to the Africans themselves. Slaves were not at all reticent about condemning the participation of their fellow Africans. "I must own to the shame of my own countrymen," wrote Ottobah Cugoano, who was sold into slavery in the mid-eighteenth century, "that I was first kidnapped and betrayed by those of my own complexion."

Most Africans were enslaved through warfare. Sometimes large armies launched massive attacks, burning whole towns and taking hundreds of prisoners. More common were smaller raids in which a group of armed men attacked at nightfall, seized everyone within reach, then escaped with their captives. Kidnapping, called *panyaring* in the jargon of the slave trade, was also common.

As the demand for slaves increased in the eighteenth century with the expansion of the plantation system in the Americas, raids extended deeper and deeper into the

African interior. The march to the coast was filled with terrors. One account describes a two-month trip in which many captives died of hunger, thirst, or exhaustion, several attempted suicide, and the whole party was forced to hide to avoid being seized by a rival band of raiders. The captives finally arrived on the coast, where they were sold to an American vessel bound for South Carolina.

Enslavement was an unparalleled shock. Venture Smith, an African born in Guinea in 1729, was eight years old when he was captured. After many years in North American slavery, he still vividly recalled the attack on his village, the torture and murder of his father, and the long march of his people to the coast. "The shocking scene is to this day fresh in my mind," he wrote, "and I have often been overcome while thinking on it."

On the coast, European traders and African raiders assembled their captives. Prisoners waited in dark dungeons or in open pens called *barracoons*. To lessen the possibility of collective resistance traders split up families and ethnic groups. Captains carefully inspected each man and woman, and those selected for transport were branded on the back or buttocks with the mark of the buyer. Olaudah Equiano remembered that "those white men with horrible looks, red faces, and long hair, looked and acted . . . in so savage a manner; . . . I had never seen among any people such instances of brutal cruelty." Equiano's narrative, written during the 1780s, after he had secured his freedom, is one of the few that provide an African account of enslavement. He and his fellow captives became convinced that they "had got into a world of bad spirits," and were about to be eaten by cannibals. A French trader wrote that many prisoners were "positively prepossessed with the opinion that we transport them into our country in order to kill and eat them."

The Middle Passage

In the eighteenth century English sailors christened the voyage of slave ships the Middle Passage, the middle part of a triangle from England to Africa to America and back to England. From coastal forts and barracoons, crews rowed small groups of slaves out to the waiting ships and packed them into shelves below deck only six feet long by two and a half feet high. "Rammed like herring in a barrel," wrote one observer, slaves were "chained to each other hand and foot, and stowed so close, that they were not allowed above a foot and a half for each in breadth." People were forced to sleep "spoon fashion," and the tossing of the ship knocked them about so violently that the skin over their elbows sometimes was worn to the bone from scraping on the planks. One ship designed to carry 450 slaves regularly crossed the Atlantic with more than 600.

Their holds filled with human cargo, the ships headed toward Cape Verde to catch the trade winds blowing toward America. A favorable voyage from Senegambia to Barbados might be accomplished in as little as three weeks, but a ship from Guinea or Angola becalmed in the doldrums or driven back by storms might take as much as three months.

The voyage was marked by a daily routine. In the morning the crew opened the hatch and brought the

A slave coffle in an eighteenth century print. As the demand for slaves increased, raids extended deeper and deeper into the African interior. Tied together with forked logs or bark rope, men, women, and children were marched hundreds of miles toward the coast, where their African captors traded them to European traders.

captives on deck, attaching their leg irons to a great chain running the length of the bulwarks. After a breakfast of beans came a ritual known as dancing the slave: while an African thumped an upturned kettle or plucked a banjo, the crew commanded men and women to jump up and down in a bizarre session of exercise. A day spent chained on deck was concluded by a second bland meal and then the stowing away. During the night, according to one seaman, there issued from below "a howling melancholy noise, expressive of extreme anguish." Down in the hold, the groans of the dying, the shrieks of women and children, and the suffocating heat and stench were, in the words of Olaudah Equiano, "a scene of horror almost inconceivable."

Among the worst of the horrors was the absence of adequate sanitation. There were "necessary tubs" set below deck, but Africans, "endeavoring to get to them, tumble over their companions," one eighteenth-century ship's surgeon wrote, "and as the necessities of nature are not to be resisted, they ease themselves as they lie." Efficient captains ordered crews to scrape and swab the holds daily, but so sickening was the task that on many ships it was rarely performed and Africans were left to wallow in their urine and feces. When first taken below deck, the boy Equiano remembered, "I received such a salutation in my nostrils as I had never experienced in my life," and "became so sick and low that I was not able to eat." Many captives sickened and died in these conditions. Many others contracted dysentery, known as the "flux." Frequent shipboard epidemics of smallpox, measles, and yellow fever added to the misery.

The unwilling voyagers offered plenty of resistance. As long as ships were still within sight of the African coast, hope remained alive and the danger of revolt was great. One historian has found references to fifty-five slave revolts on British and American ships from 1699 to 1845. Once on the open sea, however, captives' resistance took more desperate form. The sight of the disappearing coast of Africa "left me abandoned to despair," wrote Equiano; "I now saw myself deprived of all chance of returning to my native country, or even the least glimpse of hope of gaining the shore." He witnessed several Africans jump overboard and drown, "and I believe many more would very soon have done the same if they had not been prevented by the ship's crew." Captains took the precaution of spreading netting along the sides of their ships. "Could I have got over the nettings," Equiano declared, "I would have jumped over the side."

Arrival in the New World

As the ship approached its destination the crew prepared the human cargo for market. All but the most rebellious were freed from their chains and allowed to wash themselves and move about the deck. Captains did what they could to get their Africans into presentable condition. To impress buyers, slavers might parade Africans off the ship to the tune of an accordion or the beat of a drum. But the toll of the Middle Passage was difficult to disguise. One observer described a disembarking group as "walking skeletons covered over with a piece of tanned leather."

Some cargoes were destined for a single wealthy planter, or consigned to a merchant who sold the captives in return for a commission; in other cases the captain himself was responsible. Buyers painstakingly examined the Africans, who once again suffered the indignity of probing eyes and poking fingers. In ports such as Charleston, sales were generally made by auction, or by a method known as the *scramble*. In the scramble, standard prices were set in advance for men, women, boys, and girls. The Africans were then driven into a corral, and at a signal the buyers rushed among them, grabbing their pick of the lot. The noise, clamor, and eagerness of the buyers, Equiano remembered, renewed all the terrible apprehensions of the Africans. Bought by a Virginian, Equiano was taken to an isolated tobacco plantation where he found himself unable to communicate with any of his fellow slaves, who came from other ethnic groups.

Political and Economic Effects on Africa

Africa began the sixteenth century with genuine independence. But as surely as Europe and America grew stronger as a result of the trade and the labor of slaves, so Africa grew weaker by their loss. In the short term, slave-trading kingdoms on the coast increased their power at the expense of interior states. But these coastal states found that the slave trade was a viper that could easily strike back at them. "Merchants daily seize our own subjects, sons of the land and sons of our noblemen, they grab them and cause them to be sold," King Dom Affonso of the Kongo wrote to the Portuguese monarch in the sixteenth century, "and so great, Sir, is their corruption and licentiousness that our country is being utterly depopulated."

More serious still, however, than the loss of millions of men and women over the centuries was the long-term stagnation of the West African economy. Labor was drawn away from farming and other productive activities, and imported consumer goods such as textiles and metalwares stifled local manufacturing. African traders were expert at driving a hard bargain for slaves, but even when they appeared to get the best of the exchange, the ultimate advantage lay with the Europeans, who received wealth-producing workers in return for mere consumer goods.

For every man or woman taken captive, as many as two more died in the chronic slave raiding. Many of the new West African states became little more than machines for supplying captives to European traders, and a "gun–slave cycle" pushed neighboring kingdoms into a destructive arms race. The resulting political and cultural demoralization prepared the way for the European conquest of Africa in the nineteenth century.

The Development of North American Slave Societies

New World slavery was nearly two centuries old before it became an important system of labor in North America. There were slaves in each of the British colonies during the seventeenth century, but in 1700 they were only 11 percent of the colonial population. During the eighteenth century slavery greatly expanded, and by 1770 Africans and African Americans in British North America numbered 460,000, or more than 20 percent of the colonial population. The ethnic structure of the South diverged radically from that of the North during this period.

Slavery Comes to North America

The first Africans arrived in Virginia in 1619, but only a small number were brought to Virginia over the next several decades. In fact, there are indications that the Africans who worked in the tobacco fields were not slaves at all, but servants.

In the last quarter of the seventeenth century, however, a number of developments encouraged the expansion of true slavery. In colonies such as Pennsylvania, European immigrants discovered good opportunities as free farmers, so it became increasingly difficult to recruit them as indentured servants. Moreover, after Bacon's Rebellion and the other social conflicts of the 1670s, a number of colonial leaders became concerned about potential rebellions among former indentured servants. Because people were living longer, possibly the result of being better fed and more resistant to disease, more servants were surviving their indentures. But these im-

provements in living conditions also affected Africans, increasing their rates of survival, and planters began to see more advantage in the purchase of slaves. During these same years, the supply of slaves in North America increased when the Royal African Company inaugurated direct shipments from West Africa to the mainland. Thus the work force of indentured servants was gradually replaced by a work force of slaves.

As the proportions of slaves in the colonial population rose, colonists wrote slavery into law, a process best observed in the case of Virginia. In 1662 colonial officials declared that children inherited the status of their slave mothers; five years later they added that baptism could no longer alter conditions of servitude. Two important avenues to freedom were thus closed. The colony then placed life-threatening violence in the hands of masters, declaring in 1669 that the death of a slave during punishment "shall not be accounted felony." Such regulations accumulated piecemeal until 1705, when Virginia gathered them into a comprehensive slave code that became a model for other colonies.

Thus the institution of slavery was strengthened just as the Atlantic slave trade reached flood tide in the eighteenth century. During that century's first decade, more Africans were imported into North America than the total number for the previous ninety-three years of colonial history. The English colonies were primed for an unprecedented growth of plantation slavery.

The Tobacco Colonies

During the eighteenth century the European demand for tobacco increased more than tenfold. This demand was supplied largely by increased production in the Chesapeake. Tobacco was far and away the single most important commodity produced in North America, accounting for more than a quarter of the value of all colonial exports.

The expansion of tobacco production could not have taken place without an enormous growth in the size of the slave labor force. Unlike sugar, tobacco did not require large plantations and could be produced successfully on small farms. But it was a crop that demanded a great deal of hand labor and close attention, and from the beginnings of Chesapeake colonization its cultivation had been the responsibility of indentured servants and slaves. As tobacco farming grew, slaveholding became widespread. By 1770 more than a quarter million slaves labored in the colonies of the Upper South, and because of the exploding market for to-

An Overseer Doing His Duty, *a watercolor sketch made by Benjamin Henry Latrobe during a trip to Virginia in 1798. The majority of masters in the tobacco region owned only one or two slaves and worked with them in the fields. In his portrayal of this overseer, relaxing as he supervises his workers, Latrobe clearly expressed his disgust for slavery.*
Watercolor on paper. Collection of the Maryland Historical Society, Baltimore.

bacco, their numbers were expanding at about double the rate of the general population.

Shipments from Africa accounted for part of the growth of the slave population. In the Caribbean and Brazil, where profits from sugar were high, many sugar planters preferred to work their slaves to death, replenishing them with a constant stream of new arrivals from Africa. In Virginia, however, lower rates of profit may have caused tobacco planters to pay more attention to the health of their labor force, establishing work routines that were not so deadly. Food supplies were plentiful in North America, which made the Chesapeake populations of Africans resistant to disease. Thus self-sustained population growth among Chesapeake slaves had begun by the 1730s, and by the 1770s the majority were "country-born."

The Lower South

For fifty years after the founding of the South Carolina colony in 1670, the area outside the immediate region of Charleston remained a rough and dangerous frontier. English settlers raised cattle, often using slaves with experience in the pastoral economies of West Africa. But the most valuable part of the early Carolina economy was the Indian slave trade. Practicing a strategy of divide and conquer, using Indian tribes to fight one another, Carolinians enslaved tens of thousands of Indians before the 1730s.

As the chapter opening illustrates, by 1715, however, rice production had become the most dynamic sector of the South Carolina economy and like cattle grazing, it depended on the expertise of West Africans. Another important crop was added in the 1740s, when a young South Carolina woman named Elizabeth Lucas Pickney successfully adapted West Indian indigo to the low-country climate. It is likely that the assistance of West Indian slaves skilled in indigo culture was crucial. The indigo plant, native to India, produced a deep blue dye important in textile manufacture. Rice grew in the lowlands, but indigo could be cultivated on the high ground. And because they had different seasonal growing patterns, the two crops harmonized perfectly. Rice and indigo production rose steadily over the next thirty years. By the 1770s they were among the most valuable commodities exported from the mainland colonies of North America.

Like tobacco, the expansion of rice and indigo production depended on the growth of African slavery. Before the international slave trade to the United States was ended in 1807, at least 100,000 Africans had arrived at Charleston. One of every five ancestors of today's African Americans passed through Charleston on his or her way to the rice and indigo fields.

By the 1740s many of the arriving Africans were being taken to Georgia, a colony created by an act of the English Parliament in 1732. Its leader, James Edward Oglethorpe, hoped to establish a buffer against Spanish invasion from Florida and make it a haven for poor British farmers, who could then sell their products in the markets of South Carolina. Under Oglethorpe's influence, Parliament agreed to prohibit slavery in Georgia. Soon, however, Georgia's coastal regions were being colonized by South Carolina planters with their slaves. In 1752 Oglethorpe and Georgia's trustees abandoned their experiment, and the colony was opened to slavery under royal authority. The Georgia coast had already become an extension of the Carolina low-country slave system.

By 1770 there were nearly 90,000 African Americans in the Lower South, about 80 percent of the coastal population of South Carolina and Georgia. The slave economy of the Lower South was dominated by large plantations, which had fifty to seventy-five slaves each. The work was hard, but because of the task system described at the beginning of the chapter, slaves exercised a measure of control over their own lives. The African American communities of the Lower South, like those of the Chesapeake, achieved self-sustained growth by the middle of the eighteenth century.

Slavery in the Spanish Colonies

Slavery was basic to the Spanish colonial labor system, yet doubts about the enslavement of Africans were raised by both church and the crown. The papacy denounced slavery many times as a violation of Christian principles. But the institution of slavery remained intact, and later in the eighteenth century, when sugar production expanded in Cuba, the slave system there was as brutal as any in the history of the Americas.

The character of slavery varied with local conditions. One of the most benign forms operated in Florida. In 1699 the Spanish declared Florida a refuge for escaped slaves from the English colonies, offering free land to any fugitives who would help defend the colony. Over the next half-century, refugee Indians and fugitive Africans established many communities in the countryside surrounding St. Augustine.

In New Mexico the Spanish depended on Indian slavery. In the sixteenth century the colonial governor sent Indian slaves to the mines of Mexico. The enslavement of Indians was one of the causes of the Pueblo Revolt (see Chapter 3). During the eighteenth century, the Spanish were much more cautious in their treatment of the Pueblos, who were officially considered Catholics. But they captured and enslaved "infidel Indians" such as the Apaches or nomads from the Great Plains, using them as house servants and field workers.

French Louisiana

Slavery was also important in Louisiana, the colony founded by the French in the lower Mississippi Valley in the early eighteenth century. By 1750 several thousand French colonists had established farms and plantations on the Gulf Coast and in a narrow strip of settlement along the Mississippi River. Soon they were exporting rice, indigo, and tobacco, in addition to furs and skins, which they traded with the backcountry Indians. Like the Spanish in St. Augustine, however, the French were more interested in defending their access to the Mississippi against rival colonial threats than in commerce or export. Consequently, African slaves amounted to no more than a third of the colonial population of 10,000. It was not until the end of the eighteenth century that the colony of Louisiana became an important North American slave society.

Slavery in the North

North of the Chesapeake, slavery was much less important. Slaves worked on some farms, but almost never in groups, and they were principally concentrated in port cities. Slaves were first shipped to Philadelphia in the 1680s, and a visitor to the city in 1750 noted that slaves were bought "by almost everyone who could afford [them]."

The Quakers, many of whom had themselves kept slaves, voiced the first antislavery sentiment in the colonies. In *Considerations on the Keeping of Negroes* (1754), John Woolman urged his readers to imagine themselves in the place of the African people. Suppose, he wrote,

> that our ancestors and we had been exposed to constant servitude in the more servile and inferior employments of life; that we had been destitute of the help of reading and good company; that amongst ourselves we had had few wise and pious instructors; that the religious amongst our superiors seldom took notice of us; that while others in ease have plentifully heaped up the fruit of our labour, we had received barely enough to relieve nature, and being wholly at the command of others had generally been treated as a contemptible, ignorant part of mankind. Should we, in that case, be less abject than they now are?

It was not until the Revolution, however, that antislavery sentiment became more widespread.

In New York slavery was somewhat more important. By 1770 New York and New Jersey were home to some 27,000 African Americans, about 10 percent of the population. Black people were concentrated even more highly in New York City. In 1770, 3,000 slaves and 100 free blacks, about 17 percent of the population, lived in the city.

The most important center of slavery in the North, however, was Newport, Rhode Island. In 1760 African

Americans there made up about 20 percent of the population, a concentration resulting from that port's dominance of the midcentury slave trade.

Becoming African American

The majority of Africans transported to North America arrived during the eighteenth century. They were met by a rapidly growing population of country-born slaves, or *creoles,* a term first used by slaves in Brazil to distinguish their children, born in the New World, from newly arrived Africans. The perspective of creoles was shaped by their having grown up under slavery, and that perspective helped them to determine which elements of African culture they would incorporate into the emerging culture of the African American community. That community was formed out of the relationship between creoles and Africans, and between slaves and their European masters.

The Daily Life of Slaves

Because slaves made up the overwhelming majority of the labor force that made the plantation colonies so profitable, it is fair to say that Africans built the South. As an agricultural people, Africans—both men and women—were accustomed to the routines of rural labor, and this was put to use on the plantations. Most Africans were field hands, and even domestic servants labored in the fields when necessary. As crop production expanded during the eighteenth century and plantations became larger and more extensive, labor became specialized. On the eighteenth-century Virginia plantation of George Mason, for example, slaves worked as carpenters, coopers, sawyers, blacksmiths, tanners, curriers, shoemakers, spinners, weavers, knitters, and even distillers.

Masters provided their workers with rude clothing, sufficient in the summer but nearly always inadequate in the winter. Stiff shoes were a necessity in the cold months, but they so cramped the feet that everyone looked forward to shedding them in the spring and going barefoot all summer and fall. Hand-me-down clothes from the master's family offered slaves an opportunity to brighten their costumes, and many of them dressed in a variety of styles and colors. Similarly, they relieved the monotony of their rations of corn and pork with vegetables from their small gardens, game and fish from field and stream, and wild plant foods from the forests.

The growing African population, and larger plantations on which larger numbers lived and worked together, created the concentration necessary for the emergence of African American communities and African American culture. On small farms, Africans might work side by side with their owners and, depending on the character of the master, might enjoy living conditions not too different from those of other family members. But plantations offered possibilities for a more autonomous cultural life.

Families and Communities

The family was the most important institution for the development of community and culture. Slave codes did not provide for legal slave marriages, for that would have contradicted the master's freedom to dispose of his property as he saw fit. "The endearing ties of husband and wife are strangers to us," declared the Massachusetts slaves who petitioned for their freedom in 1774, "for we are no longer man and wife than our masters or mistresses think proper." Despite the barriers, however, by the 1730s Africans in both the Chesapeake and the Lower South had created the stable families that were essential for the development of African American culture.

On large plantations throughout the southern colonies, travelers found Africans living in nuclear family households. In many cases men and women lived together in the slave quarters, and this was clearly the ideal. But on smaller plantations, men often married women from neighboring farms, and with the permission of both owners visited their families in the evenings or on Sundays.

Emotional ties to particular places, connections between the generations, and relations of kinship and friendship linking neighboring plantations and farms were the foundation stones of African American community life. Kinship was especially important. African American parents encouraged their children to use family terms in addressing unrelated persons: *auntie* or *uncle* became a respectful way of addressing older men and women, *brother* and *sister* affectionate terms for agemates. *Fictive kinship* may have been one of the first devices enslaved Africans used to humanize the world of slavery. During the Middle Passage, it was common for children to call their elders aunt and uncle, for adults to address all children as son or daughter.

African American Culture

The eighteenth century was the formative period in the development of the African American community, for it was then that the high birth rate and the growing numbers of country-born provided the necessary stability for the evolution of culture. During this period, men and women from dozens of African ethnic groups molded themselves into a new people. Distinctive patterns in music and dance, religion, and oral tradition illustrate the resilience of the human spirit under bondage as well as the successful struggle of African Americans to create a spiritually sustaining culture of their own.

Eighteenth-century masters were reluctant to allow their slaves to become Christians, fearing that baptism would open the way to claims of freedom or give Africans dangerous notions of universal brotherhood and equality with masters. One frustrated missionary was told by a planter that a slave was "ten times worse when a Christian than in his state of paganism." The majority of black southerners before the American Revolution practiced some form of African religion. Large numbers of African Americans were not converted to Christianity until the Great Awakening, which swept across the South after the 1760s (see Chapter 5).

One of the most crucial areas of religious practice concerned the rituals of death and burial. African Americans, often decorated graves with shells and pottery, an old African custom. The African custom of covering graves with shells and pottery was continued in the colonies. African Americans generally believed that the spirits of their dead would return to Africa. The burial ceremony was often held at night to keep it secret from masters, who objected to the continuation of African traditions. The deceased was laid out, and around the body men and women would move counterclockwise in a slow dance step while singing ancestral songs. The pace gradually increased, finally reaching a frenzied but joyful conclusion. The circle dance was a widespread custom in West Africa, and in America it became known as the *ring shout*. As slaves from different backgrounds joined together in the circle, they were beginning the process of cultural unification.

Music and dance may have formed the foundation of African American culture, coming even before a common language. Many eighteenth-century observers commented on the musical and rhythmic gifts of Africans. Olaudah Equiano remembered his people, the Ibos, as "a nation of dancers, musicians, and poets." Thomas Jefferson, raised on a Virginia plantation, wrote that blacks "are more generally gifted than the whites, with accurate ears for tune and time." Many Africans were accomplished players of stringed instruments and drums, and their style featured improvisation and rhythmic complexity—elements that would become prominent in African American music. In America, slaves recreated African instruments, as in the case of the banjo, and mastered the art of the European violin and guitar. Fearing that slaves might communicate by code, authorities often outlawed drums. But using bones, spoons, or sticks or simply "patting juba" (slapping their thighs), slaves produced elaborate multirhythmic patterns.

One of the most important developments of the eighteenth century was the invention of an African American language. An English traveler during the

An African stringed instrument called mbanza—*an animal skin stretched across a gourd with an unfretted wooden neck—evolved in America into the banjo. The "dirty" sound of the instrument and the style in which it was played echoed the tonic and rhythmic complexity associated with African music. Introduced by slave musicians, by the nineteenth century the banjo had become an American folk instrument used by black and white alike.*

1770s complained he could not understand Virginia slaves, who spoke "a mixed dialect between the Guinea and English." But such a language made it possible for country-born and "saltwater" Africans to communicate. The two most important dialects were Gullah and Geechee, named after two of the African peoples most prominent in the Carolina and Georgia low country, the Golas and Gizzis of the Windward Coast. These creole languages were a transitional phenomenon, gradually giving way to distinctive forms of black English, although in certain isolated areas, such as the sea islands of the Carolinas and Georgia, they persisted into the twentieth century.

The Africanization of the South

The African American community often looked to recently arrived Africans for religious leadership and medical magic. Throughout the South, many whites had as much faith in slave conjurers and herb doctors as the slaves themselves did. This was one of many ways in which white and black southerners came to share a common culture. Acculturation was by no means a one-way street; English men and women in the South were also being Africanized.

Slaves worked in the kitchens of their masters, and thus introduced an African style of cooking into colonial diets already transformed by the addition of Indian crops. African American culinary arts are responsible for such southern perennials as barbecue, fried chicken, black-eyed peas, and collard greens. And the liberal African use of red pepper, sesame seeds, and other sharp flavors established the southern preference for highly spiced foods. In Louisiana a combination of African, French, and Indian elements produced a distinguished American regional cuisine, exemplified by gumbos (soups) and jambalayas (stews).

Mutual acculturation is also evident in many aspects of material culture. African architectural designs featuring high, peaked roofs (to drain off the heat) and broad, shady porches gradually became part of a distinctive southern style. The West African iron-working tradition was evident throughout the South, especially in the ornamentation of the homes of Charleston and New Orleans.

Even more important were less tangible aspects of culture. Slave mothers nursed white children as well as their own. As one English observer wrote, "each child has its [black] Momma, whose gestures and accent it will necessarily copy, for children, we all know, are imitative beings." In this way many Africanisms passed into the English language of the South: *goober* (peanut), *yam, banjo, okay, tote*. Some linguists have argued that the southern "drawl," evident among both black and white speakers, derived from the incorporation of African intonations of words and syllables.

Violence and Resistance

Slavery was a system based on the use of force and violence. Fear underlay the daily life of both masters and slaves. Owners could be humane, but slaves had no guarantees of benevolent treatment, and the kindest master could turn cruel. Even the most cultured plantation owners of the eighteenth century thought nothing about floggings of fifty or seventy-five lashes. "Der prayer was answered," sang the Africans of South Carolina, "wid de song of a whip." Although the typical planter punished slaves with extra work, public humiliation, or solitary confinement, the threat of the lash was omnipresent. There were also sadistic masters who stabbed, burned, maimed, mutilated, raped, or castrated their slaves.

Yet African Americans demonstrated a resisting spirit. In their day-to-day existence they often refused to cooperate: they malingered, they mistreated tools and animals, they destroyed the master's property. Flight was also an option, and judging from the advertisements placed by masters in colonial newspapers, even the most trusted Africans ran away.

Runaways sometimes collected together in communities called *maroons,* from the Spanish *cimarron,* meaning wild and untamed. The African communities in Spanish Florida were often called maroons. Indeed, as a whole these mixed African and Creek Indian Florida peoples called themselves Seminoles, a name deriving from their pronunciation of *cimarron.* Maroons also settled in the backcountry of the Lower South, and although they were less common in the Upper South, a number of fugitive communities existed in the Great Dismal Swamp between Virginia and North Carolina. In the 1730s a group of escaped Africans built a community of grass houses and set up a tribal government there, but they were soon dispersed by the authorities.

The most direct form of resistance was revolt. In the Lower South, where slaves were a majority of the population, there were isolated but violent slave uprisings in 1704, 1720, and 1730. Then in 1738 there were a series of violent revolts throughout South Carolina and Georgia. Then in September 1739, the largest slave rebellion of the colonial period took place when a group of twenty Angolans sacked the armory in

Stono, South Carolina. They armed themselves and began a march toward Florida and freedom. Beating drums to attract other slaves to their cause, they grew to nearly one hundred. They plundered a number of planters' homes along the way and killed some thirty colonists. Pausing in a field to celebrate their victory with dance and song, they were overtaken by the militia and destroyed in a pitched battle. That same year there was an uprising in Georgia. Another took place in South Carolina the following year. Attributing these revolts to the influence of newly arrived Africans, colonial officials shut off the slave trade through Charleston for the next ten years.

Wherever masters held slaves there were persistent fears of uprisings. But compared with such slave colonies as Jamaica, Guiana, or Brazil, there were few slave revolts in North America. The conditions favoring revolt—large African majorities, brutal exploitation with correspondingly low survival rates and little acculturation, and geographic isolation—prevailed only in some areas of the Lower South. Indeed, the very success of African Americans in British North America at establishing families, communities, and a culture of their own inevitably made them less likely to take the risks that rebellions required.

Slavery and the Structure of Empire

Slavery contributed enormously to the economic growth and development of Europe during the colonial era, and it was an important factor in Great Britain, just before the Industrial Revolution of the eighteenth century. Slavery was the most dynamic force in the Atlantic economy during that century, creating the conditions for industrialization. But because slave colonists single-mindedly committed their resources to the expansion and extension of the plantation system, they derived very little benefit from the economic diversification that characterized industrialization.

Slavery the Mainspring

The slave colonies—the sugar islands of the West Indies and the colonies of the South—were responsible for 95 percent of the exports of the British colonies in the Americas during the eighteenth century. Although the slave colonies of the South constituted considerably less than half the population of Britain's mainland North American possessions, they accounted for more than 80 percent of the value of their exports. Moreover, there was the prime economic importance of the slave trade itself. In the words of one Englishman, slavery was "the strength and sinews of this western world." The labor of African slaves was largely responsible for the economic success of the British Empire in the Americas.

The most obvious and direct effect of slavery on economic development was on the growth of transport. Ships had to be outfitted and provisioned, trade goods had to be manufactured, and the commodities produced on slave plantations had to be processed. The multiplier effects of these activities are best seen in the growth of English ports such as Liverpool and Bristol. There the African and American trades provided employment for ships' crews, dockmen, construction workers, traders, shopkeepers, lawyers, clerks, factory workers, and officials of all ranks down to the humblest employees of the custom house. It was said of Bristol that "there is not a brick in the city but what is cemented with the blood of a slave."

The profits of the slave trade and slave production resulted in huge accumulations of capital, much of it invested in enterprises in these same cities. This capital funded the first modern banks and insurance companies, and eventually found its way into a wide range of economic activities. In the countryside surrounding Liverpool, capital acquired through slavery was invested in the cotton textile industry. Later, the demand for raw cotton to supply cotton textile factories led to the further expansion of American plantation slavery. The connections between slavery and the growth of industry were clear and dramatic.

The Politics of Mercantilism

When imperial officials argued that colonies existed solely for the benefit of the mother country, they had in mind principally the great wealth produced by slavery. To ensure that this wealth benefited their states, European imperial powers created a system of regulations that later became known as *mercantilism*. The essence of mercantile policy was the political control of the economy by the state. First advanced in France in the seventeenth century under the empire of Louis XIV, in the eighteenth centry mercantilist politics were most successfully applied by Great Britain. The monarchy and Parliament established a uniform national monetary system, regulated wages, encouraged agriculture and manufacturing, and erected tariff barriers to protect themselves from foreign competition. England also sought to organize and control colonial trade to the maximum advantage of its own shippers, merchants, manufacturers, and bureaucrats.

The mercantilists viewed the economy as a zero-sum game, in which total economic gains were equal to total losses. Profits were thought to result from successful speculation, crafty dealing, or simple plunder—all forms of stealing wealth. The institution of slavery confirmed the theory, for it was nothing more than a highly developed system by which some stole the labor of others. The essence of the competition between states, the mercantilists argued, was the struggle to acquire and hoard the fixed amount of wealth that existed in the world. The nation that accumulated the largest treasure of gold and silver would be the most powerful.

Wars for Empire

The mercantilist era was thus a period of intense and violent competition among European states. Wars usually arose out of Old World issues, spilling over into the New, but they also originated in conflicts over the colonies themselves.

In the southern region, these wars had everything to do with slavery. The first fighting of the eighteenth century took place during Queen Anne's War (known in Europe as the War of the Spanish Succession), a conflict that pitted Great Britain and its allies against France and Spain. In 1702 troops from South Carolina invaded Florida, plundering and burning St. Augustine in an attempt to destroy the refuge for fugitive slaves there. A combined French and Spanish fleet took revenge in 1706 by bombarding Charleston. The British finally prevailed, and in 1713, as part of the Peace of Utrecht, Spain ceded to the English the exclusive right to supply slaves to its American colonies, a very lucrative business.

The entrance of British slavers into Spanish ports provided an opportunity for illicit trade, and sporadic fighting between the two empires broke out a number of times over the next two decades.

In the northern region, the principal focus of the imperial struggle was control of the Indian trade. In 1704, during Queen Anne's War, the French and their Algonquian Indian allies raided New England frontier towns such as Deerfield, Massachusetts, dragging men, women, and children into captivity in Canada. In turn, the English mounted a series of expeditions against the strategic French fortress of Port Royal, which they captured in 1710. At the war's conclusion in 1713, France was forced to cede Acadia, Newfoundland, and Hudson's Bay to Great Britain in exchange for guarantees of security for the French-speaking residents of those

provinces. Nearly thirty years of peace followed, but from 1740 to 1748 England again went to war against France and Spain. During King George's War (known in Europe as the War of the Austrian Succession), the French attacked the British in Nova Scotia, Indian and Canadian raids again devastated the border towns of New England and New York, and hundreds of British subjects were killed or captured.

British Colonial Regulation

Mercantilists used means other than war to win the wealth of the world. The British monarchy, for example, chartered the East India Company, the Hudson's Bay Company, and the Royal African Company as trading monopolies in their respective regions.

English manufacturers complained that the merchant-dominated trading monopolies paid too little attention to the export of their products to colonial markets. Reacting to these charges, between 1660 and 1696 Parliament passed the Navigation Acts (see also Chapter 3), which created the legal and institutional structure of Britain's eighteenth-century colonial system. The Acts defined the colonies as both suppliers of raw materials and markets for English manufactured goods. Merchants from other nations were expressly forbidden to trade in the colonies, and all trade had to be conducted in ships built in England or the British colonies themselves. The regulations specified a list of *enumerated goods,* colonial products that could be shipped only to England. These included the products of the southern slave colonies (sugar, molasses, rum, tobacco, rice, and indigo), those of the northern Indian trade (furs and skins), and those essential for supplying the shipping industry (masts, tar, pitch, resin, and turpentine). The bulk of these products were not destined for English consumption; at great profit they were reexported elsewhere.

England also placed limitations on colonial enterprises that might compete with those at home. A series of enactments—including the Wool Act of 1699, the Hat Act of 1732, and the Iron Act of 1750—forbade the manufacture of those products. Moreover, colonial assemblies were forbidden to impose tariffs on English imports as a way to protect colonial industries. Banking was disallowed, local coinage prohibited, and the export of coin from England forbidden. Badly in need of a circulating medium, Massachusetts illegally minted copper coin, and several colonies issued paper currency, forcing Parliament to explicitly legislate against the practice. The colonists depended mostly on "commodity money"

SUMMARY TABLE	*The Colonial Wars*	
King William's War	1689–97	France and England battle on the northern frontiers of New England and New York.
Queen Anne's War	1702–13	England fights France and Spain in the Caribbean and on the northern frontier of New France. Part of the European conflict known as the War of the Spanish Succession.
War of Jenkins's Ear	1739–43	Great Britain versus Spain in the Caribbean and Georgia. Part of the European War of the Austrian Succession.
King George's War	1744–48	Great Britain and France fight in Acadia and Nova Scotia; the second American round of the War of the Austrian Succession.
French and Indian War	1754–63	Last of the great colonial wars pitting Great Britain against France and Spain. Known in Europe as the Seven Years' War.

(furs, skins, or hogsheads of tobacco) and the circulation of foreign currency. Official rates of exchange between commodity money, colonial paper, foreign currency, and English pounds allowed this chaotic system to operate without too much difficulty.

As the trade in colonial products increased, the British came to agree that it made little sense to tamper with such a prosperous system. Prime Minister Walpole pursued a policy later characterized as one of "salutory neglect": any colonial rules and regulations deemed contrary to good business practice were simply ignored and not enforced. Between 1700 and 1760 the quantity of goods exported from the colonies to the mother country rose 165 percent, while imports from Britain to North America increased by more than 400 percent. In part because of the lax enforcement, but mostly because the system operated to the profit of colonial merchants, colonists complained very little about the operation of the mercantilist system before the 1760s.

The Colonial Economy

Despite the seemingly harsh mercantilist regulations, the economic system operated to the benefit of planters, merchants, and white colonists in general. Southern slave owners made healthy profits on the sale of their commodities. They enjoyed a protected market in which competing goods from outside the empire were heavily taxed. Planters found themselves with steadily increasing purchasing power. Pennsylvania, New York, and New England, and increasingly the Chesapeake as well, produced grain, flour, meat, and dairy products. None of these were included in the list of enumerated goods, and they could thus be sold freely abroad. They found their most ready market in the British West Indies

and the Lower South, where food production was slighted in favor of sugar and rice. Most of this trade was carried in New England ships. Indeed, the New England shipbuilding industry was greatly stimulated by the allowance under the Navigation Acts for ships built and manned in the colonies. So many ships were built for English buyers that by midcentury nearly a third of all British tonnage was American made.

The greatest benefits for the port cities of the North came from their commercial relationship to the slave colonies. New England merchants had become important players in the slave trade by the early eighteenth century, and soon thereafter they began to make inroads into the export trade of the West Indian colonies. It was in the Caribbean that northern merchants most blatantly ignored mercantilist regulations. In violation of Spanish, French, and Dutch regulations prohibiting foreign trade, New Englanders traded foodstuffs for sugar in foreign colonies. They illegally sent it to England. By 1750 more than sixty distilleries in Massachusetts Bay were exporting over 2 million gallons of rum, most of it produced from sugar obtained illegally. Because the restrictive rules and regulations enacted by Britain for its colonies were not enforced, such growth and prosperity among the merchants and manufacturers of the port cities of the North prospered.

By the mid-eighteenth century, the Chesapeake and Lower South regions were major exporters of tobacco, rice, and indigo, and the middle colonies major exporters of grain to Europe.

The carrying trade in the products of slave labor made it possible for the northern and middle colonies to earn the income necessary to purchase British imports despite the lack of valuable products from their own regions. Gradually, the commercial economies of

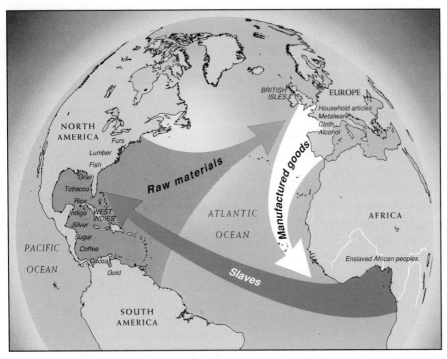

Triangular Trade Across the Atlantic

The pattern of commerce among Europe, Africa, and the Americas became known as the Triangular Trade. Sailors called the voyage of slave ships from Africa to America the Middle Passage because it formed the crucial middle section of this trading triangle.

the Northeast and the South were becoming integrated. From the 1730s to the 1770s, for example, while the volume of trade between Great Britain and Charleston doubled, the trade between Charleston and northern ports grew sevenfold. The same relationship was developing between the Chesapeake and the north. Merchants in Boston, Newport, New York, and Philadelphia increasingly provided southern planters not only with shipping services but also with credit and insurance. Like London, Liverpool, and Bristol—though on a smaller scale—the port cities of the North became pivots in the expanding trade network linking slave plantations with Atlantic markets. This trade provided northern merchants with the capital that financed commercial growth and development in their cities and the surrounding countryside. Slavery thus contributed to the growth of a score of northern port cities, forming an indirect but essential part of their economies.

Slavery and Freedom

The prosperity of the eighteenth-century plantation economy thus improved the living conditions for the residents of northern cities as well as for a large segment of the population of the South, providing them with the opportunity for a kind of freedom unknown in the previous century. The price of prosperity and freedom was the oppression and exploitation of millions of Africans

and African Americans. Freedom for white men based on the slavery of African Americans is the most important contradiction of American history.

The Social Structure of the Slave Colonies

At the summit of southern colonial society stood a small elite of wealthy planters, in contrast with the mass of slave men and women who formed the working population. Slavery had produced a society in which property was concentrated in the hands of a wealthy few. The richest 10 percent of colonists owned more than half the cultivated land and over 60 percent of the wealth. Although there was no colonial aristocracy—no nobility or royal appointments—the landed elite of the slave colonies came very close to constituting one.

The typical wealthy Virginia planter lived in a Tidewater county; owned several thousand acres of prime farmland and more than a hundred slaves; resided in a luxurious plantation mansion, built perhaps in the fashionable Georgian style; and had an estate valued at more than 10,000 pounds. Elected to the House of Burgesses and forming the group from which the magistrates and counselors of the colony were chosen, these "first families of Virginia"—the Carters, Harrisons, Lees, Fitzhughs, Washingtons, Randolphs, and others—were a self-perpetuating governing class.

A similar elite ruled the Lower South, although wealthy landowners spent little time on their plantations.

They lived instead in fashionable Charleston, where they made up a close-knit group who controlled the colonial government. "They live in as high a style here, I believe, as any part of the world," wrote a visitor to Charleston.

A considerable distance separated this slave-owning elite from typical southern landowners. About half the adult white males were small planters and farmers. But while the gap between rich and middling colonists grew larger during the eighteenth century, the prosperity of the plantation economy created generally favorable conditions for this large landed class. Slave ownership, for example, became widespread among this group during the eighteenth century. In Virginia at midcentury, 45 percent of heads of household held one to four slaves and even poorer farmers kept one or two.

Despite the prosperity that accompanied slavery in the eighteenth century, however, a substantial portion of colonists owned no land or slaves at all. Some rented land or worked as tenant farmers, some hired out as overseers or farm workers, and still others were indentured servants. Throughout the plantation region, landless men constituted about 40 percent of the population. A New England visitor found a "much greater disparity between the rich and poor in Virginia" than at home.

White Skin Privilege

But all the white colonists of eighteenth-century North America shared the privileged status of their skin color. As slavery became increasingly important, Virginia officials took considerable care to create legal distinctions between the status of colonists and that of Africans. Beginning in 1670, free Africans were prohibited from owning Christian servants. Ten years later, another law declared that any African, free or slave, who struck a Christian would receive thirty lashes on his bare back. One of the most important measures was designed to suppress intimate interracial contacts. Although there were many cases of masters forcing themselves on African women, most sexual intimacy occured between white servants and enslaved Africans. A 1691 act "for prevention of that abominable mixture and spurious issue which hereafter may encrease in this dominion" established severe penalties for interracial sexual relationships. Virginia policy thus deliberately encouraged the growth of racism.

In the Chesapeake relationships between indentured servants and African slaves had by 1700 produced a rather large group of mulattoes. Because by law children inherited the bond or free status of their mothers, the majority of those of mixed ancestry were slaves; a minority, the children of European women and African men, were free. According to a Maryland census of 1755, over 60 percent of mulattoes were slaves. But Maryland mulattoes also made up three-quarters of a small free African American population. This group, numbering about 4,000 in the 1770s, was denied the right to vote, to hold office, or to testify in court—all on the basis of racial background. Denied the status of citizenship enjoyed by even the poorest white men, free blacks were a pariah group who raised the status of white colonials by contrast.

Racial distinctions thus served as a constant reminder of the common freedom of white colonists and the common debasement of all blacks, slave or free. Racism set up a wall of contempt between colonists and African Americans. Despite their close association, said Thomas Jefferson, the two peoples were divided by "deep rooted prejudices entertained by the whites" and "ten thousand recollections, by the blacks, of the injuries they have sustained." "I tremble for my country when I reflect that God is just," he concluded in a deservedly famous passage, and remember "that his justice cannot sleep forever."

Conclusion

During the eighteenth century nearly half a million Africans were kidnapped from their homes, marched to the African coast, and packed into ships for up to three months before arriving in British North America. They provided the labor that made colonialism pay. Southern planters, northern merchants, and especially British traders and capitalists benefited greatly from the commerce in slave-produced crops, and that prosperity filtered down to affect many of the colonists of British North America. Slavery was fundamental to the operation of the British empire in North America. Mercantilism was a system designed to channel colonial wealth produced by slaves to the nation-state, but as long as profits were high, the British tended to wink at colonists' violations of mercantilist regulations.

Although African Americans received little in return, their labor helped build the greatest accumulation of capital that Europe had ever seen. But despite enormous hardship and suffering, African Americans survived by forming new communities in the colonies, rebuilding families, restructuring language, and reforming culture. African American culture added important components of African knowledge and experience to colonial agriculture, art, music, and cuisine. The African Americans of the English colonies lived better lives than the slaves worked to death on Caribbean sugar plantations, but lives of misery compared to the men they were forced to serve. As the slaves sang on the Georgia coast, "Dah Backrow Man go wrong you, Buddy Quow."

CHRONOLOGY

1441	African slaves first brought to Portugal
1518	Spain grants official license to Portuguese slavers
1535	Africans constitute a majority on Hispaniola
1619	First Africans brought to Virginia
1655	English seize Jamaica
1662	Virginia law makes slavery hereditary
1670	South Carolina founded
1672	Royal African Company organized
1691	Virginia prohibits interracial sexual contact
1698	Britain opens the slave trade to all its merchants
1699	Spanish declare Florida a refuge for escaped slaves
1702	South Carolinians burn St. Augustine
1705	Virginia Slave Code established
1706	French and Spanish navies bombard Charleston
1710	English capture Port Royal
1712	Slave uprising in New York City
1713	Peace of Utrecht
1722–48	Robert Walpole leads British cabinet
1733	Molasses Act
1739	Stono Rebellion War of Jenkins's Ear
1740–48	King George's War
1741	Africans executed in New York for conspiracy
1752	Georgia officially opened to slavery
1770s	Peak period of the English colonies' slave trade
1808	Importation of slaves into the United States ends

Review Questions

1. Trace the development of the system of slavery and discuss the way it became entrenched in the Americas.
2. Describe the effects of the slave trade both on enslaved Africans and on the economic and political life of Africa.
3. Describe the process of acculturation involved in becoming an African American. In what ways did slaves Africanize the South?
4. Explain the connection between the institution of slavery and the building of a commercial empire.
5. In what ways did colonial policy encourage the growth of racism?

Recommended Reading

MICHAEL CRATON, *Sinews of Empire: A Short History of British Slavery* (1974). An introduction to the British mercantilist system that emphasizes the importance of slavery. Includes a comparison of the mainland colonies with the Caribbean.

PHILIP D. CURTIN, *The African Slave Trade: A Census* (1969). The pioneer work in the quantitative history of the slave trade. All subsequent histories of the slave trade are indebted to Curtin.

HERBERT G. GUTMAN, *The Black Family in Slavery and Freedom, 1750–1925* (1976). A path-breaking history of the development of the African American community in North America. The sections on the eighteenth century provide evidence of the development of multigenerational family and kin networks.

WINTHROP D. JORDAN, *White over Black: American Attitudes Toward the Negro, 1550–1812* (1968). Remains the best and most comprehensive history of racial values and attitudes. A searching examination of British and American literature, folklore, and history.

PETER KOLCHIN, *American Slavery, 1619–1877* (1993). This survey features comparisons with slavery in Brazil and the Caribbean and serfdom in Russia. Includes a comprehensive bibliographic essay.

DANIEL P. MANNIX AND MALCOLM COWLEY, *Black Cargoes: A History of the Atlantic Slave Trade* (1962). An overview of the slave trade with a focus on the Middle Passage. Rich with horrifying historical testimony.

GERALD W. MULLIN, *Flight and Rebellion: Slave Resistance in Eighteenth-Century Virginia* (1972). Details how the acculturation of Africans in America made resistance possible. Evidence is drawn from colonial manuscripts and newspapers.

WALTER RODNEY, *How Europe Underdeveloped Africa* (1974). This highly influential book traces the relationship between Europe and Africa from the fifteenth to the twentieth century, and demonstrates how Europe's industrialization became Africa's impoverishment.

MECHAL SOBEL, *The World They Made Together: Black and White Values in Eighteenth-Century Virginia* (1987). Demonstrates the ways in which both Africans and Europeans shaped the formation of American values, perceptions, and identities.

IAN K. STEELE, *Warpaths: Invasions of North America* (1994). A new synthesis of the colonial wars from the sixteenth to the eighteenth century that places Indians as well as empires at the center of the action.

STERLING STUCKEY, *Slave Culture: Nationalist Theory and the Foundations of Black America* (1987). By concentrating on folklore, the author illuminates the African origins of African American culture. Includes important evidence on African American religion in the era before Christianization.

PETER H. WOOD, *Black Majority: Neogroes in Colonial South Carolina from 1670 through the Stono Rebellion* (1974). The classic study of the Lower South in the colonial period. Wood describes now the region was shaped by the interaction of Africans and Europeans.

5

THE CULTURES OF COLONIAL NORTH AMERICA, 1700–1780

AMERICAN COMMUNITIES

FROM DEERFIELD TO KAHNAWAKE: CROSSING CULTURAL BOUNDARIES

Two hours before daylight on February 29, 1704, Reverend John Williams and his wife, Eunice, of Deerfield, Massachusetts, awoke to "horrid shouting and yelling" and the crash of axes and hatchets breaking open the doors and windows of their house. Leaping out of bed they knew immediately that the town was under attack by Indians and their French allies; this frontier settlement on the northwestern fringe of New England had already been attacked six times in the perennial fighting with New France. Never before, however, had the enemy penetrated the town's stockade. Suddenly the door burst open and "with painted faces and hideous exclamations" Indians began pushing inside. "I reached up my hands for my pistol," Williams remembered, "cocked it, and put it to the breast of the first Indian that came up." It misfired, and as the couple stood trembling in their nightclothes, they were bound and dragged into the central hall with their seven children. In horror they were forced to watch the invaders club and kill their resisting six-year-old son, their screaming newborn infant daughter, and the black nursemaid. The family was hustled out into the frigid dawn and, with more than a hundred other captives, marched north through snow and ice toward Canada, leaving the frightful sight of the burning town behind.

The Deerfield raid became one of the most infamous events in the long series of colonial wars. One hundred and forty residents of the town managed to hold off the invasion and survive, but fifty others died in the attack. Among the captives, twenty-one were murdered along the way, in most cases because they were too weak to travel; the murdered included Mrs. Williams, who had not yet recovered from a difficult childbirth just six weeks before.

Most of the Deerfield captives were delivered to the French authorities in Montreal. Within two years, fifty-nine of them had been ransomed and returned home to Deerfield, the Reverend Williams and four of his surviving children among them. Williams soon published an account of his captivity, *The Redeemed Captive Returning to Zion*.

Among the Deerfield captives, thirty-one—including ten-year-old Eunice Williams, her mother's namesake—remained in Canada. Eunice and many of the other Deerfield captives lived at Kahnawake, a community of Catholic Indians near

Montreal. Like Deerfield, Kahnawake was a farming town of fifty or sixty homes clustered around a central church and surrounded by a stockade to protect it from enemy raiders. The differences between the two communities, however, were more striking than the similarities.

Founded in the seventeenth century by Jesuit missionaries as a refuge for Iroquois converts, Kahnawake not only became home to a great variety of Native American Catholics but also welcomed people of mixed Indian and European ancestry. Such mixing was also evident in the community's culture, the exotic mélange of European and Indian clothing, the use of both Indian and French names, and the special ways the community bent Catholic ritual to fit traditional Iroquois practices. Community members crossed boundaries in other ways, too: many residents were smugglers who engaged in the illegal trade of furs and other Indian products across the frontier into New York. According to the frustrated authorities in Montreal, Kahnawake operated as "a sort of republic," insisting on its freedom and independence.

As the historian John Demos writes, Kahnawake was "a unique experiment in bicultural living." Its residents were skilled at offering sympathetic sanctuary to traumatized captive children, and by the time Eunice Williams's father and siblings were ransomed she told the man who had come to fetch her that she was "unwilling to return." Soon she converted to Catholicism. Over the years the father sent several emissaries to retrieve her, but all she would say were two words of Iroquois: *jaghte oghte,* meaning "maybe not." She refused to acknowledge her English name, having taken another: *A'ongonte,* which in Iroquois means "she has been planted as a person." In 1713, at the age of sixteen, she married a Kahnawake Mohawk. Father and daughter would meet only once more, the following year, when he went to Kahnawake a final time to beg her to return. But she would "not so much as give me one pleasant look," Williams wrote mournfully.

John Williams died in 1729, surrounded by his children and grandchildren but longing for his "unredeemed" daughter. It was not until 1739 that A'ongonte found the courage to bring her family south for a visit, for she feared being held in New England against her will. Her brother Stephen wrote in his diary that at long last "we had ye joyfull, Sorrowfull meeting of our poor Sister that we had been Sepratd from fer above 36 years." After that A'ongonte visited only rarely because of the continuing warfare. "We have a great desire of going down to see you," she wrote to her brother through an interpreter near the end of their lives in the 1770s, "but do not know when an oppertunity may offer. . . . I pray the Lord that he may give us grace so to Live in this as to be prepared for a happey meeting in the woreld to Come." And, perhaps as a sign of reconciliation, she signed the letter, "Loving Sister until death, Eunice Williams."

KEY TOPICS

- **The similarities and differences among eighteenth-century Spanish, French, and English colonies**
- **The impact on British colonial culture of increasing European immigration**
- **Cultural changes in Indian America brought about by contact with European customs and lifestyles**
- **Patterns of work and class in eighteenth-century America**
- **Tensions between Enlightenment thought and the Great Awakening's call to renewed religious devotion**

North American Regions

American colonial history too often is written as if only the British colonists along the Atlantic coast really mattered. But as the experience of the Deerfield community and the Williams family suggests, this is a mistake eighteenth-century colonists could not afford to make. In the first place, Indian America was a critically important part of the eighteenth-century world. From the fringes of colonial societies into the native heart of the continent, from the eastern foothills of the Appalachians to the western flank of the Sierra Nevada in California, hundreds of Indian cultures—despite being deeply affected by the spread of colonial culture—remained firmly in control of their homelands. And in addition to

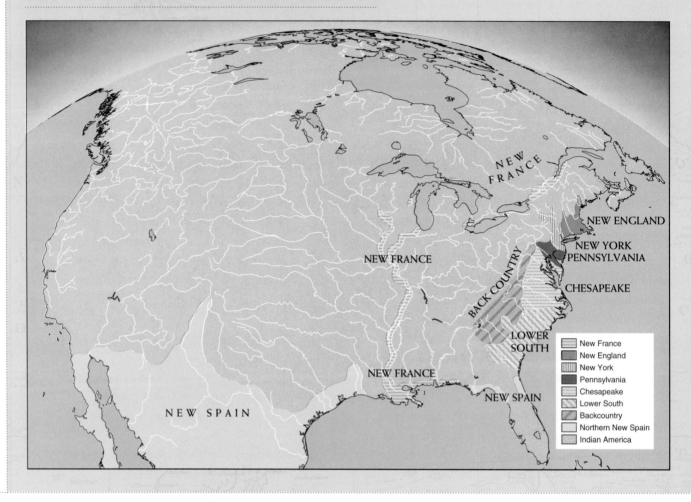

the British provinces stretching along the Atlantic coast, there were Hispanic colonists who defended the northern borderlands of the Spanish Caribbean and Mexican empire in isolated communities from Florida to California, and French communities that occupied the valley of the St. Lawrence River and scattered down the Mississippi Valley from the Great Lakes to the Gulf of Mexico. There were impressive similarities among these colonial societies, representing a continuation in the New World of traditional Old World beliefs, customs, and institutions, as well as a general pattern of European adaptation to American conditions.

Indian America

As the native peoples of the Atlantic coastal plain lost their lands to colonists through battles or treaties, and moved into or beyond the Appalachian Mountains, they became active in the European fur trade and dependent on firearms, metal tools, and other manufactured goods to maintain their way of life. Yet through the American Revolution they continued to assert a proud independence and gained considerable skill at playing colonial powers off against each other.

In general, the French had significantly better relations with native peoples than the English, but inevitably as they pursued their expansionist plans they came into conflict with a number of Indian groups, and when opposed they could be just as cruel and violent as any other power. In the early eighteenth century the Fox Indians blocked French passage between the Great Lakes and the upper Mississippi, attempting to make themselves into middlemen in the fur trade. Sporadic fighting continued until the French defeated the tribe in 1716. But Fox warriors rose again in 1726, and it took massive violence before the French were able to force the tribe into signing a treaty in 1738. On the lower Mississippi the Natchez and Chickasaw tribes opposed

REGION	POPULATION
New France	70,000
New England	400,000
New York	100,000
Pennsylvania	230,000
Chesapeake	390,000
Lower South	100,000
Backcountry	100,000
Northern New Spain	20,000
Indian America	1,500,000

REGIONS IN EIGHTEENTH-CENTURY NORTH AMERICA

By the middle of the eighteenth century, European colonists had established a number of distinctive colonial regions in North America. The northern periphery of New Spain, the oldest and most prosperous European colony, stretched from Baja California to eastern Texas, then jumped to the settlements on the northern end of the Florida peninsula; cattle ranching was the dominant way of life in this thinly populated region. New France was like a great crescent, extending from the plantation communities along the Mississippi near New Orleans to the French colonial communities along the St. Lawrence; in between were isolated settlements and forts, connected only by the extensive French trading network.

the arrival of the French, engaging them in a series of bloody conflicts during the 1720s that concluded only when the French decimated the Natchez in 1731.

The preeminent concern of the Indians of the eastern half of the continent was the tremendous growth of colonial population in the British Atlantic coastal colonies, especially the movement of settlers westward. In the 1730s and 1740s Pennsylvania perpetrated a series of fraudulent seizures of western lands from the Delawares. Particularly in the light of Pennsylvania's previous history of fair dealing with Indian peoples, these acts were yet another disturbing sign of things to come. Thus Indian alliances with the French resulted not from any great affection but from their great fear of British expansion.

Meanwhile, a long-term population decline continued among the Indian peoples of North America. Indian America continued to take a terrific beating from epidemics of European disease. There was no systematic census of North American Indians before the nineteenth century, but historians estimate that from a high of 7 to 10 million native Americans north of Mexico in 1500 the population had probably fallen to around a million by 1800. Thus, during the eighteenth century colonial population overtook and began to overwhelm the native population of the continent. Population loss did not affect all Indian tribes equally, however. Native peoples with a century or more of colonial contact and interaction had lost 50 percent or more of their numbers, but most Indian societies in the interior had yet to be struck by the horrible epidemics.

Colonization introduced other, less distressing changes in Indian cultures. By the early eighteenth century, Indians on the southern fringe of the Great Plains were using horses stolen from the Spanish in New Mexico. Horses enabled Indian hunters to exploit the buffalo herds much more efficiently, and on the base of this more productive subsistence strategy a number of groups built a distinctive and elaborate nomadic culture. Vast numbers of Indian peoples moved onto the plains during the eighteenth century, pulled by this new way of life, pushed by colonial invasions and disruptions radiating southwest from Canada and north from the Spanish borderlands. The invention of nomadic Plains Indian culture was another of the dramatic cultural amalgamations and innovations of the eighteenth century. The mounted Plains Indian, so often used as a symbol of native America, was actually a product of the colonial era.

The Spanish Borderlands

Mexico City, the administrative capital of New Spain, was the most sophisticated metropolis in the Western Hemisphere, the site of one of the world's great universities, with broad avenues and spectacular baroque architecture. New Spain's northern provinces of Florida, Texas, New Mexico, and California, however, were far removed from this opulence. Officials of the viceroyalty of New Spain, who oversaw these colonies, thought of them as buffer zones, protecting New Spain from the expanding colonial empires of Spain's New World rivals.

In Florida, the oldest European colonies in North America, fierce fighting among the Spanish, the British, and the Indians had by the early eighteenth century reduced the colonial presence to little more than the forts of St. Augustine on the Atlantic and Pensacola on the Gulf of Mexico, each surrounded by small colonized territories populated with the families of Spanish troops. In their weakened condition, the Spanish had no choice but to establish cooperative relations with the Creek and Seminole Indians who dominated the region, as well as the hundreds of African American runaways who considered St. Augustine a refuge from the cruel slave regimes in Georgia and Carolina. Like the community of Kahnawake, eighteenth-century Florida included a growing mestizo population and a considerable number of free African Americans and Hispanicized Indians from the old missions.

Nearly 2,000 miles to the west, New Mexico was similarly isolated from the mainstream of New Spain. At midcentury New Mexico included some 20,000 Pueblo Indians (their numbers greatly reduced by disease since their first contact with Europeans) and perhaps 10,000 colonists, who were able to support themselves with subsistence agriculture but whose prosperity was severely constrained by a restrictive colonial economic policy that forced them to exchange their wool, pottery, buffalo hides, and buckskin for imported goods at very unfavorable rates. Unlike the colonial population of Florida, however, the settlements of New Mexicans were gradually expanding, following the valleys and streams that led east and north from the original colonial outposts scattered along the upper Rio Grande.

The Spanish also founded new northern outposts during the eighteenth century. Concerned about French colonization of the Mississippi Valley, they established a number of military posts or *presidios* on the fringes of the colony of Louisiana and in 1716 began the construction of a string of Franciscan missions among the Indian peoples of Texas. By 1750 the settlement of San Antonio had become the center of a developing frontier province. The Spanish also established new colonial outposts west of New Mexico, in what is today southern Arizona. In the 1690s, Jesuit missionaries, led by Father Eusebio Kino, founded missions among the desert Indians of the lower Colorado and Gila River Valleys. Mission San Xavier del Bac near Tucson is acclaimed the most striking example of Spanish colonial architecture in the United States. Cattle ranching, introduced by the Jesuits, and farming spread along the lower Rio Grande Valley; in fact, ranching continued to define the region's economy for the next 200 years.

Midcentury also found the Spanish considering new settlements along the California coast. Juan Cabrillo, an associate of Hernán Cortés, had first explored the coastal waters in 1542 and was the first European to sail into the fine harbor at San Diego. In 1603 explorer Sebastián Vizcaíno had come upon Monterey Bay. The Spanish did little to follow up on these finds, but in 1769, acting on rumors of Russian expansion along the northern Pacific coast (for a discussion of Russian America, see Chapter 9), officials in Mexico City ordered Gaspar de Portolá, governor of what is now Baja California, to establish a Spanish presence in the North. With him were Franciscan missionaries led by Junípero Serra, president of the missions in Baja. At the harbor of San Diego, Portolá and Serra founded the first mission and pueblo complex in present-day California. Portolá then proceeded overland, becoming the first European to explore the interior valleys and mountains, and in 1770 he and Serra established their headquarters at Monterey Bay on the central coast. Two years later Juan Bautista de Anza established an overland route across the blistering deserts connecting Arizona and California, and in 1776 he led a colonizing expedition that founded the pueblo of San Francisco. Over the next fifty years the number of California settlements grew to include twenty-one missions and a half-dozen presidios and pueblos, including the town of Los Angeles.

Founded in 1781 by a group of mestizo settlers from Sinaloa, Mexico, by the end of the century Los Angeles had a population of only 300, but it was California's largest town.

For the Spanish, conquest demanded conversion, which, according to theory, would lead Indians toward "civilization." Like the efforts of the Jesuits at Kahnawake and elsewhere in New France, the Spanish experiment in cultural transformation was designed to make Indians into Christians and loyal subjects by educating them and putting them to work raising cattle and crops. The most extensive mission project took place in California, where under the direction of priests thousands of Indian laborers produced a flourishing local economy based on irrigated farming as well as horse, cattle, and sheep ranching. Indian people also constructed the adobe and stone churches, built on Spanish and Moorish patterns, whose ruins symbolize California's colonial society.

To keep the system functioning, the Franciscan missionaries resorted to cruel and sometimes violent means of controlling their Indian subjects: shackles, solitary confinement, and whipping posts. Indians resisted from the very beginning, but the arms and organization of Spanish soldiers were usually sufficient to suppress their uprisings. Another form of protest was flight: whole villages sometimes fled to the mountains.

Overwork, inadequate nutrition, overcrowding, poor sanitation, and epidemic disease contributed to death rates that exceeded birth rates. Over the fifty years of the mission system the native population of California fell by at least 25 percent.

The French Crescent

In France, as in Spain, church and state were closely interwoven. During the seventeenth century the French prime ministers, Cardinal Richelieu and Cardinal Mazarin, laid out a fundamentally Catholic imperial policy, and under their guidance colonists constructed a second Catholic empire in North America. In 1674 church and state collaborated in establishing the bishopric of Quebec. Under aggressive leadership that office founded local seminaries, oversaw the appointment and review of priests, and laid the foundation of the resolutely Catholic culture of New France. Meanwhile, Jesuit missionaries continued to carry Catholicism deep into the continent.

The number of French colonists rose from fewer than 15,000 in 1700 to more than 70,000 at midcentury, an impressive rate of growth. During the eigh-

teenth century the French used their trade network and alliances with the Indians to establish a great crescent of colonies, military posts, and settlements that extended from the mouth of the St. Lawrence River, southwest through the Great Lakes, then down the Mississippi River to the Gulf of Mexico. The maritime colony of Acadia, populated by fishermen and farmers, anchored the crescent on the northeast; the slave colony of Louisiana held the other end at the mouth of the Mississippi. Over this vast territory the French laid a thin colonial veneer, the beginning of what they planned as a great continental empire that would contain the Protestant British to a narrow strip of Atlantic coastline.

At the heart of the French empire in North America were the farming communities of the colony of Quebec along the banks of the St. Lawrence, including the towns of Montreal and Quebec City. There were also farming communities in the Illinois country, which shipped wheat down the Mississippi to supply the booming sugar plantations of Louisiana. By the mid-eighteenth century, those plantations—extending along

The persistence of French colonial long lots in the pattern of modern landholding is clear in this enhanced satellite photograph of the Mississippi River near New Orleans. Long lots, the characteristic form of property holding in New France, were designed to offer as many settlers as possible a share of good bottomland as well as a frontage on the waterways, which served as the basic transportation network.

the river from Natchez and Baton Rouge to New Orleans—had become the most profitable French enterprise in North America.

One of the most distinctive French stamps on the North American landscape were the "long lots" stretching back from the rivers that provided each settler family a share of good bottomland to farm as well as frontage on the waterways, the "interstate highway system" of the French Crescent. Long lots were laid out along the lower Mississippi in Louisiana and at sites on the upper Mississippi such as Kaskaskia and Prairie du Chien, as well as at the strategic passages of the Great Lakes, the communities of Mackinac, Sault Ste. Marie, and Detroit. In 1750 Detroit was a stockaded town with a military garrison, a small administrative center, several stores, a Catholic church, and 100 households of *métis* (French for mestizo) families. French and métis farmers worked the land along the Detroit River, not far from communities inhabited by more than 6,000 Ottawa, Potawatomi, and Huron Indians.

Communities of this sort that combined both French and Indian elements were in the tradition of the inclusive frontier. Detroit looked like "an old French village," said one observer, except that its houses were "mostly covered with bark," in Indian style. Detroit had much of the character of the mixed community of Kahnawake on the St. Lawrence.

Family and kinship were also cast in the Indian pattern. Households often consisted of several related families, but wives limited their births, having on average only two or three children. There were arranged marriages and occasional polygamy, but women had easy access to divorce and enjoyed property rights. Yet the people focused their activities on commerce and identified themselves overwhelmingly as Catholic.

New England

Just as New Spain and New France had their official church, so did the people of New England: local communities in all the New England colonies but Rhode Island were governed by Puritan congregations. Under the plan established in Massachusetts, the local church of a community was free to run its own affairs under the guidance of the General Court (the governor and the representatives selected by the towns). The Puritan colonies allotted each congregation a tract of communal land. Church members divided this land among themselves on the basis of status and seniority, laying out central villages such as Deerfield and building churches (called meetinghouses) that were maintained through

taxation. Adult male church members constituted the freemen of the town, and thus there was very little distinction between religious and secular authority. At the town meeting the freemen chose their minister, voted on his salary and support, and elected local men to offices ranging from town clerk to fence viewer.

The Puritan tradition was a curious mix of freedom and repression. Although local communities had considerable autonomy, they were tightly bound by the restrictions of the Puritan faith and the General Court. Contrary to the beliefs of many, the Puritans did not come to America to create a society where religion could be freely practiced but to establish their own version of the "right and perfect way," which placed severe restraints on individuals. Not only did the Puritans exile dissidents such as Roger Williams and Anne Hutchinson (see Chapter 3), they banned Anglicans and Baptists and jailed, tortured, and even executed members of the Society of Friends, commonly known as the Quakers.

One of the first formal arguments for religious toleration was made by New Englander Roger Williams, leader of dissenting Rhode Island. "Forced worship," he wrote, "stinks in God's nostrils." After the religious excesses of the English civil war this was an argument that began to have an appeal. In 1661, King Charles II ordered a stop to religious persecution in Massachusetts. The Toleration Act, passed by Parliament in 1689, was at first resisted by the Puritans, but under pressure from English authorities, Massachusetts and Connecticut reluctantly allowed other Protestant denominations to begin practicing their religions openly in 1700, although Congregationalism (as the Puritan Church had become known because congregations governed themselves) continued to be supported officially through taxation. By the 1730s there were Anglican, Baptist, and Presbyterian congregations in many New England towns.

As towns grew too large for the available land, groups of residents left together, "hiving off" to form new churches and towns elsewhere, and the region was knit together by an intricate network of roads and rivers. Seventy-five years after the Indians of southern New England suffered their final defeat in King Philip's War (see Chapter 3), Puritan farm communities had taken up most of the available land of Massachusetts, Connecticut, and Rhode Island, leaving only a few communities of Pequots, Narragansets, and Wampanoags on restricted reservations. Northern Algonquians and Catholic Iroquois allied with the French in Quebec, however, maintained a defensive barrier preventing New Englanders from expanding northward into Maine,

New Hampshire, and the region later called Vermont. Deerfield represented the far northern limit of safe settlement. By midcentury, then, as the result of growing population, New England was reaching the limit of its land supply.

The Middle Colonies

The colony of New York had one of the most ethnically diverse populations on the continent, in striking contrast to the ethnically homogeneous neighboring New England colonies of Connecticut and Massachusetts. At midcentury, society along the lower Hudson River, including the counties in northern New Jersey, was a veritable mosaic of ethnic communities: the Dutch of Flatbush, the Huguenots of New Rochelle, the Flemish of Bergen County, and the Scots of Perth Amboy were but a few. African Americans, both slave and free, made up more than 15 percent of the lower Hudson population. Congregations of Puritans, Baptists, Quakers, Catholics, and Jews worshiped without legal hindrance. There was a great deal of intermingling (as there was at places such as Kahnawake), but these different communities would long retain their ethnic and religious distinctions, which made New York something of a cultural salad bowl rather than a melting pot.

New York City grew by leaps and bounds in the eighteenth century, but because the elite who had inherited the rich lands and great manors along the upper Hudson chose to rent to tenants rather than to sell, this region was much less attractive to immigrants. By contrast, Pennsylvania was what one German immigrant called "heaven for farmers." The colony's Quaker proprietors were willing to sell land to anyone who could pay the modest prices. Thus as the region around New York City filled up, immigrants by the thousand made the decision to land at Philadelphia, Pennsylvania's port of entry on the Delaware River. During the eighteenth century the population of this region and an extended area that encompassed portions of New Jersey, Delaware, and Maryland grew more dramatically than any other in North America. Boasting some of the best farmland in North America, the region was soon exporting abundant produce through the growing port city of Philadelphia.

The Quakers who had founded Pennsylvania quickly became a minority, but, unlike the Puritans, they were generally comfortable with religious and ethnic pluralism. Many of the founders of the Society of Friends had been imprisoned for their beliefs in pre-Restoration England, and they were determined to prevent a repeti-

tion of this injustice in their own province. Indeed, the Quakers were opposed to all signs of rank, and among American Friends, women preached equally with men.

These Quaker attitudes were well suited to the ethnically and religiously diverse population of Pennsylvania. Although the Society of Friends remained the affiliation of the governing elite, it never became an established church. Most German immigrants were Lutherans or Calvinists, most North Britons were Presbyterians, and there were plenty of Anglicans and Baptists as well.

The institutions of government were another pillar of community organization. Colonial officials appointed justices of the peace from among the leading local men, and these justices provided judicial authority for the countryside. Property-owning farmers chose their own local officials. Country communities were tied together by kinship bonds and by bartering and trading among neighbors. The substantial stone houses and great barns of the Pennsylvania countryside testified to the social stability and prosperity of this system. However, the communities of the middle colonies were more loosely bound than those of New England. Rates of mobility were considerably higher, with about half the population moving on in any given decade. Because land was sold in individual lots rather than in communal parcels, farmers tended to disperse themselves at will over the open countryside. Villages gradually developed at crossroads and ferries but with little forethought or planning. It was Pennsylvania, which emphasized individual settlement, that provided the basic model for American expansion.

The Backcountry

By 1750 Pennsylvania's exploding population had pushed beyond the first range of the Appalachian highlands. Settlers occupied the northern reaches of the Great Valley, which extended southwest from Pennsylvania into Virginia. Although they hoped to become commercial farmers, these settlers began more modestly, planting Indian corn and raising hogs, hunting in the woods for meat and furs, and building log cabins. This strategy had originated with the settlers of the New Sweden colony on the lower Delaware River.

The movement into the Pennsylvania and Virginia backcountry that began during the 1720s was the first of the great pioneer treks that would take Americans into the continental interior. Many, perhaps most, of these pioneers held no legal title to the lands they occupied; they simply hacked out and defended their squat-

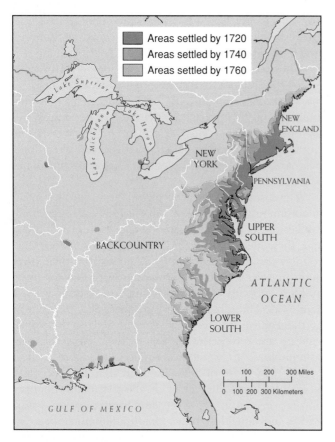

Spread of Settlement: Movement into the Backcountry, 1720–1760

The spread of settlement from 1720 to 1760 shows the movement of population into the backcountry in the midcentury.

ters' claims from Indian tribes and all other comers. Coming from the northern borders of England and Ireland, where there was considerable clan and ethnic violence, these people adapted well to the violence of the backcountry. To the Delawares and Shawnees, who had been pushed into the interior, or the Cherokees, who occupied the Appalachian highlands to the south, these pioneers presented a new and deadly threat to homelands. Rising fears and resentments over this expanding population would cause much eighteenth-century warfare.

In the eighteenth century the people of the backcountry forged another distinctive American region. The settlers cared little for rank. But the myth of frontier equality was simply that. Most pioneers owned little or no land, whereas "big men" held great tracts and dominated local communities with their bombastic style

of personal leadership. Here the men were warriors, the women workers.

The South

The Chesapeake and the Lower South were triracial societies, with intermingled communities of white colonists and black slaves, along with substantial Indian communities living on the fringes of colonial settlement. Much of the population growth of the region resulted from the forced migration of enslaved Africans, who by 1750 made up 40 percent of the population. Colonial settlement had filled not only the Tidewater area of the southern Atlantic coast but a good deal of the Piedmont as well. Specializing in rice, tobacco, and other commercial crops, these colonies were overwhelmingly rural. Farms and plantations were dispersed across the countryside, and villages or towns were few.

English authorities made the Church of England the state religion in the Chesapeake colonies. Residents paid taxes to support the Church and were required to attend services. No other churches were allowed into Virginia and Maryland, and dissenters were excluded or exiled. Before the 1750s, the Toleration Act was little enforced in the South; at the same time, the Anglican establishment was internally weak. It maintained neither a colonial bishop nor local institutions for training clergy.

Along the rice coast, the dominant institution of social life was the large plantation. The heavy investment required to transform the tangle of woods and swamps along the rivers into the order of dams, dikes, and flooded fields determined that rice cultivation was undertaken only by men of means. By midcentury, established plantations typically were dominated by a large main house, generally located on a spot of high ground overlooking the fields. Nearby, but a world apart, were the slave quarters, rough wooden cabins lining two sides of a muddy pathway near the outbuildings and barns.

Because tobacco, unlike rice, could be grown profitably in small plots, the Chesapeake included a greater variety of farmers and a correspondingly diverse landscape. Tobacco quickly drained the soil of its nutrients, and plantings had to be shifted to fresh ground every few years. Former tobacco land could be planted with corn for several years but then required twenty years or more of rest before reuse. The landscape was thus a patchwork of fields, many in various stages of ragged second growth. The poorest farmers lived in wooden cabins little better than the shacks of the slaves. More prosperous farm families lived with two or three slaves in houses that were nevertheless considerably smaller than the substantial homes of New England.

In the Lower South, where the plantations were little worlds unto themselves, there was little community life outside the plantation. But by midcentury the Chesapeake had given rise to well-developed neighborhoods based on kinship networks and economic connections. Encouraging the developing sense of community more than any other institution was the county court, which held both executive and judicial power. On court day, white people of all ranks held a great gathering that included public business, horse racing, and perhaps a barbecue. The gentleman justices of the county, appointed by the governor, included the heads of the leading planter families. These men in turn selected the grand jury, composed of substantial freeholders. One of the most significant bonding forces in this free white population was a growing sense of racial solidarity in response to the increasing proportion of African slaves dispersed throughout the neighborhoods.

Traditional Culture in the New World

In each of these North American colonial societies the family and kinship, the church, and the local community were the most significant factors in everyday life. Throughout the continent, colonists tended to live much as they had in their European homelands at the time their colonies were settled. Thus the residents of New Mexico, Quebec, and New England continued to be attached to the religious passions of the seventeenth century long after their mother countries had put those religious controversies aside in favor of imperial geopolitics. Nostalgia for Europe helped to fix a conservative colonial attitude toward culture.

These were oral cultures, depending on the transmission of information by the spoken word rather than through print, on the passage of traditions through storytelling and song, music and crafts. North American colonial folk cultures, traditional and suspicious of change, preserved an essentially medieval worldview. The rhythms of life were regulated by the hours of sunlight and the seasons of the year. People rose with the sun and went to bed soon after it went down. The demands of the season determined their working routines. They farmed with simple tools and were subject to the whims of nature, for drought, flood, or pestilence might quickly sweep away their efforts. Experience told them that the natural world imposed limitations within which men and women had to learn to live. Even patterns of

reproduction conformed to nature's cycle: in nearly every European colonial community of North America the number of births peaked in late winter, then fell to a low point during the summer; for African Americans, by contrast, births peaked in early summer. Historians have not yet accounted for this intriguing pattern or provided an explanation for the differences between white and black families, but apparently there was some "inner" seasonal clock tied to old European and African patterns. Human sexual activity itself seemed to fluctuate with the rural working demands created by the seasons.

These were also communal cultures. In Quebec villagers worked side by side to repair the roads, in New Mexico they collectively maintained the irrigation canals, and in New England they gathered in town meetings to decide the dates when common fields were to be plowed, sowed, and harvested. Houses offered little privacy, with families often sleeping together in the same chamber, sitting together on benches rather than in chairs, and taking their supper from a common bowl or trencher.

Throughout North America, most colonists continued the traditional European occupation of working the land. Plantation agriculture was designed to be a commercial system, in which crops were commodities for sale. Commercial farming also developed in some particularly fertile areas, notably southeastern Pennsylvania, which became known as the breadbasket of North America, as well as the country surrounding colonial cities such as New York, Boston, and Quebec. However, the majority of the farmers of eighteenth-century North America, grew crops and raised livestock for their own needs or for local barter, and communities were largely self-sufficient. Most farmers attempted to produce small surpluses as well, which they sold to pay their taxes and buy some manufactured goods. But rather than specializing in the production of one or two crops for sale, they attempted to remain as independent of the market as possible, diversifying their activities. The primary goal was ownership of land and the assurance that children and descendants would be able to settle within the community on lands nearby.

Rural households often practiced crafts or trades as a sideline. Farm men were also blacksmiths, coopers, weavers, or carpenters. Some farm women were independent traders in dairy products or eggs. Others became midwives and medicinal experts serving the community.

In colonial cities, artisans and craftsmen worked at their trades full time, organizing themselves according to the European craft system. In the colonial cities of the Atlantic coast, carpenters, ironmakers, blacksmiths, shipwrights, and scores of other tradesmen had their own self-governing associations. Young men who wished to pursue a trade served several years as apprentices, working in exchange for learning the skills and secrets of the craft. After completing their apprenticeships they sought employment in a shop. Their search often required them to migrate to some other area, thus becoming "journeymen." As in farming, the ultimate goal was independence.

With the exception of midwifery, there were few opportunities for women outside the household. By law, husbands held managerial rights over family property, but widows received support in the form of a one-third lifetime interest, known as "dower," in a deceased husband's real estate (the rest of the estate being divided among the heirs). And in certain occupations, such as printing (which had a tradition of employing women), widows succeeded their husbands in business.

The Frontier Heritage

The colonial societies of eighteenth-century North America also shared perspectives unique to their frontier heritage. European colonists came from Old World societies in which land was scarce and monopolized by property-owning elites. They settled in a continent where, for the most part, land was abundant and cheap. This was probably the most important distinction between North America and Europe. American historians once tied the existence of this "free land" directly to the development of democracy. But the colonial experience encouraged assumptions that were anything but democratic.

One of the most important of those colonial assumptions was the popular acceptance of forced labor. A woman of eighteenth-century South Carolina once offered advice on how to achieve a good living. "Get a few slaves," she declared, and "beat them well to make them work hard." There was a labor shortage throughout all the colonies. In a land where free men and women could work for themselves on their own plot of ground, there was little incentive to work for wages. Thus the use of forced labor was one of the few ways a landowner could gain control over an agricultural work force. In the Spanish borderlands, captured Apache children were made lifetime servants, and the Indian slave trade flourished through the eighteenth century. In Quebec one could see African American slaves from the French Caribbean working side-by-side with enslaved Indians captured by other tribes in the West and sold to

French traders. The colonists came from European cultures that believed in social hierarchy and subordination, and involuntary servitude was easily incorporated into their worldview.

At least half the immigrants to eighteenth-century British America arrived as indentured servants. This system allowed poor immigrants to arrange passage across the Atlantic in exchange for four or five years of service in America. Usually indentured servants were single men, often skilled artisans. Sometimes families without means emigrated as "redemptioners." Under this system, they arranged with the ship's owner to pay their passage upon arrival in North America. If no one in the colonies stepped forth to pay, they sold themselves into service for the payment. Thus family members were sometimes separated. In addition, during the eighteenth century the British sent over, mostly to the Chesapeake, some 50,000 convicts sentenced to seven or fourteen years at hard labor. One historian, accounting for the cost of passage and upkeep, estimates that indentured servants earned their masters, on average, about fifty pounds sterling over their terms of service, the equivalent of something like four or five thousand dollars in today's values.

All classes of bound laborers remained on board ship after arrival in America, awaiting inspection by potential buyers, who poked muscles, peered into open mouths, and pinched women. Although servants were not slaves, to the men and women lined up for inspection that distinction may have seemed irrelevant. There were other similarities between indentured servitude and slavery. The ocean crossing was often traumatic. One immigrant described a passage across the Atlantic to Philadelphia in which several hundred people were packed like sardines in the ship's hold. "The ship is filled with pitiful signs of distress," he wrote, "smells, fumes, horrors, vomiting, various kinds of sea sickness, fever, dysentery, headaches, heat, constipation, boils, scurvy, cancer, mouth-rot, and similar afflictions. In such misery all the people on board pray and cry pitifully together."

Unlike slaves, however, servants who endured had a chance of freedom. "Freedom dues" might include a suit of clothes, tools, money, and sometimes land. Of the thousands of men who came to the British colonies under indenture during the seventeenth and early eighteenth centuries, only about 20 percent achieved positions of moderate comfort. The majority died before their terms were completed, returned to England, or continued in miserable poverty. But opportunities for advancement increased somewhat with the overall prosperity of the eighteenth-century British colonies. By midcentury, the chances of moderate success for former servants were probably better than fifty–fifty. The majority of redemptioners, for example, appear to have become small farmers.

The common expectation of property ownership in all the colonial regions was part of the second fundamental colonial expectation. It led to rising popular demands in all regions that more and more land be taken from the Indian inhabitants and opened to white settlement. Some colonists justified such wars of dispossession by arguing, as Puritans did, that Indians deserved to lose their lands because they had failed to use them to their utmost capacity. Others simply maintained that Indians should be dispossessed because they were "savages." But whatever their specific justifications, the majority of colonists— whether British, Spanish, or French—accepted the violence and brutality directed against the Indians as an essential aspect of colonial life. With this as the prevailing attitude, one can understand why Eunice Williams was hesitant to return to Deerfield after she had married an Indian.

Diverging Social and Political Patterns

Despite these important similarities among the colonial regions of North America, in the eighteenth century the experience of the British colonies began to diverge sharply from that of the French and Spanish. Immigration, economic growth, and provincial political struggles all pushed British colonists in a radically new direction.

Population Growth and Immigration

All the colonial regions of North America experienced unprecedented growth in the eighteenth century. "Our people must at least be doubled every twenty years," wrote Benjamin Franklin in a remarkable 1751 essay on population, and he was nearly right. In 1700 there were 290,000 colonists north of Mexico; fifty years later they had grown to approximately 1.3 million, an average annual growth rate of about 3 percent. Typical preindustrial societies grow at rates of less than 1 percent per year, approximately the pace of Europe's expansion in the eighteenth century.

High fertility played an important role in this extraordinary growth. It was common for women in the British colonies to bear seven or more children during their childbearing years, and colonial women in the French villages along the St. Lawrence or the towns of New Mexico were equally fertile. In addition, mortality

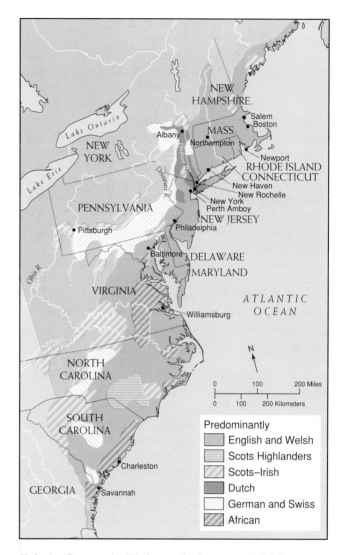

Ethnic Groups in Eighteenth-Century British North America

The first federal census, taken in 1790, revealed remarkable ethnic diversity. New England was filled with people from the British Isles, but the rest of the colonies were a patchwork. Most states had at least three different ethnic groups within their borders, and although the English and Scots–Irish were heavily represented in all colonies, in some they had strong competition from Germans (eastern and southern Pennsylvania) and from African peoples (Virginia and South Carolina).

rates were low: in most colonial areas there were fewer than 30 deaths for every 1,000 persons, a death rate 15 or 20 percent lower than rates in Europe. Moreover, levels of infant mortality were low. Blessed with fertile lands and the effectiveness of Indian agricultural techniques, North America had no famines. For the colonists, North America was a remarkably healthy environment.

Yet despite the high fertility of all North American colonial societies, in New France and New Spain restrictive policies curbed the number of European immigrants. Dedicated to keeping its North American colonies exclusively Catholic, France turned down the requests of thousands of Protestant Huguenots who desperately sought to emigrate to Canada. The Spanish, fearful of depleting their population at home, severely limited the migration of their own subjects to their colonies and absolutely forbade the immigration of foreigners. To supply the demand for labor in their Caribbean and Gulf coast settlements, they imported thousands of African slaves.

By contrast, English authorities allowed a massive immigration of their own subjects to North America in the seventeenth century. A total of 150,000 English men and women had relocated to the colonies by 1700, providing a substantial population base for further growth. In addition, the British became the only colonial power to encourage the immigration of foreign nationals to their colonies. In the 1680s, William Penn had sent agents to recruit settlers in Holland, France, and the German principalities along the Rhine River. Further encouraging this development, most of the British colonies enacted liberal naturalization laws in the early eighteenth century, allowing immigrants who professed Protestantism and swore allegiance to the British crown to become free denizens with all the freedoms and privileges of natural-born subjects. In 1740 Parliament passed a general naturalization law that extended these policies to all the colonies, although continuing to prohibit the naturalization of Catholic and Jewish immigrants, tiny minorities in the British colonies.

Before the Revolution at least 100,000 Germans settled in the British colonies, where they were known as the Dutch (from *Deutsch,* the German-language term for *German*). Another area of substantial emigration was the northern British Isles. Squeezed by economic hardship, an estimated 250,000 Highland Scots and Protestant Irish from the Ulster region (known in America as the Scots–Irish) emigrated to North America before the end of the colonial period. Concerned that they would dilute the purity of their brand of Protestantism, Puritan New Englanders did all they could to prevent the settlement of these new immigrants in their region, although Britian's naturalization law of 1740 forced New England to open its door to immigrants.

The first federal census in 1790 provides a snapshot of this significant experiment in ethnic diversity and cultural encounter. Less than 50 percent of the population of the thirteen states was English in origin, and nearly 20 percent was African; 15 percent was Irish or Scots, and 7 percent German, with other ethnic backgrounds making up the remainder. There were significant differences by region. New England remained more than three-quarters English, but Pennsylvania was only a quarter English and nearly 40 percent German. The backcountry—the backside of the colonies running along the Appalachian Mountains from western Pennsylvania to Georgia—was populated largely by North Britons. The population of the coastal South was nearly half African. The legacy of eighteenth-century immigration to the British colonies was thus a population of unprecedented diversity.

Social Class

Although traditional working roles were transferred to North America, attempts to transplant the European class system by creating land monopolies were far less successful. In New France the landowning seigneurs claimed privileges similar to those enjoyed by their aristocratic counterparts at home; the Spanish system of encomienda and the great manors created by the Dutch and continued by the English along the Hudson River also represented attempts to bring the essence of European feudalism to North America. But in most areas, because settlers had free access to land, these monopolies proved difficult or impossible to maintain. There was a system of economic rank and an unequal distribution of wealth, prestige, and power. North American society was not aristocratic, but neither was it without social hierarchy.

In New Spain the official criterion for status was racial purity. *Españoles* (Spaniards) or *gente de razón* (literally, "people of reason") occupied the top rung of the social ladder, with mestizos, mulattoes, and others on descending levels; African slaves and Indians were at the bottom. In the isolated northern borderlands, however, these distinctions tended to disappear, with *castas* (persons of mixed background) enjoying considerably more opportunity. Mestizos who acquired land might suddenly be reclassified as españoles. Spanish and French colonial societies were cut in the style of the Old World, with its hereditary ranks and titles. The landlords of New France and the Spanish borderlands may have lacked the means to accumulate real wealth, but they lived lives of elegance compared to the hard toil of the people who owed them labor service or rent.

Despite their lack of titles, the wealthy planters and merchants in the British colonies lived far more extravagantly than the seigneurs of New France or the dons of the Spanish borderlands. What separated the culture of class in the British colonies from that of New France or New Mexico was not so much the material conditions of life as the prevailing attitude toward social rank. In the Catholic cultures, the upper class attempted to obscure its origins, claiming descent from European nobility. But in British North America people celebrated social mobility. The class system was remarkably open, and the entrance of newly successful planters, commercial farmers, and merchants into the upper ranks was not only possible but common, although by midcentury most upper-class families had inherited, not earned, their wealth.

To be sure, there was a large lower class in the British colonies. Slaves, bound servants, and poor laboring families made up at least 40 percent of the population. For them the standard of living did not rise above bare subsistence. Most lived from hand to mouth, often suffering through seasons of severe privation. A small proportion of poor whites could expect their condition to improve during their lifetimes, but slaves were a permanently servile population. Enslaved African Americans stood apart from the gains in the standard of living enjoyed by immigrants from Europe. Their lives had been degraded beyond measure from the conditions prevailing in their native lands.

The feature of the class system most often commented on by eighteenth-century observers was not the character or composition of the lower ranks but rather the size and strength of the middle class, a rank entirely absent in the colonies of France and Spain. More than half the population of the British colonies, and nearly 70 percent of all white settlers, might be so classified. Most were families of landowning farmers of small to moderate means, but the group also included artisans, craftsmen, and small shopkeepers.

Households solidly in the center of this broad ranking owned land or other property worth approximately 500 pounds and earned the equivalent of about 100 pounds per year. They enjoyed a standard of living higher than that of the great majority of people in England and Europe. The low mortality of British Americans was important testimony to generally better living conditions. Touring the British Isles at midcentury, Benjamin Franklin was shocked at the squalid conditions of farmers and workers.

Economic Growth and Increasing Inequality

One of the most important differences among North American colonial regions in the eighteenth century was the economic stagnation in New France and New Spain compared with the impressive economic growth of the British colonies. Weighed down by royal bureaucracies and overbearing regulations, neither the French Crescent nor New Spain evidenced much prosperity. In British North America, however, per capita production grew at an annual rate of .5 percent. Granted, this was considerably less than the average annual growth rate of 1.5 percent that prevailed during the era of industrialization, from the early nineteenth through the mid-twentieth century. But as economic growth steadily increased the size of the economic pie, most middle- and upper-class British Americans began to enjoy improved living conditions. Improving standards of living and open access to land encouraged British colonists to see theirs as a society where hard work and savings could translate into prosperity, thus producing an upward spiral of economic growth.

At the same time, this growth produced increasing social inequality. In the commercial cities, for example, prosperity was accompanied by a concentration of assets in the hands of wealthy families. In Boston and Philadelphia at the beginning of the century, the wealthiest 10 percent of households owned about half of the taxable property; by about midcentury this small group owned 65 percent or more. In the commercial farming region of Chester County in southeastern Pennsylvania, the holdings of the wealthiest tenth increased more modestly, from 24 to 30 percent during the first half of the century. But at the same time the share of taxable property owned by the poorest third fell from 17 to 6 percent. The general standard of living may have been rising, but the rich were getting richer and the poor poorer. The greatest concentrations of wealth occurred in the cities and in regions dominated by commercial farming, whether slave or free, while the greatest economic equality continued to be found in areas of self-sufficient farming such as the backcountry.

Another eighteenth-century trend confounded the hope of social mobility in the countryside. As population grew and as generations succeeded one another in older settlements, all the available land in the towns was taken up. Under the pressure of increased demand, land prices rose almost beyond the reach of families of modest means. As a family's land was divided among the heirs of the second and third generations, parcels became ever smaller and thus more intensively farmed. Eventually the soil was exhausted.

By the eighteenth century, many farm communities did not have sufficient land to provide those of the emerging generation with farms of their own. There were notable increases in the number of landless poor in the towns of New England as well as the disturbing appearance of the "strolling poor," homeless people who traveled from town to town looking for work or a handout. Destitute families crowded into Boston, which by midcentury was expending more than 5,000 pounds annually on relief for the poor, who were required to wear a large red *P* on their clothing. In other regions, land shortages in the older settlements almost inevitably prompted people to leave in search of cheap or free land.

Fishing and shipping had first become important during the late seventeenth century, as merchants struggled to find a successful method of earning foreign exchange. The expanding slave market in the South opened new opportunities, prompting the growth of thriving coastal ports such as New Haven, Newport, Salem, and Boston. By midcentury New England had become the most urban of all North America's regions. Boston, the largest city in the British colonies, was the metropolis of a region that included not only New England but also the maritime settlements of Nova Scotia and Newfoundland, where New England merchants dominated commerce and recruited seamen for their fishing and shipping fleets.

Contrasts in Colonial Politics

The administration of the Spanish and French colonies was highly centralized. French Canada was ruled by a superior council including the royal governor (in charge of military affairs), the *intendant* (responsible for civil administration), and the bishop of Quebec. New Spain was governed by the Council of the Indies, which sat in Spain, and direct executive authority over all political affairs was exercised by the viceroy in Mexico City. Although local communities enjoyed informal independence, the highly bureaucratized and centralized governments of the French Crescent and the Spanish Borderlands left little room for the development of vigorous traditions of self-government.

The situation in the British colonies was quite different. During the early eighteenth century the British government of Prime Minister Robert Walpole assumed that a decentralized administration would best accomplish the nation's economic goals. Contented colonies, Walpole argued, would present far fewer problems. Each of the colonies was administered by royally appointed governors, its taxes and finances set by constituent assemblies. Those who owned property could vote for representatives to the assembly. Because many people—mostly white males—owned property, the proportion of adult white men able to vote was 50 percent or higher in all the British colonies. Proportionally, the electorate of the British colonies was the largest in the world.

However, that did not mean that the British colonies were democratic. The basic principle of order in eighteenth-century British culture was the ideal of deference to natural hierarchies. The well-ordered family, in which children were to be strictly governed by their parents and wives by their husbands, was the common metaphor for civil order. Members of subordinate groups, such as women, the non-English, African American slaves, servants, and Indians—who in some colonies constituted nine of every ten adults in the population—could not vote or hold public office. Moreover, for the most part the men who did vote chose wealthy landowners, planters, or merchants to serve as their leaders. Thus, provincial assemblies were controlled by colonial elites.

To educated British colonists, the word *democracy* implied rule by the mob, the normal order of things turned upside-down. However, over the eighteenth century there was an important trend toward stronger institutions of representative government. By midcentury most colonial assemblies in British North America had achieved considerable power over provincial affairs. They collected local revenues and allocated funds for government programs, asserted the right to audit the accounts of public officers, and in some cases even acquired the power to approve the appointment of provincial officials. Because the assemblies controlled the purse strings, most royal governors were unable to resist this trend.

The royal governors who were most successful at realizing their agendas were those who became adept at playing one provincial faction off against another. All this conflict had the important effect of schooling the colonial elite in the art of politics. It was not democratic politics, but schooling in the ways of patronage, coalition-building, and behind-the-scenes intrigue had important implications for the development of American institutions.

The Cultural Transformation of British North America

Despite broad similarities, the colonial regions of North America developed along divergent lines during the eighteenth century. The British colonies were marked by increasing ethnic diversity, economic growth, social tensions, and conflictual politics that proved to be training for self-government. The middle decades of the eighteenth century also witnessed significant cultural transformation as new ideas and writings associated with the Enlightenment made their way across the Atlantic on the same ships that transported European goods. In New Spain and New France, by contrast, colonial officials worked diligently to suppress these challenging new ideas. The Catholic Church effectively banned the works of hundreds of authors. In Mexico officials of the Inquisition conducted house-to-house searches in pursuit of prohibited texts that they feared had been smuggled into the country.

The Enlightenment Challenge

Drawing from the discoveries of Galileo, Copernicus, and the seventeenth-century scientists René Descartes and Sir Isaac Newton, Enlightenment thinkers in Britain and on the Continent argued that the universe was governed by natural laws that people could understand and apply to their own advantage. John Locke, for example, articulated a philosophy of reason in proposing that the state existed to provide for the happiness and security of individuals, who were endowed with inalienable rights to life, liberty, and property. Enlightenment writers emphasized rationality, harmony, and order, themes that stood in stark contrast to folk culture's traditional emphasis on the unfathomable mysteries of God and nature and the inevitability of human failure and disorder.

Enlightenment thinking undoubtedly appealed most to those whose ordered lives had improved their lot. The colonial elite had good reason to believe in progress. They sent their sons to college, where the

Reverend Cotton Mather (1663–1728), pastor of Boston's Second Congregational Church and author of 450 books on theology, history, government, and science, combined both traditional and Enlightenment views. Although he defended the existence of witches, contributing to the hysteria of the Salem witchcraft trials, he also promoted Copernican science and inoculation against disease.

Unknown artist, portrait of Cotton Mather, ca. 1725. Oil painting. Courtesy American Antiquarian Society, Worcesster, MA.

texts of the new thinkers were promoted. Harvard, established in 1636, remained the only institution of higher education in British America until 1693, when Anglicans established the College of William and Mary at Williamsburg, soon to become the new capital of Virginia. Puritans in Connecticut, believing that Harvard was too liberal, founded Yale College in 1701. The curricula of these colleges, modeled on those of Oxford and Cambridge in England, were designed to train ministers, but gradually each institution introduced courses and professors influenced by the Enlightenment.

A mixture of traditional and Enlightenment views characterized the colonial colleges, as it did the thought of men such as Cotton Mather. A conservative defender of the old order, Mather wrote a book supporting the existence of witches. On the other hand, he was also a member of the Royal Society, an early supporter of inoculation against disease, and a defender of the Copernican sun-centered model of the universe.

About half the adult men and a quarter of the adult women of the British colonies could read, evidencing a literacy rate comparable to those of England and Scandinavia. In striking contrast, in the French and Spanish colonies reading was a skill confined to a tiny minority of upper-class men. In New England, where the Puritans were committed to Bible reading and had developed a system of public education, literacy rates were 85 percent among men and approximately 50 percent among women—the highest in the entire Atlantic world. But the tastes of ordinary readers ran to traditional rather than Enlightenment fare. Not surprisingly, the best-selling book of the colonial era was the Bible. In second place was that unique American literary form, the captivity narrative, including the Reverend John Williams's *Redeemed Captive,* cited in the opening of this chapter, most with a lot less religion and a great deal more gore.

Another popular literary form was the almanac, a combination calendar, astrological guide, and sourcebook of medical advice and farming tips reflecting the concerns of traditional folk culture. The best remembered is Benjamin Franklin's *Poor Richard's Almanac* (1732–57), although it was preceded and outlived by a great many others. But what was so innovative about Franklin's almanac, and what made it so important, was the manner in which the author used this traditional literary form to promote the new Enlightenment emphasis on useful and practical knowledge. Posing as the simple bumpkin Poor Richard, the highly sophisticated Franklin was one of the first Americans to bring Enlightenment thought to ordinary folk.

The growth of the economy in the British colonies and the development of a colonial upper class stimulated the emergence of a more cosmopolitan Anglican culture, particularly in the cities of the Atlantic coast. A rising demand for drama, poetry, essays, novels, and history was met by urban booksellers who imported British publications.

A Decline in Religious Devotion

While these new ideas flourished, religion seemed in decline. South of New England, the Anglican Church was weak, its ministers uninspiring, and many families remained "unchurched." A historian of religion has estimated that only one adult in fifteen was a member of a congregation. Although this figure may understate the impact of religion on community life, it helps keep things in perspective.

The Puritan churches of New England also suffered declining membership and falling attendance at services, and many ministers began to warn of Puritanism's "declension," pointing to the "dangerous" trend toward the "evil of toleration." By the second decade of the eighteenth century only one in five New Englanders belonged to an established congregation. When Puritanism had been a sect, membership in the church was voluntary and leaders could demand that followers testify to their religious conversion. But when Puritanism became an established church, attendance was expected of all townspeople, and conflicts inevitably arose over the requirement of a conversion experience. An agreement of 1662, known as the Half-Way Covenant, offered a practical solution: members' children who had not experienced conversion themselves could join as "half-way" members, restricted only from participation in communion. Thus the Puritans chose to manage rather than to resolve the conflicts involved in becoming an established religion. In 1708 the churches of Connecticut agreed to the Saybrook Platform, which enacted a system of governance by councils of ministers and elders rather than by congregations. This reform also had the effect of weakening the passion and commitment of church members.

In addition, an increasing number of Congregationalists began to question the strict Calvinist theology of predestination—the belief that God had predetermined the few men and women who would be saved in the Second Coming. In the eighteenth century many Puritans turned to the much more comforting idea that God had given people the freedom to choose salvation by developing their faith and good works. This belief was in harmony with the Enlightenment view that men and women were not helpless pawns but rational beings who could actively shape their own destinies. Also implicit in these new views was an image of God as a loving rather than a punishing father. These liberal ideas appealed to groups experiencing economic and social improvement, especially commercial farmers, merchants, and the comfortable middle class with its rising expectations. But among ordinary people, especially those in the countryside where traditional patterns lingered, there was a good deal of opposition to these unorthodox new ideas.

The Great Awakening

The first stirrings of a movement challenging this rationalist approach to religion occurred during the 1730s, most notably in the movement sparked by Reverend Jonathan Edwards in the community of Northampton, in western Massachusetts. As the leaders of the community increasingly devoted their energies to the pursuit of wealth, the enthusiasm seemed to go out of religion. The congregation adopted rules allowing church membership without evidence of a conversion experience and adopted a seating plan for the church that placed wealthy families in the prominent pews, front and center. But the same economic forces that made the "River Gods"—as the wealthy landowners of the Connecticut Valley were known—impoverished others. Young people from the community's poorer families grew disaffected as they were forced to postpone marriage because of the scarcity and expense of the land needed to set up a farm household. Increasingly they refused to attend church meeting, instead gathering together at night for "frolics" that only seemed to increase their discontent.

Reverend Edwards made this group of young people his special concern. Believing that they needed to "have their hearts touched," he preached to them in a style that appealed to their emotions. For the first time in a generation, the meetinghouse shook with the fire and passion of Puritan religion. "Before the sermon was done," one Northampton parishioner remembered one notable occasion, "there was a great moaning and crying through the whole house—What shall I do to be saved?—Oh I am going to Hell!—Oh what shall I do for Christ?" Religious fervor swept through the community, and church membership began to grow. There was more to this than the power of one preacher, for similar revivals were soon breaking out in other New England communities, as well as among German pietists and Scots–Irish Presbyterians in Pennsylvania. Complaining of "spiritual coldness," people abandoned ministers whose sermons read like rational dissertations for those whose preaching was more emotional.

These local revivals became an intercolonial phenomenon thanks to the preaching of George Whitefield, an evangelical Anglican minister from England, who in 1738 made the first of several tours of the colonies. By all accounts, his preaching had a powerful effect. Even Benjamin Franklin, a religious skeptic, wrote of the "extraordinary influence of [Whitefield's] oratory" after attending an outdoor service in Philadelphia where 30,000 people crowded the streets to hear him. Whitefield began as Edwards did, chastising his listeners as "half animals and half devils," but he left them with the hope that God would be responsive to their desire for salvation. Whitefield avoided sectarian differences. "God help us to forget party names and become Christians in deed and truth," he declared.

Historians of religion consider this widespread colonial revival of religion, known as the Great Awakening, to be the American version of the second phase of the Protestant Reformation. Religious leaders condemned the laxity, decadence, and officalism of established Protestantism and reinvigorated it with calls for piety and purity. People undergoing the economic and social stresses of the age, unsure about their ability to find land, marry, and participate in the promise of a growing economy, found relief in religious enthusiasm.

In Pennsylvania, two important leaders of the Awakening were William Tennent and his son Gilbert. An Irish-born Presbyterian, the elder Tennent was an evangelical preacher who established a school in Pennsylvania to train like-minded men for the ministry. His lampooned "Log College," as it was called, ultimately evolved into the College of New Jersey — later Princeton University—founded in 1746. In the early 1740s, disturbed by what he called the "presumptuous security" of the colonial church, Tennent toured with Whitefield and delivered the famous sermon "The Dangers of an Unconverted Ministry," in which he called upon Protestants to examine the religious convictions of their own ministers.

Among Presbyterians, open conflict broke out between the revivalists and the old guard, and in some regions the church hierarchy divided into separate organizations. In New England similar factions, known as the New Lights and the Old Lights, accused each other of heresy. The New Lights railed against a rationalist heresy, and called for a revival of Calvinism. The Old Lights condemned emotional enthusiasm as part of the heresy of believing in a personal and direct relationship with God outside the order of the church. Itinerant preachers appeared in the countryside, stirring up trouble. Many congregations split into feuding factions, and ministers found themselves challenged by their newly awakened parishioners. Never had there been such turmoil in New England churches.

The Great Awakening was one of the first national events in American history. It began somewhat later in the South, developing first in the mid-1740s among Scots–Irish Presbyterians, then achieving its full impact with the organization work of Methodists and particularly Baptists in the 1760s and early 1770s. The revival not only affected white Southerners but also introduced many slaves to Christianity for the first time. Local awakenings were often a phenomenon shared by both whites and blacks. The Baptist churches of the South in the era of the American Revolution included members of both races and featured spontaneous preaching by slaves as well as masters. In the nineteenth century white and black Christians would go their separate ways, but the joint experience of the eighteenth-century Awakening shaped the religious cultures of both groups.

Many other "unchurched" colonists were brought back to Protestantism by the Great Awakening. But a careful examination of statistics suggests that the proportion of church members in the general population probably did not increase during the middle decades of the century. While the number of churches more than doubled from 1740 to 1780, the colonial population grew even faster, increasing by a factor of three. The greatest impact was on families already associated with the churches. Before the Awakening, attendance at church had been mostly an adult affair, but throughout the colonies the revival of religion had its deepest effects on young people, who flocked to church in greater numbers than ever before. For years the number of people experiencing conversion had been steadily falling, but now full membership surged. Church membership previously had been concentrated among women, leading Cotton Mather, for one, to speculate that perhaps women were indeed more godly. But men were particularly affected by the Great Awakening, and their attendance and membership rose.

Great Awakening Politics

The Awakening appealed most of all to groups who felt bypassed by the economic and cultural development of the British colonies during the first half of the eighteenth century. The New Lights tended to draw their greatest strength from small farmers and less prosperous craftsmen. Many members of the upper class and the comfortable "middling sort" viewed the excesses of the Great Awakening as indications of anarchy, and became even more committed to rational religion.

A number of historians have suggested that the Great Awakening had important political implications. In Connecticut, for example, Old Lights politicized the religious dispute by passing a series of laws in the General Assembly designed to suppress the revival. In one town, separatists refused to pay taxes that supported the established church and were jailed. New Light judges were thrown off the bench, and others were denied their elected seats in the assembly. The arrogance of these actions was met with popular outrage, and by the 1760s the Connecticut New Lights had organized themselves politically and, in what amounted to a political rebellion, succeeded in turning the Old Lights out of office. These New Light politicians would provide the leadership for the American Revolution in Connecticut.

Such direct connections between religion and politics were rare. There can be little doubt, however, that for many people the Great Awakening offered the first opportunity to participate actively in public debate and public action that affected the direction of their lives. Choices about religious styles, ministers, and doctrine were thrown open for public discourse, and ordinary people began to believe that their opinions actually counted for something. Underlying the debate over these issues were insecurities about warfare, economic growth, and the development of colonial society. The Great Awakening empowered ordinary people to question their leaders, an experience that would prove critical in the political struggles to come.

Conclusion

By the middle of the eighteenth century a number of distinct colonial regions had emerged in North America, all of them with rising populations demanding that more land be seized from the Indians. Some colonies attempted to ensure homogeneity, whereas others embraced diversity, pushing them in very different directions. Within the British colonies, New England in particular seemed bound to the past, whereas the Middle Colonies and the backcountry pointed the way toward pluralism and expansion. These developments placed them in direct competition with the expansionist plans of the French and at odds with Indian peoples committed to the defense of their homelands.

The economic development of the British colonies introduced new social and cultural tensions that led to the Great Awakening, a massive revival of religion that was the first transcolonial event in American history. Thousands of people experienced a renewal of religious passions, but rather than resuscitating old traditions, the Awakening pointed people toward a more active role in their own political futures. These transformations added to the differences among the British colonies on one hand and the Spanish and French on the other.

CHRONOLOGY

1636	Harvard College founded
1644	Roger Williams's *Bloudy Tenent of Persecution*
1662	Half-Way Covenant in New England
1674	Bishopric of Quebec established
1680s	William Penn begins recruiting settlers from the European Continent
1682	Mary Rowlandson's *Sovereignty and Goodness of God*
1689	Toleration Act passed by Parliament
1690s	Beginnings of Jesuit missions in Arizona
1693	College of William and Mary founded
1700s	Plains Indians begin adoption of the horse
1701	Yale College founded
	Iroquois sign treaty of neutrality with France
1704	Deerfield raid
1708	Saybrook Platform in Connecticut
1716	Spanish begin construction of Texas missions
1730s	French decimate the Natchez and defeat the Fox Indians
1732	Franklin begins publishing *Poor Richard's Almanac*
1738	George Whitefield first tours the colonies
1740s	Great Awakening gets under way in the Northeast
1740	Parliament passes a naturalization law for the colonies
1746	College of New Jersey (Princeton) founded
1760s	Great Awakening achieves full impact in the South
1769	Spanish colonization of California begins
1775	Indian revolt at San Diego
1776	San Francisco founded
1781	Los Angeles founded

Review Questions

1. What were the principal colonial regions of North America? Discuss their similarities and differences. Contrast the development of their political systems.
2. Why did the Spanish and the French close their colonies to immigration? Why did the British open theirs? How do you explain the ethnic homogeneity of New England and the ethnic pluralism of New York and Pennsylvania?
3. What were the principal trends in the history of Indian America in the eighteenth century?
4. Discuss the development of class differences in the Spanish, French, and British colonies in the eighteenth century.
5. Discuss the effects of the Great Awakening on the subsequent history of the British colonies.

Recommended Reading

JOHN DEMOS, *The Unredeemed Captive: A Family Story from Early America* (1994). A moving history of the Deerfield captives, focusing on the experience of Eunice Williams, the unredeemed captive.

W. J. ECCLES, *The Canadian Frontier, 1534–1760* (1983). An introduction to the history of French America by a leading scholar on colonial Canada.

DAVID HACKETT FISCHER, *Albion's Seed: Four British Folkways in America* (1990). An engaging history with fascinating details on the regions of New England, Pennsylvania, Virginia, and the backcountry.

JACK P. GREENE, *Pursuits of Happiness: The Social Development of Early Modern British Colonies and the Formation of American Culture* (1986). A distillation of a tremendous amount of historical material on community life in British North America.

JAMES A. HENRETTA AND GREGORY H. NOBLES, *Evolution and Revolution: American Society, 1600–1820* (1987). A useful synthesis of the newest social history of the British colonies. Includes an excellent bibliographic essay.

RICHARD HOFSTADTER, *America at 1750* (1971). Although more than twenty years old and left unfinished by the premature death of the author, this remains the single best book on the eighteenth-century British colonies.

COLON MCEVEDY, *The Penguin Atlas of North American History to 1870* (1988). An unparalleled comparative perspective on the Spanish, French, and British regions of the continent, from precolonial times to the nineteenth century.

JACKSON TURNER MAIN, *The Social Structure of Revolutionary America* (1965). A detailed treatment of colonial social structure, with statistics, tables, and enlightening interpretations.

D. W. MEINIG, *The Shaping of America: Atlantic America, 1492–1800* (1986). A geographer's overview of the historical development of the North American continent in the era of European colonialism. Provides a survey of the British and French colonies.

DAVID J. WEBER, *The Spanish Frontier in North America* (1992). A magnificent treatment of the entire Spanish borderlands, from Florida to California. Includes important chapters on colonial government and social life.

ROBERT WELLS, *The Population of the British Colonies in America Before 1776* (1975). The standard source on colonial population growth.

6

FROM EMPIRE TO INDEPENDENCE, 1750–1776

AMERICAN COMMUNITIES

THE FIRST CONTINENTAL CONGRESS SHAPES A NATIONAL POLITICAL COMMUNITY

In September 1774, the colonies made clear their displeasure with the Empire's actions. Fifty-six elected delegates from twelve of the colonies met at Philadelphia to draft a common response to what they called Intolerable Acts—the closing of the port of Boston, the suspension of Massachusetts government, and other British measures. These were the empire's latest attempt to force the colonies to accept the power of Parliament to make laws binding them "in all cases whatsoever." This was the first intercolonial meeting since the Stamp Act Congress of 1765 (discussed later in this chapter). If the colonies now failed to act together, they would be "attacked and destroyed by piecemeal," declared Arthur Lee of Virginia. Abigail Adams, the politically astute wife of John Adams of Massachusetts, agreed. "You have before you," she wrote to her husband, "the greatest national concerns that ever came before any people."

The opening minutes of the first session, on September 5, did not bode well. One delegate moved that they begin with prayer; another responded that they were "so divided in religious sentiments, some Episcopalians, some Quakers, some Anabaptists, some Presbyterians and some Congregationalists, so that we could not join in the same act of worship." Were the delegates to be stymied from the very beginning by things that separated rather than united them? John Adams's cousin, fellow Massachusetts delegate Samuel Adams, jumped to his feet. He was no bigot, he said, "and could hear a prayer from any gentlemen of piety and virtue who was at the same time a friend to his country." This incident highlighted the most important task confronting the Continental Congress: they had to develop trust in one another, for what they were doing was considered treason by the British authorities. They had to find a way to support the common cause without compromising their local identities. At first it was as if the delegates were "ambassadors from a dozen belligerent powers of Europe," wrote John Adams. The delegates represented different colonies, whose traditions and histories were as different as those of separate countries. Moreover, these lawyers, merchants, and planters, who were leaders in their respective colonies, were strangers to one another. Their political opinions ranged from loyalty to the British crown and empire to a belief in the necessity of violent revolution. "Every man," Adams wrote, "is a great man, an orator, a critic, a statesman, and therefore every man, upon every question, must show his oratory, his criticism, and his political abilities." As a result he continued, "business is drawn and spun out to an immeasurable length. I believe that if it was moved and seconded that we should come to a resolution that three and two make five, we should be entertained with logic and rhetorick, law, history, politicks and mathematics concerning the subject for two whole days."

During seven weeks of deliberations, the men of the Continental Congress succeeded in forging an agreement on the principles and policies they would have to follow in addressing the most serious crisis in the history of Britain's North American colonies. Equally important, the delegates found ways to work together and harmonize their interests. They immediately resolved that each colony would have one vote, thereby committing themselves to preserving provincial autonomy. They sent their most vexing problems to committees, whose members could sound each other out on the issues without speaking for the public record, and they added to their daily routine a round of dinners, parties, and late-night tippling. The greatest single accomplishment of the Continental Congress was the creation of a community of leadership for the united colonies. "It has taken us much time to get acquainted," John Adams wrote to Abigail, but he left Philadelphia thinking of his fellow representatives as "a collection of the greatest men upon this continent."

Patrick Henry of Virginia, one of the delegates already committed to independence, was exuberant when the Continental Congress adjourned in late October. "The distinctions between Virginians, Pennsylvanians, New Yorkers, and New Englanders, are no more. I am not a Virginian, but an American," he declared. Henry struck at an important truth. Great Britain had forced the colonists to recognize that they shared a community of interest distinct from that of the mother country. Theirs was a first attempt to overcome local diversity and difference in pursuit of a common national goal.

KEY TOPICS

- The final struggle among Great Britain, France, and Native American tribes for control of eastern North America
- American nationalism in the aftermath of the French and Indian War
- Great Britain's changing policy toward its North American colonies
- The political assumptions of American republicanism
- The colonies' efforts to achieve unity in their confrontation with Great Britain

---

The Seven Years' War in America

The first attempt at cooperation among the leaders of the British colonies occurred in 1754, when representatives from New England, New York, Pennsylvania, and Maryland met to consider a joint approach to the French and Indian challenge. Even as the delegates met, fighting between French Canadians and Virginians began on the Ohio River, the first shots in a great global war for empire, known in Europe as the Seven Years' War, that pitted Britain (allied with Prussia) against the combined might of France, Austria, and Spain. In North America this would be the final and most destructive armed conflict between the British and the French. Ultimately it decided the imperial future of the vast region between the Appalachian Mountains and the Mississippi River, and lay the ground for the conflict between the British and the colonists led to the American Revolution.

The Albany Conference of 1754

The 1754 meeting, which included an official delegation from the Iroquois Confederacy, took place in the New York town of Albany on the Hudson River, had been convened by the British Board of Trade. British officials wanted the colonies to consider a collective response to the continuing conflict with New France and the Indians of the interior. High on the agenda was the negotiation of a settlement with the leaders of the Iroquois Confederacy, who had grown impatient with colonial land grabbing. Because the powerful Iroquois Confederacy, with its Covenant Chain of alliances with other Indian tribes, occupied such a strategic location between New France and the British colonies, the

British could ill afford Iroquois disaffection. But the official Iroquois delegation walked out of the conference, refusing all offers to join a British alliance.

The Albany Conference did adopt Benjamin Franklin's Plan of Union, which proposed that Indian affairs, western settlement, and other items of mutual interest be placed under the authority of a grand council composed of representatives elected by the colonial assemblies and led by a royally appointed president. But the colonial assemblies rejected the Albany Plan of Union.

Colonial Aims and Indian Interests

The absence of intercolonial cooperation in North America would prove to be one of the greatest weaknesses of the British Empire because the ensuing war would be fought at a number of widespread locations. There were three principal flash points of conflict in North America. The first was along the northern Atlantic coast. France had ceded to Britain its colony of Acadia in 1713 (which the British renamed Nova Scotia), but continued to occupy the fortress of Louisburg, from which it guarded its fishing grounds and the St. Lawrence approach to New France. The French subsequently reinforced Louisburg to such an extent that it became known as the Gibraltar of the New World.

A second zone of conflict was the border region between New France and New York, from Niagara Falls to Lake Champlain, where Canadians and New Yorkers were in furious competition for the Indian trade. Unable to compete effectively against superior English goods, the French resorted to armed might, constructing fortifications on Lake George and reinforcing their base at Niagara. In this zone the strategic advantage was held by the Iroquois Confederacy.

It was the Ohio country—the trans-Appalachian region along the Ohio River—that became the primary focus of British and French attention. This rich land was a prime target of British backcountry settlers and frontier land speculators. The French worried that their isolated settlements would be overrun by the expanding British population, and that the loss of the Ohio would threaten their entire Mississippi trading empire. To reinforce their claims, in 1749 the French sent a heavily armed force down the Ohio to warn off the British, and in 1752, supported by their northern Indian allies, they expelled a large number of British traders from the region. To prevent the British from returning to the west, they began the next year to construct a series of forts running south from Lake Erie to the junction of the Al-

The War for Empire in North America, 1754–63

The Seven Years' War in America (or the French and Indian War) was fought in three principal areas: Nova Scotia and what was then Acadia, the frontier between New France and New York, and the upper Ohio River, gateway to the Great West.

legheny and Monongahela rivers, the site known as the Forks of the Ohio River.

The French "have stripped us of more than nine parts in ten of North America," one British official cried, "and left us only a skirt of coast along the Atlantic shore." In preparation for a general war, the British established the port of Halifax in Nova Scotia as a counterpart to Louisburg. In northern New York, they strengthened existing forts and constructed new ones. And finally, the king decided to directly challenge the French claim to the upper Ohio Valley: he conferred an enormous grant of land on the Ohio Company, organized by Virginia and London capitalists, and the company made plans to build a fort at the Forks of the Ohio River.

The impending conflict did not merely involve competing colonial powers, however, for the Indian peoples of the interior had interests of their own. In addition to its native inhabitants, the Ohio country had become a refuge for Indian peoples who had fled the

Northeast, Delawares, Shawnees, Hurons, and Iroquois among them. Most of the Ohio Indians opposed the British, and were anxious to preserve the Appalachians as a barrier to westward expansion. They were also disturbed by the French movement into their country. However, the French outposts, unlike those of the British, did not become centers of expanding agricultural settlements.

The Iroquois Confederacy as a whole sought to play off one European power against the other, to its own advantage. In the South the Creeks carved out a similar role for themselves between the British, the French in Louisiana, and the Spanish in Florida. The Cherokees and Choctaws attempted, less successfully, to do the same. It was in the interests of these Indians to perpetuate the existing colonial stalemate. Their position would be greatly undermined by an overwhelming victory for either side.

Frontier Warfare

At the Albany Congress the delegates received news that Colonel George Washington, a young militia officer sent by the governor of Virginia to expel the French from the region granted to the Ohio Company, had been forced to surrender his troops to a French force near the headwaters of the Monongahela River. The Canadians now commanded the interior country from their base at Fort Duquesne.

Taking up the challenge, the British government dispatched two Irish regiments under General Edward Braddock across the Atlantic in 1755 to attack and destroy Fort Duquesne. Meanwhile, colonial militias commanded by colonial officers were to strike at the New York frontier and the north Atlantic coast. An army of New England militiamen succeeded in capturing two important French forts on the border of Nova Scotia, but the other two prongs of the campaign were failures. The offensive in New York was repulsed. And in the worst defeat of a British army during the eighteenth century, Braddock's force was destroyed by a smaller number of French and Indians on the upper Ohio, and Braddock himself was killed.

Braddock's defeat resulted in the outbreak of full-scale warfare between Britain and France in 1756. Known as the Seven Years' War in Europe, in North America it came to be called the French and Indian War. The fighting of 1756 and 1757 was a near catastrophe for Great Britain. Canadians captured the British forts in northern New York. Indians pounded backcountry settlements, killed thousands of settlers, and raided deep

into the coastal colonies, throwing British colonists into panic. The absence of colonial cooperation greatly hampered the British attempt to mount a counterattack. When British commanders tried to exert direct control over provincial troops, they succeeded only in angering local authorities.

The Conquest of Canada

In the darkest days of 1757, William Pitt, an enthusiastic advocate of British expansion, assumed the prime ministership of Great Britain. Heavily subsidizing the Prussians to fight the war in Europe, he reserved his own forces and resources for naval and colonial operations. Pitt committed the British to the conquest of Canada and the elimination of all French competition in North America. Such a goal could be achieved only with a tremendous outpouring of men and money. By promising that the war would be fought "at His Majesty's expense," Pitt was able to buy colonial cooperation. A massive infusion of British currency and credit greatly stimulated the North American economy. Pitt dispatched over 20,000 regular British troops across the Atlantic. Combining them with colonial forces, he massed over 50,000 armed men against Canada.

The British attracted Indian support for their plans by "redressing the grievances complained of by the Indians, with respect to the lands which have been fraudulently taken from them." In 1758 officials promised the Iroquois Confederacy and the Ohio Indians that the crown would "agree upon clear and fixed boundaries between our settlements and their hunting grounds, so that each party may know their own and be a mutual protection to each other of their respective possessions."

Thus did Pitt succeed in reversing the course of the war. Regular and provincial forces captured Louisburg in July 1758, setting the stage for the penetration of the St. Lawrence Valley. A month later a force of New Englanders captured the strategic French fort of Oswegoon on Lake Ontario, thereby preventing the Canadians from resupplying their western posts. Encouraged by British promises, many Indian tribes abandoned the French alliance, and the French were forced to give up Fort Duquesne. A large British force soon took control of the French fort at the Forks of the Ohio, renaming the post Fort Pitt (Pittsburgh today) in honor of the prime minister. The last of the French forts on the New York frontier fell in 1759. In the South, regular and provincial British troops invaded the homeland of the Cherokees and crushed them.

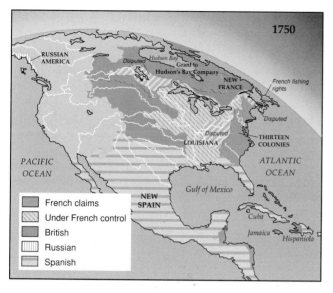
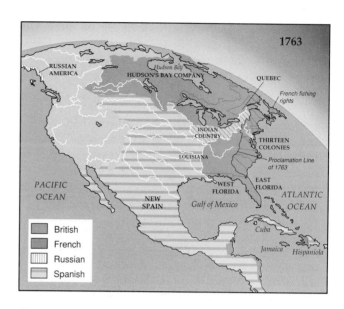

European Claims in North America, 1750 and 1763

As a result of the British victory in the Seven Years' War, the map of colonial claims in North America was fundamentally transformed.

British forces now converged on Quebec, the heart of French Canada. In the summer of 1759 British troops, responding to General James Wolfe's order to "burn and lay waste the country," plundered the farms of *habitants* and shelled the city of Quebec. Finally, in an epic battle fought on the Plains of Abraham before the city walls, more than 2,000 British, French, American, and Canadian men lost their lives, including both Wolfe and the French commander, the Marquis de Montcalm. The British army prevailed, and Quebec fell. The conquest of Montreal in 1760 marked the destruction of the French empire in America.

In the final two years of the war the British swept French ships from the seas, conquered important French and Spanish colonies in the Caribbean, achieved dominance in India, and even captured the Spanish Philippines. In the Treaty of Paris, signed in 1763, France lost all its possessions on the North American mainland. It ceded its claims east of the Mississippi to Great Britain, with the exception of New Orleans. That town, along with the other French trans-Mississippi claims, passed to Spain. For its part, Spain ceded Florida to Britain in exchange for the return of all its Caribbean and Pacific colonies. The imperial rivalry in eastern North America that had begun in the sixteenth century now came to an end with complete victory for the British empire.

Indians and Europeans Struggle over the West

Both the French and the British had long used gift-giving as a way of gaining favor with Indians. The Spanish officials who replaced the French in Louisiana made an effort to continue the old policy. But the British military governor of the western region, General Jeffery Amherst, in one of his first official actions, banned presents to Indian chiefs and tribes, demanding that they learn to live without "charity." Not only were Indians angered by Amherst's reversal of custom, but they were also frustrated by his refusal to supply them with the ammunition they required for hunting. Many were left starving.

In this climate, hundreds of Ohio Indians became disciples of an Indian visionary named Neolin ("The Enlightened One" in Algonquian), known to the English as the Delaware Prophet. The core of Neolin's teaching was that Indians had been corrupted by European ways and needed to purify themselves by returning to their traditions and preparing for a holy war.

In May 1763 a confederacy of Indians, under the political leadership of the Ottawa chief Pontiac, simultaneously attacked all the British forts in the west. They sacked and burned eight British posts, but failed to take the key forts of Niagara, Detroit, and Pitt. Pontiac fought on for another year, but most of the Indians sued for peace, fearing the destruction of their villages. The British came to terms because they knew they could not overwhelm the Indian peoples. The war thus ended in stalemate.

Even before the uprising, the British had been at work on a policy they hoped would help to resolve frontier tensions. In the Royal Proclamation of 1763, the British government set aside the region west of the crest of the Appalachian Mountains as "Indian Country," and required the specific authorization of the crown for any purchase of these protected Indian lands.

Colonists had expected that the removal of the French threat would allow them to move unencumbered into the West, regardless of the wishes of the Indian inhabitants. They could not understand why the British would award territory to Indian enemies who had slaughtered more than 4,000 settlers during the previous war. In fact, the British proved unable and ultimately unwilling to prevent the westward migration that was a dynamic part of the colonization of British North America. Within a few years of the war, New Englanders by the thousands were moving into the northern Green Mountain district, known as Vermont. In the middle colonies, New York settlers pushed ever closer to the homeland of the Iroquois, while others located within the protective radius of Fort Pitt in western Pennsylvania. Hunters, stock herders, and farmers crossed over the first range of the Appalachians in Virginia and North Carolina, planting pioneer communities in what are now West Virginia and eastern Tennessee.

Moreover, the press of population growth and economic development turned the attention of investors and land speculators to the area west of the Appalachians. In response to demands by settlers and speculators, British authorities were soon pressing the Iroquois and Cherokees for cessions of land in Indian Country. No longer able to play off rival colonial powers, Indians were reduced to a choice between compliance and resistance. Weakened by the recent war, they chose to sign away their land rights.

The individual colonies were even more aggressive. Locked in a dispute with Pennsylvania about jurisdiction in the Ohio country, in 1773 Virginia governor John Murray, Earl of Dunmore, sent a force to occupy Fort Pitt. In 1774, in an attempt to gain legitimacy for his dispute with Pennsylvania, Dunmore provoked a frontier war with the Shawnees. After defeating them he forced them to cede the region to Virginia.

The Imperial Crisis in British North America

No colonial power of the mid-eighteenth century could match Britain in projecting imperial power over the face of the globe. During the years following its victory in the Seven Years' War, Britain turned confidently to the reorganization of its North American empire. This new colonial policy plunged British authorities into a new and ultimately more threatening conflict with the colonists, who had begun to develop a sense of their own nationality.

The Emergence of American Nationalism

Despite the anger of frontiersmen over the Proclamation of 1763, the conclusion of the Seven Years' War had left most colonists proud of their place in the British empire. But during the war many had begun to note important contrasts between themselves and the mother country. The soldiers of the British army, for example, shocked Americans with their profane, lewd, and violent behavior. But the colonists were equally shocked by the swift and terrible punishment that aristocratic officers used to keep these soldiers in line. Americans who had witnessed such savage punishments found it easy to believe in the threat of British slavery.

Colonial forces, by contrast, were composed of volunteer companies. Officers tempered their administration of punishment, knowing they had to maintain the enthusiasm of these troops. Discipline thus fell considerably below the standards to which British officers were accustomed. "Riff-raff," one British general said of the colonials, "the lowest dregs of the people, both officers and men." For their part, many colonial officers believed that the British ignored the important role the Americans had played in the Seven Years' War. During that war many colonists began to see themselves as distinct from the British.

The Seven Years' War also strengthened a sense of intercolonial, American identity. Farm boys who never before had ventured outside the communities of their birth fought in distant regions with men like themselves from other colonies. Such experiences reinforced a developing nationalist perspective, as did one of the most important means of intercolonial communication, the weekly newspaper. Early in the eighteenth century the colonial press functioned as a mouthpiece for the government; editors who criticized public officials could land in jail. In 1735, for example, New York City editor

John Peter Zenger was indicted for seditious libel after printing antigovernment articles. But as it turned out, the case provided the precedent for greater freedom of the press when Zenger was acquitted by a jury. By 1760, more than twenty highly opinionated weekly newspapers circulated in the British colonies, and according to one estimate, a quarter of all male colonists were regular readers. During these years the British colonists of North America first began to use the term *American* to denote their common identity. More than any previous event, the Seven Years' War promoted a new spirit of nationalism and a wider notion of community. This was the social base of the political community later forged at the Continental Congress.

Politics, Republicanism, and the Press

The pages of the colonial press reveal the political assumptions held by informed colonists. For decades governors had struggled with colonial assemblies over their respective powers. As commentary on the meaning of these struggles, colonial editors often reprinted the writings of the radical Whigs of eighteenth-century England, pamphleteers such as John Trenchard and Thomas Gordon, political theorists such as John Locke, and essayists such as Alexander Pope and Jonathan Swift. They warned of the growing threat to liberty posed by the unchecked exercise of power. In their more emotional writings they argued that a conspiracy existed among the powerful—kings, aristocrats, and Catholics—to quash liberty and institute tyranny. Outside the mainstream of British political opinion, these ideas came to define the political consensus in the British colonies, a point of view historians call republicanism.

The Sugar and Stamp Acts

The emerging sense of American political identity was soon tested by British measures designed to raise revenues in the colonies. To quell Indian uprisings and stifle discontent among the French and Spanish populations of Quebec and Florida, 10,000 British troops remained stationed in North America at the conclusion of the Seven Years' War. The cost of maintaining this force added to the enormous debt Britain had run up during the fighting, and created a desperate need for additional revenues. In 1764 the Chancellor of the Exchequer, George Grenville, deciding to obtain the needed revenue from America, pushed through Parliament a measure known as the Sugar Act.

The Sugar Act revitalized the customs service in the colonies, introducing stricter registration procedures for ships and adding more officers. In anticipation of American resistance, the legislation also increased the jurisdiction of the vice-admiralty court at Halifax, where customs cases were heard. These courts were hated because there was no presumption of innocence and the accused had no right to a jury trial. These new regulations promised not only to squeeze the incomes of American merchants but also to cut off their lucrative smuggling operations. Moreover, colonial taxes, which had been raised during the war, remained at an all-time high. In many cities, merchants as well as artisans protested loudly. Boston was especially vocal: in response to the sugar tax, the town meeting proposed a boycott of certain English imports. This movement for nonimportation soon spread to other port towns.

James Otis, Jr., a Massachusetts lawyer fond of grand oratory, was one of the first Americans to strike a number of themes that would become familiar over the next fifteen years. A man's "right to his life, his liberty, his property" was "written on the heart, and revealed to him by his maker," he argued in language echoing the rhetoric of the Great Awakening. It was "inherent, inalienable, and indefeasible by any laws, pacts, contracts, covenants, or stipulations which man could devise." "An act against the Constitution is void," he declared; there could be "no taxation without representation."

But it was only fair, Grenville argued, that the colonists help pay the costs of the empire, and what better way to do so than by a tax? In early 1765, unswayed by American protests, he followed the Sugar Act with a second and considerably more sweeping revenue measure, the Stamp Act. This tax required the purchase of specially embossed paper for all newspapers, legal documents, licenses, insurance policies, ship's papers, and even dice and playing cards.

The Stamp Act Crisis

During the summer and autumn of 1765 the American reaction to the Stamp Act created a crisis of unprecedented proportions. The stamp tax had to be paid in hard money, and it came during a period of economic stagnation. Many colonists complained of being "miserably burdened and oppressed with taxes."

Of more importance for the longer term, however, were the constitutional implications. The British argued

Samuel Adams, a second cousin of John Adams, was a leader of the Boston radicals and an organizer of the Sons of Liberty. The artist of this portrait, John Singleton Copley, was known for setting his subjects in the midst of everyday objects; here he portrays Adams in a middle-class suit with the charter guaranteeing the liberties of Boston's freemen.

John Singleton Copley (1738–1815), *Samuel Adams,* 1772. Oil on canvas, 127 cm × 102.2 cm. Deposited by the City of Boston. Courtesy, Museum of Fine Arts, Boston.

that Americans were subject to the acts of Parliament because of *virtual representation*. That is, members of Parliament were thought to represent not just their districts, but all citizens of the empire. As one British writer put it, the colonists were "represented in Parliament in the same manner as those inhabitants of Britain are who have not voices in elections." But in an influential pamphlet of 1765, *Considerations on the Propriety of Imposing Taxes,* Maryland lawyer Daniel Dulany rejected this theory. Because Americans were members of a separate political community, he insisted, Parliament could impose no tax on them. Instead, he argued for *actual representation,* emphasizing the direct relation-

ship that must exist between the people and their political representatives.

It was just such constitutional issues that were emphasized in the Virginia Stamp Act Resolutions, pushed through the Virginia assembly by the passionate young lawyer Patrick Henry in May 1765. Although the Virginia House of Burgesses rejected the most radical of Henry's resolutions, they were all reprinted throughout the colonies. By the end of 1765 the assemblies of eight other colonies had approved similar measures denouncing the Stamp Act and proclaiming their support of "no taxation without representation."

In Massachusetts the leaders of the opposition to the Stamp Act came from a group of upper- and middle-class men who had long opposed the conservative leaders of the colony. These men had worked years to establish a political alliance with Boston craftsmen and workers who met at taverns, in volunteer fire companies, or at social clubs. One of these clubs, known as the Loyall Nine, included Samuel Adams (see this chapter's opening story), an associate and friend of James Otis who had made his career in local politics. Using his contacts with professionals, craftsmen, and laboring men, Adams helped put together an anti-British alliance that spanned Boston's social classes. In August 1765 Adams and the Loyall Nine were instrumental in organizing a protest of Boston workingmen against the Stamp Act.

Whereas Boston's elite had prospered during the eighteenth century, the conditions for workers and the poor had worsened. Unemployment, inflation, and high taxes had greatly increased the level of poverty during the depression that followed the Seven Years' War, and many were resentful. A large Boston crowd assembled on August 14, 1765, in the shade of a broad "liberty tree" and strung up effigies of several British officials, including Boston's stamp distributor, Andrew Oliver. The restless crowd then vandalized Oliver's office and home. At the order of Oliver's brother-in-law, Lieutenant Governor Thomas Hutchinson, leader of the Massachusetts conservatives, the town sheriff tried to break up the crowd, but he was pelted with paving stones and bricks. Soon thereafter, Oliver resigned his commission. The unified action of Boston's social groups had had its intended effect.

Twelve days later, however, a similar crowd gathered at the aristocratic home of Hutchinson himself. As the family fled through the back door, the crowd smashed through the front with axes. Inside they demolished furniture, chopped down the interior walls, consumed the contents of the wine cellar, and looted everything of value, leaving the house a mere shell. As these events demonstrated, it was not always possible to keep popular protests within bounds. During the fall and winter, urban crowds in commercial towns from Halifax in the north to Savannah in the south forced the resignation of British tax officials.

In many colonial cities and towns, groups of merchants, lawyers, and craftsmen sought to moderate the resistance movement by seizing control of it. Calling themselves the Sons of Liberty, these groups encouraged moderate forms of protest. They circulated petitions, published pamphlets, and encouraged crowd actions only as a last resort; always they emphasized limited political goals. There were few repetitions of mob attacks, but by the end of 1765 almost all the stamp distributors had resigned or fled, making it impossible for Britain to enforce the Stamp Act.

Repeal of the Stamp Act

In the fall of 1765, a growing number of British merchants, worried about the effects of the growing nonimportation movement among the colonists, began petitioning Parliament to repeal the Stamp Act. However, it was not until March 1766 that a bill for repeal passed the House of Commons. This news was greeted with celebrations throughout the American colonies, and the nonimportation associations were disbanded. Overlooked in the mood of optimism was Parliament's assertion in this Declaratory Act of its full authority to make laws binding the colonies "in all cases whatsoever." The notion of absolute parliamentary supremacy over colonial matters was basic to the British theory of empire. Even Pitt, friend of America that he was, asserted "the authority of this kingdom over the colonies to be sovereign and supreme, in every circumstance of government and legislation whatsoever." The Declaratory Act signaled that the conflict had not been resolved, but merely postponed.

"Save Your Money and Save Your Country"

Colonial resistance to the Stamp Act was stronger in urban than in rural communities, stronger among merchants, craftsmen, and planters than among farmers and frontiersmen. When Parliament next moved to impose its will, as it had promised to do in the Declaratory Act, imposing new duties on imported goods, the American opposition again adopted the tactic of nonimportation.

But this time resistance spread from the cities and towns into the countryside. As the editor of the *Boston Gazette* phrased the issue, "Save your money and you save your country." It became the slogan of the movement.

The Townshend Revenue Acts

During the 1760s there was a rapid turnover of government leaders that made it difficult for Britain to form a consistent and even-handed policy toward the colonies. In 1767, after several failed governments, King George III asked William Pitt to again become prime minister. Pitt enjoyed enormous good will in America, and a government under his leadership stood a good chance of reclaiming colonial credibility. But, suffering from a prolonged illness, he was soon forced to retire, and his place as head of the cabinet was assumed by Charles Townshend, Chancellor of the Exchequer.

One of the first problems facing the new government was the national debt. At home there were massive unemployment, riots over high prices, and tax protests. The large landowners forced a bill through Parliament slashing their taxes by 25 percent. The government feared continued opposition at home far more than opposition in America. So as part of his plan to close the budget gap, Townshend proposed a new revenue measure for the colonies that placed import duties on commodities such as lead, glass, paint, paper, and tea. By means of these new Revenue Acts, enacted in 1767, Townshend hoped to redress colonial grievances against *internal taxes* such as those imposed by the Stamp Act. For most colonists, however, it proved to be a distinction without a difference.

The most influential response to these Revenue Acts came in a series of articles by John Dickinson, *Letters from a Farmer in Pennsylvania,* that were reprinted in nearly every colonial newspaper. Dickinson was a wealthy Philadelphia lawyer, but in this work he posed as a humble husbandman. Parliament had the right to regulate trade through the use of duties, he conceded. It could place prohibitive tariffs, for example, on foreign products. But it had no constitutional authority to tax goods in order to raise revenues in America. As the preface to the Revenue Acts made clear, the income they produced would be used to pay the salaries of royal officials in America. Thus, Dickinson pointed out, colonial administrators would not be subject to the financial oversight of elected representatives.

Other Americans warned that this was part of the British conspiracy to suppress American liberties. Their fears were reinforced by Townshend's stringent enforcement of the Revenue Acts. He created a new and strengthened Board of Commissioners of the Customs, and established a series of vice-admiralty courts at Boston, Philadelphia, and Charleston to prosecute violators of the duties—the first time these hated institutions had appeared in the most important American port cities. To demonstrate his power, he also suspended New York's assembly. That body had refused to vote public funds to support the British troops garrisoned in the colony. Until the citizens of New York relented, Townshend declared, they would no longer be represented.

In response to these measures, some men argued for violent resistance. But it was Dickinson's essays that had the greatest effect on the public debate, not only because of their convincing argument, but because of their mild and reasonable tone. "Let us behave like dutiful children," Dickinson urged, "who have received unmerited blows from a beloved parent." As yet, no sentiment for independence existed in America.

Nonimportation: An Early Political Boycott

Associations of nonimportation and nonconsumption, revived in October 1767 when the Boston town meeting drew up a long list of British products to boycott, became the main weapon of the resistance movement. Over the next few months other port cities, including Providence, Newport, and New York, set up nonimportation associations of their own. Artisans took to the streets in towns and cities throughout the colonies to force merchants to stop importing British goods. The associations published the names of uncooperative importers and retailers. These people then became the object of protesters, who sometimes resorted to violence. Coercion was very much a part of the movement.

Adopting the language of Protestant ethics, nonimportation associations pledged to curtail luxuries and stimulate local industry. These aims had great appeal in small towns and rural districts, which previously had been uninvolved in the anti-British struggle. Nonimportation appealed to their traditional values of self-sufficiency and independence. For the first time, country people were brought into the growing community of resistance. In 1768 and 1769 colonial newspapers paid a great deal of attention to women's support for the boycott. Groups of women, some calling themselves Daughters of Liberty, organized spinning and weaving bees to produce homespun for local consumption. The actual work performed at these bees was less

important than the symbolic message. "The industry and frugality of American ladies," wrote the editor of the *Boston Evening Post,* "are contributing to bring about the political salvation of a whole continent." Other women renounced silks and satins and pledged to stop serving tea to their husbands.

Nonimportation was greatly strengthened in May 1769 when the Virginia House of Burgesses enacted the first provincial association. The association banned the importation of goods enumerated in the Townshend Acts, and slaves and luxury commodities as well. Over the next few months all the colonies but New Hampshire enacted similar associations. Because of these efforts, the value of colonial imports from Britain declined by 41 percent.

The Massachusetts Circular Letter

Boston and Massachusetts were at the center of the agitation over the Townshend Revenue Acts. In February 1768 the Massachusetts House of Representatives approved a letter, drawn up by Samuel Adams, addressed to the speakers of the other provincial assemblies. Designed largely as a propaganda device and having little practical significance, the letter denounced the Townshend Revenue Acts, attacked the British plan to make royal officials independent of colonial assemblies, and urged the colonies to find a way to "harmonize with each other." Massachusetts governor Francis Bernard condemned the document for stirring up rebellion and dissolved the legislature. In Britain Lord Hillsborough, Secretary of State for the Colonies, ordered each royal governor in America to likewise dissolve his colony's assembly if it should endorse the letter. Before this demand reached America, the assemblies of New Hampshire, New Jersey, and Connecticut had commended Massachusetts. Virginia, moreover, had issued a circular letter encouraging a "hearty union" among the colonies and urging common action against the British measures that "have an immediate tendency to enslave us."

Throughout this crisis there were rumors and threats of mob rule in Boston. Because customs agents pressed on smugglers and honest traders alike, they enraged merchants, seamen, and dockworkers. In June 1768 a crowd assaulted customs officials who had seized John Hancock's sloop *Liberty* for nonpayment of duties. So frightened were the officials that they fled the city. Hancock, reportedly the wealthiest merchant in the colonies, and a vocal opponent of the British measures, had become a principal target of the customs officers. In

September the Boston town meeting called on the people to arm themselves, and in the absence of an elected assembly it invited all the other towns to send delegates to a provincial convention. There were threats of armed resistance, but little support for it in the convention, which broke up in chaos. Nevertheless the British, fearing insurrection, occupied Boston with infantry and artillery regiments on October 1, 1768. With this action, they sacrificed a great deal of good will and respect and added greatly to the growing tensions.

The Politics of Revolt and the Boston Massacre

The British troops stationed in the colonies were the object of scorn and hostility over the next two years. There were regular conflicts between soldiers and radicals in New York City, often focusing on the Sons of Liberty. These men would erect "liberty poles" festooned with banners and flags proclaiming their cause, and the British troops would promptly destroy them. When the New York assembly finally bowed to Townshend in December 1769 and voted an appropriation to support the troops, the New York City Sons of Liberty organized a demonstration and erected a large liberty pole. The soldiers chopped it down, sawed it into pieces, and left the wood on the steps of a tavern frequented by the Sons. This led to a riot in which British troops used their bayonets against several thousand New Yorkers armed with cutlasses and clubs. Several men were wounded.

Confrontations also took place in Boston. Sam Adams played up reports and rumors of soldiers harassing women, picking fights, or simply taunting residents with versions of "Yankee Doodle." Soldiers were often hauled into Boston's courts, and local judges adopted a completely unfriendly attitude toward these members of the occupying army.

On the evening of March 5, 1770, a crowd gathered at the Customs House and began taunting a guard, calling him a "damned rascally scoundrel lobster son of a bitch." A captain and seven soldiers went to his rescue, only to be pelted with snowballs and stones. Suddenly, without orders, the frightened soldiers began to fire. Five of the crowd fell dead and six more were wounded. The soldiers escaped to their barracks, but a mob numbering in the hundreds rampaged through the streets demanding vengeance. Fearing for the safety of his men and the security of the state, Thomas Hutchinson, now governor of Massachusetts, ordered British troops out of Boston.

In Paul Revere's version of the Boston Massacre, issued three weeks after the incident, the British fire an organized volley into a defenseless crowd. Revere's print, which he plagiarized from another Boston engraver, may have been inaccurate, but was enormously effective propaganda. It hung in so many Patriot homes that the judge hearing the murder trial of these British soldiers warned the jury not to be swayed by "the prints exhibited in our houses."

The Boston Massacre became infamous throughout the colonies, in part because of the circulation of an inflammatory print produced by the Boston engraver Paul Revere, which depicted the British as firing on a crowd of unresisting civilians. But for many colonists, the incident was a disturbing reminder of the extent to which relations with the mother country had deteriorated. During the next two years, many people found themselves pulling back from the brink. "There seems," one Bostonian wrote, "to be a pause in politics."

The growth of American resistance was slowed as well by the news that Parliament had repealed most of the Townshend Revenue Acts on March 5, 1770—the same day as the Boston Massacre. In the climate of apprehension and confusion, there were few celebrations of the repeal, and the nonimportation associations almost immediately collapsed. Over the next three years, the value of British imports rose by 80 percent. The parliamentary retreat on the question of duties, like the earlier repeal of the Stamp Act, was accompanied by a face-saving measure—retention of the tax on tea "as a mark of the supremacy of Parliament," in the words of Frederick Lord North, the new prime minister.

From Resistance to Rebellion

No great issues replaced the Townshend duties during the early 1770s, and there was a lull in agitation. But the situation turned violent in 1773, when Parliament again infuriated the Americans. This time it was an ill-advised Tea Act, and it propelled the colonists on a swift track from resistance to outright rebellion.

Intercolonial Cooperation

In June 1772 Governor Hutchinson inaugurated another controversy by announcing that henceforth his salary and those of other royally appointed Massachusetts officials would be paid by the crown. In effect, this made the executive and judiciary branches of the colony's government independent of elected representatives. In October the Boston town meeting appointed a Committee of Correspondence to communicate with other towns regarding this challenge. The next month the meeting issued what became known as the *Boston Pamphlet,* a series of declarations written by Samuel Adams and other radicals, concluding that British encroachments upon colonial rights pointed to a plot to enslave Americans.

In March 1773 the Virginia House of Burgesses appointed a standing committee for intercolonial correspondence "to obtain the most early and authentic intelligence" of British actions affecting America, "and to keep up and maintain a correspondence and communication with our sister colonies." The Virginia committee, including Patrick Henry, Richard Henry Lee, and young Thomas Jefferson, served as a model, and within a year all the colonies except Pennsylvania, where conservatives controlled the legislature, had created committees of their own. These committees became the principal channel for sharing information, shaping public opinion, and building intercolonial cooperation before the Continental Congress of 1774.

The information most damaging to British influence came from the radicals in Boston. In June the Boston committee circulated a set of confidential letters from Governor Hutchinson to the ministry in Britain, obtained in London by Benjamin Franklin from friends within the British government. Because Franklin had pledged to keep the letters to himself, he became the center of a scandal in London, and was dismissed from his position as postmaster general. But the British cause in the colonies suffered much more than Franklin's reputation. The letters revealed Hutchinson's call for "an abridgement of what are called English liberties" in the colonies. "I wish to see some further restraint of liberty," he had written, "rather than the connection with the parent state should be broken." This call created a torrent of anger against the British and their officials in the colonies.

The Boston Tea Party

It was in this context that the colonists received the news that Parliament had passed a Tea Act. Colonists were major consumers of tea, but because of the tax on it that remained from the Townshend duties, the market for colonial tea had collapsed, bringing the East India Company to the brink of bankruptcy. This company was the sole agent of British power in India, and Parliament could not allow it to fail. The British therefore devised a scheme in which they offered tea to Americans at prices that would tempt the most patriotic tea drinker. The radicals argued that this was merely a device to make palatable the payment of unconstitutional taxes—further evidence of the British effort to corrupt the colonists.

In October a mass meeting in Philadelphia denounced anyone importing the tea as "an enemy of his country." The town meeting in Boston passed resolutions patterned on those of Philadelphia, but the tea agents there, including two of Governor Hutchinson's sons, resisted the call to refuse the shipments.

The first of the tea ships arrived in Boston Harbor late in November. Mass meetings in Old South Church, which included many country people drawn to the scene of the crisis, resolved to keep the tea from being unloaded. Governor Hutchinson was equally firm in refusing to allow the ship to leave the harbor. On December 16, 1773, 5,000 people crowded into the church to hear the captain of the tea ship report to Samuel Adams that he could not move his ship. "This meeting can do nothing more to save the country," Adams declared. This was the signal for a disciplined group of fifty or sixty men, including farmers, artisans, merchants, professionals, and apprentices, to march to the wharf disguised as Indians. There they boarded the ship and dumped into the harbor 45 tons of tea, valued at 18,000 pounds, all the while cheered on by Boston's citizens. "Boston Harbor's a tea-pot tonight," the crowd chanted.

Boston's was the first tea party. Other incidents of property destruction soon followed. When the Sons of Liberty learned that a cargo of tea had landed secretly in New York, they dressed themselves as Indians and dumped the tea chests into the harbor. At Annapolis a ship loaded with tea was destroyed by fire, and arson also consumed a shipment stored at a warehouse in New Jersey. But it was the action in Boston at which the British railed. The government became convinced that something had to be done about the rebellious colony of Massachusetts.

The Intolerable Acts

During the spring of 1774 an angry Parliament passed a series of acts—called by Americans the Intolerable Acts—that were calculated to punish Massachusetts and strengthen the British hand. The Boston Port Bill prohibited the loading or unloading of ships in any part of Boston Harbor until the town fully compensated the East India Company and the customs service for the destroyed tea. The Massachusetts Government Act annulled the colonial charter: delegates to the upper house would no longer be elected by the assembly, but henceforth were to be appointed by the king. Civil officers throughout the province were placed under the authority of the royal governor, and the selection of juries was given over to governor-appointed sheriffs. Town meetings, an important institution of the resistance movement, were prohibited from convening more than once a year except with the approval of the governor, who was to control their agendas. With these Acts the British terminated the long history of self-rule by communities in the colony of Massachusetts. The Administration of Justice Act protected British officials from colonial courts, thereby encouraging them to vigorously pursue the work of suppression. Those accused of committing capital crimes while putting down riots or collecting revenue, such as the soldiers involved in the Boston Massacre, were now to be sent to England for trial.

Additional measures affected the other colonies and encouraged them to see themselves in league with suffering Massachusetts. The Quartering Act legalized the housing of troops at public expense, not only in taverns and abandoned buildings, but in occupied dwellings and private homes as well.

SUMMARY TABLE	*The Thirteen Repressive British Measures*	
Legislation	**Year**	
Sugar Act	1764	Placed prohibitive duty on imported sugar; provided for greater regulation of American shipping to suppress smuggling.
Stamp Act	1765	Required the purchase of specially embossed paper for newspapers, legal documents, licenses, insurance policies, ship's papers, and playing cards; struck at printers, lawyers, tavern owners, and other influential colonists. Repealed in 1766.
Declaratory Act	1766	Parliament asserted its authority to make laws binding the colonies "in all cases whatsoever."
Townshend Revenue Acts	1767	Placed import duties, collectible before goods entered colonial markets, on many commodities including lead, glass, paper, and tea. Repealed in 1770.
Tea Act	1773	Gave the British East India Company a monopoly on all tea imports to America, hitting at American merchants.
Intolerable Acts	1774	
Boston Port Bill		Closed Boston harbor.
Massachusetts Government Act		Annulled the Massachusetts colonial charter.
Administration of Justice Act		Protected British officials from colonial courts by sending them home for trial if arrested.
Quartering Act		Legalized the housing of British troops in private homes.
Quebec Act		Created a highly centralized government for Canada.

To the American colonists this was a frightening preview of what imperial authorities might have in store for them, and it confirmed the prediction of the Committees of Correspondence that there was a British plot to destroy American liberty.

In May General Thomas Gage arrived in Boston to replace Hutchinson as governor. The same day, the Boston town meeting called for a revival of nonimportation measures against Britain. In Virginia the Burgesses declared that Boston was enduring a "hostile invasion," and made provision for a "day of fasting, humiliation, and prayer, devoutly to implore the divine interposition for averting the heavy calamity, which threatens destruction to our civil rights and the evils of civil war." For

this expression of sympathy, Governor Dunmore suspended the legislature. Nevertheless, throughout the colony on the first of June, funeral bells tolled, flags flew at half mast, and people flocked to the churches.

The First Continental Congress

It was amid this crisis that town meetings and colonial assemblies alike chose representatives for the Continental Congress described in the chapter's opening story. The delegates who arrived in Philadelphia in September 1774 included the most important leaders of the American cause. Cousins Samuel and John Adams, the radicals from Massachusetts, were joined by Patrick Henry and George Washington from Virginia and Christopher Gadsden of South Carolina. Many of the delegates were conservatives: John Dickinson and Joseph Galloway of Philadelphia and John Jay and James Duane from New York. With the exception of Gadsden, a hothead who proposed an attack on British forces in Boston, the delegates wished to avoid war and favored a policy of economic coercion.

In one of their first debates, the delegates passed a Declaration and Resolves, in which they asserted that all the colonists sprang from a common tradition and enjoyed rights guaranteed "by the immutable laws of nature, the principles of the English constitution, and the several charters or compacts" of their provinces. Thirteen acts of Parliament, passed since 1763, were declared in violation of these rights. Until these acts were repealed, the delegates pledged, they would impose a set of sanctions against the British. These would include not only the nonimportation and nonconsumption of British goods, but a prohibition on the export of colonial commodities to Britain or its other colonies.

To enforce these sanctions, the Continental Congress urged that "a committee be chosen in every county, city, and town, by those who are qualified to vote for the legislature, whose business it shall be attentively to observe the conduct of all persons." This call for democratically elected local committees in each community had important political ramifications. The following year, these groups, known as Committees of Observation and Safety, took over the functions of local government throughout the colonies. They organized militia companies, called extralegal courts, and combined to form colony-wide congresses or conventions. By dissolving the colonial legislatures, royal governors unwittingly aided the work of these committees. The committees also scrutinized the activities of fellow citi-

The Quebec Act

With the Quebec Act, Britain created a centralized colonial government for Canada, and extended that colony's administrative control southwest to the Ohio River, invalidating the sea-to-sea boundaries of many colonial charters.

zens, suppressed the expression of Loyalist opinion from pulpit or press, and practiced other forms of coercion. Throughout most of the colonies the committees formed a bridge between the old colonial administrations and the revolutionary governments organized over the next few years. Committees began to link localities together in the cause of a wider American community. It was at this point that people began to refer to the colonies as the American "states."

Lexington and Concord

On September 1, 1774, General Gage sent troops from Boston to seize the stores of cannon and ammunition the Massachusetts militia had stored at armories in Charlestown and Cambridge. In response, the Massachusetts House of Representatives, calling itself the Provincial Congress, created a Committee of Safety empowered to call up the militia. On October 15 the committee authorized the creation of special units, to be known as minutemen, who stood ready to be called at a moment's notice. The armed militia of the towns and communities surrounding Boston faced the British army, quartered in the city.

In Virginia, at almost the same moment, Patrick Henry predicted that hostilities would soon begin in New England. "Gentlemen may cry peace, peace!—but there is no peace," he thundered in prose later memorized by millions of American schoolchildren. "Is life so dear, or peace so sweet, as to be purchased at the price of chains and slavery? Forbid it, Almighty God! I know not what course others may take, but as for me give me liberty or give me death!" Three weeks later, on April 14, General Gage received instructions to strike at once against the Massachusetts militia.

On the evening of April 18, Gage ordered 700 men to capture the store of American ammunition at the town of Concord. Learning of the operation, the Boston committee dispatched two men, Paul Revere and William Dawes, to alert the militia of the countryside. By the time the British forces had reached Lexington, midway to their destination, some seventy armed minutemen had assembled on the green in the center of town, but they were disorganized and confused. "Lay down your arms, you damned rebels, and disperse!" cried one of the British officers. The Americans began to withdraw in the face of overwhelming opposition, but they took their arms with them. "Damn you, why don't you lay down your arms!" someone shouted from the British lines. "Damn them! We will have them!" No order to fire was given, but

shots rang out, killing eight Americans and wounding ten others.

The British marched on to Concord, where they burned a small quantity of supplies and cut down a liberty pole. Meanwhile, news of the skirmish at Lexington had spread through the country, and the militia companies of communities from miles around converged on the town. Seeing smoke, they mistakenly concluded that the troops were burning homes. "Will you let them burn the town!" one man cried, and the Americans moved to the Concord bridge. There they attacked a British company, killing three soldiers—the first British casualties of the Revolution. The British immediately turned back for Boston, but were attacked by Americans at many points along the way. Reinforcements met them at Lexington, preventing a complete disaster, but by the time they finally marched into Boston 73 were dead and 202 wounded or missing. The British troops were vastly outnumbered by the approximately 4,000 Massachusetts militiamen, who suffered 95 casualties. The engagement forecast what would be a central problem for the British: they would be forced to fight an armed population defending their own communities against outsiders.

Deciding for Independence

"We send you momentous intelligence," read the letter received by the Charleston, South Carolina, Committee of Correspondence on May 8, reporting the violence in Massachusetts. Community militia companies mobilized throughout the colonies. At Boston, thousands of militiamen from Massachusetts and the surrounding provinces besieged the city, leaving the British no escape but by sea; their siege would last for nearly a year. Meanwhile, delegates from twelve colonies reconverged on Philadelphia.

The Second Continental Congress

The members of the Second Continental Congress, which opened on May 10, 1775, represented twelve of the British colonies on the mainland of North America. From New Hampshire to South Carolina, Committees of Observation and Safety had elected colony-wide conventions, and these extralegal bodies in turn had chosen delegates. Consequently, few conservatives or Loyalists were among them. Georgia, unrepresented at the first session of the Continental Congress, remained absent at the opening of the second. The newest mainland colony, it depended heavily on British subsidies, and its

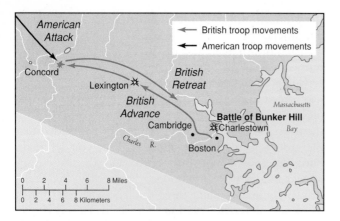

The First Engagements of the Revolution

The first military engagements of the American Revolution took place in the spring of 1775 in the countryside surrounding Boston.

leaders were cautious, fearing both slave and Indian uprisings. But in 1775 the political balance in Georgia shifted in favor of the radicals, and by the end of the summer the colony had delegates in Philadelphia.

Among the delegates at the Continental Congress were many familiar faces and a few new ones, including Thomas Jefferson, a plantation owner and lawyer from Virginia, gifted with one of the most imaginative and analytical minds of his time. All the delegates carried news of the enthusiasm for war that raged in their home provinces. They agreed that defense was the first issue on their agenda.

On May 15 the Second Continental Congress resolved to put the colonies in a state of defense, but the delegates were divided on how best to do it. They lacked the power and the funds to immediately raise and supply an army. After debate and deliberation, John Adams made the practical proposal that the delegates simply designate as a Continental Army the militia forces besieging Boston. On June 14 the Congress resolved to supplement the New England militiamen with six companies of expert riflemen raised in Pennsylvania, Maryland, and Virginia. The delegates agreed that in order to emphasize their national aspirations, they had to select a man from the South to command these New England forces. All eyes turned to George Washington. Although Washington had suffered defeat at the beginning of the Seven Years' War, he had subsequently compiled a distinguished record. On June 15 Jefferson and Adams nominated Washington to be commander in

chief of all Continental forces, and he was elected by a unanimous vote. He served without salary. The Continental Congress soon appointed a staff of major generals to support him. On June 22, in a highly significant move, the Congress voted to finance the army with an issue of $2 million in bills of credit, backed by the good faith of the Confederated Colonies. Thus began the long and complicated process of financing the Revolution.

Fighting in the North and South

Both North and South saw fighting in 1775 and early 1776. In June the Continental Congress assembled its expeditionary force against Canada. One thousand Americans moved north up the Hudson River corridor, and in November General Richard Montgomery forced the capitulation of Montreal. Meanwhile, Benedict Arnold set out from Massachusetts with another American army, and after a torturous march through the forests and mountains of Maine, he joined Montgomery outside the walls of Quebec. However, their assault failed to take the city. Montgomery and 100 Americans were killed, and another 300 were taken prisoner. Although Arnold held his position, the American siege was broken the following spring by British reinforcements who had come down the St. Lawrence. By the summer of 1776 the Americans had been forced back from Canada.

Elsewhere there were successes. Washington installed artillery on the heights south of Boston, placing the city and harbor within cannon range. General William Howe, who had replaced Gage, had little choice but to evacuate the city. In March the British sailed out of Boston harbor for the last time, heading north to Halifax with at least 1,000 American Loyalists. In the South American militia rose against the Loyalist forces of Virginia's Governor Dunmore, who had alienated the planter class by promising freedom to any slave who would fight with the British. After a decisive defeat of his forces, Dunmore retreated to British naval vessels, from which he shelled and destroyed much of the city of Norfolk, Virginia, on January 1, 1776. In North Carolina the rebel militia crushed a Loyalist force at the Battle of Moore's Creek Bridge near Wilmington in February, ending British plans for an invasion of that province. The British decided to attack Charleston, but at Fort Moultrie in Charleston harbor an American force turned back the assault. It would be more than two years before the British would try to invade the South again.

No Turning Back

Hopes of reconciliation died with the mounting casualties. The Second Continental Congress, which was rapidly assuming the role of a new government for all the states, reconvened in September and received news of the king's proclamation that the colonies were in formal rebellion. Although the delegates disclaimed any intention of denying the sovereignty of the king, they now moved to organize an American navy. They declared British vessels open to capture and authorized privateering. The Congress took further steps toward de facto independence when it authorized contacts with foreign powers through its agents in Europe. In the spring of 1776, after a period of secret negotiations, France and Spain approved the shipping of supplies to the rebellious provinces. The Continental Congress then declared colonial ports open to the trade of all nations but Britain.

The emotional ties to Britain proved difficult to break. But in 1776 help arrived in the form of a pamphlet written by Thomas Paine, a radical Englishman recently arrived in Philadelphia. In *Common Sense* Paine proposed to offer "simple fact, plain argument, and common sense" on the crisis. For years Americans had defended their actions by wrapping themselves in the mantle of British traditions. But Paine argued that the British system rested on "the base remains of two ancient tyrannies," aristocracy and monarchy, neither of which was appropriate for America. Paine placed the blame for the oppression of the colonists on the shoulders of King George. *Common Sense* was the single most important piece of writing during the Revolutionary era, selling more than 100,000 copies within a few months of its publication in January 1776. It reshaped popular thinking and put independence squarely on the agenda.

In April the North Carolina convention, which operated as the revolutionary replacement for the old colonial assembly, became the first to empower its delegates to vote for a declaration of independence. News that the British were recruiting a force of German mercenaries to use against the Americans provided an additional push toward what now began to seem inevitable. In May the Continental Congress voted to recommend that the individual states move as quickly as possible toward the adoption of state constitutions. When John Adams wrote, in the preamble to this statement, that "the exercise of every kind of authority under the said crown should be totally suppressed," he sent a strong signal that the delegates were on the verge of approving a momentous declaration.

The Declaration of Independence

On June 7, 1776 Richard Henry Lee of Virginia offered a motion to the Continental Congress: "That these united colonies are, and of right ought to be, free and independent states, that they are absolved from all allegiance to the British crown, and that all political connection between them and the state of Great Britain is, and ought to be, totally dissolved." After some debate, a vote was postponed until July, but a committee composed of John Adams, Thomas Jefferson, Roger Sherman of Connecticut, and Robert Livingston of New York was asked to prepare a draft declaration of American independence. The committee assigned the writing to Jefferson.

The intervening month allowed the delegates to sample the public discussion and debate and receive instructions from their state conventions. By the end of the month, all the states but New York had authorized a vote for independence. When the question came up for debate again on July 1, a large majority in the Continental Congress supported independence. The final vote, taken on July 2, was twelve in favor of independence, none against, with New York abstaining. The delegates then turned to the declaration itself and made a number of changes in Jefferson's draft, striking out, for example, a long passage condemning slavery. In this and a number of other ways the final version was somewhat more cautious than the draft, but it was still a stirring document.

Its central section reiterated the "long train of abuses and usurpations" on the part of King George that had led the Americans to their drastic course; there was no mention of Parliament, the principal opponent since 1764. But it was the first section that expressed the highest ideals of the delegates:

> We hold these truths to be self-evident, that all men are created equal, that they are endowed by their creator with certain unalienable rights, that among these are life, liberty, and the pursuit of happiness. That to secure these rights, governments are instituted among men, deriving their just powers from the consent of the governed. That whenever any form of government becomes destructive of these ends, it is the right of the people to alter or to abolish it, and to institute a new government, laying its foundation on such principles, and organizing its powers in such form, as to them shall seem most likely to effect their safety and happiness.

There was very little debate in the Continental Congress about these principles. The delegates, mostly men

The Manner in which the American Colonies Declared themselves INDEPENDENT of the King of ENGLAND, a 1783 English print.

of wealth and position, realized that the coming struggle for independence would require the steady support of ordinary people, so they asserted this great principle of equality and the right of revolution. There was little debate about the implications or potential consequences. Surely no statement would reverberate more through American history; the idea of equality inspired the poor as well as the wealthy, women as well as men, blacks as well as whites.

But it was the third and final section that may have contained the most meaning for the delegates: "For the support of this declaration, with a firm reliance on the protection of divine providence, we mutually pledge to each other our lives, our fortunes, and our sacred honor." In voting for independence, the delegates proclaimed their community, but they also committed treason against their king and empire. They could be condemned as traitors, hunted as criminals, and stand on the scaffold to pay for their sentiments. On July 4, 1776 these men approved the text of the Declaration without dissent.

Conclusion

Great Britain emerged from the Seven Years' War as the dominant power in North America. Yet despite its attempts at strict regulation and determination of the course of events in its colonies, it faced consistent resistance and often complete failure. Perhaps British leaders felt as John Adams had when he attended the first session of the Continental Congress in 1774: how could a motley collection of "ambassadors from a dozen belligerent powers" effectively organize as a single, independent, and defiant body? The British underestimated the political consensus that existed among the colonists about the importance of "republican" government. They also underestimated the ability of the colonists to inform one another, to work together, to build a sentiment of nationalism that cut across the boundaries of ethnicity, region, and economic status. Through newspapers, pamphlets, Committees of Correspondence, community organizations, and group protest, the colonists discovered the concerns they shared, and in so doing they fostered a new, American identity. Without that identity it would have been difficult for them to consent to the treasonous act of declaring independence, especially when the independence they sought was from an international power that dominated much of the globe.

CHRONOLOGY

1713	France cedes Acadia to Britain	1764	Sugar Act
1745	New Englanders capture Louisburg	1765	Stamp Act and Stamp Act Congress
1749	French send an expeditionary force down the Ohio River	1766	Declaratory Act
1753	French begin building forts from Lake Erie to the Ohio	1767	Townshend Revenue Acts
1754	Albany Congress	1768	Treaties of Hard Labor and Fort Stanwix
1755	British General Edward Braddock defeated by a combined force of French and Indians	1770	Boston Massacre
	Britain expels Acadians from Nova Scotia	1772	First Committee of Correspondence organized in Boston
1756	Seven Years' War begins in Europe	1773	Tea Act
1757	William Pitt becomes prime minister		Boston Tea Party
1758	Louisburg captured by the British for the second time	1774	Intolerable Acts
1759	British capture Quebec		First Continental Congress
1763	Treaty of Paris		Dunmore's War
	Pontiac's uprising	1775	Fighting begins at Lexington and Concord
	Proclamation of 1763 creates "Indian Country"		Second Continental Congress
	Paxton Boys massacre	1776	Americans invade Canada
			Thomas Paine's *Common Sense*
			Declaration of Independence

Review Questions

1. How did overwhelming British success in the Seven Years' War lead to an imperial crisis in British North America?
2. Outline the changes in British policy toward the colonies from 1750 to 1776.
3. Trace the developing sense of an American national community over this same period.
4. What were the principal events leading to the beginning of armed conflict at Lexington and Concord?
5. How were the ideals of American republicanism expressed in the Declaration of Independence?

Recommended Reading

BENEDICT ANDERSON, *Imagined Communities: Reflections on the Origin and Spread of Nationalism*, revised edition (1991). An argument that the essential first act of national consciousness is the effort to create a community that encompasses more than just local individuals and groups.

BERNARD BAILYN, *The Ideological Origins of the American Revolution* (1967). Whereas other accounts stress economic or social causes, this classic argument emphasizes the role of ideas in the advent of the Revolution. Includes an analysis of American views of the imperial crisis.

ERIC FONER, *Tom Paine and Revolutionary America* (1976). Combines a biography of Paine with a community study of the Revolution in Philadelphia and Pennsylvania.

LAWRENCE H. GIPSON, *British Empire Before the American Revolution*, 8 vols. (1936–49). Although these volumes are heavy going, they offer what is still the best and most comprehensive treatment of the Seven Years' War in America.

ROBERT A. GROSS, *The Minute Men and Their World* (1976). This fascinating and readable history examines the coming of the Revolution from the viewpoint of a New England community.

FRANCIS JENNINGS, *Empire of Fortune: Crowns, Colonies, and Tribes in the Seven Years' War in America* (1988). The French and Indian War examined from the point of view of the Iroquois Confederacy. This is opinionated but exciting history.

PAULINE MAIER, *From Resistance to Revolution: Colonial Radicals and the Development of American Opposition to Britain, 1765–1776* (1972). Argues that the American leaders were preoccupied with maintaining political and social order. An interpretation of the Revolution as a conservative movement.

RICHARD L. MERRITT, *Symbols of American Community, 1735–1775* (1966). A study of colonial newspapers that provides evidence for a rising sense of national community. The French and Indian War emerges as the key period for the growth of nationalist sentiment.

RICHARD WHITE, *The Middle Ground: Indians, Empires, and Republics in the Great Lakes Region, 1650–1815* (1991). This well-researched history provides a fascinating account of the West from the point of view of imperialists, settlers, and Indians.

THE CREATION OF THE UNITED STATES, 1776–1786

7

AMERICAN COMMUNITIES

A National Community Evolves at Valley Forge

A drum roll ushered in a January morning in 1778, summoning the Continental Army to roll call, and along a two-mile line of log cabins, doors slowly opened and ragged men stepped out onto the frozen ground of Valley Forge.

The 10,000 men of the American army were surviving on little more than "firecake," a mixture of flour and water baked hard before the fire that, according to army surgeon Albigense Waldo, turned "guts to pasteboard." Two thousand men were without shoes, others were without blankets and had to sit up all night about the fires to keep from freezing.

In the folklore of the Revolution, Valley Forge was to become the symbol of suffering and endurance. These soldiers were the seasoned veterans of one of the most arduous campaigns in American military history. After marching hundreds of weary miles and suffering three terrible defeats at the hands of a British force nearly twice their number, the soldiers of the Continental Army had retreated to this winter headquarters only to find themselves at the mercy of indifferent local suppliers. Contractors demanded exhorbitant rates for food and clothing, rates the Congress refused to pay, and as a result local farmers preferred to deal with the British, who paid in pounds sterling not depreciated Continental currency.

The 11,000 men of the Continental Army, who had not been paid for nearly six months, were divided into sixteen brigades composed of regiments from nine states. An unsympathetic observer described them as "a vagabond army of ragamuffins," and indeed many of the men were drawn from the ranks of the poor and disadvantaged: indentured servants, landless farmers, and nearly a thousand African Americans, both slave and free. Most of the men came from thinly settled farm districts or small towns where precautions regarding sanitation had been unnecessary. Every thaw revealed ground covered with "much filth and nastiness," and officers ordered sentinels to fire on any man "easing himself elsewhere than at ye vaults." Typhoid fever and other infectious diseases spread quickly: along with dysentery, malnutrition, and exposure they claimed as many as 2,500 lives that winter. More than 700 women—wives, lovers, cooks, laundresses, and prostitues—lived at Valley Forge that winter. They were kept busy nursing the sick and burying the dead.

Six months later, the force Washington marched out of Valley Forge was considerably stronger for its experience there. Most important were the strong relationships that formed among the men, twelve of whom bunked together in each cabin, grouped by state regiments and brigade. Washington referred to his general staff as his "family," and during the coming trials of battle his officers would rely greatly on the bonds of affection that had developed during the hard winter. Psychologists studying men in modern warfare have learned that it is this sense of community that contributes most to success in warfare.

To some American Patriots—as the supporters of the revolution called themselves—the European-style Continental Army betrayed the ideals of the citizen-soldier and the autonomy of local communities—central tenets of the Revolution. Washington argued strongly, however, that the Revolution could not be won without a national army, one insulated from politics and able to withstand the shifting popular mood. Through the developing sense of community among these men—who came from hundreds of localities and a variety of ethnic backgrounds—the Continental soldiers became living examples of the egalitarian ideals of the Revolution. They were a popular democratic force that counterbalanced the conservatism of the new republic's elite leadership. The national spirit they built at Valley Forge would sustain them through four more years of war and provide momentum for the long process of forging a national political system out of the persistent localism of American politics. "I admire them tremendously!" wrote one European officer serving with Washington. "It is incredible that soldiers composed of men of every age, even children of fifteen, of whites and blacks, almost naked, unpaid, and rather poorly fed, can march so well and withstand fire so steadfastly." Asked to explain why his men served, another officer declared: "Nothing but virtue and that great principle, the love of our country."

KEY TOPICS

◆ **The major alignments and divisions among Americans during the American Revolution**

◆ **Major military campaigns of the Revolution**

◆ **The Articles of Confederation and the role of the Confederation Congress during the Revolutionary War**

◆ **The states as the setting for significant political change**

◆ **The economic crisis in the aftermath of the American Revolution**

The War for Independence

At the beginning of the Revolution, the British had the world's best-equipped and most disciplined army and a navy that was unopposed in American waters. But they greatly underestimated the American capacity to fight. They also misperceived the sources of the conflict. They believed that the rebellion was the work of a small group of disgruntled conspirators, and initially defined their objective as defeating the organized Patriot opposition. In the wake of a military victory, they believed, they could easily reassert political control. But the geography of eastern North America offered no single vital center whose conquest would end the war. The Americans had the advantage of fighting on their own ground, among a population thinly spread over a territory stretching along 1,500 miles of coastline and extending 100 miles or more into the interior. When the British succeeded in defeating the Patriots in one area, resistance sprang up in another. The key factor in the outcome of the war, then, was the popular support for the American cause.

The Patriot Forces

Most American men of fighting age had to face the call to arms. From a population of approximately 350,000 eligible men, more than 200,000 saw action, though no more than 25,000 were engaged at any one time. More than 100,000 served in the Continental Army, under Washington's command and the authority of the Continental Congress; the other soldiers served in Patriot militia companies.

These militias—armed bodies of men drawn from local communities—proved most important in the defense of their own areas, for they had homes as well as local reputations to protect. Because men preferred to serve with their neighbors in local companies rather than subject themselves to the discipline of the regular army, the states failed to meet their quotas for regiments in the Continental Army. However, serving short terms of enlistment, often with officers of their own choosing, militiamen resisted discipline. Indeed, in the face of battle, militia companies demonstrated appalling rates of desertion.

The final victory, rather, resulted primarily from the steady struggle of the Continental Army. The American Revolution had little in common with modern national liberation movements in which armed populations engage in guerrilla warfare. Washington and his officers required a force that could directly engage the British, and from the beginning of the war he argued with a skeptical Congress that victory could be won only with a full commitment to a truly national army. His views conflicted with popular fears of a standing army. Congress initially refused to invoke a draft, or mandate army enlistments exceeding one year.

The failings of the militias in the early battles of the war sobered Congress and it greatly enlarged state quotas for the army and extended the term of service to three years or the war's duration. To spur enlistment Congress offered bounties, regular wages, and promises of free land after victory.

Discipline was essential in a conflict in which men fired at close range, charged each other with bayonets, and engaged in hand-to-hand combat. After being cut down by cannon, wounded Americans were slaughtered by British troops. The best estimate is that 25,674 American men died in the Revolution, approximately 6,000 from wounds suffered in battle, 10,000 from the effects of disease, the rest as prisoners of war or missing in action. Regiments of the Continental Army experienced the highest casualty rates, sometimes 30 or 40 percent. Indeed, the casualty ratio overall was higher than in any other American conflict except the Civil War. In most areas the war claimed few civilian lives, for it was confined largely to direct engagements between the armies, although in the backcountry and in regions of the South where Patriot and Loyalist militias waged vicious campaigns, noncombatant casualties were considerable.

Both the Continentals and the militias played important political roles as well. At a time when Americans identified most strongly with their local communities or perhaps their states, the Continental Army, through experiences such as the Vally Forge winter, evolved into a powerful force for nationalist sentiment. Shortages of food and pay led to a number of army mutinies in. In the most serious incident, among the Pennsylvania Line in January 1781, enlisted men killed one officer, wounded two others, and set off from their winter quarters in New Jersey for Philadelphia to ask Congress to uphold its commitments. As they marched they were joined by British agents who encouraged them to go over to the king. Enraged at this attempt at subversion, the mutineers hanged the Tories. Angry as they were at Congress, they were Americans first and hated the British. Over 100,000 men from every state served in the Continental Army, contributing mightily to the unity of purpose—the formation of a national community—that was essential to the process of nation making.

In most communities Patriots seized control of local government during the period of committee organizing in 1774 and 1775 (see Chapter 6), and with war imminent they pressed the obligation to serve in a Patriot militia on most eligible men. Probably the most important role of the Patriot militias was to force even the most apathetic of Americans to think seriously about the Revolution, and to choose sides under the scrutiny of their neighbors.

As men marched off to war, many women assumed the management of family farms and businesses; Abigail Adams, for example, ran the Adams family's farm at Quincy for years. The Boston home of Mercy Otis Warren, daughter of James Otis, was a center of Patriot political activiity. When the fighting shited to their locales, women volunteered as seamstresses, cooks, nurses, and even spies.

When the months of fighting lengthened into years, many women left their homes to join husbands and lovers, fathers and brothers in army encampments. Some were officially employed, but most took care of their own men, and many fought with them side by side. The best known women who stayed by their husbands' sides even in camp were Martha Washington and Catherine Greene, wives of the two most important American generals. But less socially prominent women were remembered as well. Mary Ludwig Hays (later

McCauley) earned the name Molly Pitcher for her courage in bringing water to the Patriots during the Battle of Monmouth in June 1778. When her husband was overcome by heat, Mary Hays took his place at the cannon. When Margaret Corbin's husband died in battle she stepped into his position. Other women, such as Deborah Sampson of Massachusetts, disguised themselves as men and enlisted.

The Loyalists

Not all Americans were Patriots. Many sat on the fence, confused by the conflict and waiting for a clear turn in the tide of the struggle before declaring their allegiance. About a fifth of the population, perhaps as many as half a million people, remained loyal to the British crown. They called themselves Loyalists, but were known to Patriots as Tories, the popular name for the conservative party in England, which traditionally supported the authority of the King over parliament. Loyalism was strongest in the Lower South, weakest in New England. Loyalists included members of ethnic minorities that had been persecuted by the dominant majority, such as the Highland Scots of the Carolinas and western New York, and southern tenant farmers who had Patriot landlords. Moreover, many slaves and most Indians, the latter fearing aggressive expansion by independent American states, identified with the Loyalists.

Patriots passed state treason acts that prohibited speaking or writing against the Revolution. They also punished Loyalists by issuing bills of attainder, a legal process by which Loyalists lost their civil rights and their property. In some areas, notably New York, South Carolina, Massachusetts, and Pennsylvania, Loyalists faced mob violence.

The most infamous American supporter of the British cause was Benedict Arnold. Arnold was a hero of the early battles of the Revolution. But in 1779, angry and resentful about what he perceived to be assignments and rank below his station, he became a paid informer of General Clinton, head of the British army in New York City. In 1780 Patriots uncovered Arnold's plot to betray the strategic post of West Point, which he commanded. After fleeing to the British, who paid him a handsome stipend and pension, he became the most hated man in America. During the last two years of the war he led British raids against his home state of Connecticut as well as Virginia, and after the Revolution he lived in England until his death in 1801.

The British strategy for suppressing the Revolution depended on mobilizing the Loyalists, but in most areas this proved impossible. However as many as 50,000 fought for the king during the Revolution. As many as 80,000 Loyalists fled the country during and after the Revolution, taking up residence in England, the British West Indies, or Canada, where they are venerated as the founding fathers of the province of Ontario. Their property was confiscated by the states and sold at public auction. Although the British government compensated many for their losses, as a group they were reluctant and unhappy exiles. Despite their disagreement with the Patriots on essential political questions, they remained Americans and mourned the loss of their country.

The Campaign for New York and New Jersey

During the winter of 1775–76 the British developed a strategic plan for the war. From his base at Halifax, Nova Scotia, Sir William Howe was to take his army to New York City, which the British navy would make impregnable. From there Howe was to drive north along the Hudson, while another British army marched south from Canada to Albany. The two armies would converge, cutting New England off from the rest of the colonies, then turn eastward to reduce the rebellious Yankees into submission. Washington, who had arrived at Boston to take command of the militia forces there in the summer of 1775, anticipated this strategy, and in the spring of 1776 he shifted his forces southward toward New York.

In early July, as Congress was taking its final vote on the Declaration of Independence, the British began

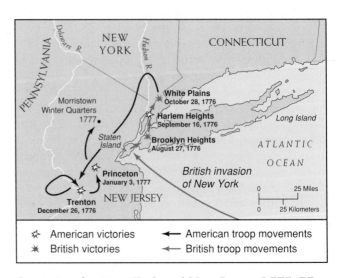

Campaign for New York and New Jersey, 1775–77

their operation at New York City, landing 32,000 men, a third of them Hessian mercenaries (from the German state of Hesse), on Staten Island. The Americans, meanwhile, set up fortified positions across the harbor in Brooklyn. Attacking in late August, the British inflicted heavy casualties on the Americans, and the militia forces under Washington's command proved unreliable under fire.

The British now offered Congress an opportunity to negotiate, and on September 6, Benjamin Franklin, John Adams, and Edward Rutledge sat down with General Howe and his brother, Admiral Richard Howe, on Staten Island. But the meeting broke up when the Howes demanded revocation of the Declaration of Independence. Six days later the British invaded Manhattan Island, and only an American stand at Harlem Heights prevented the destruction of a large portion of the Patriot army. Enjoying naval control of the harbor, the British quickly outflanked the American positions. In a series of battles over the next few months, they forced Washington back at White Plains and overran the American posts of Fort Washington and Fort Lee, on either side of the Hudson River. By November the Americans were fleeing south across New Jersey in a frantic attempt to avoid the British under General Charles Cornwallis.

With morale desperately low, whole militia companies deserted; others, announcing the end of their terms of enlistment, left for home. American resistance seemed to be collapsing all around Washington. But rather than fall back further, which would surely have meant the dissolution of his entire force, Washington decided to risk a counterattack. On Christmas night he led 2,400 troops back across the Delaware, and the next morning defeated the Hessian forces in a surprise attack on their headquarters at Trenton, New Jersey. The Americans inflicted further heavy losses on the British at Princeton, then drove them all the way back to the environs of New York.

Although these small victories of 1776 had little tactical importance, they salvaged American morale. As Washington settled into winter headquarters at Morristown, he realized he had to pursue a defensive strategy, avoiding direct confrontations with the British while checking their advances and hurting them wherever possible.

The Northern Campaigns of 1777

The fighting with the American forces had prevented Howe from moving north up the Hudson, and the British advance southward from Canada had been stalled by American resistance at Lake Champlain. In

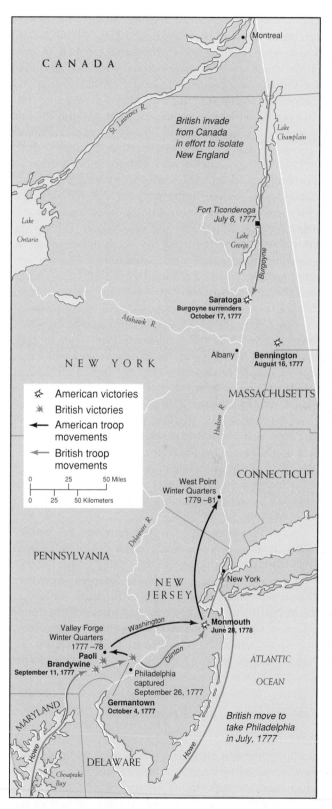

Northern Campaigns, 1777–78

1777, however, the British decided to replay their strategy. From Canada they dispatched General John Burgoyne with nearly 8,000 British and German troops. Howe was to move his force from New York, first taking the city of Philadelphia, capital of the Continental Congress, then moving north to meet Burgoyne.

Fort Ticonderoga fell to Burgoyne on July 6, but by August the general found himself bogged down and harassed by Patriot militias in the rough country south of Lake George. After several defeats in September at the hands of an American army commanded by General Horatio Gates, Burgoyne retreated to Saratoga. There his army was surrounded by a considerably larger force of Americans, and on October 19, lacking alternatives, he surrendered his nearly 6,000 men. It would be the biggest British defeat until Yorktown, decisive because it forced the nations of Europe to recognize that the Americans had a fighting chance to win their Revolution.

The Americans were less successful against Howe. A force of 15,000 British troops left New York in July, landing a month later at the northern end of Chesapeake Bay. At Brandywine Creek the British outflanked the Americans, inflicting heavy casualties and forcing a retreat. Ten days later the British routed the Americans a second time with a frightful bayonet charge at Paoli that cost many Patriot lives. When British troops occupied Philadelphia on September 26, Congress had already fled. Washington attempted a valiant counterattack at Germantown on October 4, but his initial success was followed by miscoordination that eventually doomed the operation.

After this campaign the Continentals headed for winter quarters at Valley Forge, a few dozen miles from Philadelphia, the bitterness of their defeats muted somewhat by news of the surrender at Saratoga. In taking Philadelphia, the British had taken the most important city in North America, but it proved to have little strategic value. Central government was virtually nonexistent, and so the unified effort suffered little disruption. At the end of two years of fighting, the British strategy for winning the war had to be judged a failure.

The Politics of the French and Spanish Alliance

During these first two years of fighting, the Americans were sustained by loans from France and Spain, both of which saw an opportunity to win back some of the North American territories lost to Great Britain in the Seven Years' War. The Continental Congress maintained a diplomatic delegation in Paris headed by Benjamin Franklin. Through 1777 Franklin was unable to convince France to commit to an alliance.

In England, meanwhile, the Whig opposition argued strongly against the war. When, in December 1777, Lord North received the news of Burgoyne's surrender, he dispatched agents to begin peace discussions with Franklin in Paris. Fears of British conciliation with the revolutionaries, in addition to word of the victory at Saratoga, finally persuaded Vergennes to tie France to the United States. In mid-December he informed Franklin that the king's council had decided to recognize American independence.

In February 1778 the American delegation submitted to Congress a treaty of commerce and alliance it had negotiated with the French. In the treaty, to take effect upon a declaration of war between France and Britain, the French pledged to "maintain effectually the liberty, sovereignty, and independence" of the United States. France was compelled to guarantee to the United States all the "northern parts of America" as well as other "conquests" made in the war, while the United States promised to recognize French acquisitions of British islands in the West Indies. Warfare between France and Britain broke out in June.

France was allied with Spain in the "family compact" of monarchs, and a year later Spain also entered the war. But Spain pursued its own strategy: raising funds for the Revolution and at the same time attacking and taking Natchez, Baton Rouge, Mobile and Pensacola. The first French ambassador to the United States arrived with instructions to do everything he could to prevent the Americans from enlarging their territory at the expense of the Spanish empire. The French also feared the potential power of an independent United States. American leaders understood that the treaty with the French was an expedient for both sides, and they recognized the dangers that France and Spain posed to the United States. But far more important was the prospect the treaty offered of victory over Britain.

In the spring of 1778 Congress rejected a new British offer of negotiations. Lord North's government had sent a peace commission to America with promises to repeal the parliamentary legislation that had provoked the crisis and never again to impose revenue taxes on the colonies. But the Continental Congress now declared that any person coming to terms with the peace commission was a traitor; the only possible topics of negotiation were the withdrawal of British forces and the recognition of American independence.

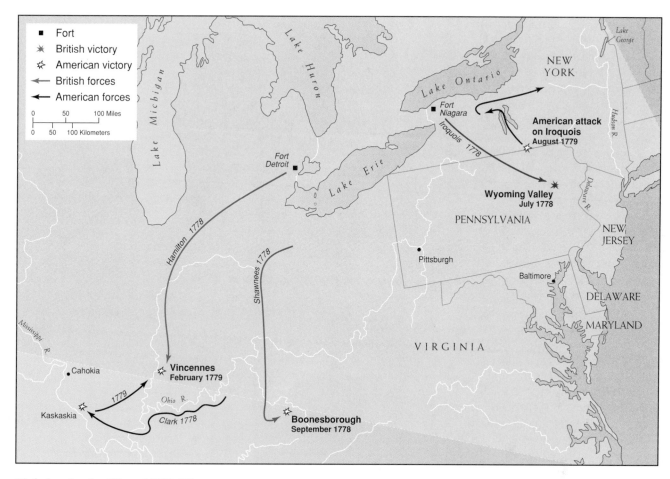

Fighting in the West, 1778–79

The entry of France into the war forced the British to rethink their strategy. The West Indies were now at risk, and the British shipped 5,000 men from New York to the Caribbean, where they beat back a French attack. Fearing the arrival of the French fleet along the North American coast, the new British commander in America, General Henry Clinton, evacuated Philadelphia in June 1778. In hot pursuit were Washington's Continentals, fresh out of Valley Forge. At the Battle of Monmouth on June 28, the British blunted the American drive and retreated to New York. The Americans, centered at West Point, took up defensive positions surrounding the lower Hudson. Confidence in an impending victory now spread through the Patriot forces. But after a failed campaign with the French against the British forces at Newport, Rhode Island, Washington settled for a defensive strategy. Although the Americans enjoyed a number of small successes in the Northeast over the next two years, the war there stalled.

The War in the South

The most important fighting of these years took place in the South. General Clinton regained the initiative for Britain in December 1778 by sending a force from New York against Georgia, the weakest of the colonies. The British crushed the Patriot militia at Savannah and began to organize the Loyalists in an effort to reclaim the colony. Several American counterattacks failed, including one in which the French fleet bombarded Savannah in September and October. Encouraged by their success in Georgia, the British decided to apply the lessons learned there throughout the South. This involved a fundamental change from a strategy of military conquest to one of pacification: territory would be retaken step by step, then handed over to Loyalists who would reassert colonial authority loyal to the crown. In early 1780 Clinton evacuated Rhode Island, the last British stronghold in New England, and

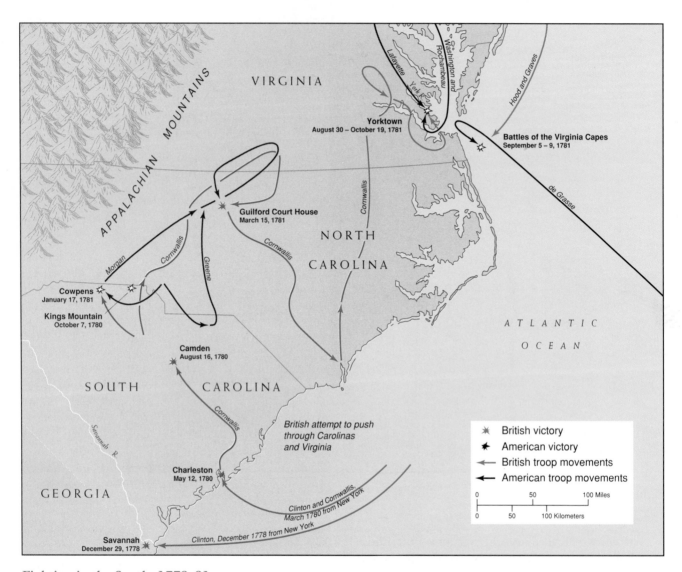

Fighting in the South, 1778–81

proceeded with 8,000 troops for a campaign against Charleston.

The siege of Charles Town (Charleston) began in February 1780. Outflanking the American defenders, Clinton forced the surrender of over 5,000 troops in May—the most significant American defeat of the war. Horatio Gates, the hero of Saratoga, led a detachment of Continentals southward, but in August they were defeated by Cornwallis at Camden, South Carolina. Patriot resistance collapsed in the Lower South, and American fortunes were suddenly at their lowest ebb since the beginning of the war.

The southern campaign was marked by vicious violence between partisan militias of Patriots and Loyalists.

The violence peaked in September 1780 with Cornwallis's invasion of North Carolina, where the Patriots were stronger and better organized. There the British found their southern strategy untenable: plundering towns and farms in order to feed the army in the interior had the effect of producing angry support for the Patriots.

Into 1781 the Continentals and militias waged what General Greene called a fugitive war of hit and run against the British. "I am quite tired of marching about the country in quest of adventures," Cornwallis wrote. Finally deciding he would not be able to hold the Carolinas as long as Virginia remained a base of support and supply for the Americans, he led his army north in the summer of 1781. After marauding the Virginia countryside he reached the Chesapeake, where he expected reinforcements from New York. The British withdrawal from North Carolina allowed Greene to reestablish Patriot control of the Lower South.

Yorktown

While the British raged through the South the stalemate continued in the Northeast. In the summer of 1780, taking advantage of the British evacuation of Rhode Island, the French landed 5,000 troops at Newport under the command of General Rochambeau. But it was not until the spring of 1781 that the general risked joining his force to Washington's Continentals north of New York. They planned a campaign against the city, but in August Washington learned that the French Caribbean fleet was headed for the Chesapeake. Washington sensed the possibility of a coup de grâce if only he and Rochambeau could move their troops south in coordination with the French naval operation, locking Cornwallis into his camp at Yorktown. Leaving a small force behind as a decoy, Washington and Rochambeau moved quickly down the coast to the Virginia shore.

Over 16,000 American and French troops had converged on the almost 8,000-man British garrison at Yorktown by mid-September. French and American heavy artillery hammered the British unmercifully until the middle of October. Cornwallis found it impossible to break the siege, and after the failure of a planned retreat across the York River, he opened negotiations for the surrender of his army. Two days later, on October 19, 1781, Cornwallis, pleading illness, sent his second-in-command, General O'Hara, to surrender. O'Hara first approached General Rochambeau, but the Frenchman waved him toward Washington. It was almost incomprehensible to the British that they would be surrendering to former subordinates. Everyone knew this was an event of incalculable importance, but few guessed it was the end of the war, for the British still controlled New York.

In London, at the end of November, Lord North received the news "as he would have taken a ball in the breast," reported the colonial secretary. "Oh God!" he moaned. "It is all over!" British fortunes were at low ebb in India, the West Indies, Florida, and the Mediterranean; the cost of the war was enormous; and there was little support among the public and members of Parliament for it. King George wished to press on, but North submitted his resignation, and in March 1782 the king was forced to accept the counsel of Lord Rockingham, who favored granting Americans their independence.

The United States in Congress Assembled

The motion for independence, offered to the Continental Congress by Richard Henry Lee on June 7, 1776, called for a confederation of the states. The Articles of Confederation, the first written constitution of the United States, created a national government of sharply limited powers. This arrangement reflected the concerns of people fighting to free themselves from a coercive central government.

The Articles of Confederation

The debate over confederation that took place in the Continental Congress following the Declaration of Independence made it clear that the delegates favoring a loose union of autonomous states outnumbered those who considered themselves nationalists. The following year a consensus finally emerged. In November 1777 the Articles of Confederation were formally adopted by the Continental Congress and sent to the states for ratification. The Articles created a national assembly, called the Congress, in which each state had a single vote. Delegates, selected annually in a manner determined by the individual state legislatures, could serve no more than three years out of six. A presiding president elected annually by Congress was eligible no more than one year out of three. Votes would be decided by a simple majority of the states, except for major questions, which would require the agreement of nine states.

Congress was granted national authority in the conduct of foreign affairs, matters of war and peace, and maintenance of the armed forces. It could raise loans, issue bills of credit, establish a coinage, and regulate trade with Indian peoples, and it was to be the final authority in jurisdictional disputes between states. It was charged with establishing a national postal system as well as a common standard of weights and measures. Lacking the power to tax citizens directly, however, the national government was to apportion its financial burdens among the states according to the extent of their surveyed land. The Articles explicitly guaranteed the sovereignty of the individual states, reserving to them all powers not expressly delegated to Congress. Ratification or amendment required the agreement of all thirteen states. This constitution thus created a national government of specific yet sharply circumscribed powers.

The legislatures of twelve states soon voted in favor of the Articles, but final ratification was held up for over three years by the state of Maryland. Representing the interests of states without claims to lands west of the Appalachians, Maryland demanded that states cede to Congress their western claims, the new nation's most valuable resource, for "the good of the whole." It was 1781 before all eight states with western claims voted to cede them. Maryland then agreed to ratification, and in March the Articles of Confederation took effect.

Financing the War

Congress financed the Revolution through grants and loans from friendly foreign powers and by issuing paper currency. The total foreign subsidy by the end of the war approached $9 million, but this was insufficient to back the circulating Continental currency that Congress had authorized, the face value of which had risen to $200 million. Congress called on the states to raise taxes, payable in Continental dollars, so that this currency could be retired. But most of the states were unwilling to do this. In fact, the states resorted to printing currency of their own, which totaled another $200 million by the end of the war. The results of this growth in the money supply were rapid depreciation of Continental currency and runaway inflation. People who received fixed incomes for services—Continental soldiers, for example, as well as merchants, landlords, and other creditors—were devastated. When Robert Morris, one of the wealthiest merchants in the country, became secretary of finance in May 1781, Continental currency had ceased to circulate; things of no value were said to be "not worth a Continental."

Morris persuaded Congress to charter the Bank of North America in Philadelphia, the first private commercial bank in the United States. There he deposited large quantities of gold and silver coin and bills of exchange obtained through loans from Holland and France. He then issued new paper currency backed by this supply. Once confidence in the bank had developed, Morris was able to begin supplying the Continental Army through private contracts. He was also able to meet the interest payments on the debt, which in 1783 he estimated to be about $30 million.

Morris was associated with the nationalists who controlled Congress in the early 1780s. With their support, he proposed amending the Articles of Confederation to empower Congress to levy a 5 percent duty on imports. The Confederation would then have a source of revenue independent of state requisitions. Localists, who continued to believe in a decentralized Confederation, voiced much opposition to the Morris plan for an independent

congressional revenue. When his plan failed to gain acceptance, Morris resigned office in 1784.

Negotiating Independence

Peace talks between the United States and Great Britain opened in July 1782, when Benjamin Franklin sat down with the British emissary in Paris. Congress had issued its first set of war aims in 1779. The fundamental demands were recognition of American independence and withdrawal of British forces. Negotiators were to press for as much territory as possible, including Canada, and guarantees of the American right to fish the North Atlantic. As for its French ally, Congress instructed the commissioners to be guided by friendly advice, but also by "knowledge of our interests, and by your own discretion, in which we repose the fullest confidence." In June 1781, partly as a result of French pressure, Congress issued a new set of instructions: the commissioners were to settle merely for a grant of independence and withdrawal of troops, and to be subject to the guidance and control of the French in the negotiations.

Franklin, John Jay, and John Adams, the peace commissioners in Paris, were aware of French attempts to manipulate the outcome of negotiations and to limit potential American power. In violation of instructions and treaty obligations, and without consulting the French, they signed a preliminary treaty with Britain in November. In the treaty Britain acknowledged the United States as "free, sovereign & independent," and agreed to withdraw its troops from all forts within American territory "with all convenient speed." They guaranteed Americans "the right to take fish" in northern waters. The American commissioners had pressed the British for Canada, but settled for territorial boundaries that extended to the Mississippi. Britain received American promises to erect "no lawful impediments" to the recovery of debts, to cease confiscating Loyalist property, and to try to persuade the states to fairly compensate Loyalist exiles. Finally, the two nations agreed to unencumbered navigation of the Mississippi. The American commissioners had accomplished an astounding coup. The new boundaries, they wrote to Congress, "appear to leave us little to complain of and not much to desire."

France was thus confronted with a *fait accompli*. When the French criticized the commissioners, the Americans responded by hinting that resistance to the treaty provisions could result in a British–American alliance. France thereupon quickly made an agreement of its own with the British.

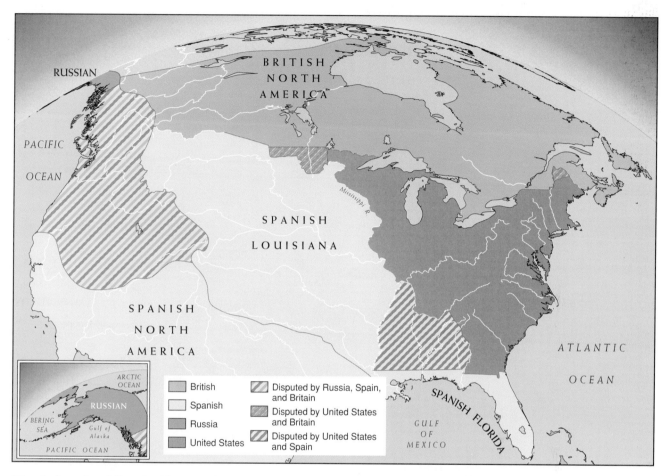

North America After the Treaty of Paris, 1783

The map of European and American claims to North America was radically altered by the results of the American Revolution.

Though left out of the negotiations, Spain claimed sovereignty over much of the trans-Appalachian territory granted to the United States as a result of its successful campaign against the British in the west. Spain also arranged a separate peace with Great Britain, in which it won the return of Florida. The final Treaty of Paris—actually a series of separate agreements among the United States, Great Britain, France, and Spain—was signed at Versailles on September 3, 1783.

The Crisis of Demobilization

During the two years between the surrender at Yorktown and the signing of the Treaty of Paris, the British continued to occupy New York City, Charleston, and a series of western posts. The Continental Army remained on wartime alert, with some 10,000 men and

an estimated 1,000 women encamped at Newburgh, New York, north of West Point. The soldiers had long been awaiting their pay, and were very concerned about the postwar bounties and land warrants promised them. The most serious problem, however, lay not among the enlisted men but in the officer corps.

Continental officers had extracted a promise from Congress of life pensions at half pay in exchange for enlistment for the duration of the war. By 1783, however, Congress had still not made specific provisions for the pensions. With peace at hand, officers began to fear that the army would be disbanded before the problem was resolved, and they would lose whatever power they had to pressure Congress. In January 1783 a group of prominent senior officers petitioned Congress, demanding that pensions be converted to a bonus equal to five

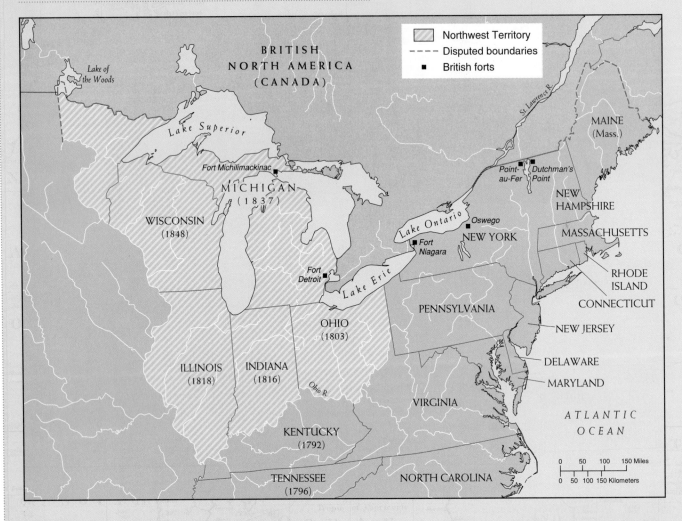

THE NORTHWEST TERRITORY AND THE LAND SURVEY SYSTEM OF THE UNITED STATES

The greatest achievement of the Confederation government was the passing of the Land Ordinance of 1785 and the Northwest Ordinance of 1787. The first act made provision for the federal survey of newly incorporated lands. To avoid the problem of overlapping surveys that could occur under the old system of "metes and bounds" surveying, the authors of the ordinance created an ordered system of survey, dividing the land into townships composed of thirty-six sections of one square mile (640 acres) each. (The differences are clearly evident in the contrast between the patterns of landholding in Ohio, on the left side of the photo, and Pennsylvania, on the right.) The income from section 16 was reserved for the support of local schools, and sections 8, 11, 26, and 29 were held off the market for later sale. First used in the territory north of the Ohio River, this survey system was used for all the western territory of the United States and has been adopted by many other nations.

With the Northwest Ordinance, Congress established a system of government for the Territory North of the Ohio. This legislation established the important principle

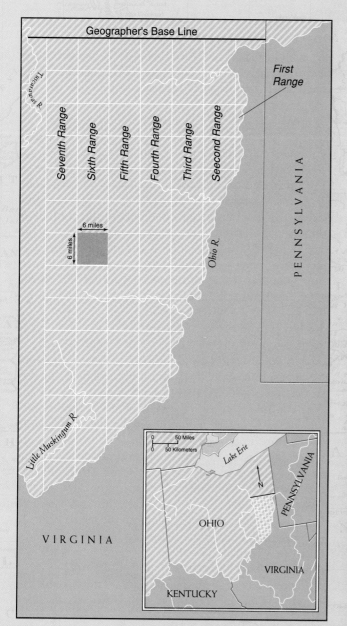

Geographer's Base Line

First Range

Seventh Range
Sixth Range
Fifth Range
Fourth Range
Third Range
Seecond Range

Tuscarawas R.

PENNSYLVANIA

Ohio R.

6 miles

6 miles

Little Muskingum R.

VIRGINIA

0 50 Miles
0 50 Kilometers

Lake Erie

N

OHIO

PENNSYLVANIA

VIRGINIA

KENTUCKY

6 miles

Income from section 16
reserved for school support

16 One section (1 sq. mi.)

6	5	4	3	2	1
7	8	9	10	11	12
18	17	16	15	14	13
19	20	21	22	23	24
30	29	28	27	26	25
31	32	33	34	35	36

6 miles

THE SURVEY SYSTEM
A township (36 square miles)

Half-section
(320 acres)

Quarter-section
(160 acres)

Half-quarter-section
(80 acres)

Quarter-quarter-sections
(40 acres)

of eventually bringing new territory into the states on an equal basis with the original thirteen states. The Northwest Territory was eventually divided into the five states that are the focus of this map, and each was admitted to the Union on the date that appears below its name. The Northwest Ordinance also outlawed slavery north of the Ohio River.

Before that process could begin, however, the United States had to establish sovereignty over the country. The British did not abandon the posts that they had continued to occupy after 1783 until June 1, 1796, following the agreement between the U.S. and Great Britain in Jay's Treaty (1794).

years of full pay. On Washington's urging, Congress agreed to do this.

As for the common soldiers, they wanted simply to be discharged. In May 1783 Congress voted the soldiers three months' pay as a bonus and instructed Washington to begin dismissing them. Some troops remained at Newburgh until the British evacuated New York in November, but by the beginning of 1784 the Continental Army had shrunk to no more than a few hundred men.

The Problem of the West

Even during the Revolution, thousands migrated west, and after the war, settlers poured over the mountains and down the Ohio River. Thousands of Americans pressed against the Indian country north of the Ohio River, and destructive violence continued along the frontier. British troops continued to occupy posts in the Northwest, and encouraged Indian attacks on vulnerable settlements. To the southwest, Spain, refusing to accept the territorial settlement of the Treaty of Paris, closed the Mississippi River to Americans. Westerners who saw that route as their primary access to markets were outraged.

John Jay, appointed secretary for foreign affairs in 1784, attempted to negotiate with the British, but was told that British troops would not evacuate the Northwest until all outstanding debts from before the war were settled. Jay negotiated with the Spanish for guarantees of territorial sovereignty and commercial relations, but they insisted that the United States in return would have to relinquish free navigation of the Mississippi. Congress would approve no treaty under those conditions. Under these frustrating circumstances, some westerners considered leaving the Confederation. Kentuckians threatened to rejoin the British. The Spanish secretly employed a number of prominent westerners, including George Rogers Clark and General James Wilkinson, as informants and spies. The people of the West "stand as it were upon a pivot," wrote Washington in 1784 after a trip down the Ohio. "The touch of a feather would turn them any way." In the West, local community interest continued to override the fragile development of national community sentiment.

In that year, Congress took up the problem of extending national authority over the West. Legislation was drafted, principally by Thomas Jefferson, providing for "Government for the Western Territory." The legislation was a remarkable attempt to create a democratic colonial policy. The public domain was to be divided into states, and Congress guaranteed the settlers in them immediate self-government and republican institutions. Once the population of a territory numbered 20,000, the residents could call a convention and establish a constitution and government of their own choosing. And once the population grew to equal that of the smallest of the original thirteen states, the territory could obtain statehood, provided it agreed to remain forever a member of the Confederation. Congress accepted these proposals, but it also rejected, by a vote of seven to six, Jefferson's clause prohibiting slavery.

Passed the following year, the Land Ordinance of 1785 provided for the survey and sale of western lands. To avoid the chaos of overlapping surveys and land claims that had characterized Kentucky, the authors of the ordinance created an ordered system of survey, dividing the land into townships composed of thirty-six sections of one square mile (640 acres) each. This measure would have an enormous impact on the North American landscape, as can be seen by anyone who has flown over the United States and looked down at the patchwork pattern. Jefferson argued that land ought to be given away to actual settlers. But Congress, eager to establish a revenue base for the government, provided for the auction of public lands for not less than one dollar per acre. In the treaties of Fort Stanwix in 1784 and Fort McIntosh in 1785, congressional commissioners forced the Iroquois and some of the Ohio Indians to cede a portion of their territory in what is now eastern Ohio, and surveyors were sent there to divide up the land. These treaties were not the result of negotiation; the commissioners dictated the terms by seizing hostages and forcing compliance. The first surveyed lands were not available for sale until the fall of 1788. In the meantime, Congress, desperate for revenue, sold a tract of more than 1.5 million acres to a new land company, the Ohio Company, for a million dollars.

Thousands of westerners chose not to wait for the official opening of the public land north of the Ohio River, but settled illegally. In 1785 Congress raised troops and evicted many of them, but once the troops left the squatters returned. The persistence of this problem convinced many congressmen to revise Jefferson's democratic territorial plan. In the Northwest Ordinance of 1787, Congress established a system of government for the territory north of the Ohio. Three to five states were to be carved out of the giant Northwest Territory and admitted "on an equal footing with the original states in all respects whatsoever." Slavery was prohibited. But the guarantee of initial self-government in Jefferson's plan was replaced by the rule of a court of judges and a governor appointed by Congress. Once the free white male population of the territory had grown to 5,000, these citizens would be permitted to choose an assembly, but the governor was to have the power of absolute veto on all territorial legislation. National interest would be imposed on the localistic western communities.

The creation of the land system of the United States was the major achievement of the Confederation government. But there were other important accomplishments. Under the Articles of Confederation, Congress led the country through the Revolution and its commissioners negotiated the terms of a comprehensive peace treaty. In organizing the departments of war, foreign affairs, the post office, and finance, the confederation government created the beginnings of the origins of the national bureaucracy.

Revolutionary Politics in the States

Despite these accomplishments, most Americans focused not on the Confederation goverment in Philadelphia, but on the goverments of their own states. During the revolutionary era, most Americans identified politically and socially with their local communities and states rather than with the American nation. The national community feeling of the Revolution was overwhelmed by persistent localism. People spoke of "these United States," emphasizing the plural. The states were the setting for the most important political struggles of the Confederation period and for long after.

The Broadened Base of Politics

The political mobilization that took place in 1774 and 1775 greatly broadened political participation. Mass meetings in which ordinary people expressed their opinions, voted, and gained political experience were common, not only in the cities but in small towns and rural communities as well. During these years, a greater proportion of the population began to participate in elections. Compared with the colonial assemblies, the new state legislatures included more men from rural and western districts—farmers and artisans as well as lawyers, merchants, and large landowners. Many delegates to the Massachusetts provincial congress of 1774 were men from small farming communities who lacked formal education and owned little property.

This transformation was accompanied by a dramatic shift in the political debate. During the colonial period, when only the upper crust of society had been truly engaged in the political process, the principal argument had been between the Tory and Whig positions. The

Tory position, argued by royal officials, was that colonial governments were simply convenient instruments of the king's prerogative, serving at his pleasure. Colonial elites, seeking to preserve and increase their own power, had argued for stronger assemblies, using traditional Whig arguments about the need for a balanced government, represented by the governor, the upper house, and the assembly. This debate was ended by the Revolution. The Tory position lost all legitimacy. For the first time in American history, democracy became a term of approval. Patriots who took a Whig position on balanced government found themselves challenged by farmers, artisans, and other ordinary people armed with a new and radical democratic ideology.

One of the first post-Revolution debates focused on the appropriate governmental structure for the new states. The thinking of democrats was indicated by the title of a New England pamphlet of 1776, *The People the Best Governors.* Power, the anonymous author argued, should be vested in a single, popularly elected assembly. The people, the pamphlet said, "best know their wants and necessities, and therefore are best able to govern themselves." The ideal form of government, according to democrats, was the community or town meeting, in which the people set their own tax rates, created a militia, controlled their own schools and churches, and regulated the local economy. State government was necessary only for coordination among communities.

Conservative Americans took up the Whig argument on the need for a balanced government. The "unthinking many," wrote another pamphleteer, should be checked by a strong executive and an upper house. Both of these would be insulated from popular control by property qualifications and long terms in office, the latter designed to draw forth the wisdom and talent of the country's wealthiest and most accomplished men. The greatest danger, according to conservatives, was the possibility of majority tyranny, which might lead to the violation of property rights and to dictatorship. "We must take mankind as they are," one conservative wrote, "and not as we could wish them to be."

The First State Constitutions

Fourteen states—the original thirteen plus Vermont—adopted constitutions between 1776 and 1780. Each of these documents was shaped by debate between radicals and conservatives, democrats and Whigs, and reflected a political balance of power. The constitutions of Pennsylvania, Maryland, and New York typified the political range of the times. Pennsylvania instituted a radical democracy, Maryland created a conservative set of institutions designed to keep citizens and rulers as far apart as possible, and New York adopted a system somewhere in the middle.

Declarations of Rights

One of the most important innovations of the state constitutions was a guarantee of rights patterned on the Virginia Declaration of Rights of June 1776. Written by George Mason—a wealthy planter, democrat, and brilliant political philosopher—the Virginia declaration set a distinct tone in its very first article: "That all men are by nature equally free and independent, and have certain inherent rights, . . . namely, the enjoyment of life and liberty, with the means of acquiring and possessing property and pursuing and obtaining happiness and safety." The fifteen articles declared, among other things, that sovereignty resided in the people, that government was the servant of the people, and that the people had the "right to reform, alter, or abolish" that government. There were guarantees of due process and trial by jury in criminal prosecutions, and prohibitions of excessive bail and "cruel and unusual punishments." Freedom of the press was guaranteed as "one of the great bulwarks of liberty," and the people were assured of "the free exercise of religion, according to the dictates of conscience."

Eight state constitutions included a general declaration of rights similar to the first article of the Virginia declaration; others incorporated specific guarantees. A number of states proclaimed the right of the people to engage in free speech and free assembly, to instruct their representatives, and to petition for the redress of grievances—rights either inadvertently or deliberately omitted from Virginia's declaration. These declarations were important precedents for the Bill of Rights, the first ten amendments to the federal constitution. Indeed, George Mason of Virginia was a leader of the democrats who insisted that the Constitution stipulate such rights.

A Spirit of Reform

The political upheaval of the Revolution raised the possibility of other reforms in American society. The 1776 Constitution of New Jersey, by granting the vote to "all free inhabitants" who met the property requirements, enfranchised women as well as men. The number of women voters eventually led to male protests and a new state law explicitly limiting the right to vote to "free white male citizens."

The New Jersey controversy may have been an anomaly, but women's participation in the Revolution wrought subtle but important changes. In 1776 Abigail Adams wrote to her husband John Adams, away at the Continental Congress, "In the new code of laws which I suppose it will be necessary for you to make I desire you would remember the ladies, and be more generous and favourable to them than your ancestors." In the aftermath of the Revolution, there was evidence of increasing sympathy in the courts for women's property rights and fairer adjudication of women's petitions for divorce. And the postwar years witnessed an increase in opportunities for women seeking an education. From a strictly legal and political point of view, the Revolution may have done little to change women's role in society, but it did seem to help change expectations.

The most steadfast reformer of the day was Thomas Jefferson, who after completing work on the Declaration of Independence returned to Virginia to take a seat in its House of Delegates. In 1776 he introduced a bill that abolished the law of entails, which had confined inheritance to particular heirs in order that landed property remain undivided. Jefferson believed that entail and primogeniture (inheritance of all the family property by the firstborn son)—legal customs long in effect in aristocratic England—had no place in a republican society. The legislation had little practical effect because few estates were entailed, but the repeal was symbolically important, for its repudiated an aristocratic custom. By 1790, every state but one had followed Virginia's lead (Rhode Island acted in 1798).

Jefferson's other notable success was his Bill for Establishing Religious Freedom. Indeed, he considered this document one of his greatest accomplishments. At the beginning of the Revolution, there were established churches in nine of the thirteen colonies: the Congregationalists in Massachusetts, New Hampshire, and Connecticut and the Anglicans in New York and the South. (See also Chapter 5 for a discussion of colonial religion.) Established religion was increasingly opposed in the eighteenth century, in part because of Enlightenment criticism of the power it had over free and open inquiry, but more importantly because of the growing sectarian diversity produced by the religious revival of the Great Awakening.

African Americans and the Revolution

For most African Americans there was little to celebrate in the American victory, for it perpetuated the institution of slavery. Few people were surprised when thousands of black fighters and their families departed with the British at the end of the war, settling in the West Indies, Canada, and Africa. Virginia and South Carolina were said to have lost 30,000 and 25,000 slaves, respectively, as a result of the war.

To many white Americans there was an obvious contradiction in waging a war for liberty while continuing to support the institution of slavery. Slavery was first abolished in the state constitution of Vermont in 1777, and in Massachusetts and New Hampshire in 1780 and 1784, respectively. Pennsylvania, Connecticut, and Rhode Island adopted systems of gradual emancipation during these years, freeing the children of slaves at birth. By 1804 every northern state had provided for abolition or gradual emancipation, although as late as 1810, 30,000 African Americans remained enslaved in the North.

In the Upper South, revolutionary idealism, the Christian egalitariansim of Methodists and Baptists, and a shift from tobacco farming to the cultivation of cereal grains such as wheat and corn combined to weaken the commitment of many planters to the slave system. There was a great increase in manumissions—grants of freedom to slaves by individual masters. In the Upper South there was a small but important movement to encourage gradual emancipation by convincing masters to free their slaves in their wills. George Washington not only freed several hundred of his slaves upon his death but developed an elaborate plan for apprenticeship and tenancy for the able-bodied and lodging and pensions for the aged. However, planters in the Lower South, heavily dependent as they were on slave labor, resisted the growing calls for an end to slavery. Between 1776 and 1786 all the states but South Carolina and Georgia prohibited or heavily taxed the international slave trade, and this issue became an important point of contention at the Constitutional Convention in 1787 (see Chapter 8).

Perhaps the most important result of these developments was the growth of the free African American population. From a few thousand in 1750, the free African American population grew to more than 200,000 by the end of the century. Largely excluded from the institutions of white Americans, the African American community now had sufficient strength to establish schools, churches, and other institutions of its own. Initially this development was opposed. But by the 1790s the Williamsburg African Church had grown to over 500 members, and the Baptist Association reluctantly recognized it. In Philadelphia Reverend Absalom Jones established St. Thomas's African Episcopal Church. The incorporation of the word *African* in the names of churches, schools, and mutual benefit societies reflected the pride African Americans took in their heritage.

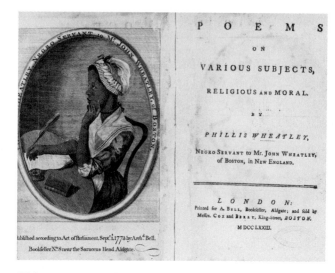

This portrait of African American poet Phyllis Wheatley was included in the collection of her work published in London in 1773, when she was only twenty. Kidnapped in Africa when a girl, then purchased off the Boston docks, she was more like a daughter than a slave to the Wheatley family, and later married and lived as a free woman before her untimely death in 1784.

A small group of African American writers rose to prominence in the revolutionary era. Benjamin Banneker published a popular almanac that both white and black Americans consulted. The most famous African American writer, however, was Phyllis Wheatley, who came to public attention when her *Poems on Various Subjects, Religious and Moral* appeared in London in 1773, while she was still a domestic slave in Boston. Kidnapped as a young girl and converted to Christianity during the Great Awakening, Wheatley wrote poems that combined her piety and a concern for her people.

Economic Problems

During the Revolution, the shortage of goods resulting from the British blockade, the demand for supplies by the army and militias, and the flood of paper currency issued by Congress and the states combined to create the worst inflation that Americans have ever experienced. The first Continental dollars were worth roughly one silver dollar (the Spanish peso) in 1777. By 1779 they were worth 21 to 1, and 400 to 1 by 1781. There was a popular outcry at the incredible increase in prices, and communities and states in the North responded with laws regulating wages and prices.

The sponsors of wage and price schedules often attributed high prices to hoarding and profiteering. Although it is doubtful that such practices caused the inflation, many merchants did gouge their customers. Many communities experienced demonstrations and food riots; men and women demanded fair prices, and when they did not receive them, they broke into storehouses and took what they needed. People organized local committees to monitor economic activity and punish wrongdoers.

After the war the primary economic problem was no longer inflation but depression. Political revolution could not alter economic realities: the independent United States continued to be a supplier of raw materials and an importer of manufactured products, and Great Britain remained its most important trading partner.

With few exports to offset all the imports, the trade deficit with Britain for the period 1784–86 rose to approximately 5 million pounds. The deficit acted like a magnet, drawing hard currency from American accounts. Short of hard currency, the commercial banks in the United States insisted on immediate repayment of old loans and refused to issue new ones. The country was left with very little coin in circulation. It all added up to a serious depression, lasting from 1784 to 1788. At their lowest level, in 1786, prices had fallen 25 percent.

The depression struck while the country was burdened with the huge debt incurred during the Revolution. The total debt owed by the national and state governments amounted to more than $50 million in 1785. Not allowed to raise taxes on its own, the Confederation Congress requisitioned the states for the funds necessary for debt repayment. The states in turn taxed their residents. At a time when there was almost no money in circulation, people rightly feared being crushed by the burden of private debt and public taxes. Thus the economic problem became a political problem.

State Remedies

Where there were manufacturing interests, as in the Northeast, states erected high tariffs to curb imports and protect infant industries. But shippers could avoid these duties simply by unloading their cargo in nearby seaboard states that lacked tariffs; domestic merchants then distributed the products overland. To be effective, commercial regulation had to be national. Local sentiment had to give way to the unity of a national community.

The most controversial economic remedies were those designed to relieve the burden on debtors and ordinary taxpayers. In some areas, farmers called for laws permitting payment of taxes or debts in goods and commodities, a kind of institutionalized barter. More commonly, farmers and debtors pressed their state governments for legal tender laws, which would require creditors to accept at specified rates of exchange a state's paper currency—regardless of its worth—for all debts public and private. Understandably, creditors opposed such a plan. But farmers were strong enough to enact currency laws in seven states during the depression. For the most part, these were modest programs that worked rather well, caused little depreciation, and did not result in the problems feared by creditors. In most instances, the notes were loaned to farmers, who put up the value of their land as collateral.

Shays' Rebellion

In 1786 a rural uprising of communities in Massachusetts shook the nation. Farmers in the western part of the state had been hit particularly hard during the depression, when country merchants pressed them to pay their debts in hard currency they didn't have. About a third of all male heads of household were sued for debt during the 1780s, and the county jails filled with debtors who couldn't pay. Dozens of towns petitioned the state government for relief, but the legislature, dominated by urban and merchant interests, rejected legal tender and paper currency laws. During the spring and summer of 1786, farmers throughout the rural parts of the state mustered their community militia companies and closed the courts—precisely what they had done during the Revolution.

This uprising quickly became known as Shays' Rebellion, after Daniel Shays, one of the leaders of the "committee of the people" who had also been a leader in the Revolution. Although the rebellion was most widespread in Massachusetts, similar disorders occurred in every other New England state except Rhode Island, where the farmers had already taken power. There were a number of incidents outside New England as well.

The crisis ended when a militia force raised in communities from eastern Massachusetts marched west and crushed the Shaysites in January 1787 as they marched on the armory in Springfield. Fifteen of the leaders were subsequently sentenced to death; two were hanged before the remainder were pardoned, and several hundred farmers had to swear an oath of allegiance to the state. In fact, these men had wanted little more than temporary relief from their indebtedness, and rural discontent quickly disappeared once the depression began to lift in 1788.

The most important consequence of Shays' Rebellion was its effect on conservative nationalists unhappy with the distribution of power between the states and national government under the Articles of Confederation. The uprising "wrought prodigious changes in the minds of men respecting the powers of government," wrote Henry Knox. "Everybody says they must be strengthened and that unless this shall be effected, there is no security for liberty and property." It was time, he declared, "to clip the wings of a mad democracy."

Conclusion

The Revolution was a tumultuous era, marked by violent conflict between Patriots and Loyalists, masters and slaves, settlers and Indian peoples. But the advocates of independence emerged successful, largely because of their ability to pull together and begin to define their national community. But fearful of the power of central authority, Americans created a weak national government. By the mid-1780s, however, many nationalists were paraphrasing Washington's question of 1777: "What then is to become of this nation?" Most Americans would seek to answer that question not by retreating to the security of their localities and states, but by attempting to reform the national government and build a strong new national community.

CHRONOLOGY

1775	Lord Dunmore, royal governor of Virginia, appeals to slaves to support Britain
1776	July: Declaration of Independence
	August: battle of Long Island initiates retreat of Continental Army
	September: British land on Manhattan Island
	December: George Washington counterattacks at Trenton
1777	Slavery abolished in Vermont
	September: British General William Howe captures Philadelphia
	October: British General John Burgoyne surrenders at Saratoga
	November: Continentals settle into winter quarters at Valley Forge
	December: France recognizes American independence
1778	June: France enters the war
	June: battle of Monmouth hastens British retreat to New York
	July: George Rogers Clark captures Kaskaskia
	December: British capture Savannah
1779	Spain enters the war
1780	February: British land at Charleston
	July: French land at Newport
	September: British General Charles Cornwallis invades North Carolina
1781	February: Robert Morris appointed superintendent of finance
	March: Articles of Confederation ratified
	October: Cornwallis surrenders at Yorktown
1782	Peace talks begin
1783	March: Washington mediates issue of officer pensions
	September: Treaty of Paris signed
	November: British evacuate New York
1784	Treaty of Fort Stanwix
	Postwar depression begins
1785	Land Ordinance of 1785
	Treaty of Fort McIntosh
1786	Jefferson's Bill for Establishing Religious Freedom
	Rhode Island currency law
	Shays' Rebellion

Review Questions

1. Assess the relative strengths of the Patriots and the Loyalists in the American Revolution.
2. What roles did Indian peoples and African Americans play in the Revolution?
3. Describe the structure of the Articles of Confederation. What were its strengths and weaknesses?
4. How did the Revolution affect politics within the states?
5. What were the issues in Shays' Rebellion? How do they help to illustrate the political conflict in the nation during the 1780s?

Recommended Reading

EDWARD COUNTRYMAN, *The American Revolution* (1985). The best short introduction to the social and political history of the Revolution. Informed by the great outpouring of studies during the twenty years preceding its publication.

MERRILL JENSEN, *The New Nation: A History of the United States During the Confederation, 1781–1789* (1950). Still the standard work on the 1780s.

ROBERT MIDDLEDAUFF, *The Glorious Cause: The American Revolution, 1763–1789* (1982). A good account of the military and diplomatic side of the conflict.

MARY BETH NORTON, *Liberty's Daughters: The Revolutionary Experience of American Women, 1750–1800* (1980). A provocative and comprehensive history of women in the Revolutionary era. Treats not only legal and institutional change but also the more subtle changes in habits and expectations.

CHARLES ROYSTER, *A Revolutionary People at War* (1979). A pathbreaking study of the Continental Army and popular attitudes toward it. Emphasizes the important role played by the officer corps and the enlisted men in the formation of the first nationalist constituency.

JOHN SHY, *A People Numerous and Armed* (1976). A series of studies of the local and state militias, demonstrating that their most important contribution was political, not military.

DAVID P. SZATMARY, *Shays' Rebellion: The Making of an Agrarian Insurrection* (1980). An excellent study of the famous farmers' rebellion that stimulated conservatives to write the Constitution. Includes a great deal of general background material on the Confederation period, as well as excellent coverage of the specifics of the revolt.

ALFRED F. YOUNG, ED., *The American Revolution: Explorations in American Radicalism* (1976). Includes provocative essays on African Americans, Indians, and women.

AMERICAN COMMUNITIES

MINGO CREEK SETTLERS REFUSE TO PAY THE WHISKEY TAX

It was a hot July afternoon in 1794 when the federal marshall and the tax collector arrived at the backcountry farm of William Miller in Mingo Creek, a community south of Pittsburgh. Like most of his neighbors, Miller had failed to pay the federal excise tax on his homemade whiskey still, and these men had come to serve him with a notice to appear in federal court in Philadelphia. "I felt myself mad with passion," said the farmer, knowing that the fine and the cost of the trip back east would ruin him. As the men argued, thirty or forty of Miller's neighbors suddenly appeared, armed with muskets and pitchforks. Members of the Mingo Creek Democratic Society, they had come to fight off this infringement upon liberty. There was an angry confrontation, and someone fired a gun into the air. No one was hit, and after a heated verbal confrontation, the two officials rode off unmolested. But the farmers were fuming, and decided to make a "citizen's arrest" of the officials the next day.

At Mingo Creek, poverty was the outstanding fact of life. A third of the farm families owned no land, but rented or simply squatted on the acres of others. The tax collector was one of the great landlords of Mingo Creek, not only controlling most of the local wealth but monopolizing political office as well. Other landlords lived outside the community, the most powerful being President George Washington himself, who owned thousands of acres in the West, much of it in the vicinity of Mingo Creek. The president had evicted so many squatters from his land that local people considered him a grasping speculator. Washington returned the compliment by describing these frontier settlers as "a parcel of barbarians" who lived little better than "dogs or cats."

In the Ohio region farm families lived in miserable mud-floored log huts scattered along the creeks of the Monongahela Valley. But despite appearances, the farmers of Mingo Creek were bound together in networks of family and clan, work and barter, religion and politics. The militiamen acted together in what they perceived to be the interests of their community.

Like all the Western Territories, this was a violent place in a violent time. No-holds-barred fights at local taverns were common, and travelers remarked on the presence of one-eyed men, the victims of brutal gougings. Everyone knew of men or women lost in the continuing Indian wars. The new federal government had committed over 80 percent of its operating budget to defeating the Indians, but the failure of its campaigns left backcountry families resentful.

It was to help pay the costs of these campaigns that Congress placed the tax on whiskey in 1791. The tax applied to the owners of stills, whether they produced commercially or simply for family and neighbors. Farmers throughout America protested that the excise ran counter to Revolutionary principles. "Internal taxes upon consumption," declared the citizens of Mingo Creek, are "most dangerous to the civil rights of freemen, and must in the end destroy the liberties of every country in which they are introduced."

Protest followed the course familiar from the Revolution. At first citizens gathered peacefully and petitioned their representatives, but when the tax collectors appeared, there was vigilante action. Faces blackened or covered with handkerchiefs, farmers tarred and feathered the tax men. Although the immediate issue was taxation, larger matters were at stake. The Mingo Creek Democratic Society was part of Thomas Jefferson's political movement that supported republicanism and the French Revolution, in opposition to the conservative principles of the Washington administration. The tax protesters made this linkage explicit when they raised banners proclaiming the French slogan of "Liberty, Equality, Fraternity" and adding their own phrase, "and No Excise!"

But it was only in western Pennsylvania that the protests turn to riot. When the Mingo Creek militia went to arrest the tax man, several of their number were killed in the confrontation. In a community meeting afterward, the protesters resolved to attack and destroy Pittsburgh, where the wealthy and powerful local landlords resided. Terrified residents of the town saved the day by welcoming the rebels with free food and drink. "It cost me four barrels of whiskey that day," declared one man, but "I would rather spare that than a single quart of blood." Destruction was averted, but an angry farmer rode through the street waving a tomahawk and warning, "It is not the excise law only that must go down. A great deal more is to be done. I am but beginning yet."

Declaring the Whiskey Rebellion "the first ripe fruit" of the democratic sentiment sweeping the country, Washington organized a federal army of 13,000 men, larger than the one he had commanded during the Revolution, and ordered the occupation of western Pennsylvania. Soldiers dragged half-naked men from their beds and forced them into open pens, where they remained for days in the freezing rain. Authorities arrested twenty people, and a judge convicted two of treason. The protest gradually died down. Washington pardoned the felons, sparing their lives.

Federal power had prevailed over the local community. In his Farewell Address, Washington warned of an excessive spirit of localism that "agitates the community with ill-founded jealousies and false alarms; kindles the animosity of one part against another; foments occasionally riot and insurrection." But resistance to the excise remained widespread, and no substantial revenue was ever collected from the tax on whiskey. More important, the whiskey rebels had raised some of the most important issues of the day: the power and authority of the new federal government, the relationship of the West to the rest of the nation, the nature of political dissent, and the meaning of the Revolutionary tradition.

KEY TOPICS

- **The tensions and conflicts between local and national authorities in the decades after the American Revolution**
- **The struggle to draft the Constitution and to achieve its ratification**
- **Establishment of the first national government under the Constitution**
- **The beginning of American political parties**
- **The first stirrings of an authentic American national culture**

Forming a New Government

Eight years before the Whiskey Rebellion, Shays's Rebellion (see Chapter 7) had helped pull together a nationalist movement that ultimately replaced the Articles of Confederation with a powerful new central government.

Nationalist Sentiment

Nationalists had long argued for a strengthened union of the states. In general, the nationalists were drawn from the elite circles of American life. "Although there are no nobles in America, there is a class of men denominated 'gentlemen,'" the French ambassador to America wrote home in 1786. "They are creditors, and therefore interested in strengthening the government, and watching over the execution of the law. The majority of them being merchants, it is for their interest to establish the credit of the United States in Europe on a solid foundation by the exact payment of debts, and to grant to Congress powers extensive enough to compel the people to contribute for this purpose."

The economic crisis that followed the Revolutionary War (see Chapter 7) provided the nationalists with their most important opportunity to organize. In March 1785 a group of men from Virginia and Maryland, including James Madison, George Mason, and George Washington, drafted an agreement to present to legislatures uniform commercial regulations, duties, and currency laws. Early the next year, at Madison's urging, the Virginia legislature invited all the states to send representatives to a commercial conference to be held at Annapolis in the fall. Only five states sent strong nationalist delegates to the Annapolis Convention in September 1786. But this time, most Americans agreed that the Articles needed strengthening, especially in regard to commercial regulation and the generation of revenue. Early in 1787 the Confederation Congress cautiously endorsed the plan for a convention "for the sole and express purpose of revising the Articles of Confederation."

The Constitutional Convention

Fifty-five men from twelve states assembled at the Pennsylvania State House in Philadelphia in late May 1787. Rhode Island, where radical localists held power (see Chapter 7), refused to send a delegation. A number of prominent men were missing. Thomas Jefferson and John Adams were serving as ambassadors in Europe, and crusty localist Patrick Henry declared that he "smelt a rat." But most of America's best-known leaders

This cartoon appeared during the protests over the congressional tax (or excise) on whiskey passed in 1791. In western Pennsylvania the opposition to the exciseman turned to popular rebellion in 1794, arousing conservative fears that the United States might be on the brink of the same kind of disorder that characterized the French Revolution.

Courtesy of Atwater Kent Museum.

were present: George Washington, Benjamin Franklin, Alexander Hamilton, James Madison, George Mason, Robert Morris. Twenty-nine of them were college educated, thirty-four were lawyers, twenty-four had served in Congress, and twenty-one were veteran officers of the Revolution. At least nineteen owned slaves, and there were also land speculators and merchants. But there were no ordinary farmers or artisans present, and no women, African Americans, or Indians. The Constitution was framed by men who represented America's social and economic elite.

On their first day of work, the delegates agreed to vote by states, as was the custom of Congress, and chose Washington to chair the meeting. James Madison, a young, conservative Virginian with a profound knowledge of history and political philosophy, took voluminous daily minutes of the entire convention. Madison and his fellow Virginians had arrived early and drafted what became known as the Virginia Plan. Presented by Governor Edmund Randolph of Virginia on May 29, it set the convention's agenda.

The authors of the Virginia Plan proposed scrapping the Articles of Confederation in favor of a "consolidated government" having the power to tax and to enforce its laws directly rather than through the states. "A spirit of locality," Madison declared, was destroying "the aggregate interests of the community," by which he meant the great community of the nation. Madison's plan would have reduced the states to little more than administrative districts. Representation in the bicameral national legislature was to be based on population districts, the members of the House of Representatives elected by popular vote, but senators chosen indirectly so that they might be insulated from democratic pressure. The Senate would lead, controlling foreign affairs and the appointment of officials. An appointed chief executive and a national judiciary would together form a Council of Revision having the power to veto both national and state legislation.

The main opposition to these proposals came from the delegates from small states, who feared being swallowed up by the large ones. After two weeks of debate, William Paterson of New Jersey introduced an alternative, a set of "purely federal" principles known since as the New Jersey Plan. He proposed increasing the powers of the central government but retaining a single-house Congress in which the states were equally represented. After much debate, and a series of votes that split the convention down the middle, the delegates finally agreed to what has been called the Great Compromise: proportional representation in the House, representation by states in the Senate. The compromise allowed the creation of a strong national government while still providing an important role for the states.

Part of this agreement was a second, fundamental compromise that brought together the delegates from North and South. In the matter of counting population for purposes of representation, southern delegates insisted on including their slaves. Ultimately it was agreed that five slaves would be counted as the equal of three freemen—the "three-fifths rule." Furthermore, the representatives of South Carolina and Georgia demanded protection for the slave trade, and after bitter debate the delegates included a provision preventing any prohibition of the trade for twenty years. Another article legitimized the return of fugitive slaves from free states. The word *slave* was nowhere used in the text of the Constitution, but these provisions amounted to national guarantees for southern slavery. Although many delegates were opposed to slavery, and regretted having to give in on this issue, they agreed with Madison, who wrote that "great as the evil is, a dismemberment of the union would be worse."

In the ensuing debate on the role of the branches of government the delegates favored a strong federal judiciary with the implicit power to declare acts of Congress unconstitutional. There was also considerable support for a president with veto power to check the legislature.

In early September the delegates turned their rough draft of the Constitution over to a Committee of Style that shaped it into an elegant and concise document providing the general principles and basic framework of government. The delegates voted their approval on September 17, 1787, and transmitted the document to Congress, agreeing that it would become operative after ratification by nine states. Despite some congressmen who were outraged that the convention had exceeded its charge of simply modifying the Articles of Confederation, Congress called for a special ratifying convention in each of the states.

Ratifying the New Constitution

The supporters of the new Constitution immediately adopted the name *Federalists* to describe themselves. In this, as in much of the subsequent process of ratification, the Federalists grabbed the initiative, and their opponents had to content themselves with the label *Anti-Federalists*. These critics of the Constitution were by no means a unified group. Because most of them were localists, they represented a variety of social and regional interests. But most believed the Constitution granted far too much power to the center, weakening the autonomy of communities and states. As local governments "will always possess a better representation of the feelings and interests of the people at large," one critic wrote, "it is obvious that these powers can be deposited with much greater safety with the state than the general government."

All the great political thinkers of the eighteenth century had argued that a republican form of government could work only for small countries. As French philosopher Montesquieu had observed, "In an extensive republic, the public good is sacrificed to a thousand private views." But in *The Federalist,* a brilliant series of essays in defense of the Constitution written in 1787 and 1788 by Madison, Hamilton, and John Jay, Madison stood Montesquieu's assumption on its head. Rhode Island had demonstrated that the rights of property might not be protected in even the smallest of states. Asserting that "the most common and durable source of factions has been the various and unequal distribution of property," Madison concluded that the best way to control such factions was to "extend the sphere" of government. Rather than a disability, Madison argued, great size is an advantage: interests are so diverse that no single faction is able to gain control of the state, threatening the freedoms of others.

It is doubtful whether Madison's sophisticated argument, or the arguments of the Anti-Federalists for that matter, made much of a difference in the popular voting in the states to select delegates for the state ratification conventions. The alignment of forces generally followed the lines laid down during the fights over economic issues in the years since the Revolution. Agrarian–localist and commercial–cosmopolitan alignments characterized most of the states. The most critical convention took place in Massachusetts in early 1788. Five states—Delaware, Pennsylvania, New Jersey, Georgia, and Connecticut—had already voted to ratify, but the states with the strongest Anti-Federalist movements had yet to convene. If the Constitution lost in Massachusetts, its fate would be in great danger. At the convention, Massachusetts opponents of ratification enjoyed a small majority. But several important Anti-Federalist leaders, including Samuel Adams, were swayed by the enthusiastic support for the Constitution among Boston's townspeople, and on February 16 the convention voted narrowly in favor of ratification. To no one's surprise, Rhode Island rejected in March, but Maryland and South Carolina approved in April and May. On June 21 New Hampshire became the ninth state to ratify.

New York, Virginia, and North Carolina were left with the decision of whether to join the new Union. Anti-Federalist support was strong in each of these states. North Carolina voted to reject. (It did not join the Union until the next year, followed by a still reluctant Rhode Island in 1790.) In New York the delegates were moved to vote their support by a threat from New York City to secede from the state and join the Union separately if the convention failed to ratify. The Virginia convention was almost evenly divided, but promises to amend the Constitution to protect individual rights persuaded enough delegates to produce a victory for the Constitution. The promise of a Bill of Rights was important in the ratification vote of five of the states.

The Bill of Rights

Although the Bill of Rights—the first ten amendments to the Constitution—was adopted during the first session of the new federal Congress, it was first proposed during the debates over ratification. The various state ratification conventions had proposed a grab bag of over two hundred potential amendments. Madison set about transforming these into a series that he introduced into the new Congress on June 8, 1789. Congress passed twelve and sent them to the states, and ten survived the ratification process to become the Bill of Rights in 1791.

The First Amendment prohibits Congress from establishing an official religion and provides for the freedoms of assembly, speech, and the press and the right of petition. The other amendments guarantee the right to bear arms, limit the government's power to quarter troops in private homes, and restrain the government from unreasonable searches or seizures; they assure the people their legal rights under the common law, including the prohibition of double jeopardy, the right not to be compelled to testify against oneself, and due process of law before life, liberty, or property can be taken. Finally, the unenumerated rights of the people are protected, and the powers not delegated to the federal government are reserved to the states.

The first ten amendments to the Constitution have been a restraining influence on the growth of government power over American citizens. Their provisions have become an admired aspect of the American political tradition throughout the world. The Bill of Rights is the most important constitutional legacy of the Anti-Federalists.

The New Nation

Ratification of the Constitution was followed by the first federal elections—for the Congress and the presidency—and in the spring of 1789 the new federal government assumed power in the temporary capital of New York City. The inauguration of George Washington as the first president of the United States took place on April 30, 1789, on the balcony of Federal Hall, at the corner of Wall and Broad streets. The first years under the new federal Constitution were especially important for the future because they shaped the structure of the American state in ways that would be enormously significant for later generations.

The Washington Presidency

Although he dressed in plain American broadcloth at his inauguration and claimed to be content with the plain republican title of "president" (John Adams's proposed title of "His Highness the President of the United States" had been rejected by a majority of the House of Representatives as too monarchial), Washington was counted among the nationalists. By nature reserved and solemn, choosing to ride about town in a grand carriage drawn by six horses and escorted by uniformed livery-men, he was anything but a man of the people. In the tradition of British royalty, delivered his addresses personally to Congress, and received from both houses an official reply. These customs were continued by John Adams, Washington's successor, but ended by Thomas Jefferson, who considered them "rags of royalty." On the other hand, Washington worked hard to adhere to the letter of the Constitution, refusing, for example, to use the veto power except where he thought the Congress had acted unconstitutionally, and personally seeking the "advice and consent" of the Senate.

Congress quickly moved to establish departments to run the executive affairs of state, and Washington soon appointed Jefferson his secretary of state, Alexander Hamilton to run the Treasury, Henry Knox the War Department, and Edmund Randolph the Justice Department as attorney general. The president consulted each of these men regularly, and during his first term met with them as a group to discuss matters of policy. By the end of Washington's presidency the secretaries had coalesced into what came to be known as the Cabinet, a group that has survived to the present despite the absence of constitutional authority or enabling legislation. Washington was a powerful and commanding personality, but he understood the importance of national unity, and in his style of leadership, his consultations, and his appointments he sought to achieve a balance of conflicting political perspectives and sectional interests. These intentions would be sorely tested during the eight years of his administration.

An Active Federal Judiciary

The most important piece of legislation to emerge from the first session of Congress was the Judiciary Act of 1789, which implemented the judicial clause of the Constitution and set up a system of federal courts. Congress provided that the Supreme Court consist of six members, and established three circuit and thirteen district courts. Strong nationalists argued for a powerful federal legal system that would provide a uniform code of civil and criminal justice throughout the country. But the localists in Congress fought successfully to retain the various bodies of law that had developed the states. The act gave federal courts limited original jurisdiction, restricting them mostly to appeals from state courts. But it thereby established the principle of federal judicial review of state legislation, despite the silence of the Constitution on this point.

Under the leadership of Chief Justice John Jay, the Supreme Court heard few cases during its first decade. Still, it managed to raise considerable political controversy. In *Chisholm* v. *Georgia* (1793) it ruled in favor of two South Carolina residents who had sued the state of Georgia for the recovery of confiscated property. Thus did the Court overthrow the common law principle that a sovereignty could not be sued without its consent, and supported the Constitution's grant of federal jurisdiction over disputes "between a state and citizens of another state." Many localists feared that this nationalist ruling threatened the integrity of the states. In response, they proposed the Eleventh Amendment to the Constitution, ratified in 1798, which declared that no state could be sued by citizens from another state.

Hamilton's Controversial Fiscal Program

Fiscal and economic affairs pressed upon the new government. Lacking revenues and faced with the massive national debt contracted during the Revolution, it took power in a condition of virtual bankruptcy. At the urging of James Madison, Congress passed the Tariff of 1789, a compromise between advocates of protective tariffs (duties so high that they made foreign products prohibitively expensive, thus "protecting" American products) and those who wanted moderate tariffs that produced income. Duties on imported goods, rather than direct taxes on property or incomes, would constitute the bulk of federal revenues until the twentieth century. After setting this system of duties in place, Congress turned to the problem of the debt. In January 1790 Hamilton submitted a "Report on the Public Credit" in which he recommended that the federal government assume the obligations accumulated by the states during the previous fifteen years and redeem the national debt—owed to both domestic and foreign leaders—by agreeing to a new issue of interest-bearing bonds.

By this means, Hamilton sought to inspire the confidence of domestic and foreign investors in the public credit of the new nation. Congress endorsed his plan to pay off the $11 million owed to foreign creditors, but balked at funding the domestic debt of $27 million and assuming the state debts of $25 million. Necessity had forced many individuals to sell off at deep discounts the notes, warrants, and securities the government had issued them during the Revolution. Yet Hamilton now advocated paying these obligations at face value, providing any speculator who held them with fabulous profits. An even greater debate took place over the assumption of the state debts, for some states, mostly those in the South, had already arranged to liquidate their debts, whereas others had left theirs unpaid. Congress remained deadlocked on this issue for six months, until congressmen from Pennsylvania and Virginia arranged a compromise.

Final agreement, however, was stalled by a sectional dispute over the location of the new national capital. Southerners supported Washington's desire to plant it on the Potomac River, but northerners argued for Philadelphia. In return for Madison's pledge to obtain enough southern votes to pass Hamilton's assumption plan—which Madison had earlier opposed as a "radically immoral" windfall for speculators—northern congressmen agreed to a location for the new federal district on the boundary of Virginia and Maryland. In July 1790 Congress passed legislation moving the temporary capital from New York to Philadelphia until the expected completion of the federal city in the District of Columbia in 1800. Two weeks later it adopted Hamilton's credit program. This was the first of many sectional compromises.

Hamilton now proposed the second component of his fiscal program, the establishment of a Bank of the United States. The bank, a public corporation funded by private capital, would serve as the depository of government funds and the fiscal agent of the Treasury. Congress narrowly approved it, but Madison's opposition raised doubts in the president's mind about the constitutionality of the measure, and Washington solicited the opinion of his Cabinet. Here for the first time were articulated the classic interpretations of constitutional authority. Jefferson took a *strict constructionist* position, arguing that the powers of the federal government must be limited to those specifically enumerated in the Constitution. This position came closest to the basic agreement of the men who had drafted the document. Hamilton, on the other hand, reasoned that the Constitution "implied" the power to use whatever means were "necessary and proper" to carry out its enumerated powers—a *loose constructionist* position. Persuaded by Hamilton's opinion, Washington signed the bill, and the bank went into operation in 1791.

The third component of Hamilton's fiscal program was an ambitious plan (called the "Report on Manufactures") involving the use of government securities as investment capital for infant industries and high protective tariffs to encourage the development of an industrial economy. Many of Hamilton's specific proposals for increased tariff protection became part of a revision of duties that took place in 1792. Moreover, his fiscal program as a whole dramatically restored the financial health of the United States. The notes of the Bank of the United States became the most important circulating medium of the North American commercial economy, and their wide acceptance greatly stimulated business enterprise. "Our public credit," Washington declared toward the end of his first term, "stands on that ground which three years ago it would have been considered as a species of madness to have foretold."

The Beginnings of Foreign Policy

The Federalist political coalition, forged during the ratification of the Constitution, was sorely strained by these debates over fiscal policy. By the middle of 1792, Jefferson, representing the southern agrarians, and Hamilton, speaking for northern capitalists, were locked in a full-scale feud within the Washington administration. Hamilton conducted himself more like a prime minister than a Cabinet secretary, greatly offending Jefferson, who considered himself the president's heir apparent. But the dispute went deeper than a mere conflict of personalities. Hamilton stated the difference clearly when he wrote that "one side appears to believe that there is a serious plot to overturn the State governments, and substitute a monarchy to the present republican system," while "the other side firmly believes that there is a serious plot to overturn the general government and elevate the separate powers of the States upon its ruins." The conflict between Hamilton and Jefferson was to grow even more bitter over the issue of American foreign policy.

The commanding event of the Atlantic world during the 1790s was the French Revolution, which had begun in 1789. Most Americans enthusiastically welcomed the fall of the French monarchy. After the people of Paris stormed the Bastille, Lafayette sent Washington the key to its doors as a symbol of the relationship between the two revolutions. But with the beginning of the Reign of Terror in 1793, which claimed upon the guillotine the lives of hundreds of aristocrats, American conservatives began to voice their opposition. The execution of King Louis XVI, and especially the onset of war between revolutionary France and monarchical Great Britain in 1793, firmly divided American opinion.

Most at issue was whether the Franco-American alliance of 1778 required the United States to support France in its war with Britain. All of Washington's Cabinet agreed on the importance of American neutrality. With France and Britain prowling for each other's vessels on the high seas, the vast colonial trade of Europe was delivered up to neutral powers, the United States prominent among them. In other words, neutrality meant windfall profits. Jefferson believed it highly unlikely that the French would call upon the Americans to honor the 1778 treaty; the administration should simply wait and see. But Hamilton argued that so great was the danger, Washington should immediately declare the treaty "temporarily and provisionally suspended."

These disagreements revealed two contrasting perspectives on the course the United States should chart in international waters. Hamilton believed in the necessity of an accommodation with Great Britain, the most important trading partner of the United States and the world's greatest naval power. Jefferson and Madison, on the other hand, looked for more international independence, pinning their hopes on the future of western expansion.

The debate in the United States grew hotter with the arrival in early 1793 of French ambassador Edmond Genêt. Large crowds of supporters greeted him throughout the nation. Understandably, a majority of Americans still nursed a hatred of imperial Britain, and these people expressed a great deal of sympathy for republican France. Conservatives such as Hamilton, however, favored a continuation of traditional commercial relations with Britain and feared the antiaristocratic violence of the French. Washington sympathized with Hamilton's position, but most of all he wished to preserve American independence and neutrality. Knowing he must act before "Citizen" Genêt (as the ambassador was popularly known) compromised American sovereignty and involved the United States in a war with Britain, the president issued a proclamation of neutrality on April 22, 1793. In it he assured the world that the United States intended to pursue "a conduct friendly and impartial towards the belligerent powers," while continuing to do business with all sides.

Hamilton's supporters applauded the president, but Jefferson's were outraged. Throughout the country those sympathetic to France organized Democratic Societies, political clubs modeled after the Sons of Liberty. Society members corresponded with each other, campaigned on behalf of candidates, and lobbied with congressmen. People interpreted the international question in the light of issues of local importance. Thus the members of the Mingo Creek Democratic Society used enthusiasm for the French Revolution as a way of organizing political opposition to the Washington administration. In a speech to Congress, President Washington denounced what he called these "self-created societies," declaring them "the most diabolical attempt to destroy the best fabric of human government and happiness."

Citizen Genêt miscalculated, alienating even his supporters, when he demanded that Washington call Congress into special session to debate neutrality. Jefferson, previously a confidant of the ambassador, now denounced Genêt as "hotheaded" and "indecent towards the President." But these words came too late to save his reputation in the eyes of Washington, and at the end of 1793 Jefferson left the administration. The continuing upheaval in France soon swept Genêt's party from power and he was recalled, but fearing the guillotine, he claimed sanctuary and remained in the United States. During his time in the limelight, however, he furthered the division of the Federalist coalition into a faction identifying with Washington, Hamilton, and conservative principles and a faction supporting Jefferson, Madison, democracy, and the French Revolution.

The United States and the Indian Peoples

Among the many problems of the Washington presidency, one of the most pressing concerned the West. The American attempt to treat the western tribes as conquered peoples after the Revolution had resulted only in further violence and warfare. The Northwest Ordinance of 1787 (see Chapter 7) signaled a new approach. "The utmost good faith shall always be observed towards the Indians," it read. "Their lands and property shall never be taken from them without their consent; and in their property, rights, and liberty, they shall never be invaded or disturbed, unless in just and lawful wars authorized by Congress." Although the Constitution was silent regarding Indian policy, this statutory recognition of the largely independent character of the Indian tribes was endorsed by Congress in the Intercourse Act of 1790, the basic law by which the United States would "regulate trade and intercourse with the Indian tribes." To eliminate the abuses of unscrupulous traders, the act created a federal licensing system; subsequent amendments authorized the creation of subsidized trading houses, or "factories," where Indians could obtain goods at reasonable prices. Trade abuses continued unabated for lack of adequate policing power, but these provisions indicated the good intentions of the Washington administration.

To clarify the question of Indian sovereignty, the Indian Intercourse Act declared public treaties between the United States and the Indian nations to be the only legal means of obtaining Indian land. Treaty making

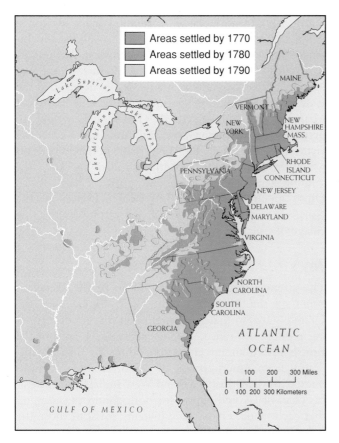

Areas settled by 1770
Areas settled by 1780
Areas settled by 1790

Spread of Settlement: The Backcountry Expands, 1770–90

From 1770 to 1790 American settlement moved across the Appalachians for the first time. The Ohio Valley became the focus of bitter warfare between Indians and settlers.

thus became the procedure for establishing and maintaining relations. Although the federal government often applied military pressure to facilitate the signing of such treaties, the process preserved a semblance of legality. In the twentieth century a number of Indian tribes have successfully appealed for the return of lands obtained by states or individuals in violation of this provision of the Intercourse Act.

Yet conflict continued to characterize the relationship of Americans and Indians, for one of the government's highest priorities was the acquisition of Indian land to supply a growing population of farmers. In defense of their homelands, villages of Shawnees, Delawares, and other Indian peoples confederated with the Miamis under their war chief Little Turtle. In the fall of 1790 Little Turtle lured an American expedi-

tionary force led by General Josiah Harmar into the confederacy's stronghold in Ohio and badly mauled them. In November 1791 the confederation inflicted an even more disastrous defeat on a large American force under General Arthur St. Clair, governor of the Northwest Territory. More than 900 Americans were killed or wounded, making this the worst defeat of an army by Indians in North American history.

Spanish and British Hostility

The position of the United States in the West was made even more precarious by the hostility of Spain and Great Britain, who controlled the adjoining territory. Under the dynamic leadership of King Carlos III and his able ministers, Spain introduced liberal reforms to revitalize the rule-bound economy of its American empire; as a result the economy of New Spain grew rapidly in the 1780s. Moreover, Spain claimed for itself most of the territory south of the Ohio River and pursued a policy designed to block the expansion of the new republic.

Spain's anti-American policy in the West had several facets. Controlling both sides of the lower Mississippi, they closed the river to American shipping, making it impossible for western American farmers to market their crops through the port of New Orleans. They also sought to create a barrier to American settlement by promoting immigration to Louisiana and Florida. They succeeded in attracting several thousand of the Acadians whom the British had deported during the Seven Years' War. Reassembling their distinctive communities in the bayou country of Louisiana, these tough emigrants became known as the Cajuns. But otherwise the Spanish had little success with immigration and relied mostly on creating a barrier of pro-Spanish Indian nations in the lower Mississippi Valley. To consolidate these gains, in the early 1790s the Spanish constructed two new Mississippi River forts at sites that would later become the cities of Vicksburg and Memphis.

North of the Ohio River the situation was much the same. Thousands of Loyalists had fled the United States in the aftermath of the Revolution and settled in the country north of lakes Ontario and Erie. In 1791 the British Parliament passed the Canada Act, creating the province of Upper Canada (later renamed Ontario) and granting the Loyalists limited self-government. To protect this province British troops remained at a number of posts within American territory at places such as Detroit, where they supplied the Indian nations with arms and ammunition, hoping to create a buffer to American expansion.

Domestic and International Crises

Washington faced the gravest crisis of his presidency in 1794. In the West the inability of the federal government to subdue the Indians, eliminate the British from the fur trade or arrange with the Spanish for unencumbered use of the Mississippi River, stirred frontiersmen to loud protests. There were rumblings of rebellion and secession from western communities. As the opening to this chapter illustrates, this discontent was strengthened by the federal excise tax on whiskey, which hit back-country farmers hardest. In the Northwest and Southwest, English and Spanish secret agents gave liberal bribes to entice American settlers to quit the Union and join themselves to Canada or Florida. In the Atlantic Great Britain declared a blockade of France and seized vessels trading with the French West Indies. From 1793 to the beginning of 1794, the British confiscated the cargoes of more than 250 American ships, threatening hundreds of merchants with ruin. The United States was being "kicked, cuffed, and plundered all over the ocean," declared Madison, and in Congress he introduced legislation imposing retaliatory duties on British ships and merchandise.

The Whiskey Rebellion, which broke out in the summer of 1794, thus came at a time when President Washington considered the nation to be under siege. The combination of Indian attack, international intrigue, and domestic insurrection, he believed, made for the greatest threat to the nation since the Revolution. In April the president had dispatched Chief Justice John Jay to London to arrange a settlement with the British. At the same time, war seemed increasingly likely, and Washington feared that any sign of federal weakness in the face of western rebellion would invite British or Spanish intervention. With Hamilton's urging, he took the decisive course described in the opening vignette: he raised a large militia even as he pursued halfhearted negotiations with local authorities and made preparations to occupy the area around Pittsburgh, including Mingo Creek. It is clear that the president overreacted, for although there were riots and violence in western Pennsylvania, there was no organized insurrection. Nevertheless, his mobilization of federal military power dramatically demonstrated the federal commitment to the preservation of the Union, the protection of the western boundary, and the supremacy of the national over the local community.

This action was reinforced by an impressive American victory against the Indian confederacy. Following the disasterous defeat of St. Clair by Little Turtle, Washington appointed General Anthony Wayne to lead a greatly strengthened American force to subdue the Indian confederacy and secure the Northwest. At the Battle of Fallen Timbers, fought in the Maumee country of northern Ohio on August 20, 1794, Wayne crushed the Indians. Retreating, the warriors found the gates of Fort Miami closed and barred, the British inside thinking better of engaging the powerful American force. The victory set the stage for the Treaty of Greenville, in which the representatives of twelve Indian nations ceded a huge territory encompassing most of present-day Ohio, much of Indiana, and other enclaves in the Northwest, including the town of Detroit and the tiny village of Chicago.

Jay's and Pinckney's Treaties

The strengthened American position in the West encouraged the British to settle their dispute with the United States so that they might concentrate on defeating republican France. In November 1794 Jay and the British signed an agreement providing for British withdrawal from American soil by 1796, limited American trade with the British East and West Indies, and the status of most favored nation for both countries (meaning that each would enjoy trade benefits equal to those the other accorded any other state). The treaty represented a solid gain for the young republic. Having only a small army and no navy to speak of, the United States was in no position to wage war.

Details of Jay's Treaty leaked out in a piecemeal fashion that inflamed public debate. The treaty represented a victory for Hamilton's conception of American neutrality. The Jeffersonians, on the other hand, were enraged over this accommodation of Great Britain at France's expense. The absence in the treaty of any mention of compensation for the slaves who had fled to the British side during the Revolution alienated southerners. Throughout the country Democratic Societies and Jeffersonian partisans organized protests and demonstrations. Upon his return to the United States, Jay joked, he could find his way across the country by the light of his burning effigies. Despite these protests, the Senate, dominated by supporters of Hamilton, ratified the agreement in June 1795. In the House a coalition of southerners, westerners, and friends of France attempted to stall the treaty by threatening to withhold the appropriations necessary for its implementation. They demanded that they be allowed to examine the diplomatic correspondence regarding the whole affair, but the president refused, establishing the precedent of *executive privilege* in matters of state.

The deadlock continued until late in the year, when word arrived in Philadelphia that the Spanish had abandoned their claims to the territory south of the Ohio River. Having declared war on revolutionary France, Spain had suffered a humiliating defeat and fearing the loss of its American empire, the Spanish had suddenly found it expedient to mollify the quarrelsome Americans. In 1795 Spain agreed to a treaty setting the boundary with the United States at the thirty-first parallel and opened the Mississippi to American shipping. This treaty fit the Jeffersonian conception of empire, and congressmen from the West and South were delighted with its terms. But administration supporters demanded their acquiescence in Jay's Treaty before its approval.

These two important treaties finally established American sovereignty over the land west of the Appalachians and opened to American commerce a vast market extending from Atlantic ports to the Mississippi Valley. From a political standpoint, however, the events of 1794 and 1795 brought Washington down from his pedestal. Vilified by the opposition press, sick of politics, and longing to return to private life, Washington rejected the offer of a third term.

Washington's Farewell Address

During the last months of his term, Washington published his farewell address to the nation. In it he argued, not for American isolation, but rather for American disinterest in the affairs of Europe. "The great rule of conduct for us in regard to foreign nations is, in extending our commercial relations, to have with them as little *political* connection as possible." Why, he asked, "entangle our peace and prosperity in the toils of European ambition, rivalship, interest, humor, or caprice?" Later, Thomas Jefferson, in his inaugural address of 1801, paraphrased this principle of American foreign policy as "peace, commerce, and honest friendship with all nations, *entangling alliances with none.*"

Federalists and Republicans

The framers of the Constitution envisioned a one-party state in which partisan distinctions were absorbed by patriotism and public virtue. "Among the numerous advantages promised by a well constructed Union," Madison had written in *The Federalist,* is "its tendency to break and control the violence of faction." Not only did he fail to anticipate the rise of political parties or factions, but he saw them as potentially harmful to the new nation. Despite the framers' intentions, in the twelve years between the ratification of the Constitution and the federal election of 1800, political parties became a fundamental part of the American system of government.

The Rise of Political Parties

Evident in the debates and votes of Congress from 1789 to 1795 were a series of shifting coalitions. These shifting coalitions first began to polarize into political factions during the debate over Jay's Treaty in 1795, when agrarians, westerners, southerners, and supporters of France came together in opposition to the treaty. By the elections of 1796, people had begun to label these factions. The supporters of Hamilton claimed the mantle of Federalism. Forced to find another term, the opposition chose *Republican,* implying that the Federalists were really monarchists at heart. Hamilton persisted in calling his opponents Anti-Federalists, but gradually the Jeffersonian coalition came to be known as the Republicans.

These two political coalitions played a fitful role in the presidential election of 1796, which pitted John Adams, Washington's vice president, against Thomas Jefferson. Partisan organization was strongest in the

SUMMARY TABLE	*The First American Party System*
Federalist Party	Organized by figures in the Washington administration who were in favor of a strong federal government, friendship with the British, and opposition to the French Revolution; its power base was among merchants, property owners, and urban workers tied to the commercial economy. A minority party after 1800, it was regionally strong only in New England.
Democratic Republican Party	Arose as the opposition to the Federalists; its adherents were in favor of limiting federal power, sympathetic to the French Revolution, and hostile to Great Britain; it drew strength from southern planters and northern farmers. The majority party after 1800.

middle states, where there was a real contest of political forces, and weakest in New England and the South, where sectional loyalty prevailed and organized opposition was weaker. The absence of party discipline was demonstrated when the ballots of the presidential electors, cast in their respective state capitals, were counted in the Senate. Adams was victorious, but the electors chose Jefferson rather than a Federalist for vice president. Thus the new administration was born divided.

The Adams Presidency

Adams was put in the difficult situation of facing a political opposition led by his own vice president. He nevertheless attempted to conduct his presidency along the lines laid down by Washington, and retained most of the former president's appointees. This presented Adams with another problem. Although Hamilton had retired the year before, the Cabinet remained committed to his advice, actively seeking his opinion and following it. As a result, Adams's authority was further undercut.

On the other hand, Adams benefited from the rising tensions between the United States and France. Angered by Jay's Treaty, the French suspended diplomatic relations at the end of 1796 and inaugurated a tough new policy toward American shipping. During the next two years they seized more than 300 American vessels and confiscated cargoes valued at an estimated $20 million. Hoping to resolve the crisis, Adams sent an American delegation to France. But in dispatches sent back to the United States the American envoys reported that agents of the French foreign ministry had demanded a bribe before any negotiations could be undertaken. Pressed for copies of these dispatches by suspicious Republicans in Congress, in 1798 Adams released them after substituting the letters *X, Y,* and *Z* for the names of the French agents. The documents proved a major liability for the Republicans, producing powerful anti-French sentiment throughout the country. To the demand for a bribe, the American delegates had actually answered "Not a sixpence," but in the inflated rhetoric of the day the response became the infinitely more memorable "Millions for defense, but not one cent for tribute!" The XYZ Affair, as it became known, sent Adams's popularity soaring.

Adams and the Federalists prepared the country for war with France during the spring of 1798. Congress authorized tripling the size of the army, and Washington came out of retirement to command the force. Fears of a French invasion declined after word arrived of

the British naval victory over the French in August 1798 at Aboukir Bay in Egypt, but the "Quasi-war" between France and the United States continued.

The Alien and Sedition Acts

In the summer of 1798 the Federalist majority in Congress, with the acquiescence of President Adams, passed four acts severely limiting both freedom of speech and freedom of the press and threatening the liberty of foreigners in the United States. Embodying the fear that immigrants, in the words of one Massachusetts Federalist, "contaminate the purity and simplicity of the American character" by introducing dangerous democratic and republican ideas, the Naturalization Act extended the period of residence required for citizenship from five to fourteen years. The Alien Act and the Alien Enemies Act authorized the president to order the imprisonment or deportation of suspected aliens during wartime. Finally, the Sedition Act provided heavy fines and imprisonment for anyone convicted of writing, publishing, or speaking anything of "a false, scandalous and malicious" nature against the government or any of its officers.

The Federalists intended these repressive laws as weapons to defeat the Republicans. Led by Albert Gallatin, a Swiss immigrant and congressman from Pennsylvania (replacing Madison, who had retired from politics to devote his time to his plantation), the Republicans contested all the Federalist war measures and for the first time acted as a genuine opposition party, complete with caucuses, floor leaders, and partisan discipline. For the first time, the two parties contested the election of Speaker of the House of Representatives, which became a partisan office. The more effective the Republicans became, the more treasonous they appeared in the eyes of the Federalists. Disagreement with the administration was misconstrued by the Federalists as opposition to the state itself.

The Federalists thus pursued the prosecution of dissent, indicting leading Republican newspaper editors and writers, fining and imprisoning at least twenty-five of them. The most infamous victim of the Sedition Act was Congressman Matthew Lyon of Vermont, imprisoned for publishing libelous statements about President Adams in July 1798. Later that year, after a campaign conducted from his cell, he was reelected to Congress.

The Revolution of 1800

The Alien and Sedition Acts were overthrown by the Republican victory in the national elections of 1800. As the term of President Adams drew to a close, Federalists

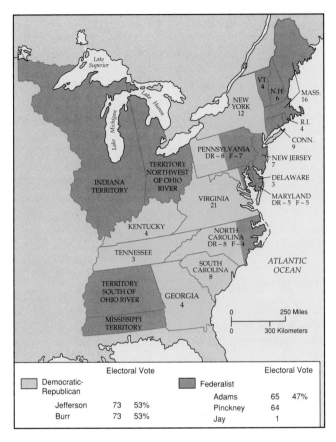

The Election of 1800

In the presidential election of 1800, Democratic Republican victories in New York and the divided vote in Pennsylvania threw the election to Jefferson. The combination of the South and these crucial middle states would keep the Democratic Republicans in control of the federal government for the next generation.

found themselves seriously divided. In 1799, by releasing seized American ships and requesting negotiations, the French convinced Adams that they were ready to settle their dispute with the United States. The president also sensed the public mood running toward peace. But the Hamiltonian wing of the party, always scornful of public sentiment, continued to beat the drums of war. When Federalists in Congress tried to block the president's attempt to negotiate, Adams threatened to resign and turn the government over to Vice President Jefferson. "The end of war is peace," Adams declared, "and peace was offered me." Adams considered the settlement of this conflict with France to be one of the greatest accomplishments of his career, but it earned him the scorn of conservative Federalists.

The presidential campaign of 1800 was the first in which Republicans and Federalists operated as two national political parties. Caucuses of congressmen nominated respective slates: Adams and Charles Cotesworth Pinckney of South Carolina, for the Federalist party, and Jefferson and Aaron Burr of New York for the Republicans. Both tickets represented attempts at sectional balance. The Republicans presented themselves as the party of traditional agrarian purity, of liberty and states' rights, of "government rigorously frugal and simple," in the words of Jefferson. They were optimistic, convinced that they were riding the wave of the future. Divided and embittered, the Federalists waged a defensive struggle for strong central government and public order, and often resorted to negative campaigning. They denounced Jefferson as an athiest, a Jacobin, and the father of mulatto children, all charges without foundation (although the last has been repeated many times since).

The balloting for presidential electors took place between October and December 1800. Adams took all the New England states, while Jefferson captured the South and West. The outcome in New York and Pennsylvania threw the election to Jefferson. Jefferson called it the Revolution of 1800. Party discipline was so effective that one of the provisions of the Constitution was shown to be badly outmoded. By this provision, the candidate receiving a majority of electoral votes became president and the runner-up became vice president. But by casting all their ballots for Jefferson and Burr, Republican electors unintentionally created a tie and forced the election into the House of Representatives. Because the new Republican-controlled Congress would not convene until March 1801, the Federalist majority was given a last chance to decide the election. They attempted to make a deal with Burr, who refused but would not withdraw his name from consideration. Finally, on the thirty-fifth ballot the Federalists gave up and arranged with their opponents to elect Jefferson without any of them having to cast a single vote in his favor. Congressman Lyon cast the symbolic final vote in a gesture of sweet revenge. The Twelfth Amendment, creating separate ballots for president and vice president, was ratified in time for the next presidential election.

With the rise of partisan politics came a transformation in political participation. In 1789 state regulations limited the franchise to a small percentage of the adult population. Women, African Americans, and Indians could not vote, but neither could a third to a half of all free adult males, who were excluded by taxpaying or property-owning requirements. Moreover, among the eligible, the turnout was generally low. The traditional manner of voting was *viva voce*, by voice. At the polling place in each community individuals announced their selections aloud to the clerk of elections, who wrote them down. Not surprisingly, this system allowed wealthy men, landlords, and employers of the community to pressure voters.

These practices changed with the increasing competition between Republicans and Federalists. Popular pressure resulted in the introduction of universal white manhood suffrage in four states by 1800 and the reduction of property requirements in others. Thus was inaugurated a movement that would sweep the nation over the next quarter century. The growth of popular interest in politics was a transformation as important as the peaceful transition from Federalists to Republicans in national government.

"The Rising Glory of America"

In 1771, Philip Freneau and Henry Hugh Brackenridge read their epic poem, "The Rising Glory of America," to their graduating class at Princeton, admitting that thus far American contributions to learning had been slim, but expressing their optimism about their country's potential. Indeed, judged against the record of the colonial period, the Revolutionary generation accomplished a great deal in their effort to build a national culture.

The Liberty of the Press

At the beginning of the Revolution in 1775 there were thirty-seven weekly or semiweekly newspapers in the thirteen colonies, only seven of which were Loyalist in sentiment. By 1789 the number of papers in the United States had grown to ninety-two, including eight dailies; three papers were being published west of the Appalachians. Relative to population, there were more newspapers in the United States than in any other country in the world—a reflection of the remarkably high literacy rate of the American people (see Chapter 5). In New England readers approached 90 percent of the population, and even on the frontier about two-thirds of the male population were literate. During the political controversy of the 1790s, the press became the principal medium of Federalist and Republican opinion, and papers came to be identified by their politics.

The prosecutions under the Sedition Act, however, threatened to curb the further development of the media, and in their opposition to these measures Republicans played an important role in establishing the principle of a free press. In *An Essay on Liberty of the Press* (1799), Virginia lawyer George Hay, later appointed to the federal bench by President Jefferson, wrote that "a man may say everything which his passions suggest." Were this not true, would he argued, the First Amendment would have been "the grossest absurdity that was ever conceived by the human mind." In his first inaugural address Jefferson echoed this early champion of the freedom of expression. "Error of opinion may be tolerated," he declared, "where reason is left free to combat it."

The Birth of American Literature

The literature of the Revolution understandably reflected the dominating political concerns of the times. The majority of best-sellers during the Revolutionary era were political. The most important were Thomas Paine's *Common Sense* (1776) and his series of stirring pamphlets, published under the running title *The American Crisis* (1776–83), the first of which began with the memorable phrase "These are the times that try men's souls."

During the post-Revolutionary years there was an enormous outpouring of American publications. In the cities the number of bookstores grew in response to the demand for reading matter. Perhaps even more significant was the appearance in the countryside of numerous book peddlers who supplied farm households with Bibles, gazettes, almanacs, sermons, and political pamphlets.

Some of the most interesting American books of the postwar years examined the developing American character and proposed that the American, a product of many cultures, was a "new man" with ideas new to the world. John Filson, the author of the *Discovery, Settlement, and Present State of Kentucke* (1784), presented the narrative of one such new man, Kentucky pioneer Daniel Boone. In doing so he took an important step toward the creation of the most American literary genre, the western.

Mason Locke Weems, a man trained as a doctor and ordained an Anglican minister, gave up both these careers in the 1790s for bookselling and writing. Parson Weems, as he was known, wrote a short biography of the first president. His *Life of Washington* (1800, enlarged edition 1806), became the most popular history

In this 1792 cartoon from The Lady's Magazine *the allegorical figure of "Columbia" receives a petition for the "Rights of Woman." Many Federalists condemned "women of masculine minds," but there was general agreement among both conservatives and democrats that the time had come for better education for American women.*

of the Revolution and introduced a series of popular and completely fabricated anecdotes, including the story of young Washington and the cherry tree. Condemned by serious writers and scholars, even at the time of its publication, Weem's biography was loved by ordinary Americans of all political persuasions. In the mid-nineteenth century Abraham Lincoln recalled that he had read Weems "away back in my childhood, the earliest days of my being able to read," and had been profoundly impressed by "the struggles for the liberties of the country."

Women on the Intellectual Scene

One of the most interesting literary trends of the 1790s was the growing demand for books that appealed to women readers. Although women's literacy rates continued to be lower than men's, they rose steadily as girls joined boys in common schools. This increase was one of the most important social legacies of the democratic struggles of the Revolutionary era.

Some writers argued that the new republican order ought to provide new roles for women as well as for men. The first avowed feminist in American history was Judith Sargent Murray, who publicly stated her belief that women "should be taught to depend on their own efforts, for the procurement of an establishment in life." She was greatly influenced by English feminist Mary Wollstonecraft.

There seemed to be general agreement among all parties that the time had come for better-educated and -informed women. Republican institutions of self-government were widely thought to depend on the wisdom and self-discipline of the American people. Civic virtue, so indispensable for the republic, must be taught at home. Thus were women provided the opportunity to be not simply "helpmates," but people "learned and wise." But they were also expected to be content with a narrow role, to not wish for fuller participation in American democracy.

Conclusion

In 1800 Canada numbered about 500,000 persons. Those of European background in New Mexico and the other Spanish North American colonies constituted approximately 25,000. The Indian people of the continent made up anywhere from 500,000 to a million. Overwhelming all these groups was the population of the United States, which stood at 5.3 million and was growing at the astounding annual rate of 3 percent. During the last decade of the eighteenth century the United States had adopted a new constitution and established a new national government. It had largely repaid the debt run up during the Revolution and made peace with adversaries abroad and Indian peoples at home. Americans had begun to learn how to channel their disagreements into political struggle. The nation had withstood a first decade of stress, but tensions continued to divide the people. At the beginning of the new century it remained uncertain whether the new nation would find a way to control and channel the energies of an expanding people.

CHRONOLOGY

1786	Annapolis Convention
1787	Constitutional Convention
1787–88	*The Federalist* published
1788	Constitution ratified
	First federal elections
1789	President George Washington inaugurated in New York City
	Judiciary Act
	French Revolution begins
1790	Agreement on site on the Potomac River for the nation's capital
	Indian Intercourse Act
	Judith Sargent Murray publishes "On the Equality of the Sexes"
1791	Bill of Rights ratified
	Bank of the United States chartered
	Alexander Hamilton's "Report on Manufactures"
	Ohio Indians defeat General Arthur St. Clair's army
1793	England and France at war; America reaps trade windfall
	Citizen Genêt affair
	President Washington proclaims American neutrality in Europe
	British confiscate American vessels
	Supreme Court asserts itself as final authority in *Chisholm* v. *Georgia*
1794	Whiskey Rebellion
	Battle of Fallen Timbers
	Jay's Treaty with the British concluded
1795	Pinckney's Treaty negotiated with the Spanish
	Treaty of Greenville
	Thomas Paine publishes *The Age of Reason*
1796	President Washington's farewell address
	John Adams elected president
1797–98	French seize American ships
1798	XYZ Affair
	"Quasi-war" with France
	Alien and Sedition Acts
	Kentucky and Virginia Resolves
1799	Fries's Rebellion
1800	Convention of 1800
	Thomas Jefferson elected president
	Mason Locke Weems publishes *Life of Washington*

Review Questions

1. Discuss the conflicting ideals of local and national authority in the debate over the Constitution.
2. What were the major crises faced by the Washington and Adams administrations?
3. Describe the roles of Madison and Hamilton in the formation of the first American political parties.
4. What did Jefferson mean when he talked of "the Revolution of 1800"?
5. Discuss the contributions of the Revolutionary generation to the construction of a national culture.

Recommended Reading

WILLIAM N. CHAMBERS, *Political Parties in a New Nation: The American Experience, 1776–1809* (1963). An introduction to the formation of the American party system. Though several decades old, it remains essential.

STANLEY ELKINS AND ERIC MCKITRICK, *The Age of Federalism* (1993). A massive and informative account of the politics of the 1790s, from the ratification of the Constitution to the election of Jefferson.

JOSEPH J. ELLIS, *After the Revolution: Profiles of Early American Culture* (1979). A series of portraits of the more important cultural innovators in the young republic.

JAMES T. FLEXNER, *Washington, The Indispensable Man* (1974). The best one-volume biography of "the Father of His Country."

REGINALD HORSMAN, *The Frontier in the Formative Years, 1783–1815* (1970). A sensitive survey of developments in the West, emphasizing that the "western question" was one of the most important facing the young republic.

JACKSON TURNER MAIN, *The Antifederalists: Critics of the Constitution, 1781–1788* (1961). A detailed examination of the localist tradition in early American politics. Includes a discussion of the ratification of the Constitution from the point of view of its opponents.

THOMAS P. SLAUGHTER, *The Whiskey Rebellion: Frontier Epilogue to the American Revolution* (1986). A detailed history of the rebellion in western Pennsylvania during the 1790s. Includes a thorough examination of the politics and culture of both the backcountry and the federal government at a moment of crisis.

JAMES M. SMITH, *Freedom's Fetters: The Alien and Sedition Laws and American Civil Liberties* (1966). Remains the best overview of the Federalist threat to liberty, as well as the Democratic Republican counterattack.

GERALD STOURZH, *Alexander Hamilton and the Idea of Republican Government* (1970). A solid biography of the ultimate Federalist man and his politics.

GORDON WOOD, *The Creation of the American Republic, 1776–1787* (1969). This general survey provides the best overview of the Constitutional Convention.

9 AN AGRARIAN REPUBLIC, 1790–1824

AMERICAN COMMUNITIES

EXPANSION TOUCHES MANDAN VILLAGES ON THE UPPER MISSOURI

It was mid-October 1804 when the news arrived at the Mandan villages on the upper Missouri: an American expedition was coming up the river. Meriwether Lewis and William Clark guided their three boats and forty-four men toward the villages, prominently situated on the Missouri bluffs. "Great numbers on both sides flocked down to the bank to view us as we passed," wrote Clark, and that evening the Mandans welcomed the Americans with an enthusiastic dance and gifts of food.

Since the fourteenth century, when they migrated from the East, the Mandans had lived along the Missouri, in what is now North Dakota. The women grew corn, beans, squash, sunflowers, and tobacco on the fertile soil of the river bottom. The men hunted buffalo and traded crops with the nomadic tribes of the plains. Well before any of them had ever met a European they were trading with other tribes for French and English kettles, knives, and guns, and exchanging them for leatherwork, glassware, and horses brought by nomads from the Spanish in the Southwest. The Mandan villages were the central marketplace of the Northern Plains.

The eighteenth century was a golden age for this communal people, who with their closely related Hidasta neighbors numbered about 3,000 people in 1804. In each of their five villages, earth lodges surrounded a central plaza. One large ceremonial lodge was used for community gatherings, and each of the other earth lodges was home to a senior woman, her husband, her sisters (perhaps married to the same man as she, for the Mandans practiced polygamy), their daughters, and their unmarried sons, along with numerous grandchildren. Matrilineal clans, the principal institution of the community, distributed food to the sick, adopted orphans, cared for the dependent elderly, and punished wrongdoers. Male clan leaders made up a village council that selected chiefs, who led solely on the basis of consensus; they lost power when the people no longer accepted their opinions.

Sent by President Jefferson to survey the Louisiana Purchase, and to find an overland route to the Pacific Ocean, Lewis and Clark were also instructed to challenge British economic control over the lucrative North American fur trade by informing the Indians that they now owed loyalty—and trade—to the American government. Meeting with the Council Chiefs the Americans offered the Mandans a military and economic alliance. His people would like nothing better, responded Chief Black Cat, for the Mandans had fallen on hard times over the past decade. "The smallpox [had] destroyed the greater part of the nation" some twenty years before, he said. "All the nations before this malady [were] afraid of them, [but] after they were reduced the Sioux and other Indians waged war, and killed a great many." Black Cat was skeptical that the Americans would deter the Sioux, but Clark reassured him.

Before they resumed their westward journey the next spring, the Americans had become part of the social life that bound the Mandan communities together. There were dances and joint hunting parties. There were frequent visits to the earth lodges, long talks around the fire, and, for many of the men, pleasant nights in the company of Mandan women. The Mandans drew charts and maps from which Lewis and Clark gained critical information on the course and distances of the Missouri, the ranges of the Rocky Mountains, and the crossing of the Continental Divide. The information and support of the Mandans and other Indian peoples to the West was vital to the success of the expedition. Lewis and Clark's voyage of discovery depended largely on the willingness of Indian peoples to tell the Americans about geographical matters that were familiar to the natives themselves.

Before long the Americans had established Fort Clark at the Mandan villages, giving American traders a base for challenging British dominance of the western fur trade. The permanent American presence brought increased contact, and with it much more disease. In 1837 a terrible smallpox epidemic carried away the vast majority of the Mandans, reducing the population to fewer than 150. In return for the kindness of the Mandans, the Americans had brought this plague.

In sending Lewis and Clark on their momentous journey to claim the land and the loyalty of the Mandans and other western Indian communities, President Jefferson was motivated by his vision of an expanding American republic of self-sufficient farmers. During his and succeeding presidencies, expansion became a key element of national policy and pride. Yet, as the experience of the Mandans showed, expansion was paradoxical. What Jefferson viewed as enlargement of "the empire for liberty" caused the death and destruction of the communities created by America's first peoples. The effects—economic, political, and social—of continental expansion dominate the history of American communities in the first half of the nineteenth century.

KEY TOPICS

◆ **The development of America's economy in a world of warring great powers**

◆ **The role of Jefferson's presidency and his agrarian republicanism in forging a national identity**

◆ **The ending of colonial dependency by the divisive War of 1812**

◆ **Westward expansion becomes a nationalizing force**

The Growth of American Communities from Coast to Coast

At first glance, the United States of America in 1800 seemed little changed from the scattered colonies of the pre-Revolution era. A long, thin line of settlements still clung to the eastern seacoast and two-thirds of the nation's people still lived within fifty miles of the Atlantic Ocean. From New Hampshire to Georgia, most people lived on farms or in small towns. Because few people had traveled far from home, their horizons were limited and local.

Nevertheless, the new nation was already transforming itself, not held back by nature but plunging more deeply into it. Between 1790 and 1800, according to the first and second federal censuses, the American population grew from 3.9 to 5.3 million. Growth was most rapid in the trans-Appalachian west, a region that was home to about 100,000 Indians. From 1800 to 1850, in an extraordinary burst of territorial expansion, Americans surged westward all the way to the Pacific. Few people in the 1800 would have imagined that in fifty years America would be a continental nation.

A National Economy

In 1800 the United States was a producer of raw materials. The new nation forced the same challenge that confronts developing nations today. Such countries are at the mercy of fluctuating world commodity prices that they cannot control, and have great difficulty protecting their domestic economies from the economic dominance of stronger, more established nations.

The Economy of the Young Republic

The United States was predominantly rural and agricultural in 1800. According to the census of 1800, 94 in 100 Americans lived in communities of fewer than 2,500 people and four in five families farmed the land, either for themselves or for others. Farming families followed centuries-old traditions of working with hand tools and draft animals, producing most of their own food and fiber. Crops were generally intended for home use. Commodities such as whiskey and hogs (both easy to transport, one in kegs and the other on the hoof) provided small and irregular cash incomes or items for barter. As late as 1820, only 20 percent of the produce of American farms was consumed outside the local community.

By contrast with the farms of the North, the plantation agriculture of the South was wholly commercial and international. The demand for cotton grew rapidly, accompanying the boom in the industrial production of textiles in England and Europe. The cotton gin, invented in 1793, enabled the South to increase production of this export commodity, for which there was an almost infinitely expanding demand.

The century turned, however, before cotton assumed a commanding place in the foreign trade of the United States. In 1790 increasing foreign demand for American goods and services hardly seemed likely. Trade with Britain, still the biggest customer for American raw materials, was considerably less than it had been before the Revolution. Americans were largely excluded by the British from the lucrative West Indian trade, and their ships were taxed with discriminatory duties.

Shipping and the Economic Boom

Despite these restrictions, the strong shipping trade begun during the colonial era and centered in the Atlantic ports unexpectedly became a major asset in the 1790s, when events in Europe provided America with extraordinary opportunities. The French Revolution, which began in 1789, marked the start of twenty-five years of continual warfare between Britain and France. All along the Atlantic seaboard, urban centers thrived as American ships carried European goods that could no longer be transported on British ships without danger of French attack (and vice versa). Because America was neutral, its merchants had the legal right to import European goods and promptly reexport them to other European countries without breaking international neutrality laws. Total exports tripled in value from 1793 to 1807, with reexports accounting for half of the total.

The vigorous international shipping trade had dramatic effects within the United States. The coastal cities all grew substantially in the period 1790–1820. This rapid urbanization was a sign of vigorous economic growth, rather than a sign that poverty was pushing rural workers off the farms (as occurs in some Third World countries today). It reflected expanding opportunities in the cities. In fact, the rapid growth of cities stimulated farmers to produce the food to feed the new urban dwellers.

The long series of European wars also allowed enterprising Americans to seize such lucrative international opportunities as the China trade. In 1784 the *Empress of China* set sail from New York for Canton with forty tons of ginseng. When it returned in 1785 with a cargo of teas, silks, and chinaware, the sponsors of the voyage made a 30 percent profit. Other merchants were quick to follow.

The active American participation in international trade fostered a strong and diversified shipbuilding industry. All of the major Atlantic ports boasted expanding shipbuilding enterprises. Demands for speed increased as well, resulting in what many people have regarded as the flower of American shipbuilding, the clipper ship. Built for speed, the narrow-hulled, many-sailed clipper ships of the 1840s and 1850s set records unequaled by any other ships of their size. In 1854 *Flying Cloud,* built in the Boston shipyards of Donald McKay, sailed from Boston to San Francisco—a 16,000-mile trip that usually took 150 to 200 days—in a mere 89 days.

The Jefferson Presidency

At noon on March 4, 1801, Thomas Jefferson walked from his modest boardinghouse through the swampy streets of the new federal city of Washington to the unfinished Capitol to begin his presidency. Washington and Adams had ridden in carriages to their inaugurals. Jefferson, refusing even a military honor guard, demon-

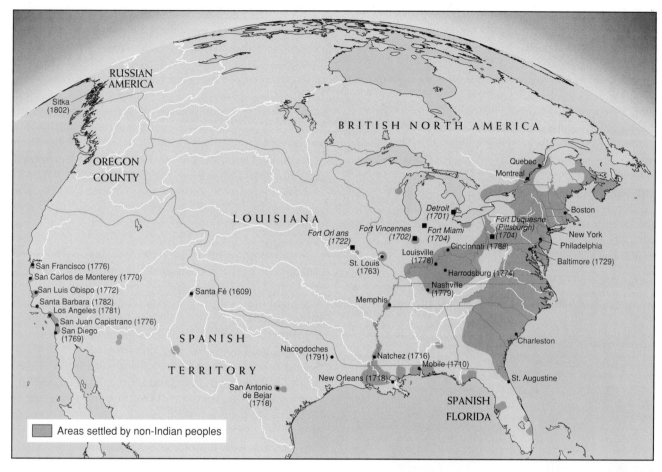

America in 1800

In 1800, the new United States of America was surrounded by territories held by the European powers: British Canada, French Louisiana (secretly ceded that year to France by Spain), Spanish Florida, Spanish Mexico, and Russian Alaska expanding southward along the Pacific coast. Few people could have imagined that by 1850 the United States would span the continent. But the American settlers who had crossed the Appalachians to the Ohio River Valley were already convinced that opportunity lay in the West.

strated by his actions that he rejected the elaborate, quasi-monarchical style of the two Federalist presidents, and their (to his mind) autocratic style of government as well.

For all its lack of pretension, Jefferson's inauguration as the third president of the United States was a truly momentous occasion in American history, for it marked the peaceful transition from one political party, the Federalists, to their hated rivals, the Republicans. One of the greatest achievements of Jefferson's presidency was to demonstrate that a strongly led party system could shape national policy without leading to dictatorship or revolt.

Republican Agrarianism

Jefferson brought to the presidency a clearly defined political philosophy. Behind all the events of his administration (1801–9) and those of his successors in what became known as the Virginia Dynasty (James Madison, 1809–17, and James Monroe, 1817–25) was a clear set of beliefs that embodied Jefferson's interpretation of the meaning of republicanism for Americans.

During his years as ambassador to France in the 1780s, Jefferson came to believe that it was impossible for Europe to achieve a just society that could guarantee to most of its members the "life, liberty and . . .

pursuit of happiness" of which he had written in the Declaration of Independence. Only America, Jefferson believed, provided fertile earth for the true citizenship necessary to a republican form of government. Governments that encouraged concentrations of wealth and inequalities between rich and poor, as the Europeans did, destroyed the possibility of republicanism.

Jefferson envisaged a nation of small family farms clustered together in rural communities—an agrarian republic. He believed that only a nation of roughly equal yeoman farmers, each secure in his own possessions and not dependent on someone else for his livelihood, would exhibit the concern for the community good that was essential in a republic. Indeed, Jefferson said that "those who labor in the earth are the chosen people of God," and so he viewed himself, though his "farm" was the large slave-owning plantation of Monticello.

Jefferson's pessimism about the inevitable injustice of European societies seemed to be confirmed by the failure

Tall, ungainly, and diffident in manner, Thomas Jefferson was nonetheless a man of genius, an architect, naturalist, political philosopher, and politician.

Charles Wilson Peale, "The Artist in His Museum." Oil on canvas, 103 ¾″ × 79 ⅞″. Courtesy of the Pennsylvania Acadamy of the Fine Arts. Gift of Mrs. Sarah Harrison. (The Joseph Harrison, Jr. Collection)

of the French Revolution. By 1799, the electrifying revolutionary cry of "*Liberté, égalité, fraternité*" had been replaced by the military dictatorship of Napoleon Bonaparte. Another European development, the growth of the factory system in England, seemed almost as horrifying. Jefferson was not alone in deploring the environmental and personal squalor of teeming new factory towns such as Manchester in the north of England. He opposed industrialization in America: in the 1790s, when Alexander Hamilton and the Federalists had proposed fostering manufactures in the United States, Jefferson had responded with outrage (see Chapter 8). He was convinced that the Federalist program would create precisely the same extremes of wealth and poverty and the same sort of unjust government that prevailed in Europe.

Jefferson's vision of an expanding agrarian republic remains one of the most compelling statements of American uniqueness and special destiny. But expansionism contained some negative aspects. The lure of the western lands fostered constant mobility and dissatisfaction rather than the stable, settled communities of yeoman farmers that Jefferson envisaged. Expansionism caused environmental damage, in particular soil exhaustion—a consequence of abandoning old lands, rather than conserving them, and moving on to new ones. Finally, expansionism bred a ruthlessness toward the Indian peoples, who were pushed out of the way for white settlement or who, like the Mandans, were devastated by the diseases that accompanied European trade and contact. Jeffersonian's agrarianism thus bred some of the best and some of the worst traits of the developing nation.

Jefferson's Government

Thomas Jefferson came to office determined to reverse the Federalist policies of the 1790s and to ensure an agrarian "republic of virtue." Accordingly he proposed a program of "simplicity and frugality," promising to cut all internal taxes, reduce the size of the army (from 4,000 to 2,500 men), navy (from twenty-five ships to seven), and government staff, and to eliminate the national debt. He kept all of these promises, even the last, although the Louisiana Purchase of 1803 cost the Treasury $15 million. This diminishment of government was a key republican principle to Jefferson. If his ideal yeoman farmer was to be a truly self-governing citizen, the federal government must not, he believed, be large or powerful.

Perhaps one reason for Jefferson's success was that the federal government he headed was small and unimportant by today's standards. The national government's main function for ordinary people was mail delivery. Everything else—law and order, education, welfare, road maintenance, economic control—rested with state or local governments. Power and political loyalty were still local, not national.

This limited authority also explains why for years the nation's capital was so small and unimpressive. Construction lagged on the president's House and the Capitol. Instead of the imposing dome we know so well today, the early Capitol consisted of two white marble boxes connected by a boardwalk. It is a telling indicator of the true location of national power that a people who had no trouble building new local communities across the continent should have had such difficulty establishing their federal city.

An Independent Judiciary

Despite his desire to revise Federalist fiscal policies, Jefferson allowed 132 Federalists to remain at their posts. However, this leniency did not extend to the notorious Federalist appointees, the so-called midnight judges.

In the last days of the Adams administration, the Federalist-dominated Congress passed a Judiciary Act that created new judgeships and circuit courts. In one of his last acts before leaving office, President Adams appointed Federalists—"midnight judges"—to the new positions. This last-minute action angered the Republicans, who had won control of Congress as well as the presidency in the 1800 election. In 1801 the Republican Congress repealed the Judiciary Act, rendering the new Federalist judges unemployed.

At issue was a fundamental constitutional point: was the judiciary independent of politics? In his celebrated 1803 decision, *Marbury* v. *Madison,* Chief Justice John Marshall, himself a strong Federalist and an Adams appointee, unequivocally defended the independence of the judiciary and the principle of judicial review. On the other hand, he conceded that the Supreme Court could not force the executive branch to appoint judges to positions that no longer existed. At first glance, Jefferson's government appeared to have won the battle. But in the long run, Marshall established the principle that only the federal judiciary could decide what was constitutional. This was a vital step in realizing the three-part balance of power envisaged in the Constitution among the executive, legislative, and judicial branches of government. During his long tenure in office (1801–35) Chief Justice Marshall consistently led the Supreme Court in a series of decisions that favored the federal government over state

governments. Under Marshall's direction, the Supreme Court became a powerful nationalizing and unifying force.

Opportunity: The Louisiana Purchase

In 1800 the United States was a new and fragile democracy in a world of contending great powers: Great Britain and France. This rivalry appeared to threaten American commerce and national security.

In 1799 the young general Napoleon Bonaparte seized control of France and began a career of military conquests. As had his predecessors, Napoleon looked at North America as a potential battleground on which to fight the British. In 1800, in a secret treaty, Napoleon acquired the Louisiana Territory, the vast western drainage of the Mississippi and Missouri rivers, from Spain, which had held the region since 1763. From Louisiana, if he chose, Napoleon could launch an attack to regain Canada from the British.

When President Jefferson learned of the secret agreement in 1801, he feared that French control would choke the growing American trade on the Mississippi River and force the young nation to take military action. In fact, in 1802 the Spanish commander at New Orleans (the French had not yet taken formal control) closed the port to American shippers, thus disrupting commerce as far away as Cincinnati. As Jefferson feared, Federalists in Congress clamored for military action to reopen it.

Responding to these events, Jefferson instructed James Monroe and Robert R. Livingston to buy New Orleans and the surrounding area (then known as West Florida) from France for $2 million (or up to $10 million, if necessary). Meanwhile Napoleon had decided that there were better military opportunities closer to hand in Europe. He offered the entire Louisiana Territory, including the crucial port of New Orleans, to the Americans for $15 million. Exceeding their instructions, Monroe and Livingston seized the opportunity and bought the entire Louisiana Territory from Napoleon in Paris in April 1803. The size of the United States doubled overnight. It was the largest peaceful acquisition of territory in United States history. Jefferson now argued that the Louisiana Purchase was vital to the nation's republican future. "By enlarging the empire of liberty," Jefferson wrote, "we . . . provide new sources of renovation, should its principles, at any time, degenerate, in those portions of our country which gave them birth." In other words, expansion was essential to liberty.

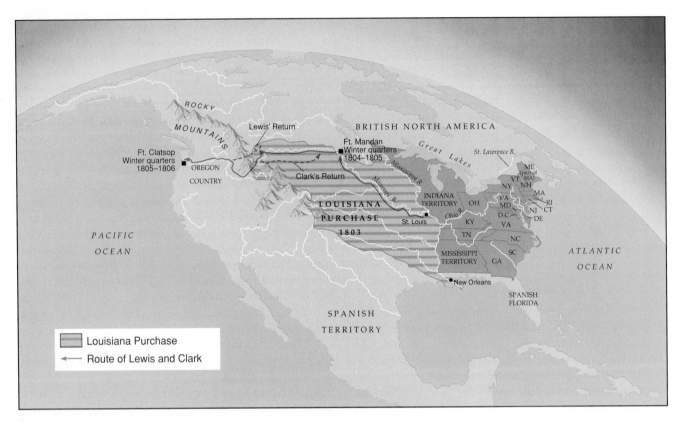

Louisiana Purchase

The Louisiana Purchase of 1803, the largest peaceful acquisition of territory in United States history, more than doubled the size of the nation. The Lewis and Clark Expedition, (1804–6) was the first to survey and document the area.

Incorporating Louisiana

The immediate issue following the Louisiana Purchase was how to treat the French and Spanish inhabitants of Louisiana Territory. Many people thought that the only way to deal with a population so "foreign" was to wipe out its customs and laws and impose American ones as quickly as possible. But this did not happen. The incorporation of Louisiana into the American federal system was a remarkable story of adaptation between two different communities—American and French.

In 1803, when the region that is now the state of Louisiana became American property, it had a racially and ethnically diverse population of 43,000 people, of whom only 6,000 were American. The French community of New Orleans effectively challenged the initial American plan of rapidly supplanting French culture and institutions with American ones. Over the next four years William Claiborne, governor of Lower Louisiana Territory, came to accept the value of French institutions to the region. As a result, with Claiborne's full

support, the Louisiana legal code established in 1808 was based on French civil law rather than English common law. This was not a small concession. French law differed from English law in many fundamental respects, such as family property (communal versus male ownership), inheritance (forced heirship versus free disposal), and even contracts, which were much more strictly regulated in the French system. Remnants of the French legal system remain part of Louisiana state law to this day. In 1812, with the required 60,000 inhabitants Louisiana was admitted to the Union. New Orleans remained for years a distinctively French city, illustrating the flexibility possible under a federal system.

Texas and the Struggle for Mexican Independence

Spain objected, in vain, to Napoleon's 1803 sale of Louisiana to America. For years Spain had attempted to seal off its rich colony of Mexico from commerce with other nations. Now, however, American Louisiana shared a vague and disputed boundary with Mexico's northern province of Texas (a parcel of land already coveted by some Americans).

In 1808, as Napolean's wars for European domination convulsed Spain, the country's long-prized New World empire began to slip away. Mexico, divided between royalists loyal to Spain and populists seeking social and economic justice for mestizos and Indians, edged bloodily toward independence. In 1810 and 1813, two populist revolts—led by Father Miguel Hidalgo and Father José Maria Morelos, respectively—were suppressed by the royalists. In 1812 a small force led by Mexican republican Bernardo Gutiérrez but composed mostly of American adventurers invaded Texas, capturing San Antonio, assassinating provincial governor Manuel Salcedo, and declaring Texas independent. A year later, however, the Mexican republicans were defeated by a royalist army that then killed suspected collaborators and pillaged Texas so thoroughly that the local economy was devastated and the Mexican population declined to fewer than 2,000. Mexico's difficult path toward independence seemed, at least to some Americans, to offer a ripe opportunity for expansion.

Renewed Imperial Rivalry in North America

Fresh from the triumph of the Louisiana Purchase, Jefferson scored a major victory over Federalist Charles Coteswoth Pinckney in the presidential election of 1804, garnering 162 electoral votes to Pinckney's 14. Jefferson's shrewd wooing of moderate Federalists had been so successful that the remaining Federalists dwindled to a highly principled but sectional group unable to attract voters outside of its home base in New England. Jefferson's Louisiana success was not repeated, however, few other consequences of the ongoing power struggle between Britain and France were so easy to solve.

Problems with Neutral Rights

In his first inaugural address in 1801, Jefferson had announced a foreign policy of "peace, commerce, and honest friendship with all nations, entangling alliance with none." This was a difficult policy to pursue after 1803, when the Napoleonic Wars resumed. By 1805 Napoleon had conquered most of Europe, but Britain, the victor at the great naval battle of Trafalgar, controlled the seas. The United States, trying to profit from

trade with both countries, was caught in the middle. The British did not look kindly on their former colonists trying to evade their blockade of the French by claiming neutrality. Beginning in 1805, the British targeted the American reexport trade between the French West Indies and France by seizing American ships bringing such goods to Europe. Angry Americans viewed such seizures as violations of their neutral rights as shippers.

An even more contentious issue arose from the substantial desertion rate of British sailors. Many deserters promptly signed up on American ships, where they drew better pay and sometimes obtained false naturalization papers as well. As many as a quarter of the 50,000 to 100,000 seamen on American ships were British. Soon the British were stopping American merchant vessels and removing any man they believed to be British, regardless of his papers.

At least 6,000 innocent American citizens suffered this impressment from 1803 to 1812. In 1807 impressment turned bloody when the British ship *Leopard* fired on the American ship *Chesapeake* in American territorial waters during the search for deserters. An indignant public protested British interference and the death of innocent sailors.

The Embargo Act

Jefferson, indignant as anyone, could not find a solution to the controversy over neutral rights. He first tried diplomatic protests, then negotiations, and finally threats, all to no avail. In 1806 Congress passed the Non-Importation Act, hoping that a boycott of British goods, which had worked so well during the Revolutionary War, would be effective once again. It was not: the British would not negotiate. Finally, in desperation, Jefferson imposed the Embargo Act in December 1807, forbidding American ships to sail to any foreign port, thereby cutting off all exports as well as imports. In addition to loss of markets, British industry was now deprived of the raw materials the ships customarily bought from the United States.

The Embargo Act proved a disaster for American trade. Exports fell from $108 million in 1807 to $22 million in 1808, and the nation was driven into a deep depression. There was widespread evasion of the embargo. A remarkable number of ships in the coastal trade found themselves "blown off course" to the West Indies or Canada. Other ships simply left port illegally. Smuggling flourished. Pointing out that the American navy's weakness was largely caused by the deep cuts

HISTORY AND THE LAND

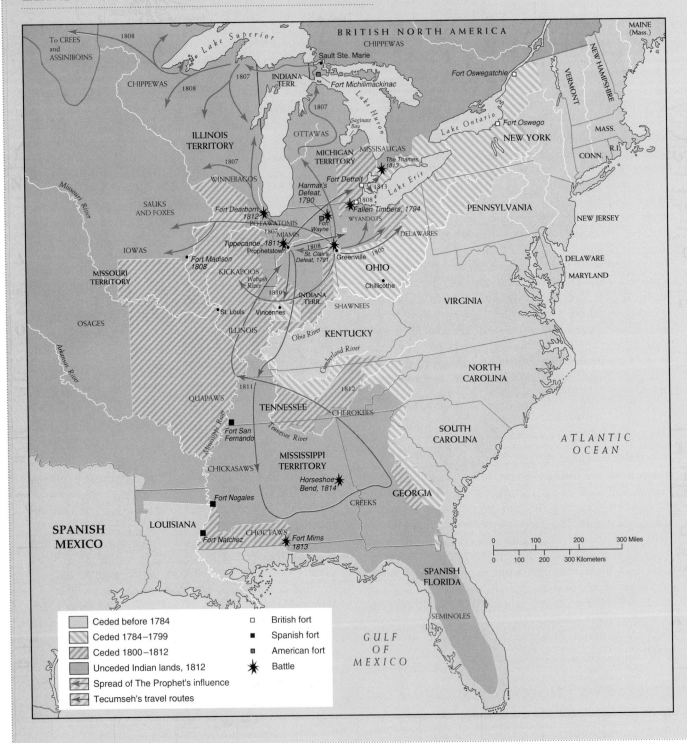

To CREES and ASSINIBOINS

1808

1808

CHIPPEWAS

BRITISH NORTH AMERICA

Lake Superior

CHIPPEWAS

Sault Ste. Marie

Fort Michilimackinac

Fort Oswegatchie

MAINE (Mass.)

VERMONT

NEW HAMPSHIRE

1807

1807

INDIANA TERR.

ILLINOIS TERRITORY

OTTAWAS

Saginaw Bay

Lake Huron

Lake Ontario

Fort Oswego

NEW YORK

MASS.

CONN.

R.I.

MICHIGAN TERRITORY

MISSISAUGAS

The Thames, 1813

Fort Detroit

1813

Lake Erie

PENNSYLVANIA

NEW JERSEY

WINNEBAGOS

1807

SAUKS AND FOXES

Fort Dearborn 1812

POTAWATOMIS

1807

MIAMIS

Harmar's Defeat, 1790

1808

Fallen Timbers, 1794

WYANDOTS

Fort Wayne

DELAWARES

1805

DELAWARE

MARYLAND

IOWAS

Tippecanoe, 1811 Prophetstown

1808

St. Clair's Defeat, 1791

Greenville

OHIO

MISSOURI TERRITORY

Fort Madison 1808

KICKAPOOS

Wabash River

1810

INDIANA TERR.

Chillicothe

VIRGINIA

Missouri River

OSAGES

St. Louis

Vincennes

ILLINOIS

SHAWNEES

Ohio River

KENTUCKY

Cumberland River

NORTH CAROLINA

Arkansas River

QUAPAWS

1811

1812

TENNESSEE

CHEROKEES

Tennessee River

SOUTH CAROLINA

ATLANTIC OCEAN

Fort San Fernando

CHICKASAWS

MISSISSIPPI TERRITORY

Horseshoe Bend, 1814

GEORGIA

SPANISH MEXICO

LOUISIANA

Fort Nogales

CHOCTAWS

Fort Natchez

Fort Mims 1813

CREEKS

SPANISH FLORIDA

SEMINOLES

GULF OF MEXICO

	Scale
0 100 200 300 Miles	
0 100 200 300 Kilometers	

Legend:
- Ceded before 1784
- Ceded 1784–1799
- Ceded 1800–1812
- Unceded Indian lands, 1812
- Spread of The Prophet's influence
- Tecumseh's travel routes
- □ British fort
- ■ Spanish fort
- ▪ American fort
- ✴ Battle

INDIAN RESISTANCE, 1790–1816

American westward expansion put relentless pressure on the Indian nations in the trans-Appalachian South and West. The Trans-Appalachian region was marked by constant warfare from the time of the earliest settlements in Kentucky in the 1780s to the War of 1812. Tecumseh's Alliance in the Northwest (1809–11) and the Creek Rebellion in the Southwest (1813–14) were the culminating struggles in Indian resistance to the American invasion of the Trans-Appalachian region. Tecumseh, a Shawnee military leader (left), and his brother Tenskwatawa, a religious leader called the Prophet (right), led a pan-Indian revitalization and resistance movement that posed a serious threat to American westward expansion. As the map shows,

Tenskwatawa's message had wide appeal in the Northwest. Tecumseh traveled widely, attempting to build a military alliance on his brother's spiritual message. He achieved considerable success in the Northwest, but less in the Southwest, where large numbers of Indian peoples put their faith in accommodation. British abandonment of their Shawnee allies at the end of the War of 1812 and Tecumseh's death at the Battle of Thames (1813) marked the end of organized Indian resistance in the Old Northwest. In the South, Andrew Jackson crushed Creek resisters in the Battle of Horseshoe Bend in 1814, and then demanded the cession of 23 million acres of land from both hostile and friendly Creek peoples.

Jefferson had inflicted on it, the Federalists sprang to life with a campaign of outspoken opposition to Jefferson's policy and found a ready audience in New England, hardest hit by the embargo.

Madison and the Failure of "Peaceable Coercion"

In this troubled atmosphere, Thomas Jefferson despondently ended his second term, acknowledging the failure of what he called "peaceable coercion." He was followed in office by his friend and colleague, James Madison of Virginia. Madison received 122 electoral votes to only 47 for the Federalist ticket of Charles Pinckney and Rufus King. Nevertheless the Federalists' total marked a threefold increase over their share of the 1804 vote.

In March 1809 Congress admitted failure, and the Embargo Act was repealed. But the struggle to remain neutral in the confrontation between the European giants continued. The next two years saw passage of several acts—among them the Non-Intercourse Act of 1809 and Macon's Bill Number 2 in 1810—that unsuccessfully attempted to prohibit trade with Britain and France unless they ceased their hostile treatment of U.S. shipping. Frustration with the ineffectiveness of government policy mounted.

A Contradictory Indian Policy

Arguments with Britain and France over neutral shipping rights were not the only military troubles the United States faced. In the West the powerful Indian nations of the Ohio Valley were determined to resist the wave of expansion that had carried thousands of white settlers onto their lands. North of the Ohio River lived the Northwest Confederation of the Shawnee, Delaware, Miami, Potawatomi, and a number of smaller tribes. To the south of the Ohio were five major groups: the Cherokees, Creeks, Choctaws, Chickasaws, and (in Florida) the Seminoles.

According to United States policy toward Indian peoples since the Intercourse Act of 1790, Indian lands must be ceded by treaty rather than simply seized. But the reality of westward expansion was much harsher. Commonly, settlers pushed ahead of treaty boundaries. When Indian peoples resisted the invasion of their lands, the pioneers fought back and called for military protection. Defeat of an Indian people led to further land cessions and made almost inevitable a cycle of invasion, resistance, and military defeat.

Thomas Jefferson was deeply concerned with the fate of the western Indian peoples. Convinced that Indians had to give up hunting in favor of the yeoman-farmer lifestyle he so favored for all Americans, Jefferson directed the governors of the Northwest Territory, Michigan Territory, and Indiana Territory to "promote energetically" his vision of civilizing the Indians, which included Christianizing them and teaching them to read. Many Indian peoples actively resisted these efforts at conversion. In addition, Jefferson's Indian civilization plan was never fully supported by territorial governors and settlers.

Indian Resistance

The Shawnees, a hunting and farming tribe (the men hunted, the women farmed) of the Ohio Valley, had resisted white settlement in Kentucky and Ohio since the 1750s.

The decisive defeat at Fallen Timbers in 1794 and the continuing pressure of American settlement split the Shawnees. One group, led by Black Hoof, accepted assimilation. Soon Quaker and Moravian missionaries were converting Black Hoof's band and teaching them farming. Most of the other Shawnees broke into small bands and tried to eke out a living by hunting, but they were struck down by disease and by alcohol offered them illegally by private traders. One group of traditional Shawnees, led by the warrior Tecumseh moved farther west and attempted to continue their traditional seminomadic life of hunting and farming.

But there was no escape from white encroachment. Between 1801 and 1809, William Henry Harrison, governor of Indiana Territory, concluded fifteen treaties with the Delaware, Potawatomi, Miami, and other tribes. These treaties opened eastern Michigan, southern Indiana, and most of Illinois to white settlement and compressed the Indians into ever-smaller reservations. Many of these treaties were obtained by coercion, bribery, and outright trickery, and most Indians did not accept them.

In 1805 Tecumseh's brother, Tenskwatawa, known as the Prophet, began preaching a message of Indian revitalization: a return to traditional ways and a rejection of all contact with the Americans. Tenskwatawa urged his listeners to reject American alcohol, clothing, and trade goods and to return to traditional practices of hunting and farming. If the Northwest Indians returned to traditional ways, he promised, "the land will be overturned so that all the white people will be covered and you alone shall inhabit the land."

Tenskwatawa's message enabled Tecumseh to mold his brother's religious following into a powerful pan-Indian resistance movement. With each new treaty that Harrison concluded, Tecumseh gained new followers among the Northwest Confederation tribes. Importantly, he also had the support of the British in nearby Canada.

The pan-Indian strategy was at first primarily defensive, aimed at preventing further westward expansion. But the Treaty of Fort Wayne in 1809, in which the United States gained 3 million acres of Delaware and Potawatomi land in Indiana, led to active resistance. Confronting Harrison directly, Tecumseh argued that the land belonged to the larger community of all the Indian peoples; no one tribe could give away the common property of all. He then warned that any surveyors or settlers who ventured into the 3 million acres would be risking their lives.

Tecumseh took his message of common land ownership and military resistance to all the Indian peoples of the Northwest Confederacy. He was not uniformly successful even among the Shawnees. Black Hoof, for example, refused to join.

Tecumseh also recruited among the tribes south of the Ohio River. In councils with Choctaws, Chickasaws, Creeks, and Cherokees, he preached a stark message of resistance to the white man's destructive culture. But the southern tribes, who had chosen assimilation, refused to join with Tecumseh.

In November of 1811, while Tecumseh was still recruiting among the southern tribes, Harrison marched to the pan-Indian village of Tippecanoe with 1,000 soldiers. The 600 to 700 Indian fighters at the town, urged on by Tenskwatawa, attacked Harrison's forces before dawn on November 7, hoping to surprise them. The attack failed, and in the battle that followed, the Americans inflicted about 150 Indian casualties while sustaining about as many themselves. Although Harrison claimed victory, the truth was far different. Dispersed from Tippecanoe, Tecumseh's angry followers fell upon American settlements in Indiana and southern Michigan, killing many pioneers and forcing the rest to flee to fortified towns. Tecumseh entered into a formal alliance with the British. For western settlers, the Indian threat was greater than ever.

The War of 1812

Many westerners blamed the British for Tecumseh's attacks on pioneer settlements in the Northwest. British support of western Indians and the long-standing difficulties over neutral shipping rights were the two grievances cited by President Madison when he asked Congress for a declaration of war against Britain on June 1, 1812; Congress obliged him on June 18. But the war had other, more general causes as well.

A rising young generation of political leaders, first elected to Congress in 1810, felt a strong sense of colonial resentment against Britain, the former mother country. These War Hawks, who included such future leaders as Henry Clay of Kentucky and John C. Calhoun of South Carolina, were young Republicans from the South and West. They found all aspects of continuing British dominance, such as impressment and the support of western Indians, intolerable. The War Hawks were eager to strike a blow for national honor by assert-

The War of 1812

On land, the War of 1812 was fought to define the nation's boundaries. In the north, American armies attacked British forts in the Great Lakes region with little success, and the invasion of Canada was a failure. On the sea, British dominance was so complete and their blockade so effective that British troops were able to invade the Chesapeake and burn the capital of the United States.

ing complete independence from England once and for all. They also wanted to occupy Florida to prevent runaway slaves from seeking refuge with the Seminole Indians. Westerners wanted to invade Canada, hoping thereby to end threats from British-backed Northwest Indians such as Tecumseh. What powered these dreams of expansion, then, was a desire to control peoples of other races at the edges of the national boundaries.

President James Madison yielded to the War Hawks' clamor for action in June of 1812. Not realizing that the British, hurt by the American trade embargo, were on the verge of adopting a more conciliatory policy, he declared war.

Madison's declaration of war passed the U.S. Senate by the close vote of 19 to 13 and the House by 79 to 49. All the Federalists voted against the war. (The division along party lines continued in the 1812 presidential election, in which Madison garnered 128 electoral votes to 89 for his Federalist opponent, DeWitt Clinton.) The vote was sectional, with New England and the Middle Atlantic states in opposition and the West and South strongly prowar. Thus the United States entered the War of 1812 more deeply divided along sectional lines than in any other foreign war in American history.

The Americans had a few glorious moments, but on the whole the War of 1812 was an ignominious struggle that gained them little. As a result of Jefferson's economizing, the American army and navy were small and weak. In contrast, the British, fresh from almost ten years of Napoleonic Wars, were in fighting trim. The British navy quickly established a strong blockade, harassing coastal shipping along the Atlantic seaboard and attacking coastal settlements at will. In the most humiliating attack, the British burned Washington in the summer of 1814, forcing the president and Congress to flee. There were a few American military successes. Commodore Oliver Perry's ships defeated a British fleet on Lake Erie in 1813, whereupon Perry sent the famous message "We have met the enemy and they are ours." In early 1815 (after the peace treaty had been signed) Andrew Jackson improbably won a lopsided victory over veteran British troops in the Battle of New Orleans.

The New England states opposed the war. Massachusetts, Rhode Island, and Connecticut refused to provide militia or supplies, and other New England governors turned a blind eye to the flourishing illegal trade across the U.S.–Canadian border. Opposition to the war culminated in the Hartford Convention of 1814, where Federalist representatives from the five New England states met to discuss their grievances. At first the air was full of talk of secession from the Union, but soon cooler heads prevailed.

The convention did insist, however, that a state had the right "to interpose its authority" to protect its citizens against unconstitutional federal laws. This *nullification* threat from Hartford was ignored, for peace with Britain was announced as delegates from the convention made their way to Washington to deliver their message to Congress. There the convention's grievances were treated not as serious business but as an anticlimactic joke.

By 1814 the long Napoleonic Wars in Europe were slowly drawing to a close. and the British decided to end their war with the Americans. The peace treaty, after months of hard negotiation, was signed at Ghent, Belgium, on Christmas Eve in 1814. Like the war itself, the treaty was inconclusive. The major issues of impressment and neutral rights were not mentioned, but the British did agree to evacuate their western posts, and late in the negotiations they abandoned their insistence on a buffer state for neutral Indian peoples in the Northwest.

For all its international inconsequence, the war did have an important effect on national morale. Andrew Jackson's victory at New Orleans allowed Americans to believe that they had defeated the British. It would be more accurate to say that by not losing the war the Americans had ended their own feelings of colonial dependency. Equally important, they convinced the British government to stop thinking of America as its colony.

The War of 1812 was one of America's most divisive wars, arousing more intense opposition than any other American conflict, including Vietnam. Today most historians regard the war as both unnecessary and a dangerous risk to new and fragile ideas of national unity. Fortunately for its future, the United States as a whole came out unscathed, and the Battle of New Orleans had provided last-minute balm for its hurt pride.

The only clear losers of the war were the northwestern Indian nations and their southern allies. With the death of Tecumseh at the Battle of the Thames in 1813 and the defeat of the Southern Creeks in 1814, the last hope of a united Indian resistance to white expansion perished forever. Britain's abandonment of its Indian allies in the Treaty of Ghent sealed their fate. By 1815 American settlers were on their way west again.

Defining the Boundaries

With the War of 1812 behind them, Americans turned, more seriously than ever before, to the tasks of expansion and national development.

Another Westward Surge

The end of the War of 1812 was followed by a westward surge to the Mississippi River and beyond, which populated the Old Northwest (Ohio, Indiana, Illinois) and the Old Southwest (western Georgia, Alabama, Mississippi, Louisiana). The extent of the population redistribution was dramatic: in 1790, 95 percent of the nation's population had lived in states bordering the Atlantic Ocean; by 1820 fully 25 percent of the population lived west of the Appalachians.

What accounted for the westward surge? There were both push and pull factors. Between 1800 and 1820, the nation's population almost doubled, increasing from 5.3 million to 9.6 million. Overpopulated farmland in all of the seaboard states pushed farmers off the land, while new land pulled them westward. Defeat and removal of the Indians by the War of 1812 was another important pull factor.

Geography facilitated lateral westward movement (northerners tended to migrate to the Old Northwest, southerners to the Old Southwest). Except in southern Ohio and parts of Kentucky and Tennessee, there was very little contact between regional cultures. New Englanders carried their values and lifestyles directly west and settled largely with their own communities, and southerners did the same, as the following two examples show.

One section of northern Ohio known as the Western Reserve had been Connecticut's western land claim since the days of its colonial charter. Revolutionary general Moses Cleaveland led one of the first groups of Yankees, fifty-two in all to the Western Reserve. In 1795 they settled the community that bears his name (though not his spelling of it). Many other groups followed, naming towns such as Norwalk after those they had left in Connecticut. These New Englanders brought to the Western Reserve their religion (Congregational), their love of learning (tiny Norwalk soon boasted a three-story academy), and their adamant opposition to slavery.

A very different migration occurred in the South. Even before the War of 1812, plantation owners in the Natchez district of Mississippi had made fortunes growing cotton, which they shipped to Britain from New Orleans. After the war, as cotton growing expanded, hopeful slave owners from older parts of the South (Virginia, North and South Carolina, Georgia) flooded into the Old Southwest, and so, involuntarily, did their slaves. The movement was like a gold rush, characterized by high hopes, land speculation, and riches for a few. Most of the settlers in the Old Southwest were small farmers living in forest clearings. Most did not own slaves, but they hoped to, for ownership of slaves was the means to wealth. Quickly, the lifestyle and values of older southern states were replicated on this new frontier. More than half of the people who flooded into the Old Southwest after 1812 were enslaved African Americans.

This western transplantation of distinctive regional cultures explains why, although by 1820 western states accounted for over a third of all states (eight out of twenty-three), the West did not form a third unified political region. In general, communities in the Old Northwest shared New England political attitudes, whereas those in the Old Southwest shared southern attitudes.

The Election of 1816 and the Era of Good Feelings

In 1816 James Monroe, the last of the Virginia Dynasty was easily elected president over his Federalist opponent, Rufus King (183 to 34 electoral votes). This was the last election in which the Federalists ran a candidate. Monroe had no opponent in 1820 and was reelected nearly unanimously (231 to 1). The triumph of the Republicans appeared complete.

Tall, dignified, dressed in the old-fashioned style of knee breeches and white-topped boots that Washington had worn, Monroe looked like a traditional figure. But he exemplified a new mood. A Boston newspaper characterized the mood as an Era of Good Feelings, a phrase that has been applied to Monroe's presidency (1817–25) ever since.

Monroe sought a government of national unity, and he chose men from North and South, Republicans and Federalists, for his Cabinet. He selected John Quincy Adams, a former Federalist, as his secretary of state, virtually ensuring that Adams, like his father, would become president. To balance Adams, Monroe picked John C. Calhoun of South Carolina, a prominent War Hawk, as secretary of war. And Monroe supported the American System, a program of national economic development that became identified with westerner Henry Clay, speaker of the House of Representatives.

In supporting the American System, Monroe was following President Madison, who had proposed the program in his message to Congress in December 1815. Madison and Monroe broke with Jefferson's agrarianism to embrace much of the Federalist program for economic development, including the chartering of a national bank, a tax on imported goods to protect American manufacturers, and a national system of roads and canals. All three of these had first been proposed by Alexander Hamilton in the 1790s (see Chapter 8). At the time they had met with bitter Republican opposition. The support that Madison and Monroe gave to Hamilton's ideas following the War of 1812 was a crucial sign of the dynamism of the American commercial economy. Many Republicans now acknowledged that the federal government had a role to play in fostering the economic and commercial circumstances in which both yeoman farmer and merchant could succeed.

In 1816 Congress chartered the Second Bank of the United States for twenty years. Located in Philadelphia, the bank was to provide large-scale financing that the smaller state banks could not handle, and to create a strong national currency. Because they feared concentrated economic power, Republicans had allowed the charter of the original Bank of the United States, founded in 1791, to expire in 1811. The Republican about-face in 1816 was a sign that the strength of commercial interests had grown to rival that of farmers, whose distrust for central banks persisted.

The Tariff of 1816 was the first substantial protective tariff in American history. In 1815 British exports, which had been excluded for eight years, flooded the United States. American manufacturers complained that the British were dumping their goods below cost to prevent the growth of American industries. Congress responded with a tariff on imported woolens and cottons, iron, leather, hats, paper, and sugar. The measure had southern as well as northern support, although in later years the passage of higher tariffs would become one of the most persistent sources of sectional conflict.

The third item in the American System, funding for roads and canals—internal improvements, as they came to be known—was also destined for long-standing contention. Monroe and Madison both believed it was unconstitutional for the federal government to pay for anything but genuinely national (that is, interstate) projects. Congressmen, however, aware of the urgent need to improve transportation in general and scenting the possibility of funding for their districts, proposed spending federal money on local projects. Both Madison and Monroe vetoed such proposals. Thus it was that some of the most famous projects of the day, such as the Erie Canal (see Chapter 10) and the early railroads, were financed by state or private money.

The support of Madison and Monroe for measures initially identified with their political opposition was an indicator of their realism. The three aspects of the American System—bank, tariff, roads—were all parts of the basic infrastructure that the American economy needed to develop. Despite the support for them during the Era of Good Feelings, they would later become hot sources of partisan argument.

Diplomatic Achievements

The diplomatic achievements of the Era of Good Feelings were due almost entirely to the efforts of one man, John Quincy Adams, Monroe's secretary of state. Adams set himself the task of tidying up the borders of the United States. In two accords with Britain, the Rush–Bagot Treaty of 1817 and the Convention of 1818, the border between the United States and Canada was demilitarized and fixed at the forty-ninth parallel; west of the Rocky Mountains, joint occupancy of Oregon was agreed upon for ten (eventually twenty) years. The American claim to Oregon (present-day Washington, Oregon, northern Idaho, and parts of Montana) was based on China trader Robert Gray's discovery of the Columbia River in 1792, and on the Lewis and Clark expedition of 1804–6.

Adams's major diplomatic accomplishment, however, was his skill at wresting concessions from the faltering Spanish Empire. In the Adams–Onis Treaty of 1819, Spain, preoccupied with revolts in its Latin American Empire, ceded not only Florida, but all previous claims to the entire Louisiana Territory. In return, the U.S. assumed $5 million in U.S. citizens' claims against Spain and relinquished an American claim to Texas.

Finally, Adams picked his way through the minefield of Spain's disintegrating Latin American empire to the policy that bears his president's name, the Monroe Doctrine. The United States was the first country outside Latin America to recognize the independence of Spain's former colonies, Argentina, Chile, Columbia, and Mexico, all of which had broken free by 1822. When the European powers (France, Austria, Russia, and Prussia) began talk of a plan to help Spain recover these lost colonies, what was the United States to do? The British, always suspicious of Continental European powers, proposed a British–American declaration against European intervention in the hemisphere. Some Americans might have been flattered by an approach from the British empire, but Adams would have none of it. Showing the national pride that was so characteristic of the era, he insisted on an independent American policy. He therefore drafted for the president the hemispheric policy that the United States has followed ever since.

On December 2, 1823, the president presented the Monroe Doctrine to Congress and the world. It called for the end of colonization of the Western Hemisphere by European nations (this was aimed as much at Russia and its West Coast settlements as at other European powers). It declared that intervention by European powers in the affairs of the independent New World nations would be considered by the United States a danger to its own peace and safety. Finally, the Monroe Doctrine pledged that the United States would not interfere in the affairs of European countries or in the affairs of their remaining New World colonies.

All of this was a very large bark from a very small dog. In 1823 the United States lacked the military and economic force to back up its grand statement. In fact, what kept the European powers out of Latin America was British opposition to European intervention, enforced by the Royal Navy.

This string of diplomatic achievements—the treaties with Britain and Spain and the Monroe Doctrine—were a fitting end to the period dominated by the Virginia Dynasty, the enlightened revolutionaries who did so much to shape the new nation.

The Panic of 1819

Across this impressive record of political and economic nation building fell the shadow of the Panic of 1819. A delayed reaction to the end of the War of 1812 and the Napoleonic Wars, the panic forced Americans to come to terms with their economic place in a peaceful world. The American shipping boom came to an end as British merchant ships resumed their earlier trade routes. American farmers, as well as American shippers, were hurt by diminished international demand for American foodstuffs as European farms resumed production after the long wars.

Domestic economic conditions made matters worse. The western land boom that began in 1815 turned into a speculative frenzy that ended with a sharp contraction of credit by the Second Bank of the United States in 1819. State banks were forced to foreclose on many bad loans. Many western farmers were ruined, and they blamed the faraway Bank of the United States for their troubles. In the 1830s Andrew Jackson would build a political movement on their resentment.

Urban workers suffered both from the decline in international trade and from manufacturing failures caused by competition from British imports. As they lobbied for local relief, they became deeply involved in urban politics, where they could express their resentment against the merchants and owners who had laid them off. Thus developed another component of Andrew Jackson's new political coalition.

Another confrontation arose over the tariff. Southern planters, hurt by a decline in the price of cotton, began to actively protest the protective tariff, which kept the price of imported goods high even when cotton prices were low. Manufacturers, hurt by British competition, lobbied for even higher rates, which they achieved in 1824 over southern protests. Southerners then began to raise doubts about the fairness of a political system in which they were always outvoted.

The Panic of 1819 was a symbol of this transitional time. It showed how far the country had moved since 1800 from Jefferson's republic of yeoman farmers toward commercial activity. And the anger and resentment expressed by the groups harmed by the depression—farmers, urban workers, and southern planters—were portents of the politics of the upcoming Jackson era.

The Missouri Compromise

In the Missouri crisis of 1819–21 the nation confronted for the first time a momentous issue that had been buried in the general enthusiasm for expansion: as America expanded, would slavery expand as well? Until 1819, this question was decided regionally. The Northwest Ordinance of 1787 explicitly banned slavery in the northern section of trans-Appalachia but made no mention of it elsewhere. Because so much of the expansion into the Old Northwest and Southwest was lateral (northerners stayed in the north, southerners in the south), there was little conflict over sectional differences. In 1819, however, the sections collided in Missouri, which applied for admission to the Union as a slave state.

The northern states, most of which had abolished slavery by 1819, looked askance at the extension of slavery. Southerners, on the other hand, did not believe that Congress had the power to limit the expansion of slavery. They were alarmed that northerners were considering national legislation on the matter. Slavery, in southern eyes, was a question of property, and therefore was a matter for state rather than federal legislation. Thus, from the very beginning, the expansion of slavery raised constitutional issues. Indeed, the aging politician of Monticello, Thomas Jefferson, immediately grasped the seriousness of the question of the expansion of slavery. As he prophetically wrote to a friend, "This momentous question like a fire bell in the night, awakened and filled me with terror. I considered it at once the [death] knell of the Union."

In 1819 Representative James Tallmadge, Jr., of New York began more than a year of congressional controversy when he demanded that Missouri agree to the gradual end of slavery as the price of entering the Union. At first, the public paid little attention, but northern religious reformers (Quakers prominent among them) organized a number of antislavery rallies

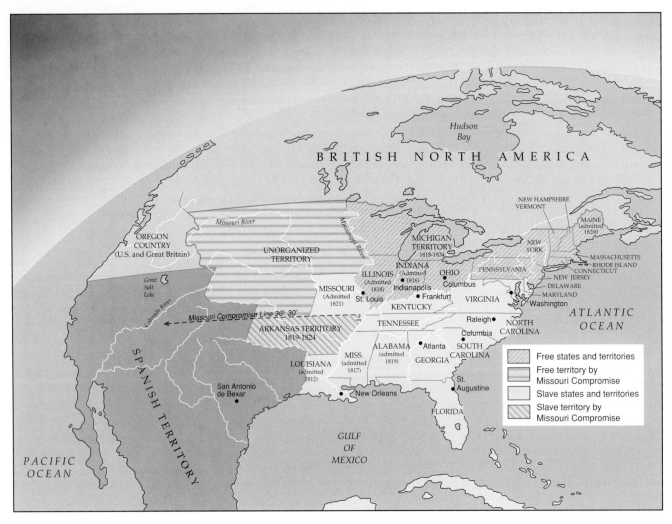

The Missouri Compromise, 1820

Before the Missouri Compromise of 1820, the Ohio River was the dividing line between the free states of the Old Northwest and the slaveholding states of the Old Southwest. The Compromise stipulated that Missouri would enter the Union as a slave state (balanced by Maine, a free state), but slavery would be prohibited in the Louisiana Territory north of 36°30' (Missouri's southern boundary). This awkward compromise lasted until the Mexican-American War of 1846 reopened the issue of the expansion of slavery.

that made politicians take notice. Former Federalists in the North, who had seen their party destroyed by the achievements of Jefferson and his successors in the Virginia Dynasty, seized upon the Missouri issue eagerly. This was the first time that the growing northern reform impulse had intersected with sectional politics. It was also the first time that southern threats of secession were made openly in Congress.

The Senate debate over the admission of Missouri, held in the early months of 1820, was the nation's first extended debate over slavery. Observers noted the high proportion of free African Americans among the listeners in the Senate gallery. But the full realization that the future of slavery was central to the future of the nation was not apparent to the general public until the 1850s.

In 1820 Congress achieved a compromise over the sectional differences when Henry Clay forged the first of the many agreements that were to earn him the title of the Great Pacificator (peacemaker). The Missouri Compromise maintained the balance between free and slave states by admitting Maine (which had been part of Massachusetts) as a free state in 1820 and Missouri as a slave state in the following year. It also enacted a policy with respect to slavery in the rest of the Louisiana Purchase: slavery was to be prohibited north of 36 degrees north latitude—the southern boundary of Missouri—and permitted south of that line. This meant that the vast majority of the Louisiana Territory would be free. In reality, then, the Missouri Compromise could be only a temporary solution because it left open the question of how the balance between slave and free states would be maintained.

Conclusion

In complex ways a developing economy, geographical expansion, and even a minor war helped shape American unity. Locally, small, settled face-to-face communities in both the North and the South began to send their more mobile, expectant members to new occupations in urban centers or west to form new settlements, where they displaced Indian communities in the process.

The westward movement was the novel element in the American national drama. Europeans believed that large size and a population in motion bred instability and political disintegration. Thomas Jefferson thought otherwise, and the Louisiana Purchase was the gamble that confirmed his guess. The westward population movement dramatically changed the political landscape and Americans' view of themselves.

Expansion would not create the settled communities of yeoman farmers Jefferson had hoped for. Rather, it would breed a nation of restless and acquisitive people and a new kind of national democratic politics that reflected their search for broader definitions of community.

CHRONOLOGY

1790s	Second Great Awakening begins
1800	Thomas Jefferson elected president
1803	Louisiana Purchase
	Marbury v. *Madison*
	Ohio admitted to the Union
1804	Lewis and Clark expedition begins
	Thomas Jefferson reelected president
1807	*Chesapeake–Leopard* incident
	Embargo Act
1808	James Madison elected president
1809	Tecumseh forms military alliance among Northwest Confederacy peoples
1811	Battle of Tippecanoe
1812	War of 1812 begins
	James Madison reelected president
	Louisiana admitted to the Union
1814	Hartford Convention
	Treaty of Ghent
1815	Battle of New Orleans
1816	James Monroe elected president
	Congress charters Second Bank of the United States
	Indiana admitted to the Union
1817	Mississippi admitted to the Union
1818	Illinois admitted to the Union
1819	Panic of 1819
	Adams–Onís Treaty
	Alabama admitted to the Union
1819–20	Missouri Crisis and Compromise
1820	James Monroe reelected president
	Maine admitted to the Union
1821	Missouri admitted to the Union as a slave state
1823	Monroe Doctrine

Review Questions

1. What economic and political problems did the United States face as a new nation in a world dominated by war between Britain and France? How successful were the efforts by the Jefferson, Madison, and Monroe administrations to solve these problems?

2. The anti-European cast of Jefferson's republican agrarianism made it appealing to many Americans who wished to believe in their nation's uniqueness, but how realistic was it in the real world of politics during Jefferson's administration?

3. Some Federalists opposed the Louisiana Purchase, warning of the dangers of westward expansion. What are arguments for and against expansion?

4. The confrontations between Tecumseh's alliance and soldiers and settlers in the Old Northwest reveal the contradictions in American Indian policy. What were these contradictions? Can you suggest solutions to them?

5. What did the War of 1812 accomplish?

6. What issues made it impossible for the Era of Good Feelings to last?

Recommended Reading

FRANK BERGON, ED., *The Journals of Lewis and Clark* (1989). A handy abridgment of the fascinating history of the expedition. (For more intensive study, Gary Moulton's six-volume unabridged edition of the expedition journals is unsurpassed.)

GEORGE DRAGO, *Jefferson's Louisiana: Politics and the Clash of Legal Traditions* (1975). Illuminating example of the cultural flexibility of the federal system.

R. DAVID EDMUNDS, *Tecumseh and the Quest for Indian Leadership* (1984). A sympathetic portrait.

JOHN MACK FARAGHER, *Sugar Creek* (1987). The fullest examination of the lives of pioneers in the Old Northwest.

DONALD HICKEY, *The War of 1812: A Forgotten Conflict* (1989). Takes a fresh look at the events and historiography of the war.

DREW McCOY, *The Elusive Republic: Political Economy in Jeffersonian America* (1980). The most useful discussion of the ties between expansion and republican agrarianism.

GLOVER MOORE, *The Missouri Controversy, 1819–1821* (1953). The standard account.

CURTIS P. NETTELS, *The Emergence of a National Economy, 1775–1815* (1962). A useful overview.

MERRILL PETERSON, *Thomas Jefferson and the New Nation* (1970). A good one-volume biography of Jefferson. (The major biography, by Dumas Malone, is a multivolume work.)

JAMES RONDA, *Lewis and Clark Among the Indians* (1984). An innovative look at the famous explorers through the eyes of the Indian peoples they encountered.

AMERICAN COMMUNITIES

MARTIN VAN BUREN FORGES A NEW KIND OF POLITICAL COMMUNITY

When Martin Van Buren left Albany for Washington in the fall of 1821 to take up his new position as junior senator from New York, he left behind more than ten years of intense activity in New York State politics in which he and his allies, nicknamed the Bucktails (for the Indian-inspired insignia, the tail of a buck, that members wore on their hats), created one of the first modern democratic political parties. How could it be, Washington politicians asked, that this short, invariably pleasant but rather nondescript man had triumphed over the renowned DeWitt Clinton?

Tall, handsome, arrogant DeWitt Clinton, governor of New York since 1817, represented old-style politics. An aristocrat in wealth, connections, and attitude, Clinton ran the New York Democratic Republican Party as though it was his personal property, dispensing patronage to his relatives and friends on the basis of their loyalty to him rather than their political principles. Swept into office in 1817 on a tide of popularity generated by his promotion of a statewide canal, Clinton soon gained legislative approval for the project. The result was the Erie Canal, the most ambitious and successful canal project of the era.

Martin Van Buren, the man who engineered Clinton's downfall, was a new kind of politician. Van Buren was the son of a tavern keeper, not a member of the wealthy elite. Raised in the small Dutch-dominated town of Kinderhook, New York, Van Buren never lost his resentment of the aristocratic landowning families who had disdained him when he was young. Masking his anger with charming manners, Van Buren took advantage of the growing strength of the Democratic Republican Party in New York State to make a different kind of career in politics. By 1819, Van Buren had gathered together enough other disgruntled Democratic Republicans to form the Bucktail faction and openly challenge Clinton for control of the party. Two years later, the state constitutional convention of 1821 (three-fourths of whose delegates were Bucktails) sealed their victory.

The convention voted to streamline the organization of state government and sharply curtail the patronage powers of the governor. To cement these changes, delegates enacted nearly total manhood suffrage: all adult male citizens who paid state or local taxes, served in the militia, or worked on state roads—more than four-fifths of the adult male population—were now eligible to vote directly for state legislators, governor, and members of Congress. This dramatic democratization of politics reflected the state's changing population. Already the bustling port of New York was the nation's largest city, and commercial opportunity was attracting shrewd Yankee traders from New England. The old ruling families, failing to recognize the new commercial and social attitudes of the newcomers, were losing their grip on politics.

Responding to the state's diverse and growing population, Martin Van Buren and the Bucktails formulated a new kind of political community. The Bucktails asserted that a political party should be a democratic organization, expressing the will of all its members. Party loyalty, rather than personal opinion or friendship, became the bond that kept the party together. Leaders were now the most loyal, not the most aristocratic.

Van Buren's friends and allies, called the Albany Regency, ran New York State politics for twenty years. For all those years Martin Van Buren was in Washington, where he was a major architect of the new democratic politics of mass participation that has been called the Second American Party System. This new movement created, for the first time in American history, national communities of political partisans. The sources and expression of the new politics were linked to wider economic and cultural factors that encouraged national cohesion.

KEY TOPICS

◆ **The role of Andrew Jackson's presidency in affirming and solidifying the new democratic politics**

◆ **The part played by the transportation revolution in unifying the nation**

◆ **Establishment of the basic two-party pattern of American political democracy**

◆ **The creation of a distinctive American cultural identity by writers and artists**

The New Democratic Politics

The early years of the nineteenth century were a time of extraordinary growth and change for the new republic. Economic development in the early nineteenth century increased the difference between the nation's two major regions: the South committed itself to cotton growing and the slave system, and the North moved rapidly to a commercial, industrializing economy. Although North and South were still economically interconnected, the two sections were on very different paths. Had the United States of America consisted only of the thirteen original states, North–South compromises might well have broken down by the 1820s and split the nation into two parts.

Westward expansion, however, became a nationalizing force. Because of developments in transportation, in 1840 the larger United States was more closely knit than the original thirteen states had been in 1787. And the nine new states west of the Appalachians that entered the Union between 1800 and 1840 contributed their own regional perspective to national politics. Although settlement patterns tended to align people in what is now called the Old Northwest (Ohio, Indiana, Illinois, Wisconsin, and Michigan) with New England and those in the Old Southwest (Mississippi and Alabama) with the South, westerners as a whole shared common concerns and attitudes that national politicians from the two older areas could not ignore.

The Expansion and Limits of Suffrage

Before 1800 most of the original thirteen states limited the vote to property owners or taxpayers, thus permitting less than half the white male population to vote.

Westward expansion changed the nature of American politics. The new western states extended the right to vote to all white males over the age of twenty-one. Kentucky entered the Union with universal manhood suffrage in 1792, Tennessee (1796) and Ohio (1803) with low taxpayer qualifications that approached universal suffrage. Soon older states such as New Jersey (1807) and Maryland (1810) dropped their property qualification for voting. By 1820, most of the older states had followed suit. Some states liberalized voting in the hopes of dissuading disgruntled nonvoters from moving west or because it seemed unfair to recruit men to fight in the War of 1812 but not allow them to vote. There were laggards—Rhode Island, Virginia, and Louisiana did not liberalize their voting qualifications

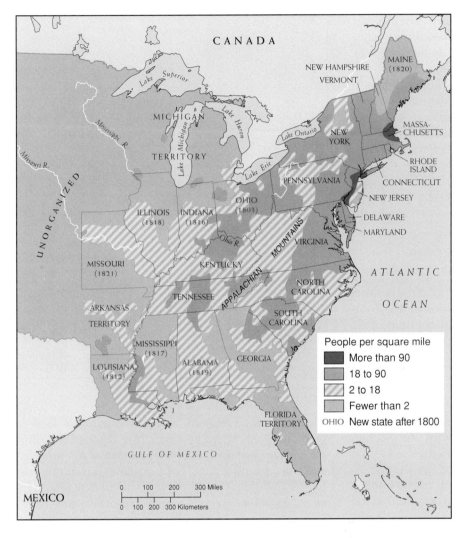

Population Trends: Westward Expansion, 1830

Westward population movement, a trickle in 1800, had become a flood by 1830. Between 1800 and 1830 the U.S. population more than doubled (from 5.3 million to 12.9 million), but the trans-Appalachian population grew tenfold (from 370,000 to 3.7 million). By 1830 more than a third of the nation's inhabitants lived west of the original thirteen states.

until later—but by 1840, more than 90 percent of adult white males in the nation could vote. Governors and (most important) presidential electors were now elected by direct vote, rather than chosen by small groups of state legislators.

However, the right to vote was by no means universal; it was limited to adult white males, and neither free black men nor women of any race could vote. Only in five New England states (Maine, New Hampshire, Vermont, Massachusetts, and Rhode Island) could free black men vote before 1865. Elsewhere in the North the right of free African American men to vote was limited. In 1821 in New York, for example, men had to own property valued at $250 or more, a very high amount at the time. Only 68 of the nearly 13,000 African Americans in New York City in 1825 qualified to vote.

In the new western states, the civil rights of free African Americans were even more restricted. The Ohio constitution of 1802 denied African Americans the rights to vote, hold public office, and testify against white men in court cases. The constitutions of other western states—Illinois, Indiana, Michigan, Iowa, Wisconsin, and, later, Oregon—attempted to solve the "problem" of free African Americans by simply denying them entry into the state at all.

The denial of suffrage to white women stemmed from patriarchal beliefs that men were always heads of their households and represented the interests of all of its members. Women were always subordinate, so even wealthy single women who lived alone were denied the vote, except in New Jersey, where some women voted until 1807. The extension of suffrage to all classes of white males effectively denied women a role in public affairs. Increasingly, as "manhood" rather than property became the qualification for voting, women's participation in politics came to be regarded as inappropriate. Thus, in this period famous for democratization and "the rise of the common man," the exclusion of important groups—women of all races and African American men—marked the limits of liberalization.

All the same, it remained true that nowhere else in the world was the right to vote so widespread as it was in the United States. The extension of suffrage to propertyless farm workers and members of the laboring poor in the nation's cities left European observers wondering: could "mob rule" succeed? The election of 1824 provided the first outline of the answer.

The Election of 1824

The 1824 election marked a dramatic end to the political truce that James Monroe had established in 1817. Of four candidates, all were of the same party (Democratic Republicans): William H. Crawford of Georgia, John Quincy Adams of Massachusetts, Henry Clay of Kentucky, and Andrew Jackson of Tennessee. Jackson was able to use his reputation as a military hero to run as a national candidate. He won the most electoral votes: 99. John Quincy Adams was the runner up with 84.

Because no candidate had a majority, the election was thrown into the House of Representatives, as the election of 1800 had been. Clay threw his support to Adams, the candidate whose political and economic opinions were closest to his own. This was customary: the Constitution gave the House the power to decide, and Clay had every right to advise his followers how to vote. When Adams named Clay his secretary of state, Jackson's supporters promptly accused Clay and Adams of a corrupt bargain, and popular opinion, the new element in politics, agreed. John Quincy Adams served four miserable years as president, knowing that Jackson would challenge him, and win, in 1828.

Organizing Popular Politics

As the election of 1824 showed, the spread of universal manhood suffrage meant a change in popular attitudes that spelled the end of personal, elitist politics. Politicians in other states shared Van Buren's vision of tightly organized, broad-based political groups. In Virginia a group known as the Richmond Junto had control of state politics by 1816, and in Tennessee the Nashville Junto, masterminded by John Overton, held sway by 1822. In New Hampshire, Isaac Hill's Concord Regency was firmly in control by 1825.

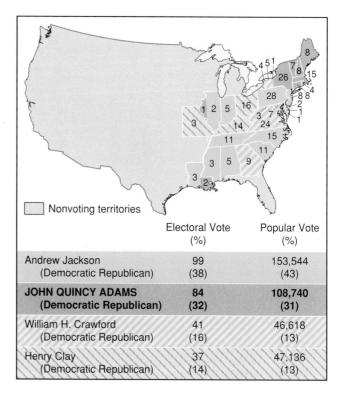

	Electoral Vote (%)	Popular Vote (%)
Andrew Jackson (Democratic Republican)	99 (38)	153,544 (43)
JOHN QUINCY ADAMS (Democratic Republican)	**84 (32)**	**108,740 (31)**
William H. Crawford (Democratic Republican)	41 (16)	46,618 (13)
Henry Clay (Democratic Republican)	37 (14)	47,136 (13)

Nonvoting territories

The Election of 1824

The presidential vote of 1824 was clearly sectional. John Quincy Adams carried his native New England and little else, Henry Clay carried only his own state of Kentucky and two adjoining states, and Crawford's appeal was limited to Virginia and Georgia. Only Andrew Jackson moved beyond the regional support of the Old Southwest to wider appeal and the greatest number of electoral votes. Because no candidate had a majority, however, the election was thrown into the House of Representatives, which chose Adams.

The techniques of mass campaigns—huge political rallies, parades, and candidates with wide name recognition such as military heroes—were quickly adopted by the new political parties. So were less savory techniques such as lavish food and (especially) drink at polling places, which often turned elections into rowdy, brawling occasions.

The spirit that motivated the new mass politics was democratic pride in participation. The party provided some of the same satisfactions that popular sports offer today: excitement, entertainment, and a sense of belonging. But the glue that held political parties together went beyond the appeal of a particular leader or loyalty to one's friends. Political parties were based on genuine differences of political opinion. The task of politicians, as Van Buren recognized, was to emphasize those differences in ways that forged support not just for one election but for permanent, national communities of political interest.

The Election of 1828

The election of 1828 was the first to demonstrate the power and effectiveness of the new party system. With the help of Martin Van Buren, his campaign manager, Andrew Jackson rode the wave of the new democratic politics to the presidency. Jackson's party, the Democratic Republicans (they soon dropped "Republicans" and became simply the Democrats), spoke the language of democracy, and they opposed the special privilege personified for them by President John Quincy Adams and his National Republicans.

Jackson won 56 percent of the popular vote (well over 80 percent in much of the South and West) and a decisive electoral majority of 178 votes to Adams's 83. The vote was interpreted as a victory for the common man. But the most important thing about Jackson's victory was the coalition that achieved it. The new democratically based political organizations—the Richmond and Nashville Juntos, the Albany and Concord Regencies, with help from Calhoun's organization in South Carolina—worked together to elect him. Popular appeal, which Jackson the military hero certainly possessed, was not enough to ensure victory. To be truly national, a party had to create and maintain a coalition of North, South, and West. The Democrats were the first to do this.

The Jackson Presidency

Andrew Jackson's election ushered in a new era in American politics, an era that has been called the Age of the Common Man. Historians have determined that Jackson himself was not a "common" man: he was a military hero, a rich slave owner, and an imperious and decidedly undemocratic personality. Yet he had a mass appeal to ordinary people unmatched—and indeed unsought—by earlier presidents. The secret to Jackson's extraordinary appeal lies in the changing nature of American society. Jackson was the first to respond to the ways in which westward expansion and the extension of the suffrage were changing politics at the national as well as the local and state levels.

A Popular President

On March 4, 1829, Andrew Jackson was inaugurated as president of the United States. The small community of Washington was crowded with strangers, many of them westerners and common people who had come especially for Jackson's inauguration. Jackson's brief inaugural address was almost drowned out by the cheering of the crowd, and after the ceremony the new president was mobbed by well-wishers. The same unrestrained enthusiasm was evident at a White House reception, where the crowd was large and disorderly. People stood on chairs and sofas to catch glimpses of Jackson and shoved and pushed to reach the food and drink, which was finally carried out to the lawn. In the rush to follow, some people exited through windows rather than the doors. All in all, a disapproving observer noted, this behavior indicated the end of proper government and the beginning of "the reign of King Mob." Indeed, Jackson's administration was different from all those before it.

The Nation's Leader vs. Sectional Spokesmen

For all of his western origins, Jackson was a genuinely national figure. He was more interested in asserting strong national leadership than promoting sectional

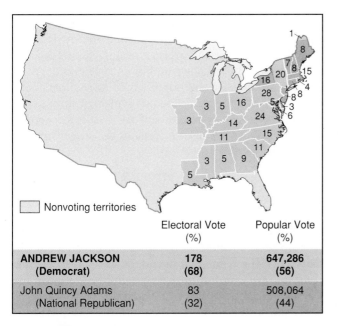

	Electoral Vote (%)	Popular Vote (%)
ANDREW JACKSON (Democrat)	**178** **(68)**	**647,286** **(56)**
John Quincy Adams (National Republican)	83 (32)	508,064 (44)

▢ Nonvoting territories

The Election of 1828

Andrew Jackson's victory in 1828 was the first success of the new national party system. The coalition of state parties that elected him was national, not regional. Although his support was strongest in the South and West, voters in Pennsylvania and New York demonstrated his national appeal.

Until 1829, presidential inaugurations had been small, polite, and ceremonial occasions. Jackson's popularity brought a horde of well-wishers to Washington. As they all arrived to attend Jackson's frontier-style open house at the White House, conservative critics claimed that "the reign of King Mob" had begun.

compromise. He believed that the president, who symbolized the popular will of the people, ought to dominate the government. Voters were much more accustomed to thinking of politics in sectional terms. Jackson faced a Congress full of strong and immensely popular sectional figures. Three stood out: northerner Daniel Webster, southerner John C. Calhoun, and westerner Henry Clay.

Intense, dogmatic, and uncompromising, John C. Calhoun of South Carolina had begun his political career as an ardent nationalist and expansionist in his early days as a War Hawk before the War of 1812. Since the debate over the Missouri Compromise in 1820, however, Calhoun had wholeheartedly identified with southern interests, which were first and foremost the expansion and preservation of slavery.

Senator Daniel Webster of Massachusetts was the outstanding orator of the age. Large, dark, and stern, Webster delivered his speeches in a deep, booming voice that, listeners said, "shook the world." A lawyer for business interests, Webster became the main spokesman for the new northern commercial interests, supporting a high protective tariff, a national bank, and a strong federal government.

In contrast with the other two, Henry Clay of Kentucky, spokesman of the West, was charming, witty, and always eager to forge political compromises. Clay held the powerful position of Speaker of the House of Representatives from 1811 to 1825 and later served several terms in the Senate. A spellbinding storyteller and well known for his ability to make a deal, Clay worked to incorporate western desires for good, cheap transporta-

tion into national politics. He put forward a political agenda that became known as the American System: a national bank, a protective tariff, and internal improvements, by which he meant substantial federal money for roads, canals, and railroads (see Chapter 9). Clay might well have forged a political alliance between the North and the West if not for the policies of President Jackson, his fellow westerner and greatest rival. Jackson's preeminence thwarted Clay's own ambition to be president.

The prominence and popularity of these three politicians show that sectional interests remained strong even under a president as determined as Jackson to override sectional politics and disrupt politics as usual by imposing his own personal style.

A Strong Executive

Andrew Jackson dominated his own administration. With the exception of Secretary of State Van Buren, Jackson ignored most of the heads of government departments who composed his official cabinet. Instead he consulted with an informal group, dubbed the Kitchen Cabinet, made up of Van Buren and old western friends; it did not include John C. Calhoun, the vice-president. Nor was Jackson any friendlier with the two other great sectional representatives: he never forgave Henry Clay for his role in the "corrupt bargain" of 1825, and Daniel Webster represented the privileged elite who were Jackson's favorite target.

Jackson freely used the tools of his office to strengthen the executive branch of government at the expense of the legislature and judiciary. By using the veto more often than all previous presidents combined (twelve vetoes compared with nine by the first six presidents), Jackson forced Congress to constantly consider his opinions. Even more important, Jackson's negative activism restricted federal activity, thereby allowing more power to remain in state hands.

In one of his most famous and unexpected actions, the veto of the Maysville Road Bill of 1830, Jackson refused to allow federal funding of a southern spur of the National Road in Kentucky. Like Presidents James Madison and James Monroe before him, Jackson believed that federal funding for extensive and expensive transportation measures referred to as internal improvements was unconstitutional because it infringed on the reserved powers specified by the Constitution for the states. What made the veto surprising was that Jackson's western supporters strongly desired better transportation. His veto risked that support. But by aiming his message to a popular audience, not just to Congress, and by dramatizing his objection by portraying federal funding as a threat to the popular political principle of states' rights (and by making it clear that he was not opposed to federal funding of all internal improvements), Jackson actually gained political support. He also had the satisfaction of defeating a measure central to the American System proposed by his western rival, Henry Clay.

Internal Improvements: Building an Infrastructure

Despite the ongoing constitutional debate over who should fund internal improvements, this was not an argument over whether they should be funded. Politicians of all persuasions and ordinary people agreed that both federal and state governments had an important role in encouraging economic growth and fostering the development of a national market. Indeed, people expected the state and federal governments to subsidize the costs of building the basic infrastructure—the canals and railroads that tied the national market together.

The Transportation Revolution

The remarkable changes that occurred in transportation in the years from 1800 to 1840 truly constituted a revolution. No single development did more than the improvement of the means of transportation to encourage Americans to look beyond their local communities or to foster the enterprising commercial spirit for which Americans became so widely known.

The commitment of the federal government to the improvement of interregional transportation had significant effects. The National Road, the greatest single federal transportation expense (an eventual total of $7 million), built of gravel on a stone foundation, crossed the Appalachian Mountains at Cumberland, Maryland, thereby opening up the West. Built in stages (to Wheeling by 1818, to Columbus by 1833, to Vandalia, Illinois—almost at the Mississippi River—by 1850), the National Road was strong evidence of the nation's commitment to both expansion and cohesion, for by tying the East and the West together it helped to foster a national community.

Canals and Steamboats

However much they helped the movement of people, the National Road and other roads were unsatisfactory for commercial purposes. Shipment of bulky goods such as grain was too slow and expensive by road. Waterborne transportation was much cheaper, but before the 1820s most water routes were north–south or coastal (Boston to Charleston, for example); east–west links were urgently needed. Canals turned out to be the answer.

The Erie Canal, the most famous canal of the era, was the brainchild of New York governor DeWitt Clinton, who envisioned a link between New York City and the Great Lakes through the Hudson River and a 364-mile-long canal stretching from Albany to Buffalo. When Clinton proposed the canal in 1817 it was derisively called Clinton's Ditch; the longest then existing American canal was only 27 miles long and had taken nine years to build. Nevertheless, Clinton convinced the New York legislature to approve a bond issue, and investors (New York and British merchants) subscribed to the tune of $7 million, an immense sum for the day.

Building the canal—40 feet wide, 4 feet deep, 364 miles long, with 83 locks and more than 300 bridges along the way—was a vast engineering and construction challenge. In the early stages nearby farmers worked for $8 a month, but when malaria hit the work force in the summer of 1819, many went home. They were replaced by 3,000 Irish contract laborers, who were much more expensive—50 cents a day plus room and board—but more reliable (if they survived). The importation of foreign contract labor for this job was a portent of the future. Much of the heavy construction work on later canals and railroads was performed by immigrant labor.

DeWitt Clinton had promised, to general disbelief, that the Erie Canal would be completed in less than ten years, and he made good on his promise. The canal was the wonder of the age. On October 26, 1825, Clinton declared it open in Buffalo and sent the first boat, the *Seneca Chief,* on its way to New York at the incredible speed of four miles an hour. (Ironically, the Seneca Indians, for whom the boat was named, had been "removed" from the path of the canal and confined to a small reservation.) The Erie Canal provided easy passage to and from the interior, both for people and for goods. It drew settlers like a magnet from the East and, increasingly, from overseas: by 1830, 50,000 people a year were moving west on the canal to the rich farmland of Indiana, Illinois, and territory farther west. Earlier settlers now had a national, indeed an international, market for their produce. Moreover, farm families themselves became consumers.

Towns along the canal—Utica, Rochester, Buffalo—became instant cities, each an important commercial center in its own right. Perhaps the greatest beneficiary was the city of New York, which quickly established a commercial and financial supremacy no American city could match. The Erie Canal decisively turned New York's merchants away from Europe and toward America's own heartland, building both interstate commerce and a feeling of community.

The phenomenal success of the Erie Canal prompted other states to construct similar waterways. Between 1820 and 1840, $200 million was invested in canal building. No other waterway achieved the success of the Erie—in its first nine years, the Erie collected $8.5 million in tolls—but most contributed to the building of east–west links.

An even more important improvement in water transportation, was the steamboat. Robert Fulton first demonstrated the commercial feasibility of steamboats in 1807, and they were soon operating in the East. Redesigned with more efficient engines and shallower, broader hulls, steamboats transformed commerce on the country's great inland river system: the Ohio, the Mississippi, the Missouri, and their tributaries. Steamboats were extremely dangerous: frequent boiler explosions led to one of the first public demands for regulation of private enterprise in 1838.

Dangerous as they were, steamboats greatly stimulated trade in the nation's interior. Downstream trade along the Mississippi River system had long been possible, but the long return trip overland on the Natchez Trace had been too arduous and dangerous for most. Cities such as Cincinnati, already notable for its rapid growth, experienced a new economic surge that, like New England shipping of a generation before, increased urbanization and commerce of all kinds. A frontier outpost in 1790, Cincinnati was by the 1830s a center of

steamboat manufacture and machine tool production as well as a central shipping point for food for the southern market. The steamboat was soon a powerful symbol of energy and international commerce.

Railroads

The most remarkable transportation improvement was still to come. Railroads, new in 1830 (when the Baltimore and Ohio Railroad opened with 13 miles of track), grew to an astounding 31,000 miles by 1860. By that date, New England and the Old Northwest had laid a dense network of rails, and several lines had reached west beyond the Mississippi. The South, the least industrialized section of the nation, had fewer railroads. Railroad mania surpassed even canal mania, as investors, as many as one-quarter of them British, rushed to invest in the new invention.

Early railroads, like the steamboat, were forced to solve technological and supply problems.

Until the 1850s, in fact, canalboats and coastal steamers carried more freight than the railroads, and at lower cost. But in the 1850s consolidation of local railroads into larger systems began in earnest, and it was clear that this youngest transportation innovation would have far-reaching social consequences in the future.

Commercial Agriculture in the Old Northwest

Every advance in transportation—better roads, canals, steamboats, railroads—made it easier for farmers to get their produce to market. Improvements in agricultural machinery increased the amount of acreage a farmer could cultivate. These two developments, added to the availability of rich, inexpensive land in the heartland, moved American farmers permanently away from subsistence agriculture and into production for sale.

The impact of the transportation revolution on the Old Northwest was particularly marked. In the 1830s, after the opening of the Erie Canal, migrants from New England streamed into northern Ohio, Illinois, Indiana, southern Wisconsin, and Michigan and began to reach into Iowa. Government policy strongly encouraged western settlement by offering easy terms for federal land sales. Terms by 1820 had eased to $1.25 an acre for 80 acres. Still, this was too much for most settlers to pay all at once. Some people simply squatted, taking their chances that they could make enough money to buy the land before someone else bought it. Less daring settlers relied on credit, which was extended by banks, storekeepers, speculators, promoters,

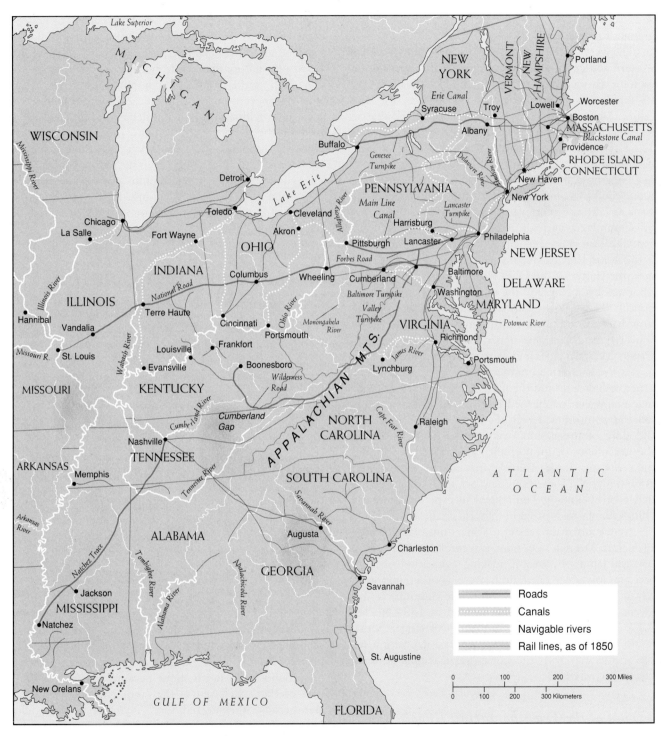

Commercial Links: Rivers, Canals, Roads, 1830, and Rail Lines, 1850

By 1830, the United States was tied together by a network of roads, canals, and rivers. This transportation revolution fostered a great burst of commercial activity and economic growth. Transportation improvements accelerated the commercialization of agriculture by getting farmers' products to wider, nonlocal markets and by providing access to such markets it encouraged new textile and other manufacturers to increase their scale of production. By 1850, another revolutionary mode of transportation, railroads, added another vital link to the transportation infrastructure.

and, somewhat later, railroads, which received large grants of federal lands.

The very need for cash to purchase land involved western settlers in commercial agriculture from the beginning. Farmers, and the towns and cities that grew up to supply them, needed access to markets for their crops. Canals, steamboats, and railroads ensured that access, immediately tying the individual farm into national and international commercial networks. The long period of subsistence farming that had characterized colonial New England and the early Ohio Valley frontier was superseded by commercial agriculture stimulated by the transportation revolution.

Commercial agriculture in turn encouraged regional specialization. Ohioans shipped corn and hogs first by flatboat and later by steamboat to New Orleans. Cincinnati, the center of the Ohio trade, earned the nickname "Porkopolis" because of the importance of its slaughterhouses. By 1840, the national center of wheat production had moved west of the Appalachians to Ohio. Wheat flowed from the upper Midwest along the Erie Canal to eastern cities and increasingly to Europe.

At the same time, farmers who grew wheat or any other cash crop found themselves at the mercy of far-off markets, which established crop prices; distant canal or railroad companies, which set transportation rates; and the state of the national economy, which determined the availability of local credit. This direct dependence on economic forces outside the control of the local community was something new. So, too, was the dependence on technology, embodied in expensive new machines that farmers often bought on credit.

New tools made western farmers unusually productive. John Deere's steel plow (invented in 1837) cut in half the labor of plowing, making cultivation of larger acreages possible. Seed drills were another important advance. But the most remarkable innovation was Cyrus McCormick's reaper, patented in 1834. Earlier, harvesting had depended on manpower alone. A man could cut two or three acres of wheat a day with a cradle scythe, but with the horse-drawn reaper he could cut twelve acres.

Effects of the Transportation Revolution

Every east–west road, canal, and railroad helped to reorient Americans away from the Atlantic and toward the heartland. This new focus was decisive in the creation of national pride and identity. Transportation improvements such as the Erie Canal and the National Road linked Americans together in larger communities of interest beyond the local community in which they lived. Other results were less positive. The technological triumphs of canal building and rail laying fostered a brash spirit of conquest over nature that was to become part of the American myth of the frontier. Furthermore, although every new transportation or communication link broke down local and regional isolation and helped to build a spirit of pride in the nation, it also refocused attention on questions of national politics. The new transportation system caused a subtle political shift, for it strengthened the influence of the North by improving the North's ties with the West more than those of the South. In this way, the new modes of communication and transportation served to heat up the politics of the era.

Jackson and His Opponents: The Rise of the Whigs

As transportation improvements increased commercialization, and the new politics drew the people of the United States out of localism into larger networks, fundamental questions about national unity arose. What was the correct balance between local interests—the rights of the states—and the powers of the central government? Because the Constitution deliberately left the federal structure ambiguous, all subsequent sectional disagreements automatically became constitutional arguments that carried a threat to national unity. The great issues of Jackson's presidency expressed this continuing tension between nationalism and sectionalism. Jackson's responses to these issues created such controversy that from them a permanent opposition—another political party, known as the Whigs—was born.

The Nullification Crisis

The political issue that came to symbolize the divergent sectional interests of North and South—and the rights of individual states versus a federal majority—was the protective tariff. As a group, wealthy southern planters were opposed to tariffs, both because tariffs raised the cost of the luxury goods they imported from Europe and because they feared that American tariffs would cause other countries to retaliate with tariffs against southern cotton. Most southern congressmen, assured that the 1816 tariff was a temporary postwar recovery measure, voted for it. But as the North industrialized and new industries demanded protection, the tariff bills of 1824 and 1828, nicknamed the Tariff of Abominations, raised rates still higher and covered more items.

A nationalist and expansionist in the War of 1812, John C. Calhoun of South Carolina increasingly identified with southern regional interests. While serving as Jackson's vice-president (1829–32), Calhoun supported South Carolina's nullification doctrine because he believed that the Constitution guaranteed states' rights. But his open defiance of the president earned him Jackson's undying enmity.

Southerners protested, but they were outvoted in Congress by northern and western representatives.

Southerners in Congress faced the bleak prospect that their economic interests would always be ignored by the majority. They insisted that the tariff was not a truly national measure but a sectional one that helped only some groups while harming others. Thus it was unconstitutional because it violated the rights of some of the states.

South Carolina reacted to the tariff of 1828 with the doctrine of nullification, which upheld the right of a state to declare a federal law null and void and to refuse to enforce it within the state. This was not a new argument. Thomas Jefferson and James Madison had used it in the Kentucky and Virginia Resolves of 1798, which they wrote in opposing the Alien and Sedition Acts (see Chapter 8). The Hartford Convention of 1814–15, at which Federalists protested grievances related to the War of 1812, had considered the same doctrine (see Chapter 9). At issue was the constitutional power of the state versus that of the federal government.

South Carolina had an important supporter of nullification in John C. Calhoun, who wrote a widely circulated defense of nullification, the *Exposition and Protest,* in 1828. Because Calhoun was soon to serve as Andrew Jackson's vice-president, he wrote the *Exposition* anonymously. He hoped to use his influence with Jackson to gain support for nullification, but he was disappointed.

Jackson saw nullification as a threat to national unity. As he said in a famous exchange of toasts at the annual Jefferson Day dinner in 1830, "Our Federal Union, *it must be preserved.*" In response to Jackson, Calhoun offered his own toast: "The Union—next to our liberty most dear. May we always remember that it can only be preserved by distributing equally the benefits and burdens of the Union." The president and the vice-president were thus in open disagreement on a matter of crucial national importance. The outcome was inevitable: Calhoun lost all influence with Jackson, and two years later he took the unusual step of resigning the vice-presidency. Martin Van Buren was elected to the office for Jackson's second term. Calhoun, his presidential aspirations in ruins, became a senator from South Carolina, and in that capacity participated in the last act of the nullification drama.

In 1832 the nullification controversy became a full-blown crisis. In passing the tariff of 1832, Congress (despite Jackson's urging) retained high taxes on woolens, iron, and hemp, although it reduced duties on other items. South Carolina responded with a special convention and an Ordinance of Nullification, in which it rejected the tariff and refused to collect the required taxes. The state further issued a call for a volunteer militia and threatened to secede from the Union if Jackson used force against it. Jackson responded vehemently, denouncing the nullifiers—"Disunion by armed force is *treason*"—and obtaining from Congress a Force Bill authorizing the federal government to collect the tariff in South Carolina at gunpoint if necessary. Intimidated, the other southern states refused to follow South Carolina's lead. More quietly, Jackson also asked Congress to revise the tariff. Henry Clay, the Great Pacificator, swung into action and soon, with Calhoun's support, had crafted the Tariff Act of 1833. This measure met southern demands by pledging a return to the tariff rate of 1816 (an average of 20 percent) by 1842. The South Carolina legislature, unwilling to act without the support of other southern states, quickly accepted this face-saving compromise and repealed its nullification of the tariff of 1832. In a final burst of bravado, the legislature nullified the Force Bill, but Jackson defused the crisis by ignoring this second nullification.

This episode was the most serious threat to national unity that the United States had ever experienced. South Carolinians, by threatening to secede, had forced concessions on a matter they believed of vital economic importance. They and a number of other southerners believed that the resolution of the crisis illustrated the success of their uncompromising tactics. Most of the rest of the nation simply breathed a sigh of relief, echoing Daniel Webster's sentiment, spoken in the heat of the debate over nullification, "Liberty and Union, now and forever, one and inseparable!"

Indian Removal

The official policy of the United States government from the time of Jefferson's administration was to promote the assimilation of Indian peoples. To those who resisted "civilization" or who needed more time to adapt, Jefferson offered the alternative of removal from settled areas to the new Indian Territory west of the Mississippi River. Following this logic, at the end of the War of 1812 the federal government signed removal treaties with the Indian nations of the Old Northwest, thereby opening up large tracts of land for white settlement (see Chapter 9), but in the Southwest, the "Five Civilized Tribes"—the Cherokees, Chickasaws, Choctaws, Creeks, and Seminoles—remained. By the 1830s, under constant pressure from settlers, each of the five tribes had ceded most of its lands, but sizable self-governing groups lived in Georgia, Alabama, Mississippi, and Florida. All of these (except the Seminoles) had moved far in the direction of coexistence with whites, and they resisted suggestions that they should voluntarily remove themselves.

Despite the evidence of successful adaptation, in the 1820s the legislatures of Georgia, Alabama, and Mississippi, responding to pressures from land-hungry whites, voted to invalidate federal treaties granting special self-governing status to Indian lands. Because the federal government, not the states, bore responsibility for Indian policy, these state actions constituted a challenge to federal authority. In this instance, however, unlike the Nullification Crisis, the resisting states had presidential support.

In 1830, at President Jackson's urging, the U.S. Congress passed the hotly debated Indian Removal Act, which appropriated funds for relocation, by force if necessary. Jackson helped increase the pressure by sending federal officials to negotiate removal treaties with the southern tribes. The Cherokees fought their removal by using the white man's weapon: the law. At first they seemed to have won: in *Cherokee Nation* v. *Georgia* (1831) and *Worcester* v. *Georgia* (1832) Chief Justice John Marshall ruled that the Cherokees, though not a state or a foreign nation, were a "domestic dependent nation" that could not be forced by the state of Georgia to give up its land against its will. Ignoring the decision, Jackson continued his support for removal.

Faced by the Cherokees' de facto defeat, most of the Choctaws moved west in 1830; the last of the Creeks were forcibly moved by the military in 1836, and the Chickasaws a year later. The last and most infamous removal, was that of the Cherokees, who were driven west to Oklahoma along the Trail of Tears in 1838. A 7,000-man army escorting them watched thousands (perhaps a quarter of the 16,000 Cherokees) die along the way. Another futile effort to resist removal, the Black Hawk "war," occurred in the Old Northwest. In 1832, Sac and Fox Indians, led by Black Hawk, attempted to move back to their old tribal grounds in Illinois following removal, but settlers saw the move as an invasion and demanded military protection. Federal troops chased the Black Hawk band to Wisconsin, where more than 300 Indians died in a final battle, and Black Hawk himself was taken prisoner. As in the South, the last of the remaining Indians east of the Mississippi were removed by the end of the 1830s.

The Bank War

In 1816 Congress granted a twenty-year charter to the Second Bank of the United States. Like its predecessor, the Bank played a powerful role in the expanding American economy, encouraging the growth of strong and stable financial interests and curbing less stable and irresponsible ones.

The Bank was not a government agency but a private institution, the majority of whose directors were appointed by the government. Its stockholders were some of the nation's richest men (New York's John Jacob Astor and Philadelphia's Stephen Girard among them). The bank was directed by the erudite and aristocratic Nicholas Biddle of Philadelphia. Biddle, a friend of Thomas Jefferson and an avid amateur scientist, was the editor of the journals of Lewis and Clark.

The Bank, with thirty branches, was the nation's largest, and performed a variety of functions: it held the

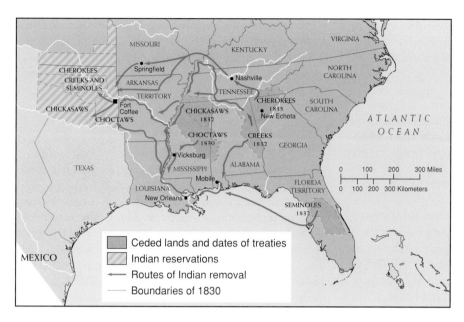

Southern Indian Cessions and Removals, 1830s

Pressure on the five major southern Indian peoples that began during the War of 1812 culminated with their removal in the 1830s. Some groups from every tribe ceded their southern homelands peacefully and moved to the newly established Indian Territory west of Arkansas and Missouri. Some, like the Seminoles, resisted by force. Others, like the Cherokees, resisted in the courts but finally lost. The Cherokees, the last to move, were forcibly removed by the U.S. Army along the Trail of Tears in 1838.

government's money (about $10 million), sold government bonds, and made commercial loans. But its most important function was the control it exercised over state banks. At the time, America lacked a national currency. The money in circulation was a mixture of paper money (U.S. notes and the notes of state banks) and gold and silver coins (specie), many of them of foreign origin. Because state banks tended to issue more paper money than they could back with hard currency, the Bank always demanded repayment of its loans to them in coin. This policy forced state banks to maintain adequate reserves, curbed inflationary pressures (overprinting of banknotes), and restricted speculative activities such as risky loans. In times of recession, the bank eased the pressure on state banks, demanding only partial payment in coin. Thus the Bank acted as a currency stabilizer by helping to control the money supply. It brought a semblance of order to what we today would consider a chaotic money system: coins of various weights and a multitude of state banknotes, many of which were discounted (not accepted at full face value) in other states.

The concept of a strong national bank was supported by the majority of the nation's merchants and businessmen and was a key element in Henry Clay's American System. Nevertheless, the Bank had many opponents. Western land speculators, many western farmers, and state bank directors chafed at the bank's tight control over the currency reserves of state banks, claim-

ing it slowed western development. Urban workers had bitter memories of the Panic of 1819, which the Bank had caused (at least in part) by sharply contracting credit. Many ordinary people were uneasy not only about the Bank but about banks of all kinds. They believed that a system based on paper currency would be manipulated by bankers in unpredictable and dangerous ways. Among those who held that opinion was Andrew Jackson, who had hated and feared banks ever since the 1790s, when he had lost a great deal of money in a speculative venture.

Nicholas Biddle, urged on by Henry Clay and Daniel Webster, precipitated the conflict with Jackson by making early application for rechartering the Bank, believing the president would not risk a veto in an election year. He was wrong. Jackson immediately decided on a stinging veto, announcing to Van Buren, "The bank . . . is trying to kill me, *but I will kill it!*"

And kill it he did that same July, with one of the strongest veto messages in American history. Denouncing the Bank as unconstitutional, harmful to states' rights, and "dangerous to the liberties of the people," Jackson presented himself as the spokesman for the majority of ordinary people and the enemy of special privilege. Asserting that the Bank's "exclusive privileges" were benefiting only the rich, Jackson claimed to speak for the "humble members of society—the farmers, mechanics and laborers"—and to oppose injustice and inequality. In short, the veto spoke directly to many of the fears and resentments that Americans felt at this time of exceptionally rapid economic and social change.

Jackson's Reelection in 1832

Jackson's veto message was a great popular success, and it set the terms for the presidential election of 1832. Democrats successfully painted his opponent, Henry Clay, as the defender of the Bank and of privilege. Clay's defeat was decisive: he drew only 49 electoral votes, to Jackson's 219.

Although the election was a triumph for Jackson, the Bank War continued. The Bank charter did not expire until 1836, but Jackson, declaring that "the hydra of corruption is only scotched, not dead," decided to kill the Bank by transferring its $10 million in government deposits to favored state banks ("pet banks," critics called them). Cabinet members objected, as did the U.S. Senate, but Jackson responded that the election had given him a popular mandate to act against the Bank. Short of impeachment, there was nothing Congress could do to prevent Jackson's vast, novel interpretation of presidential powers.

Whigs, Van Buren, and the Election of 1836

But there was someone outside Congress with power to respond: the Bank's director, Nicholas Biddle. "This worthy President thinks that because he has scalped Indians . . . he is to have his way with the Bank," Biddle commented. "He is mistaken." As the government withdrew its deposits, Biddle abruptly called in the Bank's commercial loans, thereby causing a sharp panic and recession in the winter of 1833–34. Merchants, businessmen, and southern planters were all furious at Jackson. His opponents, only a loose coalition up to this time, coalesced into a formal opposition party that called itself the Whigs. Evoking the memory of the Patriots who had resisted King George III in the American Revolution, the new party called on everyone to resist tyrannical "King Andrew." Just as Jackson's own calls for popular democracy had appealed to voters in all regions, so his opponents overcame their sectional differences to unite in opposition to his economic policies and arbitrary methods.

Vice-President Martin Van Buren, Jackson's designated successor, won the presidential election of 1836 because the Whigs, unable to agree on a common presidential candidate, ran four sectional candidates. The

Whig defeat drove home the weakness of the traditional sectional politics, but the closeness of the popular vote (50.9 percent for Van Buren, 49.1 for the Whigs) showed that the basis for a united national opposition did exist. In 1840, the Whigs would prove that they had learned this lesson.

The Panic of 1837

Meanwhile, the consequences of the Bank War continued. The recession of 1833–34 was followed by a wild speculative boom, caused as much by foreign investors as by the expiration of the Bank. Many new state banks were chartered that were eager to give loans, the price of cotton rose rapidly, and speculation in western lands was feverish (in Alabama and Mississippi, the mid-1830s were known as "the Flush Times"). A government surplus of $37 million distributed to the states in 1836 made the inflationary pressures worse. Jackson became alarmed at the widespread use of paper money (which he blamed for the inflation), and in July 1836 he issued the Specie Circular, announcing that the government would accept payment for public lands only in hard currency. At the same time, foreign investors, especially British banks, affected by a world recession, called in their American loans. The sharp contraction of credit led to the Panic of 1837 and a six-year recession, the worst the American economy had ever known.

In 1837, 800 banks suspended business, refusing to pay out any of the $150 million of their deposits. The collapse of the banking system led to business closures and outright failures. In the winter of 1837–38 in New York City alone, one-third of all manual laborers were unemployed and an estimated 10,000 were living in abject poverty. New York laborers took to the streets. Four or five thousand protesters carrying signs reading "Bread, Meat, Rent, Fuel!" gathered at City Hall on February 10, 1838, then marched to the warehouse of a leading merchant, Eli Hart. Breaking down the door, they took possession of the thousands of barrels of flour Hart had stored there rather than sell the flour at what the mob considered a fair price. Policemen and state militia who tried to prevent the break-in were beaten by the angry mob. Nationwide, the unemployment rate was estimated at more than 10 percent. Not until 1843 did the economy show signs of recovery.

In neither 1837 nor 1819 did the federal government take any action to aid victims of economic recession. No banks were bailed out, no bank depositors were saved by federal insurance, no laid-off workers got unemployment payments. Nor did the government undertake any public works projects or pump money into the economy. All of these steps, today seen as essential to prevent economic collapse and to alleviate human suffering, were unheard of in 1819 and 1837. Soup kitchens and charities were mobilized in major cities, but only by private, volunteer groups, not by local or state governments. Panics and depressions were believed to be natural stages in the business cycle, and government intervention was considered unwarranted—although it was perfectly acceptable for government to intervene to promote growth. As a result, workers, farmers, and members of the new business middle class suddenly realized that participation in America's booming economy was very dangerous. The rewards were great, but so were the penalties.

Martin Van Buren (quickly nicknamed Van Ruin) spent a dismal four years in the White House presiding over bank failures, bankruptcies, and massive unemployment. Van Buren, who lacked Jackson's compelling personality, could find no remedies to the depression. His misfortune gave the opposition party, the newly formed Whigs, their opportunity.

The Second American Party System

The political struggles of the Jackson era, coupled with the dramatic social changes caused by expansion and economic growth, created the basic pattern of American politics: two major parties, each with at least some appeal among voters of all social classes and in all sections of the country. That pattern, which we call the Second American Party System, remains to this day.

Whigs and Democrats

There were genuine differences between the Whigs and the Democrats, but they were not sectional differences. Instead, the two parties reflected just-emerging class and cultural differences. The Democrats, as they themselves were quick to point out, had inherited Thomas Jefferson's belief in the democratic rights of the small, independent yeoman farmer. They had nationwide appeal, especially in the South and West, the most rural regions. Most Democratic voters were opposed to the rapid social and economic changes that accompanied the transportation revolution.

The Whigs were more receptive to economic change, in which they were often participants. Heirs of the Federalist belief in the importance of a strong federal government in the national economy (see Chapter 8), they supported Henry Clay's American System: a strong central government, the Bank of the United States, a protective tariff, and internal improvements. In fact, Whigs wanted to improve not only roads but people as well. Religion was an important element in political affiliation, and many Whigs were members of evangelical reforming denominations. Whigs were in favor of education and social reforms such as temperance that aimed to improve the ordinary citizen. Whigs favored government intervention both in economic and in social affairs. The Whigs' greatest strength was in New England and the northern part of the West (the Old Northwest). Their strength reflected rather accurately those areas most affected by commercial agriculture and factory work.

The Campaign of 1840

In 1840, the Whigs set out to beat the Democrats at their own game. Passing over the ever-hopeful Henry Clay, the Whigs nominated a man as much like Andrew

SUMMARY TABLE	*The Second American Party System*
Democrats	First organized to elect Andrew Jackson to the presidency in 1828. The Democratic Party spoke for Jeffersonian democracy, expansion, and the freedom of the "common man" from interference from government or from financial monopolies such as the Bank of the United States. It found its power base in the rural South and West and among some northern urban workers. The Democratic Party was the majority party from 1818 to 1860.
Whigs	Organized in opposition to Andrew Jackson in the early 1830s. Heir to Federalism, the Whig Party favored a strong role for the national government in the economy (for example, it promoted Henry Clay's American System) and supported active social reform. Its power base lay in the North and Northwest among voters who benefited from increased commercialization and among some southern planters and urban merchants. The Whigs won the elections of 1840 and 1848.

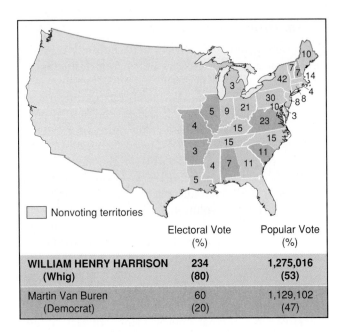

	Electoral Vote (%)	Popular Vote (%)
WILLIAM HENRY HARRISON (Whig)	**234 (80)**	**1,275,016 (53)**
Martin Van Buren (Democrat)	60 (20)	1,129,102 (47)

The Election of 1840

The 1840 Whig electoral triumph was achieved by beating the Democrats at their own game. Whigs could expect to do well in the commercializing areas of New England and the Old Northwest, but their adopted strategy of popular campaigning worked well in the largely rural South and West, contributing to Harrison's victory. The Whigs' choice of John Tyler as vice-presidential candidate, another strategy designed to appeal to southern voters, backfired when Harrison died and Tyler, who did not share Whig principles, became America's first accidental president.

Jackson as possible, the aging Indian fighter William Henry Harrison, former governor of Indiana Territory from 1801 to 1812. In an effort to duplicate Jackson's winning appeal to the South as well as the West, the Whigs balanced the ticket by nominating a southerner, John Tyler, for vice-president. The campaign slogan was "Tippecanoe and Tyler too" (Tippecanoe was the site of Harrison's famous victory over Tecumseh's Indian confederation in 1811). As if this were not enough, Whigs made Harrison out to be a humble man who would be happy to live in a log cabin, although he actually lived in a large and comfortable house. The Whigs reached out to ordinary people with torchlight parades, barbecues, songs, coonskin caps, bottomless jugs of (hard) cider, and claims that Martin Van Buren, Harrison's hapless opponent, was a man of privilege and aristocratic tastes. Nothing could be further from the truth: Van Buren was the son of a tavern keeper.

The Whigs' campaign tactics, added to the popular anger at Van Buren because of the continuing depression, gave Harrison a sweeping electoral victory, 234 votes to 60. Even more remarkable, the campaign achieved the greatest voter turnout up to that time (and rarely equaled since), 80 percent.

Whig Victory Turns to Loss: The Tyler Presidency

Although the Whig victory of 1840 was a milestone in American politics, the triumph of Whig principles was short-lived. William Henry Harrison, who was sixty-eight, died of pneumonia a month after his inauguration. For the first time in American history the vice-president stepped up to the presidency. Not for the last time, important differences between the dead president and his successor reshaped the direction of American politics.

John Tyler of Virginia was a former Democrat who had left the party because he disagreed with Jackson's autocratic style. The Whigs had sought him primarily for his sectional appeal and had not inquired too closely into his political opinions, which turned out to be anti-Whig as well as anti-Jackson. President Tyler vetoed a series of bills embodying all the elements of Henry Clay's American System: tariffs, internal improvements, and a new Bank of the United States. In exasperation, congressional Whigs read Tyler out of the party, and his entire cabinet of Whigs resigned. To replace them, Tyler appointed former Democrats. Thus the Whig triumph of 1840, one of the clearest victories in American electoral politics, was negated by the stalemate between Tyler and the Whig majority in Congress. The Whigs were to win only one more election, that of 1848.

American Arts and Letters

Jackson's presidency was a defining moment in the development of an American identity. His combination of western belligerency and combative individualism was the strongest statement of American distinctiveness since Thomas Jefferson's agrarianism. The definitions of American identity that were beginning to emerge in popular culture and in intellectual circles, however, were more complex than the message coming from the White House.

The Spread of the Written Word

The transportation revolution facilitated communication. The rapidly growing number of newspapers, magazines, and books played an important role in broadening people's horizons beyond their own community. A print revolution began in 1826 when a reform organization, the American Tract Society, installed the country's first steam-powered press. Three years later the new presses had turned out 300,000 Bibles and 6 million religious tracts. The greatest growth, however, was in newspapers that reached a mass audience. Most newspapers were published by political parties and were openly partisan. Packed with articles that today would be considered libelous and scandalous, newspapers were entertaining and popular reading. For western readers, the popular Crockett almanacs offered a mix of humorous stories and tall tales attributed to Davy Crockett (the boisterous Tennessee "roarer" who died defending the Alamo in 1836) along with meteorological and climate information. Throughout the country, religious literature was still the most widely read, but a small middle-class audience existed for literary magazines and, among women especially, for sentimental magazines and novels.

Accompanying all these changes in print communication was an invention that outsped them all: the telegraph. Samuel F. B. Morse sent his first message from Washington to Baltimore in 1844. Soon messages in Morse code would be transmitted instantaneously across the continent. The impact of this revolutionary invention, the first to separate the message from the speed at which a human messenger could travel, was immediate. Distant events gained new and exciting immediacy. Everyone's horizon and sense of community was widened.

Creating an American Culture

For all the improvements in communication, the United States was a provincial culture, still looking to Britain for values, standards, and literary offerings. In the early years of the nineteenth century, eastern seaboard cities actively built the cultural foundation that would nurture American art and literature. Philadelphia's American Philosophical Society, founded by Benjamin Franklin in 1743, boasted a distinguished roster of scientists, including Thomas Jefferson, concurrently its president and president of the United States. Culturally, Boston ran a close second to Philadelphia, founding the Massachusetts General Hospital (1811) and the Boston Athenaeum (1807), a gentlemen's library and reading room. Southern cities were much less successful in supporting culture. Charleston had a Literary and Philosophical Society (founded in 1814), but the widely dispersed residences of the southern elite made urban cultural institutions difficult to sustain. Unwittingly, the South ceded cultural leadership to the North.

The cultural picture was much spottier in the West. A few cities, such as Lexington, Kentucky, and Cincinnati, had civic cultural institutions, and a number of transplanted New Englanders maintained cultural connections. Most pioneers were at best uninterested and at worst actively hostile to traditional literary culture. This was neither from lack of literacy nor from failure to read. Newspaper and religious journals both had large readerships: the Methodist *Christian Advocate,* for example, reached 25,000 people yearly (compared with the *North American Review's* 3,000). The frontier emphasis on the practical was hard to distinguish from anti-intellectualism.

Thus in the early part of the nineteenth century, the gap between the intellectual and cultural horizons of a wealthy Bostonian and a frontier farmer in Michigan widened. Part of the unfinished task of building a national society was the creation of a national culture that could fill this gap. For writers and artists, the challenge was to find distinctively American themes.

Of the eastern cities, New York produced the first widely recognized American writers. In 1819, Washington Irving published *The Sketch Book,* thus immortalizing Rip Van Winkle and the Headless Horseman. Within a few years James Fenimore Cooper's *Leatherstocking* novels (of which *The Last of the Mohicans,* published in 1826, is the best known) achieved wide success in both America and Europe. In Cooper's novels the westward expansion, of which the conquest of the Indians was a vital part, became established as a serious and distinctive American literary theme.

It was New England, however, that saw itself as the home of American cultural independence from Europe, a claim voiced in 1837 by Ralph Waldo Emerson in his lecture to the Harvard faculty, "The American Scholar": "Our day of dependence, our long apprenticeship to the learning of other lands, draws to a close," Emerson announced, encouraging American writers to find inspiration in the ordinary details of daily life. Emerson was the star of the lyceum circuit, a lecture network that sent speakers on cultural subjects to all parts of the country. His message of cultural self-sufficiency was one that Americans were eager to hear.

Artists and Builders

Artists were as successful as novelists in finding American themes. Thomas Cole, who came to America from England in 1818, applied the British romantic school of landscape painting to American scenes. He founded the Hudson River school of American painting, a style and subject frankly nationalistic in tone.

Asher Durand, a member of the Hudson River school of landscape painting, produced this work, Kindred Spirits, in 1849 as a tribute to Thomas Cole, the leader of the school. Cole is one of the figures depicted standing in a romantic wilderness.

The western painters—realists such as Karl Bodmer and George Catlin and romantics such as Albert Bierstadt and Thomas Moran—drew on the dramatic western landscape and its peoples. Another unusual western painter, John James Audubon, made striking and sometimes grotesque etchings of American birds. George Caleb Bingham, an accomplished genre painter, produced somewhat tidied-up scenes of American workers, such as flatboatmen on the Missouri River. All these painters found much to record and to celebrate in American life. Ironically, the inspiration for the most prevalent theme, the American wilderness, was profoundly endangered by the rapid western settlement of which the nation was so proud.

The haste and transiency of American life are nowhere so obvious as in the architectural record of this era, which is sparse to say the least. The neoclassical style that Jefferson had recommended for official buildings in Washington continued to be favored for public buildings elsewhere and by private concerns trying to be imposing, such as banks. But in general Americans were in too much of a hurry to build for the future, and in balloon-frame construction they found the perfect technique for the present. The basic frame of wooden studs fastened with crosspieces top and bottom could be put up quickly, cheaply, and without the help of a skilled carpenter. Covering the frame with wooden siding was equally simple, and the resultant dwelling was as strong, although not as well insulated, as a house of solid timber or logs. Balloon-frame construction, first used in Chicago in the 1830s, created an almost instant city. The four-room balloon-frame house became standard in that decade, making houses affordable to many who could not have paid for a traditionally built dwelling. This was indeed housing for the common family.

Conclusion

Andrew Jackson's presidency witnessed the building of a strong national party system based on nearly universal white manhood suffrage. As the nation expanded politically (nine new western states were admitted between 1800 and 1840), construction of new roads, canals, and railroads and other improvements in transportation and communication created the infrastructure that united the nation physically and intellectually. Sectionalism and localism seemed to have been replaced by a more national consciousness. The party system, exemplified by Van Buren and the Bucktails, created new kinds of national communities based on political belief. But the forces of sectionalism existed despite the strong nationalizing tendencies of the era. As the next two chapters show, economic and social forces continued to push the South and the North apart.

CHRONOLOGY

1817	Erie Canal construction begins
1818	National Road completed to Wheeling
1821	Martin Van Buren's Bucktails oust DeWitt Clinton in New York
1824	John Quincy Adams elected president by the House of Representatives
1825	Erie Canal opens
1826	First American use of the steam-powered printing press
1828	Congress passes Tariff of Abominations
	Andrew Jackson elected president
	John C. Calhoun publishes *Exposition and Protest*
1830	Jackson vetoes Maysville Road Bill
	Congress passes Indian Removal Act
	Baltimore and Ohio Railroad opens
1832	Nullification Crisis begins
	Jackson vetoes renewal of Bank of the United States charter
	Jackson reelected president
1833	National Road completed to Columbus, Ohio
1834	Cyrus McCormick patents the McCormick reaper
	Whig party organized
1836	Jackson issues Specie Circular
	Martin Van Buren elected president
1837	John Deere invents steel plow
	Ralph Waldo Emerson first presents "The American Scholar"
	Panic of 1837
1838	Cherokee removal along Trail of Tears
1840	Whig William Henry Harrison elected president
1841	John Tyler assumes presidency at the death of President Harrison
1844	Samuel F. B. Morse operates first telegraph

Review Questions

1. Why would a person *oppose* universal white manhood suffrage? suffrage for free African American men? for women of all races?
2. Opponents believed that Andrew Jackson was unsuited in both political experience and temperament to be president of the United States, yet his presidency is considered one of the most influential in American history. Explain the changes in political organization and attitude that made his election possible.
3. Both the Nullification Crisis and Indian Removal raised the constitutional issue of the rights of a minority in a nation governed by majority rule. What rights, in your opinion, does a minority have, and what kinds of laws are necessary to defend those rights?
4. Why was the issue of government support for internal improvements so controversial? Who benefitted from the transportation revolution? Who lost ground?
5. What were the key differences between Whigs and Democrats? What did each party stand for? Who were their supporters? What is the link between the party's programs and party supporters?
6. What distinctive American themes did the writers, artists, and builders of the 1820s and 1830s express in their works? Are they still considered American themes today?

Recommended Reading

DONALD B. COLE, *Martin Van Buren and the American Political System* (1984). An excellent study of Van Buren's key role in the transformation of politics.

DONALD B. COLE, *The Presidency of Andrew Jackson* (1993). In this recent work, Jackson is seen as just as influential, but less commanding and more ambiguous in his political attitudes than in earlier studies.

RONALD P. FORMISANO, *Transformation of Political Culture: Massachusetts Parties, 1790s–1840s* (1983). One of many detailed studies that have contributed to our understanding of the development of the second party system.

WILLIAM W. FREEHLING, *Prelude to Civil War* (1966). An examination of the Nullification Crisis that stresses the centrality of slavery to the dispute.

PAUL W. GATES, *The Farmer's Age: Agriculture, 1815–1860* (1966). The standard source on the growth of commercial agriculture.

JEAN V. MATTHEWS, *Toward a New Society: American Thought and Culture, 1800–1830* (1991). A valuable survey of American attitudes toward religion, politics, science, nature, and culture in the early nineteenth century.

JOHN NIVEN, *Martin Van Buren: The Romantic Age of American Politics* (1983). More interesting insights into the life of "the Little Magician," as Van Buren was nicknamed.

MERRILL D. PETERSON, *The Great Triumvirate: Webster, Clay, and Calhoun* (1987). A biography of the famous trio that is also a "life and times."

ROBERT REMINI, *Andrew Jackson and the Source of American Freedom* (1981). An account of Jackson's White House years by his major biographer.

GEORGE ROGERS TAYLOR, *The Transportation Revolution, 1815–1860* (1951). The indispensable book on all aspects of the American economy during this period.

HARRY L. WATSON, *Liberty and Power: The Politics of Jacksonian America* (1990). An excellent recent overview of Jacksonian politics.

THE SOUTH AND SLAVERY, 1790s–1850s

11

AMERICAN COMMUNITIES

NATCHEZ-UNDER-THE-HILL

The wharfmaster had just opened the public auction of confiscated cargoes in the center of Natchez when a great cry was heard. All present turned to see an angry crowd of flatboatmen, Bowie knives in hand, storming up the bluffs from the Mississippi shouting, as the local newspaper reported, "threats of violence and death upon all who attempted to sell and buy their property." It was November 1837, and the town council had just enacted a restrictive tax of $10 per flatboat, a measure designed to rid the wharf district known as Natchez-Under-the-Hill of the most impoverished and disreputable of the riverboatmen. The council had made its first confiscation of cargo after nine captains refused to pay this tax. As the boatmen approached, merchants and onlookers shrank back in fear. But the local authorities had taken the precaution of calling out the militia, and a company of farmers and planters now came marching into the square with their rifles primed and lowered. "The cold and sullen bayonets of the Guards were too hard meat for the Arkansas toothpicks," reported the local press, and "there was no fight." The boatmen sullenly turned back down the bluffs. It was the first confrontation in the "Flatboat Wars" that erupted as Mississippi ports tried to bring their troublesome riverfronts under regulation.

The first European to take notice of this "land abundant in subsistence" was a member of Hernando de Soto's expedition in the sixteenth century. The area was "thickly peopled" by the Natchez Indians, he wrote. It was not until the French established the port of Fort Rosalie in the 1720s, however, that Europeans settled in the area. The French destroyed the highly organized society of the Natchez Indians in the 1730s and the port became a major Mississippi River trading center. From Fort Rosalie, the French conducted an extensive frontier trade that brought peoples of different races into contact with one another, leading ultimately to considerable intermarriage and the growth of a mixed-race population. French traders bought deerskins, for which there was a large export market from Choctaw, Chickasaw, and Creek hunters.

When the Spanish took control of the territory in 1763 they laid out the new town of Natchez high on the bluffs, safe from Mississippi flooding. Fort Rosalie, rechristened Natchez-Under-the-Hill, continued to flourish as the produce grown by American farmers in Kentucky and Tennessee moved downriver on flatboats. When

Americans took possession of Mississippi in 1798, this abundant land of rich, black soil became thickly peopled, but this time with cotton planters and their African American slaves.

Under-the-Hill became renowned as the last stop for boatmen before New Orleans. Mingling among American rivermen of all descriptions were trappers and hunters in fur caps, Spanish shopkeepers in bright smocks, French gentlemen from New Orleans in velvet coats, Indians wrapped in their trade blankets, African Americans both free and slave—a pageant of nations and races.

On the bluffs, meanwhile, the town of Natchez had become the winter home to the southwestern planter elite. They built their mansions with commanding views of the river. Sustaining this American aristocracy was the labor of thousands of enslaved men and women, who lived in the squalid quarters behind the great house and worked the endless fields of cotton. It was they who made possible the greatest accumulations of wealth in early-nineteenth-century America.

In the late 1830s the district was jolted by rumors that a group of African Americans and Under-the-Hill desperadoes were conspiring to rebel against the Natchez elite on a Fourth of July. The planters were to be murdered by their slaves as they gathered for the celebration, and the Under-the-Hill crowd would loot the mansions. It is unlikely that there was any conspiracy, but the rumors illustrated the growing conviction among planters that they could no longer tolerate the polyglot community of the riverfront. The measures that ultimately provoked the flatboatmen's threats in November 1837 soon followed.

In response to these threats, the planters issued an extralegal order giving all the gamblers, pimps, and whores of Under-the-Hill twenty-four hours to evacuate the district. As the Mississippi militia sharpened their bayonets, panic swept the wharves, and that night dozens of flatboats loaded with a motley human cargo headed for the more tolerant community of New Orleans. But there were similar orders of expulsion in other river ports. Thus, one resident remembered, "the

towns on the river became purified from a moral pestilence which the law could not cure."

These two communities—Natchez, home to the rich slave-owning elite, and Natchez-Under-the-Hill, the bustling polyglot trading community—epitomize the paradox of the American South in the early nineteenth century. Enslaved African Americans grew the region's most profitable crop, cotton. On these profits, aristocratic southerners built a sumptuous and distinctive lifestyle for themselves. The boatmen and traders of Natchez-Under-the-Hill were a vital part of their prosperity, for they carried cotton and other products of slave labor to market. But the slave owners' system of control over slavery, built on a rigid distinction between free white people and enslaved black people, was threatened by the more open community formed in the polyglot racial and social mixing of Natchez-Under-the-Hill. Because the slave owners could not control the boatmen, they expelled them. This defensive reaction—the effort to seal off the world of slavery from the wider commercial world—exposed the vulnerability of the slave system at the very moment of its greatest commercial success.

> **KEY TOPICS**
>
> ◆ **The domination of southern life by the slave system**
>
> ◆ **The economic implications of "King Cotton"**
>
> ◆ **The creation of African American communities under slavery**
>
> ◆ **The social structure of the white South and its increasing defensiveness**

King Cotton and Southern Expansion

Slavery had long dominated southern life. African American slaves grew the great export crops of the colonial period—tobacco, rice, and indigo—on which slave owners' fortunes were made, and their presence shaped southern society and culture (see Chapter 4). In the early days of American independence, the slave system waned, only to be revived by the immense profitability of cotton in a newly industrializing world. The overwhelming economic success of cotton and of the slave system on which it depended created a distinctive regional culture quite different from that developing in the North.

The Cotton Gin and Expansion into the Old Southwest

Short-staple cotton, long recognized as a crop ideally suited to southern soils and growing conditions, had one major drawback: the seeds were so difficult to remove from the lint that it took an entire day to hand-clean a single pound of cotton. The invention in 1793 that made cotton growing profitable was the result of collaboration between a young northerner named Eli Whitney, recently graduated from Yale College, and Catherine Greene, a South Carolina plantation owner and widow who hired Whitney to tutor her children. Whitney built a prototype cotton engine, dubbed "gin" for short, a simple device consisting of a hand-cranked cylinder with teeth that tore the lint away from the seeds. At Greene's suggestion, the teeth were made of wire. With the cotton gin it was possible to clean more than fifty pounds of cotton a day. Soon large and small planters in the inland regions of Georgia and South Carolina had begun to grow cotton. By 1811 this area was producing 60 million pounds of cotton a year, and exporting most of it to England.

Other areas of the South quickly followed South Carolina and Georgia into cotton production. New land was most suitable, for cotton growing rapidly depleted the soil. The profits to be made from cotton growing drew a rush of southern farmers into the so-called black belt, an area stretching through western Georgia, Alabama, and Mississippi that was blessed with exceptionally fertile soil.

This migration caused the population of Mississippi to double and that of Alabama to grow sixteenfold in the decade 1810–20. Southerners had historically taken the lead in westward expansion, but on this frontier African American pioneers (albeit involuntary ones) cleared the forests, drained the swamps, broke the ground, built houses and barns, and planted the first crops.

Like the simultaneous expansion into the Old Northwest, settlement of the Old Southwest took place at the expense of the region's Indian population (see Chapter 9). Beginning with the defeat of the Creeks at Horseshoe Bend in 1814 and ending with the Cherokee forced migration along the Trail of Tears in 1838, the "Five Civilized Tribes"—the Cherokees, Chickasaws, Choctaws, Creeks, and Seminoles—were forced to give up their lands and move to Indian Territory (see Chapter 10).

A major reason for Indian removal was the European hunger for land and profit, present throughout the nation. On every American frontier, white expansion and

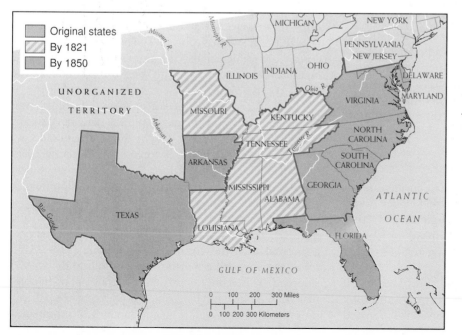

The South Expands, 1790–1850

This map shows the dramatic effect cotton production had on southern expansion. From the original six states of 1790, westward expansion, fueled by the search for new cotton lands, added another six states by 1821, and three more by 1850.

settlement meant the killing, confining, or removal of Indian peoples. In these respects the expansion into the Old Southwest fit the national pattern. But another reason was rooted in slavery: there was simply no room in the southern social order for anything other than white and black, master and slave. Literate, slave-owning Indians confused this simple picture: they were too "civilized" to be like slaves, but the wrong color to be masters. Thus southern Indian removal, like southern expansion, was dictated by the needs of the slave system.

The Question of Slavery

White southerners believed that only African slaves could be forced to work day after day, year after year, at the rapid and brutal pace required in the cotton fields of large plantations in the steamy southern summer. As the production of cotton climbed higher every year, so did the demand for slaves.

But at the very moment that the South committed its future to cotton, opinion about slavery was changing. Britain outlawed the international slave trade in 1807. In the preceding quarter century, all the northern states had abolished slavery or passed laws for gradual emancipation (see Chapter 7).

Following the invention of the cotton gin in 1793 and the realization of the riches to be made from cotton, southern attitudes hardened. Between 1804 and 1808, Charleston boomed as one of the world's largest slaving ports: at least 40,000 Africans were imported. It was clear, however, that national opinion found the international slave trade abhorrent, and on January 1, 1808, the earliest date permitted by the Constitution, a bill to abolish the importation of slaves became law. Although a small number of slaves continued to be smuggled from Africa, the growth of the slave labor force after 1808 depended primarily on natural increase. The ban on foreign importations vastly increased the importance of the internal slave trade.

The Internal Slave Trade

The cotton boom caused a huge increase in the domestic slave trade. Plantation owners in the Upper South (Delaware, Kentucky, Maryland, Virginia, and Tennessee) sold their slaves to meet the demand for labor in the new and expanding cotton-growing regions of the Old Southwest.

Cumulatively, between 1820 and 1860 nearly 50 percent of the slave population of the Upper South took part against their will in southern expansion. Purchased by slave traders from owners in the Upper South, slaves were gathered together in notorious slave pens such as the ones in Richmond and Charleston and then moved south by train or boat. In the interior, they were carried as cargo on steamboats on the Mississippi River, hence the phrase "sold down the river." Often slaves moved on foot, chained together in groups of fifty or more known as coffles. Arriving at a central market in the Lower South such as Natchez, New Orleans, or Mobile, the slaves, after being carefully inspected by potential buyers, were sold at auction to the highest bidder.

Although popular stereotype portrayed slave traders as unscrupulous outsiders who persuaded kind and reluctant masters to sell their slaves, the historical truth is much harsher. Traders, far from being shunned by slave-owning society, were often respected community members. Similarly, the sheer scale of the slave trade makes it impossible to believe that slave owners only reluctantly parted with their slaves at times of economic distress. Instead, it is clear that many owners sold slaves and separated slave families not out of necessity but to increase their profits.

The Economics of Slavery

The insatiable demand for cotton was a result of the technological and social changes that we know today as the industrial revolution. Beginning early in the eighteenth century, a series of small inventions mechanized spinning and weaving in the world's first factories in the north of England. The ability of these factories to produce unprecedented amounts of cotton cloth revolutionized the world economy. The invention of the cotton gin came at just the right time. British textile manufacturers were eager to buy all the cotton the South could produce.

Indeed, the export of cotton from the South was the dynamic force in the developing American economy in the period 1790–1840. Just as the international slave trade had been the dynamic force in the Atlantic economy of the eighteenth century (see Chapter 4), southern slavery financed northern industrial development in the nineteenth century.

The connection between southern slavery and northern industry was direct. Most mercantile services associated with the cotton trade (insurance, for example) were in northern hands and, significantly, so was shipping. This economic structure was not new. In colonial times, New England ships dominated the African slave trade. Some New England families invested some of their profits in the new technology of textile manufacturing in the 1790s. Other merchants made their money from cotton shipping and brokerage.

Cotton Culture

Northerners, who were caught up in rapid industrialization and urbanization, failed to recognize this economic connection between regions and increasingly regarded the South as a backward region.

Concentration on plantation agriculture did divert energy and resources from the South's cities. At a time when the North was experiencing the greatest spurt of urban growth in the nation's history, southern cities did not keep pace. Charleston, for example, one of America's five largest cities in 1800, had a population of only 41,000 in 1860, compared with Boston's 177,840 and Baltimore's 212,418. The one exception was New Orleans. In 1860 New Orleans was the nation's fifth largest city, with a population of 169,000. The nine other leading cities were all northern or western. Most of the South remained rural: less than 3 percent of Mississippi's population lived in cities of more than 2,500 residents, and only 10 percent of Virginia's did.

The failure of the South to industrialize at the northern rate was not a matter of ignorance but of choice. Southern capital was tied up in land and slaves, and southerners, buoyed by the world's insatiable demand for cotton, saw no reason to invest in economically risky railroads, canals, and factories. Nor were they eager to introduce the disruptive factor of free wage work into the tightly controlled slave system. Cotton was safer.

Thus the cotton boom created a distinctive regional culture. Although cotton was far from being the only crop (the South actually devoted more acreage to corn than to cotton in 1860), its vast profitability affected all aspects of society.

To Be a Slave

The slave population, estimated at 700,000 by 1790, grew to more than 4 million. After 1808 (when official American participation in the international slave trade ceased) the growth occurred because of natural increase—that is, births within the slave population. Despite the burden of slavery, a distinctive African American community, begun in the eighteenth century (see Chapter 4), flourished in the years before the Civil War.

The Maturing of the American Slave System

In 1850, 55 percent of all slaves were engaged in cotton growing. Another 20 percent labored to produce other crops: tobacco (10 percent), rice, sugar, and hemp. About 15 percent of all slaves were domestic servants, and the remaining 10 percent worked in mining, lumbering, industry, and construction.

Slavery had become distinctively southern: by 1820, as a result of laws passed after the Revolution, all of the northern states had abolished slaveholding (see Chapter 7). Slaves were increasingly clustered in the Lower South, as Upper South slave owners sold slaves downriver or migrated westward with their entire households.

Slaves were not distributed equally among southern slave owners. More than half of all slave owners owned five slaves or fewer, but 75 percent of all slaves lived in groups of ten or more. This disproportionate distribution could have a major impact on a slave's life, for it was a very different matter to be the single slave of a small farmer than a member of a 100-person black community on a large plantation.

Finally, of all the New World slave societies, the one that existed in the American South was the only one that grew by natural increase rather than the constant importation of captured Africans. This fact alone made the African American community of the South different from the slave societies of Cuba, the Caribbean islands, and Brazil. The first thing to understand, then, are the circumstances of survival.

The Challenge to Survive

The primary challenge facing African Americans was survival. Mortality rates for slave children under five were twice those for their white counterparts. Pregnant black women were inadequately nourished, worked too hard, or were too frequently pregnant, birthing six to eight children at year-and-a-half intervals.

Health remained a lifelong issue for slaves. Malaria and infectious diseases such as yellow fever and cholera were endemic in the South. White people as well as black died, as the life expectancy figures for 1850 show: 25.5 years for white people and 21.4 years for African Americans. Slaves were more at risk because of the circumstances of slave life: poor housing, poor diet, and constant, usually heavy work. Sickness was chronic: 20 percent or more of the slave labor force on most plantations were sick at any one time. Many owners believed their slaves were not sick but only malingering.

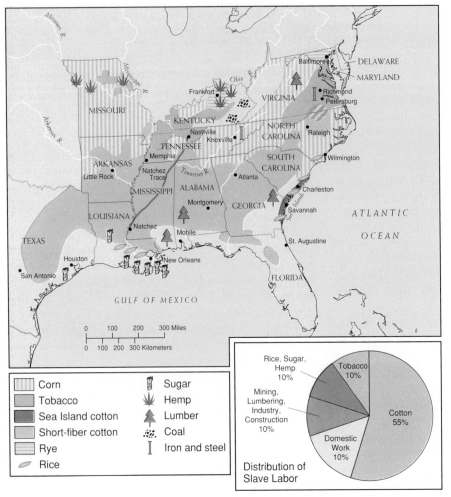

Agriculture, Industry, and Slavery, 1850

The distribution of the slave population in the South was determined by agricultural and industrial patterns. In 1850, 55 percent of all slaves worked in cotton, 10 percent in tobacco, and another 10 percent in rice, sugar, and hemp. Ten percent worked in mining, lumbering, industry, and construction, and 15 percent worked as domestic servants. Slaves were not generally used to grow corn, the staple crop of the yeoman farmer.

They failed to realize that adequate diet, warm housing, and basic sanitation might have prevented the pneumonia and dysentery that killed or weakened many slaves.

From Cradle to Grave

Slavery was a lifelong labor system, and the constant and inescapable issue between master and slave was how much work the latter would do. Southern white slave owners claimed that by housing, feeding, and clothing their slaves from infancy to death they were acting more humanely than northern industrialists, who employed people only during their working years. But despite occasional instances of manumission, or the freeing of a slave, the child born of a slave was destined to remain a slave.

Children lived with their parents (or with their mother if the father was a slave on another farm or plantation) in housing provided by the owner. Slaves owned by small farmers usually had only a bed or mattress to sleep on in the attic or a back room. Larger slave owners housed slaves in one-room cabins with dirt floors and few furnishings (a table, stools, a cooking pot and a few dishes, a bed or corn-shuck mattresses).

Masters supplied food to their slaves. One common ration for a week was three pounds of meat, a quart of corn meal, and some molasses for each person. Often slaves were encouraged to supplement their diet by keeping their own gardens, and by hunting (though not, of course, with guns). Slaves were also provided with clothes, usually of rough homespun cloth: two shirts, two pairs of pants, and a pair of shoes a year for men, and enough cloth for women to make an equal number of smocks for themselves and their children yearly. This clothing was barely adequate, and in severe winters slaves suffered badly.

From birth to about age seven, slave children played with one another and with white children, observing and learning how to survive. They saw the penalties: black adults, perhaps their own parents, whipped for disobedience; black women, perhaps their own sisters, violated by white men. And they might see one or both parents sold away as punishment or for financial gain. They would also see signs of white benevolence: special treats for children at holidays, appeals to loyalty from the master or mistress, perhaps friendship with a white child.

The children would learn slave ways of getting along: apparent acquiescence in white demands; pilfering; and malingering, sabotage, and other methods of slowing the relentless work pace. Fanny Kemble, an accomplished actress, was quick to note the pretense in the "outrageous flattery" she received from her husband's slaves. But many white southerners genuinely believed that their slaves were both less intelligent and more loyal than they really were.

Most slaves spent their lives as field hands, working in gangs with other slaves under a white overseer, who was usually quick to use his whip to keep up the work pace. But there were other occupations. In the "big house" there were jobs for women as cooks, maids, seamstresses, laundresses, weavers, and nurses. Black men became coachmen, valets, and gardeners, or skilled craftsmen (carpenters, mechanics, and blacksmiths). Some children began learning these occupations at age seven or eight, often in an informal apprentice system. Other children, both boys and girls, were expected to take full care of younger children while the parents were working. Of course black children had no schooling of any kind: in most of the southern states, it was against the law to teach a slave to read, although indulgent owners often rewarded their "pet" slaves by teaching them despite the law. At age twelve, slaves were considered full grown and put to work in the fields or in their designated occupation.

House Servants

At first glance, working in the big house might seem to have been preferable to working in the fields. Physically it was much less demanding, and house slaves were often better fed and clothed. They also had much more access to information, for white people, accustomed to servants and generally confident of their loyalty, often forgot their presence and spoke among themselves about matters of interest to the slaves: local gossip, changes in laws or attitudes, policies toward disobedient or rebellious slaves.

For many white people, one of the worst surprises of the Civil War was the eagerness of their house slaves to flee. Considered by their masters the best treated and the most loyal, these slaves were commonly the first to leave or to organize mass desertions. Even the Confederacy's first family, President Jefferson Davis and his wife Varina, were chagrined by the desertion of their house servants in 1864.

From the point of view of the slave, the most unpleasant thing about being a house servant (or the single slave of a small owner) was the constant presence of white people. There was no escape from white supervision. Many slaves who were personal maids and children's nurses were required to live in the big house and rarely saw their own families. Cooks and other house servants were exposed to the tempers and whims of all members of the white family, including the children. And house servants, more than any others, were forced to act grateful and ingratiating. The demeaning images of Uncle Tom and the ever-smiling mammy derive from the roles slaves learned as the price of survival. Genuine intimacy was possible, especially between black nurses and white children, but these were bonds that the white children were ultimately forced to reject as the price of joining the master class.

Artisans and Skilled Workers

A small number of slaves were skilled workers: weavers, seamstresses, carpenters, blacksmiths, and mechanics. More slave men than women achieved skilled status (partly because many jobs considered appropriate for women, such as cooking, were not thought of as skilled). Solomon Northup, a northern free African American kidnapped into slavery, explained in his 1853 narrative, *Twelve Years a Slave,* that he had had three owners and had been hired out repeatedly as a carpenter and as a driver of other slaves in a sugar mill; he had also been hired out to clear land for a new Louisiana plantation and to cut sugar cane. Black people worked as lumberjacks (of the 16,000 lumber workers, almost all were slaves), as miners, as deckhands and stokers on Mississippi riverboats, as stevedores loading cotton on the docks of Charleston, Savannah, and New Orleans, and in the handful of southern factories. Because slaves were their masters' property, the wages of the slave belonged to the owner, not the slave.

The extent to which slaves made up the laboring class was most apparent in cities. A British visitor to Natchez in 1835 noted slave "mechanics, draymen, hostelers, labourers, hucksters and washwomen and the heterogeneous multitude of every other occupation." In the North, all these jobs were performed by white workers. In part because the South failed to attract as much immigrant labor as the North, southern cities offered both enslaved and free black people opportunities in skilled occupations such as blacksmithing and carpentering that free African Americans in the North were denied.

Field Work

A full 75 percent of all slaves were field workers. Field hands, both men and women, worked from "can see to can't see" (sunup to sundown) summer and winter, and often longer at harvest, when eighteen-hour days were common. On most plantations, the bell sounded an hour before sunup, and slaves were expected to be on their way to the fields as soon as it was light. The usual pattern of working in groups of twenty to twenty-five harked back to African communal systems of agricultural work. Many work gangs had black drivers in addition to white overseers. Work continued till noon, and after an hour or so for lunch and rest the slaves worked nearly until dark. Work days were shorter in the winter, perhaps only ten hours.

Work was tedious in the hot and humid southern fields, and the overseer's whip was never far away. Cotton growing was hard work: plowing and planting, chopping weeds with a heavy hoe, and picking the ripe cotton from the stiff and scratchy bolls at the rate of 150 pounds a day. In the rice fields, slaves worked knee-deep in water. On sugar plantations, harvesting the cane and getting it ready for boiling was exceptionally heavy work. A strong, hardworking slave—a "prime field hand"—was valuable property, worth at least $1,000 to the master. Slaves justifiably took pride in their strength, but aged fast. Poor diet and heavy labor undermined health. When they were too old to work, they took on other tasks within the black community, such as caring for young children. Honored by the slave community, the elderly were tolerated by white owners, who continued to feed and clothe them until their deaths. Few actions show the hypocrisy of southern paternalism more clearly than the speed with which white owners evicted their elderly slaves in the 1860s when the end of the slave system was in sight.

The African American Community

Surely no group in American history has faced a harder job of community building than the black people of the antebellum South. Living in intimate, daily contact with

Five generations of one family on a South Carolina plantation are gathered together for this 1862 picture, providing living evidence of the importance of kinship in the building of African American communities.

their oppressors, African Americans nevertheless created an enduring culture of their own, a culture that had far-reaching and lasting influence on all of southern society (see Chapter 4). Within their own communities, African American values and attitudes, and especially their own forms of Christianity, played a vital part in shaping a culture of endurance and resistance.

Few African Americans were unfortunate enough to live their lives alone among white people. Over half of all slaves lived on plantations with twenty or more other slaves, and others, on smaller farms, had links with slaves on nearby properties. Urban slaves were able to make and sustain so many secret contacts with other African Americans in cities or towns that slave owners wondered whether slave discipline could be maintained in urban settings. There can be no question that the bonds among African Americans were what sustained them during the years of slavery.

In law, slaves were property, to be bought, sold, rented, worked, and otherwise used (but not abused or killed) as the owner saw fit. But slaves were also human beings, with feelings, needs, and hopes. Even though most white southerners believed black people to be members of an inferior, childish race, all but the most brutal masters acknowledged the humanity of their slaves. Furthermore, as a practical matter, white owners had long since learned that unhappy or rebellious slaves were poor workers. White masters learned to live with the two key institutions of African American community life: the family and the African American church.

Slave Families

No southern state recognized slave marriages in law. However, most owners not only recognized but encouraged them, sometimes even performing a kind of wedding ceremony for the couple. Masters sometimes tried to arrange marriages, but slaves usually found their own mates, sometimes on their own plantation, sometimes elsewhere. Masters encouraged marriage among their slaves, believing it made the men less rebellious, and for economic reasons they were eager for women to have children.

Whatever marriages meant to the masters, to slaves they were a haven of love and intimacy in a cruel world and the basis of the African American community. Husbands and wives had a chance, in their own cabins, to live their own lives among loved ones. The relationship between slave husband and wife was different from that of the white husband and wife. The patriarchal system dictated that the white marriage be unequal, for the man had to be dominant and the woman dependent and submissive. Slave marriages were more equal, for husband and wife both knew that neither could protect the other from abuse at the hands of white people.

Husband and wife cooperated in loving and sheltering their children and teaching them survival skills. Above all, family meant continuity. Parents made great efforts to teach their children the family history. As Alex Haley's *Roots* illustrated, many African American families today maintain strong oral traditions dating back to their African origins. Parents did their best to surround children with a supportive and protective kinship network.

The strength of these ties is shown by the great numbers of husbands, wives, children, and parents who searched for each other after the Civil War when slavery came to an end. As the ads in black newspapers indicate, some family searches went on into the 1870s and 1880s, and many ended in failure.

Separations of slave families were common. One in every five slave marriages was broken, and one in every three children sold away from their families. These figures clearly show that slave owners' support for slave marriages was secondary to their desire for profits.

In the face of constant separation, slave communities attempted to act like larger families. Following practices developed early in slavery, children were taught to respect and learn from all the elders, to call all adults of a certain age "aunt" or "uncle," and to call children of their own age "brother" or "sister" (see Chapter 4). Thus, in the absence of their own family, separated children could quickly find a place and a source of comfort in the slave community to which they had been sold.

The kinship of the entire community, where old people were respected and young ones cared for, represented a conscious rejection of white paternalism. The slaves' ability, in the most difficult of situations, to structure a community that expressed *their* values, not those of their masters, was extraordinary. Equally remarkable was the way in which African Americans reshaped Christianity to serve their needs.

African American Religion

Slaves brought religions from Africa but were not allowed to practice them, for white people feared religion would create a bond among slaves that might lead to rebellion. African religions managed to survive in the slave community in forms that white people considered "superstition" or "folk belief," such as the medicinal use of roots by conjurers. Religious ceremonies survived, too, in late-night gatherings deep in the woods where the sound of drumming, singing, and dancing could not reach white ears (see Chapter 4).

Most masters of the eighteenth century made little effort to Christianize their slaves, afraid they might take the promises of universal brotherhood and equality too literally. The Great Awakening, which swept the South after the 1760s, introduced many slaves to Christianity, often in mixed congregations with white people (see Chapter 5). The transformation was completed by the Second Great Awakening, which took root among black and white southerners in the 1790s. The number of African American converts, preachers, and lay teachers grew rapidly, and a distinctive form of Christianity took shape.

The first African American Baptist and Methodist churches were founded in Philadelphia in 1794. In 1816, the African Methodist Episcopal (AME) denomination was formed. By the 1830s, free African American ministers such as Andrew Marshall of Savannah and many more enslaved black preachers and lay ministers preached, sometimes secretly, to slaves. Their message was one of faith and love, deliverance, and the coming of the promised land.

African Americans found in Christianity a powerful vehicle to express their longings for freedom and justice. But why did their white masters allow it? Some white people, converted by the revivals, doubtless believed that they should not deny their slaves the same religious experience. But the evangelical religion of the early nineteenth century was also a powerful form of social control. Southern slave owners, seeking to counteract the appeal of African American religion, expected *their* Christianity to make their slaves obedient and peaceful. Forbidding their slaves to hold their own religious gatherings, owners insisted that their slaves attend white church services. Slaves were quick to realize the owners' purpose. As a former Texas slave recalled: "We went to church on the place and you ought to heard that preachin'. Obey your massa and missy, don't steal chickens and eggs and meat, but nary a word 'bout havin' a soul to save." But at night, away from white eyes, they held their own prayer meetings.

In churches and in spontaneous religious expressions, the black community made Christianity its own. Fusing Christian texts with African elements of group activity such as the circle dance, the call-and-response pattern, and, above all, group singing, black people created a unique community religion full of emotion, enthusiasm, and protest. Nowhere is this spirit more compelling than in the famous spirituals: "Go Down Moses," with its mournful refrain "Let my people go"; the rousing "Didn't My Lord Deliver Daniel . . . and why not every man"; the haunting "Steal Away."

Nevertheless, this was not a religion of rebellion, for that was unrealistic for most slaves. Black Christianity was an enabling religion: it helped slaves to survive, not as passive victims of white tyranny but as active opponents of an oppressive system that they daily protested in small but meaningful ways.

Freedom and Resistance

Whatever their dreams, most slaves knew they would never escape. Almost all successful escapes in the nineteenth century (approximately 1,000 a year) were from the Upper South (Delaware, Maryland, Virginia, Kentucky, Missouri). A slave in the Lower South or the Southwest simply had too far to go to reach freedom. In addition, white southerners were determined to prevent escapes. Slave patrols were a common sight on southern roads. Any black person without a pass from his or her master was captured (usually roughly) and returned home to certain punishment. But despite almost certain recapture, slaves continued to flee and

to help others do so. Escaped slave Harriet Tubman of Maryland, who made nineteen rescue missions freeing 300 slaves in all, had extraordinary determination and skill.

Slaves who knew they could not reach freedom often demonstrated their desire for liberty or their discontent over mistreatment by taking unauthorized leave from their plantation. Hidden in nearby forests or swamps, provided with food smuggled by other slaves from the plantation, the runaway might return home after a week or so, often to rather mild punishment. Temporary flight by any slave was a warning sign of discontent that a wise master did not ignore.

Slave Revolts

The ultimate resistance, however, was the slave revolt. Southern history was dotted with stories of former slave conspiracies and rumors of current plots (see Chapter 4). Every white southerner knew about the last-minute failure of Gabriel Prosser's insurrection in Richmond in 1800 and the chance discovery of Denmark Vesey's plot in Charleston in 1822. But when in 1831 Nat Turner actually started a rebellion in which a number of white people were killed, southern fears were greatly magnified.

A literate man, Nat Turner was a lay preacher, but he was also a slave. It was Turner's intelligence and strong religious commitment that made him a leader in the slave community and, interestingly, these very same qualities led his master, Joseph Travis, to treat him with kindness even though Turner had once run away for a month after being mistreated by an overseer. Turner began plotting his revolt after a religious vision in which he saw "white spirits and black spirits engaged in battle"; "the sun was darkened—the thunder rolled in the Heavens, and blood flowed in streams." Turner and five other slaves struck on the night of August 20, 1831, first killing Travis, who, Turner said, "was to me a kind master, and placed the greatest confidence in me; in fact, I had no cause to complain of his treatment of me."

Moving from plantation to plantation and killing a total of fifty-five white people, the rebels numbered sixty by the next morning, when they fled from a group of armed white men. More than forty blacks were executed after the revolt, including Turner, who was captured accidentally after he had hidden for two months in the woods. Thomas R. Gray, a white lawyer to whom Turner dictated a lengthy confession before his death, was impressed by Turner's composure. "I looked on him," Gray said, "and my blood curdled in my veins." If

Harriet Tubman escaped in 1849 from slavery in Maryland, and returned nineteen times to free almost 300 other slaves. Here Tubman (at left), the most famous "conductor" on the Underground Railroad, is shown with some of those she led to freedom.

intelligent, well-treated slaves such as Turner could plot revolts, how could white southerners ever feel safe? After 1831, fear of slave insurrection was never far from southern minds.

Free African Americans

Another source of white disquiet was the growing number of free African Americans. By 1860 nearly 250,000 free black people lived in the South. For most, freedom dated from before 1800, when antislavery feeling among slave owners in the Upper South was widespread and cotton cultivation had yet to boom.

Most free black people lived in the countryside of the Upper South, where they worked as tenant farmers or farm laborers. Urban African Americans were much more visible. Life was especially difficult for female-headed families because only the most menial work—street peddling and laundry work, for example—was available to free black women. The situation for African American males was somewhat better. Although they were discriminated against in employment and social life, there were opportunities for skilled black craftsmen in trades such as blacksmithing and carpentering. Cities such as Charleston, Savannah, and Natchez were home to flourishing free African American communities that formed their own churches and fraternal orders.

Throughout the South in the 1830s, state legislatures tightened black codes (laws concerning free black people). Free African Americans could not carry firearms, could not purchase slaves (unless they were members of their own family), and were liable to the criminal penalties meted out to slaves (that is, whippings

and summary judgments without a jury trial). They could not testify against whites, hold office, vote, or serve in the militia. In other words, except for the right to own property, free blacks had no civil rights.

Yeomen and Poor Whites

Two-thirds of all southerners did not own slaves, yet slave owners dominated the social and political life of the region. Who were the two-thirds of white southerners who did not own slaves, and how did they live? Throughout the south, slave owners occupied the most productive land: tobacco-producing areas in Virginia and Tennessee, coastal areas of South Carolina and Georgia where rice and cotton grew, sugar lands in Louisiana, and large sections of the cotton-producing black belt, which stretched westward from South Carolina to Texas. Small farmers, usually without slaves, occupied the rest of the land. This ranged from adequate to poor, from depleted, once-rich lands in Virginia to the Carolina hill country and the pine barrens of Mississippi.

Yeomen

The word *yeoman*, originally a British term for a farmer who works his own land, is often applied to independent farmers of the South, most of whom lived on family-sized farms. Although yeoman farmers sometimes owned a few slaves, in general they and their families worked their land by themselves. Typical of the yeoman-farmer community was northwestern Georgia, once home to the Creeks and Cherokees, but now populated by communities of small farmers who grew enough vegetables to feed their families, including corn, which they either ate themselves or fed to hogs. In addition, these farmers raised enough cotton every year (usually no more than one or two bales) to bring in a little cash.

Where yeomen and large slave owners lived side by side, as in the Georgia black belt, where cotton was the major crop, slavery provided a link between richer and poorer. Large plantation owners often bought food for their slaves from small local farmers, ground the latter's corn in the plantation mill, ginned their cotton, and transported and marketed it as well. But although planters and much smaller yeomen were part of a larger community network, in the black belt the large slave owners were clearly dominant. Only in their own up-country communities did yeomen feel truly independent.

Poor White People

Not all small farmers were on an equal footing. One-third of the farmers in the Georgia up country were tenant farmers. Some were farmers' sons, striking out on their own while waiting to inherit their fathers' land. But others were poor whites with little hope of improving their condition. From 30 to 50 percent of all southern white people were landless, a proportion similar to that in the North. But the existence of slavery affected the opportunity of southern poor white people. Slaves made up the permanent, stable work force in agriculture and in many skilled trades. Many poor white people led highly transient lives in search of work, such as farm labor at harvest time, which was only temporary. Others were tenant farmers working under share-tenancy arrangements that kept them in debt to the landowner.

Poor white men and women often worked side by side with black slaves in the fields and were socially and sexually intimate with enslaved and free African Americans. White people engaged in clandestine trade to supply slaves with prohibited items such as liquor, helped slaves to escape, and in one case were executed for their participation in planning a slave revolt. At the same time, the majority of poor white people insisted, sometimes violently, on their racial superiority over blacks. For their part, many African American slaves, better dressed, better nourished, and healthier, dismissed them as "poor white trash." But the fact was that the difficult lives of poor whites, whom one contemporary described

as "a third class of white people," served to blur the crucial racial distinction between independent whites and supposedly inferior, dependent black people on whom the system of slavery rested.

Yeoman Values

In 1828 and 1832, southern yeomen and poor white men voted overwhelmingly for Andrew Jackson. They were drawn variously to his outspoken policy of ruthless expansionism, his appeals to the common man, and his rags-to-riches ascent from poor boy to rich slave owner. It was a career many hoped to emulate. The dominance of the large planters was due at least in part to the ambition of many yeomen, especially those with two or three slaves, to expand their holdings and become rich. These farmers, enthusiastic members of the lively democratic politics of the South, supported the leaders they hoped to join.

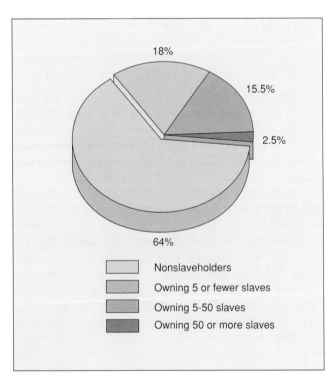

Slaveholding and Class Structure in the South, 1830

The great mass of the southern white population were yeoman farmers. In 1830, slave owners made up only 36 percent of the southern white population; owners of more than fifty slaves constituted a tiny 2.5 percent.

Source: U.S. Bureau of the Census.

But for a larger group of yeomen, independence, not wealth, was most important. The very high value southern yeomen placed on freedom grew directly from their own experience as self-sufficient property-owning farmers in small, family-based communities. This was a way of life that southern "plain folk" were determined to preserve. It made them resistant to the economic opportunities and challenges that capitalism and industrialization posed for northern farmers, which southern yeomen perceived as encroachments on their freedom.

The irony was that the freedom yeomen so prized rested on slavery. White people could count on slaves to perform the hardest and worst labor, and the degradation of slave life was a daily reminder of the freedom they enjoyed in comparison. Slavery meant that all white people, rich and poor, were equal in the sense that they were all free. This assumption of white skin privilege had formed in the eighteenth century as slavery became the answer to the South's labor problem (see Chapter 4). The democratization of politics in the early nineteenth century and the enactment of nearly universal white manhood suffrage perpetuated the belief in white skin privilege, in spite of the fact that the gap between rich and poor white people was widening.

Planters

Remarkably few slave owners fit the popular stereotype of the rich and leisured plantation owner with hundreds of acres of land and hundreds of slaves. Only 36 percent of southern white people owned slaves in 1830, and only 2.5 percent owned fifty slaves or more. Just as yeomen and poor whites were diverse, so, too, were southern slave owners.

Small Slave Owners

The largest group of slave owners were small yeomen taking the step from subsistence agriculture to commercial production. To do this in the South's agricultural economy, they had to own slaves. But owning one or two slaves increased farm production only slightly, and it was hard to accumulate the capital to buy more. One common pattern was for a slave owner to leave one or two slaves to farm while he worked another job (this arrangement usually meant that his wife had unacknowledged responsibility for their supervision). In other cases, small farmers worked side by side with their slaves in the fields. In still other cases, owners hired out their slaves to larger slave owners.

In every case, the owner was economically vulnerable: a poor crop or a downturn in cotton prices could wipe out his gains and force him to sell his slaves. When times improved, he might buy a new slave or two and try again, but getting a secure footing on the bottom rung of the slave owner ladder was very difficult. The roller-coaster economy of the early nineteenth century did not help matters, and the Panic of 1837 was a serious setback to many small farmers.

For a smaller group of slave owners, the economic struggle was not so hard. Middle-class professional men—lawyers, doctors, and merchants—often managed to become large slave owners because they already had capital (the pay from their professions) to invest in land and slaves. Sometimes they received payment for their services not in money but in slaves. These owners were the most likely to own skilled slaves—carpenters, blacksmiths, other artisans—and to rent them out for profit. By steady accumulation, the most successful members of this middle class were able to buy their way into the slave-owning elite and to confirm that position by marrying their sons or daughters into the aristocracy.

The Planter Elite

The slave-owning elite, the 2.5 percent who owned fifty slaves or more, enjoyed the prestige, political leadership, and lifestyle to which many white southerners aspired. Almost all great slave owners inherited their wealth. They were rarely self-made men, although most tried to add to the land and slaves they had inherited. Men of wealth and property had led southern politics since colonial times, but increasingly after 1820 it was men from the middle classes who were most often elected to political office. As the nation moved toward universal manhood suffrage, planters tried to learn how to appeal to the popular vote, but most never acquired the common touch. The smaller slave owners formed a clear majority in every southern state legislature before 1860.

As southerners and slave owning spread westward, membership in the elite broadened to include the new wealth of Alabama, Mississippi, Louisiana, and Texas. The rich planters of the Natchez community were popularly called "nabobs" (from a Hindi word for Europeans who had amassed fabulous wealth in India).

The extraordinary concentration of wealth in Natchez—in 1850 it was the richest county in the nation—fostered a self-consciously elite lifestyle that derived not from long tradition but from suddenly acquired riches.

Plantation Life

The urban life of the Natchez planters was unusual. Many wealthy planters, especially those on new lands in the Old Southwest, lived in isolation on their plantations with their families and slaves. Through family networks, common boarding school experience, political activity, and frequent visiting, the small planter elite consciously worked to create and maintain a distinctive lifestyle that was modeled on that of the English aristocracy, as southerners understood it. This entailed a large estate, a spacious, elegant mansion, and lavish hospitality. For men, the gentlemanly lifestyle meant immersion in masculine activities such as hunting, soldiering, or politics and a touchy concern with "honor" that could lead to duels and other acts of bravado. Women of the slave-owning elite, in contrast, were expected to be gentle, charming, and always welcoming of relatives, friends, and other guests.

But this gracious image was at odds with the economic reality. Large numbers of black slaves had to be forced to work to produce the wealth of the large plantations. A large plantation was an enterprise that required many hands, many skills, and a lot of management. Large plantation owners might have overseers or black drivers to supervise field work, but often they themselves had direct financial control of daily operations.

A paternalistic ideology infused the life of large plantations and enabled the planter elite to rationalize their use of slaves and the submissiveness they demanded of wives. In this paternalistic theory, each plantation was a family composed of both black and white. The master, as head of the plantation, was head of the family, and the mistress was his "helpmate." The master was obligated to provide for all of his family, both black and white, and to treat them with humanity. In return, slaves were to work properly and do as they were told, as children would. Most elite slave owners spoke of their position of privilege as a duty and a burden. (Their wives were even more outspoken about the burdensome aspects of supervising slave labor, which they bore more directly than their husbands.) John C. Calhoun spoke for many slave owners when he described the plantation as "a little community" in which the master directed all operations so that the abilities and needs of every member, black and white, were "perfectly harmonized." Convinced of their own benevolence, slave owners expected not only obedience but gratitude from all members of their great "families."

The Plantation Mistress

Southern paternalism not only laid special burdens on plantation mistresses but put restrictions on their lives and activities not experienced by northern women of the same social rank. The difficulties experienced by these women illustrate the way the slave system affected every aspect of the personal life of slave owners.

Plantation mistresses spent most of their lives tending family members, including slaves, in illness and in childbirth, and supervising their slaves' performance of such daily tasks as cooking, housecleaning, weaving, and sewing. In addition, the plantation mistress often had to spend hours, even days, of behind-the-scenes preparation for the crowds of guests she was expected to welcome in her role as elegant and gracious hostess.

Despite the reality of the plantation mistress's daily supervision of an often extensive household, she did not rule it: her husband did. A wife who challenged her husband or sought more independence from him threatened the entire paternalistic system of control. After all, if she were not dependent and obedient, why should slaves be? In addition, although many southern women were deeply affected by evangelical religion and exhortations to care for those in need, enlisting in reform movements like their northern counterparts would have been far too threatening to the system of slave control to be tolerated in the South, for it might have led slaves to believe that their lives, too, could be improved.

Many southern women also suffered deeply from isolation from friends and kin. Sometimes the isolation of life on rural plantations could be overcome by long visits, but women with many small children and extensive responsibilities found it difficult to leave. Plantation masters, on the other hand, often traveled widely for political and business reasons.

Plantation women in the Old Southwest, many of whom had moved unwillingly and now were far from their families on the eastern seaboard, were particularly lonely. Mary Kendall wrote, "For about three weeks I did not have the pleasure of seeing one white female face, there being no white family except our own upon the plantation." The irony is that she was surrounded by women, but the gap between the white mistress and her black slave was generally unbridgeable.

Although on every plantation black women served as nursemaids to young white children and as lifelong maids to white women, usually accompanying them when they moved as brides into their own homes, there are few historical examples of genuine sympathy and understanding of black women by white women of the slave-owning class. Few of the latter seemed to understand the sadness, frustration, and despair often experienced by their lifelong maids, who were forced to leave their own husbands and children to serve in their mistresses' new homes. A number of southern women did rail against "the curse of slavery," but few meant the inhumanity of the system; most were actually complaining about the extra work entailed by housekeeping with slaves. Many former slaves remembered their mistresses as being kinder than their masters, but fully a third of such accounts mention cruel whippings and other punishments by white women.

Coercion and Violence

There were generous and benevolent masters, but most large slave owners believed that constant discipline and coercion were necessary to make slaves work hard. Some slave owners used their slaves with great brutality. Owners who killed slaves were occasionally brought to trial (and usually acquitted), but no legal action was taken in the much more frequent cases of excessive punishment, general abuse, and rape.

One of the most common violations of the paternalistic code of behavior (and of southern law) was the sexual abuse of female slaves by their masters. Usually, masters forcibly raped their women slaves at will, and slave women had little hope of defending themselves from these attacks. Sometimes, however, long-term intimate relationships between masters and slaves developed.

It was rare for slave owners to publicly acknowledge fathering slave children or to free these children, and black women and their families were helpless to protest their treatment. Equally silenced was the master's wife, who for reasons of modesty as well as her subordinate position was not supposed to notice either her husband's infidelity or his flagrant crossing of the color lines. As Mary Boykin Chesnut, wife of a South Carolina slave owner, vehemently confided to her diary: "God forgive us, but ours is a monstrous system. . . . Like the patriarchs of old, our men live all in one house with their wives and their concubines, and the mulattoes one sees in every family partly resemble the white children."

The Defense of Slavery

"Slavery informs all our modes of life, all our habits of thought, lies at the basis of our social existence, and of our political faith," announced South Carolina planter William Henry Trescot in 1850, explaining why the

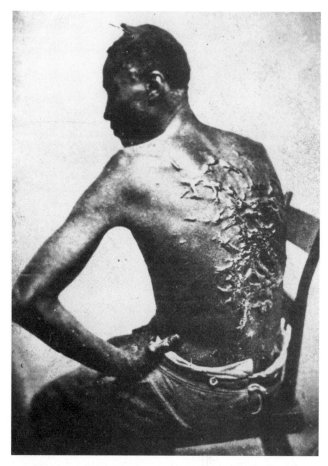

This Louisiana slave named Gordon was photographed in 1863 after he had escaped to Union lines during the Civil War. Few slaves were so brutally marked, but all lived with the threat of beatings if they failed to obey.

South would secede from the Union before giving up slavery. Slavery bound white and black southerners together in tortuous ways that eventually led, as Trescot had warned, to the Civil War.

The sheer numbers of African Americans reinforced white people's perpetual fears of black retaliation for the violence exercised by the slave master. Every rumor of slave revolts, real or imagined, kept those fears alive. The basic question was this: what might slaves do if they were not controlled?

Developing Proslavery Arguments

Southerners increasingly sought to justify slavery. Apologists found justifications for slavery in the Bible and in the histories of Greece and Rome, both slave-owning

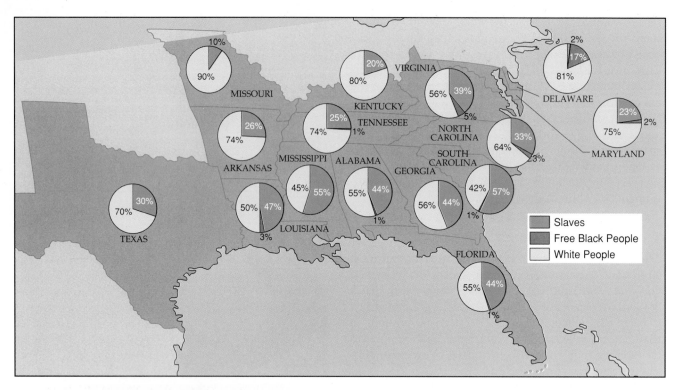

Population Patterns in the South

In South Carolina and Mississippi the enslaved African American population outnumbered whites; in four other Lower South states the percentage was above 40 percent. These ratios frightened many white southerners. Whites also feared the free black population, although only three states in the Upper South and Louisiana had free black populations of 3 percent or more. Six states had free black populations that were so small (less than 1 percent) as to be statistically insignificant.

societies. The strongest defense was a legal one: the Constitution allowed slavery. Though never specifically mentioned in the final document, slavery had been a major issue between North and South at the Constitutional Convention in 1787. In the end, the delegates agreed that seats in the House of Representatives would be apportioned by counting all of the white population and three-fifths of the black people (Article I, Section 2, Paragraph 3); they included a clause requiring the return of runaway slaves who had crossed state lines (Article IV, Section 2, Paragraph 3) and they agreed that Congress could not abolish the international slave trade for twenty years (Article I, Section 9, Paragraph 1). There was absolutely no question: the Constitution did recognize slavery.

The Missouri Crisis of 1819–20 alarmed most southerners, who were shocked by the evidence of widespread antislavery feeling in the North. South Carolinians viewed Denmark Vesey's conspiracy, occurring only two years after the Missouri debate, as an

example of the harm that irresponsible northern antislavery talk could cause. After Nat Turner's revolt in 1831, Governor John Floyd of Virginia blamed the uprising on "Yankee peddlers and traders" who supposedly told slaves that "all men were born free and equal." Thus northern antislavery opinion and the fear of slave uprisings were firmly linked in southern minds.

After Nat Turner

In 1831 the South began to close ranks in defense of slavery. Nat Turner's revolt was linked in the minds of many southerners with antislavery agitation from the North. Militant abolitionist William Lloyd Garrison began publishing the *Liberator,* the newspaper that was to become the leading antislavery organ, in 1831. The British gave notice that they would soon abolish slavery on the sugar plantations of the West Indies, an action that seemed to many southerners much too close to home. Emancipation for West Indian slaves came in 1833. Finally, 1831 was the year before the Nullification Crisis (see Chapter 10) was resolved. Although the other southern states did not support the hotheaded South Carolinians who called for secession, they did sympathize with the argument that the federal government had no right to interfere with a state's special interest (namely, slavery).

In 1835, a crowd broke into a Charleston post office, made off with bundles of antislavery literature, and set an enormous bonfire, to fervent state and regional acclaim. By 1835 many southern legislatures tried to blunt the effect of abolitionist literature by passing stringent laws forbidding slaves to learn how to read. These laws were so effective that by 1860, it is estimated, only 5 percent of all slaves could read. Slaves were forbidden to gather for dances, religious services, or any kind of organized social activity without a white person present. Other laws made manumission illegal and placed even more restrictions on the lives of free black people (as in Natchez).

Attempts were made to stifle all open debate about slavery within the South; dissenters were pressured to remain silent or to leave. A few, such as James G. Birney and Sarah and Angelina Grimké of South Carolina, left for the North to act on their antislavery convictions, but most chose silence.

Southern politicians painted melodramatic pictures of a beleaguered white South hemmed in on all sides by "fanatic" antislavery states, while at home southerners were forced to contemplate what might happen when they had "to let loose among them, freed from the wholesome restraints of patriarchal authority . . . an idle, worthless, profligate set of free negroes" whom they feared would "prowl the . . . streets at night and [haunt] the woods during the day armed with whatever weapons they could lay their hands on."

Finally, southern apologists moved beyond defensiveness to develop proslavery arguments. One of the first to do this was James Henry Hammond, elected a South Carolina congressman in 1834. In 1836 Hammond delivered a major address to Congress in which he denied that slavery was evil. Rather, he claimed, it had produced "the highest toned, the purest, best organization of society that has ever existed on the face of the earth."

In 1854 another southern spokesman, George Fitzhugh, asserted that "the negro slaves of the South are the happiest, and, in some sense, the freest people in the world" because all the responsibility for their care was borne by concerned white masters. Fitzhugh contrasted southern paternalism with the heartless individualism that ruled the lives of northern "wage slaves."

Changes in the South

Despite these defensive and repressive proslavery measures, which made the South seem monolithic in northern eyes, there were some surprising indicators of dissent. Most came from up-country nonslaveholders. One protest occurred in the Virginia state legislature in 1832, when nonslaveholding delegates, alarmed by the Nat Turner rebellion, forced a two-week debate on the merits of gradual abolition. In the final vote, abolition was defeated 73 to 58. The subject was never raised again.

In North Carolina, disputes between slave owners and nonslaveholders erupted in print in 1857, when Hinton Helper published a book attacking slavery titled *The Impending Crisis*. His protest was an indicator of the growing tensions between the haves and the have-nots in the South. Equally significant, though, Helper's book was published in New York, where he was forced to move once his views became known.

Despite these signs of tension and dissent, the main lines of the southern argument were drawn in the 1830s and remained fixed thereafter. The defense of slavery stifled debate within the South, prevented a search for alternative labor systems, and narrowed the possibility of cooperation in national politics. In time, it made compromise impossible.

Conclusion

The amazing growth of cotton production after 1793 transformed the South and the nation. Physically, the South expanded explosively westward. Cotton production was based on the labor of African American slaves, who built strong communities under extremely difficult circumstances. The cohesion of African American families and the powerful faith of African American Christianity were the key community elements that bred a spirit of endurance and resistance. White southerners, two-thirds of whom did not own slaves, denied their real dependence on slave labor by claiming equality in white skin privilege, while slave owners boasted of their own paternalism. In the 1830s, the South defensively closed ranks against real and perceived threats to the slave system. In defending the slave system, the South was increasingly different from the dynamic capitalist free labor system that was gaining strength in the North.

CHRONOLOGY

1790s	Second Great Awakening
	Black Baptist and African Methodist Episcopal churches founded
1793	Cotton gin invented
1800	Gabriel Prosser's revolt discovered in Virginia
1806	Virginia tightens law on manumission of slaves
1808	Congress prohibits U.S. participation in the international slave trade
1816–20	"Alabama Fever": migration to the Old Southwest
1819–20	Missouri Crisis
1822	Denmark Vesey's conspiracy in Charleston
1831	Nat Turner's revolt in Virginia
	William Lloyd Garrison begins publishing antislavery newspaper, the *Liberator*
1832	Nullification Crisis
1832–38	"Flush Times": second wave of westward expansion
1832	Virginia legislature debates and defeats a measure for gradual emancipation
1833	Britain frees slaves throughout the empire, including the West Indies
1835	Charleston crowd burns abolitionist literature
	Tightening of black codes completed by southern legislatures
1836	Congress passes "gag rule" to prevent discussion of antislavery petitions
	James Henry Hammond announces to Congress that slavery is not evil
1854	George Fitzhugh publishes *Sociology for the South,* a defense of slavery
1857	Hinton Helper publishes *The Impending Crisis,* an attack on slavery

Review Questions

1. How did cotton production after 1793 transform the social and political history of the South? How did the rest of the nation benefit? In what way was it an international phenomenon?
2. What were the two key institutions of the African American slave community? How did they function, and what beliefs did they express?
3. The circumstances of three very different groups—poor whites, educated and property-owning American Indians, and free African Americans—put them outside the dominant southern equation of white equals free and black equals slave. Analyze the difficulty each group encountered in the slave-owning South.
4. Who were the yeoman farmers? What was their interest in slavery?
5. Southern slaveholders claimed that their paternalism justified their ownership of slaves, but paternalism implied obligations as well as privileges. How well do you think slaveholders lived up to their paternalistic obligations?
6. How did slaveowners justify slavery? How did their defense change over time?

Recommended Reading

IRA BERLIN, *Slaves Without Masters* (1974). A full portrait of the lives of free black people in the South before the Civil War.

CHARLES C. BOLTON, *Poor Whites of the Antebellum South: Tenants and Laborers in Central North and Northeast Mississippi* (1994). A careful consideration of a hitherto "invisible" population.

B. A. BOTKIN, ED., *Lay My Burden Down: A Folk History of Slavery* (1945). One of the first of many volumes drawing on the words of former slaves concerning their memories of slavery.

ORVILLE VERNON BURTON, *In My Father's House Are Many Mansions: Family and Community in Edgefield, South Carolina* (1985). A detailed community study that considers the farms, families, and everyday relations of white and black people in the period 1850–80.

THOMAS D. CLARK AND JOHN D. W. GUICE, *Frontiers in Conflict: The Old Southwest, 1795–1830* (1989). Considers the Indian nations and their removal, white settlement, and the economic development of the region.

CATHERINE CLINTON, *The Plantation Mistress: Woman's World in the Old South* (1982). Illustrates how slavery shaped the lives of elite white women. The exclusive focus on white women, however, neglects the black women with whom they lived on a daily basis.

DREW GILPIN FAUST, *James Henry Hammond and the Old South* (1982). This outstanding biography uses the complex and interesting story of one man's life and ambitions to tell a larger story about southern attitudes and politics.

LACY K. FORD JR., *Origins of Southern Radicalism: The South Carolina Upcountry, 1800–1860* (1988). One of a growing number of studies of up-country non-slaveholders and their commitment to liberty and equality.

EUGENE GENOVESE, *Roll, Jordan, Roll: The World the Slaves Made* (1974). The landmark book that redirected the attention of historians from slaves as victims to the slave community as an active participant in the paternalism of the southern slave system.

HERBERT GUTMAN, *The Black Family in Slavery and Freedom, 1750–1925* (1977). A sometimes overly statistical study that proves the centrality and durability of the African American family under slavery and after emancipation.

STEVEN HAHN, *The Roots of Southern Populism: Yeoman Farmers and the Transformation of the Georgia Upcountry, 1850–1890* (1983). One of the first studies of the changing world of southern yeomen.

BRUCE LEVINE, *Half Slave and Half Free: The Roots of Civil War* (1992). A useful survey of the different lines of development of the northern and southern economies and the political conflicts between the regions.

JAMES OAKES, *The Ruling Race: A History of American Slaveholders* (1982). Oakes disagrees with Genovese's characterization of paternalism and sees slave owners instead as entrepreneurial capitalists. Especially useful for distinguishing the various classes of slave owners.

PETER J. PARISH, *Slavery: History and Historians* (1989). A useful survey and synopsis of a large literature.

MICHAEL TADMAN, *Speculators and Slaves: Masters, Traders, and Slaves in the Old South* (1989). Examines the extent, organization, and values of the internal slave trade.

12 INDUSTRY AND THE NORTH, 1790s–1840s

AMERICAN COMMUNITIES

WOMEN FACTORY WORKERS FORM A COMMUNITY IN LOWELL, MASSACHUSETTS

In the 1820s and 1830s, young farm women from all over New England flocked to Lowell, to work a twelve-hour day in one of the first cotton textile factories in America. Living six to eight to a room in nearby boardinghouses, they earned an average of three dollars a week. Some also attended inexpensive nighttime lectures and classes. Lowell was considered a model factory town and its educated workers drew worldwide attention.

The Boston investors who financed Lowell were businessmen, not philanthropists, but they wanted to keep Lowell free of the dirt, poverty, and social disorder that made English factory towns notorious. Built in 1823, Lowell boasted six neat factory buildings grouped around a central clock tower, the area pleasantly landscaped with flowers, shrubs, and trees. Housing was similarly well ordered, including supervised boarding houses for the model work force that made Lowell famous: young New England farm women.

The choice of young women as factory workers seemed shockingly unconventional in the 1820s and 1830s. Young unmarried women lived and worked with their parents until they married. In these years of growth and westward expansion, however, America was chronically short of labor, and the Lowell manufacturers were shrewd enough to realize that young farm women were an untapped labor force. For farmers' sons the lure of a farm of one's own was much stronger than factory wages, but for their sisters, escaping from rural isolation and earning wages was an appealing way to spend a few years before marriage. To attract respectable young women, Lowell offered supervision both on the job and at home, with strict rules of conduct, compulsory religious services, cultural opportunities such as concerts and lectures, and cash wages. The adjustment of new arrivals was eased by other women, often their own sisters or neighbors, who had preceded them into the mill. In the factory itself women helped women: as a matter of company policy, senior women carefully trained the newcomers.

The most novel aspect of textile mills was the rigid work schedule required to keep pace with the uniform pace of the power-driven machinery. Every mill published elaborate schedules and insisted that the workers adhere to them; there were fines and penalties for latecomers. Every mill also had one or two overseers per floor to make sure the pace was maintained. Men held these positions and the skilled mechanic positions, and they earned more than the women and children who made up most of the work force.

Some came to Lowell to supplement their family's income, but most regarded Lowell as an opportunity to escape rural isolation and parental supervision. Working side by side and living in company boarding houses with six to twelve other women, some of whom might be relatives or friends from home, the Lowell women built a close, supportive community for themselves.

The owners of Lowell made large profits. They also derived substantial acclaim for their carefully managed community with its intelligent and independent work force. But their success was short-lived. In the depression of the 1830s, the owners imposed wage cuts and work speedups that their model work force did not take lightly. The Lowell women joined in concerted protests in the form of spontaneous "turnouts" and even sustained strikes. By 1850, all thoughts of a "philanthropic manufacturing college" had ended. The original Lowell work force of New England farm girls had been replaced by impoverished Irish immigrants, who worked much harder and for much less pay than their predecessors. Now Lowell was simply another mill town.

The history of Lowell epitomizes the process by which the North (both New England and the Middle Atlantic states) began to change from a society composed largely of self-sufficient farm families (Jefferson's "yeoman farmers") to one of urban wageworkers in an industrial economy. In this chapter we will examine the effects of commercialization and industrialization on the lives of ordinary people.

KEY TOPICS

- **Preindustrial ways of working and living**
- **The nature of the market revolution**
- **The effects of industrialization on workers in early factories**
- **Ways the market revolution changed the lives of ordinary people**
- **The emergence of the middle class**

Preindustrial Ways of Working

At the beginning of the nineteenth century, 97 percent of all Americans lived on farms, and most work was done in or near the home. There was a community network of barter and mutual obligation. Lack of cash was the common experience. Work was slow, unscheduled, and task-oriented. A rural artisan worked when he had orders, responding to demand, not to the clock. The "just price" for an item was set by agreement among neighbors, not by an impersonal market.

Urban Artisans and Workers

In urban areas skilled craftsmen had controlled preindustrial production since the early colonial period.

A young man became a skilled worker—an artisan—by starting as an apprentice in a trade at the age of twelve or fourteen. Contracts bound the apprentice to the master for three to seven years. During that time, the master housed, fed, and clothed the boy while teaching him the trade. Sometimes the master also agreed to make sure the boy went to school. In return, the master had the full use of the boy's labor for no wages. At the end of the term, the apprentice, now in his late teens or early twenties, became a journeyman craftsman. As the name implies, he could travel anyplace he could find work in his trade. Journeymen worked for wages in the shop of a master craftsman until they had enough capital to set up shop for themselves.

Although women as well as men did task-oriented skilled work, they were excluded from the formal apprenticeship system because it was assumed they would marry and so needed only domestic skills. However some women needed or wanted work, and they found a small niche as domestic servants, laundresses, or seamstresses. Some owned boardinghouses. All these were considered respectable occupations, unlike prostitution, another common female occupation in seaport cities.

Patriarchy in Family, Work, and Society

Like the farm family, an entire urban household was commonly organized around one kind of work. Usually the family lived at the shop or store and everyone did part of the work. For example, although a printer was the artisan, his wife was perfectly capable of carrying out some of the operations in his absence and supervising the work of their children or apprentices. She would also be responsible for feeding and clothing apprentices who lived with the family. In a bakery the husband might bake (which often meant getting up in the middle of the night) and relied on his wife to sell the goods during the day.

In both urban and rural settings, working families were organized along strictly patriarchal lines. The husband had the unquestioned authority to direct the lives and the work of the family members and apprentices and to decide on occupations for his sons and marriages for his daughters. His wife had many crucial responsibilities: feeding, clothing, child rearing, and all the other domestic affairs of the household. But in all these activities she was subject to the direction of her husband. The father was head of the family as well as boss of the work. Men were heads of families and bosses of artisanal shops; family assistance was informal and generally unrecognized.

The patriarchal organization of the family was reflected in society as a whole. Legally, men had all the power: neither women nor children had property or legal rights. For example, a married woman's property belonged to her husband, a woman could not testify on her own behalf in court; and in the rare cases of divorce, the husband kept the children, for they were considered his property. When a man died, his son or sons inherited his property. The underlying principle, in both legal and voting rights, was that the man, as head of the household, represented the common interests of everyone for whom he was responsible—women, children, servants, and apprentices. He controlled everything of value, and he alone could vote for political office.

The Social Order

In this preindustrial society everyone, from the smallest yeoman farmer to the largest urban merchant, had a fixed place in the social order. The social status of artisans was below that of wealthy merchants but decidedly above that of common laborers. Yeoman farmers, less grand than large landowners, ranked above tenant farmers and farm laborers. Although men of all social ranks mingled in their daily work, they did not mingle as equals. Great importance was placed on rank and status, which were distinguished by dress and manner. Although by the 1790s many artisans who owned property were voters and vocal participants in politics, few directly challenged the traditional authority of the rich and powerful to run civic affairs. The rapid spread of universal white manhood suffrage after 1800 democratized politics (see Chapter 10). At the same time, economic changes undermined the preindustrial order. There were also a few wealthy artisans in the seacoast cities who were beginning to upset the social order.

New York cabinetmaker Duncan Phyfe and sailmaker Stephen Allen amassed fortunes in their operations. Allen, when he retired, was elected mayor of New York, customarily a position reserved for gentlemen. These artisans owed much of their success to the economic changes brought on by the market revolution discussed next.

The Market Revolution

It encompassed three broad, interrelated economic changes: exceptionally rapid improvements in transportation (discussed in Chapter 10), which allowed both people and goods to move with new ease and speed; commercialization, the production of goods for a cash market rather than home use or local barter; and industrialization, in which power-driven machinery produced goods previously made by hand. Commercialization, exemplified by the putting-out system, preceded industrialization.

The Accumulation of Capital

In the northern states the business community was largely confined to the seaboard cities: Boston, Providence, New York, Philadelphia, and Baltimore. Many merchants had made substantial profits in the international shipping boom of the period 1790–1807 (as discussed in Chapter 9). Such extraordinary opportunities in shipping attracted enterprising people. John Jacob Astor, who had arrived penniless from Germany in 1784, made his first fortune in the Pacific Northwest fur trade with China and eventually through his American Fur Company, he came to dominate the fur trade in the United States as well. He made his second fortune in New York real estate. When he retired in 1834 with $25 million, he was reputed to be the wealthiest man in America. Many similar stories of success, though not so fabulous as Astor's, demonstrated that risk-takers might reap rich rewards in international trade.

When the early years of the nineteenth century posed difficulties for international trade, some of the nation's wealthiest men turned to local investments. In Providence, Rhode Island, Moses Brown and his son-in-law William Almy invested some of the family profits from their worldwide trade in iron, candles, rum, and slaves in the new cotton textile trade. Cincinnati merchants banded together to finance the building of the first steamboats to operate on the Ohio River.

Much of the capital for the new investments came from banks that had been established for international

Wealth in Boston, 1687–1848

Percent of the Population	1687	Percent of Wealth Held		
		1771	1833	1848
Top 1 percent	10%	16%	33%	37%
Top 10 percent	42	65	75	82
Lowest 80 percent	39	29	14	4

This table tracing the distribution of wealth in Boston reflects the gains made by merchants during the international shipping boom of 1790–1807 and the way in which intermarriage between wealthy families consolidated these gains.

trade. But an astonishing amount of capital was raised through family connections. In the late eighteenth century, members of the business communities in the seaboard cities had begun to consolidate their position and property by intermarriage. In Boston such a strong community developed that when Francis Cabot Lowell needed $300,000 in 1813 to build the world's first automated cotton mill in Waltham, Massachusetts, (the prototype for the Lowell mill), he had only to turn to his family network.

Southern cotton provided much of the capital for continuing development. Because the northerners built the ships and controlled shipping trade, they profited almost as much as the south did. For example, in 1825, of the 204,000 bales of cotton shipped from New Orleans, nearly a third (69,000) were shipped via the northern ports of New York, Philadelphia, and Boston.

The Putting-Out System

Initially, the American business community invested not in machinery but in the small putting-out system of home manufactures. In this significant departure from preindustrial work, people still produced goods at home, but under the direction of a merchant who "put out" the raw materials to them, paid them a certain amount per piece, and sold the finished item to a distant market. A look at the shoe trade in Lynn, Massachusetts, shows how the change from preindustrial manufacture occurred.

Long one of the major centers of the American shoe trade, in 1800, Lynn produced 400,000 pairs of shoes, enough for every fifth person in the country. Lynn boasted 200 master artisans and their families, each with a number of journeymen and apprentices, organized in hundreds of small home workshops. The entire family worked on shoes. The artisan and journeymen cut the leather, wives and daughters did the binding of the upper parts of the shoe, the men stitched the shoe together, and children and apprentices helped where needed. The artisan might barter his shoes with a local shopkeeper, or sell them to larger retailers in Boston or Salem. Although the production of shoes in Lynn increased yearly from 1780 to 1810 as markets widened, shoes continued to be made in traditional artisanal ways.

The investment of merchant capital in the shoe business changed everything. A small group of Quaker shopkeepers and merchants, connected by family, religious, and business ties, took the lead in reorganizing the shoe trade in Lynn. Financed by the bank they founded in 1814, Lynn capitalists such as Micajah Pratt built large, two-story central workshops to replace the scattered workshops. Pratt employed a few skilled craftsmen to cut leather for shoes, but he put out the rest of the shoemaking to less skilled workers who were no longer connected by family ties. Individual farm women and children sewed the uppers and the completed uppers were then soled by rural men and boys. These workers were paid more per piece than the women and children who did the sewing, but much less than a master craftsman or a journeyman. As a result of these savings, capitalists could employ more labor. Production increased enormously: the largest central shop in 1832 turned out ten times more shoes than the largest shopkeeper had sold in 1789. Slowly apprentiship and the artisanal system of production were destroyed.

The putting-out system moved the control of production from the individual artisan households to the merchant capitalists, who could now control labor costs, production goals, and shoe styles to fit certain markets. For example, the Lynn trade quickly monopolized the market for cheap boots for southern slaves and western farmers. This specialization of the national market—indeed, even thinking in terms of a national market—was new. Most important from the merchant's point of view was the ability to cut back or expand the labor force as economic conditions or competition warranted. The unaccustomed severity of economic slumps such as the panic of 1819 (see Chapter 9) made this flexibility especially desirable.

The putting-out system first became prevalent in New England around 1805, in the making of shoes. Soon thereafter it was applied to textiles. Other crafts that rapidly became organized on an outwork basis were flax and wool spinning, straw braiding, glove making, and stocking knitting. Many New England farm households were drawn into the cash economy for the first time when the women and children began doing outwork. Wages for piecework replaced the barter system, and many families experienced a sudden new prosperity. They used their new wages to buy mass-produced goods—among them shoes, boots, hats, buttons, stockings, suspenders, horsewhips, machine-made textiles and men's work clothes—at the store. In this way, farm families moved away from self-sufficiency and into the market economy.

British Technology and American Industrialization

Important as the transportation revolution and the commercialization made possible by the putting-out system were, the third component of the market revolution, industrialization, was the greatest change of all. Industrialization began in Britain and was the result of a series of technological changes in the textile trade that mechanized the spinning and weaving of cotton and woolen yarn. In contrast to the decentralized putting-out system, industrialization required workers to work in factories at the pace of power-driven machinery.

The simplest and quickest way for America to industrialize was to copy the British but the British, aware of the value of their machinery, enacted laws forbidding the export of textile machinery and even the emigration of skilled textile workers. But over the years a number of British artisans, lured by American offers, emigrated in disguise to the United States.

One of the first of these workers was young Samuel Slater, who had just finished an apprenticeship in the most up-to-date cotton spinning factory in England when he disguised himself as a farm laborer and slipped out of England. In Providence, Rhode Island, he met Moses Brown and William Almy, who had been trying without success to duplicate British industrial technology. Having carefully committed the designs to memory before leaving England, Slater promptly built copies of the latest British machinery for Brown and Almy. Slater's Mill, as it became known, began operation in 1790. It was the most advanced cotton mill in America.

Following British practice, Slater built a work force primarily of young children (ages seven to twelve) and women, who could be paid much less than the handful of skilled male mechanics who kept the machines working. The yarn spun at Slater's Mill, much more than could be produced by home spinning, was then put out to local home weavers, who turned it into cloth on handlooms. Home weaving flourished, for it repre-

Slater's Mill, the first cotton textile mill in the United States, depended on the water power of Pawtucket Falls for its energy. New England was rich in swiftly flowing streams that could provide power to spinning machines and power looms.

sented a new opportunity for families to make money at a task with which they were already familiar.

Soon many other merchants and mechanics followed Slater's lead, and the rivers of New England were dotted with mills wherever water power could be tapped.

The Lowell Mills

Another way to deal with British competition was to design better machinery. This was the approach of a proper young Bostonian, Francis Cabot Lowell, who made an apparently casual tour of British textile mills in 1811. His hosts were pleased by his interest and by his intelligent questions. They didn't know that each night, in his hotel room, Lowell made sketches from memory of the machines he had inspected during the day.

When Lowell returned to the United States, he worked closely with a Boston mechanic, Paul Moody, to improve on the British models. They not only made the machinery for spinning cotton more efficient, but they also invented a power loom. This was a great advance, for it allowed all aspects of textile manufacture to be gathered together in the same factory. But it also represented a much larger capital investment than that required by a small spinning mill such as Slater's. With help from his family network, Lowell opened the world's first integrated cotton mill in Waltham, near Boston, in 1814. It was a great success: in 1815, the Boston Associates (Lowell's family partners) made profits of 25 percent, and their efficiency allowed them to survive the intense British competition. Many smaller New England mills did not survive. The lesson was clear: size mattered.

The Boston Associates took the lesson to heart, and when they moved their enterprise to a new location in 1823, they thought big. They built an entire town at the junction of the Concord and Merrimack rivers, and named it Lowell (in memory of Francis, who had died, still a young man, in 1817). As described earlier, the new industrial community boasted six mills and company housing for all the workers. In 1826 the town had 2,500 inhabitants; ten years later the population was 17,000.

Family Mills

Lowell was unique. No other textile mill was so large or integrated so many tasks or relied on such a homogenous work force. Nor were most mills situated in new towns. Much more common in the early days of industrialization were small rural spinning mills, on the model of Slater's first mill, built on swiftly running streams near existing farm communities. Often the owners of these mills hired entire families (hence the name *family mills*). The customary job for children (ages eight to twelve) was doffing (changing) spindles on the spinning machines. Children made up an estimated 50 percent of the work force, women about 25 percent, and men (who usually had more skilled jobs and were paid more) the rest.

Relations between these small rural mill communities and the surrounding farming communities were often difficult, as the history of the towns of Dudley and Oxford, Massachusetts, shows. Near these two towns (but not in them) Slater (now a millionaire) built three small mill communities, each consisting of a small factory, a store, and cottages and a boardinghouse for workers. Slater's mills provided a substantial amount of work for local people, putting out to them work such as cleaning the raw cotton and weaving the spun yarn. But despite this economic link, relations between Slater and his workers on one side and the farmers and shopkeepers of the Dudley and Oxford communities on the other were stormy. They disagreed over the building of mill dams, over taxes, schools, and the upkeep of local roads. The debates were so constant and so heated that in 1831 Slater petitioned the Massachusetts General Court to create a separate town that would encompass his three mill communities. For their part, the residents of Dudley and Oxford became increasingly hostile to Slater's authoritarian control, which they regarded as undemocratic, and his workers, whom they disdained for their poverty and transiency. People in the rural communities began referring to millworkers as *operatives,* a sort of worker different from themselves. Industrial work thus led to new social distinctions.

The American System of Manufactures

Not all American technology was copied from British inventions; there were many homegrown inventors.

In 1798 Eli Whitney contracted with the government to make 10,000 rifles in twenty-eight months, an incredibly short period had Whitney produced each rifle in the traditional way, individually and by hand. Instead, he broke down the rifle into standard components and made an exact mold for each. All pieces from the same mold matched a uniform standard and thus were interchangeable. The concept of interchangeability not only hastened production but also meant that a broken part could be easily replaced.

Whitney's ideas far outran his performance. It took him ten years, rather than twenty-eight months, to fulfill his contract. This second crucial step, the invention of milling machines that would grind each part to exact specifications, was achieved by another New Englander, Simeon North, in 1816. A third New Englander, John Hall, brought the idea to fruition in 1824. When the system of interchangeable machine-made parts was quickly adopted by the national armory at Springfield, Massachusetts the Springfield rifle got its name.

The concept of interchangeable parts, realized first in gun manufacturing, was so unusual that the British soon dubbed it the American system. Standardized production quickly revolutionized the manufacture of items as simple as nails and as complicated as clocks. American buinesses mass-produced high-quality goods for ordinary people earlier in America than in Britain or any European country. The availability of these goods was a practical demonstration of American beliefs in democracy and equality.

Other Factories

Although cotton textile mills were the first and best known of the early factories, a number of early factories produced other items, among them metal and iron. Like the textile mills, many of these factories were rural rather than urban because they depended on natural water sources for power or because they needed to be near raw materials such as iron ore. And like the early textile mills, these first heavy industries initially coexisted with the traditional artisanal system.

The rapid development of the steamship industry in Cincinnati illustrates both the role of merchant capital and the coexistence of old and new production methods. Cincinnati's first steamboat, financed by local merchant capital, was commissioned in 1816. It proved so successful that by 1819 one-quarter of all western steamboats were being built in Cincinnati. At the same time, much of the detail work on the steamboat was performed by traditional artisans such as cabinetmakers, upholsterers, tinsmiths, and blacksmiths, who did record-breaking amounts of work in their small, independent shops. In this way, new factory methods and industrial techniques were often coupled with old craft techniques.

From Artisan to Worker

The changes in methods of production caused by industrialization had permanent effects on ordinary Americans. The proportion of wage laborers in the nation's labor force rose from 12 percent in 1800 to 40 percent by 1860. Most of these workers were employed in the North, and almost half were women, performing outwork in their homes. The young farm woman who worked at Lowell for a year or two, then returned home; the master craftsman in Lynn who expanded his shop with the aid of merchant capital; the home weaver who prospered on outwork from Slater's Mill—all of these people were participating, often unknowingly, in fundamental personal and social changes. This section examines these changes.

Personal Relationships

The putting-out system, with its division of each craft into separate tasks, effectively destroyed artisan production and the apprenticeship system. For example, in New York by the mid-1820s, tailors and shoemakers were teaching apprentices only a few simple operations, in effect using them as helpers. Printers undercut the system by hiring partly trained apprentices as journeymen. In almost every trade, apprentices no longer lived with the master's family, but in their own homes. Instead, artisans paid a cash amount to the boy's parents, effectively creating a child labor system. The pressure of cheaper competition forced artisans to accept the central shop and the putting-out system.

The breakdown of the patriarchal relationship between the master and his workers soon became an issue in the growing political battle between the North and the South over slavery. Southern defenders of slavery compared their cradle-to-grave responsibility to their slaves with northern employers' "heartless" treatment of their "wage slaves." Certainly the new northern employer *did* show less responsibility for individual workers than had the traditional artisan. Although the earliest textile manufacturers such as those at Lowell provided housing for their workers, workers became responsible for their own food and housing. Moreover, northern employers felt no obligation to help or care for old or disabled workers. Southerners were right: this *was* a heartless system. But northerners were also right: industrialization was certainly freer than the slave system, freer even than the hierarchical craft system, though it sometimes really offered only the freedom to starve.

Mechanization and Women's Work

Industrialization posed a major threat to the status and independence of male workers. In trade after trade, mechanization meant that most tasks could be performed by unskilled labor. Work in the textile mills was so simple, in fact, that children came to form a large part of the work force.

Mechanization adversely affected women's work as well. The industrialization of textiles—first in spinning, then in weaving—robbed women of their most reliable home occupation. Women now had the choice of following textile work into the factory for low pay or finding other kinds of home work.

The 1820s saw the birth of the garment industry: in New York City, employers began hiring women to sew ready-made clothing (at first rough, unfitted clothing for sailors and southern slaves, later overalls and shirts for westerners and finer items such as men's shirts). In 1860, Brooks Brothers had 70 "inside" workers in a central workshop, but put out work to 3,000 "outside" workers, all women. The division of labor, the basic principle of factory work, disadvantaged women outworkers. The low pay and seasonal nature of the industry became notorious. Manufacturers in the garment trade made their profits not from efficient production, but by obtaining intensive labor for very low wages. Because women were banned from many occupations deemed inappropriate, they were pushed into the garment industry and their oversupply led to wage cutting. The lower the piece rate, the more each woman, sewing at home, had to produce to earn enough to live. Ironically, the invention of the sewing machine, which immensely speeded up work formerly done by hand, only made matters worse. Some women found themselves working fifteen to eighteen hours a day to meet the high output required.

The Cash Economy

Another effect of the market revolution was the transformation of a largely barter system into a cash economy. For example a farm woman might pay in butter and eggs for a pair of shoes from the local shoemaker. A few years later, the same woman, now part of the vast New England outwork industry, might buy new shoes with cash she earned by braiding straw for hats. Community economic ties were replaced by distant and national ones.

The pay envelope became the only connection between factory worker and (often absentee) owner. Workers were no longer part of a settled, orderly, and familiar community; now they were free to labor wherever they could, at whatever wages their skills or their bargaining power could command. That workers took their freedom seriously is evidenced by the very high turnover—50 percent a year—in the New England textile mills.

While moving on was often a sign of workers' increased freedom of opportunity, the economic changes caused by the market revolution forced mobility on others. In New England, for example, many prosperous farmers and artisans faced disruptive competition from factory goods and western commercial agriculture. They could remain where they were only if they became factory workers or commercial farmers. Often the more conservative choice was to move west and try to re-establish one's tradional lifestyle on the frontier.

Free Labor

At the heart of the industrializing economy was the notion of free labor. Originally, *free* referred to individual economic choice—that is, the right of workers to move to another job rather than be held to a position by customary obligation or the formal contract of apprenticeship or journeyman labor. But *free labor* soon came to encompass the range of attitudes—hard work, self-discipline, and a striving for economic independence—that were necessary for success in a competitive, industrializing economy. These were profoundly individualistic attitudes, and owners cited them in opposing labor unions and the use of strikes to achieve wage goals.

For their part, many workers were inclined to define freedom more collectively, arguing that their just grievances as free American citizens were not being heard. As a group of New Hampshire female workers rhetorically asked, "Why [is] there . . . so much want, dependence and misery among us, if forsooth, we are *freemen* and *freewomen?*"

Early Strikes

Rural women workers led some of the first strikes in American labor history. One of the earliest actions occurred at a Pawtucket, Rhode Island, textile mill in 1824. Women protesting wage cuts and longer hours led their co-workers, female and male, out on strike. They had the support of many townspeople.

More famous were the strikes that the women at the model mill in Lowell led. The first serious trouble came in 1834, when 800 women participated in a spontaneous turnout to protest a wage cut of 25 percent. The owners were shocked and outraged by the strike, considering it both unfeminine and ungrateful. The workers, however, were bound together by a sense of sisterhood and were protesting not just the attack on their economic independence but also the blow to their position as "daughters of freemen still." Nevertheless,

Eight hundred women "operatives," followed by four thousand workmen, participate in a strike for higher wages in Lynn in 1860. The women's banner expresses a demand for rights that was a recurrent theme of women's strikes: "American Ladies Will Not Be Slaves."

the wage cuts were enforced, as were more cuts in 1836, again in the face of a turnout. Many women simply packed their clothes in disgust and returned home to the family farm.

A New Social Order

The market revolution reached into every aspect of life, from the social structure to the most personal family decisions. It also fundamentally changed the social order, creating a new middle class with distinctive habits and beliefs.

Wealth and Class

There had always been social classes in America. Since the early colonial period a wealthy elite made up of planters in the South and merchants in the North had existed. Somewhere below the elite but above the mass of people were the "middling sort": a small professional group that included lawyers, ministers, schoolteachers, doctors, public officials, some prosperous farmers, prosperous urban shopkeepers and innkeepers, and a few wealthy artisans such as Boston silversmith Paul Revere. The political and social dominance of the small, wealthy elite was largely unquestioned, as was the "natural" social order that fixed most people in the social rank to which they were born.

The market revolution ended the old social order, creating the dynamic and unstable one we recognize today: upper, middle, and working classes, whose members all share the hope of climbing as far up the social ladder as they can. This social mobility was new.

The major change came in the lives of the "middling sort." The market revolution downgraded many independent artisans to the role of worker, but elevated others such as Duncan Phyfe and Stephen Allen of New York. Other formerly independent artisans or farmers (or more often, their children) joined the rapidly growing ranks of managers and white-collar workers such as accountants, bank tellers, clerks, bookkeepers, and insurance agents. Occupational opportunities shifted dramatically in just one generation. In Utica, New York, for example, 16 percent of the city's young men held white-collar jobs in 1855, compared with only 6 percent of their fathers. At the same time, 15 percent fewer younger men filled artisanal occupations than older men.

These new white collar workers owed not only their jobs but their lifestyles to the new structure and organization of industry. The new economic order demanded certain habits and attitudes: sobriety, responsibility, steadiness, and hard work. Thus a new middle class with distinctively new attitudes was formed.

Religion and Personal Life

Religion, which had undergone dramatic changes since the 1790s, played a key role in the development of these new attitudes. The orderly and intellectual Puritan religion of early New England had been supplanted by a new evangelistic religious spirit, which stressed the achievement of salvation through personal faith. It was more democratic and more enthusiastic than the Puritan religion. Original sin, the cornerstone of Puritan belief, was replaced by the optimistic belief that a willingness to be saved was enough to ensure salvation. Conversion and repentance were now community experiences, often taking place in huge revival meetings where the eyes and emotions of the entire congregation were focused on the sinners about to be saved. The converted bore a heavy personal responsibility to demonstrate their faith in their daily lives through morally respectable behavior. In this way the new religious feeling fostered individualism and self-discipline.

In 1825 in Utica, New York, and other towns along the recently opened Erie Canal, evangelist Charles G. Finney held a series of dramatic revival meetings. His spellbinding message reached both rich and poor, converting members of all classes to the new evangelistic religion. In 1830, made famous by the revivals, Finney was invited by businessmen to preach in Rochester. Prayer meetings were held in schools and businesses, impromptu religious services in people's homes. Middle-class women in particular carried Finney's message by prayer and pleading to the men of their families, who found that evangelism's stress on self-discipline and individual achievement helped them adjust to the new business conditions.

The New Middle-Class Family

The market revolution and the new evangelism also affected women's family roles. Women took the lead in making certain their families joined them in converting to the new, more emotional approach to religion. And when production moved into the hands of paid factory workers, the husband's direct connection with the household was broken: he became a manager of workers, and was no longer the undisputed head of a family unit that combined work and personal life.

Wives, on the other hand, remained at home, where they were still responsible for cooking, cleaning, and other domestic tasks, but no longer contributed directly to what had been the family enterprise. Instead, women took on a new responsibility, that of providing a quiet, well-ordered, relaxing refuge from the pressures of the industrial world. Catharine Beecher's *Treatise on Domestic Economy,* first published in 1841, became the standard housekeeping guide for a generation of middle-class American women. In it, Beecher combined innovative ideas for household design (especially in the kitchen, where she introduced principles of organization) with medical information, child-rearing advice, recipes, and numerous discussions of the mother's moral role in the family. The book clearly filled a need: for many pioneer women, it was the only

The invention of photography made possible family portraits that earlier were too expensive for all but the wealthiest. This portrait of the Edward Miner Gallaudet family, photographed by Mathew Brady in the 1860s, exhibits the gender differences expected in the middle-class family: strong, self-reliant men and softer, more clinging women.

book besides the Bible that they carried west with them.

As the work of middle-class men and women diverged, so did social attitudes about appropriate male and female roles and qualities. Men were expected to be steady, industrious, responsible, and painstakingly attentive to their business. In the competitive, uncertain, and rapidly changing business conditions of the early nineteenth century, these qualities were essential for men who hoped to hold their existing positions or to get ahead. In contrast, women's nurturing qualities were stressed. Gentleness, kindness, morality, and selfless

devotion to family became the primary virtues for fe-
males, who were expected to exercise them within the
"woman's sphere"—the home.

The maintenance or achievement of a middle-class
lifestyle required more cooperation between husband
and wife than was called for in the preindustrial patriarchal family. This new relationship, *companionate marriage*, was yet another result of the market revolution.
The new family cooperation showed most clearly in decisions concerning children.

Family Limitation

Middle-class couples chose to have fewer children than
their predecessors. Children raised to succeed in the
middle class required more care, training, and education
than children who could be put to work at traditional
tasks at an early age. The dramatic fall in the birth rate
during the nineteenth century (from an average of seven
children per woman in 1800 to four in 1900) is evidence of conscious decisions about family limitation,
first by members of the new middle class and later by
working-class families. Few couples used mechanical
methods of contraception such as the condom, partly
because these were difficult to obtain and partly because
most people associated their use with prostitution and
the prevention of venereal disease rather than with family planning. Instead people used birth control methods
that relied on mutual consent: coitus interruptus (withdrawal before climax), the rhythm method (intercourse
only during the woman's infertile period), and, most
often, abstinence or infrequent intercourse.

When mutual efforts at birth control failed, married
women often sought a surgical abortion, a new technique that was much more reliable than the folk remedies women had always shared among themselves.
Surgical abortions were widely advertised and used after
1830, especially by middle-class married women seeking
to limit family size. In fact, some historians estimate that
one out of every four pregnancies was aborted. The rising rate of abortion prompted the first legal bans. By
1860, twenty states had outlawed abortions.

Accompanying the interest in family limitation was a
redefinition of sexuality. Doctors generally recommended that sexual urges be controlled, but they believed that men would have much more difficulty
exercising such control than women, partly because
they also believed women were uninterested in sex. It
was the task of middle-class women to help their husbands and sons restrain their sexuality by appealing to
their higher, moral natures. Women who were visibly

interested in sexual matters ran the risk of being considered immoral or "fallen," and thereupon shunned by
the middle class.

Many women of the late eighteenth century wanted
to be free of the medical risks and physical disability that
too-frequent childbearing brought, but they had little
chance of achieving that goal until men became equally
interested in family limitation. The rapid change in attitudes toward family size that occurred in the early nineteenth century has been repeated around the world as
other societies undergo the dramatic experience of industrialization. It is a striking example of the ways economic changes affect our most private and personal
decisions.

Motherhood

New responsibilities toward children led to another
major redefinition of women's roles. The children of the
new middle class needed a new kind of upbringing, one
that involved a long period of nurturing in the moral
beliefs and personal habits necessary for success. Mothers assumed primary responsibility for this training, in
part because fathers were too busy, but also because
people believed that women's superior qualities of gentleness, morality, and loving watchfulness were essential
to the task.

Fathers retained a strong role in major decisions
concerning children, but mothers commonly turned to
other women for advice on daily matters. Through their
churches, women formed maternal associations for help
in raising their children to be religious and responsible.

Middle-class families sacrificed to keep their sons in
school or in training for their chosen profession. They
housed and fed their sons until the young men had established themselves financially and could marry. A
mother had an important role in making sure her family
had friends and contacts that would be useful when her
children were old enough to consider careers and marriage. Matters such as these, rarely considered by earlier
generations living in small communities, now became
important in the new middle-class communities of
America's towns and cities.

Contrary to the growing myth of the self-made
man, middle-class success was *not* a matter of individual
achievement. Instead it was usually based on a family
strategy in which women's efforts were essential. Although boys were trained for success, this was not an
acceptable goal for their sisters. Women were trained to
be the nurturing, silent "support system" that under-
girded male success. They were also expected to ease

the tensions of the transition to new middle-class behavior by acting as models and monitors of traditional values. The great wave of reform that we will examine in Chapter 13 owed much to women's search for an acceptable outlet for the conflicts created by their new middle-class role.

Conclusion

The market revolution had three aspects: improvements in transportation, commercialization, and industrialization. Each began at different times. The transportation revolution (discussed in Chapter 10) is usually dated from 1825 (the year of the opening of the Erie Canal), accelerating with the building of railroads in the 1830s and 1840s. Commercialization began earlier, as a consequence of the reoganization of manufacturing, the putting-out system, by northern merchants that began around 1805. After that date, local barter arrangements were slowly eroded by case purchase of items manufactured elsewhere. American industrialization began with Samuel Slater's small cotton spinning mill in Rhode Island in 1790, but the most famous early example was the mill town of Lowell, which opened in 1823. These three events, taken together, made up the market revolution that, by changing the ways people worked, changed how they thought.

CHRONOLOGY

1790	Samuel Slater's first mill opens in Rhode Island	1815	War of 1812 ends; British competition in manufactures resumes
1793	Cotton gin invented	1816	First protective tariff
1798	Eli Whitney contracts with the federal government for 10,000 rifles, which he produces with interchangeable parts	1820s	Large-scale outwork networks develop in New England
		1823	Lowell mills open
1807	Embargo Act excludes British manufactures	1824	John Hall successfully achieves interchangeable parts at Harpers Ferry armory
1810	Francis Cabot Lowell tours British textile factories		Women lead strike at Pawtucket textile mill
	First steamboat on the Ohio River	1825	Erie Canal opens
1812	Micajah Pratt begins his own shoe business in Lynn, Massachusetts	1830	Charles G. Finney's revivals in Rochester
1813	Francis Cabot Lowell raises $300,000 to build his first cotton textile factory at Waltham, Massachusetts	1834	First strike at Lowell mills
		1841	Catharine Beecher's *Treatise on Domestic Economy* published

Review Questions

1. What changes in preindustrial life and work were caused by the market revolution?
2. This chapter argues that when people begin doing new kinds of work, their beliefs and attitudes change. Give three examples of such changes described in the chapter. Can you think of other examples?
3. Discuss the opinion offered by historian David

Potter that mass production has been an important democratizing force in American politics. Do you agree? Why or why not?

4. Consider the portrait of the nineteenth-century middle-class family offered in this chapter and imagine yourself as a member of such a family. What new aspects of family relations would you welcome? Which would be difficult? Why?

Recommended Reading

CHRISTOPHER CLARK, *The Roots of Rural Capitalism: Western Massachusetts, 1780–1860* (1990). The most thorough examination to date of how the commercial spirit changed rural life.

ALAN DAWLEY, *Class and Community: The Industrial Revolution in Lynn* (1976). A pathbreaking study of the shift from artisanal to wage labor.

THOMAS DUBLIN, *Women at Work: The Transformation of Work and Community in Lowell, Massachusetts, 1826–1860* (1979). A careful look at the female workers of Lowell and their changing conditions.

KAREN HALTTUNEN, *Confidence Men and Painted Women: A Study of Middle-Class Culture in America* (1982). Explores the development and importance of sentimentalism to the new middle class.

DAVID HOUNDSHELL, *From the American System to Mass Production, 1800–1932* (1984). Shows how not only Eli Whitney but an entire network of New England "mechanics" contributed to the invention of interchangeable parts.

PAUL JOHNSON, *A Shopkeeper's Millennium: Society and Revivals in Rochester, New York, 1815–1837* (1978). A study of the changing relationship between masters and workers in Rochester.

BRUCE LAURIE, *Artisans into Workers: Labor in Nineteenth-Century America* (1989). Using many specific examples, traces the changes in labor described in this chapter.

JONATHAN PRUDE, *The Coming of Industrial Order: Town and Factory Life in Rural Massachusetts, 1810–1860* (1983). A major source of information on family mills.

STEVEN J. ROSS, *Workers on the Edge: Work, Leisure and Politics in Industrializing Cincinnati, 1788–1890* (1985). Studies the growth of wage labor in a major western city.

MARY RYAN, *The Making of the Middle Class* (1981). A study of Utica, New York, that was the first to clearly discern the role of women in the family strategies of the new middle class.

CHARLES SELLERS, *The Market Revolution: Jacksonian America 1815–1846* (1991). A synthesis of the political, religious, and economic change of the period.

CHRISTINE STANSELL, *City of Women: Sex and Class in New York, 1789–1860* (1983). Exceptionally useful in exploring the range of women's work and the social dynamics of rapidly growing New York City.

13 COMING TO TERMS WITH THE NEW AGE, 1820s–1850s

AMERICAN COMMUNITIES

SENECA FALLS: WOMEN REFORMERS RESPOND TO THE MARKET REVOLUTION

In the summer of 1848, a small advertisement appeared in an upstate New York newspaper:

WOMAN'S RIGHTS CONVENTION.—A Convention to discuss the social, civil, and religious condition and rights of woman, will be held in the Wesleyan Chapel, at Seneca Falls, N.Y., on Wednesday and Thursday, the 19th and 20th of July, current; commencing at 10 o'clock A.M. During the first day the meeting will be exclusively for women, who are earnestly invited to attend. The public generally are invited to be present on the second day, when Lucretia Mott of Philadelphia, and other ladies and gentlemen, will address the convention.

Charlotte Woodward, a nineteen-year-old glove maker who did outwork in her rural home, saw the advertisement and persuaded six friends to travel to the convention with her. To the surprise of the convention organizers, almost 300 people—men as well as women—attended the two-day meeting, where they discussed a document modeled on the Declaration of Independence. It began thus: "We hold these truths to be self-evident: That all men and women are created equal. . . ."

The resolutions accompanying the declaration pointed out that men had deprived women of legal rights, of the right to own their own property, of custody of their children in cases of divorce, of the right to higher education (at that time only Oberlin College and Mount Holyoke College admitted women), of full participation in religion, and of the right to vote. As the delegates to the Seneca Falls convention discussed and voted on each resolution, all were passed unanimously except the last, which a minority found too radical to support. "Why Lizzie, thee will make us ridiculous!" Quaker Lucretia Mott had exclaimed when Elizabeth Cady Stanton proposed the voting rights measure. Yet, for the group assembled in the Wesleyan Chapel, this first women's rights convention was so successful that they promptly planned another one three weeks later in New York's most important upstate city, Rochester.

What impelled Charlotte Woodward and her friends to ride forty miles to attend this meeting? And what attracted the other participants? They were responding to the many changes brought about recently in their own work and communities and by the market revolution. The Seneca Falls region, a farming frontier in 1800, had plunged into national commerce when it was linked to an off-shoot of the Erie Canal in 1828. It was drawn even further into the modern age when the railroad arrived in 1841. Seneca Falls itself had become a center for flour milling and manufacturing, and a hub of the outwork network of which Charlotte Woodward was a part. Swamped by newcomers (among them a growing number of poor and foreign-sounding Irish Catholics), the inhabitants of Seneca Falls struggled to maintain the sense of community of the earlier, smaller town by grouping together in volunteer organizations of all kinds—religious, civic, social, educational, and recreational—and to undertake active reforms to counteract the effects of industrialization, rapid growth and the influx of newcomers in the community. The town of Seneca Falls, like many others beset by rapid social change, became home to a number of active reform organizations whose members hoped to improve community life through social change.

Many reformers belonged to liberal religious groups with wide social perspectives. Both the Wesleyan Methodist Society of Seneca Falls and the Progressive Quakers of the nearby town of Waterloo had broken away from the national organizations of the Methodists and Quakers because they would not take a strong stand against slavery. Both groups were outspoken in their belief in the moral equality of all humankind and in their commitment to social activism. Perhaps as many as a third of those attending the Woman's Rights Convention were members of the Wesleyan Chapel, and another quarter or so were Waterloo Quakers. Others were members of temperance societies. Seneca Falls had been the site of a "temperance reformation" in the early 1840s, when the enthusiasm generated in large revival-like meetings had convinced hundreds to sign pledges of abstinence from alcohol.

Family connections and personal friendships bound the reform community together. In July 1848 Lucretia Mott, the Philadelphia Quaker who was the nation's best-known woman reformer, visited her sister in Waterloo (after a reform-related tour of the new penitentiary at Auburn and a nearby Indian reservation). Elizabeth Cady Stanton of Seneca Falls, wife of a well-known antislavery

orator and niece of a leading reform philanthropist, came to have tea and to renew her acquaintance with Mott. As she and Mott spoke about the difficulties of women's lives, the idea of a women's rights convention was born. Initially, women's rights was just one of many reforms, but it was to be exceptionally long-lasting. Stanton, soon to form a working partnership with former temperance worker Susan B. Anthony, devoted the rest of her life to women's rights.

But what of Charlotte Woodward, a local farm girl, unaware of the national reform community? Why was she there? Because in this age of hopefulness and change she wanted a better life for herself. She was motivated, she said, by

> all the hours that I sat and sewed gloves for a miserable pittance, which, after it was earned, could never be mine. [By law and custom her father, as head of the household, was entitled to her wages.] I wanted to work, but I wanted to choose my task and I wanted to collect my wages.

The reforming women of Seneca Falls, grouped together on behalf of social improvement, had found in the first women's rights convention a way to speak for the needs of working women such as Charlotte Woodward as well as for their own.

All over the North, local communities such as Seneca Falls as well as cities such as New York became places where Americans gathered together in reform organizations to try to solve the problems that the market revolution posed for work, family life, personal and social values, and urban growth. Through their reform organizations local women and men became participants in wider communities of concern. From their many local efforts a national reform movement grew.

KEY TOPICS

◆ **The new social problems that accompanied immigration and urbanization**

◆ **The responses of reformers**

◆ **The origins and political effects of the abolitionist movement**

◆ **The involvement of women in reform efforts**

Immigration

Previous chapters described the personal and political effects of the market revolution. This chapter focuses on the urban and community problems caused by the market revolution and the response to them. One of the most fundamental changes was in the ethnic composition of the American people.

Patterns of Immigration

Although the United States is a nation of immigrants, the rate of immigration had varied greatly from year to year. For example, between 1790 and 1820 the Napoleonic wars prevented a lot of immigration. But beginning in 1830, immigration to the United States soared, increasing fivefold in the period 1831–40, tripling in the next decade, and then peaking at nearly 450,000 in 1854. In 1860 one out of three white males in the North was foreign-born (one out of four in the South—an indication of the greater economic diversity and attractiveness of the North).

Many of the immigrants to the United States before the Civil War were from Ireland and Germany; they represented the largest influx of non-English immigrants the country had known. They were also the poorest: Most of the Irish arrived destitute. In addition, most of the Irish and half of the Germans were Catholics, another unwelcome novelty to many Protestant Americans.

There was a demand for immigrant labor to fuel the expanding American economy and to turn wilderness into farmland. Some projects simply could not have been accomplished without immigrant labor. The Erie Canal, finished in the 1820s, is a case in point: the labor of Irish contract workers was essential to its completion (see Chapter 10). For the rest of the century, industries that demanded heavy physical labor (steelmaking, mining, railroads) drew on the labor of immigrant men. Immigrant women, meanwhile, found jobs as domestic servants and in the needle trades.

Few immigrants found life in the United States pleasant or easy. In addition to the psychological difficulties of leaving a home and familiar ways behind, most immigrants endured harsh living and working conditions. America's cities were unprepared for the social problems posed by large numbers of immigrants. There was no significant federal regulation or responsibility for immigration until the 1880s; the burden fell completely on cities and states.

Irish Immigration

The first major immigrant wave to test American cities was caused by the catastrophic Irish Potato Famine of 1845–49. The Irish, held in unwilling colonial status by the British, subsisted poorly on small plots of farmland on which they grew grain for British landlords and potatoes for their own food. In 1845 Ireland's green fields of potatoes turned black with blight. The British government could not cope with the scale of the disaster, leaving the Irish with two choices: starve or leave. One million people died, and another 1.5 million emigrated, the majority to the United States. Starving, diseased (thousands died of typhus during the voyage), and destitute, hundreds of thousands disembarked at East Coast ports. Lacking the money to go inland and begin farming, they remained in the cities. Crowded together in miserable housing, desperate for work at any wages, foreign in their religion and pastimes (drinking and fighting, their critics said), tenaciously nationalistic and bitterly anti-British, they created ethnic enclaves of a kind new to American cities.

The largest numbers of Irish came to New York, which managed to absorb them. But Boston, a much smaller and more homogeneous city, was overwhelmed by the Irish influx. By 1850, a quarter of Boston's population was Irish, most of them recent immigrants. Boston, the home of Puritanism and the center of American intellectualism, did not welcome illiterate Irish Catholic peasants. All over the city in places of business and in homes normally eager for domestic servants the signs went up: "No Irish Need Apply." The Irish were able to get only the worst and poorest-paying jobs.

The Irish Community

Isolated partly by their own beliefs (for Catholics fully reciprocated the hatred and fear Protestants showed them), the Irish created their own community within Boston. They raised the money to erect Catholic churches staffed by Irish priests. They established parochial schools with Irish nuns as teachers, and sent their children there in preference to the openly anti-Catholic public schools. They formed mutual aid societies based on kinship or town of origin in Ireland. Men and women formed religious and social clubs, as well as lodges and brotherhoods and their female auxiliaries. This dense network of associations provided help in time of need and companionship in a hostile environment. And, almost from the moment of their arrival, the Irish sent huge sums of money back to Ireland so that relatives could join them in America. As one newcomer wrote, "There is a great many ill conveniences here, but no empty bellies."

For such large amounts of money to be raised from such a poor community, family work strategies were

HISTORY AND THE LAND

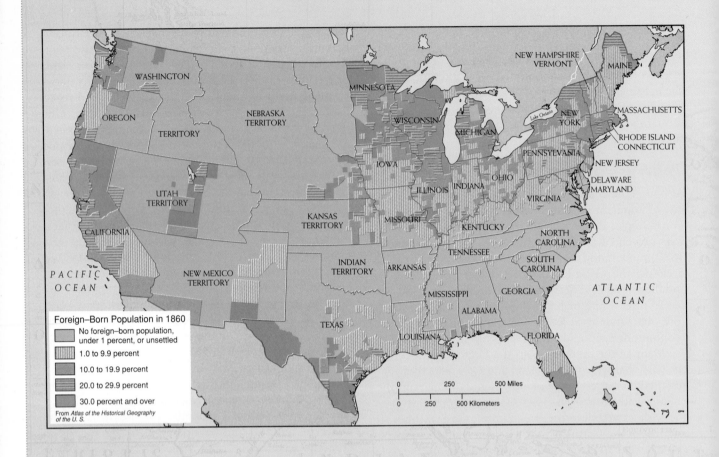

Foreign–Born Population in 1860

- No foreign–born population, under 1 percent, or unsettled
- 1.0 to 9.9 percent
- 10.0 to 19.9 percent
- 20.0 to 29.9 percent
- 30.0 percent and over

From *Atlas of the Historical Geography of the U. S.*

SOARING IMMIGRATION
IN THE NINETEENTH CENTURY

Immigration soared in the period 1830–54, and the ethnic composition of the immigrant stream changed. The Irish Potato Famine of 1845 and economic troubles in Germany caused the numbers of Irish and German immigrants to rise sharply. The Irish impact was predominantly urban. By 1860, Irish-born immigrants made up 25 percent of the populations of Boston and New York and Jersey City (across the Hudson River from New York) and nearly 20 percent of the population of Philadelphia and Providence, Rhode Island. The Irish worked primarily as unskilled laborers and were the first large Catholic ethnic group in a predominantly Protestant country. They were also politically active, and bitter contests between Irish necessary. Families were generally large, and every member contributed to the family income. Young men might work far away on railroad construction or in mines, but most of their wages were sent home. Young women worked in textile mills or as live-in domestic servants for Bostonians.

Irish men made their way in two occupations: the priesthood and politics. The Irish quickly took over the local Democratic party, opposing that city's traditional power structure, made up mostly of Whigs, the heirs of the Federalists. Their strength lay at the neighborhood level, where politicians knew everyone personally. Often the neighborhood politicians were saloon keepers, for the tavern was the secular center of Irish society—much to the horror of Bostonians, many of whom sternly advocated temperance. Political popularity and loyalty were ensured by the small gestures of aid (a job for a son, a small loan, even a

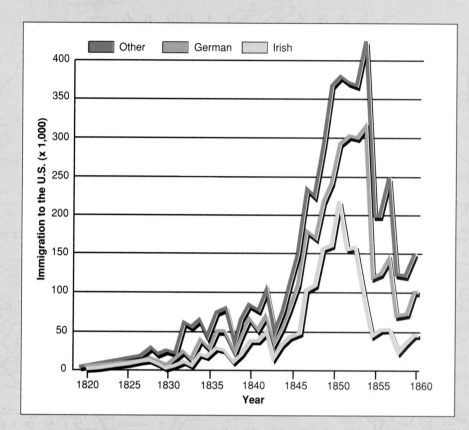

Immigration to the U.S. (x 1,000)

Legend: Other, German, Irish

agricultural communities in Texas. Western cities with large German populations were New Orleans, St. Louis, Cincinnati, and Milwaukee, while the eastern cities of New York, Philadelphia, and Baltimore boasted "little Germanies." Although many German immigrants, like the Irish, were Catholic, more of them were artisans and able to move quickly into skilled labor positions. Less active politically than the Irish, many Germans were attracted to the new Republican Party in the 1850s.

Other areas attracting immigrants were Gold Rush California, which drew many Chinese, and Utah Territory, where the Mormon Church recruited many former English factory workers to their new Zion. The high proportion of foreign-born in Texas and New Mexico in 1860 reflects not immigration but the fact that Mexicans living in the territories acquired from Mexico in 1848 were now classified as foreign-born in what had formerly been their homeland.

Most of the immigration labeled "other" on this chart came from Britain. The increase in their numbers in 1845–60 was due in part to intensive Mormon missionary efforts in Britain.

Democratic "machine" politicians and Whig reformers quickly became a part of urban politics.

The impact of German immigration was more diffused. Because many Germans arrived in America via New Orleans, they settled in the American interior. Following the Mississippi River north, many took up farming in Michigan and Wisconsin; others formed

round of free drinks) on which a poor community depends. By these methods, the first Irish mayor of Boston, Hugh O'Brien, was elected in 1884. One Irish saloon keeper, Patrick Joseph Kennedy, founded one of America's most famous political dynasties. Barely a century after Patrick's birth into a poor immigrant family, his grandson, John Fitzgerald Kennedy, was elected the first Irish Catholic president of the United States.

German Immigration

The nineteenth-century immigration of Germans began somewhat later and more slowly than that of the Irish, but by 1854 it had surpassed the Irish influx. Some German peasants, like the Irish, were driven from their homeland by potato blight in the mid-1840s. But the typical German immigrant was a small farmer or artisan dislodged by the same market forces at work in America: industrialization of production and consolidation and commercialization of farming. There was also a small group of middle-class liberal intellectuals who left the German states (Germany was not yet a unified nation) after 1848 when attempts at revolution had failed. German migrants were thus a more diverse group than the Irish, and their settlement patterns were more diffuse. Nevertheless, like the Irish, they formed their own communities and encountered American hostility for their "foreign" ways.

After their arrival in Baltimore or New Orleans, many Germans made their way to the Mississippi and Ohio river valleys—where they settled in Pittsburgh, Cincinnati, and St. Louis—and to farms in Ohio, Indiana, Missouri, and Texas. Few Germans settled in northeastern cities or in the South.

These immigrants formed predominantly German farm communities by *clustering*, or taking up adjoining land. A small cluster could support German churches, German-language schools, and German customs and thereby attract other Germans, some directly from Europe and some from other parts of the United States. Such communities reinforced the traditional values of German farmers, such as persistence, hard work, and thrift. Non-German neighbors often sold out and moved on, but the Germans stayed and improved the land so they could pass it on to the next generation. They used soil conservation practices, for example, that were unusual for the time. Persistence paid: German cluster communities exist to this day in Texas, the Midwest, and the Pacific Northwest, and families of German origin are still the single largest ethnic group in agriculture.

Little Germanies

Germans who settled in urban areas built ethnic enclaves in which they sought to duplicate the rich cultural life of German cities. Like the Irish, the Germans formed church societies, mutual benefit societies, and fire and militia companies for the purpose of mutual support. The Germans also formed a network of leisure organizations: singing societies, debating and political clubs, and *turnvereine* (gymnastics associations).

"Little Germanies" often boasted German-language schools theater groups, and a flourishing German-language press. In the summer entire families frequented beer gardens, which were usually in semirural settings and always had music. This flourishing community culture, with its emphasis on music, intellectual interests, and love of nature, had an impact on American urban life, especially in Baltimore and Cincinnati. At first the Germans were greeted with hostility (temperance societies were especially unhappy about the beer gardens), but by 1860 not only the beer gardens but other German customs such as gymnasiums and candlelit Christmas trees were shared by Germans and non-Germans alike. German ideas about education led to the adoption by public schools of kindergartens, music programs, gymnastics, and vocational training, and influenced the structure of high schools. The construction of ethnic neighborhoods and communities by German and Irish immigrants eased their adjustment to American circumstances, but the poverty and strangeness of the new immigrants added to the list of social problems that America's urban centers were unable to solve in the early nineteenth century.

Urban America

The market revolution left no aspect of American life unaffected. Nowhere was the impact so obvious as in the cities.

The Growth of Cities

In 1820 only 6 percent of the American population lived in cities. Between 1820 and 1860, the market revolution caused cities to grow at a more rapid rate than at any other time in American history. By 1860, almost 20 percent of the population was urban. The great seaports continued to lead the way in population growth.

The nation's five largest cities in 1850 were the same as in 1800, with one exception. New York, Philadelphia, Baltimore, and Boston still topped the list, but Charleston had been replaced by New Orleans (see Chapter 9). The rate of urban growth was extraordinary for the nation's five largest cities. Between 1800 and 1860, all four Atlantic seaports—New York, Philadelphia, Baltimore, and Boston—grew at least 25 percent each decade, and often much more. New York's growth was by far the greatest: 64 percent between 1820 and 1830. New York was not only America's largest city (60,500 in 1800, 202,600 in 1830, over 1 million in 1860) but also its largest port and financial center. It had far outstripped its rival American seaports on the Atlantic coast.

Philadelphia, the nation's largest city in 1800, was half the size of New York in 1850. Nevertheless, its growth was substantial: from 70,000 in 1800 to 389,000 in 1850 and to 565,529 in 1860. Philadelphia became as much an industrial as a commercial city.

Baltimore was half the size of Philadelphia (212,418 in 1860). Baltimore merchants, attempting to protect trade links with the trans-Appalachian West that were threatened by the Erie Canal, built the first important railroad, the Baltimore and Ohio, in 1830. Although Baltimore remained the East Coast center of the tobacco trade with Europe, by 1850 its major foreign trade consisted of shipping flour to and importing coffee from Brazil.

Boston had 177,840 people in 1860. In colonial times Boston had dominated the triangular trade between Britain and the West Indies. Now Boston merchants had a new triangular trade: ships carried New England cotton cloth, shoes, and other manufactured goods to the South, delivered southern cotton to British and European ports, and returned to Boston with European manufactured goods. Boston still dominated the China trade as well.

By 1860 New Orleans had become the fifth largest city, with a population of 168,675. Fed by the expansion of cotton throughout the South and commercial agriculture in the Mississippi Valley, New Orleans increased its exports from $5 million in 1815 to $107 million in 1860. By the 1850s New Orleans handled about half the nation's cotton exports.

Each of these ports had turned its back to the oceans by 1860 to reach far into the American interior for trade. Prosperous merchants in these cities now depended on American exports rather than European imports for their profits.

Another result of the market revolution was the appearance of "instant" cities, which sprang up at critical points on the new transportation network. Utica, New York, once a frontier trading post, was transformed by the opening of the Erie Canal into a commercial and manufacturing center. Railroads made the fortune of Chicago, located on the shores of Lake Michigan at a junction of water and rail transport. By the 1850s Chicago was a trade hub boasting grain storage facilities, slaughterhouses, and warehouses of all kinds to service the trade that passed through the city and manufacturing plants to serve the needs of Midwestern farmers. By 1860 Chicago had a population of 100,000, making it the nation's eighth largest city (after Cincinnati and St. Louis).

Class Structure in the Cities

Although economists estimate that per capita income doubled between 1800 and 1850, the growing gap between rich and poor was glaringly apparent in the nation's cities. The benefits of the market revolution were unequally distributed. In the cities there was a very small group of wealthy people worth more than $5,000 (about 3 percent of the population), a very large group of poor people who owned $100 or less (nearly 70 percent), and a middle class with incomes in between (25 to 30 percent).

Differences in income affected every aspect of urban life. Very poor families, including almost all new immigrants, performed unskilled labor, lived in cheap rented housing, moved frequently, and depended on more than one income to survive. Artisans and skilled workers with incomes of $500 or more could live adequately, though often in cramped quarters that also served as their shops. Middle-class life was comfortable if a family earned more than $1,000 a year. Then it could afford a larger house of four to six rooms complete with carpeting, wallpaper, and good furniture. The very rich built mansions and large town houses and staffed them with many servants. In the summer they left the cities for country estates or homes at seaside resorts such as Newport, Rhode Island, which attracted wealthy families from all over the country.

Sanitation and Living Patterns

Early-nineteenth-century cities lacked municipal water supplies, sewers, and garbage collection. People drank water from wells, used outdoor privies that often contaminated the water supply, and threw garbage and slop out the door to be foraged by roaming herds of pigs. Every American city suffered epidemics of sanitation-related diseases such as yellow fever, cholera, and typhus. Philadelphia's yellow fever epidemic of 1793 caused 4,000 deaths and stopped all business with the outside world for over a month.

Yet the cities were slow to take action. In response to the yellow fever epidemic, Philadelphia completed a city water system in 1801, but it was not free of charge, and only the richest subscribed in the early days. Neither New York nor Boston had public water systems until the 1840s. Garbage collection remained a private service, and cities charged property owners for the costs of sewers, water mains, and street paving. Poorer areas of the cities could not afford the new sanitation costs.

Provision of municipal services led to residential segregation. Richer people clustered in neighborhoods having the new amenities, or escaped to the new suburbs. Increasingly, the poor gathered in bad neighborhoods—slums. The worst New York slum in the nineteenth century was Five Points, a stone's throw from City Hall. There, immigrants, free black people, and criminals were crammed into rundown buildings known in the slang of the time as *rookeries*. Notorious gangs of thieves and pickpockets with names such as the Plug Uglies and the Shirt Tails dominated the district. Starvation and murder were common.

After 1830, when urban growth was augmented by increasing immigration from Europe, slums were perceived by middle-class Americans as the home of strange and foreign people who deserved less than American-born citizens. In this way, residential patterns came to embody larger issues of class and citizenship in American life.

Urban Popular Culture

The size, diversity, and changing working conditions in American cities bred a new, rougher, urban popular culture. Taverns, which served as neighborhood centers of drink and sociability, were also frequent centers of brawls and riots. Community groups such as fire engine companies that had once included men of all social classes now attracted rough young laborers who formed their own youth gangs and defended "their" turf against other gangs. Some tradesmen, such as butchers, became notorious for starting fights in taverns and grog shops.

Theaters, which had been frequented by men of all social classes, provided another setting for violence. By the 1830s, middle-class men withdrew to more respectable theaters to which they could bring their wives and daughters. Workers found new amusements in theaters such as the Lafayette Circus that featured dancing girls and horseback riders as well as theatrical acts. Another popular urban working-class amusement was the blackface minstrel show. White actors (often Irish) blacked their faces and entertained audiences with songs (including the famous "Dixie," written by an Irishman as a blackface song), dances, theatrical skits, and antiblack political jokes.

Another challenge to middle-class respectability came from the immensely popular penny papers (so called from their price), the New York *Morning Post* and the *Sun*, which began appearing in 1833. These papers, with lurid headlines such as "Double Suicide," "Secret Tryst," and "Bloody Murder," fed the same popular appetite for scandal, as did dime novels such as *Franklin Evans; or, The Inebriate* written in 1842 by struggling young newspaperman Walter (later Walt) Whitman. Whitman distilled his passionate love for the variety and commonness of the American people in *Leaves of Grass*, a book of free-verse poems published in 1855. Regarded at the time as scandalous because of its frank language, Whitman's poetry nevertheless captured the driving energy and democratic spirit of the new urban popular culture. In a rather more sinister way, so did the writings of Edgar Allan Poe of Baltimore, who found the inspiration for his gothic horror stories in contemporary American crimes.

Urban Life of Free African Americans

By 1860 there were nearly half a million free African Americans in the United States, constituting about 11 percent of the total black population. More than half of all free African Americans lived in the North, mostly in cities. Philadelphia and New York had the largest black communities: 22,000 African Americans in Philadelphia and 12,500 in New York (another 4,313 lived just across the East River in Brooklyn). There were much smaller but still significant black communities in the New England cities of Boston, Providence, and New Haven and in Ohio cities such as Cincinnati.

Free black people in northern cities faced residential segregation, pervasive job discrimination, segregated

Free African Americans suffered many forms of discrimination, but as this 1850 daguerreotype of an unknown woman shows, they sought to achieve the same levels of education and economic comfort as other Americans.

public schools, and severe limitations on their civil rights. In addition to these legal restrictions, African Americans of all economic classes endured daily affronts such as exclusion from public concerts, lectures, and libraries and segregation or exclusion from public transportation.

Like the German and Irish immigrants discussed earlier, African Americans created their own community structures. They formed associations for aiding the poorest members of the community, for self-improvement, and for socializing. Tired of being insulted by the white press, African American communities supported their own newspapers. The major community organization was the black Baptist or African Methodist Episcopal (AME) church, which served, as one historian put it, as "a place of worship, a social and cultural center, a political meeting place, a hiding place for fugitives, a training ground for potential community leaders, and one of the few places where blacks could express their true feelings."

Employment prospects for black men deteriorated from 1820 to 1850. Free African American men who had held jobs as skilled artisans were forced from their positions, and their sons denied apprenticeships, by white mechanics and craftsmen who were themselves hurt by industrialization (see Chapter 12). Limited to day labor, African Americans found themselves in direct competition with the new immigrants, especially the Irish, for jobs. One of the major areas of competition was the waterfront, where black men lost their jobs as longshoremen and carters to the Irish. One of the few occupations still open was that of seaman. Perhaps half of all American sailors in 1850 were black. Mothers, wives, and daughters were left ashore to work as domestic servants (in competition with Irishwomen), washerwomen, and seamstresses. In addition to rioting (in 1801, 1819, 1826, and 1832) in support of their slave counterparts in the south and against slave catchers taking escaped slaves back to slavery, free African Americans were themselves targets of urban violence. An 1829 riot in Cincinnati sent a thousand black people fleeing to Canada in fear for their lives, a three-day riot in Providence in 1831 destroyed a black district, and an 1834 New York riot destroyed a church, a school, and a dozen homes. Philadelphia, home to the largest free African American community in the North, was repeatedly rocked by antiblack riots in the period 1820–49. A riot in 1834 destroyed two churches and thirty-one homes; one African American was killed and many injured. Other cities had similar stories. Urban riots of all kinds had cost 125 lives by 1840, by 1860 more than 1,000.

The Labor Movement and Urban Politics

Universal white manhood suffrage and the development of mass politics (see Chapter 10), coupled with the rapid growth of cities, changed urban politics. The traditional leadership of the wealthy elite waned. In their place were professional politicians whose job it was to make party politics work. In New York and in other large cities, this change was spurred by working-class activism.

The Tradition of Artisanal Politics

Protests by urban workers had been an integral part of the older social order controlled by the wealthy elite. In the eighteenth century, when only men of property could vote, demonstrations usually indicated widespread discontent or economic difficulty among workers. They served as a warning signal that the political elite rarely ignored.

By the 1830s the status of artisans and independent craftsmen in the nation's cities had changed. Workers' associations came to include defensive and angry workers who were acutely conscious of their declining status in the economic and social order. Tentatively at first, but then with growing conviction, they became active defenders of working-class interests.

What was new was the open antagonism between workers and employers. The community of interest between master and workers in preindustrial times broke down. Workers quickly came to see that they must turn to other workers, not to employers, for support. In their turn, employers and members of the middle class began to take urban disorders much more seriously than their grandfathers might have done.

The Union Movement

Urban worker protest against changing conditions quickly took the form of party politics. The Workingmen's party began in Philadelphia in 1827 and chapters quickly formed in New York and Boston as well. Using the language of class warfare, the "Workies" campaigned for the ten-hour day and the preservation of the small artisanal shop. They also called for the end of government-chartered monopolies—banks were high on the list—and for a public school system and cheap land in the West. Although the "Workies" themselves did not survive as a party, Jacksonian Democrats were quick to pick up on some of their themes, and the Democrats attracted a number of workers' votes in 1832.

Both major parties competed for the votes of urban workers. For their part, the Whigs assuring workers that Henry Clay's American System, and tariff protection in particular, would be good for the economy and for workers' jobs. Nevertheless, neither major political party really spoke to the primary need of workers: well-paid, stable jobs.

Between 1833 and 1837 a wave of strikes in New York City cut the remaining ties between master craftsmen and the journeymen who worked for them. In 1833 journeymen carpenters struck for higher wages. Workers in fifteen other trades came to their support, and within a month the strike was won. The lesson was obvious: if skilled workers banded together across craft lines, they could improve their conditions. The same year, representatives from nine different craft groups formed the General Trades Union (GTU) of New York. By 1834 similar groups had sprung up in over a dozen cities. In 1834 representatives of several local GTUs met in Baltimore and organized the National Trades Union (NTU). In its founding statement the NTU criticized the "unjustifiable distribution of the wealth of society in the hands of a few individuals," which had created for working people "a humiliating, servile dependency, incompatible with . . . natural equality."

Convinced that unions were dangerous, New York employers took striking journeymen tailors to court in 1836. Judge Ogden Edwards pronounced the strikers guilty of conspiracy and declared unions un-American. The GTU responded with a mass rally at which Judge Edwards was burned in effigy. A year later, stunned by the effects of the Panic of 1837, the GTU collapsed. The founding of these general unions, a visible sign of a class-based community of interest among workers, is generally considered to mark the beginning of the American labor movement. However, these early unions included only white men in skilled trades; the majority of workers—men in unskilled occupations, all free African Americans, and all women—were excluded.

Big-City Machines

As America's cities experienced unprecedented growth, the electorate mushroomed. In New York, for example, the number of voters grew from 20,000 in 1825 to 88,900 in 1855. Furthermore, by 1855 half of the voters were foreign-born. The job of serving this electorate and making the new mass political party work at the urban level fell to a new kind of career politician and a new kind of political organization.

In New York City the Tammany Society slowly evolved into the key organization of the new mass politics. (Named after the Delaware chief described in Chapter 3, the society met in a hall called the Wigwam and elected "sachems" as their officers.) Tammany, which was affiliated with the national Democratic party, reached voters by using many of the techniques of mass appeal made popular by craft organizations—parades, rallies, current songs, and party newspapers. Tammany also used a tight system of political control beginning at the neighborhood level with ward committees and topped by a chairman of a citywide general committee. At the citywide level, ward leaders—bosses—bartered the loyalty and votes of their followers for positions on the city payroll for party members and community services for their neighborhoods. This was machine politics.

The new system of machine politics reflected the class structure of the rapidly growing nineteenth-century cities. Feelings of community now had to be cultivated politically. In America's big cities the result was apparent by midcentury: the political machine controlled by the boss (the politician who represented the interests of his group and delivered their votes in exchange for patronage and favors). The machines themselves offered personal ties and loyalties—community feeling—to recent arrivals in the big cities (increasingly, immigrants from Europe) and help in hard times to workers who cast their vote correctly.

Social Reform Movements

As the chapter introduction described, the earliest response to the dislocations caused by the market revolution was community-based and voluntary. The reform message was vastly amplified by inventions such as the steam printing press, which made it possible to publish reform literature in great volume. Soon there were national networks of reform groups.

Alexis de Tocqueville, the famous French observer who wrote *Democracy in America* after visiting the United States in 1831–32, remarked on the vast extent of voluntary associations and their many purposes. "In no country in the world," he noted, "has the principle of association been more successfully used, or more unsparingly applied to a multitude of different objects, than in America."

Evangelism, Reform, and Social Control

Evangelical religion was fundamental to social reform. Men and women who had been converted to the enthusiastic new faith assumed personal responsibility for making changes in their own lives. Members of evangelistic religions expected to convert the world and create the perfect moral and religious community on earth. Much of America was swept by the fervor of moralistic reform and it was the new middle class, who applied new notions of morality to the movement, that set the agenda for reform.

Reform efforts arose from the recognition that the traditional methods of small-scale local relief were no longer adequate. Reformers realized that large cities had to make large-scale provisions for social misfits, and that institutional rather than private efforts were needed. This thinking was especially true of the institutional reform movements that began in the 1830s, such as the push for insane asylums, which at the time did not exist.

A second aspect of reform efforts was a belief that the unfortunate—the poor, the insane, the criminal—would be reformed, or at least improved, in a good environment. Thus insane asylums were built in rural areas, away from the noise and stress of the cities, and orphanages had strict rules that were meant to encourage discipline and self-reliance. Prison reform carried this sentiment to the extreme. On the theory that it was largely bad social influences that were responsible for crime, some model prisons completely isolated prisoners from one another, making them eat, sleep, work, and do their required Bible reading in their own cells. The failure of these prisons to achieve dramatic changes for the better in their inmates (a number of isolated prisoners went mad, and some committed suicide) or to reduce the incidence of crime was one of the first indications that reform was not a simple task.

A third characteristic of the reform movements was their moralistic dogmatism. Reformers knew what was right, and were determined to see their improvements enacted. Their reforms were measures of *social control.* Lazy, sinful, intemperate, or unfit members of society were to be reformed for their own good, whether they wanted to be or not. This attitude was bound to cause controversy; by no means were all Americans members of reform groups, nor did many take kindly to being objects of reform.

Indeed, some aspects of the social reform movements were harmful. The intense religious feeling of the revival movement helped to foster the hostility experienced by Catholic immigrants from Ireland and Germany beginning in the 1830s. The temperance movement targeted immigrants whose drinking habits were freer than those of most older inhabitants. Thus social reform helped to foster the virulent nativism of American politics in the period 1840–60 (see Chapter 15).

The extent of reform efforts was unprecedented. Regional and national organizations quickly grew from local efforts to deal with social problems such as drinking, prostitution, mental illness, and crime. In 1828 Congregationalist minister Lyman Beecher joined other ministers in forming a General Union for Promoting the Observance of the Christian Sabbath; the aim was to prevent business on Sundays. The sabbath reformers engaged in political action but remained aloof from direct electoral politics, stressing their religious mission. Workingmen (who usually worked six days a week) were angered when the General Union forced the Sunday closure of their favorite taverns, and were quick to vote against the Whigs, the party most sympathetic to reform thinking.

Education and Women Teachers

Women were deeply involved in reform efforts. Nearly every church had a Maternal Association, where mothers gathered to discuss ways to raise their children as true Christians. The efforts of these women were evidence of a new and more positive definition of childhood. In contrast to the Puritans, who had believed that

Catharine Beecher, a member of one of America's leading families of religious reformers, advocated teaching as a suitable employment for young single women because it called for the nurturing skills and moral values she claimed all women possessed.

children were born sinful and that their wills had to be broken before they could become godly, educational reformers tended to believe that children were born innocent and needed gentle nurturing and encouragement if they were to flourish. At home, mothers began to play the central role in child rearing. Outside the home, women helped spread the new public education pioneered by Horace Mann, secretary of the Massachusetts State Board of Education.

Although literacy had long been valued, especially in New England, schooling since colonial times had been a private enterprise and a personal expense. In 1827 Massachusetts pioneered compulsory education by legislating that public schools be supported by public taxes. Soon schooling for white children between the ages of five and nineteen was common. Uniformity in curriculum and teacher training, and the grading of classes by ability—measures pioneered by Horace Mann in the 1830s—quickly caught on in other states. In the North and West more and more children went to school, and more and more teachers, usually young single women, were hired to teach them.

The spread of public education thus created the first real career opportunity for women. The great champion of teacher training for women was Catharine Beecher, who clearly saw her efforts as part of the larger work of establishing "the moral government of God." By 1850 women dominated primary school teaching, which had come to be regarded as an acceptable occupation for educated young women during the few years between their own schooling and marriage. For some women, teaching was a great adventure: They enthusiastically volunteered to be "schoolmarms" on the distant western frontiers of Wisconsin and Iowa or to be missionary teachers in distant lands. For others, a few years of teaching was quite enough. The low pay (half of what male schoolteachers earned) and community supervision (the teacher had to board with families in the community) were probably enough to make almost any marriage proposal look appealing.

Temperance

The largest reform organization of the period, the American Temperance Society, founded in 1826, boasted over 200,000 members by the mid-1830s. Dominated by evangelicals, local chapters used revival methods—lurid temperance tracts detailing the evils of alcohol, large prayer and song meetings, and heavy group pressure—to encourage young men to stand up, confess their bad habits, and "take the pledge" (not to drink). Here again, women played an important role.

Traditionally, drinking had been a basic part of men's working lives. It concluded occasions as formal as the signing of a contract and accompanied such informal activities as card games. Alcohol was a staple offering at political speeches, rallies, and elections. Much of the drinking was well within the bounds of sociability, but the widespread use (upwards of five gallons of hard liquor per capita in 1830—more than twice as much as today's rate) must have encouraged drunkeness.

There were a number of reasons to support temperance. Men drank hard liquor—whiskey, rum, and hard cider—in abundance. Heavy-drinking men hurt their families economically by spending their wages on drink. Excessive drinking also led to violence and crime, both within the family and in the larger society. But there were other reasons for the temperance movement. The new middle class, preoccupied with respectability and morality, found the old easygoing drinking ways unacceptable. As work patterns changed, employers banned alcohol at work and increasingly considered drinking men not only unreliable but immoral. Temperance became a social and political issue. Whigs, who embraced the new morality, favored it; Democrats (who in northern cities consisted increasingly of immigrant workers) were opposed.

The Panic of 1837 affected the temperance movement. Whereas most temperance crusaders in the 1820s had been members of the middle class, the long recession of 1837–44 prompted artisans and skilled workers to give up or at least cut down substantially on drinking. Forming associations known as Washington Temperance Societies, these workers spread the word that temperance was the workingman's best chance to survive economically and maintain his independence. Their wives, gathered together in Martha Washington Societies, were often even more committed to temperance than their husbands. By the mid-1840s alcohol consumption had been more than halved, to less than two gallons per capita, about today's level. But concern over drinking was constant throughout the nineteenth century and into the twentieth.

Moral Reform, Asylums, and Prisons

Alcohol was not the only "social evil" reform groups attacked. Another was prostitution, which was common in the nation's port cities. The customary approach of evangelical reformers was to "rescue" prostitutes, offering them the salvation of religion, prayer, and temporary shelter. The success rate was not very high. As an alternative to prostitution, reformers usually offered domestic work, a low-paying and restrictive occupation that many women scorned. Nevertheless, campaigns against prostitution, generally organized by women, continued throughout the nineteenth century. One of the earliest and most effective antiprostitution groups was the Female Moral Reform Society. Founded by evangelical women in New York in 1834 (the first president was Charles Finney's wife, Lydia), it boasted 555 affiliates throughout the country by 1840.

Another dramatic example of reform was the asylum movement, spearheaded by an evangelist, Dorothea Dix. In 1843, Dix horrified the Massachusetts state legislature with the results of several years of investigating the condition of mentally ill women: graphically she described women incarcerated with ordinary criminals. Dix's efforts led to the establishment of a state asylum in Massachusetts, and to similar institutions in other states. Between 1843 and 1854 Dix traveled more than 30,000 miles to publicize the movement for humane treatment of the mentally ill. By 1860 twenty-eight states had public mental institutions.

Other reformers were active in related causes, such as prison reform and the establishment of orphanages, homes of refuge, and hospitals. Model penitentiaries were built in Auburn and Ossining, New York (known as "Sing Sing"), and in Philadelphia and Pittsburgh. Characterized by strict order and discipline, these prisons were supposed to reform rather than simply incarcerate their inmates but their regimes of silence and isolation caused despair more often than rehabilitation.

Utopianism and Mormonism

Amid the political activism and reform fervor of the 1830s, a small number of people chose another route: escape into utopian communities and new religions. The upstate New York area along the Erie Canal was the seedbed for this movement just as it was for evangelical revivals and reforms such as those described in this chapter's opening story on Seneca Falls. In fact, the area was so notable for its enthusiasms that it has been called the Burned-Over District (referring to the waves of reform that swept through like forest fires).

Apocalyptic religions tend to spring up at times of rapid social change. The early nineteenth century was such a time. A second catalyst is hard times, and the prolonged depression that began with the Panic of 1837 led some people to embrace a belief in imminent catastrophe. The Millerites (named for their founder, William Miller) believed that the Second Coming of Christ would occur on October 22, 1843. In anticipation, members of the church sold their belongings and bought white robes for their ascension to heaven. When the Day of Judgment did not take place as expected, most of Miller's followers drifted away. But a small group persisted. Revising their expectations, they formed the core of the Seventh-Day Adventist faith, which is still active today.

The Shakers, founded by "Mother" Ann Lee in 1774, were the oldest utopian group. An offshoot of the Quakers, the Shakers espoused a radical social philosophy that called for the abolishment of the traditional family in favor of a family of brothers and sisters joined in equal fellowship. Although a basic rule of the sect was celibacy, the simple and highly structured lifestyle, isolation from the changing world, and the lure of equality drew new followers, especially among women. After 1850 new recruits declined and the communities withered. Several communities survived into the twentieth century, however, and a few elderly Shaker women are still alive today.

The most successful nineteenth-century communitarian movement was also a product of the Burned-Over District. In 1830 a young man named Joseph Smith organized a church based on the teachings of the Book of Mormon, which he claimed to have received from an angel in a vision. Smith founded the Church of Jesus Christ of Latter-Day Saints, popularly known as the Mormons.

Mormonism rapidly became distinctive because of its extraordinary communitarianism, achieved under the benevolent but absolute authority of the patriarch, Joseph Smith. Close cooperation and hard work made the Mormon community very successful, attracting both new followers and the animosity of neighbors, who resented Mormon exclusiveness and economic success. The Mormons were harassed in New York and driven west to Ohio and then Missouri. Finally they seemed to find an ideal home in Nauvoo, Illinois, where in 1839 they built a model community, achieving almost complete self-government and isolation from non-Mormon neighbors. But in 1844 dissension within the community over Joseph Smith's new doctrine of polygamy (marriage between one man and more than one woman simultaneously) gave outsiders a chance to intervene. Smith and his brother were arrested peacefully, but were killed by a mob from whom their jailers failed to protect them.

The beleaguered Mormon community decided to move again, this time beyond reach of harm. Led by

Brigham Young, the Mormons migrated in 1846 to the Great Salt Lake in present-day Utah. After several lean years, the Mormon method of communal settlement proved successful. Their hopes of solation were dashed, however, by the California gold rush of 1848.

Antislavery and Abolitionism

The antislavery feeling that was to play such an important role in the politics of the 1840s and 1850s also had its roots in the religious reform movement that began in the 1820s and 1830s. Three groups—the Quakers, free African Americans, and militant white reformers—worked to bring an end to slavery, but each in different ways.

The American Colonization Society

The first attempt to "solve" the problem of slavery was a plan for gradual emancipation of slaves and their resettlement in Africa, proposed by the American Colonization Society, formed in 1817 by northern religious reformers and a number of southern slave owners. The Society was ineffective, sending only 1,400 black people to Africa by 1830.

African Americans' Fight Against Slavery

Most free African Americans rejected colonization, insisting instead on a commitment to the immediate end of slavery and the equal treatment of African Americans. By 1830 there were at least fifty African American abolitionist societies in the North. These organizations held yearly national conventions, where famous African American abolitionists such as Frederick Douglass, Harriet Tubman, and Sojourner Truth spoke. The first African American newspaper, founded in 1827 by John Russwurm and Samuel Cornish, announced its antislavery position in its title, *Freedom's Journal.*

In 1829 David Walker, a free African American in Boston, wrote a widely distributed pamphlet, *Appeal . . . to the Colored Citizens,* that encouraged slave rebellion. White southerners blamed pamphlets such as these for stirring up trouble among southern slaves. They held up the 1831 Nat Turner revolt (see Chapter 11) as a horrifying example of northern interference. The vehemence of their protests is a testament to the courage of a handful of determined free African Americans to speak for their enslaved brothers and sisters.

This poignant engraving of a chained female slave was made by Patrick Reason, a black artist, in 1835. The accompanying message, "Am I Not a Woman and a Sister?" spoke especially to female abolitionists in the North.

Abolitionists

The third and best-known group of antislavery reformers was headed by William Lloyd Garrison. In 1831 Garrison broke with the gradualists of the American Colonization Society and began publishing his own paper, *The Liberator.* Garrison, the embodiment of moral indignation, was totally incapable of compromise. His approach was to mount a sweeping crusade condemning slavery as sinful and demanding its immediate abolishment. He took the radical step of demanding full social equality for black people, referring to them individually as "a man and a brother" and "a woman and a sister." Garrison's determination electrified the antislavery movement, but his inability to compromise interfered with his effectiveness as a leader.

Moral horror over slavery deeply engaged many northerners in the abolitionist movement. They flocked to hear firsthand accounts of slavery by Frederick Douglass and Sojourner Truth, and by two white sisters from South Carolina, Angelina and Sarah Grimké. Northerners eagerly read slave narratives and books such as Theodore Weld's 1838 *American Slavery as It Is* (based in part on the recollections of Angelina Grimké, whom Weld had married) that provided graphic details of abuse. Lyman Beecher's daughter, Harriet Beecher

Stowe, was to draw on the Grimké-Weld book for her immensely popular antislavery novel, *Uncle Tom's Cabin*, published in 1852.

The style of abolitionist writings and speeches was similar to the oratorical style of the religious revivalists. The abolitionists were confrontational, denunciatory, and personal in their message, much like the evangelical preachers. They also adopted the revivalists' and temperance workers' tactic of mass publishing of tracts. In 1835 alone, abolitionists mailed over a million pieces of antislavery literature to southern states. This tactic drew a backlash: Southern legislatures banned abolitionist literature, encouraged the harassment and abuse of anyone distributing it, and looked the other way when proslavery mobs seized and burned it. Most seriously, most Southern states reacted by toughening laws concerning emancipation, freedom of movement, and all aspects of slave behavior. Ironically, then, the immediate impact of abolitionism in the South was to stifle dissent and make the lives of slaves harder (see Chapter 11).

Even in the North controversy over abolitionism was common. A tactic abolitionists had borrowed from revivalists—holding large and emotional meetings—opened the door to mob action. Crowds of people often disrupted the meetings, especially those addressed by Theodore Weld, whose oratorical style earned him the title of "the most mobbed man in the United States." William Lloyd Garrison was stoned, dragged through the streets, and on one occasion almost hanged by a Boston mob.

Abolitionism and Politics

Antislavery began as a social movement but soon intersected with sectional interests and became a national political issue. In the 1830s, massive abolitionist petition drives—nearly 700,000 petitions—requesting the abolition of slavery and the slave trade in the District of Columbia were rebuffed by Congress. At southern insistence and with President Andrew Jackson's approval, Congress passed a "gag rule" in 1836 that prohibited discussion of antislavery petitions.

The gag rule and censorship of the mails, which southerners saw as necessary defenses against abolitionist frenzy, alarmed many in the North. Former president John Quincy Adams, now a congressman from Massachusetts, so publicly and persistently denounced the gag rule as a violation of the constitutional right to petition that it was repealed in 1844.

Although abolitionist groups raised the nation's emotional temperature, they failed to achieve the moral unity they had hoped for, and they began to splinter. Frederick Douglass and William Lloyd Garrison parted ways when Douglass, refusing to be limited to a simple recital of his life as a slave, began to make specific suggestions for improvements in the lives of free African Americans. When Douglass chose the path of political action, Garrison denounced him as "ungrateful." Douglass and other free African Americans worked under persistent discrimination, even from antislavery whites, some of whom refused to hire African Americans or meet with them as equals. Although many white reformers eagerly pressed for *civil* equality for African Americans, they did not accept the idea of *social* equality. On the other hand, black and white "stations" worked closely in the risky enterprise of passing fugitive slaves north over the famous Underground Railroad (the name for the various routes by which slaves made their way to freedom). Contrary to abolitionist legend, however, it was free African Americans, rather than whites, who played the major part in helping the fugitives.

In 1840 the abolitionist movement formally split. The majority moved toward party politics (which Garrison abhorred), founding the Liberty Party and choosing James G. Birney (whom Theodore Weld had converted to abolitionism) as their presidential candidate. Thus the abolitionist movement, which began as an effort at moral reform, took its first major step toward the eventual formation of the Republican party and the Civil War (see Chapter 15).

The Women's Rights Movement

American women, without the vote or a role in party politics, found a field of activity in social reform movements. Although men were often the official leaders of such movements, women often formed all-female chapters (for example, in temperance, moral reform, and abolition), so they could define their own reform policies and programs. The majority of women did not participate in reform, for they were fully occupied with housekeeping and child rearing (families with five children were the average). A small number of women, usually members of the new middle class who could afford servants, had the time and energy to look beyond their immediate tasks. Led thereby to challenge social restrictions, some, such as the Grimké sisters, found that their commitment carried them beyond the limits of what was considered acceptable activity for women.

The Grimké Sisters

Sarah and Angelina Grimké, members of a prominent South Carolina slaveholding family, rejected slavery out of religious conviction and moved north to join a Quaker community near Philadelphia. In the 1830s these two sisters found themselves drawn into the growing antislavery agitation in the North. Because they knew about slavery firsthand, they were in great demand as speakers. At first they spoke to parlor meetings of women only, as was considered proper, but as the meetings got larger and larger, they became the first female public speakers in America. In 1837 Angelina Grimké became the first woman to address a meeting of the Massachusetts state legislature.

Whereas male antislavery orators were criticized by the press and by conservative ministers for their abolitionist position, the Grimké sisters were criticized for speaking out simply because they were women. A letter from a group of ministers cited the Bible in reprimanding the sisters for stepping out of "woman's proper sphere" of silence and subordination. Sarah Grimké answered the ministers in her 1837 *Letters on the Condition of Women and the Equality of the Sexes*. She claimed that "men and women were CREATED EQUAL. . . . Whatever is right for a man to do, is *right* for woman."

Women in the antislavery movement found it a constant struggle to be heard. They solved the problem by forming their own groups such as the Philadelphia Female Anti-Slavery Society. Still, in the antislavery movement and other reform groups as well, men accorded women a secondary role, even when, as was often the case, women constituted a majority of the members.

Women's Rights

The Seneca Falls Convention of 1848, the first women's rights convention in American history, was an outgrowth of almost twenty years of female activity in social reform. Every year after 1848 women gathered to hold women's rights conventions and to work for political, legal, and social equality. Over the years, in response to persistent lobbying, states passed property laws more favorable to women and changed divorce laws to allow women to retain custody of children. Higher education opened up to women, and women gained the vote in some states, beginning with Wyoming in 1869. Nationally, female suffrage was finally enacted in 1920 in the Nineteenth Amendment to the Constitution, seventy-two years after it was first proposed at Seneca Falls.

Women played a vital role in all of the social movements of the day. In doing so, they implicitly challenged the popular notion of separate spheres for men and women—the public world for him, home and family for her. The separate-spheres argument, although it heaped praise on women for their allegedly superior moral qualities, was meant to exclude women from political life. But women reformers clearly believed they had a right and a duty to propose solutions for the moral and social problems of the day. Empowered by their own religious beliefs and activism, the Seneca Falls reformers spoke for all American women when they demanded an end to the unfair restrictions they suffered as women.

Conclusion

Beginning in the 1820s, the market revolution changed the size and social order of America's preindustrial cities and towns. Immigration, rapid population growth, and changes in working life created a host of new urban problems. Older face-to-face methods of social order no longer worked to fill the gap, so various associations (the political party, the religious crusade, the reform movement) sprang up in the first half of the 1800s. They were new manifestations of the deep human desire for connection, for continuity, and, especially in the growing cities, for social order. But a striking aspect of these associations was the uncompromising nature of the attitudes and beliefs on which much of the politics and many of the reform efforts were based. Most groups were bands of like-minded people who wanted to impose their will on others. Such intolerance boded ill for the future. If political parties, religious bodies, and reform groups were to splinter along sectional lines (as happened in the 1850s), political compromise would be very difficult. In the meantime, however, Americans came to terms with the market revolution by engaging in a passion for improvement. As a perceptive foreign observer, Francis Grund, noted, "Americans love their country not as it is but as it will be."

CHRONOLOGY

1817	American Colonization Society founded
1820s	Shaker colonies grow
1826	American Society for the Promotion of Temperance founded
1827	Workingmen's Party founded in Philadelphia *Freedom's Journal* begins publication Public school movement begun in Massachusetts
1829	David Walker, *Appeal . . . to the Colored Citizens*
1830	Joseph Smith founds Church of Jesus Christ of Latter-Day Saints (Mormon Church) Finney's revivals in Rochester Immigration begins to increase
1831	William Lloyd Garrison begins publishing antislavery newspaper, *The Liberator*
1833	American Anti-Slavery Society founded by Garrison and Theodore Weld
1834	First Female Moral Reform Society founded in New York National Trades Union formed

1836	Congress passes "gag rule" to prevent discussion of antislavery petitions
1837	Angelina Grimké addresses Massachusetts legislature Sarah Grimké, *Letters on the Equality of the Sexes and the Condition of Women* Panic begins seven-year recession
1840s	New York and Boston complete public water systems
1840	Liberty Party founded
1843	Millerites await the end of the world Dorothea Dix spearheads asylum reform movement
1844	Mormon leader Joseph Smith killed by mob
1845	Beginning of Irish Potato Famine and heavy Irish immigration
1846	Mormons begin migration to the Great Salt Lake
1848	Woman's Rights Convention at Seneca Falls

Review Questions

1. What was new about the immigration of the 1840s and 1850s?
2. Why did urbanization produce so many problems?
3. What motivated the social reformers of the period? Were they benevolent helpers or dictatorial social controllers? Study several reform causes and discuss similarities and differences among them.
4. Abolitionism differed little from other reforms in its tactics, but the effects of antislavery activism were politically explosive. Why was this so?

Recommended Reading

ARTHUR BESTOR, *Backwoods Utopias* (1950). The standard work on utopian communities.

PAUL BOYER, *Urban Masses and Moral Order in America, 1820–1920* (1978). Interprets reform as an effort to reestablish the moral order of the preindustrial community.

AMY BRIDGES, *A City in the Republic: Antebellum New York and the Origins of Machine Politics* (1984). An innovative look at the transition from elite political control to machine politics.

PAUL A. GILJE, *The Road to Mobocracy: Popular Disorder in New York City, 1763–1834* (1987). Provides an interesting and entertaining description of the many varieties of civic disorder of the day.

OSCAR HANDLIN, *Boston's Immigrants: A Study in Acculturation* (rev. ed., 1959). A pathbreaking exploration of conflict and adaptation among Boston's Irish community.

DANIEL WALKER HOWE, "The Evangelical Movement and Political Culture in the North During the Second Party System," *Journal of American History* 78:1 (March 1991). An award-winning article that explores the connections among religion, politics, and reform.

LEON LITWACK, *North of Slavery: The Negro in the Free States, 1790–1860* (1961). The standard source on free black people in the North.

ERIC LOTT, *Love and Theft: Blackface Minstrelsy and the American Working Class* (1993). Explores the complicated relationships between working-class amusements and racial attitudes.

DAVID ROEDIGER, *The Wages of Whiteness* (1991). Explores the links between artisanal republicanism, labor organization, and white racism.

DAVID ROTHMAN, *The Discovery of the Asylum: Social Order and Disorder in the New Republic* (1971). Explores institutional reforms.

KATHRYN SKLAR, *Catharine Beecher: A Study in American Domesticity* (1973). An absorbing "life and times" that explores the possibilities and limits of women's roles in the early nineteenth century.

SEAN WILENTZ, *Chants Democratic: New York City and the Rise of the American Working Class, 1788–1850* (1983). An important book, rooted in social history, that reveals how workers acted upon their understanding of republicanism in confronting the changes wrought by the market revolution.

14

THE TERRITORIAL EXPANSION OF THE UNITED STATES, 1830s–1850s

AMERICAN COMMUNITIES

TEXANS AND TEJANOS "REMEMBER THE ALAMO!"

For thirteen days in February and March 1836 a force of 187 Texans held the mission fortress known as the Alamo against a siege by 5,000 Mexican troops under General Antonio López de Santa Anna, president of Mexico. Santa Anna had come north to subdue rebellious Texas, the northernmost part of the Mexican province of Coahuila y Texas, and place it under central authority. On March 6 he ordered a final assault, and in brutal fighting that claimed over 1,500 Mexican lives, his army took the mission. All the defenders were killed, including Commander William Travis and well-known frontiersmen Jim Bowie and Davy Crockett. It was a crushing defeat for the Texans, but the cry "Remember the Alamo!" rallied the survivors who, less than two months later, routed the Mexican army and forced Santa Anna to grant Texas independence from Mexico.

But memory is selective: some things tend to be forgotten. Within a generation of the uprising few remembered that many *Tejanos,* Spanish-speaking people born in Texas, had joined with American settlers fighting for Texas independence. The Americans were concentrated in the central and eastern portions of the huge Texas territory, where during the 1820s the Mexican government had authorized several colonies managed by *empresarios* (land agents) such as Stephen F. Austin. These settler communities consisted mostly of farmers from the Mississippi Valley, who introduced slavery and cotton growing to the rich lands of coastal and upland Texas.

The Tejano community, descended from eighteenth-century Spanish and Mexican settlers, included wealthy *rancheros* who raised cattle on the shortgrass prairies of south Texas, as well as the cowboys known as *vaqueros* and the *peónes,* or poor tenant farmers. Although there was little contact between the Americans and Tejanos, their leaders interacted in San Antonio, the center of regional government. The Tejano elite welcomed the American immigrants and were enthusiastic about their plans for the economic development of Texas. Many Americans married into elite Tejano families, who hoped that by thus assimilating and sharing power with the Americans they could not only maintain but strengthen their community.

In 1832 the Tejano elite of San Antonio and a number of prominent rancheros went on record in favor of provincial autonomy and a strong role for the Americans.

One of the leaders of the San Antonio community was wealthy ranchero Juan Nepomuceno Seguín. As Santa Anna's army approached from the south, Seguín recruited a company of Tejano volunteers and joined the American force inside the walls of the Alamo. During the siege, Commander Travis sent Seguín and some of his men for reinforcements. Stopped by Mexican troops on his way across the lines, Seguín called out, "¡Somos paisanos!" ("We are countrymen"), confusing the guards just long enough for Seguín and his men to make their escape despite the hail of gunfire that quickly ensued. Seguín returned from his unsuccessful mission to find the burned bodies of the Alamo defenders, including seven San Antonio Tejanos. "*Texas será libre!*" Seguín called out as he directed the burial of the Alamo defenders—"Texas shall be free!" In April, Seguín led a regiment of Tejanos in the decisive battle of San Jacinto that won independence for Texas.

At first Tejanos were pleased with independence and played an important political role in the new Republic of Texas. But soon things began to change, illustrating a recurring pattern in the American occupation of new lands: a striking shift in the relations between different cultures in frontier areas. Most commonly, in the initial stage newcomers blended with native peoples, creating a frontier of inclusion. The first hunters, trappers, and traders on every American frontier—west of the Appalachians, in the Southwest, and in the Far West—married into the local community and tried to learn native ways. Outnumbered Americans adapted to local societies as a matter of simple survival.

A second, unstable stage occurred when the number of Americans increased and they began occupying more and more land, overrunning native communities. The usual result was warfare and the rapid growth of hostility and racial prejudice, which was largely absent in earlier days. A third stage—that of stable settlement—occurred when the native community had been completely "removed" or isolated. In this frontier of exclusion, racial mixing was rare. Generally, when Europeans pushed American Indians onto reservations they cut themselves off from sources of human history that could have helped them more fully understand the country into which they had moved. And in Texas, American settlers—initially invited in by Mexicans and Tejanos—developed an anti-

Mexican passion, regarding all Spanish-speakers as Mexican enemies rather than Tejano allies.

Unscrupulous Americans exploited these prejudices to acquire Tejano property. If the rancheros were "sufficiently scared," one wrote, they would "make an advantageous sale of their lands," and if "two or three hundred of our troops should be stationed here, I have no doubt but a man could make some good speculations." Tejanos were attacked and forced from their homes; some of their villages were burned to the ground.

Thus the Tejanos became symbols of a romanticized past rather than full participants in the building of western communities. Like the communities of Indians throughout the West, the first settlers of the American Southwest had become foreigners in the land their people had lived in for two centuries.

> ### KEY TOPICS
>
> ◆ **Continental expansion and the concept of Manifest Destiny**
>
> ◆ **The contrasting examples of frontier development in Oregon, Texas, and California**
>
> ◆ **How the political effects of expansion heightened sectional tensions**

Exploring the West

There seemed to be no stopping the expansion of the American people. By 1840 they had occupied all of the land east of the Mississippi River and had organized all of it (except for Florida and Wisconsin) into states. Of the ten states admitted to the Union between 1800 and 1840, all but one were west of the Appalachian Mountains. Less than sixty years after the United States gained its independence, the majority of its population lived west of the original thirteen states.

Many Americans looked eagerly westward to the vast unsettled reaches of the Louisiana Purchase; to Texas, Santa Fé, and trade with Mexico; and even to the Far West, where New England sea captains had been trading for furs since the 1790s. By 1848 the United States had gained all of these coveted western lands.

This chapter examines the way the United States became a continental nation, forming many frontier communities in the process, and begins as American settlers had to begin, with an understanding of the geography of the new land.

The Fur Trade

The fur trade, which flourished from the 1670s to the 1840s, was an important spur to exploration on the North American continent. In the 1670s the British Hudson's Bay Company and its French Canadian rival, Montreal's North West Company, began exploring beyond the Great Lakes in the Canadian West in search of beaver pelts. Both groups were dependent on the good will and cooperation of the native peoples of the region.

Not until the 1820s were American companies able to challenge British dominance of the trans-Mississippi fur trade. In 1824 William Henry Ashley of the Rocky Mountain Fur Company instituted the "rendezvous" system. This yearly trade fair was a boisterous, polyglot, many-day affair at which trappers of many nationalities—Americans and Indian peoples, French Canadians and métis, as well as Mexicans from Santa Fé and Taos—gathered to trade, drink, and gamble.

Artist Alfred Jacob Miller, a careful observer of the western fur trade, shows us a mountain man and his Indian wife in his 1837 Bourgeois Walker and His Wife. *Both worked together to trap and prepare beaver pelts for market.*

Most trappers sought accommodation and friendship with Indian peoples: nearly half of them contracted long-lasting marriages with Indian women, who not only helped in the trapping and curing of furs but also acted as vital diplomatic links between the white and Indian worlds.

For all its adventure, the American fur trade was short-lived. By the 1840s the population of beaver in western streams was virtually destroyed. The day of the mountain man was over.

Government-Sponsored Exploration

The federal government played a major role in the exploration and development of the West. The exploratory and scientific aspects of the Lewis and Clark expedition in 1804–6 set a precedent for many government-financed quasi-military expeditions. In 1806 and 1807, Lieutenant Zebulon Pike led an expedition to the Rocky Mountains in Colorado. Major Stephen Long's exploration and mapping of the Great Plains in the years 1819–20 was part of a show of force meant to frighten British fur trappers out of the West. Then, in 1843 and 1844 another military explorer, John C. Frémont, mapped the overland trails to Oregon and California.

Beginning with Long's expedition, the results of these surveys were published by the government, complete with maps, illustrations, and, after the Civil War, photographs. These publications fed a strong popular appetite for pictures of the breathtaking scenery of the Far West and information about its inhabitants. These images of the American West made a powerful contribution to the emerging American self-image. American pride in the land—the biggest of this, the longest of that, the most spectacular of something else—was founded on the images brought home by government surveyors and explorers. In the wake of the pathfinders came hundreds of government geologists and botanists as well as the surveyors who mapped and plotted the West for settlement according to the Land Ordinance of 1785. The basic pattern of land survey and sale established by these measures (see Chapter 7) was followed all the way to the Pacific Ocean.

Expansion and Indian Policy

While American artists were painting the way of life of western Indian peoples, eastern Indian tribes were being removed from their homelands to Indian Territory on the eastern edge of the Great Plains, a region widely regarded as unfarmable and popularly known as the Great American Desert. The justification for this western removal was the creation of a space where Indian people could live undisturbed by white people while they slowly adjusted to "civilized" ways. But the government officials who negotiated the removals failed to predict the tremendous speed at which white people would settle the West.

Encroachment on Indian Territory was not long in coming. The territory was crossed by the Santa Fé Trail, established in 1821; in the 1840s the northern part was crossed by the heavily traveled Overland Trails to California, Oregon, and the Mormon community in Utah. And in 1854, the government abolished the northern half of Indian Territory and established the Kansas and Nebraska Territories, which were immediately opened to white settlement. The tribes of the area signed treaties accepting either vastly reduced reservations or allotments (the latter were sections of private land, which Indian people often sold, under pressure, to white people). Thus many of the Indian people who had hoped for independence and escape from white pressures in Indian Territory lost both their autonomy and their tribal identity.

The southern part of Indian Territory, in what is now Oklahoma, fared somewhat better. The members of the southern tribes—the Cherokees, Chickasaws, Choctaws, Creeks, and Seminoles—who had survived the trauma of forcible removal from the Southeast in the 1830s quickly created impressive new communities. The five tribes divided up the territory and established self-governing nations with their own schools and churches. The societies they created were not so different from the American societies from which they had been expelled. The five tribes even carried slavery west with them. These southern tribes were able to remain the self-governing communities that treaties had assured them they would be until after the Civil War.

The Politics of Expansion

America's rapid expansion had many consequences, but perhaps the most significant was that it reinforced Americans' sense of themselves as pioneering people. In the 1890s Frederick Jackson Turner, America's most famous historian, observed that the repeated experience of settling new frontiers across the continent had shaped Americans into a uniquely adventurous, optimistic, and democratic people. Other historians have disagreed with Turner, but his view of the frontier long ago won the battle for popular opinion. Ever since the time of Daniel Boone, venturing into the wilderness has held a special place in the American imagination, seen almost as an American right.

Manifest Destiny, an Expansionist Ideology

How did Americans justify their restless expansionism? In 1845 newspaperman John O'Sullivan coined the phrase by which expansionism became famous. It was, O'Sullivan said, "our *manifest destiny* to overspread the continent allotted by Providence for the free development of our yearly multiplying millions." Sullivan argued that Americans had a God-given right to bring the benefits of American democracy to other, more backward peoples—meaning Mexicans and Indian nations—by force, if necessary. The notion of manifest destiny summed up the thinking of many expansionists. Pride in what America had achieved along with missionary zeal and racist attitudes toward other peoples made for a powerful combination.

Behind the bravado was concern about the economic future of the United States. After the devastating Panic of 1837 (see Chapter 10), a number of politicians became convinced that the nation's prosperity depended on vastly expanded trade with Asia. Senator Thomas Hart Benton of Missouri had been advocating trade with India by way of the Missouri and Columbia Rivers since the 1820s (not the easiest of routes, as Lewis and Clark had shown). Soon Benton and others were pointing out how greatly Pacific trade would increase if the United States held the magnificent harbors of the West Coast, among them Puget Sound in the Oregon Country, held jointly with Britain, and the bays of San Francisco and San Diego, both in Mexican-held California.

In one sense, manifest destiny was evangelical religion on a larger scale. Just as many eastern evangelists mounted reform movements aimed at changing the lives of workers, so did the western missionaries attempt to "civilize" the Indian peoples. They believed that the only way to do so was to destroy their cultures and to surround them with good American examples.

Expansionism was also tied to national politics. Most Democrats were wholehearted supporters of expansion, whereas many Whigs (especially in the North) were opposed. Democrats feared the industrialization that the Whigs welcomed. Where the Whigs saw economic progress, Democrats saw economic depression (the Panic of 1837 was the worst the nation had experienced), uncontrolled urban growth, and growing social unrest. For many Democrats, the answer to the nation's social ills was to continue to follow Thomas Jefferson's vision of establishing agriculture in the new territories in order to counterbalance industrialization (see Chapter 9). Another factor in the political struggle over expansion in the 1840s was that many Democrats were south-

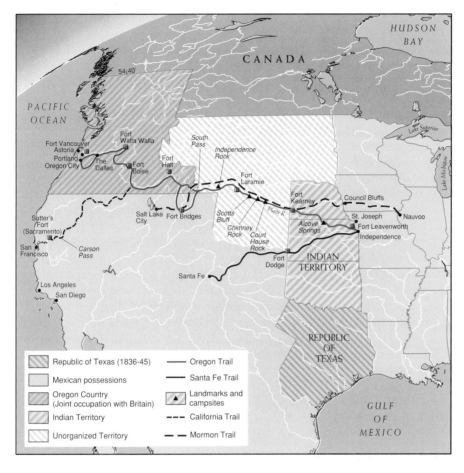

The Overland Trails, 1840

All the great trails west started at the Missouri River. The Oregon, California, and Mormon Trails followed the Platte River into Wyoming, crossed South Pass, and divided in western Wyoming. The Santa Fé Trail, a much harsher trip, stretched 900 miles southwest across the Great Plains. All of the trails crossed Indian Territory and, to a greater or lesser extent, Mexican possessions as well.

erners, for whom the continual expansion of cotton-growing lands was a matter of social faith as well as economic necessity.

The Overland Trails

The 2,000-mile trip on the Overland Trails from the banks of the Missouri River to Oregon and California usually took seven months, sometimes more. Travel was slow, dangerous, tedious, and exhausting. Pioneers often arrived at their destination with little food and few belongings, having been forced to lighten their loads as animals died and winter weather threatened. Uprooted from family and familiar surroundings, pioneers faced the prospect of being, in the poignant nineteenth-century phrase, "strangers in a strange land." Yet despite these risks, settlers streamed west: 5,000 to Oregon by 1845 and about 3,000 to California by 1848 (before the discovery of gold).

Pioneers had a number of motives for making the trip. Glowing reports from Oregon's Willamette Valley, for example, seemed to promise economic opportunity and healthy surroundings, an alluring combination to farmers in the malaria-prone Midwest who had been hard hit by the Panic of 1837. Many men were motivated by a sense of adventure, by a desire to experience the unknown, or, as they put it, to "see the elephant." Women were more likely to think of the trip as *A Pioneer's Search for an Ideal Home,* the title Phoebe Judson chose for her account of her family's 1852 trip to Oregon.

Few pioneers traveled alone, partly because they feared Indian attack (which was rare) but largely because they needed help fording rivers or crossing mountains with heavy wagons. Most Oregon pioneers traveled with their families and usually also joined a larger group, forming a "train." In the earliest years, when the route was still uncertain, trains hired a "pilot," generally a former fur trapper. Often the men of the wagon train drew up semimilitary constitutions, electing a leader. Democratic as this process appeared, not everyone was willing to obey the leader, and many trains experienced dissension and breakups along the trail. But in essence all pioneers—men, women, and children—were part of a new, westward-moving community in which they had to accept both the advantages and disadvantages of community membership.

Wagon trains started westward as soon as the prairies were green (thus ensuring feed for the livestock). The daily routine was soon established. Men took care of the moving equipment and the animals, while the women cooked and kept track of the children. Slowly, at a rate of about fifteen miles a day, the wagon trains moved west along the Platte River, crossing the Continental Divide at South Pass in present-day Wyoming. West of the Rockies the climate was much drier. The long, dusty stretch along the Snake River in present-day southern Idaho finally gave way to Oregon's steep and difficult Blue Mountains and to the dangerous rafting down the Columbia River, in which many drowned and all were drenched by the cold winter rains of the Pacific Northwest. California-bound migrants faced even worse hazards: the complete lack of water in the Humbolt Sink region of northern Nevada and the looming Sierra Nevadas, which had to be crossed before the winter snows came.

In addition to the predominant experiences of tedium and exhaustion, there were other trail hazards such as illness and accidents. Danger from Indian attack, which all pioneers feared, was actually very small. It appears that unprovoked white attacks on Indians were more common than the reverse.

In contrast, cholera killed at least a thousand people a year in 1849 and the early 1850s when it stalked sections of the trail along the Platte River. Spread by contaminated water, cholera caused vomiting and diarrhea, which in turn led to extreme dehydration and death, often in one night. In the afflicted regions, trailside graves were a common sight. Drownings were not uncommon, nor were accidental ax wounds or shootings, and children sometimes fell out of wagons and were run over.

By 1860 almost 300,000 people had traveled the Overland Trails to Oregon or California. Ruts from the wagon wheels can be seen in a number of places along the route even today. In 1869 the completion of the transcontinental railroad marked the end of the wagon train era.

Oregon

The American settlement of Oregon provides a capsule example of the stages of frontier development. The first contacts between the region's Indian peoples and Europeans were commercial. Spanish, British, Russian, and American ships traded for sea otter skins from the 1780s to about 1810. In this first frontier of inclusion there were frequent, often sexual contacts between Indians and Europeans.

The first permanent European settlers in Oregon were retired fur trappers and their Indian wives and families. They favored a spot in the lush and temperate Willamette Valley that became known as French Prairie, although the inhabitants were a mixed group of Americans, British, French Canadians, Indian peoples, and métis. The next to arrive were Protestant and Catholic missionaries. None of these missionaries was very successful. Disease took the lives of many of the region's peoples, and those who were left were disinclined to give up their nomadic life and settle down as the missionaries wanted them to do.

Finally, in the 1840s, the Midwest farmers who made up the majority of Oregon's permanent settlers arrived, carried on the wave of enthusiasm known as Oregon fever and lured by free land and patriotism. Eager for land and political control, they quickly established a frontier of exclusion on lands to which as yet they had no legal claim, for although Britain and the United States jointly claimed the region, neither government had concluded land treaties with the region's Indian peoples. Nevertheless, Oregon's Donation Land Claim Act of 1850 codified the practice of giving 320 acres to each white male age eighteen or over and 640 acres to each married couple (African Americans, Hawaiians, and American Indians were excluded). By 1845 Oregon boasted 5,000 American settlers, most of them living in the Willamette Valley.

For these early settlers, life was at first very difficult. Most arrived in late autumn, exhausted from the strenuous overland journey. They could not begin to farm until the spring, and so they depended on the earlier settlers for their survival over the winter. Ironically, in the earliest years American settlers got vital help from the Hudson's Bay Company, even though its director, John McLoughlin, had been ordered by the British government not to encourage American settlement. McLoughlin disregarded his orders, motivated both by sympathy for the plight of the newcomers and by a keen sense of the dangers his enterprise would face if he were outnumbered by angry Americans.

Joint occupancy of Oregon by the Americans and the British continued until 1846. Initially, a peaceful outcome seemed doubtful. President James K. Polk coined the belligerent slogan "Fifty-Four Forty or Fight" (meaning the United States wanted all the land south of 54°40', which was the border between Russian Alaska and British Canada) but in fact he was willing to compromise. In the spring of 1846, the British offered to accept the forty-ninth parallel as the U.S.-Canada border if the island of Vancouver remained in their hands, and both countries signed a treaty peacefully on June 15 of that year. In 1849 the Hudson's Bay Company closed Fort Vancouver and moved its operations to Victoria, thus ending the Pacific Northwest's largely successful experience with joint occupancy.

The handful of American settlers in Oregon found themselves in possession of a remote frontier. One of the first things they did (even before the American claim was finally settled) was to draw up their own constitution. When the first Oregon settlers met in the summer of 1843 to draft a constitution, they prohibited African Americans (both free and enslaved) from settling in the territory. By avoiding the divisive issue of slavery, they hoped to build community feeling between white settlers from the North and the South. Despite the law, some southerners did bring their slaves to Oregon with them, but when an early free African American pioneer, George Bush, came to Oregon, he deliberately settled north of the Columbia River, in what later became Washington Territory.

The white settlers realized that they had to forge strong community bonds if they hoped to survive on their distant frontier. Cooperation and mutual aid were the rule. Until well into the 1850s, residents organized yearly parties that traveled back along the last stretches of the trail to help straggling parties making their way to Oregon. Kinship networks were strong and vital: many pioneers came to join family who had migrated before them.

Relations with the small, disease-thinned local Indian tribes were generally peaceful until 1847, when Cayuse Indians killed missionaries Marcus and Narcissa Whitman. Their deaths initiated a series of attacks against the remaining native people. A frontier of exclusion had been achieved. Oregon thus became part of the United States (admitted as a state in 1859) in a more peaceful fashion than the U.S. expansion into the Spanish provinces of New Mexico and Texas.

The Santa Fé Trade

Santa Fé, first settled by colonists from Mexico in 1609 and the center of the Spanish frontier province of New Mexico, had long attracted American frontiersmen and traders. But Spain had forcefully resisted American penetration. For example, Lieutenant Zebulon Pike's Great Plains and Rocky Mountain exploration of 1806–7 ended ignominiously with his capture by Spanish soldiers.

When Mexico gained its independence from Spain in 1821, this exclusionary policy changed. American traders were now welcome in Santa Fé, but the trip over the legendary Santa Fé Trail from Independence, Missouri, was a forbidding 900 miles of arid plains, deserts, and mountains. There was serious danger of Indian attack, for neither the Comanches nor the Apaches of the southern high plains tolerated trespassers. In 1825, at the urging of Senator Benton and others, Congress voted federal protection for the Santa Fé Trail, even though much of it lay in Mexican territory. The number of people venturing west in the trading caravans increased yearly because the profits were so great (the first American trader to reach Santa Fé, William Becknell, realized a 1000 percent profit). By the 1840s a few hundred American trappers and traders (called *extranjeros,* or foreigners) lived permanently in New Mexico. In Santa Fé, a number of American merchants married daughters of important local families.

Settlements and trading posts soon grew up along the long Santa Fé Trail. One of the most famous was Bent's Fort, on the Arkansas River in what is now eastern Colorado, which did a brisk trade in beaver skins and buffalo robes. Like most trading posts, it had a multiethnic population. In the 1840s the occupants included housekeeper Josefa Tafoya of Taos, whose husband was a carpenter from Pennsylvania; an African American cook; a French tailor from New Orleans; Mexican muleteers; and a number of Indian women, including the two Cheyenne women who were the (successive) wives of William Bent, cofounder of the fort. The three small communities of Pueblo, Hardscrabble, and Greenhorn, spinoffs of Bent's Fort, were populated by men of all nationalities and their Mexican and Indian wives. All three communities lived by trapping, hunting, and a little farming. This racially and economically mixed existence was characteristic of all early trading frontiers except for Texas.

Mexican Texas

In 1821, when Mexico gained its independence from Spain, there were 2,240 *Tejano* (Spanish-speaking) residents of Texas. Begun in 1716 as a buffer against possible French attack on New Spain, the main Texas settlements of Nacogdoches, Goliad, and San Antonio remained small, far-flung frontier outposts (see Chapter 5). As was true everywhere in New Spain, society was divided into two classes: the *ricos* (rich), who claimed Spanish descent, and the mixed-blood *pobres* (poor). Tejano town life was traditionally hierarchical, dominated by the ricos, who were connected by blood or marriage with the great ranching families. The most colorful figures on the ranchos were mestizo (mixed-blood) vaqueros, renowned for their horsemanship; Americanization of their name made "buckaroos" of the American cowboys to whom they later taught their skills. Most Tejanos were neither ricos nor vaqueros but small farmers or common laborers who led hardscrabble frontier lives. But all Tejanos, rich and poor, faced the constant threat of raids by Comanche Indians.

Legendary warriors, the Comanches raided the small Texas settlements at will and even struck deep into Mexico itself. The nomadic Comanches followed the immense buffalo herds on which they depended for food and clothing. Their relentless raids on the Texas settlements rose from a determination to hold onto this rich buffalo territory, for the buffalo provided all that they wanted. They had no interest in being converted by mission priests or incorporated into mixed-race trading communities.

Americans in Texas

In 1821, seeking to increase the strength of its buffer zone between the heart of Mexico and the marauding Comanches, the Mexican government granted Moses Austin of Missouri an area of 18,000 square miles within the territory of Texas. Moses died shortly thereafter, and the grant was taken up by his son Stephen F., who became the first American *empresario* (land agent). From the beginning the American settlement of Texas differed markedly from other frontiers. Elsewhere, Americans often settled on land to which Indian peoples still held title or, as in the case of Oregon, they occupied lands to which other countries also made claim. In contrast, the Texas settlement was fully legal: Austin and other *empresarios* owned their lands as a result of formal contracts with the Mexican government. In exchange, Austin agreed that he and his colonists would become Mexican citizens and would adopt the Catholic religion.

Additionally, in startling contrast with the usual frontier free-for-all, Austin's community was populated with handpicked responsible settlers. He had no trouble finding Americans to apply, for the simple reason that Mexican land grants were magnificent: a square league (4,605 acres) per family. Soon Americans (including African American slaves, to whose presence the Mexican government turned a blind eye) outnumbered Tejanos: in 1830 there were an estimated 7,000 Americans and 4,000 Tejanos living in Texas.

The Austin settlement of 1821 was followed by others, twenty-six in all, concentrating in the fertile river

Painted by George Catlin about 1834, this scene, Comanche Village, *shows how everyday life of the Comanches was tied to buffalo. The women in the foreground are scraping buffalo hide, and buffalo meat can be seen drying on racks. The men and boys may be planning their next buffalo hunt.*

bottoms of east Texas (along the Sabine River) and south central Texas (the Brazos and the Colorado). These large settlements were highly organized farming enterprises whose principal crop was cotton, grown by African American slave labor, that was sold in the international market. By the early 1830s, Americans in Texas were exporting an estimated $500,000 worth of goods yearly to New Orleans, two-thirds of it cotton.

Austin's colonists and those who settled later were predominantly southerners who viewed Texas as a natural extension of settlement in Mississippi and Louisiana. These settlers created enclaves (self-contained communities) that had little contact with Tejanos or Indian peoples. Most Americans never bothered to learn Spanish, nor did they become Mexican citizens or adopt the Catholic religion. Yet because of the nature of agreements made by the empresarios, the Americans could not set up local American-style governments like the one created by settlers in Oregon. Like the immigrants who flooded into East Coast cities (see Chapter 13) the Americans in Texas were immigrants to another country, but one to which they did not intend to adapt.

For a brief period Texas was big enough to hold three communities: Comanche, Tejano, and American. The nomadic Comanches rode the high plains of northern and western Texas, raiding settlements primarily for horses.

The Tejanos maintained their ranchos and missions mostly in the South, while American farmers occupied the eastern and south central sections. Each group would fight to hold its land: the Comanches, their rich hunting grounds, the Mexicans, their towns and ranchos; and the newcomers, the Americans, their rich land grants.

The Texas Revolt

The balance between the three communities in Texas was broken in 1828, when centrists gained control of the government in Mexico City and, in a dramatic shift of policy, decided to exercise firm control over the northern province. As the Mexican government restricted American immigration, outlawed slavery, levied customs duties and taxes, and planned other measures, Americans seethed with rebellious talk—which was backed up by the presence of as many as 20,000 more Americans, many of them openly expansionist, who flooded into Texas after 1830. These settlers did not intend to become Mexican citizens. Instead, they planned to take over Texas.

Between 1830 and 1836, despite the mediation efforts of Austin (who was imprisoned for eighteen months by the Mexican government for his pains), the mood on both the Mexican and the American-Texan sides became more belligerent. In the fall of 1835 war finally broke out. After the disastrous defeat at the Alamo, Santa Anna pursued the remaining army of American and Tejano volunteers commanded by General Sam Houston. On April 21, 1836, at the San Jacinto River in eastern Texas, Santa Anna thought he had Houston trapped at last. Confident of victory against the exhausted Texans, Santa Anna's army rested in the afternoon, failing even to post sentries. Shouting "Remember the Alamo!" for the first time, the Texans completely surprised their opponents and won an overwhelming victory. Santa Anna signed a treaty fixing the southern boundary of the newly independent Republic of Texas at the Rio Grande on May 14, 1836. However, the Mexican Congress repudiated the treaty and refused to recognize Texan independence.

The Republic of Texas

In the eyes of the Mexicans, the American insistence on the Rio Grande boundary was little more than a blatant effort to stake a claim to New Mexico, an older and completely separate Spanish settlement. An effort by the Texas Republic in 1841 to capture Santa Fé was easily repulsed.

The Texas Republic was unexpectedly rebuffed in another quarter as well. The U.S. Congress refused to grant it statehood when, in 1837, Texas applied for admission to the Union. Petitions opposing the admission of a fourteenth slave state (there were then thirteen free states) poured into Congress. Congressman John Quincy Adams of Massachusetts, the former president widely regarded as the conscience of New England, led the opposition to the admission of Texas. Although President Jackson was sympathetic to the Texan cause, he knew that he did not have the power to quell the controversy that the admission of Texas would arouse. But he did manage to extend diplomatic recognition to the Texas Republic, on March 3, 1837, less than twenty-four hours before he left office.

The unresolved situation with Mexico put heavy stress on American–Tejano relations. Following a temporary recapture of San Antonio by Mexican forces in 1842, positions hardened. Many of the Tejano elite fled to Mexico, and Americans discussed banishing or imprisoning all Tejanos until the border issue was settled. This was, of course, impossible. Culturally, San Antonio remained a Mexican city long after the Americans had declared independence. The Americans in the Republic of Texas were struggling to reconcile American ideals of democracy with the reality of subordinating the Tejanos to the status of a conquered people.

American control over the other Texas residents, the Indians, was also slow in coming. Although the coastal Indian peoples were soon killed or removed, the Comanches still rode the high plains of northern and western Texas. West of the Rio Grande, equally fierce Apache bands were in control. Both groups soon learned to distrust American promises to stay out of their territory, and they did not hesitate to raid and to kill trespassers. Not until after the Civil War and major campaigns by the U.S. Army were these fierce Indian tribes conquered.

Texas Annexation and the Election of 1844

Texans continued to press for annexation to the United States while at the same time seeking recognition and support from Great Britain. The idea of an independent and expansionist republic on its southern border that might gain the support of America's traditional enemy alarmed many Americans. Annexation thus became an urgent matter of national politics. This issue also added to the troubles of a governing Whig Party. John Tyler, who had become president by default when William Harrison died in office (see Chapter 10), raised the issue of annexation in 1844, hoping to ensure his reelection, but the strategy backfired. Presenting the annexation treaty to Congress, Secretary of State John Calhoun awakened sectional fears by connecting Texas with the urgent need of southern slave owners to extend slavery.

In a storm of antislavery protest, Whigs rejected the treaty proposed by their own president, and ejected Tyler himself from the party. In his place they chose Henry Clay, the party's longtime standard-bearer, as their presidential candidate. Clay took a noncommittal

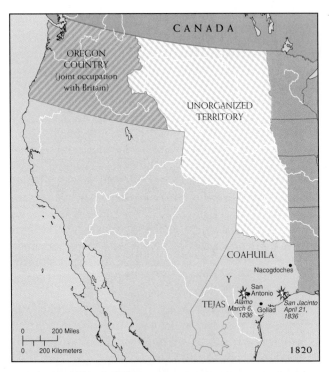

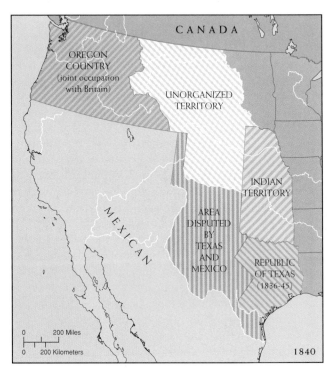

Texas: From Mexican Province to U.S. State

In the space of twenty years, Texas changed shape three times. Initially part of the Mexican province of Coahuila y Tejas, it became the Republic of Texas in 1836, following the Texas Revolt, and was annexed to the United States in that form in 1845. Finally, in the Compromise of 1850 following the Mexican–American War, it took its present shape.

stance on Texas, favoring annexation, but only if Mexico approved. Because Mexico's emphatic disapproval was well known, Clay's position was widely interpreted as a politician's effort not to alienate voters on either side of the fence.

In contrast, in the Democratic Party wholehearted and outspoken expansionists seized control. Sweeping aside their own senior politician, Van Buren, who like Clay tried to remain uncommitted, the Democrats nominated their first "dark horse" candidate, James K. Polk of Tennessee. They enthusiastically endorsed Polk's platform, which called for "the re-occupation of Oregon and the re-annexation of Texas at the earliest practicable period."

Polk won the 1844 election by the narrow margin of 40,000 popular votes (although he gained 170 electoral votes to Clay's 105). An ominous portent for the Whigs was the showing of James G. Birney of the Liberty Party, who polled 62,000 votes, largely from northern antislavery Whigs. Birney's third-party campaign was the first political sign of the growing strength of antislavery opinion. Nevertheless, the 1844 election was widely interpreted as a mandate for expansion. Thereupon John Tyler, in one of his last actions as president, pushed through Congress a joint resolution (which did not require the two-thirds approval by the Senate necessary for treaties) for the annexation of Texas.

The Mexican–American War

James K. Polk lived up to his campaign promises. In 1846 he peacefully added Oregon south of the forty-ninth parallel to the United States; in 1848, following the Mexican–American War, he acquired Mexico's northern provinces of California and New Mexico as well. With the annexation of Texas, in the short space of three years, the United States added 1.5 million square miles of territory, an increase of nearly 70 percent. Polk was indeed "the manifest destiny president."

Origins of the War

In the spring of 1846, just as the controversy over Oregon was drawing to a peaceful conclusion, tensions with Mexico grew more serious. Because the United States accepted the Texas claim of all land north of the Rio Grande, it found itself embroiled in a border dispute with Mexico. In June 1845, Polk sent General Zachary Taylor to Texas, and by October a force of 3,500 Americans were on the Nueces River with orders to defend Texas in the event of a Mexican invasion.

Polk had something bigger than border protection in mind. He coveted the continent clear to the Pacific Ocean. At the same time that he sent Taylor to Texas, Polk secretly instructed the Pacific naval squadron to seize the California ports if Mexico declared war. He also wrote to the American consul in Monterey, Thomas Larkin, that a peaceful takeover of California by its residents—Spanish Mexicans and Americans alike—would not be unwelcome.

In November 1845, Polk sent a secret envoy, John Slidell, to Mexico with an offer of $30 million or more for the Rio Grande border in Texas and Mexico's provinces of New Mexico and California. When the Mexican government refused even to receive Slidell, an angry Polk ordered General Taylor and his forces south to the Rio Grande, into the territory that Mexicans considered their soil. In April 1846 a brief skirmish between American and Mexican soldiers broke out in the disputed zone. Polk seized upon the event, sending a war message to Congress: "War exists, and, notwithstanding all our efforts to avoid it, exists by the act of Mexico herself." This claim of President Polk's was, of course, contrary to fact. On May 13, 1846, Congress declared war upon Mexico.

Mr. Polk's War

From the beginning, the Mexican–American War was politically divisive. Whig critics in Congress, among them a gawky young congressman from Illinois named Abraham Lincoln, questioned Polk's account of the border incident. They accused the president of misleading Congress and maneuvering the country into an unnecessary war. Congressional concern over the president's misuse of his war powers—an issue that recurred more than a hundred years later in the Vietnam War and again in the Reagan years—begins here in the suspicious opening of the Mexican-American War. As the war dragged on and casualties and costs mounted—13,000 American and 50,000 Mexican lives, $97 million in American military costs—opposition increased, especially among northern antislavery Whigs.

The northern states witnessed both mass and individual protests against the war. In Massachusetts, the legislature passed a resolution condemning Polk's declaration of war as unconstitutional, and philosopher–writer Henry David Thoreau went to jail rather than pay the taxes he believed would support the war effort. Thoreau's dramatic gesture was undercut by his aunt, who paid his fine after he had spent only one night in jail. Thoreau then returned to his cabin on Walden Pond, where he wrote his classic essay "Civil Disobedience," justifying the individual's moral right to oppose an immoral government.

Whigs called the war with Mexico "Mr. Polk's War," but the charge was not just a Whig jibe. Polk assumed the overall planning of the war's strategy. By the end of 1846 the northern provinces that Polk had coveted were now secured, but contrary to his expectations, Mexico refused to negotiate. In February 1847, General Santa Anna attacked American troops led by General Taylor at Buena Vista but failed to defeat Taylor's small force. A month later, in March 1847, General Winfield Scott launched an amphibious attack on the coastal city of Veracruz and rapidly captured it. After six months of

brutal fighting against stubborn Mexican resistance and American troops reacting bitterly to their high casualty rates by retaliating against Mexican citizens with acts of murder, robbery, and rape, Scott took Mexico City, and Mexican resistance came to an end.

With the American army went a special envoy, Nicholas Trist, who delivered Polk's terms for peace. In the Treaty of Guadalupe Hidalgo, signed February 2, 1848, Mexico ceded its northern provinces of California and New Mexico (which included present-day Arizona, Utah, Nevada, and part of Colorado) and accepted the

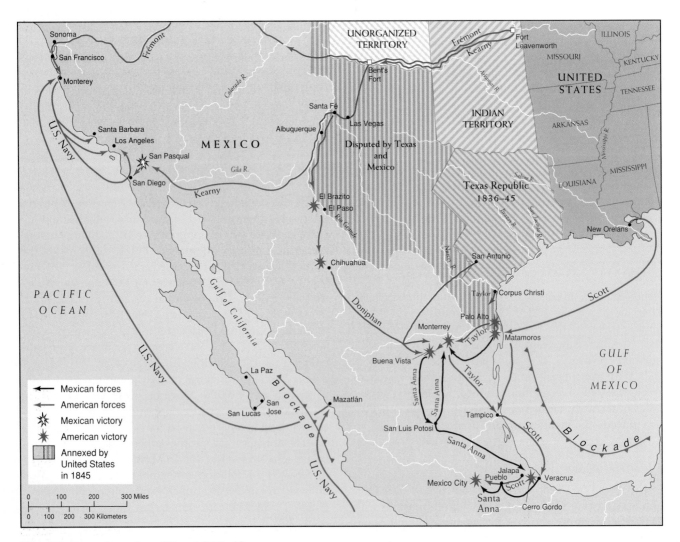

The Mexican–American War, 1846–48

The war's major battles were fought by General Zachary Taylor in northern Mexico and General Winfield Scott in Veracruz and Mexico City. Meanwhile, Colonel Stephen Kearny secured New Mexico and, with the help of the U.S. Navy and John C. Frémont's troops, California.

Rio Grande as the boundary of Texas. The United States agreed to pay Mexico $15 million and assume about $2 million in individual claims against that nation.

When Trist returned to Washington with the treaty, however, Polk was furious. He had actually recalled Trist after Scott's sweeping victory, intending to send a new envoy with greater demands, but Trist had ignored the recall order. "All Mexico!" had become the phrase widely used by those in favor of further expansion, Polk among them. But two very different groups opposed further expansion. The first group of northern Whigs included such notables as Ralph Waldo Emerson, who grimly warned, "The United States will conquer Mexico, but it will be as the man swallows arsenic, which brings him down in turn. Mexico will poison us." The second group was composed of southerners who realized that racially mixed Mexicans could not be kept as conquered people but would have to be offered their own territorial government, thus posing a challenge to white supremacy. Bowing to these political protests, Polk reluctantly accepted the treaty. A later addition, the $10 million Gadsden Purchase of parts of present-day New Mexico and Arizona, added another 30,000 square miles to the United States in 1853.

The Press and Popular War Enthusiasm

The Mexican–American War was the first war in which regular, on-the-scene reporting by representatives of the press engaged the mass of ordinary citizens in the war's daily events. Thanks to the recently invented telegraph, newspapers could get the latest news from their reporters, who were among the world's first war correspondents. The penny press, with more than a decade's experience of reporting urban crime and scandals, was quick to realize that the public's appetite for sensational war news was apparently insatiable. For the first time in American history, accounts by journalists, not the opinions of politicians, became the major shapers of popular attitudes toward a war.

The reports from the battlefield united Americans in a new way: they became part of a temporary but highly emotional community linked by newsprint and buttressed by public gatherings. In the spring of 1846, news of Zachary Taylor's victory at Palo Alto prompted the largest meeting ever held in the cotton textile town of Lowell, Massachusetts. In May 1847, New York City celebrated the twin victories at Veracruz and Buena Vista with fireworks, illuminations, and a grand procession estimated at 400,000 people. Generals Taylor and Scott became overnight heroes, and in time, both became

presidential candidates. Exciting, sobering, and terrible, war news had a deep hold on the popular imagination. It was a lesson newspaper publishers never forgot.

California and the Gold Rush

In the early 1840s California was inhabited by many seminomadic Indian tribes, whose people numbered approximately 50,000. There were also some 7,000 Californios, descendants of the Spanish Mexican pioneers who had begun to settle in 1769.

Russian–Californio Trade

The first outsiders to penetrate the isolation of Spanish California were not Americans but Russians. Evading Spanish regulations, Californios traded with the Russian American Fur Company in Sitka, Alaska. A mutually beneficial barter of California food for iron tools and woven cloth from Russia was established in 1806. This arrangement became even brisker after the Russians settled Fort Ross (near present-day Mendocino) in 1812. Agricultural productivity declined after 1832, when the Mexican government ordered the secularization of the California missions, and the Russians regretfully turned to the rich farms of the Hudson's Bay Company in the Pacific Northwest for their food supply. In 1841, they sold Fort Ross, and the Russian–Californio connection came to an end.

Early American Settlement

Johann Augustus Sutter, a Swiss who had settled in California in 1839, becoming a Mexican citizen, served as a focal point for American settlement in the 1840s. In the Sacramento Valley he built Sutter's Fort, a walled compound that was part living quarters and part supply shop for his vast cattle ranch, which was run largely on forced Indian labor. In the 1840s Sutter offered valuable support to the handful of American overlanders who chose California over Oregon, the destination preferred by most pioneers. Most of these Americans, keenly aware that they were interlopers in Mexican territory, settled near Sutter in California's Central Valley, away from the Californios clustered along the coast.

The 1840s immigrants made no effort to intermarry with the Californios or conform to Spanish ways. They were bent on taking over the territory. In June 1846 these Americans banded together at Sonoma in the Bear Flag Revolt (so called because their flag bore a bear emblem), declaring independence from Mexico.

The American takeover of California was not confirmed until the Treaty of Guadalupe Hidalgo in 1848. In the meantime, California was regarded by most Americans merely as a remote, sparsely populated frontier, albeit one with splendid potential.

Gold!

In January 1848 carpenter James Marshall noticed small flakes of gold in the millrace at Sutter's Mill (present-day Coloma). In the autumn of 1848, the East Coast heard the first rumors about the discovery of gold in California. The reports were confirmed in mid-November when an army courier arrived in Washington carrying a tea caddy full of gold dust and nuggets. The spirit of excitement and adventure so recently aroused by the Mexican–American War was now directed toward California, the new El Dorado. Thousands left farms and jobs and headed west, by land and by sea, to make their fortune. Later known as "forty-niners" for the year the Gold Rush began in earnest, these people came from all parts of the United States—and indeed, from all over the world. They transformed what had been a quiet ranching paradise into a teeming and tumultuous community in search of wealth in California's rivers and streams.

In 1849, as the Gold Rush began in earnest, San Francisco, the major entry port and supply point, sprang to life. From a settlement of 1,000 in 1848 it grew to a city of 35,000 in 1850. This surge of growth suggested that the real money to be made in California was not in panning for gold but in providing for the miners, who needed to be fed, clothed, housed, supplied with tools, and entertained. Among the first to learn that lesson was German Jew Levi Strauss, who sold so many tough work pants to miners that his name became synonymous with his product. The white population of California jumped from an estimated pre–Gold Rush figure of 11,000 to more than 100,000. California was admitted as a state in 1850.

Mining Camps

Most mining camps, though they shared San Francisco's instant beginnings, were empty again within a few years. Despite the aura of glamor that surrounds the names of the famous camps—Poker Flat, Angels Camp, Whiskey Bar, Placerville, Mariposa—they were generally dirty and dreary places. Most miners lived in tents or hovels, unwilling to take time from mining to build themselves decent quarters. They cooked monotonous meals of beans, bread, and bacon or, if they had money, bought meals at expensive restaurants and boardinghouses. Many migrants traveled to the mines with relatives or fellow townspeople. But often they split up in California—each man with his own idea of where he could find gold the easiest—and ended up on their own. They led a cheerless, uncomfortable, and unhealthy existence, especially during the long, rainy winter, with few distractions apart from the saloon, the gambling hall, and the prostitute's crib.

Most miners were young, unmarried, and unsuccessful. Only a small percentage ever struck it rich in California. Increasingly, those who stayed on in California had to give up the status of independent miners and become wage earners for large mining concerns.

As in San Francisco, a more reliable way to earn money was to supply the miners. Every mining community had its saloonkeepers, gamblers, prostitutes, merchants, and restaurateurs. Like the miners themselves, these people were transients, always ready to pick up and move at the word of a new gold strike. The majority of women in the early mining camps were prostitutes. Some grew rich or married respectably, but most died young of drugs, disease, or violence. Most of the other women were hardworking wives of miners, and in this predominantly male society they made good money doing domestic work: keeping boardinghouses, cooking, doing laundry.

Partly because few people put any effort into building communities—they were too busy seeking gold—violence was endemic in mining areas, and much of it was racial. Discrimination, especially against Chinese, Mexicans, and African Americans, was common. Often miners' claims were "jumped": thieves would rob them of the gold they had accumulated, kill them, or chase them away, and then file their own claim for the victims' strike. When violence failed, thieves used legal means to achieve illegal gains, among them a prohibitively high mining tax on foreigners.

By the mid-1850s, the immediate effects of the Gold Rush had passed. California had a booming population, a thriving agriculture, and a corporate mining industry. The Gold Rush also left California with a population that was larger, more affluent, and (in urban San Francisco) more culturally sophisticated than that in other newly settled territories. It was also significantly more multicultural than the rest of the nation, for many of the Chinese and Mexicans, as well as immigrants from many European countries, remained in California after the Gold Rush subsided. But the Gold Rush left some permanent scars, and not just on the foothills landscape: the virtual extermination of the California Indian peoples, the dis-

Chinese came to California in 1849, attracted by the Gold Rush. Often they were forced off their claims by intolerant whites. Rather than enjoy an equal chance in the gold fields, they were often forced to work in menial occupations.

possession of many Californios who were legally deprived of their land grants, and the growth of racial animosity toward the Chinese in particular.

The Politics of Manifest Destiny

In three short years, from 1845 to 1848, the United States grew an incredible 70 percent and became a continental nation. This expansion and the concept of manifest destiny quickly became the dominant issue in national politics.

The Wilmot Proviso

In 1846, almost all the northern members of the Whig Party opposed Democratic president James Polk's belligerent expansionism on antislavery grounds. Northern Whigs correctly feared that expansion would reopen the issue of slavery in the territories. But the outpouring of enthusiasm for the Mexican–American War convinced most Whig congressmen that they needed to vote military appropriations for the war despite their misgivings.

Ironically, it was not the Whigs but a freshman Democratic congressman from Pennsylvania, David Wilmot, who opened the door to sectional controversy over expansion. In August 1846, only a few short months after the beginning of the Mexican-American War, Wilmot proposed, in an amendment to a military appropriations bill, that slavery be banned in all the territories acquired from Mexico. He was ready, Wilmot said, to "sustain the institutions of the South as they exist," but not to extend them. In the debate and voting that followed, something new and ominous occurred: southern Whigs joined southern Democrats to vote against the measure, while northerners of both parties supported it. Sectional interest had triumphed over party loyalty. Wilmot's Proviso triggered the first breakdown of the national party system and reopened the debate about the place of slavery in the future of the nation.

The Wilmot Proviso was so controversial that it was deleted from the necessary military appropriations bills during the Mexican–American War. But in 1848, following the Treaty of Guadalupe Hidalgo, the question of the expansion of slavery could no longer be avoided or postponed. Antislavery advocates from the North argued with proslavery southerners in a debate that was much more prolonged and more bitter than the Missouri Crisis of 1819. Civility quickly wore thin: threats were uttered and fistfights broke out on the floor of the House of Representatives. The Wilmot Proviso posed a fundamental challenge to the party system. Neither the Democrats nor the Whigs could get its northern and southern wings to agree.

SUMMARY TABLE *Expansion Causes the First Splits in the Second American Party System*	
1844	Whigs reject President John Tyler's move to annex Texas and expel him from the Whig Party.
	Southern Democrats choose expansionist James K. Polk as their presidential candidate, passing over Martin Van Buren, who is against expansion.
	Liberty Party runs abolitionist James Birney for president, attracting northern antislavery Whigs.
1846	The Wilmot Proviso, proposing to ban slavery in the territories that might be gained in the Mexican–American War, splits both parties: southern Whigs and Democrats oppose the measure; northern Whigs and Democrats support it.
1848	The new Free-Soil Party runs northern Democrat Martin Van Buren for president, gaining 10 percent of the vote from abolitionists, antislavery Whigs, and some northern Democrats. This strong showing by a third party causes Democrat Lewis Cass to lose the electoral votes of New York and Pennsylvania, allowing Whig Zachary Taylor to win.

The Free-Soil Movement

Why did David Wilmot, a Democrat, propose this controversial measure? He was propelled not by ideology but by the pressure of practical politics. The dramatic rise of the Liberty Party, founded in 1840 by abolitionists, threatened to take votes away from both the Whig and the Democratic parties. The Liberty Party won 62,000 votes—all in the North—in the 1844 presidential election, more than enough to deny victory to the Whig candidate, Henry Clay.

The Liberty Party took an uncompromising stance against slavery. The party proposed to prohibit the admission of slave states to the Union, end slavery in the District of Columbia, and abolish the interstate slave trade that was vital to the expansion of cotton growing into the Old Southwest (see Chapter 11). Liberty Party members also favored denying office to all slaveholders (a proposal that would have robbed all the southern states of their senators). Liberty Party doctrine was too

uncompromising for the mass of northern voters, who immediately realized that the southern states would leave the Union before accepting it. Still, as the 1844 vote indicated, many northerners opposed slavery. From this sentiment the Free-Soil Party was born.

Free-soilers were willing to allow slavery to continue in the existing slave states because they supported the Union, not because they approved of slavery. However, they were unwilling to allow the extension of slavery to new and unorganized territory. If the South were successful in extending slavery, they argued, northern farmers who moved west would find themselves competing at an economic disadvantage with large planters using slave labor. Free-soilers also insisted that the northern values of freedom and individualism would be destroyed if the slave-based southern labor system were allowed to spread. In reality many free-soilers really meant "antiblack" when they said "antislavery." They proposed to ban all African American people from the new territories (a step that four states—Indiana, Illinois, Iowa, and Oregon—took but did not always enforce), thus "solving" the race issue by ignoring it.

The Election of 1848

A swirl of emotions—pride, expansionism, sectionalism, abolitionism, free-soil sentiment—surrounded the election of 1848. The Treaty of Guadalupe Hidalgo had been signed earlier in the year, and the vast northern Mexican provinces of New Mexico and California and the former Republic of Texas had been incorporated into the United States. But the issues raised by the Wilmot Proviso remained: every candidate had to have an answer to the question of whether slavery should be admitted in the new territories.

Lewis Cass of Michigan, the Democratic nominee for president (Polk, in poor health, declined to serve a second term) proposed to apply the doctrine of popular sovereignty to the crucial slave-free issue. This democratic-sounding notion of leaving the decision to the citizens of each territory was based on the Jeffersonian faith in the common man's ability to vote both his own self-interest and the common good. In fact, however, popular sovereignty was an admission of the nation's failure to resolve sectional differences. Moreover, the doctrine of popular sovereignty was deliberately vague about when a territory would choose its status. Would it do so during the territorial stage? at the point of applying for statehood? Clearly, this question was crucial, for no slave owner would invest in new land if the territory could later be declared free, and no abolitionist would move to a territory that was destined to become a slave state. Cass hoped his ambiguity on this point would win him votes in both North and South.

For their part, the Whigs passed over perennial candidate Henry Clay and turned once again to a war hero, General Zachary Taylor. Taylor, a Louisiana slaveholder, refused to take a position on the Wilmot Proviso, allowing both northern and southern voters to hope that he agreed with them. Privately, Taylor opposed the expansion of slavery. In public, he evaded the issue by running as a war hero and a national leader who was above sectional politics.

The deliberate vagueness of the two major candidates displeased a number of northern voters. An uneasy mixture of disaffected Democrats (among them David Wilmot) and Whigs joined former Liberty Party voters to support the candidate of the Free-Soil Party, former president Martin Van Buren. Van Buren, angry at the Democratic Party for passing him over in 1844 and displeased with the growing southern dominance of the Democratic Party, frankly ran as a spoiler. He knew he could not win the election, but he could divide the Democrats. In the end, Van Buren garnered 10 percent of the vote (all in the North). The vote for the Free-Soil Party cost Cass the electoral votes of New York and Pennsylvania, and General Taylor won the election with only 47 percent of the popular vote. This was the second election after 1840 that the Whigs had won by running a war hero who could duck hard questions by claiming to be above politics. Uncannily, history was to repeat itself: Taylor, like William Henry Harrison, died before his term was completed, and the chance for national unity—if ever it existed—was lost.

Conclusion

In the 1840s, westward expansion took many forms, from peaceful settlement in Oregon, to war with Mexico over Texas, to the overwhelming numbers of gold rushers who changed California forever.

The election of 1848, virtually a referendum on manifest destiny, yielded ironic results. James K. Polk, who presided over the unprecedented expansion, did not serve a second term and thus the Democratic Party gained no electoral victory to match the military one. The electorate that had been so thrilled by the war news voted for a war hero, who led the antiexpansionist Whig Party. The election was decided by Martin Van Buren, the Free-Soil candidate who voiced the sentiments of the abolitionists, a reform group that had been insignificant just a few years before. The amazing expansion achieved by the Mexican-American War—America's manifest destiny—made the United States a continental nation but stirred up the issue that was to tear it apart. Sectional rivalries and fears now dominated every aspect of politics. Expansion, once a force for unity, now divided the nation into northerners and southerners, who could not agree on the community they shared: the federal Union.

CHRONOLOGY

1609	First Spanish settlement in New Mexico
1670s	British and French Canadians begin fur trade in western Canada
1716	First Spanish settlements in Texas
1769	First Spanish settlement in California
1780s	New England ships begin sea otter trade in Pacific Northwest
1790	First American ship visits Hawaii
1803	Louisiana Purchase
1804–6	Lewis and Clark expedition
1806	Russian–Californio trade begins
1806–7	Zebulon Pike's expedition across the Great Plains to the Rocky Mountains
1819–20	Stephen Long's expedition across the Great Plains
1821	Hudson's Bay Company gains dominance of western fur trade
	Mexico seizes independence from Spain
	Santa Fé Trail opens, soon protected by U.S. military
	Stephen F. Austin becomes first American empresario in Texas
1824	First fur rendezvous sponsored by Rocky Mountain Fur Company
	Hudson's Bay Company establishes Fort Vancouver in Oregon Country
1830	Indian Removal Act moves eastern Indians to Indian Territory
1835	Texas revolts against Mexico
1836	Battles of the Alamo and San Jacinto
	Republic of Texas formed
1843–44	John C. Frémont maps trails to Oregon and California
1844	Democrat James K. Polk elected president on an expansionist platform
1845	Texas annexed to the United States as a slave state
	John O'Sullivan coins the phrase *manifest destiny*
1846	Oregon question settled peacefully with Britain
	Mexican–American War begins
	Bear Flag Revolt in California
	Wilmot Proviso
1847	Cayuse Wars begin in Oregon
	Americans win battles of Buena Vista, Veracruz, and Mexico City
1848	Treaty of Guadalupe Hidalgo
	Free-Soil Party captures 10 percent of the popular vote in the North
	General Zachary Taylor, a Whig, elected president
1849	California Gold Rush

Review Questions

1. Define and discuss the concept of manifest destiny.
2. Trace the different ways in which the frontiers in Oregon, Texas, and California moved from frontiers of inclusion to those of exclusion.
3. Take different sides (Whig and Democrat) and debate the issues raised by the Mexican–American War.
4. Referring back to Chapter 13, compare the positions of the Liberty Party and the Free-Soil Party. Examine the factors that made the free-soil doctrine politically acceptable to many, abolitionism so controversial.

Recommended Reading

ARNOLDO DE LEON, *The Tejano Community, 1836–1900* (1982). Traces the changing status of Tejanos after Texas came under the control of American Texans.

JOHN MACK FARAGHER, *Women and Men on the Overland Trail* (1979). One of the first books to consider the experience of women on the journey west.

T. R. FEHRENBACH, *Lone Star: A History of Texas and Texans* (1968). A long and leisurely study that focuses primarily on the history of Americans in Texas.

WILLIAM GOETZMAN, *Exploration and Empire: The Explorer and the Scientist in the Winning of the American West* (1966). Considers the many government-sponsored explorations of the West.

THOMAS R. HIETALA, *Manifest Design: Anxious Aggrandizement in Late Jacksonian America* (1985). An interesting reassessment of manifest destiny from the perspective of party politics.

JULIE ROY JEFFREY, *Converting the West: A Biography of Narcissa Whitman* (1991). Makes a clear connection between the missionary Whitman's evangelical upbringing and her failure to understand the culture of Oregon's Cayuse Indians.

ROBERT W. JOHANNSEN, *To the Halls of the Montezumas: The Mexican War in the American Imagination* (1985). A lively book that explores the impact of the Mexican–American War on public opinion.

JANET LECOMPTE, *Pueblo, Hardscrabble, Greenhorn: The Upper Arkansas, 1832–1856* (1978). A social history that portrays the racial and ethnic diversity of the trading frontier.

CARLOS SCHWANTES, *The Pacific Northwest: An Interpretive History* (1989). A good regional history.

DAVID J. WEBER, *The Mexican Frontier, 1821–1846: The American Southwest Under Mexico* (1982). A fine study of the history of the Southwest before American conquest. The author is a leading borderlands historian.

RICHARD WHITE, *"It's Your Misfortune and None of My Own": A History of the American West* (1991). A major reinterpretation that focuses on the history of the region itself rather than on the westward expansion of Americans. Pays much more attention to Spanish Mexicans and Indian peoples than earlier texts.

15

THE COMING CRISIS, THE 1850s

AMERICAN COMMUNITIES

ILLINOIS COMMUNITIES DEBATE SLAVERY

In the late summer and autumn of 1858, thousands of Illinois farmers and townspeople put aside their daily routines and customary chores, climbed into carriages, farm wagons, carts, and conveyances of all sorts, and converged on seven small Illinois towns: Ottawa, Freeport, Jonesboro, Charleston, Galesburg, Quincy, and Alton. Gathering on village greens, where they were entertained by brass bands, pageantry, and vast quantities of food and local gossip, they waited impatiently for the main event, the chance to take part in the debate on the most urgent question of the day: slavery. Two Illinois politicians, Democratic senator Stephen A. Douglas and his Republican challenger, Springfield lawyer Abraham Lincoln, the principal figures in the debates, presented their views in three hours of closely reasoned argument. But they did not speak alone. Cheers, boos, groans, and shouted questions from active, engaged listeners punctuated all seven of the now famous confrontations between the two men. Although commonly called the Lincoln–Douglas debates, these were really community events in which Illinois citizens—people who, like Americans everywhere, held varying political beliefs—took part. Some were proslavery, some antislavery, and many were undecided, but all agreed that democratic politics gave them the means to air their opinions and resolve their differences.

"The prairies are on fire," announced the *New York Evening Post* correspondent who covered the debates. "It is astonishing how deep an interest in politics this people take." The reason was clear: by 1858, the American nation was in deep political crisis. The decade-long effort to solve the problem of the future of slavery had failed.

Stephen Douglas was the leading Democratic contender for the 1860 presidential nomination, but before he could mount a campaign for national office he had first to win reelection to the Illinois seat he had held in the U.S. Senate for twelve years. His vote against allowing slavery in Kansas had alienated him from the strong southern wing of his own party and had put him in direct conflict with its top leader, President James Buchanan. Because the crisis of the Union was so severe and Douglas's role so pivotal, his reelection campaign clearly previewed the 1860 presidential election. For the sake of its future, the Republican Party had to field a strong opponent; it found its candidate in Abraham Lincoln.

Lincoln had represented Illinois in the House of Representatives in the 1840s but had lost political support in 1848 because he opposed the Mexican–American War. Developing a prosperous Springfield law practice, he had been an influential member of the Illinois Republican Party since its founding in 1856. Although he had entered political life as a Whig, Lincoln was radicalized by the issue of slavery extension. Despite the fact that his wife's family were Kentucky slave owners, Lincoln's commitment to freedom and his resistance to the spread of slavery had now become absolute: for him, freedom and Union were inseparable.

Much less well known than Douglas, Lincoln was the underdog in the 1858 Senate race and thus it was he who challenged Douglas to debate. As they squared off in the seven Illinois small towns, Douglas and Lincoln were an amusing sight. Douglas was short (five feet, four inches) and very square; his nickname was the Little Giant. Lincoln, on the other hand, was very tall (6 feet, 4 inches) and very thin. Both were eloquent and powerful speakers, and they had to be. The three-hour debates were held without amplification of any kind. Nevertheless, in every town, audiences of 10,000 to 15,000 listened attentively and vocally to each speaker's long and thought-packed argument and to the opponent's lengthy rebuttal.

Douglas had many strengths going into the debates. He spoke for the Union, he claimed, pointing out that the Democratic Party was a national party whereas the Republican Party was only sectional. He repeatedly appealed to the racism of much of his audience with declarations such as, "I would not blot out the great inalienable rights of the white men for all the negroes that ever existed!" He repeatedly called his opponent a "Black Republican," implying that Lincoln and his party favored the social equality of whites and blacks, even race mixing.

Lincoln did *not* believe in the social equality of the races, but he did believe wholeheartedly that slavery was a moral wrong. Pledging the Republican Party to the "ultimate extinction" of slavery, Lincoln continually warned that Douglas's position would lead to the opposite result: the spread of slavery everywhere.

The first of the seven debates, held in Ottawa on Saturday, August 21, 1858, showed not only the seriousness but the exuberance of the democratic politics of the time. By early morning the town was jammed with people. By one o'clock the town square was filled to overflowing. At two o'clock, just as the debate was about to begin, the wooden awning over the speakers' platform collapsed under the weight of those sitting on it, delaying the start for half an hour. But then the debate got under way, enthralling an estimated 12,000 people. Ottawa, in northern Illinois, was pro-Republican, and the audience heckled Douglas unmercifully. At the second debate, a week later in Freeport, Douglas's use of the phrase "Black Republicans" drew angry shouts of "White, white" from the crowd. But as the debates moved to the southern part of the state, where Democrats predominated, the tables were turned, and Lincoln sometimes had to plead for a chance to be heard.

Although Douglas won the 1858 senatorial election in Illinois, the acclaim that Lincoln achieved in the famous debates helped establish the Republicans' claim to be the only party capable of stopping the spread of slavery and made Lincoln himself a strong contender for the Republican presidential nomination in 1860. But the true winners of the Lincoln–Douglas debates were the people of Illinois who showed the strong faith Americans held in their democratic institutions and the hope—finally shattered in the election of 1860—that a lasting political solution to the problem of slavery could be found.

KEY TOPICS

- **The failure of efforts by the Whigs and the Democrats to find a lasting political compromise on the issue of slavery**
- **The end of the Second American Party System and the rise of the Republican Party**
- **The secession of the southern states following the Republican Party victory in the election of 1860**

America in 1850

In 1850, after half a century of rapid growth and change, America was a very different nation from the republic of 1800. Geographic expansion, population increase, economic development, and the changes wrought by the market revolution had transformed the struggling new nation. Economically, culturally, and politically Americans had forged a strong sense of national identity.

Expansion and Growth

America was a much larger nation than it had been in 1800. Through war and diplomacy, the country had grown to continental dimensions, more than tripling in size from 890,000 to 3 million square miles. Its popula-

tion had increased enormously: from 5.3 million in 1800 to more than 23 million, 4 million of whom were African American slaves and 2 million new immigrants, largely from Germany and Ireland. Just sixteen states in 1800, in 1850 there were thirty-one.

America was also a much richer nation: it is estimated that real per capita income doubled between 1800 and 1850. The development of manufacturing in the Northeast and the increased economic importance of the Midwest had serious domestic political implications. As the South's share of responsibility for economic growth waned, so did its political importance—at least in the eyes of many northerners—and hastened the day of open conflict between the slave South and the free-labor North and Midwest.

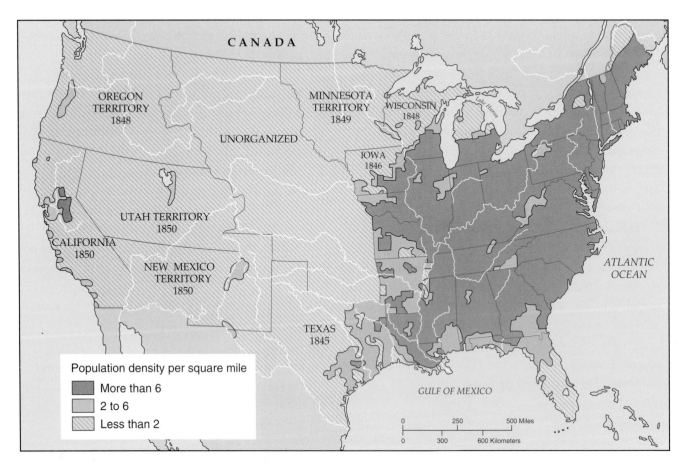

U.S. Population and Settlement, 1850

By 1850, the United States was a continental nation. The population, which Thomas Jefferson had once thought would not reach the Mississippi River for forty generations, had not only passed the river but leapfrogged to the West Coast. In comparison to the America of 1800 the growth was astounding.

The Webbs, a free African American family, performed dramatic readings from Harriet Beecher Stowe's Uncle Tom's Cabin. *Published in 1851, an all-time best seller, the novel outlasted the Civil War to become one of the most popular plays of the nineteenth century.*

Political Parties and Slavery

The Second American Party System, forged in the great controversies of Andrew Jackson's presidency (see Chapter 10), was a national party system. In their need to mobilize great masses of recently enfranchised voters to elect a president every four years, politicians created organized party structures that overrode deeply rooted sectional differences. Politicians from all sections of the country cooperated because they knew their parties could not succeed without national appeal. At a time when the ordinary person still had very strong sectional loyalties, the mass political party created a national community of like-minded voters. Yet by the election of 1848 sectional interests were eroding the political glue in both parties. Although each party still appeared united, sectional fissures already ran deep.

Political splits were preceded by divisions in other social institutions. Disagreements about slavery had already split the country's great religious organizations into northern and southern groups, the Presbyterians in 1837, the Methodists in 1844, and the Baptists in

1845. (Some of these splits turned out to be permanent. The Southern Baptist Convention, for example, is still a separate body.) The abolitionists had been posing a simple yet uncompromising choice between slavery or freedom since the 1830s. Moreover, they had been insisting on a compelling distinction: as Liberty Party spokesman Salmon P. Chase said, "Freedom is national; slavery only is local and sectional."

States' Rights and Slavery

But was freedom national and slavery sectional, or was it the other way around? Southern politicians took the latter view, as their foremost spokesman, South Carolina's John C. Calhoun, made ringingly clear throughout his long career.

In 1828 Calhoun had provoked the Nullification Crisis by asserting the constitutional right of states to nullify national laws that were harmful to their interests (see Chapter 10). Calhoun argued, as others have since, that the states' rights doctrine protected the legitimate rights of a minority in a democratic system governed by majority rule.

In 1847 Calhoun responded to the Wilmot Proviso with an elaboration of the states' rights argument. Despite the apparent precedents of the Northwest Ordinance of 1787 and the Missouri Compromise, Calhoun argued that Congress did not have a constitutional right to prohibit slavery in the territories. The territories, he said, were the common property of all the states, North and South, and Congress could not discriminate against slave owners as they moved west. On the contrary, Calhoun argued, slave owners had a constitutional right to the protection of their property wherever they moved. Of course, Calhoun's legally correct description of African American slaves as property enraged abolitionists. But on behalf of the South, Calhoun was expressing the belief—and the fear—that his interpretation of the Constitution was the only protection for slave owners whose right to own slaves (a fundamental right in southern eyes) was being attacked. Calhoun's position on the territories quickly became southern dogma: anything less than full access to the territories was unconstitutional. Slavery, Calhoun and other southerners insisted, had to be national.

As Congressman Robert Toombs of Georgia put the case in 1850, there was very little room for compromise:

> I stand upon the great principle that the South has the right to an equal participation in the territories of the United States. . . . She will divide with you if you

wish it, but the right to enter all or divide I shall never surrender. . . . Deprive us of this right and appropriate the common property to yourselves, it is then your government, not mine. Then I am its enemy. . . . Give us our just rights, and we are ready . . . to stand by the Union. . . . Refuse [them], and for one, I will strike for independence.

Northern Fears of "The Slave Power"

Speeches such as those by Calhoun and Toombs seemed to many northern listeners to confirm the warning by antislavery leaders of political danger from "the slave power." Liberty Party leader James Birney was the first to add this menacing image to the nation's political vocabulary, declaring in 1844 that southern slave owners posed a danger to free speech and free institutions throughout the nation. "The slave power," Birney explained, was a

The strident poster warns that "the Slave Power" aims "to control the government of the nation, and make it subservient to its wicked designs." For good measure, the poster also appeals to nativist fears and to workers.

group of aristocratic slave owners who not only dominated the political and social life of the South but conspired to control the federal government as well.

Birney's warnings about "the slave power" seemed in 1844 merely the overheated rhetoric of an extremist group of abolitionists. But the defensive southern political strategies of the 1850s—in particular the Fugitive Slave Law and the Kansas–Nebraska Act—convinced an increasing number of northern voters that "the slave power" did in fact exist. Thus in northern eyes the South became a demonic monolith that threatened the national government.

Two Communities, Two Perspectives

Ironically, it was a common belief in expansion that made the arguments between northerners and southerners so irreconcilable. Southerners had been the strongest supporters of the Mexican–American War, and they still hoped to expand into Cuba, believing that the slave system must grow or wither. On the other hand, although many northern Whigs had opposed the Mexican–American War, most did so for antislavery reasons, not because they opposed expansion. The strong showing of the Free-Soil Party (which evolved out of the Liberty Party) in the election of 1848 (10 percent of the popular vote) was proof of that. Basically, both North and South believed in manifest destiny, but each on its own terms.

Similarly, both North and South used the language of basic rights and liberties in the debate over expansion. But free-soilers were speaking of personal liberty, whereas southerners meant their right to own a particular kind of property (slaves) and to maintain a way of life based on the possession of that property.

By 1850, North and South had created different communities. To antislavery northerners, the South was an economic backwater dominated by a small slave-owning aristocracy that lived off the profits of forced labor and deprived poor whites of their democratic rights and the fruits of honest work. The slave system was not only immoral but a drag on the entire nation, for, in the words of Senator William Seward of New York, it subverted the "intelligence, vigor and energy" that were essential for national growth. In contrast, the dynamic and enterprising commercial North boasted a free-labor ideology that offered economic opportunity to the common man and ensured his democratic rights (see Chapter 12).

In southern eyes the South, through its export of cotton, was the great engine of national economic growth from which the North benefitted. Slavery was

SUMMARY TABLE		*The Great Sectional Compromises*
Missouri Compromise	1820	Admits Missouri to the Union as a slave state and Maine as a free state; prohibits slavery in the rest of the Louisiana Purchase Territory north of 36° 30′.
		Territory covered: The entire territory of the Louisiana Purchase, exclusive of the state of Louisiana, which had been admitted to the Union in 1812.
Compromise of 1850	1850	Admits California to the Union as a free state, settles the borders of Texas (a slave state); sets no conditions concerning slavery for the rest of the territory acquired from Mexico.
		Territory covered: The territory that had been part of Mexico before the end of the Mexican–American War and the Treaty of Guadalupe Hidalgo (1848): part of Texas, California, Utah Territory (now Utah, Nevada, and part of Colorado), and New Mexico Territory (now New Mexico and Arizona).

not only a blessing to an inferior race but the cornerstone of democracy, for it ensured the freedom and independence of all white men without entailing the bitter class divisions that marked the North. Slave owners accused northern manufacturers of hypocrisy for practicing "wage slavery" without the paternalism.

By the early 1850s, these vastly different visions of the North and the South—the result of many years of political controversy—had become fixed, and the chances of national reconciliation were very slim.

The Compromise of 1850

By 1850 the issue raised by the Wilmot Proviso—whether slavery should be extended to the new territories—could no longer be ignored. Overnight, the California Gold Rush had turned a remote frontier into a territory with a booming population. In 1849 both California and Utah applied for statehood. Should these territories be admitted as slave or free states? A simmering border war between Texas (a slave state) and New

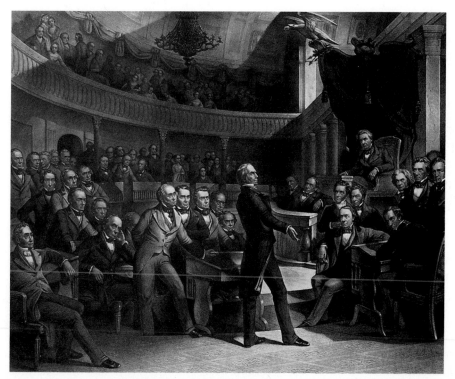

In 1850, the three men who had long represented America's three major regions attempted to resolve the free-slave crisis brought on by the applications of California and Utah for statehood. Henry Clay is speaking; John C. Calhoun stands third from right; and Daniel Webster is seated at the left with his head in his hand. Both Clay and Webster were ill, and Calhoun died before the issue was settled by a younger group of politicians led by Stephen A. Douglas.

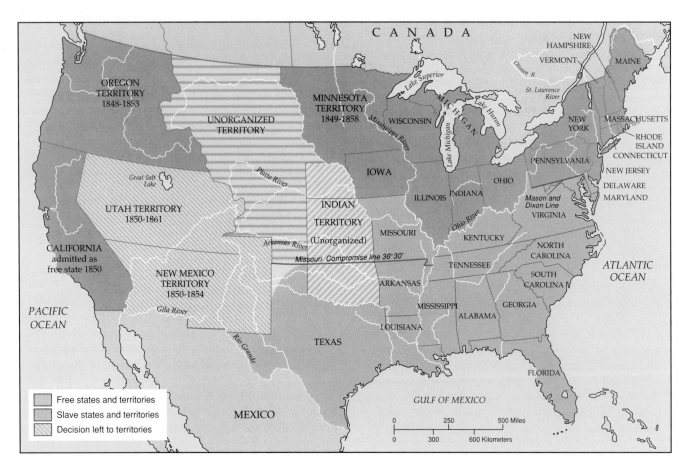

The Compromise of 1850

The Compromise of 1850 reflected heightened sectional tensions by being even messier and more awkward than the Missouri Compromise of 1820. No consistent majority voted for the five separate bills that made up the compromise.

Mexico, which seemed likely to be a free state, had to be settled, as did the issue of the debts Texas had incurred as an independent republic. Closer to home, antislavery forces demanded the end of slavery in the District of Columbia, while slave owners complained that northerners were refusing to return escaped slaves, as federal law mandated.

Debate and Compromise

The Compromise of 1850 was the final act in the political careers of the three men who in the public mind best represented America's sections: westerner Henry Clay, now seventy-three; southerner John C. Calhoun, in the final year of his life; and Daniel Webster, spokesman for the North. It was sadly appropriate to the bitter sectional argument of 1850 that the three men contributed great words to the debate but that the compromise itself was enacted by younger men.

On July 9, 1850, in the midst of the debate, President Zachary Taylor died of acute gastroenteritis. When Vice-President Millard Fillmore, a moderate northern Whig and more prosouthern than the southern-born Taylor had been, assumed the presidency, he became instrumental in arranging the Compromise of 1850 to southern liking. Although Clay had assembled all the necessary parts of the bargain, members of a younger political generation, particularly the rising young Democrat from Illinois, Stephen Douglas, drove the Compromise of 1850 through Congress. The final product consisted of five separate bills (it had been impossible to obtain a majority for a comprehensive measure), embodying three separate compromises:

First, California was admitted as a free state, but the status of the remaining former Mexican possessions was to be decided by popular sovereignty (a vote of the territory's inhabitants) when they applied for statehood.

(Utah's application for statehood was not accepted until 1896 because of controversy over the practice of polygamy by the territory's principal settlers, the Mormons.) Without Utah, the balance between states was fifteen slave states and sixteen free states. The second compromise settled some issues left over from Texas's period as an independent republic: Texas (a slave state) was required to cede land to New Mexico Territory (free-slave status undecided). In return, the federal government assumed $10 million of Texan debts incurred before statehood. Finally, the slave trade, but not slavery itself, was ended in the District of Columbia, but a stronger fugitive slave law was enacted.

Jubilation and relief greeted the news that compromise had been achieved. In Washington, where the anxiety and concern had been greatest, drunken crowds serenaded Congress, shouting, "The Union is saved!" That was certainly true for the moment, but analysis of the votes on the five bills that made up the compromise revealed no consistent majority. The sectional splits within each party that had existed before the compromise remained. In the country as a whole, the feeling was that the problem of slavery in the territories had been solved. Senator Salmon P. Chase of Ohio soberly noted, "The question of slavery in the territories has been avoided. It has not been settled." He was correct. The most immediately inflammatory measure of the compromise was the Fugitive Slave Act.

The Fugitive Slave Act

From the early days of their movement, northern abolitionists had urged slaves to escape, promising assistance and support when they reached the North. Northerners had long been appalled by professional slave catchers, who zealously seized African Americans in the North and took them south into slavery again. Most abhorrent in northern eyes was that captured black people were at the mercy of slave catchers because they had no legal right to defend themselves. In more than one case, a northern free African American was captured in his own community and helplessly shipped into slavery.

The Fugitive Slave Law, enacted in 1850, dramatically increased the power of slave owners to capture escaped slaves. The full force of the federal government now supported slave owners, and although fugitives were guaranteed a hearing before a federal commissioner, they were not allowed to testify on their own behalf. Furthermore, the new law imposed federal penalties on citizens who protected or assisted fugitives, or who did not cooperate in their return. In Boston, the center of the abolitionist movement, reaction to the new law was fierce. When an

escaped slave named Shadrach was seized in February 1851, a group of African American men broke into the courtroom, overwhelmed the federal marshals, seized Shadrach, and sent him safely to Canada. Although the action had community support—a Massachusetts jury defiantly refused to convict the perpetrators—a number of people, including Daniel Webster and President Fillmore, condemned this episode of "mob rule."

The federal government responded with overwhelming force. In April 1851, 300 armed soldiers were mobilized to prevent the rescue of Thomas Sims, who was being shipped back into slavery. In the most famous case in Boston, a biracial group of armed abolitionists led by Unitarian clergyman Thomas Wentworth Higginson stormed the federal courthouse in 1854 in an attempt to save escaped slave Anthony Burns. The rescue effort failed, and a federal deputy marshal was killed. President Pierce sent marines, cavalry, and artillery to Boston to reinforce the guard over Burns and ordered a federal ship to be ready to deliver the fugitive back into slavery. When the effort by defense lawyers to argue for Burns's freedom failed, Bostonians raised money in the community to buy his freedom. But the U.S. attorney, ordered by the president to enforce the Fugitive Slave Law in all circumstances, blocked the purchase. The case was lost, and Burns was marched to the docks through streets lined with sorrowing abolitionists. Buildings were shrouded in black and draped with American flags hanging upside down, while bells tolled as if for a funeral.

The Burns case radicalized many northerners. Conservative Whig George Hilliard wrote to a friend, "When it was all over, and I was left alone in my office, I put my face in my hands and wept. I could do nothing less." During the 1850s, 322 black fugitives were sent back into slavery; only 11 were declared free. Northern popular sentiment and the Fugitive Slave Law, rigorously enforced by the federal government, were increasingly at odds.

In this volatile atmosphere, escaped African Americans wrote and lectured bravely on behalf of freedom. Frederick Douglass, the most famous and eloquent of the fugitive slaves, spoke out fearlessly in support of armed resistance. Openly active in the underground network that helped slaves reach safety in Canada, Douglass himself had been constantly in danger of capture until his friends bought his freedom in 1847. Harriet Jacobs, who escaped to the North after seven years in hiding in the South, wrote bitterly in her *Incidents in the Life of a Slave Girl* (1861) that the Fugitive Slave Law made her feel that "I was, in fact, a slave in New York, as subject to slave laws as I had been in a slave state. . . . I had been chased during half my life, and it seemed as if the chase was never to end."

The Fugitive Slave Law made slavery national and forced northern communities to confront what that meant. Although most people were still unwilling to grant social equality to the free African Americans who lived in the northern states, more and more had come to believe that the institution of slavery was wrong. Northern protests against the Fugitive Slave Law bred suspicion in the South and encouraged secessionist thinking. These new currents of public opinion were reflected in the election of 1852.

The Election of 1852

The first sign of the weakening of the national party system in 1852 was the difficulty both parties experienced at their nominating conventions. After fifty-two ballots, the Whigs nominated General Winfield Scott (their third military hero in four elections) rather than sitting President Fillmore. Many southern Whigs were angered and alienated by the choice and either abstained, like Georgia's Alexander Stephens, or, like Robert Toombs, cast a protest vote for the Democratic candidate. The Whigs never again fielded a presidential candidate.

The Democrats had a wider variety of candidates: Lewis Cass of popular sovereignty fame; Stephen Douglas, architect of the Compromise of 1850; and James Buchanan, described as a Northern man with Southern principles. Cass, Douglas, and Buchanan competed for forty-nine ballots, each strong enough to block the others but not strong enough to win. Finally the party turned to a handsome, affable nonentity, Franklin Pierce of New Hampshire, who was thought to have southern sympathies. Uniting on a platform pledging "faithful execution" of all parts of the Compromise of 1850, including the Fugitive Slave Law, Democrats polled well in the South and in the North. Most Democrats who had voted for the Free-Soil Party in 1848 voted for Pierce. So, in record numbers, did immigrant Irish and German voters, who were eligible for citizenship after three years' residence. The strong immigrant vote for Pierce was a sign of the strength of the Democratic machines in northern cities (see Chapter 13). Pierce easily won the 1852 election, 254 electoral votes to 42.

"Young America": The Politics of Expansion

Pierce entered the White House in 1853 on a wave of good feeling. Massachusetts Whig Amos Lawrence reported, "Never since Washington has an administration commenced with the hearty [good]will of so large a portion of the country." This good will was soon strained by Pierce's support for the expansionist adventures of the "Young America" movement.

The "Young America" movement was a group within the Democratic Party who used manifest destiny to justify their desire for conquest of Central America and Cuba. During the Pierce administration, a number of private "filibusters" (from the Spanish *filibustero*, meaning an "adventurer" or "pirate") invaded Caribbean and Central American countries, usually with the declared intention of extending slave territory. The best-known of the filibusters was also the most improbable: short, slight, soft-spoken William Walker invaded Nicaragua not once but four times. After his first invasion in 1855, Walker became ruler of the country. Unseated by a regional revolt, Walker mounted three other expeditions before reaching Nicaragua again in 1860, but was captured and met his death by firing squad in Honduras.

The Pierce administration, not directly involved in the filibustering, *was* deeply involved in an effort to obtain Cuba. In 1854 Pierce authorized his minister to Spain, Pierre Soulé, to try to force the unwilling Spanish to sell Cuba for $130 million. Soulé met in Ostend, Belgium, with the American ministers to France and England to compose the offer. At first appealing to Spain to recognize the deep affinities between the Cubans and American southerners that made them "one people with one destiny," the document went on to threaten to "wrest" Cuba from Spain if necessary. This amazing document, which became known as the Ostend Manifesto, was supposed to be secret but was soon leaked to the press. Deeply embarrassed, the Pierce administration was forced to repudiate the document.

The complicity between the Pierce administration and proslavery expansionists was foolhardy and lost it the northern good will with which it had begun. The sectional crisis that preceded the Compromise of 1850 had made obvious the danger of reopening the territorial issue. Ironically, it was not the Young America expansionists but the prime mover of the Compromise of 1850 himself, Stephen A. Douglas, who reignited the sectional struggle over slavery expansion.

The Crisis of the National Party System

In 1854 Stephen A. Douglas introduced the Kansas–Nebraska Act and thereby reopened the question of slavery in the territories. Douglas knew he was taking a political risk, but he believed he could satisfy

One of the most notable casualties of the looting and burning in 1856 of the Lawrence community was the Free State Hotel, built by the New England Emigrant Aid Society to house antislavery migrants to Kansas. This illustration made the events in Lawrence national news.

both his expansionist aims and his presidential ambitions. He was wrong. Instead, he pushed the national party system into crisis, first killing the Whigs and then destroying the Democrats.

The Kansas–Nebraska Act

Douglas introduced the Kansas–Nebraska Act opening the territory to white settlement because he was an ardent advocate of a transcontinental railroad that he believed would foster American democracy and commerce. He wanted the rail line to terminate in Chicago (in his own state of Illinois) rather than in St. Louis (a rival city), and to achieve that aim, the land west of Iowa and Missouri had to be organized into territories (the first step toward statehood). To open the territory, however, he needed the votes of southern Democrats, who were unwilling to support him unless the new territory was open to slavery.

Douglas's master stroke (as he thought) was to open up the lands under the principle of popular sovereignty. By espousing popular sovereignty for Kansas and Nebraska, Douglas expected to gain favor with the southern branch of the Democratic Party—which he would need to be nominated for president in 1856—and to obtain northern support because of the railroad route.

Douglas's Kansas–Nebraska bill passed, but at a great price. Southern Whigs voted with southern Democrats in favor of the measure, northern Whigs rejected it absolutely, and the split within the party was irreconcilable. The Whigs were unable to field a presidential candidate in

1856. The damage to the Democratic Party was almost as great. In the congressional elections of 1854, northern Democrats lost two-thirds of their seats (a drop from ninety-one to twenty-five), giving the southern Democrats (who were solidly in favor of slavery extension) the dominant voice both in Congress and within the party.

Douglas had committed one of the greatest miscalculations in American political history. A storm of protest arose throughout the North. More than 300 large anti-Nebraska rallies occurred during congressional consideration of the bill, and the anger did not subside. Douglas, who confidently believed that "the people of the north will sustain the measure when they come to understand it," found himself shouted down more than once at public rallies in his efforts to explain. "I could travel from Boston to Chicago," he ruefully commented, "by the light of my own [burning] effigy."

The Kansas–Nebraska bill shifted a crucial sector of northern opinion: the wealthy merchants, bankers, and manufacturers (called "Cotton Whigs") who had economic ties with southern slave owners and had always disapproved of abolitionist activity. Convinced that the bill would encourage antislavery feeling in the North, Cotton Whigs urged southern politicians to vote against it, only to be ignored. Passage of the Kansas–Nebraska Act convinced a number of northern Whigs that compromise with the South was impossible.

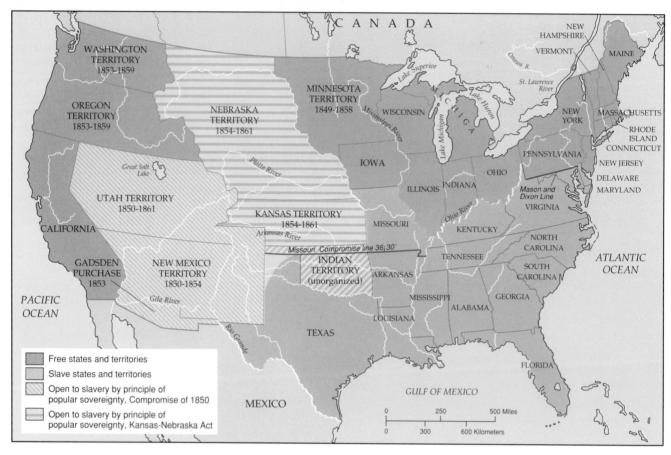

The Kansas–Nebraska Act, 1854

The Kansas–Nebraska Act, proposed by Stephen A. Douglas in 1854, opened the central and northern Great Plains to settlement. The act had two major faults: it robbed Indian peoples of half the territory guaranteed to them by treaty, and, because it repealed the Missouri Compromise Line, it opened up the lands to warring proslavery and antislavery factions.

In Kansas itself in 1854, hasty treaties were concluded with the Indian tribes who owned the land. Some, such as the Kickapoos, Shawnees, Sauks, and Foxes, agreed to relocate to small reservations. Others, such as the Delawares, Weas, and Iowas, agreed to sell their lands to whites. Still others, such as the Cheyennes and Sioux, kept the western part of Kansas Territory (now Colorado) until gold was discovered there in 1859. Once the treaties were signed, both proslavery and antislavery white settlers began to pour in, and the battle was on.

Kansas soon became the bloody battleground where the contest for popular sovereignty was fought out between the two factions. Free-soilers in Lawrence received shipments of heavy crates, innocuously marked "BOOKS" but actually containing Sharps repeating rifles, sent by eastern supporters. For their part, the proslavery "border ruffians" from nearby Missouri—

already heavily armed with Bowie knives, revolvers, rifles, and swords—called for reinforcements. David Atchison exhorted Alabamans: "Let your young men come forth to Missouri and Kansas! Let them come well armed!"

In the summer of 1856 these lethal preparations exploded into open warfare. First, proslavery forces burned and looted the town of Lawrence. The Free State Hotel, among other buildings, was burned to the ground. In retaliation, a grim old man named John Brown led his sons in killing five unarmed proslavery neighbors at Pottawatomie Creek. In the wave of the burnings and killings that followed Lawrence and Pottawatomie, John Brown and his followers became merely one of a number of bands of marauding murderers who were never arrested, never brought to trial, and never stopped from committing further violence. Armed bands roamed the countryside, and killings be-

Cartoons like this one sought to couple concerns about temperance (shown by the barrels of Irish whiskey and German lager beer) with nativist claims that immigrant voters were voting illegally (indicated by the struggle in the background).

came common. Peaceful residents of large sections of rural Kansas were repeatedly forced to flee to the safety of military forts when rumors of one or another armed band reached them.

The Politics of Nativism

Meanwhile, sectional pressures continued to reshape national politics. The breakup of the Whig Party coincided with one of the strongest bursts of nativism, or anti-immigrant feeling, in American history. The rapid rise in the number of foreign-born Democratic voters drew an equally rapid nativist backlash. The wave of German and Irish newcomers had tripled the immigration rate in the decades 1845–55 (see Chapter 13). Most of these immigrants were poor Catholics who clustered in urban centers, where they provided votes for Democratic Party bosses. Legally, immigrants could become U.S. citizens after three years' residence, but in Democrat-controlled big cities, where ward bosses sought votes, the time span was often much shorter.

The reformist and individualistic attitudes of many Whigs inclined them toward nativism and toward the new American Party, which formed in 1850 to give political expression to anti-immigrant feeling. Many Whigs disapproved of the new immigrants because they were poor, intemperate Catholics, whereas Whigs were strong supporters of temperance. The inability of urban governments to deal with the sudden growth in urban

population in the 1830s and 1840s was another cause of nativism: Whigs resented the increases in crime and the rising expenditures on relief for the poor that they blamed solely on immigration.

For all of these reasons, former Whigs, especially young men in white-collar and skilled blue-collar occupations, were strongly drawn to the new American Party. At the core of the party were several secret fraternal societies open only to native-born Protestants who pledged never to vote for a Catholic (on the grounds that all Catholics took their orders straight from the pope in Rome—a fear that was to be voiced again by Southern Baptists in 1960 when John F. Kennedy ran for president). When questioned about their beliefs, party members maintained secrecy by answering, "I know nothing," hence the popular name for American Party members: Know-Nothings.

Know-Nothings scored startling victories in northern state elections in 1854, winning control of the legislature in Massachusetts and polling 40 percent of the vote in Pennsylvania. But in the 1850s, no party could ignore slavery, and in 1855 the American Party split into

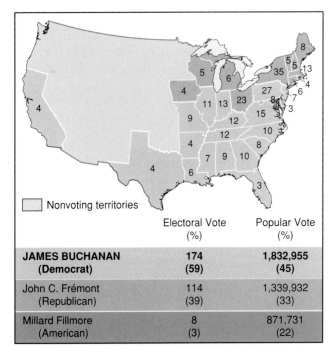

	Electoral Vote (%)	Popular Vote (%)
JAMES BUCHANAN (Democrat)	**174** (59)	**1,832,955** (45)
John C. Frémont (Republican)	114 (39)	1,339,932 (33)
Millard Fillmore (American)	8 (3)	871,731 (22)

The Election of 1856

Because three parties contested the 1856 election, Democrat James Buchanan was a minority president. Although Buchanan alone had national support, Republican John Frémont won most of the free states, and Millard Fillmore of the American Party gained 40 percent of the vote in most of the slave states.

SUMMARY TABLE	*Political Parties Split and Realign*
Whig Party	Ran its last presidential candidate in 1852. The candidate, General Winfield Scott, alienated many southern Whigs and the party was so split it could not field a candidate in 1856.
Democratic Party	Remained a national party through 1856, but Buchanan's actions as president made southern domination of the party so clear that many northern Democrats were alienated. Stephen Douglas, running as a Northern Democrat in 1860, won 29 percent of the popular vote; John Breckinridge, running as a Southern Democrat, won 18 percent.
Liberty Party	Antislavery party ran James G. Birney for president in 1844. He won 62,000 votes, largely from northern antislavery Whigs.
Free-Soil Party	Ran Martin Van Buren, former Democratic president, in 1848. Gained 10 percent of the popular vote, largely from Whigs but also from some northern Democrats.
American (Know-Nothing) Party	Nativist party made striking gains in 1854 congressional elections, attracting both northern and southern Whigs. In 1856, its presidential candidate, Millard Fillmore, won 21 percent of the popular vote.
Republican Party	Founded in 1854. Attracted many northern Whigs and northern Democrats. Presidential candidate John C. Frémont won 33 percent of the popular vote in 1856; in 1860 Abraham Lincoln won 40 percent and was elected in a four-way race.

northern (antislavery) and southern (proslavery) wings. Soon after this split, many people who had voted for the Know-Nothings changed their support, giving it to another political combination of many of the same Whig attitudes and a westward-looking, expansionist, free-soil policy. This was the Republican Party, founded in 1854.

The Republican Party and the Election of 1856

Many constituencies found room in the new Republican Party. There were many former northern Whigs who opposed slavery absolutely, many Free-Soil Party supporters who opposed the expansion of slavery but were willing to tolerate it in the South, and many northern reformers concerned about temperance and Catholicism. The Republicans also attracted the economic core of the old Whig Party: the merchants and industrialists who wanted a strong national government to promote economic growth by supporting a protective tariff, transportation improvements, and cheap land for western farmers. In quieter times it would have taken this party a while to sort out all its differences and become a true political community. But because of the sectional crisis, the fledgling party nearly won its first presidential election.

The immediate question facing the nation in 1856 was which new party, the Know-Nothings or the Republicans, would emerge the stronger. But the more important question was whether the Democratic Party could hold together. The two strongest contenders for the Dem-

ocratic nomination were President Pierce and Stephen A. Douglas. Douglas had proposed the Kansas–Nebraska Act and Pierce had actively supported it. Both men therefore had the support of the southern wing of the party. But it was precisely their support of this act that made northerners oppose both of them. The Kansas–Nebraska Act's divisive effect on the Democratic Party now became clear: no one who had voted on the bill, either for or against, could satisfy both wings of the party. A compromise candidate was found in James Buchanan of Pennsylvania, the "Northern man with Southern principles." Luckily for him, he had been ambassador to Great Britain at the time of the Kansas–Nebraska Act and thus had not had to commit himself.

The election of 1856 appeared to be a three-way contest that pitted Buchanan against explorer John C. Frémont of the Republican Party and the American (Know-Nothing) Party's candidate, former president Millard Fillmore. In fact, the election was two separate contests, one in the North and one in the South. The southern race was between Buchanan and Fillmore, the northern race between Buchanan and Frémont. Buchanan won the election with only 45 percent of the popular vote because he was the only national candidate. But the Republicans, after studying the election returns, claimed "victorious defeat," for they realized that in 1860 the addition of just two more northern states to their total would mean victory. Furthermore, the Republican Party had clearly defeated the American Party in the battle to win designation as a major party.

These were grounds for great optimism—and for great concern, for the Republican Party was a sectional rather than a national party; it drew almost all its support from the North. Southerners viewed its very existence as an attack on their vital interests. Thus the rapid rise of the Republicans posed a growing threat to national unity.

The Differences Deepen

In one dreadful week in 1856 the people of the United States heard, in quick succession, about the looting and burning of Lawrence, Kansas, about John Brown's retaliatory massacre at Pottawatomie, Kansas, and about unprecedented violence on the Senate floor. In the last of these incidents, Senator Charles Sumner of Massachusetts suffered permanent injury in a vicious attack by Congressman Preston Brooks of South Carolina. Trapped at his desk, Sumner was helpless as Brooks beat him so hard with his cane that it broke. A few days earlier, Sumner had given an insulting antislavery speech. Using the abusive, accusatory style favored by abolitionists, he had singled out for ridicule Senator Andrew Butler of South Carolina, Preston Brooks's uncle. In Brooks's mind, he was simply avenging an intolerable affront to his uncle's honor. So far had the behavioral codes of North and South diverged that each man found his own action perfectly justifiable and the action of the other outrageous.

The Dred Scott Decision

Although James Buchanan firmly believed that he alone could hold together the nation so riven by hatred and violence, his self-confidence outran his abilities. He was so deeply indebted to the strong southern wing of the Democratic Party that he could not take the impartial actions necessary to heal "Bleeding Kansas." Equally unfortunate, his support of the prosouthern *Dred Scott* decision encouraged further sectional differences.

On March 6, 1857, two days after James Buchanan was sworn in, the Supreme Court announced one of its most momentous opinions. In *Dred Scott* v. *Sandford,* a southern-dominated court attempted—and failed—to solve the political controversy over slavery. Declaring the Missouri Compromise unconstitutional, Chief Justice Roger B. Taney asserted that the federal government had no right to interfere with the free movement of property throughout the territories. This was John C. Calhoun's states' rights position, always before considered an extremist southern argument. Taney then dismissed the *Dred Scott* case, which had been in the

These sympathetic portraits of Harriet and Dred Scott and their daughters in 1857 helped to shape the northern reaction to the Supreme Court decision that denied the Scotts' claim for freedom. The infamous Dred Scott *decision, which was intended to resolve the issue of slavery expansion, instead heightened angry feelings in both North and South.*

courts for eleven years, on the grounds that only citizens could bring suits before federal courts and that black people, slave or free, were not citizens. With this bold judicial intervention into the most heated issue of the day, Taney intended to settle the controversy over the expansion of slavery once and for all. Instead, he enflamed the conflict.

Dred Scott had been a slave all his life. His owner, army surgeon John Emerson, had taken Scott on his military assignments during the 1830s to Illinois (a free state) and Wisconsin Territory (a free territory by the Missouri Compromise line). During that time Scott married another slave, Harriet, and their daughter, Eliza, was born in free territory. Emerson and the Scotts then returned to Missouri (a slave state) and there, in 1846, Dred Scott sued for his freedom and that of his wife and the daughter born in Wisconsin Territory (who as women had no legal standing of their own) on the grounds that residence in free lands had made them free.

The five southern members of the Supreme Court concurred in Taney's decision, as did one northerner, Robert C. Grier. Historians have found that President-elect Buchanan had pressured Grier, a fellow Pennsylvanian, to support the majority. Two of the three other northerners vigorously dissented, and the last voiced other objections. This was clearly a sectional decision, and the response to it was sectional. Southerners expressed great satisfaction and strong support for the Court. Many northerners disagreed so strongly with the *Dred Scott* decision that for the first time they found themselves seriously questioning the power of the Supreme Court to establish the law of the land.

For the Republican Party, the *Dred Scott* decision represented a formidable challenge. By invalidating the Missouri Compromise, the decision swept away the free-soil foundation of the party. But to directly challenge a Supreme Court decision was a weighty matter. The most sensational Republican counterattack—made by both Abraham Lincoln and William Seward—was the accusation that President Buchanan had conspired with the southern Supreme Court justices to subvert the American political system by delaying the decision until after the presidential election. Lincoln also raised the frightening possibility that "the next *Dred Scott* decision" would legalize slavery even in free states that abhorred it. President Buchanan's response to events in Kansas, including the drafting of a proslavery constitution, also stoked political antagonisms.

The Lecompton Constitution

In Kansas, the doctrine of popular sovereignty led to continuing civil strife and the political travesty of two territorial governments. The first election of officers to a territorial government in 1855 produced lopsided proslavery results that were clear evidence of illegal voting by Missouri border ruffians. Free-soilers protested by forming their own government, so Kansas had both a proslavery territorial legislature in Lecompton and a free-soil government in Topeka. A proslavery majority wrote the proslavery Lecompton constitution and applied to Congress for admission to the Union in 1857. In the meantime, in October honest elections for the territorial legislature had returned a clear free-soil majority. Nevertheless, Buchanan, in the single most disastrous mistake of his administration, endorsed the proslavery constitution because he feared to lose the support of southern Democrats. It seemed that Kansas would enter the Union as a slave state and that the free–slave balance of states would thereby be equalized at sixteen to sixteen.

Unexpected congressional opposition came from Stephen Douglas. In 1857, in what was surely the bravest step of his political career, Douglas opposed the Lecompton constitution on the grounds that it violated the principle of popular sovereignty. He insisted that the Lecompton constitution must be voted upon by Kansas voters in honest elections (as Buchanan had initially promised). Defying his own president, Douglas carried the congressional vote in April 1858 that refused admission to Kansas under the Lecompton constitution. The people of Kansas also rejected the Lecompton constitution, 11,300 to 1,788. Kansas was finally admitted as a free state in January 1861.

The defeat of the Lecompton constitution did not come easily. There was more bloodshed in Kansas, more violence in Congress, and conflict on still another level: the Democratic Party was breaking apart. Douglas had intended to preserve the Democrats as a national party, but instead he lost the support of the southern wing. Summing up these events, Congressman Alexander Stephens of Georgia wrote glumly to his brother, "All things here are tending my mind to the conclusion that the Union cannot and will not last long."

The Panic of 1857

Adding to the growing political tensions was the short but sharp depression of 1857 and 1858. Technology played a part: in August 1857, the failure of an Ohio investment house—the kind of event that had formerly taken weeks to be widely known—was the subject of a news story flashed immediately over telegraph wires to Wall Street and other financial markets. A wave of panic selling ensued, leading to business failures and slowdowns that threw thousands out of work. The major cause of the panic was a sharp but temporary downturn in agricultural exports to Britain, and recovery was well under way by early 1859.

Because cotton exports were affected less than northern exports, the Panic of 1857 was less harmful to the South than to the North. Southerners took this as proof of the superiority of their economic system to the free-labor system of the North. It seemed that all matters of political discussion were being drawn into the sectional dispute. The next step toward disunion was an act of violence perpetrated by the grim abolitionist from Kansas, John Brown.

This painting by Charles G. Rosenberg and James H. Cafferty shows a worried crowd exchanging the latest news on Wall Street during the Panic of 1857. This was the first economic depression in which the telegraph played a part by carrying bad financial news in the West to New York much more rapidly than in the past.

John Brown's Raid

In the heated political mood of the late 1850s, some improbable people became heroes. None was more improbable than John Brown, the self-appointed avenger who slaughtered unarmed proslavery men in Kansas in 1856. In 1859 Brown proposed a wild scheme to raid the South and start a general slave uprising. He believed, as did most northern abolitionists, that discontent among southern slaves was so great that such an uprising needed only a spark to get going. Significantly, free African Americans—among them Frederick Douglass—did not support Brown, thinking his first planned foray, to raid the federal arsenal at Harpers Ferry, Virginia, was doomed to failure. They were right. On October 16, 1859, Brown led a group of twenty-two white

and African American men against the arsenal. However, he had made no provision for escape. Even more incredible, he had not notified the Virginia slaves whose uprising it was supposed to be. In less than a day the raid was over. Eight of Brown's men (including two of his sons) were dead, no slaves had joined the fight, and Brown himself was captured. Moving quickly to prevent a lynching by local mobs, the state of Virginia tried and convicted Brown of treason, murder, and fomenting insurrection while he was still weak from the wounds of battle.

Ludicrous in life, possibly insane, Brown was nevertheless a noble martyr. In his closing speech before sentencing, Brown was magnificently eloquent: "Now, if it is deemed necessary that I should forfeit my life for the furtherance of the end of justice, and mingle my blood

John Brown's death provoked almost unprecedented mourning in the North, a reaction that horrified the South.

further with the blood of my children and with the blood of millions in this slave country whose rights are disregarded by wicked, cruel, and unjust enactments, I say, let it be done."

Brown's death by hanging on December 2, 1859, was marked throughout northern communities with public rites of mourning not seen since the death of George Washington. Ralph Waldo Emerson said that Brown would "make the gallows as glorious as the cross," and Henry David Thoreau called him "an angel of light." Not all northerners supported Brown's action, but many people did support the antislavery cause he represented.

Brown's raid shocked the South because it aroused the greatest fear, that of slave rebellion. Southerners believed that northern abolitionists were provoking slave revolts, a suspicion apparently confirmed when documents captured at Harpers Ferry revealed that Brown

had the financial support of half a dozen members of the northern elite. These "Secret Six"—Gerrit Smith, George Stearns, Franklin Sanborn, Thomas Wentworth Higginson, Theodore Parker, and Samuel Gridley Howe—had been willing to finance armed attacks on the slave system.

Even more shocking to southerners than the raid itself was the extent of northern mourning for Brown's death. Although the Republican Party disavowed Brown's actions, southerners simply did not believe the party's statements. Senator Robert Toombs of Georgia warned that the South would "never permit this Federal government to pass into the traitorous hands of the Black Republican party." Talk of secession as the only possible response became common throughout the South.

The South Secedes

By 1860, sectional differences had caused one national party, the Whigs, to collapse. The second national party, the Democrats, stood on the brink of dissolution. Ordinary people in both the North and the South were coming to believe there was no way to avoid what in 1858 William Seward (once a Whig, now a Republican) had called an "irrepressible conflict."

The Election of 1860

The split of the Democratic Party into northern and southern wings that had occurred during President Buchanan's tenure became official at the Democratic nominating conventions in 1860. The party convened first in Charleston, South Carolina, the center of secessionist agitation. It was the worst possible location in which to attempt to reach unity. Although Stephen Douglas had the support of the plurality of delegates, he did not have the two-thirds majority necessary for nomination. As the price of their support, southerners insisted that Douglas support a federal slave code—a guarantee that slavery would be protected in the territories. Douglas could not agree without violating his own belief in popular sovereignty and losing his northern support. After ten days, fifty-nine ballots, and two southern walkouts, the convention ended where it had begun: deadlocked.

In June, the Democrats met again in Baltimore. The Douglasites, recognizing the need for a united party, were eager to compromise wherever they could, but most southern Democrats were not. More than a third of the delegates bolted. Later, holding a convention of their own, they nominated Buchanan's vice-president, John C. Breckinridge of Kentucky. The remaining two-thirds of the Democrats nominated Douglas, but everyone knew that a Republican victory was inevitable. To make matters worse, some southern Whigs joined with some border-state nativists to form the Constitutional Union Party, which nominated John Bell of Tennessee.

Republican strategy was built on the lessons of the 1856 "victorious defeat." The Republicans planned to carry all the states Frémont had won, plus Pennsylvania, Illinois, and Indiana. The two leading Republican contenders were Senator William H. Seward of New York and Abraham Lincoln of Illinois. Seward, the party's best-known figure, had enemies among party moderates, who thought he was too radical, and among nativists with whom he had clashed in the New York Whig

Party. Lincoln, on the other hand, appeared new, impressive, more moderate than Seward, and certain to carry Illinois. Lincoln won the nomination on the third ballot.

The election of 1860 presented voters with one of the clearest choices in American history. On the key issue of slavery, Breckinridge supported its extension to the territories; Lincoln stood firmly for its exclusion. Douglas attempted to hold the middle ground with his principle of popular sovereignty; Bell vaguely favored compromise as well. The Republicans offered other platform planks designed to appeal to northern voters: a homestead act (free western lands), support for a transcontinental railroad, other internal improvements, and a higher tariff. Although they spoke clearly against the extension of slavery, Republicans devoted most of

SUMMARY TABLE	*The Irrepressible Conflict*	
Declaration of Independence	1776	Thomas Jefferson's denunciation of slavery deleted from the final version.
Northwest Ordinance	1787	Slavery prohibited in the Northwest Territory (north of the Ohio River).
Constitution	1787	Slavery unmentioned but acknowledged in Article I, section 2, counting three-fifths of slaves in a state's population, and in Article I, section 9, in which the international slave trade could not be prohibited for twenty years.
Louisiana Purchase	1803	Louisiana admitted as a slave state in 1812; no decision about the rest of Louisiana Purchase.
Missouri Compromise	1820	Missouri admitted as a slave state, but slavery prohibited in Louisiana Purchase north of 36°30′.
Wilmot Proviso	1846	Proposal to prohibit slavery in territory that might be gained in Mexican–American War causes splits in national parties.
Compromise of 1850	1850	California admitted as free state; Texas (already admitted, 1845) is a slave state, the rest of Mexican Cession to be decided by popular sovereignty. Ends the slave trade in the District of Columbia but stronger Fugitive Slave Law, leading to a number of violent recaptures, arouses northern antislavery opinion.
Kansas–Nebraska Act	1854	At the urging of Stephen A. Douglas, Congress opens Kansas and Nebraska Territories for settlement under popular sovereignty. Open warfare between proslavery and antislavery factions breaks out in Kansas.
Lecompton Constitution	1857	President James Buchanan's decision to admit Kansas to the Union with a proslavery constitution is defeated in Congress.
Dred Scott Decision	1857	The Supreme Court's denial of Dred Scott's case for freedom is welcomed in the South, condemned in the North.
John Brown's raid and execution	1859	Northern support for John Brown shocks the South.
Democratic Party Nominating Conventions	1860	The Democrats are unable to agree on a candidate; two candidates, one northern (Stephen A. Douglas) and one southern (John C. Breckinridge) split the party and vote, thus allowing Republican Abraham Lincoln to win.

The Republican Party poster for the election of 1860 combines the party's major themes: free land, free soil, opposition to "the Slave Power" (the slogan "Free Speech"), and higher tariffs. But above all was the message, "THE UNION MUST AND SHALL BE PRESERVED."

their other efforts to dispelling their radical abolitionist image. The Republican platform condemned John Brown's raid as "the gravest of crimes," repeatedly denied that Republicans favored the social equality of black people, and strenuously affirmed that they sought to preserve the Union. In reality, Republicans simply did not believe the South would secede if Lincoln won. In this the Republicans were not alone: few northerners believed southern threats—southerners had threatened too many times before.

The only candidate who spoke urgently and openly about the impending threat of secession was Douglas. Breaking with convention, Douglas personally campaigned in both the North and the South, warning of the danger of dissolution and presenting himself as the only truly national candidate. Realizing that his own chances for election were slight, Douglas bravely cam-

paigned for national unity in a hostile South. As he told his private secretary, "Mr. Lincoln is the next President. We must try to save the Union. I will go South."

In accordance with tradition, Lincoln did not campaign for himself, but many other Republicans spoke for him. The Republicans did not campaign in the South; Breckinridge did not campaign in the North. Each side was therefore free to believe the worst about the other. All parties, North and South, campaigned with oratory, parades and rallies, free food and drink. Even in the face of looming crisis, this presidential campaign was the best entertainment of the day.

The mood in the Deep South was close to mass hysteria. Rumors of slave revolts in Texas, Alabama, and South Carolina swept the region, and vigilance committees sprang up to counter the supposed threat. In upcountry South Carolina, the question of secession

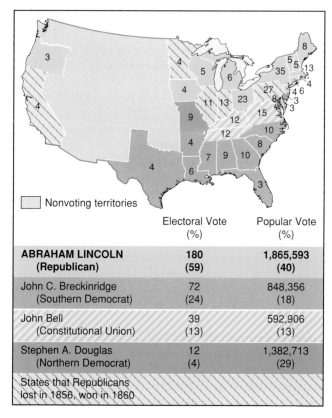

	Electoral Vote (%)	Popular Vote (%)
ABRAHAM LINCOLN (Republican)	**180 (59)**	**1,865,593 (40)**
John C. Breckinridge (Southern Democrat)	72 (24)	848,356 (18)
John Bell (Constitutional Union)	39 (13)	592,906 (13)
Stephen A. Douglas (Northern Democrat)	12 (4)	1,382,713 (29)

☐ Nonvoting territories

▨ States that Republicans lost in 1856, won in 1860

The Election of 1860

The election of 1860 was a sectional election. Lincoln won no votes in the South, Breckinridge none in the North. The contest in the North was between Lincoln and Douglas, and although Lincoln swept the electoral vote, Douglas's popular vote was uncomfortably close. The large number of northern Democratic voters opposed to Lincoln was a source of political trouble for him during the Civil War.

dominated races for the state legislature. Candidates who advocated "patriotic forbearance" if Lincoln won were soundly defeated. The very passion and excitement of the election campaign moved southerners toward extremism. Even the weather—the worst drought and heat wave the South had known for years—contributed to the tension.

The election of 1860 produced the second highest voter turnout in U.S. history (81.2 percent, topped only by 81.8 percent in 1876). The election turned out to be two regional contests: Breckinridge versus Bell in the South, Lincoln versus Douglas in the North. Breckinridge carried eleven slave states with 18 percent of the popular vote; Bell carried Virginia, Tennessee, and Kentucky with 13 percent of the popular vote. Lincoln won all eighteen of the free states (he split New Jersey with

Douglas) and almost 40 percent of the popular vote. Douglas carried only Missouri, but gained nearly 30 percent of the popular vote. Lincoln's electoral vote total was overwhelming: 180 to a combined 123 for the other three candidates. But although Lincoln had won 54 percent of the vote in the northern states, his name had not even appeared on the ballot in ten southern states. The true winner of the 1860 election was sectionalism.

The South Leaves the Union

The results of the election shocked southerners. They were humiliated and frightened by the prospect of becoming a permanent minority in a political system dominated by a party pledged to the elimination of slavery. In southern eyes the Republican triumph meant they would become unequal partners in the federal enterprise, their way of life (the slave system) existing on borrowed time.

The governors of South Carolina, Alabama, and Mississippi, each of whom had committed his state to secession if Lincoln were elected, immediately issued calls for special state conventions. At the same time, calls went out to southern communities to form vigilance committees and volunteer militia companies. Co-operationists (the term used for those opposed to immediate secession) were either intimidated into silence or simply left behind by the speed of events.

On December 20, 1860, South Carolina, with all the hoopla and excitement of bands, fireworks displays, and huge rallies, seceded from the Union. James Buchanan, the lame-duck president (Lincoln would not be inaugurated until March), did nothing. In the weeks that followed, six other southern states (Mississippi, Florida, Alabama, Georgia, Louisiana, and Texas) followed suit. In none of these state conventions was the vote for secession unanimous, as it had been in South Carolina, but on average, 80 percent of the delegates voted to leave the Union. Although there was genuine division of opinion in the South (especially in Georgia and Alabama, along customary up-country–low-country lines) none of the Deep South states held anywhere near the number of Unionists that Republicans had hoped. Throughout the South, secession occurred because southerners no longer believed they had a choice.

In every state that seceded, the joyous scenes of South Carolina were repeated as the decisiveness of action replaced the long years of anxiety and tension. People danced in the streets, most believing the North had no choice but to accept secession peacefully. They ignored the fact that eight other slave states (Delaware,

The Southern States Secede

The southern states that would compose the Confederacy seceded in two major groups. The states of the Lower South seceded before Lincoln took office and war began at Fort Sumter. Three states of the Upper South—Virginia, North Carolina, and Tennessee—and Arkansas waited until after Fort Sumter. And four border slave states: Delaware, Maryland, Kentucky, and Missouri, chose not to secede. Every southern state (except South Carolina) was divided on the issue of secession, generally along up-country–low-country lines. In Virginia this division was so extreme that West Virginia split off to become a separate nonslave state and was admitted to the Union in 1863.

Maryland, Kentucky, Missouri, Virginia, North Carolina, Tennessee, and Arkansas) had not acted—though the latter four states did join them before war broke out. Just as Republicans had miscalculated in thinking southern threats a mere bluff, so secessionists now miscalculated in believing they would be able to leave the Union in peace.

The North's Political Options

What should the North do? Buchanan continued to do nothing. The decision thus rested with Abraham Lincoln, even before he officially became president. One possibility was compromise, and many proposals were suggested, ranging from full adoption of the Breckinridge campaign platform to reinstatement of the Missouri Compromise line. Lincoln cautiously refused them all, making it clear that he would not compromise on the extension of slavery, which was the South's key demand. He hoped, by appearing firm but moderate, to discourage additional southern states from seceding while giving pro-Union southerners time to organize. He succeeded in his first aim, but not in the second. Lincoln and most of the Republican Party had seriously overestimated the strength of pro-Union sentiment in the South.

A second possibility, suggested by Horace Greeley of the *New York Tribune,* was to let the seven seceding states "go in peace," but too many northerners—including Lincoln himself—believed in the Union for this to happen. As Lincoln said, what was at stake was "the necessity of proving that popular government is not an absurdity. We must settle this question now, whether in a free government the minority have the right to break up the government whenever they choose." The third possibility was force, and this was the crux of the dilemma. Although he believed their action was wrong, Lincoln was loath to go to war to force the seceding states back into the Union. On the other hand, he refused to give up federal powers over military forts and customs posts in the South. These were precisely the powers the seceding states had to command if they were to function as an independent nation. A confrontation was bound to come.

Establishment of the Confederacy

In February, delegates from the seven seceding states met in Montgomery, Alabama, and created the Confederate States of America. They wrote a constitution that was identical to the Constitution of the United States, with a few crucial exceptions: it strongly supported states' rights and made the abolition of slavery practically impossible. These two clauses did much to define the Confederate enterprise.

The Montgomery convention passed over the fire-eaters—the men who had been the first to urge secession—and chose Jefferson Davis of Mississippi as president and Alexander Stephens of Georgia as vice-president of the new nation. Both men were known as moderates. The choice of moderates was deliberate, for the strategy of the new Confederate state was to argue that secession was a normal, responsible, and expectable course of action, and nothing for the North to get upset about. This was the theme that President Jefferson Davis of the Confederate States of America struck in his

Abraham Lincoln's inauguration on March 4, 1861, shown here in Leslie's Illustrated Newspaper, *symbolized the state of the nation. As he took the oath to become president of a divided country, Lincoln stood before a Capitol building with a half-finished dome and was guarded by soldiers who feared a Confederate attack. Politicians had long been concerned about the dangers of sectionalism in American life. But most ordinary people had taken for granted the federal Union of states—and the ability of slave and nonslave states—to coexist.*

inaugural address, delivered to a crowd of 10,000 from the steps of the State Capitol at Montgomery on February 18, 1861. "We have changed the constituent parts," Davis said, "but not the system of our Government." Secession was a legal and peaceful step that, Davis said, quoting from the Declaration of Independence, "illustrates the American idea that governments rest on the consent of the governed . . . and that it is the right of the people to alter or abolish them at will whenever they become destructive of the ends for which they were established."

Lincoln's Inauguration

The country as a whole waited to see what Abraham Lincoln would do. It appeared he was doing nothing. In Springfield, Lincoln refused to issue public statements before his inaugural (although he sent many private messages to Congress and to key military officers), for fear of making a delicate situation worse. Similarly, during a twelve-day whistle-stopping railroad trip east from Springfield, he was careful to say nothing controversial. Eastern intellectuals, already suspicious of a mere "prairie lawyer," were not impressed. Finally, hard evidence of an assassination plot forced Lincoln to abandon his whistle-stops at Harrisburg and, protected by Pinkerton detectives, to travel incognito into Washington "like a thief in the night," as he complained. These signs of moderation and caution did not appeal to an American public with a penchant for electing military heroes. Americans wanted leadership and action.

However, Lincoln continued to offer nonbelligerent firmness and moderation. And at the end of his inaugural address on March 4, 1861, as he stood ringed by federal troops called out in case of a Confederate attack, the new president offered unexpected eloquence:

> I am loath to close. We are not enemies, but friends. We must not be enemies. Though passion may have strained, it must not break our bonds of affection. The mystic chords of memory, stretching from every battlefield, and patriot grave, to every living heart and hearthstone, all over this broad land, will yet swell the chorus of the Union, when again touched, as surely they will be, by the better angels of our nature.

Conclusion

Americans had much to boast about in 1850. Their nation was vastly larger, richer, and more powerful than it had been in 1800. But the issue of slavery was slowly dividing the North and the South, two communities with similar origins and many common bonds. The decade was marked by frantic efforts at political compromise, but politics had failed: the issue of slavery was irreconcilable. The only remaining recourse was war. But although Americans were divided, they were still one people. That made the war, when it came, all the more terrible.

CHRONOLOGY

1820	Missouri Compromise
1832	Nullification Crisis
1846	Wilmot Proviso
1848	Treaty of Guadalupe Hidalgo ends Mexican–American War
	Zachary Taylor elected president
	Free-Soil Party formed
1849	California and Utah seek admission to the Union as free states
1850	Compromise of 1850
	California admitted as a free state
	American Party (Know-Nothing) formed
	Zachary Taylor dies, Millard Fillmore becomes president
1851	North reacts to Fugitive Slave Law
	Harriet Beecher Stowe's *Uncle Tom's Cabin* published
1852	Franklin Pierce elected president
1854	Ostend Manifesto
	Kansas–Nebraska Act
	Treaties with Indians in northern part of Indian Territory renegotiated

	Republican Party formed as Whig Party dissolves
1855	William Walker leads first filibustering expedition to Nicaragua
1856	Burning and looting of Lawrence, Kansas
	John Brown leads Pottawatomie massacre
	James Buchanan elected president
1857	*Dred Scott* decision
	President Buchanan accepts proslavery Lecompton constitution in Kansas
	Panic of 1857
1858	Congress rejects Lecompton constitution
	Lincoln–Douglas debates
1859	John Brown's raid on Harpers Ferry
1860	Four parties run presidential candidates
	Abraham Lincoln elected president
	South Carolina secedes from Union
1861	Six other Deep South states secede
	Confederate States of America formed
	Lincoln takes office

Review Questions

1. What aspects of the remarkable economic development of the United States in the first half of the nineteenth century contributed to the sectional crisis of the 1850s?

2. How were the violent efforts by abolitionists to free escaped slaves who had been recaptured and the federal armed enforcement of the Fugitive Slave Act viewed by different segments of the Boston population in the early 1850s? How might these events have looked to merchants (the so-called Cotton Whigs), Irish immigrants, and abolitionists?

3. Consider the course of events in "Bloody Kansas" from Douglas's Kansas–Nebraska Act to the Congressional rejection of the Lecompton constitution. Were these events the inevitable result of the political impasse in Washington, or could other decisions have been taken that would have changed the outcome?

4. The nativism of the 1850s, which surfaced so strongly in the Know-Nothing Party, was eclipsed by the crisis over slavery. But nativist sentiment has been a recurring theme in American politics. Discuss why it was strong in the 1850s and why it has emerged periodically since then.

5. Evaluate the character and actions of John Brown. Was he the hero proclaimed by northern supporters or the terrorist condemned by the South?

6. Imagine that you lived in Illinois, home state to both Douglas and Lincoln, in 1860. How would you have voted in the presidential election, and why?

Recommended Reading

WILLIAM L. BARNEY, *The Secessionist Impulse: Alabama and Mississippi in 1860* (1974). Covers the election of 1860 and the subsequent conventions that led to secession.

DON E. FEHRENBACHER, *The* Dred Scott *Case: Its Significance in American Law and Politics* (1978). A major study by the leading historian on this controversial decision.

ERIC FONER, *Free Soil, Free Labor, Free Men: The Ideology of the Republican Party Before the Civil War* (1970). A landmark effort that was among the first studies to focus on free labor ideology of the North and its importance in the political disputes of the 1850s.

LACEY K. FORD JR., *Origins of Southern Radicalism: The South Carolina Upcountry, 1800–1860* (1988). One of a number of recent studies of the attitudes of up-country farmers, who in South Carolina supported secession wholeheartedly.

HOMAN HAMILTON, *Prologue to Conflict: The Crisis and Compromise of 1850* (1964). The standard source on the Compromise of 1850.

BRUCE LEVINE, *Half Slave and Half Free: The Roots of the Civil War* (1992). Good survey of the contrasting attitudes of North and South.

ALICE NICHOLS, *Bleeding Kansas* (1954). The standard source on the battles over Kansas.

DAVID M. POTTER, *The Impending Crisis, 1848–1861* (1976). A comprehensive account of the politics leading up to the Civil War.

ANNE C. ROSE, *Voices of the Marketplace: American Thought and Culture, 1830–1860* (1995). A new study that considers the effects of the concepts of Christianity, democracy, and capitalism on American cultural life.

KENNETH M. STAMPP, *America in 1857: A Nation on the Brink* (1990). A study of the crucial year by a leading southern historian.

16 THE CIVIL WAR, 1861–1865

AMERICAN COMMUNITIES

MOTHER BICKERDYKE CONNECTS NORTHERN COMMUNITIES TO THEIR BOYS AT WAR

In May 1861 Rev. Edward Beecher interrupted his customary Sunday service at Brick Congregational Church in Galesburg, Illinois, to read a disturbing letter to the congregation. Two months earlier, Galesburg had proudly sent 500 of its young men off to join the Union army. They had not yet been in battle, yet the letter reported that an alarming number were dying of diseases caused by inadequate food, medical care, and sanitation at the crowded military camp in Cairo, Illinois. Most army doctors were surgeons, trained to operate and amputate on the battlefield. They were not prepared to treat dysentery, pneumonia, typhoid, measles—all serious, often fatal diseases that could often be cured with careful nursing. The letter writer, appalled by the squalor and misery he saw around him, complained of abuses by the army. The fact was, however, that the Union army was overwhelmed with the task of readying recruits for battle and had made few provisions for their health when not in combat.

The shocked and grieving members of Beecher's congregation quickly decided to send not only supplies but one of their number to inspect the conditions at the Cairo camp and to take action. Despite warnings from a veteran of the War of 1812 that army regulations excluded women from encampments, the congregation voted to send their most qualified member, Mary Ann Bickerdyke, a middle-aged widow who made her living as a "botanic physician." This simple gesture of community concern launched the remarkable Civil War career of "the Cyclone in Calico," who defied medical officers and generals alike in her unceasing efforts on behalf of ill, wounded, and convalescent Union soldiers.

"Mother" Bickerdyke, as she was called, let nothing stand in the way of helping her "boys." When she arrived in Cairo, she immediately set to work cleaning the hospital tents and the soldiers themselves and finding and cooking nourishing food for them. The sheer number of soldiers and the constant need to set up new field hospitals for an army on the move and to commandeer scarce food supplies required an unusual person. A plainspoken, hardworking woman, totally unrespectful of rank or tender masculine egos, Mother Bickerdyke single-mindedly devoted herself to what she called "the Lord's work." The ordinary soldiers loved her; wise generals supported her. Once, when an indignant officer's wife complained about Bickerdyke's rudeness, General William Tecumseh Sherman joked, "You've picked the one person around here who out-ranks me. If you want to lodge a complaint against her, you'll have to take it to President Lincoln."

Mother Bickerdyke's essential services exposed the fact that the War Department was unable to meet the needs of the first mass army in the nation's history. Of course, she was not the only person to realize this. Just as the Galesburg congregation recognized the need for supplies and assistance, so did communities all over the North. Women came together in their communities to make clothing for local men who had gone off to the war. A number of women, most of them experienced in earlier reform efforts, banded together to form the Women's Central Association of Relief. Eventually, 7,000 association chapters throughout the North were raising funds; making and sending bandages, food, clothing, medicine, and more than 250,000 quilts and comforters to army camps and hospitals; and providing meals, housing, and transportation to soldiers on furlough. These women's groups supplied an estimated $15 million worth of goods to the Union troops.

Convincing President Abraham Lincoln that it needed official status, in June 1861 the association gained a new name—the United States Sanitary Commission—along with the power to investigate and advise the Medical Bureau. Henry Bellows, a Unitarian clergyman, became president of the organization and Frederick Law Olmsted its executive secretary. More than 500 "sanitary inspectors" (usually men, and all volunteers) instructed soldiers in matters such as water supply, placement of latrines, and safe cooking.

Although at first she worked independently and remained suspicious of all organizations (and even of many other relief givers), in 1862 Mother Bickerdyke was persuaded to become an official agent of "the Sanitary" as it was known. She gained access to supplies and the ability to order precisely what she needed from the commission's warehouses. The Sanitary Commission gained an unequaled fundraiser. In speaking tours throughout Illinois, Bickerdyke touched her female listeners with moving stories of wounded boys whom she had cared for as if they were her own sons. Her words

to men were more forceful. It was a man's business to fight, she said. If he was too old or ill to fight with a gun, he should fight with his dollars. Bickerdyke's blunt fundraising was extremely effective. Aided by her appeals, the Sanitary Commission was able to contribute a total of $50 million to the Union war effort.

As the Civil War continued, Mother Bickerdyke became a vital intermediary between the home front and the battlefield in a practical sense as well as in her symbolic function as the soldiers' mother. Just as the Sanitary Commission itself became a major example of the way volunteers in northern civilian communities linked the home front with the battlefield, Bickerdyke came to stand for all mothers who had sent their sons to war.

The Civil War was a community tragedy. It ripped apart the national political community. The nation suffered more casualties in this internal war than in any other war in its history. Yet in another sense, the Civil War was a community triumph. Local communities directly supported and sustained their soldiers in unprecedented and massive ways. As national unity failed, the strength of local communities, symbolized by Mother Bickerdyke, continued.

KEY TOPICS

- ◆ **The social and political changes created by the unprecedented nature and scale of the Civil War**
- ◆ **A brief military history of the war**
- ◆ **The central importance of the end of slavery to the war efforts of North and South**

Communities Mobilize for War

The country in March 1861 presented to the observer an ominous series of similarities. Two nations, the United States of America (shorn of seven Deep South states) and the Confederate States of America, blamed each other for the breakup of the Union. Two new presidents, Abraham Lincoln and Jefferson Davis, were faced with the challenging task of building and maintaining national unity. Two regions, North and South, scorned each other and boasted of their own superiority. But the most basic similarity was not yet apparent: both sides and all participants were unprepared for the ordeal that lay ahead.

Fort Sumter: The War Begins

In their inaugural addresses, both Lincoln and Davis prayed for peace but positioned themselves for war. Careful listeners to both addresses realized that the two men were on a collision course.

Fort Sumter, South Carolina, a major federal military installation, sat on a granite island at the entrance to Charleston harbor. As long as it remained in Union hands, Charleston, the center of secessionist sentiment, would be immobilized. Thus it was hardly surprising that Fort Sumter should be the first crisis facing President Lincoln.

On April 6 Lincoln notified the governor of South Carolina that he was sending a relief force carrying only food and no military supplies to the fort. On April 10 Davis ordered General P. G. T. Beauregard to demand the surrender of Fort Sumter, and to use force if the garrison did not comply. On April 12, as Lincoln's relief force neared Charleston harbor, Beauregard opened fire on Fort Sumter. Two days later, the defenders surrendered and the Confederate stars and bars rose over the fort.

The Call to Arms

Even before Sumter, the Confederate Congress had authorized a volunteer army of 100,000 men to serve for twelve months. Men flocked to enlist, and their com-

Community members gather for a formal send-off to men of the First Michigan Infantry in 1861, shown drawn up to hear patriotic speeches by local officials before leaving for Washington, where they and other state regiments were mustered into the Union army.

munities sent them off with bands playing "Dixie" and other martial music. For these early recruits, war was a patriotic adventure.

The "thunderclap of Sumter" startled the North into an angry response. The apathy and uncertainty that had prevailed since Lincoln's election disappeared. On April 15 Lincoln issued a proclamation calling for 75,000 state militiamen to serve in the federal army for 90 days. Enlistment offices were swamped with so many enthusiastic volunteers that many men were sent home. Free African Americans, among the most eager to serve, were turned away.

The mobilization in Chester, Pennsylvania, was typical of the northern response to the outbreak of war. A patriotic rally was held as a company of volunteers calling themselves the Union Blues were mustered into the Ninth Regiment of Pennsylvania Volunteers, amid cheers and band music. As they marched off to Washington, companies of home guards were organized by the men who remained behind. Within a month, the women of the Chester community had organized a countywide system of war relief that sent a stream of clothing, blankets, bandages, and other supplies to the local troops, as well as providing assistance to their families at home. Relief organizations such as this, some formally organized, some informal, existed in every community, North and South, that sent soldiers off to the Civil War. These organizations not only played a vital role in supplying the troops, but also maintained the human, local link on which so many soldiers depended. In this sense, every American community accompanied its young men to war.

The Border States

The first secession, between December 20, 1860, and February 1, 1861, had taken seven Deep South states out of the Union. Now, in April, the firing on Fort Sumter and Lincoln's call for state militias forced the other southern states to take sides. Courted—and pressured—by both North and South, Virginia, Arkansas, Tennessee, and North Carolina joined the original seven in April and May 1861. The capital of the Confederacy was moved to Richmond. This meant that the two capitals, Richmond and Washington, were less than 100 miles apart.

Still undecided was the loyalty of the northernmost tier of slave-owning states: Missouri, Kentucky, Maryland, and Delaware. Each controlled vital strategic assets. Missouri bordered the Mississippi River and also controlled the routes to the west. Kentucky controlled the Ohio River. The main railroad link with the West ran through Maryland and the hill region of western Virginia (which split from Virginia to become the free state of

West Virginia in 1863). Delaware controlled access to Philadelphia. Finally, the nation's capital, already facing a Confederate enemy nearby in Virginia, was bordered on all other sides by Maryland.

Delaware was loyal to the Union (less than 2 percent of its population were slaves), but Maryland's loyalty was divided. Lincoln took swift and stern measures to secure Maryland's loyalty, stationing Union troops along the state's crucial railroads, declaring martial law in Baltimore, and arresting the suspected ringleaders of a pro-Confederate mob that had attacked Union troops in Baltimore and holding them without trial. In July Lincoln ordered the detention of thirty-two secessionist legislators and a number of sympathizers. Thus was Maryland's Union loyalty ensured. This was the first of a number of violations of basic civil rights that occurred during the war, all of which the president justified on the basis of national security.

An even bloodier division occurred in Missouri, where old foes from "Bleeding Kansas" faced off. The proslavery governor and most of the legislature fled to Arkansas, where they declared a Confederate state government in exile. Unionists remained in St. Louis and declared a provisional government that lasted until 1865. Although Missouri had been saved for the Union, the federal military was unable to stop the guerrilla warfare that raged there.

Finally, Lincoln kept Kentucky in the Union by accepting its declaration of neutrality at face value and looking the other way as it became the center of a huge illegal trade with the Confederacy through neighboring Tennessee. By the summer of 1861, Unionists controlled most of the state.

That these four border states chose to stay in the Union was a severe blow to the Confederacy. Among them, the four states could have added 45 percent to the white population and military manpower of the Confederacy and 80 percent to its manufacturing capacity. Almost as damaging, the decision of four slave states to stay in the Union punched a huge hole in the Confederate argument that the southern states were forced to secede to protect the right to own slaves.

The Battle of Bull Run

The event that shattered the early mistaken notions about a quick end to the war was the First Battle of Bull Run, at Manassas Creek in Virginia in July 1861. Confident of a quick victory, a Union army of 35,000 men marched south crying "On to Richmond!" So lighthearted and unprepared was the Washington community that the troops were accompanied not only by journalists but by a crowd of politicians and sightseers. At first the Union troops held their ground against the 25,000 Confederate troops commanded by General P. G. T. Beauregard (of Fort Sumter fame). But when 2,300 fresh Confederate troops arrived as reinforcement, northern soldiers and civilians ran all the way to Washington.

The Civil War was the most lethal military conflict in American history. More than 600,000 died, more than the nation's combined casualties in the First and Second World Wars. One out of every four soldiers did not return home. Devastation on the battlefield and desolation at home were two of the major legacies of the Civil War.

The Relative Strengths of North and South

Overall, in both population and productive capacity, the Union seemed to have a commanding edge. The North had two and a half times the South's population and enjoyed an even greater advantage in industrial capacity (nine times that of the South). The North produced almost all of the nation's firearms (97 percent), had 71 percent of its railroad mileage, and produced 94 percent of its cloth and 90 percent of its footwear. The North seemed able to feed, clothe, arm, and transport all the soldiers it chose. These advantages eventually proved decisive. But in the short term, the South had some important assets.

First, for the South, this was a defensive war, in which the most basic principle of the defense of home and community united almost all white southerners, regardless of their views toward slavery. The North would have to invade the South and control guerrilla warfare to win.

Second, the military disparity was less than it appeared. Although the North had manpower, the troops were mostly untrained. Moreover, the South, because of its tradition of honor and belligerence (see Chapter 11), appeared to have an advantage in military leaders, the most notable of whom was Robert E. Lee.

Finally, it was widely believed that the slave system would work to the South's advantage, for slaves could continue to do the vital plantation work while their masters went off to war. Because of the crucial role of southern cotton in industrialization, the South was confident that the British and French need for cotton would soon bring these governments to recognize the Confederacy as a separate nation.

The Lincoln Presidency

The Civil War forced the federal government to assume powers unimaginable just a few years before. Abraham Lincoln took as his primary task his responsibility as commander in chief to lead and unify the nation. He found the challenge almost insurmountable. Fortunately, the nation had found in Lincoln a man with the moral courage and political skill to chart a course through the many conflicting currents of northern public opinion.

Lincoln as Party Leader and War President

Lincoln's first task as president was to assert control over his own Cabinet. Because he had few national contacts outside the Republican Party, Lincoln chose to staff his Cabinet with other Republicans, including two who had been his rivals for the presidential nomination: Treasury Secretary Salmon P. Chase, a staunch abolitionist, and Secretary of State William Seward. That the Republican Party was a not-quite-jelled mix of former Whigs, abolitionists, moderate free-soilers, and even some prowar Democrats made Lincoln's task as party leader much more difficult.

Following the fall of Fort Sumter, Lincoln took a number of executive actions that were driven by military necessity: calling up the state militias, ordering a naval blockade of the South, and vastly expanding the military budget. Although James K. Polk's direction of the Mexican–American War created somewhat of a precedent, Lincoln was the first president to act as commander in chief in both a practical and a symbolic way. His involvement in military strategy sprang from his realization that a civil war presented different problems than a foreign war of conquest. Lincoln wanted above all to *persuade* the South to rejoin the Union, and his every military move was dictated by the hope of eventual reconciliation, hence his cautiousness and his acute sense of the role of public opinion.

The War Department

The greatest expansion in government power came in the War Department, which by early 1862 was faced with the task of feeding, clothing, and arming 700,000 Union soldiers. This was an organizational challenge of unprecedented size. As Mother Bickerdyke's work shows, at first the War Department was unequal to the task, and individual states agreed to equip and supply their vastly expanded militias until the Union Army could absorb the costs. In many northern cities volunteer groups such as the one in Chester, Pennsylvania, sprang up to recruit regiments, buy them weapons, and send them to Washington. After January 1862 the War Department, under the able direction of Edwin M. Stanton, was able to perform many basic functions of procurement and supply without too much delay or corruption.

Still, in procurement and supply, as in mobilization, the battlefront was related to the home front on a scale that Americans had not previously experienced.

Taxes and the Greenback Dollar

The need for money for the vast war effort was pressing. Secretary of the Treasury Chase worked closely with Congress to develop ways to finance the war. They naturally turned to the nation's private bankers, merchants, and managers of large businesses. With the help of Philadelphia financier Jay Cooke, the Treasury used patriotic appeals to sell war bonds to ordinary people in amounts as small as $50. This was the first example in American history of the mass financing of war. By war's end, the United States had borrowed $2.6 billion for the war effort. Additional sources of revenue were sales taxes and the first federal income tax (which affected only the affluent).

Most radical of all, after a bitter congressional fight Chase received authorization to print Treasury notes (paper money) and have them accepted nationally. Until then, the money in circulation had been a mixture of coins and state banknotes issued by 1,500 different state banks. The Legal Tender Act of February 1862 created a national currency that, because of the color, was popularly known as the greenback. In 1863 Congress passed the National Bank Act, which prohibited state banks from issuing their own notes and forced them to apply for federal charters.

The national currency was widely recognized as a major centralization of economic power in the hands of the federal government. Such a measure would have been unthinkable if southern Democrats, the heirs to Jackson's animosity to national banks, had still been part of the national government. The absence of southern Democrats also made possible passage of a number of Republican economic measures not directly related to the war.

Politics and Economics: The Republican Platform

The Republican Party had campaigned in 1860 on a comprehensive program of economic development. Once in office, Republicans quickly passed the Morrill Tariff Act (1861), and by 1864 subsequent measures had raised tariffs to more than double their prewar rate. In 1862 and 1864 Congress created two federally chartered corporations, the Union Pacific Railroad Company, to build a transcontinental railroad westward from Omaha, and the Central Pacific, to build eastward from California. Two other measures, both passed in 1862, had long been sought by westerners. The Homestead Act gave 160 acres of public land to any citizen who agreed to live on it for five years, improve it by building a house and cultivating some of the land, and pay a small fee. The Morrill Land Grant Act gave states public land that would allow them to finance land-grant colleges offering education to ordinary citizens in practical skills such as agriculture, engineering, and military science. Coupled with this act, the establishment of a federal Department of Agriculture in 1862 gave American farmers a big push toward modern commercial agriculture.

These were powerful nationalizing forces. They connected ordinary people to the federal government in new ways. Although many of the executive war powers lapsed when the battles ended, the accrual of strength to the federal government was never reversed.

Diplomatic Objectives

To Secretary of State William Seward fell the job of making sure that Britain and France did not extend diplomatic recognition to the Confederacy. The South had been certain that King Cotton would gain it European support, but British public opinion would not countenance the recognition of a nation based on slavery. British cotton manufacturers found alternatives to southern cotton in Egypt and India. France did take advantage of the Civil War to invade Mexico, in serious violation of the Monroe Doctrine, but for fear that France might recognize the Confederacy or invade Texas, Seward had to content himself with refusing to recognize the new Mexican government. He achieved his diplomatic goal—preventing recognition of the Confederacy by the European powers—but not until the Union victories at Vicksburg and Gettysburg in July 1863 could he be confident of success.

The Confederacy

Lincoln faced a major challenge in keeping the North unified enough to win the war, but Jefferson Davis's challenge was even greater: he had to *create* a Confederate nation. The Confederate States of America was a loose grouping of eleven states that each believed strongly in states' rights. Yet the necessities of war required central direction.

Jefferson Davis as President

Although Davis had three advantages over Lincoln—he had held national Cabinet rank, had experience as an administrator, and was a former military man—he was unable to hold the Confederacy together. Perhaps no one could have.

Davis's first Cabinet of six men, appointed in February 1861, included a representative from each of the states of the first secession except Mississippi, which was represented by Davis himself. This careful attention to the equality of the states pointed to the fundamental Confederate problem that Davis was unable to overcome. Although he saw the need for unity, he was unable to impose it. Soon his autonomous style of leadership—he wanted to decide every detail himself—angered his generals, alienated Cabinet members, and gave southern governors reason to resist his orders. After the first flush of patriotism had passed, the Confederacy never lived up to its hope of becoming a unified nation.

Diplomatic Hopes

The failure of "cotton diplomacy" was a crushing blow. White southerners were stunned that Britain and France would not recognize their claim to independence. Well into 1863, the South hoped that a decisive battlefield victory would change the minds of cautious Europeans.

In the meantime, plantations continued to grow cotton, but not to ship it, hoping that lack of raw material for their textile mills would lead the British and French to recognize the Confederacy. But the British, indignant over what they considered economic blackmail, found new sources of cotton in Egypt and India. In 1862, when the Confederacy ended the embargo and began to ship its great surplus, the result was to depress the world price of cotton. Then too, the Union naval blockade, weak at first, began to take effect. Cotton turned out to be not so powerful a diplomatic weapon after all.

The Sinews of War

Perhaps the greatest southern failure was in the area of finances. The Confederate government at first tried to raise money from the states, but governors refused to impose new taxes on their residents. By the time uniform taxes were levied (1863), it was too late. In the meantime, large amounts of borrowing and the issuance of even greater supplies of paper money had produced runaway inflation (a rate of 9,000 percent, compared

The contrast between the hope and valor of these young southern volunteer soldiers, photographed shortly before the First Battle of Bull Run, and the later advertisements for substitutes is marked.

Cook Collection, Valentine Museum, Richmond, VA (left).

SUBSTITUTE NOTICES.

WANTED—A SUBSTITUTE for a conscript, to serve during the war. Any good man over the age of 35 years, not a resident of Virginia, or a foreigner, may hear of a good situation by calling at Mr. GEORGE BAGBY'S office, Shockoe Slip, to-day, between the hours of 9 and 11 A. M. [jy 9—1t*]   A COUNTRYMAN.

WANTED—Two SUBSTITUTES—one for artillery, the other for infantry or cavalry service. Also, to sell, a trained, thoroughbred cavalry HORSE. Apply to   DR. BROOCKS,
Corner Main and 12th streets, or to
                                        T. T. BROOCKS,
jy 9—3t*   Petersburg, Va.

WANTED—Immediately, a SUBSTITUTE. A man over 35 years old, or under 18, can get a good price by making immediate application to Room No. 50, Monument Hotel, or by addressing "J. W.," through Richmond P. O.   jy 9—1t*

WANTED—A SUBSTITUTE, to go into the 24th North Carolina State troops, for which a liberal price will be paid. Apply to me at Dispatch office this evening at 4 o'clock P. M.
jy 9—1t*   R. R. MOORE.

WANTED—A SUBSTITUTE, to go in a first-rate Georgia company of infantry, under the heroic Jackson. A gentleman whose health is impaired, will give a fair price for a substitute. Apply immediately at ROOM, No. 13, Post-Office Department, third story, between the hours of 10 and 3 o'clock.   jy 9—6t*

WANTED—Two SUBSTITUTES for the war. A good bonus will be given. None need apply except those exempt from Conscript. Apply to-day at   GEORGE I. HERRING'S,
jy 9—1t*   Grocery store, No. 56 Main st.

with 80 percent in the North). This caused incalculable damage to morale and prospects for unity.

After the initial surge of volunteers, enlistment in the military fell off (as it did in the North). In April 1862 the Confederate Congress passed the first draft law in American history (the Union Congress approved a draft in March 1863). The southern law declared that all able-bodied men between eighteen and thirty-five were eligible for three years of military service. Purchase of substitutes was allowed, as in the North, but in the South the price was uncontrolled, rising eventually to $10,000 in Confederate money. The most disliked part of the draft law was a provision exempting one white man on each plantation that had twenty or more slaves. This not only seemed to disprove the earlier claim that slavery freed up more white men to fight but also aroused class resentments. In the bitter phrase of the time, "It's a rich man's war but a poor man's fight."

Contradictions of Southern Nationalism

In the early days of the war, Jefferson Davis successfully mobilized feelings of regional identity and patriotism. Many southerners felt part of a beleaguered region that had been forced to resist northern tyranny. But most people felt loyalty to their own state, not to a Confederate *nation*. Davis could not overcome his region's strong beliefs in states' rights and aristocratic privilege, beliefs that undermined the Confederate cause. The very steps necessary for unity, such as moving militias outside their home states, were resisted by some southern governors. Broader measures, such as general taxation, were widely evaded by rich and poor alike. The inequitable draft was only one of a number of steps that convinced the ordinary people of the South that this was a war for privileged slave owners, not for them. Too many people feared that centralization would destroy what was distinctively southern. As a result, the Confederacy was unable to mobilize the resources that might have prevented its destruction by northern armies.

The Fighting Through 1862

Just as political decisions were often driven by military necessity, the basic northern and southern military strategies were affected by political considerations as much as by military ones. The initial policy of limited war, thought to be the best route to ultimate reconciliation, faced public impatience for victories. But victories, as the mounting slaughter made clear, were not easy to achieve.

The War in Northern Virginia

The initial northern strategy, dubbed by critics the Anaconda Plan (after the constricting snake), envisaged slowly squeezing the South with a blockade at sea and on the Mississippi River. Lincoln accepted the basics of the plan, but public clamor for a fight pushed him to agree to the disastrous Battle of Bull Run and then to a major buildup of Union troops in northern Virginia under General George B. McClellan. Dashing in appearance, McClellan was extremely cautious in battle. In March 1862, after almost a year of drilling the raw Union recruits, and after repeated exhortations by an impatient Lincoln, McClellan finally committed 120,000 troops to the Peninsula campaign to capture Richmond, the Confederate capital. All of these troops and their supplies and support were ferried from Washington to Fortress Monroe, near the mouth of the James River. Inching up the James Peninsula, by June McClellan's troops were close enough to Richmond to hear the church bells ringing, but not close enough for victory. In a series of battles known as the Seven Days, Robert E. Lee boldly counterattacked, repeatedly catching McClellan by surprise. In August a disappointed Lincoln ordered McClellan to abandon the campaign and return to Washington.

Jefferson Davis, like Abraham Lincoln, was an active commander-in-chief. Following the Seven Days victories, he ordered a Confederate attack on Maryland. But the all-out attack failed: in September McClellan turned back Lee at Antietam, at the cost of more than 5,000 dead and 19,000 wounded. Lee retreated to Virginia, where he held off a northern attack at Fredericksburg in December. The war in northern Virginia was stalemated: neither side was strong enough to win, but each was too strong to be defeated.

Shiloh and the War for the Mississippi

Although most public attention was focused on the fighting in Virginia, battles in Tennessee and along the Mississippi River proved to be the key to eventual Union victory. The rising military figure in the West was Ulysses S. Grant, who had once resigned from the service because of a drinking problem. In February 1862 Grant captured Fort Henry and Fort Donelson, on the Tennessee and Cumberland rivers, gaining Union control of much of Tennessee.

Moving south with 63,000 men, Grant met a 40,000-man Confederate force commanded by General Albert Sidney Johnston at Shiloh Church in April. After two days of bitter and bloody fighting in the rain, the Confederates withdrew. The losses on both sides were

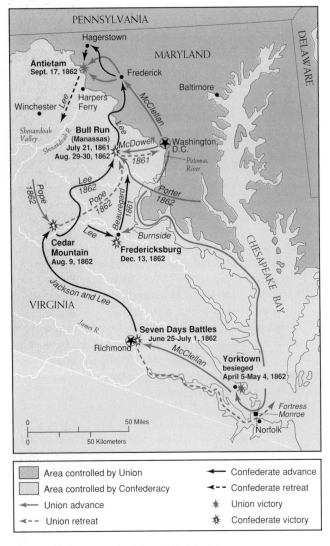

Major Battles in the East, 1861–62

Northern Virginia was the most crucial and the most constant theater of battle. The prizes were the two opposing capitals, Washington and Richmond, only 70 miles apart. By the summer of 1862, George B. McClellan, famously cautious, had achieved only stalemate in the Peninsular campaign. However, he did turn back Robert E. Lee at Antietam in September.

1862 it was clear that it was only a matter of time before the entire river would be in Union hands.

The War in the Trans-Mississippi West

Although only one western state, Texas, seceded from the Union, the Civil War was fought in small ways in many parts of the West. Southern dreams of the extension of slavery into the Southwest were reignited by the war. Texans mounted an attack on New Mexico, which

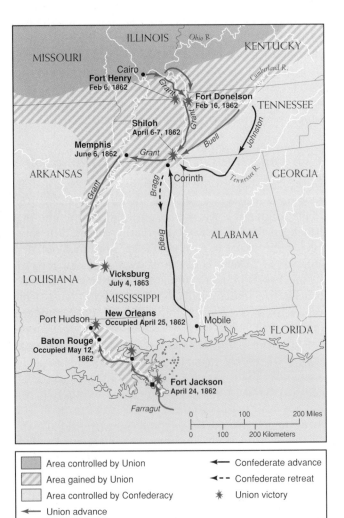

Major Battles in the West, 1862–63

Ulysses S. Grant waged a mobile war by winning at Fort Henry and Fort Donelson in Tennessee in February 1862 and at Shiloh in April and capturing Memphis in June. He then laid seige to Vicksburg, as Admiral David Farragut captured New Orleans and began to advance up the Mississippi River.

enormous: the North lost 13,000 men, the South 11,000, including General Johnston, who bled to death. Grant kept moving, capturing Memphis in June and beginning a seige of Vicksburg, Mississippi, in November. Earlier that year, naval forces under Admiral David Farragut had captured New Orleans in April and then continued up the Mississippi River. By the end of

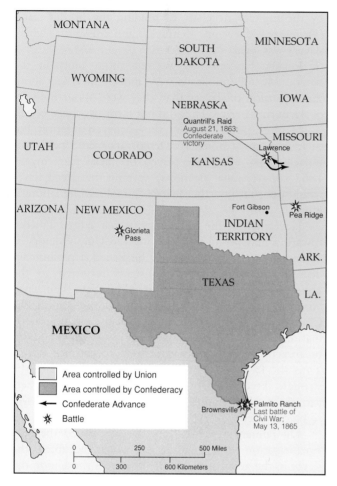

The War in the West

Far removed from the major theaters of battle, the Far West was nevertheless a rich prize in the Civil War. Battles in remote places such as Glorieta Pass, New Mexico, were decisive in holding the Far West for the Union. The battles in Kansas and Indian Territory, however, arose primarily from prewar antagonisms and settled little.

Source: Reprinted from Warren Beck and Ynez Haase, *Historical Atlas of the American West,* Copyright © 1989 University of Oklahoma Press. Reprinted by permission.

they had long coveted (see Chapter 14), and kept their eyes on the larger prizes of Arizona Territory and California beyond. A Confederate force led by General Henry H. Sibley occupied Santa Fé and Albuquerque early in 1862 without resistance, thus posing a serious Confederate threat to the entire Southwest. Confederate hopes were dashed, however, by a ragtag group of 950 miners and adventurers organized into the first Colorado Volunteer Infantry Regiment. After an epic march of 400

miles from Denver to Fort Union in thirteen days through snow and high winds, the Colorado militia stopped the unsuspecting Confederate troops in the Battle of Glorieta Pass, March 26–28, 1862. This dashing action, coupled with the efforts of California militias to safeguard Arizona and Utah from seizure by Confederate sympathizers, secured the Far West for the Union.

Other military action in the West was less decisive. The chronic fighting along the Kansas-Missouri border set a record for brutality when Quantrill's Raiders made a predawn attack on Lawrence, Kansas, in August 1863, massacring 150 inhabitants and burning the town. Another civil war took place in Indian Territory, south of Kansas. The southern Indian tribes, who had been removed there from the Old Southwest in the 1820s and 1830s (see Chapters 10 and 11), held a number of Confederate sympathizers. Among them were wealthy slave owners and many who remembered the horrors of removal by federal troops with great bitterness. Others, however, had equally bitter memories of the role of the southern states in forcing the removals. Union victories at Pea Ridge (in northwestern Arkansas) in March 1862 and near Fort Gibson (in Indian Territory) in 1863 secured the area for the Union but did little to stop the dissension among the Indian groups themselves. This internal conflict was costly, for after the Civil War the victorious federal government used the excuse of Confederate sympathies to insist on further land cessions from the tribes.

The hostilities in the West showed that no part of the country and none of its inhabitants could remain untouched by the Civil War.

The Naval War

Initially, the Union blockade of southern ships was unsuccessful. Southern blockade runners evaded Union ships with ease: only an estimated one-eighth of all Confederate shipping was stopped in 1862. Moreover, the Confederacy licensed British-made privateers to strike at northern shipping. In a two-year period one such Confederate raider, the *Alabama,* destroyed sixty-nine Union ships with cargoes valued at $6 million. Beginning in 1863, however, as the Union Navy increased in size, the naval blockade began to take effect. In 1864 a third of the blockade runners were captured, and in 1865 half of them. As a result, fewer and fewer supplies reached the South.

For the Union, the most successful naval operation in the first two years of the war was not the blockade but the seizing of exposed coastal areas. The Sea Islands of South Carolina were taken, as were some of the

North Carolina islands and Fort Pulaski, which commanded the harbor of Savannah, Georgia. Most damaging to the South was the capture of New Orleans.

The Black Response

The capture of Port Royal in the South Carolina Sea Islands in 1861 was important for another reason. Whites fled at the Union advance, but 10,000 slaves greeted the troops with jubilation and shouts of gratitude. Union troops had unwittingly freed these slaves, in advance of any official Union policy.

Early in the war, an irate southerner who saw three of his slaves disappear behind Union lines at Fortress Monroe, Virginia, demanded the return of his property, citing the Fugitive Slave Law. The Union commander, Benjamin Butler, replied that the Fugitive Slave Law no longer applied, and that the escaped slaves were "contraband of war." News of Butler's decision spread rapidly. Two days later, eight runaway slaves appeared; the next day fifty-nine black men and women arrived at the fort. Union commanders had found an effective way to rob the South of its work force. The "contrabands," as they were known, were put to work in the northern camps.

As Union troops drove deeper into the South, the black response grew. The most dramatic single example happened in 1864 during Sherman's march through Georgia, where 18,000 slaves—entire families, people of all ages—flocked to the Union lines. By war's end, nearly a million black people, fully a quarter of all the slaves in the South, had "voted with their feet."

The Death of Slavery

The overwhelming response of black slaves to Union troops changed the nature of the war. As increasing numbers of slaves flocked to Union lines, the conclusion was unmistakable: any northern policy that ignored the issue of slavery and the wishes of the slaves was unrealistic.

The Politics of Emancipation

Abraham Lincoln had always said that this was a war to preserve the Union, not a war to end slavery. In his inaugural address, he had promised to leave slavery untouched in the South. Although Lincoln personally abhorred slavery, his official policy was based on a realistic assessment of several factors. At first, he hoped to give pro-Union forces in the South a chance to consolidate and to prevent the outbreak of war. After the war began, as we have seen, Lincoln was impelled by the military necessity of holding the border states (Delaware, Maryland, Kentucky, and Missouri), where slavery was legal.

Finally, Lincoln was worried about unity in the North. Most Republicans were more concerned about the expansion of slavery than they were about the lives of slaves themselves. They did not favor the social equality of black people, whom they believed inferior. For their part, most northern Democrats were openly antiblack. They effectively played on racial fears in the 1862 congressional elections, warning that freed slaves would pour into northern cities and take white laborers' jobs.

Nevertheless, the necessities of war edged Lincoln toward a new position. Following the Union victory at Antietam in September 1862, he issued a preliminary decree: unless the rebellious states returned to the Union by January 1, 1863, he would declare their slaves "forever free." Although Lincoln did not expect the Confederate states to surrender because of his proclamation, the decree increased the pressure on the South by directly linking the slave system to the war effort. Thus the freedom of black people became part of the struggle. Frederick Douglass, the voice of black America, wrote, "We shout for joy that we live to record this righteous decree."

On January 1, 1863, Lincoln duly issued the final Emancipation Proclamation, in which he freed the slaves in the areas of rebellion—the areas the Union did not control—but specifically exempted slaves in the border states and in former Confederate areas won by the Union in battle. Lincoln's purpose was to meet the abolitionist demand for a war against slavery while retaining the support of conservatives, especially in the border states. But the proclamation was so equivocal that Lincoln's own secretary of state, William Seward, remarked sarcastically, "We show our sympathy with slavery by emancipating slaves where we cannot reach them and holding them in bondage where we can set them free."

One group greeted the Emancipation Proclamation with open celebration. On New Year's Day hundreds of African Americans gathered outside the White House and cheered the president. Realizing the symbolic importance of the proclamation, free black people predicted that the news would encourage southern slaves either to flee to Union lines or to refuse to work for their masters. Both of these things were already happening as black people seized upon wartime changes to reshape white–black relations in the South. In one sense, then, the Emancipation Proclamation simply gave a name to a process already in motion.

OVERALL STRATEGY OF THE CIVIL WAR

In 1861, the initial Union battle strategy was the so-called Anaconda Plan, which aimed to constrict and slowly squeeze the South by a blockade at sea and on the Mississippi River. By the end of 1862, signs of success were evident: the capture of the sea islands of South Carolina and Georgia and areas of North Carolina, and the victories of Ulysses S. Grant in Tennessee and Admiral David Farragut along the Mississippi. Failure for both sides occurred in the stalemated theater of battle in northern Virginia, where Confederate General Robert E. Lee consistently beat back Union attacks but lacked the strength to win.

The war's turning point occurred in 1863, with Lee's defeat at Gettysburg (July 1–3) and Grant's capture of Vicksburg (July 4). These two great victories turned the tide in favor of the Union. The Confederates never again mounted a major offensive, and total Union control of the Mississippi exposed the Lower South.

In 1864–65, Grant (now in command of all the Union armies) and General William Tecumseh Sherman abandoned the Anaconda strategy and brought the war home to the South. Sherman's destructive "March to the Sea" and Grant's hammering tactics in his frequent

battles with Lee in northern Virginia enveloped the South and drained southerners of energy to continue. Finally, on April 9, 1865, Lee surrendered to Grant at Appomattox, thus ending the bloodiest war in the nation's history.

Abolitionists set about to move Lincoln beyond his careful stance in the Emancipation Proclamation. Reformers such as Elizabeth Cady Stanton and Susan B. Anthony lobbied and petitioned for a constitutional amendment outlawing slavery. At Lincoln's urging, Congress passed and sent to the states a statement banning slavery throughout the United States. Quickly ratified by the Union states in 1865, the statement became the Thirteenth Amendment to the Constitution.

Black Fighting Men

As part of the Emancipation Proclamation, Lincoln gave his support for the first time to the recruitment of black soldiers. Early in the war, eager black volunteers had been bitterly disappointed at being turned away. Many, like Robert Fitzgerald, a free African American from Pennsylvania, found other ways to serve the Union cause. Fitzgerald first drove a wagon and mule for the

This unidentified young African American corporal is shown holding his rifle with a fixed bayonet. As Frederick Douglass commented, once black men such as this had served in the Union Army, "there is no power on earth that can deny he has earned the right to citizenship."

Quartermaster Corps, and later served in the Union Navy. After the Emancipation Proclamation, he was able to do what he had wanted to do all along: be a soldier. He enlisted in the Fifth Massachusetts Cavalry, a regiment that, like all the units in which black soldiers served, was 100 percent African American.

As was customary in black regiments, the commanding officers were white. After a scant two months of training (two years had been customary for prewar cavalry units), Fitzgerald's company was sent on to Washington and thence to battle in northern Virginia. Uncertain of the reception they would receive in northern cities with their history of antiblack riots, Fitzgerald and his comrades were pleasantly surprised. "We are cheered in every town we pass through," he wrote in his diary. White people had reason to cheer: black volunteers, eager and willing to fight, made up 10 percent of the Union Army. Nearly 200,000 African Americans (one out of five black males in the nation) served in the Union Army or Navy. A fifth of them— 37,000—died defending their own freedom and the Union.

Military service was something no black man could take lightly. African American soldiers faced prejudice within the army and had to prove themselves in battle. Furthermore, the Confederates hated and feared black troops, and threatened to treat any captured African American soldier as an escaped slave subject to execution. On at least one occasion, at Fort Pillow, Tennessee, in 1864, the threats were carried out. Confederate soldiers massacred 262 black soldiers after they had surrendered. More common were smaller episodes of hatred. On duty near Petersburg, Virginia, a picket in Robert Fitzgerald's company was wounded in the leg and Confederate soldiers smashed his skull with their musket butts.

Another extraordinary part of the story of the African American soldiers was their reception by black people in the South. The sight of armed black men, many of them former slaves themselves, wearing the uniform of the Union Army was overwhelming. As his regiment entered Wilmington, North Carolina, one African American soldier wrote of how "men and women, old and young, were running throughout the streets, shouting and praising God. We could then truly see what we have been fighting for."

African American soldiers were not treated equally by the Union Army. They were segregated in camp and given the worst jobs. Many white officers and soldiers treated them as inferiors. In addition, they were paid less than whites (ten dollars a month rather than thirteen). Although they were not able to do much about

When the family of Robert and Cornelia Fitzgerald posed for a group picture in the 1890s, Robert Fitzgerald proudly dressed in the Union Army uniform he had worn during the Civil War. Fitzgerald's pride in his war service, doubtless shared by many African American veterans, was an important family memory of the fight against slavery.

the other kinds of discrimination, they could protest the pay inequity. The Fifty-Fourth Massachusetts regiment found an unusual way to protest: they refused to accept their pay, preferring to serve the army for free until it decided to treat them as free men. The protest was effective: in June 1864 the War Department equalized wages between black and white soldiers.

The Front Lines and the Home Front

Civil War soldiers wrote millions of letters home, more proportionately than in any American war. Their letters are a testament to the patriotism of both Union and Confederate troops, for the story they told was often one of slaughter and horror.

The Toll of War

Despite early hopes for a "brotherly" war, one that avoided excessive conquest and devastation, Civil War deaths, in battle after battle, were appalling. One reason was technology: improved weapons, in particular modern rifles, had much greater range and accuracy than the muskets they replaced. Another was that almost all Union and Confederate generals were committed to the conventional military doctrine of massed infantry offensives—the Jomini doctrine—that they had learned in their military classes at West Point. In earlier military doctrine the artillery was supposed to "soften up" the defensive line before the infantry assault, but now the range of the new rifles made artillery itself vulnerable to attack. As a result, generals relied less on softening up than on assaults by immense numbers of infantrymen, hoping that enough of them would survive the withering rifle fire to overwhelm the enemy line. The enormous casualties, then, were a consequence of basic strategy.

Medical ignorance was another factor in the huge casualty rate. Because the use of antiseptic procedures was in its infancy, men often died because minor wounds became infected. Gangrene was a common cause of death. Disease was an even more frequent killer, taking twice as many men as were lost in battle. The overcrowded and unsanitary conditions of many camps were breeding grounds for disease: smallpox, dysentery, typhoid, pneumonia, and, in the summer, malaria.

Yet another factor was that both North and South were completely unprepared to handle the supply and health needs of their large armies. Twenty-four hours after the Battle of Shiloh, most of the wounded still lay on the field in the rain. Many died of exposure; some, unable to help themselves, drowned.

Army Nurses

Many medical supplies that the armies were unable to provide were donated by the United States Sanitary Commission in the North, as described in the opening of the chapter, and by women's volunteer groups in the South. In addition to supplies, an urgent need also existed for skilled nursing. At the insistence of the Sanitary, women became army nurses, despite the objections of most army doctors. Hospital nursing, which had been both minimal and disreputable, now became a suitable vocation for middle-class women. Most women had done considerable nursing for their own families; care of the sick was considered one of women's key domestic qualities. But taking care of the bodily needs of strange men in hospitals was another thing. There were strong objections that such work was "unseemly" for respectable women. Many senior army doctors objected because they realized they would now be under the critical eye of women who were no different from their own daughters and wives. Nevertheless, reforming women persisted. Under the leadership of veteran reformer Dorothea Dix (see Chapter 13) and in coopera-

Nurse Ann Bell is shown preparing medicine for a wounded soldier. Prompted by the medical crisis of the war, women such as Bell and "Mother" Bickerdyke actively participated as nurses in the war effort.

tion with the Sanitary Commission, by war's end more than 3,000 northern women had worked as paid army nurses and many more as volunteers.

One of the volunteers was Ellen Ruggles Strong of New York, who, over her husband's objections, insisted on nursing in the Peninsula campaign of 1862. "The little woman has come out amazingly strong during these two months," George Templeton Strong wrote in his diary with a mixture of pride and condescension. "Have never given her credit for a tithe of the enterprise, pluck, discretion, and force of character that she has shown. God bless her." Other women organized other volunteer efforts outside the Sanitary Commission umbrella. Perhaps the best known was Clara Barton, who organized nursing and medical supplies; she also used congressional contacts to force reforms in army medical practice, of which she was very critical.

Southern women were also active in nursing and otherwise aiding soldiers, though the South never boasted a single large-scale organization like the Sanitary Commission. The women of Richmond, Virginia, volunteered when they found the war on their doorstep in the summer of 1862. During the Seven Days Battles, thousands of wounded poured into Richmond; many died in the streets because there was no room for them in hospitals. Richmond women first established informal "roadside hospitals" to meet the need, and their activities expanded from there. As in the North, middle-class women at first faced strong resistance from army doctors and even their own families, who believed that a field hospital was "no place for a refined lady." Kate Cumming of Mobile, who nursed in Corinth, Mississippi after the Shiloh battle, faced down such reproofs, though she confided to her diary that nursing wounded men was very difficult: "Nothing that I had ever heard or read had given me the faintest idea of the horrors witnessed here." She and her companion nurses persisted and became an important part of the Confederate medical services. For southern women, who had been much less active in the public life of their communities than their northern reforming sisters, this Civil War activity marked an important break with prewar tradition.

Although women had made important advances, most army nurses and medical support staff continued to be men. One volunteer nurse was poet Walt Whitman, who visited wounded soldiers in the hospital in Washington, D.C. Horrified at the suffering he saw, Whitman also formed a deep admiration for the "incredible dauntlessness" of the common soldier in the face of slaughter and privation. While never denying the senselessness of the slaughter, Whitman nevertheless found hope in the determined spirit of the common man and woman.

The Life of the Common Soldier

The conditions experienced by the eager young volunteers of the Union and Confederate armies included massive, terrifying, and bloody battles, apparently unending, with no victory in sight. The uncertainty of supply left troops, especially in the South, without uniforms, tents, and sometimes even food. Disease was rampant in their dirty, verminous, and unsanitary camps, and hospitals were so dreadful that more men left them dead than alive.

Many soldiers had entered military service with unrealistic, even romantic, ideas about warfare. Reality was a rude shock. Desertion was common: an estimated one of every nine Confederate soldiers and one of every seven Union soldiers deserted. Absence without leave (AWOL) was another problem. At Antietam Robert E. Lee estimated that a third to a half of his troops were AWOL. In October 1861 a Louisiana man wrote to his brother-in-law, "You spoke as if you had some notion of volunteering. I advise you to stay at home." Once the initial patriotic fervor had waned, such attitudes were increasingly common on the battlefield and at home.

Wartime Politics

In the very earliest days of the war, northerners had joined together in support of the war effort. Democrat Stephen A. Douglas, Lincoln's defeated rival, paid a visit to the White House to offer Lincoln his support. Within a month, Douglas was dead at age forty-eight. The Democrats had lost the leadership of a large-minded man who might have done much on behalf of northern unity. By 1862 Democrats had split into two factions: the War Democrats and the Peace Democrats, or Copperheads (from the poisonous snake).

The Democratic Party remained a powerful force in northern politics. It had received 44 percent of the popular vote in the 1860 election. The united opposition of the Democratic Party to the emancipation of slaves explains much of Lincoln's equivocal action on this issue. But the Peace Democrats went far beyond this: they denounced the draft, martial law, and the high-handed actions of "King Abraham."

The leader of the Copperheads, Clement Vallandigham, a former Ohio congressman, advocated an armistice and a negotiated peace. Western Democrats, he threatened, might form their own union with the South, excluding New England with its radical abolitionists and high-tariff industrialists. Lincoln could not afford to take Vallandigham's threats lightly. Besides, he was convinced that some Peace Democrats were members of secret societies—the Knights of the Golden Circle and the Sons of Liberty—that had been conspiring with the Confederacy. In 1862 Lincoln proclaimed that all people who discouraged enlistments in the army or otherwise engaged in disloyal practices would be subject to martial law. In all, 13,000 people were arrested and imprisoned, including Vallandigham, who was exiled to the Confederacy. Lincoln rejected all protests, claiming that his arbitrary actions were necessary for national security.

Lincoln also faced divisions in his own party between Radicals and conservatives. As the war continued, the Radicals gained strength. The most troublesome was Salmon P. Chase, who caused a Cabinet crisis in December of 1862 when he encouraged Senate Republicans to complain that Secretary of State William Seward was "lukewarm" in his support for emancipation. This Radical–conservative split was a portent of the party's difficulties after the war, which Lincoln did not live to see.

Economic and Social Strains in the North

Wartime needs caused a surge in northern economic growth, but the gains were unequally spread. Early in the war, some industries suffered: cotton textile manufacturers could not get cotton, and shoe factories that had made cheap shoes for slaves were without a market. But other industries boomed: boots, ships, and woolen goods such as blankets and uniforms. Coal mining expanded, as did iron making, especially the manufacture of iron rails for railroads. Agricultural goods were in great demand, and this furthered the mechanization of farming. The McCormick brothers grew rich from sales of their reapers. Women, left to tend the family farm while the men went to war, found that they could manage the demanding task of harvesting with mechanized equipment.

Meeting wartime needs enriched some people honestly, but speculators and profiteers also flourished. By the end of the war, government contracts had exceeded $1 billion. Not all of this business was free from corruption. New wealth was evident in every northern city.

For most people, the war brought the day-to-day hardship of inflation. During the four years of the war, the North suffered an inflation rate of 80 percent, or nearly 15 percent a year. This annual rate, three times what is generally considered tolerable, did much to inflame social tensions in the North. For one thing, wages rose only half as much as prices. Workers responded by joining unions and striking for higher wages. Manufacturers, bitterly opposed to unions, freely hired strikebreakers (many of whom were African Americans, women, or immigrants) and formed organizations of their own to prevent further unionization and to blacklist union organizers. Thus both capital and labor moved far beyond the small and local confrontations of the early industrial period, laying the groundwork for the national battle between workers and manufacturers that dominated the last part of the nineteenth century.

Another major source of social tension was conscription, implemented for the first time in U.S. history. The Union introduced a draft in July 1863. (The Confederacy had done so the previous year.) Especially unpopular in the 1863 draft law was a provision that allowed the hiring of substitutes or the payment of a commutation fee of $300. Substitution had been accepted in all previous European and American wars, but the Democratic party made it an inflammatory issue. Pointing out that $300 was almost a year's wages for an unskilled laborer, Democrats appealed to popular resentment by calling the draft law "aristocratic legislation" and to fear by running headlines such as "Three Hundred Dollars or Your Life."

Conscription was often marred by favoritism and prejudice. Many more poor than rich men were called, and many more immigrants were selected than their proportion of the population would logically dictate. But in reality, only 7 percent of all men called to serve actually did so. About 25 percent of the draftees hired a substitute, another 45 percent were exempted for cause (usually health reasons), and another 20 to 25 percent simply failed to report to the community draft office. Nevertheless, by 1863 many northern urban workers believed that the slogan "a rich man's war but a poor man's fight," though coined in the South, applied to them as well.

The New York City Draft Riots

In the spring of 1863 there were protests against the draft throughout the North. Riots and disturbances broke out in a number of northern cities, and several federal enrollment officers were killed. But the worst trouble occurred in New York City, July 13–17, 1863, in a wave of working-class rioting, looting, fighting, and lynching that claimed the lives of 105 people, many of them black. The rioting was quelled only when five units of the U.S. Army were rushed from the battlefield at Gettysburg, where they had been fighting Confeder-

ates the week before. It was the most extensive rioting in American history.

The riots had several causes. Anger at the draft and racial prejudice were what most contemporaries saw. A longer historical view reveals that the riots had less to do with the war than with the urban growth and tensions explored in Chapter 13.

Ironically, African American men, a favored target of the rioters' anger, were a major force in easing the national crisis over the draft. Black volunteers ultimately composed one-tenth of the Union Army, though they had been barred from service until 1863. Nearly 200,000 black soldiers filled the gap that the controversial draft was meant to address.

The Failure of Southern Nationalism

The war brought even greater changes to the South. As in the North, war needs led to expansion and centralization of government control over the economy. In many cases, Jefferson Davis himself initiated government control (over railroads, shipping, and war production, for example), often in the face of protest or inaction by states' rights governors. The expansion of government brought sudden urbanization, a new experience for the predominantly rural South. Richmond, the Confederate capital, almost tripled in population, in large part because the Confederate bureaucracy grew to 70,000 people. Because of the need for military manpower, a good part of the Confederate bureaucracy was female ("government girls," the women were called). All of this—government control, urban growth, women in the paid work force—was new to southerners, but not all of it was welcomed.

The voracious need for soldiers fostered class antagonisms in the South. When small yeoman farmers went off to war, their wives and families struggled to farm on their own, without the help of mechanization or slaves. But wealthy men were exempted from the draft if they had more than twenty slaves. Furthermore, many upper-class southerners—at least 50,000—avoided military service by paying liberally ($5,000 and more) for substitutes. In the face of these inequities, desertions from the Confederate Army soared.

Worst of all was the starvation, caused by the northern blockade and the breakdown of the southern transportation system and vastly magnified by runaway inflation that reached an unbelievable 9,000 percent. Speculation and hoarding by the rich made matters even worse. In the spring of 1863 food riots broke out in four Georgia cities (Atlanta among them) and in North Carolina. In Richmond, the capital, more than a thou-

A black man is lynched during the New York City Draft Riots in July 1863. Free black people and their institutions were major victims of the most extensive rioting in American history. The riots were less a protest against the draft than an outburst of frustration over urban problems that had been festering for decades.

sand people, mostly women, broke into bakeries and snatched loaves of bread, crying "Bread! Bread! Our children are starving while the rich roll in wealth!" When the bread riot threatened to turn into general looting, Jefferson Davis himself appealed to the crowd to disperse, but found he had to threaten the rioters with gunfire before they would leave. A year later, Richmond stores sold eggs for six dollars a dozen and butter for twenty-five dollars a pound. A Richmond woman exclaimed, "My God! How can I pay such prices? I have seven children; what shall I do?"

Increasingly, the ordinary people of the South, preoccupied with staying alive, refused to pay taxes, provide food, or serve in the army. Soldiers were drawn home by the desperation of their families as well as the discouraging course of the war. By 1864 the desertion rate had climbed to 40 percent.

At the same time, the life of the southern ruling class was irrevocably changed by the changing nature of slavery. One-quarter of all slaves had fled to the Union lines by war's end, and those who remained often stood in a different relationship to their owners. As white masters and overseers left to join the army, white women were left behind on the plantation to cope with shortages, grow crops, and manage the labor of slaves. Lacking the patriarchal authority of their husbands, these women found that white–black relationships shifted, sometimes drastically (as when slaves fled) and sometimes more subtly. Slaves increasingly made their own

decisions about when and how they would work, and they refused to accept the punishments that would have accompanied this insubordination in prewar years.

Peace movements in the South were motivated by a confused mixture of realism, war weariness, and states' rights animosity toward Jefferson Davis's efforts to hold the Confederacy together. The anti-Davis faction was led by his own vice president, Alexander Stephens, who early in 1864 suggested a negotiated peace. Peace sentiment was especially strong in North Carolina, where over a hundred public meetings in support of negotiations were held in the summer of 1863. Davis would have none of it. The peace sentiment, which grew throughout 1864, flourished outside the political system in secret societies such as the Heroes of America and the Red Strings. As hopes of Confederate victory slipped away, the military battlefield expanded to include the political battles that southern civilians were fighting among themselves.

The Tide Turns

As Lincoln's timing of the Emancipation Proclamation showed, by 1863 the nature of the war was changing. The Proclamation freeing the slaves struck directly at the southern home front and the civilian work force. That same year, the nature of the battlefield war changed as well: the Civil War became the first total war.

The Turning Point of 1863

In the summer of 1863 the moment finally arrived when the North could begin to hope for victory. But for the Union Army the year opened with stalemate in the East and slow and costly progress in the West. For the South, 1863 represented its highest hopes for military success and for diplomatic recognition by Britain or France.

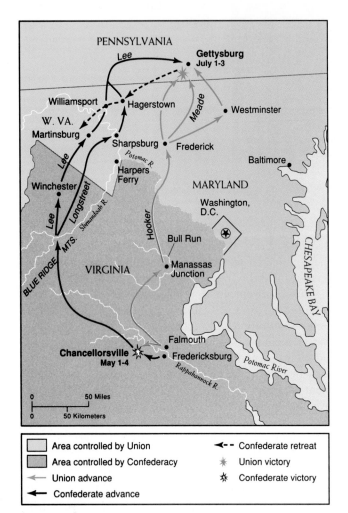

The Turning Point: 1863

In June, Lee boldly struck north into Maryland and Pennsylvania, hoping for a victory that would cause Britain and France to demand a negotiated peace on Confederate terms. Instead, he lost the hard-fought battle of Gettysburg, July 1–3. The very next day, Grant's long siege of Vicksburg succeeded. These two great Fourth of July victories turned the tide in favor of the Union. The Confederates never again mounted a major offensive. Total Union control of the Mississippi now exposed the Lower South to attack.

Attempting to break the stalemate in northern Virginia, General Joseph "Fighting Joe" Hooker and a Union army of 130,000 men attacked a Confederate army half that size at Chancellorsville in May. In response, Robert E. Lee took the daring risk of dividing his forces. He sent General Stonewall Jackson and 30,000 men on a day-long flanking movement that caught the Union troops by surprise. Although Jackson was killed (shot by his own men by mistake), Chancellorsville was a great Confederate victory. However, Confederate losses were also great: 13,000 men, representing more than 20 percent of Lee's army (versus 17,000 Union men). Though weakened, Lee moved to the attack in the war's most dangerous single thrust into Union territory.

In June Lee moved north into Maryland and Pennsylvania. His purpose was as much political as military: he hoped that a great Confederate victory would lead Britain and France to intervene in the war and demand a negotiated peace. The ensuing Battle of Gettysburg, July 1–3, 1863, was another horrible slaughter. A Union officer reported the next day, "I tried to ride over the field but could not, for dead and wounded lay too thick to guide a horse through them."

Lee retreated from the field, leaving more than one-third of his army behind—28,000 men killed, wounded, or missing. His great gamble had failed; he never again mounted a major offensive.

The next day, July 4, 1863, Ulysses S. Grant took Vicksburg, Mississippi, after a costly seven-month seige. The combined news of Gettysburg and Vicksburg dissuaded Britain and France from recognizing the Confederacy and checked the northern peace movement. It also tightened the grip of the Anaconda on the South, for the Union now controlled all of the Mississippi River. In November Generals Grant and Sherman captured Chattanooga, Tennessee, thus opening the way for the capture of Atlanta.

Grant and Sherman

In March 1864 President Lincoln called Grant east and appointed him general in chief of all the Union forces. Lincoln's critics were appalled. Grant was an uncouth westerner (like the president) and (unlike the president) was rumored to have a drinking problem. Lincoln replied that if he knew the general's brand he would send a barrel of whiskey to every other commander in the Union Army.

Grant devised a plan of strangulation and annihilation. He sent General William Tecumseh Sherman to defeat Confederate general Joe Johnston's Army of Tennessee, while he himself took on Lee in northern

Virginia. Both Grant and Sherman exemplified the new kind of warfare. They aimed to inflict maximum damage on the fabric of southern life, hoping the South would choose to surrender rather than face total destruction. This decision to broaden the war so that it directly affected civilians was new in American military history and prefigured the total wars of the twentieth century.

In northern Virginia, Grant pursued a policy of destroying civilian supplies. He said he "regarded it as humane to both sides to protect the persons of those found at their homes, but to consume everything that could be used to support or supply armies." One of those supports was slaves. Grant welcomed fleeing slaves to Union lines and encouraged army efforts to put them to work or enlist them as soldiers. But the most famous example of the new total war strategy was General Sherman's 1864 march through Georgia.

On September 2, 1864, Sherman captured Atlanta. The battle had been fierce, and the city lay in ruins, but the rest of Georgia now lay open to him. In November Sherman set out to march the 285 miles to the coastal city of Savannah, living off the land and destroying everything else in his path. His military purpose was to tighten the noose around Robert E. Lee's army in northern Virginia by cutting off Mississippi, Alabama, and Georgia from the rest of the Confederacy. But his

This striking photograph by Thomas C. Roche shows a scene of horror: a dead Confederate soldier, killed at Petersburg on April 3, 1865, only six days before the surrender at Appomattox. Photography, a new technique, gave a gruesome reality to the mounting total of dead and wounded that affected every American community.

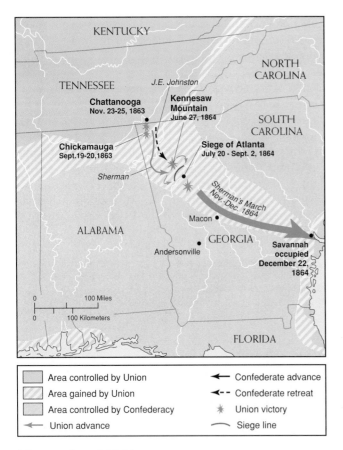

Area controlled by Union · Confederate advance
Area gained by Union · Confederate retreat
Area controlled by Confederacy · Union victory
Union advance · Siege line

The Battles of 1864

Ulysses S. Grant and William Tecumseh Sherman, two like-minded generals, commanded the Union's armies in the final push to victory. While Grant hammered away at Lee in northern Virginia, Sherman captured Atlanta in September (a victory that may have been vital to Lincoln's reelection) and began his March to the Sea in November 1864.

second purpose, openly stated, was to "make war so terrible" to the people of the South "that generations would pass away before they would again appeal to it." Accordingly, he told his men to seize, burn, or destroy everything in their path (but not to harm civilians).

Terrifying to white southern civilians, Sherman was initially hostile to black southerners as well. In the interests of speed and efficiency, he turned away many of the 18,000 slaves who flocked to him in Georgia, causing a number to be recaptured and reenslaved. This callous action caused such a scandal in Washington that Secretary of War Edwin Stanton arranged a special meeting with Sherman and twenty black ministers who spoke for the freed slaves. This in itself was extraordinary: no one

before had asked slaves what they wanted. Equally extraordinary was Sherman's response: In Special Field Order 15, issued in January 1865, he set aside more than 400,000 acres of land to be given to the freed slaves in forty-acre parcels.

The 1864 Election

The war complicated the presidential election of 1864. Lincoln was renominated during a period of war stalemate. Opposed by the Radicals, who thought he was too conciliatory toward the South, and by Republican conservatives, who disapproved of the Emancipation Proclamation, Lincoln had little support within his own party.

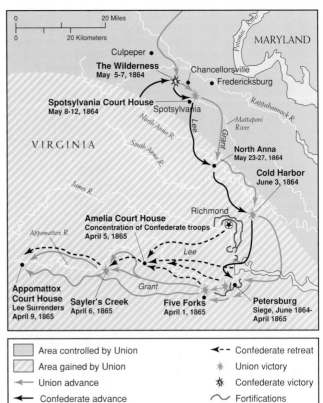

Area controlled by Union · Confederate retreat
Area gained by Union · Union victory
Union advance · Confederate victory
Confederate advance · Fortifications

The Final Battles in Virginia, 1865

In the war's final phase early in 1865, Sherman closed one arm of the pincers by marching north from Savannah while Grant attacked Lee's last defensive positions in Petersburg and Richmond. Lee retreated from them on April 2 and surrendered at Appomattox Court House on April 9, 1865, succumbing at last to the overwhelming pressures of shortage and starvation.

The Democrats had an appealing candidate: General George McClellan, who proclaimed the war a failure and proposed an armistice to end it. Other Democrats played shamelessly on the racist fears of the urban working class, accusing Republicans of being "negro-lovers" and warning that race mixing lay ahead.

A deeply depressed Lincoln fully expected to lose the election. "I am going to be beaten," he told an army officer in August of 1864, "and unless some great change takes place *badly* beaten." A great change *did* take place: Sherman captured Atlanta on September 2. Jubilation swept the North: some cities celebrated with 100-gun salutes. Lincoln won the election with 55 percent of the popular vote. The vote probably saved the Republican party from extinction. Furthermore, the election was important evidence of northern support for Lincoln's policy of unconditional surrender for the South. There would be no negotiated peace; the war would continue.

Nearing the End

As Sherman devastated the Lower South, Grant was locked in struggle with Lee in northern Virginia. Grant did not favor subtle strategies of warfare. He bluntly said, "The art of war is simple enough. Find out where your enemy is. Get at him as soon as you can. Strike at him as hard as you can, and keep moving on." Following this plan, Grant hammered Lee into submission in a year. But victory was expensive. Lee inflicted heavy losses on the Union Army: almost 18,000 at the Battle of the Wilderness, more than 8,000 at Spotsylvania, and 12,000 at Cold Harbor. At Cold Harbor, Union troops wrote their names and addresses on scraps of paper and pinned them to their backs, so certain were they of being killed or wounded in battle. Grim and terrible as Grant's strategy was, it eventually proved effective. The North's great advantage in population finally began to show. There were more Union soldiers to replace those lost in battle, but there were no more white Confederates.

In desperation, the South turned to the hitherto unthinkable: arming slaves to serve as soldiers in the Confederate Army. But—and this was the bitter irony—the African American soldiers and their families would have to be promised freedom or they would desert to the Union the first chance they had. Even though the plan had the support of Robert E. Lee, the Confederate Congress balked at first. As one congressman said, "If slaves make good soldiers our whole theory of slavery is wrong." Finally, on March 13, 1865, the Confederate Congress authorized a draft of black soldiers, but although two regiments of black soldiers were immediately organized in Richmond, it was too late—the war was lost. Thus the South never had to publicly acknowledge the paradox of having to offer slaves freedom so that they would fight to defend slavery.

Abraham Lincoln toured the ruins of Richmond, the Confederate capital, just hours after Jefferson Davis had fled. In these ruins and in others throughout the South, Lincoln saw firsthand the immense task of rebuilding and reconciliation that he did not live to accomplish.

By the spring of 1865, public support for the war simply disintegrated in the South. Starvation, inflation, dissension, and the prospect of military defeat were too much. In February, Jefferson Davis sent his vice president, Alexander Stephens, to negotiate terms at a peace conference at Hampton Roads. But Lincoln would not countenance anything less than full surrender, so the conference failed and southern resistance faded away.

Appomattox

In the spring of 1865 Lee and his remaining troops, outnumbered two to one, still held Petersburg and Richmond, the Confederate capital. Starving, short of ammunition, and losing men in battle or to desertion every day, Lee retreated from Petersburg on April 2. The Confederate government fled Richmond, stripping and burning the city. Seven days later, Lee and his 25,000 troops surrendered to Grant at Appomattox

Lincoln's assassination, just days after Lee's surrender at Appomattox, was a stunning blow. From the most elderly person to the youngest child, from the most distinguished to the obscure, the Union mourned.

Hermann Faber. *Death of Abraham Lincoln*, 1865. Pencil on paper 13 7/8 X 9 7/8". Armed Forces Institute of Pathology, Washington, D.C. Otis Historical Archives, National Museum of Health and Medicine.

Courthouse. Grant treated Lee with great respect and set a historic precedent by giving the Confederate troops parole. This meant they could not subsequently be prosecuted for treason. He then sent the starving army on its way with three days' rations for every man. Jefferson Davis, who had hoped to set up a new government in Texas, was captured in Georgia on May 10. The war was finally over.

Death of a President

Sensing the war was near its end, Abraham Lincoln visited Grant's troops when Lee withdrew from Petersburg on April 2. Thus it was that he came to visit Richmond, and to sit briefly in Jefferson Davis's presidential office, soon after Davis had left it. As Lincoln walked the streets of the burned and pillaged city, black people poured out to see him and surround him, shouting "Glory to God! Glory! Glory! Glory!" Lincoln in turn said to Admiral David Porter, "Thank God I have lived to see this. It seems to me that I have been dreaming a horrid dream for four years, and now the nightmare is gone." Lincoln had only the briefest time to savor the victory. On the night of April 14,

President and Mrs. Lincoln went to Ford's Theater in Washington. There Lincoln was shot at point-blank range by John Wilkes Booth, a Confederate sympathizer. He died the next day. For the people of the Union, the joy of victory was muted by mourning for their great war leader.

Conclusion

In 1865 a divided people were forcibly reunited by battle. Their nation, the United States of America, had been permanently changed by civil war. Devastating losses among the young men of the country affected not only their families but all of postwar society. Politically, the deepest irony of the Civil War was that only by fighting it had America become completely a nation, for it was the war that broke down local isolation and forced a national perspective on ordinary people. The question now was whether this strengthened but divided national community, forged in battle (to use Lincoln's words from the Gettysburg Address), could create a just peace.

CHRONOLOGY

1861	March: Morrill Tariff Act
	April: Fort Sumter falls; war begins
	April: Mobilization begins
	April–May: Virginia, Arkansas, Tennessee, and North Carolina secede
	June: United States Sanitary Commission established
	July: First Battle of Bull Run
1862	February: Legal Tender Act
	February: Battles of Fort Henry and Fort Donelson
	March: Battle of Pea Ridge
	March–August: George B. McClellan's Peninsular campaign
	March: Battle of Glorieta Pass
	April: Battle of Shiloh
	April: Confederate Conscription Act
	April: David Farragut captures New Orleans
	May: Homestead Act
	June–July: Seven Days Battles
	July: Pacific Railway Act
	July: Morrill Land Grant Act
	September: Battle of Antietam
	December: Battle of Fredericksburg
1863	January: Emancipation Proclamation
	February: National Bank Act
	March: Draft introduced in the North
	April: Richmond bread riot
	May: Battle of Chancellorsville
	June: French occupy Mexico City
	July: Battle of Gettysburg
	July: Surrender of Vicksburg
	July: New York City Draft Riots
	November: Battle of Chattanooga
	November: Union troops capture Brownsville, Texas
1864	March: Ulysses S. Grant becomes general in chief of Union forces
	May: Battle of the Wilderness
	May: Battle of Spotsylvania
	June: Battle of Cold Harbor
	September: Atlanta falls
	November: Abraham Lincoln reelected president
	November–December: William Tecumseh Sherman's March to the Sea
1865	April: Richmond falls
	April: Robert E. Lee surrenders at Appomattox
	April: Lincoln assassinated
	December: Thirteenth Amendment to the Constitution becomes law

Review Questions

1. At the outset of the Civil War, what were the relative advantages of the North and the South, and how did they affect the final outcome?

2. In the absence of the southern Democrats, in the early 1860s the new Republican Congress was able to pass a number of party measures with little opposition. What do these measures tell you about the historical roots of the Republican Party? More generally, how do you think we should view legislation passed in the absence of the customary opposition, debate, and compromise?

3. The greatest problem facing Jefferson Davis and the Confederacy was the need to develop a true feeling of nationalism. Can the failure of this effort be blamed on Davis's weakness as a leader alone, or are there other causes?

4. In what ways can it be said that the actions of African Americans, both slave and free, came to determine the course of the Civil War?

5. Wars always have unexpected consequences. List some of these consequences both for soldiers and for civilians in the North and in the South.

6. Today, Abraham Lincoln is considered one of our greatest presidents, but he did not enjoy such approval at the time. List some of the contemporary criticisms of Lincoln, and evaluate them.

Recommended Reading

NINA BROWN BAKER, *Cyclone in Calico: The Story of Mary Ann Bickerdyke* (1952). Mother Bickerdyke's wartime career is told in homely detail.

IVER BERNSTEIN, *The New York City Draft Riots* (1990). A social history that places the famous riots in the context of the nineteenth century's extraordinary urbanization.

PAUL ESCOTT, *After Secession: Jefferson Davis and the Failure of Confederate Nationalism* (1978). A thoughtful study of Davis's record as president of the Confederacy.

ALVIN JOSEPHY, *The Civil War in the West* (1992). A long-needed study, by a noted western historian, of the course of the war in the trans-Mississippi West.

JAMES M. MCPHERSON, *The Atlas of the Civil War* (1994). Detailed battle diagrams with clear descriptions.

———, *Battle Cry of Freedom: The Civil War Era* (1988). An acclaimed, highly readable synthesis of much scholarship on the war.

———, *The Negro's Civil War: How American Negroes Felt and Acted During the War for the Union* (1965). One of the earliest documentary collections on African American activity in wartime.

WILLIAM QUENTIN MAXWELL, *Lincoln's Fifth Wheel: The Political History of the United States Sanitary Commission* (1956). A useful study of the major northern volunteer organization.

PAULI MURRAY, *Proud Shoes: The Story of an American Family* (1956). Murray tells the proud story of her African American family and her grandfather Robert Fitzgerald.

PHILIP SHAW PALUDAN, *"A People's Contest": The Union at War, 1861–1865* (1988). A largely successful social history of the North during the war.

17 RECONSTRUCTION, 1863–1877

AMERICAN COMMUNITIES

HALE COUNTY, ALABAMA: FROM SLAVERY TO FREEDOM IN A BLACK BELT COMMUNITY

On a bright Saturday morning in May 1867, 4,000 former slaves eagerly streamed into the town of Greensboro, bustling seat of Hale County in west-central Alabama. They came to hear speeches from two delegates to a recent freedmen's convention in Mobile and to find out about the political status of black people under the Reconstruction Act just passed by Congress. In the days following this unprecedented gathering of African Americans, tension mounted throughout the surrounding countryside. Military authorities had begun supervising voter registration for elections to the upcoming constitutional convention that would rewrite the laws of Alabama. On June 13, John Orrick, a local white man, confronted Alex Webb, a politically active freedman, on the streets of Greensboro. Webb had recently been appointed a voter registrar for the district. Orrick swore he would never be registered by a black man, and shot Webb dead. Hundreds of armed and angry freedmen formed a posse to search for Orrick, but they failed to find him. Webb's murder galvanized 500 local freedmen to form a local Union League chapter, which functioned as both a militia company and a forum to agitate for political rights.

The Civil War had destroyed slavery and the Confederacy, but the political and economic status of newly emancipated African Americans remained to be worked out. The four million freed people constituted roughly one-third of the total southern population, but the black–white ratio in individual communities varied enormously. In some places the Union army had been a strong presence during the war, hastening collapse of the slave system and encouraging experiments in free labor. Other areas remained untouched by the fighting.

Large plantations dominated the economy and political life of west-central Alabama's communities. Hale county was typical of the South's black belt: African Americans constituted over three-quarters of the population. The arrival of Union troops there in the spring of 1865 emboldened African Americans to challenge the traditional arrangements by which masters had organized plantation labor.

Although the organization of work and methods of payment varied throughout the postwar South, the key transformation involved a shift from the gang labor characteristic of slavery to individual families engaged in sharecropping. The slave labor force on antebellum plantations had been typically organized into large work gangs, under the harsh and continuous supervision of white overseers. Under the sharecropping system African American families worked small plots of land and received a share of the crop from plantation owners. Sharecropping was less of a victory for newly freed African Americans than a defeat for plantation owners, who resented even the limited economic independence won by the black work force.

One owner, Henry Watson, found that his entire work force had deserted him at the end of 1865. "I am in the midst of a large and fertile cotton growing country," Watson wrote to a partner. "Many plantations are entirely without labor, many plantations have insufficient labor, and upon none are the laborers doing their former accustomed work." Black women refused to work in the fields, preferring to stay home with their children and tend garden plots. Nor would male field hands do any work, such as caring for hogs, that did not directly increase their share of the cotton crop.

Overseers and owners thus grudgingly allowed freed people to work the land "in families," letting them choose their own supervisors and find their own provisions. When Wilson O'Berry, longtime supervisor of the large Cameron plantation in Hale County, switched to a sharecropping arrangement in 1867, he reported improved productivity and better work habits among the hands. Over the next few years, the Cameron place was leased and eventually sold in small plots to families of former slaves. African Americans believed owning and farming their own land was the best way to secure their freedom, keep their family together, and get ahead. An independent black community still exists on the old Cameron plantation today.

Only a small fraction—perhaps 15 percent—of African American families were fortunate enough to be able to buy land. The majority settled for some version of sharecropping, while others managed to rent land from owners, becoming tenant farmers. Still, planters throughout Hale County had been forced to change the old routines of plantation labor.

Local African Americans also organized politically. In 1866 Congress had passed the Civil Rights Act and

sent the Fourteenth Amendment to the Constitution to the states for ratification; both promised full citizenship rights to former slaves. Hale County freedmen joined the Republican Party and local Union League chapters, which operated as the Republican Party's organizational arm in the South. Freedmen used their new political power to press for better labor contracts, demand greater autonomy for the black work force, and agitate for the more radical goal of land confiscation and redistribution. Two Hale County former slaves, Brister Reese and James K. Green, won election to the Alabama state legislature in 1869.

These new labor arrangements and aggressive black political activism prompted a white counterattack. In the spring of 1868, the Ku Klux Klan came to Hale County. A secret organization of white people devoted to terrorizing and intimidating African Americans and their white Republican allies, the Klan quickly made its presence felt. Disguised in white sheets, armed with guns and whips, and making nighttime raids on horseback, Klansmen flogged, beat, and murdered freed people. The spread of sharecropping and tenant farming dispersed African American families throughout the countryside, making them more vulnerable to violent attack. Planters used Klan terror to dissuade former slaves from leaving plantations or organizing for higher wages. The Klan was also a potent weapon for punishing African American voters and political activists.

An 1871 congressional investigation led to passage of the Ku Klux Klan Act. Federal intervention did manage to break the power of the Klan temporarily in parts of the former Confederacy. But no serious effort was made to stop Klan terror in the west Alabama black belt. Planters thus reestablished much of their social and political control.

Reconstruction was only partially successful. Not until the "Second Reconstruction" of the twentieth-century civil rights movement would the descendants of Hale County's African Americans enjoy the full fruits of freedom, and even then these would be of lesser quality. Events in Hale County typified a struggle that took place in hundreds of southern communities in the aftermath of the Civil War. The destruction of slavery and the Confederacy forced African Americans and white people to renegotiate their old economic and political roles. During the Reconstruction era, these community battles both shaped and were shaped by the victorious and newly expansive federal government in Washington.

The Politics of Reconstruction

When General Robert E. Lee's men stacked their guns at Appomattox, the bloodiest war in American history ended. Although President Abraham Lincoln insisted early on that the conflict was over the maintenance of the Union, by 1863 the contest had evolved into a war of African American liberation as well as a constitutional struggle. Indeed, slavery—as a political, economic, and moral issue—was the root cause of the war. The Civil War ultimately destroyed slavery, though not racism, once and for all.

The Civil War also settled which interpretation of the Constitution—states' rights or federalism—would prevail. The name *United States* would from now on be understood as a singular rather than a plural noun, signaling an important change in the meaning of American nationality. The old notion of the United States as a voluntary union of sovereign states gave way to the new reality of a single nation in which the federal government took precedence over the individual states.

The Defeated South

The white South paid an extremely high price for secession, war, and defeat. In addition to the battlefield casualties of 260,000, the Confederate states sustained deep

Charleston, South Carolina, in 1865, after Union troops had burned the city. In the aftermath of the Civil War, scenes like this were common throughout the South. The destruction of large portions of so many southern cities and towns contributed to the postwar economic hardships faced by the region.

material and psychological wounds. Much of the best agricultural land was destroyed. Many towns and cities, including Richmond, Atlanta, and Columbia, South Carolina, lay in ruins. By 1865 the South's most precious commodities, cotton and African American slaves, no longer were measures of wealth and prestige. Retreating Confederates destroyed most of the South's cotton to prevent its capture by federal troops. What remained was confiscated by Union agents as contraband of war. The former slaves, many of whom had fled to Union lines during the latter stages of the war, were determined to chart their own course in the reconstructed South as free men and women.

It would take the South's economy a generation to overcome the severe blows dealt by the war. In 1860 the South held 30 percent of the nation's wealth; a decade later it controlled only 12 percent.

Many white southerners resented their conquered status, and white notions of race, class, and "honor" died hard. A white North Carolinian, for example, who had lost almost everything dear to him in the war—his sons, home, and slaves—recalled in 1865 that despite the tragedy he still retained one thing. "They've left me one inestimable privilege—to hate 'em. I git up at half-past four in the morning, and sit up till twelve at night, to hate 'em."

Emancipation proved the bitterest pill for white Southerners to swallow, especially the planter elite. Conquered and degraded, and in their view robbed of their slave property, white people responded by tending more than ever to perceive African Americans as vastly inferior to themselves. However, emancipation, forced white people to redefine their world. The specter of political power and social equality for African Americans made racial order the consuming passion of most white southerners during the Reconstruction years. In fact, racism can be seen as one of the major forces driving Reconstruction, and ultimately, undermining it.

Abraham Lincoln's Plan

By late 1863 Union military victories had convinced President Lincoln of the need to fashion a plan for the reconstruction of the South (see Chapter 16). He based his reconstruction program on bringing the seceded states back into the Union as quickly as possible. His Proclamation of Amnesty and Reconstruction of December 1863 offered full pardon and the restoration of property, not including slaves, to white southerners willing to swear an oath of allegiance to the United States and its laws, including the Emancipation Proclamation. Prominent Confederate military and civil leaders were excluded from Lincoln's offer, although he indicated that he would freely pardon these officers.

The president also proposed that when the number of any Confederate state's voters who took the oath of allegiance reached 10 percent of the number who had voted in the election of 1860, this group could establish a state government that Lincoln would recognize as legitimate. Fundamental to this Ten Percent Plan was acceptance by the reconstructed governments of the abolition of slavery. Lincoln's plan was designed less as a blueprint for Reconstruction than as a way to shorten the war and gain white people's support for emancipation.

Lincoln's amnesty proclamation angered Radical Republicans, who advocated not only equal rights for the freedmen but a tougher stance toward the white South as well. In July 1864 Senator Benjamin F. Wade of Ohio and Congressman Henry W. Davis of Maryland sought to substitute a harsher alternative to the Ten Percent Plan. The Wade–Davis bill required that 50 percent of the white male citizens had to take a loyalty oath before elections for new state constitutional conventions could be held in the seceded states. The Radicals saw Reconstruction as a chance to effect a fundamental transformation of southern society. They thus wanted to delay the process until war's end and to limit participa-

FREEDOM TO SLAVES!

Whereas, the President of the United States did, on the first day of the present month, issue his *Proclamation* declaring "that *all persons held as Slaves in certain designated States, and parts of States, are, and henceforward shall be free,*" and that the Executive Government of the United States, including the Military and Naval authorities thereof, would recognize and maintain the freedom of said persons. *And Whereas*, the county of *Frederick* is included in the territory designated by the Proclamation of the President, in which the *Slaves should become free*, I therefore hereby notify the citizens of the city of Winchester, and of said County, of said Proclamation, and of my intention to maintain and enforce the same.

I expect all citizens to yield a ready compliance with the Proclamation of the Chief Executive, and I admonish all persons disposed to resist its peaceful enforcement, that upon manifesting such disposition by acts, they will be regarded as rebels in arms against the lawful authority of the Federal Government and dealt with accordingly.

All persons liberated by said Proclamation are admonished to abstain from all violence, and immediately betake themselves to useful occupations.

The officers of this command are admonished and ordered to act in accordance with said proclamation and to yield their ready co-operation in its enforcement.

R. H. Milroy,
Brig. Gen'l Commanding.

Winchester Va.
Jan. 5th, 1863.

A Union commander notifies the citizens of Winchester, Virginia, of President Abraham Lincoln's Emancipation Proclamation. Union officers throughout the South had to improvise arrangements for dealing with African Americans who streamed into Union army camps. For many newly freed slaves, the call for taking up "useful occupations" meant serving the Union forces in their neighborhoods as laborers, cooks, spies, and soldiers.

tion to a smaller number of southern Unionists. Lincoln viewed Reconstruction as part of the larger effort to win the war and abolish slavery. He wanted to weaken the Confederacy by creating new state governments that could win broad support from southern white people. The Wade–Davis bill threatened his efforts to build political consensus within the southern states, so Lincoln vetoed it.

As Union armies occupied parts of the South, commanders improvised a variety of arrangements involving confiscated plantations and the African American labor force. For example, in 1862 General Benjamin F. Butler initiated a policy of transforming slaves on Louisiana sugar plantations into wage laborers under the close supervision of occupying federal troops. Butler's policy required slaves to remain on the estates of loyal planters, where they would receive wages according to a fixed schedule, as well as food and medical care for the aged and sick. Abandoned plantations would be leased to northern investors.

In January 1865 General William T. Sherman issued Special Field Order No. 15, setting aside the Sea Islands off the Georgia coast and a portion of the South Carolina low-country rice fields for the exclusive settlement of freed people. Each family would receive forty acres of land and the loan of mules from the army—the origin, perhaps, of the famous "forty acres and a mule" idea that would soon capture the imagination of African Americans throughout the South. Sherman's intent was to relieve the demands placed on his army by the thousands of impoverished African Americans who followed his march to the sea. By the summer of 1865 some 40,000 freed people, eager to take advantage of the general's order, had been settled on 400,000 acres of "Sherman land."

Conflicts within the Republican party prevented the development of a systematic land distribution program. In March 1865 Congress established the Freedmen's Bureau. Along with offering provisions, clothing, and fuel to destitute former slaves, the bureau was charged with supervising and managing "all the abandoned lands in the South and the control of all subjects relating to refugees and freedmen." The act that established the bureau also stated that forty acres of abandoned or confiscated land could be leased to freed slaves or white Unionists, who would have an option to purchase after three years and "such title thereto as the United States can convey."

On April 14, 1865, while attending the theater in Washington, President Lincoln was shot by John Wilkes Booth. At the time of his assassination, Lincoln's Reconstruction policy remained unsettled and incomplete. In its broad outlines the president's plans had seemed to favor a speedy restoration of the southern states to the Union and a minimum of federal intervention in their affairs. But with his death the specifics of postwar Reconstruction would have to be hammered out by a new president, Andrew Johnson of Tennessee, a Democrat whose personality, political background, and racist learnings put him at odds with a Republican-controlled Congress determined to win the peace as well as the war.

Andrew Johnson and Presidential Reconstruction

Andrew Johnson, a Democrat and former slaveholder, was a most unlikely successor to the martyred Lincoln. By trade a tailor, educated by his wife, Johnson overcame his impoverished background and served as state legislator, governor, and U.S. senator. Throughout his career he had championed yeoman farmers and viewed the South's plantation aristocrats with contempt.

In 1864 the Republicans, determined to broaden their appeal to include northern and border state "War Democrats," nominated Johnson, the only southern member of the U.S. Senate to remain loyal to the Union, for vice president. But despite Johnson's success in the 1864 campaign, many Radical Republicans distrusted him. In the immediate aftermath of Lincoln's murder, however, Johnson appeared to side with the Radical Republicans who sought to treat the South as a conquered province.

But support for Johnson quickly faded as the new president's policies unfolded. Johnson defined Reconstruction as the province of the executive, not the legislative, branch, and he planned to restore the Union as quickly as possible. He blamed individual southerners—the planter elite—rather than entire states for leading the South down the disastrous road to secession.

In the spring of 1865 Johnson granted amnesty and pardon, including restoration of property rights except slaves, to all Confederates who pledged loyalty to the Union and support for emancipation. Fourteen classes of southerners, mostly major Confederate officials and wealthy landowners, were excluded. But these men could apply individually for presidential pardons. During his tenure Johnson pardoned roughly 90 percent of those who applied. Significantly, he instituted this plan while Congress was not in session. Johnson also appointed provisional governors for several former Confederate states, and set highly favorable terms for readmission to the Union. By the fall of 1865 ten of the eleven Confederate states claimed to have met Johnson's requirements to reenter the Union.

Andrew Johnson used the term *restoration* rather than *reconstruction*. A lifelong Democrat with ambitions to be elected president on his own in 1868, Johnson hoped to build a new political coalition composed of northern Democrats, conservative Republicans, and southern Unionists. Firmly committed to white supremacy, he opposed political rights for the freedmen. Johnson's open sympathy for his fellow white southerners, his antiblack bias, and his determination to control the course of Reconstruction placed him on a collision course with the powerful Radical wing of the Republican party.

The Radical Republican Vision

Most Radicals were men whose careers had been shaped by the slavery controversy. At the core of their thinking lay a deep belief in equal political rights and equal economic opportunity, both guaranteed by a powerful national government. They argued that once free labor, universal education, and equal rights were implanted in the South, that region would be able to share in the North's material wealth, progress, and social mobility.

In the Radicals' view, the power of the federal government would be central to the remaking of southern society, especially in guaranteeing civil rights and suffrage for freedmen. In the most far-reaching proposal, Representative Thaddeus Stevens of Pennsylvania called for the confiscation of 400 million acres belonging to the wealthiest 10 percent of southerners, to be redistributed to black and white yeomen and northern land buyers.

Northern Republicans were especially outraged by the "Black Codes" passed by southern states to restrict the freedom of the black labor force and keep freed people as close to slave status as possible. Laborers who left their jobs before contracts expired would forfeit wages already earned and be subject to arrest by any white citizen. Vagrancy, very broadly defined, was punishable by fines and involuntary plantation labor. Apprenticeship clauses obliged black children to work without pay for employers. Some states attempted to bar African Americans from land ownership. Other laws specifically denied African Americans equality with white people in civil rights, excluding them from juries and prohibiting interracial marriages.

The Black Codes underscored the unwillingness of white southerners to accept the full meaning of freedom for African Americans. The Radicals, although not a majority of their party, were joined by moderate Republicans as growing numbers of northerners grew suspicious of white southern intransigence and the denial of political rights to freedmen. When the Thirty-Ninth Congress convened in December 1865, the large Republican majority prevented the seating of the white southerners elected to Congress under President Johnson's provisional state governments. Republicans also established the Joint Committee on Reconstruction. After hearing extensive testimony from a broad range of witnesses, it concluded that not only were old Confederates back in power in the South, but that Black Codes and racial violence directed at African Americans necessitated increased protection for them.

As a result, in the spring of 1866 Congress passed two important bills designed to aid African Americans. The landmark Civil Rights bill, which bestowed full citizenship upon African Americans, overturned the 1857 *Dred Scott* decision and the Black Codes. It defined all people born in the United States (except Indian peoples) as national citizens, and it enumerated various rights, including the rights to make and enforce contracts, to sue, to give evidence, and to buy and sell property. Under this bill, African Americans acquired "full and equal benefit of all laws and proceedings for the security of person and property as is enjoyed by white citizens."

Congress also voted to enlarge the scope of the Freedmen's Bureau, empowering it to build schools and pay teachers, and also to establish courts to prosecute those charged with depriving African Americans of their civil rights. The bureau achieved important, if limited, success in aiding African Americans. Bureau-run schools helped lay the foundation for southern public education. The bureau's network of courts allowed freed people to bring suits against white people in disputes involving violence, nonpayment of wages, or unfair division of crops.

An angry President Johnson vetoed both of these bills. But his intemperate attacks on the Radicals—he damned them as traitors unwilling to reunite the Union—rallied the united moderate and Radical Republicans and they succeeded in overriding the vetoes. Congressional Republicans, led by the Radical faction, were now united in challenging the president's power to direct Reconstruction and in using national authority to define and protect the rights of citizens.

In June 1866, fearful that the Civil Rights Act might be declared unconstitutional and eager to settle the basis for the seating of southern representatives, Congress passed the Fourteenth Amendment. The amendment defined national citizenship to include former slaves ("all persons born or naturalized in the United States") and prohibited the states from violating the privileges of citizens without due process of law. It also empowered Congress to reduce the representation of any state that denied the suffrage to males over twenty-one. Republicans adopted the Fourteenth Amendment as their platform for the 1866 congressional elections and suggested that southern states would have to ratify it as a condition of readmission. President Johnson, meanwhile, took to the stump in August to support conservative Democratic and Republican candidates. His unrestrained speeches often degenerated into harangues, alienating many voters and aiding the Republican cause.

For their part, the Republicans began an effective campaign tradition known as "waving the bloody shirt"—reminding northern voters of the hundreds of thousands of Yankee soldiers left dead or maimed by the war. In November 1866 the Republicans increased their majority in both the House and the Senate and gained control of all the northern states.

Congressional Reconstruction and the Impeachment Crisis

United against Johnson, Radical Republicans and their moderate allies took control of Reconstruction early in 1867. In March Congress passed the First Reconstruction Act over Johnson's veto. This act divided the South into five military districts subject to martial law. To achieve restoration, southern states were first required to call new constitutional conventions, elected by universal manhood suffrage. Once these states had drafted new constitutions, guaranteed African American voting rights, and ratified the Fourteenth Amendment, they were eligible for readmission to the Union.

Congress also passed several laws aimed at limiting Johnson's power. One of these, the Tenure of Office Act, stipulated that any officeholder appointed by the president with the Senate's advice and consent could not be removed until the Senate had approved a successor. In this way, congressional leaders could protect Republicans, such as Secretary of War Edwin M. Stanton, entrusted with implementing Congressional Reconstruction. In August 1867, with Congress adjourned, Johnson suspended Stanton and appointed General Ulysses S. Grant interim secretary of war. This enabled the president to remove generals in the field that he judged to be too radical and replace them with men who were sympathetic to his own views. It also served as a challenge to the Tenure of Office Act. In January 1868, when the Senate overruled Stanton's suspension, Grant broke openly with Johnson in a bitter dispute. Stanton resumed his position and barricaded himself in his office when Johnson attempted to remove him once again.

Outraged by Johnson's relentless obstructionism and seizing upon his violation of the Tenure of Office Act as a pretext, Radical and moderate Republicans in the House of Representatives again joined forces and voted to impeach the president by a vote of 126 to 47 on February 24, 1868. To ensure the support of moderate Republicans, the articles of impeachment focused on violations of the Tenure of Office Act, leaving unstated the Republicans' real reasons for wanting the president removed: Johnson's political views, his opposition to the Reconstruction Acts, and his incompetence.

Behind the scenes during his Senate trial, Johnson agreed to abide by the Reconstruction Acts. An influential group of moderate Senate Republicans feared the damage a conviction might do to the constitutional separation of powers. They also worried about the polit-

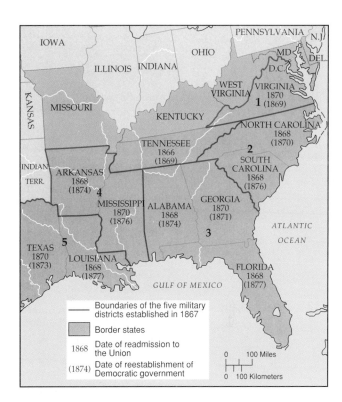

Reconstruction of the South, 1866–77

Dates for the readmission of southern states to the Union and the return of Democrats to power varied according to the specific political situation in those states.

ical and economic policies that might be pursued by the man who would succeed Johnson: Benjamin Wade, the Radical president pro tem of the Senate. In May the Senate voted thirty-five for conviction, nineteen for acquittal—one vote shy of the two-thirds necessary for removal from office. Johnson's narrow acquittal established the precedent that only criminal actions by a president—not political disagreements—warranted removal from office.

The Election of 1868

Sobered by the close impeachment vote, Johnson cooperated with Congress for the remainder of his term. In 1868 seven states (Arkansas, Alabama, Florida, Georgia, Louisiana, North Carolina, and South Carolina) ratified the revised constitutions, elected Republican governments, and ratified the Fourteenth Amendment. Having done so, they rejoined the Union. Although Mississippi, Texas, and Virginia still awaited readmission to the Union, the presidential election of 1868 offered some

SUMMARY TABLE	*Reconstruction Amendments to the Constitution, 1865–70*	
Amendment and Date Passed by Congress	**Main Provisions**	**Ratification Process (3⁄4 of all states including ex-Confederate states required)**
13 (January 1865)	Slavery prohibited in the United States	December 1865 (27 states, including 8 southern states)
14 (June 1866)	1. National citizenship for all persons born or naturalized in the United States 2. State representation in Congress reduced proportionally for any state disfranchising male citizens 3. Denied former Confederates the right to hold state or national office 4. Repudiated Confederate debt	July 1868 (after Congress makes ratification a prerequisite for readmission of ex-Confederate states to the Union)
15 (February 1869)	Prohibited denial of suffrage because of race, color, or previous condition of servitude	March 1870 (ratification required for readmission of Virginia, Texas, Mississippi, and Georgia)

hope that the Civil War's legacy of sectional hate and racial tension might finally ease.

Republicans nominated Ulysses S. Grant, the North's foremost military hero. Grant enjoyed tremendous popularity after the war, especially when he broke with Johnson. Totally lacking in political experience, Grant admitted after receiving the nomination that he had been forced into it in spite of himself.

Significantly, at the very moment that the South was being forced to enfranchise former slaves as a prerequisite for readmission to the Union, the Republicans rejected a campaign plank endorsing black suffrage in the North. Their platform left "the question of suffrage in all the loyal States . . . to the people of those States." State referendums calling for black suffrage failed in eleven northern states between 1865 and 1868, succeeding only in Iowa and Minnesota. The Democrats, determined to reverse congressional Reconstruction, nominated Horatio Seymour, former governor of New York and a long-time foe of emancipation and supporter of states' rights.

The Ku Klux Klan, founded as a Tennessee social club in 1866, threatened, whipped, and murdered black and white Republicans to prevent them from voting. This terrorism enabled the Democrats to carry Georgia and Louisiana, but such tactics ultimately cost the Democrats votes in the North. In the final tally, Grant carried twenty-six of the thirty-four states for an electoral

college victory of 214 to 80. But he received a popular majority of less than 53 percent, beating Seymour by only 306,000 votes. Significantly, more than 500,000 African American voters cast their ballots for Grant, demonstrating their overwhelming support for the Republican party. The Republicans also maintained overwhelming majorities in both houses of Congress.

In February 1869 Congress passed the Fifteenth Amendment, providing that "the right of citizens of the United States to vote shall not be abridged . . . on account of race, color, or previous condition of servitude." To enhance the chances of ratification, Congress required the three remaining unreconstructed states—Mississippi, Texas, and Virginia—to ratify both the Fourteenth and Fifteenth Amendments before readmission. They did so and rejoined the Union in early 1870. The Fifteenth Amendment was ratified in February 1870. In the narrow sense of simply readmitting the former confederate states to the Union, Reconstruction was complete.

Woman Suffrage and Reconstruction

Many women's rights advocates had long been active in the abolitionist movement. The Fourteenth and Fifteenth amendments, which granted citizenship and the vote to freedmen, both inspired and frustrated these activists. For

Susan B. Anthony (1820–1906) and Elizabeth Cady Stanton (1815–1902), the two most influential leaders of the woman suffrage movement, c. 1870. They opposed the Fifteenth Amendment, arguing that the doctrine of universal manhood suffrage it embodied would give constitutional authority to the claim that men were the social and political superiors of women.

example, Elizabeth Cady Stanton and Susan B. Anthony, two leaders with long involvement in both the antislavery and feminist movements, objected to the inclusion of the word *male* in the Fourteenth Amendment. "If that word 'male' be inserted," Stanton predicted in 1866, "it will take us a century at least to get it out."

Stanton, Anthony, and Lucy Stone founded the Equal Rights Association in 1866. The group launched a series of lobbying and petition campaigns to remove racial and sexual restrictions on voting from state constitutions. Throughout the nation, the old abolitionist organizations and the Republican party emphasized passage of the Fourteenth and Fifteenth Amendments and withdrew funds and support from the cause of woman suffrage. Disagreements over these amendments divided woman suffragists for decades.

The radical wing, led by Stanton and Anthony, opposed the Fifteenth Amendment, arguing that ratification would establish an "aristocracy of sex," enfran-

chising all men while leaving women without political privileges. They argued for a Sixteenth Amendment that would secure the vote for women. Other women's rights activists, including Lucy Stone and Frederick Douglass, asserted that "this hour belongs to the Negro." They feared a debate over woman suffrage at the national level would jeopardize passage of the two amendments.

By 1869 woman suffragists had split into two competing organizations: the moderate American Woman Suffrage Association (AWSA), which sought the support of men, and the more radical all-female National Woman Suffrage Association (NWSA). For the NWSA, the vote represented only one part of a broad spectrum of goals inherited from the Declaration of Sentiments manifesto adopted at the first women's convention held in 1848 at Seneca Falls (see Chapter 13).

Although women did not win the vote in this period, they did establish an independent suffrage movement that eventually drew millions of women into political life. The NWSA in particular demonstrated that self-government and democratic participation in the public sphere were crucial for women's emancipation. The failure of woman suffrage after the Civil War was less a result of factional fighting than of the larger defeat of Radical Reconstruction and the ideal of expanded citizenship.

The Meaning of Freedom

The deep desire for independence from white control formed the underlying aspiration of newly freed slaves. For their part, most southern white people sought to restrict the boundaries of that independence. As individuals and as members of communities transformed by emancipation, former slaves struggled to establish economic, political, and cultural autonomy. They built upon the twin pillars of slave culture—the family and the church—to consolidate and expand African American institutions and thereby laid the foundation for the modern African American community.

Emancipation greatly expanded the choices available to African Americans. It helped build confidence in their ability to effect change without deferring to white people. Freedom also meant greater uncertainty and risk. But the vast majority of African Americans were more than willing to take their chances.

Moving About

The first impulse of many emancipated slaves was to test their freedom. The simplest, most obvious way to do this

"Leaving for Kansas," Harper's Weekly, *May 17, 1879. This drawing depicts a group of southern freedpeople on their way to Kansas. Black disillusionment following the end of Reconstruction led thousands of African Americans to migrate to Kansas, where they hoped to find the political rights, economic opportunities, and freedom from violence denied them in the South. Most of these "Exodusts" (after the biblical story of the Israelite Exodus from Egypt) lacked the capital or experience to establish themselves as independent farmers on the Great Plains. Yet few chose to go back to the South, where their former masters had returned to political and economic power.*

involved leaving home. By walking off a plantation, coming and going without restraint or fear of punishment, African Americans could taste freedom. Throughout the summer and fall of 1865, observers in the South noted the enormous numbers of freed people on the move.

Yet many who left their old neighborhoods returned soon afterward to seek work in the general vicinity, or even on the plantation they had left. Many wanted to separate themselves from former owners, but not from familial ties and friendships. Others moved away altogether, seeking jobs in nearby towns and cities. A large number of former slaves left predominantly white counties, where they felt more vulnerable and isolated, for new lives in the relative comfort of predominantly black communities. Many African Americans, attracted by schools, churches, and fraternal societies as well as the army, preferred the city. Between 1865 and 1870, the African American population of the South's largest ten cities doubled while the white population increased by only 10 percent.

Disgruntled planters had difficulty accepting African American independence. During slavery, they had expected obedience, submission, and loyalty from African Americans. Now, many could not understand why so many former slaves wanted to leave despite urgent pleas to continue working at the old place. Many freed people went out of their way to reject the old subservience. Moving about freely was one way of doing this, as was refusing to tip one's hat to white people, ignoring for-

mer masters or mistresses in the streets, and refusing to step aside on sidewalks.

The African American Family

Emancipation allowed freed people the chance to strengthen family ties that had existed under slavery. For many former slaves, freedom meant the opportunity to reunite with long-lost family members. To track down relatives, freed people trekked to faraway places, put ads in newspapers, sought the help of Freedmen's Bureau agents, and questioned anyone who might have information about loved ones. Many thousands of family reunions took place after the war.

Thousands of African American couples who had lived together under slavery streamed to military and civilian authorities and demanded to be legally married. By 1870 the two-parent household was the norm for a large majority of African Americans.

Emancipation brought changes to gender roles within the African American family as well. Black men could now serve on juries, vote, and hold office; black women, like their white counterparts, could not. Freedmen's Bureau agents designated the husband as household head and established lower wage scales for women laborers. African American editors, preachers, and politicians regularly quoted the biblical injunction that wives submit to their husbands.

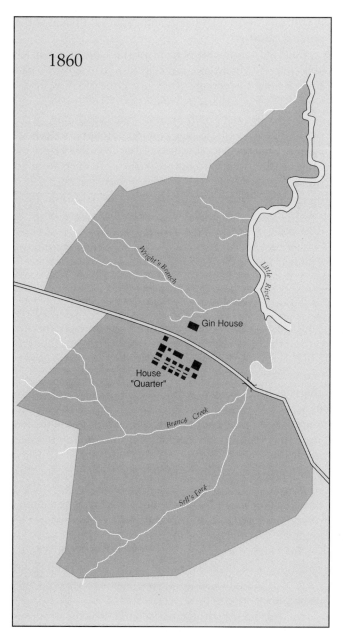

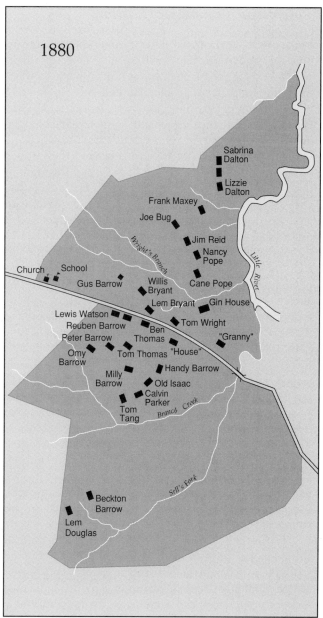

The Barrow Plantation, Oglethorpe County, Georgia, 1860 and 1881 (Appx. 2,000 acres)

These two maps, based on drawings from Scribner's Monthly, *April 1881, show some of the changes brought by emancipation. In 1860 the plantation's entire black population lived in the communal slave quarters, right next to the white master's house. In 1881 black sharecropper and tenant families lived on individual plots, spread out across the land. The former slaves had also built their own school and church.*

African American men asserted their male authority, denied under slavery, by insisting their wives work at home instead of in the fields. Yet African American women continued to work outside the home, engaging in seasonal field labor for wages or working a family's rented plot.

Most rural black families barely eked out a living, so the labor of every family member was essential to survival. The key difference from slave times was that African American families themselves, not white masters and overseers, decided when and where women and children worked.

Labor and Land After Slavery

Most newly emancipated African Americans aspired to quit the plantations and to make new lives for themselves. Leaving the plantation was not as simple as walking off. Some freed people did find jobs in railroad building, mining, ranching, or construction work. Others raised subsistence crops and tended vegetable gardens on squatters' land. The majority hoped to become self-sufficient farmers. Many former slaves believed they were entitled to the land they had worked throughout their lives. This was not a pipe dream. Frequent reference in the Congress and the press to the question of land distribution made the idea of "forty acres and a mule" a matter of serious public debate.

Above all, African Americans sought economic autonomy, and ownership of land promised the most independence. But by 1866 the federal government had already pulled back from the various wartime experiments involving the breaking up of large plantations and the leasing of small plots to individual families. President Johnson directed General Howard of the Freedmen's Bureau to evict tens of thousands of freed people settled on confiscated and abandoned land in southeastern Virginia, southern Louisiana, and the Georgia and South Carolina low country. These evictions created a deep sense of betrayal among African Americans. A former Mississippi slave, Merrimon Howard, bitterly noted that African Americans had been left with "no land, no house, not so much as a place to lay our head. . . . We were friends on the march, brothers on the battlefield, but in the peaceful pursuits of life it seems that we are strangers."

By the late 1860s, sharecropping had emerged as the dominant form of working the land. Sharecropping represented a compromise between planters and former slaves. Under sharecropping arrangements, individual families contracted with landowners to be responsible for a specific plot. Large plantations were thus broken into family-sized farms. Generally, sharecropper families received one-third of the year's crop if the owner furnished implements, seed, and draft animals, or one-half if they provided their own supplies. African Americans preferred sharecropping to gang labor—a system in which large groups of freedmen worked under labor contracts for planters, who often cheated them—as it allowed families to set their own hours and tasks and offered freedom from white supervision and control. For planters, the system stabilized the work force by requiring sharecroppers to remain until the harvest and to employ all family members. It also offered a way around the chronic shortage of cash and credit that plagued the postwar South.

By 1880 about 80 percent of the land in the black belt states—Mississippi, Alabama, and Georgia—had been divided into family-sized farms. Nearly three-quarters of black southerners were sharecroppers. Through much of the black belt, family and community were one. Often several families worked adjoining parcels of land in common, pooling their labor in order to get by. Men usually oversaw crop production. Women went to the fields seasonally during planting or harvesting, but they mainly tended to household chores and child care. In addition, women often held jobs that might bring in cash, such as raising chickens or taking in laundry. The cotton harvest engaged all members of the community, from the oldest to the youngest.

African American Churches and Schools

The creation of separate African American churches proved the most lasting and important element of the energetic institution building that went on in post-Emancipation years. Before the Civil War southern Protestant churches had relegated slaves and free African Americans to second-class membership. Black worshipers were required to sit in the back during services, they were denied any role in church governance, and they were excluded from Sunday schools. Even in larger cities, where all-black congregations sometimes built their own churches, the law required white pastors. In rural areas, slaves preferred their own preachers to the sermons of local, white ministers who quoted scripture to justify slavery and white supremacy.

In communities around the South, African Americans now pooled their resources to buy land and build their own churches. Before these structures were completed, they might hold services in a railroad boxcar, where Atlanta's First Baptist Church began, or in an outdoor arbor, the original site of the First Baptist Church of Memphis. Churches became the center not only for religious life but for many other activities that defined the African American community: schools, picnics, festivals, and political meetings. They also helped spawn a host of organizations devoted to benevolence and mutual aid, such as burial societies, Masonic lodges, temperance clubs, and trade associations.

The church became the first social institution fully controlled by African Americans. In nearly every community ministers, respected for their speaking and organizational skills, were among the most influential leaders. By 1877 the great majority of black southerners had withdrawn from white-dominated churches and belonged to black Baptist or Methodist churches.

African American communities received important educational aid from outside organizations. By 1869 the Freedmen's Bureau was supervising nearly 3,000 schools serving over 150,000 students throughout the South. Over half the roughly 3,300 teachers in these schools were African Americans, many of whom had been free before the Civil War. Other teachers included dedicated northern white women volunteers. Throughout the South in 1865 and 1866, African Americans raised money to build schoolhouses, buy supplies, and pay teachers. Black artisans donated labor for construction, and black families offered room and board to teachers. By 1870 black southerners, most of them impoverished, had managed to raise over $1 million for education, a feat that long remained a source of collective pride.

The Origins of African American Politics

Inclusion rather than separation formed the keynote of early African American political activity. In 1865 and 1866 African Americans throughout the South organized scores of mass meetings, parades, and petitions that demanded civil equality and the right to vote. In the cities the growing web of churches and fraternal societies helped bolster early efforts at political organization.

Hundreds of African American delegates, selected by local meetings or churches, attended statewide political conventions held throughout the South in 1865 and 1866. Convention debates sometimes reflected the tensions within African American communities, such as friction between poorer former slaves and better-off free black people, or between lighter- and darker-skinned African Americans. But most of these state gatherings concentrated on passing resolutions on issues that united all African Americans. The central concerns were suffrage and equality before the law.

The passage of the First Reconstruction Act in 1867 encouraged even more political activity among African Americans. The military started registering the South's electorate, ultimately enrolling approximately 735,000 black and 635,000 white voters in the ten unreconstructed states. Five states—Alabama, Florida, Louisiana, Mississippi, and South Carolina—had black electoral majorities. Fewer than half the registered white voters participated in the elections for state constitutional conventions in 1867 and 1868. In contrast, four-fifths of the registered black voters cast ballots in these elections.

The Union League, begun during the war, became the political voice of the former slaves. Union League

"Electioneering at the South," Harper's Weekly, *July 25, 1868. Throughout the Reconstruction-era South, newly freed slaves took a keen interest in both local and national political affairs. The presence of women and children at these campaign gatherings illustrates the importance of political issues to the entire African American community.*

chapters brought together local African Americans, soldiers, and Freedmen's Bureau agents to demand the vote and an end to legal discrimination against African Americans. It brought out African American voters, instructed freedmen in the rights and duties of citizenship, and promoted Republican candidates.

In 1867 and 1868 the promise of Radical Reconstruction enlarged the scope of African American political participation and brought new leaders to the fore. Many were teachers, preachers, or others possessing useful skills, such as literacy. For most ordinary African Americans, politics was inseparable from economic issues, especially the land question. Grass-roots political organizations often intervened in local disputes with planters over the terms of labor contracts. African American political groups closely followed the congressional debates over Reconstruction policy and agitated for land confiscation and distribution. Perhaps most important, politics was the only arena where black and white southerners might engage each other on an equal basis.

Southern Politics and Society

By the summer of 1868, when the South had returned to the Union, the majority of Republicans believed the task of Reconstruction to be finished. Ultimately, they put their faith in a political solution to the problems facing the vanquished South. That meant nurturing a viable two-party system in the southern states, where no Republican party had ever existed. If that could be accomplished, Republicans and Democrats would compete for votes, offices, and influence, just as they did in northern states.

Yet over the next decade the political structure created in the southern states proved too restricted and fragile to sustain itself. Federal troops were needed to protect Republican governments and their supporters from violent opposition. Congressional action to monitor southern elections and protect black voting rights became routine. Despite initial successes, southern Republicanism proved an unstable coalition of often conflicting elements, unable to sustain effective power for very long. By 1877 Democrats had regained political control of all the former Confederate states.

Southern Republicans

Three major groups composed the fledgling Republican coalition in the postwar South. The first group, African American voters, made up a large majority of southern Republicans throughout the Reconstruction era.

The second group consisted of white northerners, derisively called *carpetbaggers* by native white southerners. Most carpetbaggers combined a desire for personal gain with a commitment to reform the "unprogressive" South by developing its material resources and introducing Yankee institutions such as free labor and free public schools. Most were veterans of the Union Army who stayed in the South after the war. Others included Freedmen's Bureau agents and businessmen who had invested capital in cotton plantations and other economic enterprises. Although they made up a tiny percentage of the population, carpetbaggers played a disproportionately large role in southern politics. They won a large share of Reconstruction offices, particularly in Florida, South Carolina, and Louisiana and in areas with large African American constituencies.

The third major group of southern Republicans comprised native whites perjoratively called *scalawags.* They had more diverse backgrounds and motives than the northern-born Republicans. Loyalists during the war, traditional enemies of the planter elite (most were small farmers), these white southerners looked to the Republican party for help in settling old scores and relief from debt and wartime devastation.

Deep contradictions strained the alliance of these three groups. Republican state conventions in 1867 and 1868 voiced support for internal improvements, public schools, debt relief, and railroad building. Yet few white southerners identified with the political and economic aspirations of African Americans. Nearly every party convention split between "confiscation radicals" (generally African Americans) and moderate elements committed to white control of the party and to economic development that offered more to outside investors than to impoverished African Americans and poor whites.

Reconstructing the States: A Mixed Record

With the old Confederate leaders barred from political participation, and with carpetbaggers and newly enfranchised African Americans representing many of the plantation districts, Republicans managed to dominate the

This poster, ca. 1880, honored seven prominent ex-slaves, including U.S. Senators Hiram R. Revels and Blanche K. Bruce, both representing Mississippi. In the center is Frederick Douglass. This poster was typical of many other Reconstruction-era prints celebrating the entry of African Americans into states and national legislatures.

ten southern constitutional conventions of 1867–69. Most of these conventions produced constitutions that expanded democracy and the public role of the state. The new documents guaranteed the political and civil rights of African Americans, and they abolished property qualifications for officeholding and jury service, as well as imprisonment for debt. They created the first state-funded systems of education in the South, to be administered by state commissioners. The new constitutions also mandated establishment of orphanages, penitentiaries, and homes for the insane. In 1868, only three years after the end of the war, Republicans came to power in most of the southern states. By 1869 new constitutions had been ratified in all the old Confederate states. "These constitutions and governments," one South Carolina Democratic newspaper vowed bitterly, "will last just as long as the bayonets which ushered them into being, shall keep them in existence, and not one day longer."

Republican governments in the South faced a continual crisis of legitimacy that limited their ability to legislate change. They had to balance reform urges against ongoing efforts to gain acceptance, especially by white southerners. Their achievements were thus mixed. In the realm of race relations there was a clear thrust toward equal rights and against discrimination. Republican legislatures followed up the federal Civil Rights Act of 1866 with various antidiscrimination clauses in new constitutions and laws prescribing harsh penalties for civil rights violations. African Americans could now be employed in police forces and fire departments, serve on juries, school boards, and city councils, and hold public office at all levels of government.

However, segregation became the norm in public school systems. African American leaders often accepted segregation because they feared that insistence on integrated education would jeopardize funding for the new school systems. African Americans opposed constitutional language requiring racial segregation in schools, but most were less interested in the abstract ideal of integrated education than in ensuring educational opportunities for their children and employment for African American teachers.

Segregation in railroad cars and other public places was more objectionable to African Americans. By the early 1870s, as black influence and assertiveness grew, laws guaranteeing equal access to transportation and public accommodation were passed in many states. By and large, though, such civil rights laws were difficult to enforce in local communities.

In economic matters, Republican governments failed to fulfill African Americans' hopes of obtaining land. Few former slaves had the cash to buy land in the open market, so they looked to the state for help. Republicans tried to weaken the plantation system and promote black ownership by raising taxes on land. Yet even when state governments seized land for nonpayment of taxes, the property was never used to create black homesteads.

Republican leaders envisioned promoting northern-style capitalist development—factories, large towns, and diversified agriculture—in the South through state aid. Much Republican state lawmaking was devoted to encouraging railroad construction. Between 1868 and 1872 the southern railroad system was rebuilt and over 3,000 new miles of track added, an increase of almost 40 percent. But despite all the new laws, it proved impossible to attract significant amounts of northern and European investment capital. The obsession with railroads drew resources from education and other programs. As in the North, it also opened the doors to widespread corruption and bribery of public officials. Railroad failures eroded public confidence in the Republicans' ability to govern. The "gospel of prosperity" ultimately failed to modernize the economy or solidify the Republican party in the South.

White Resistance and "Redemption"

The emergence of a Republican Party in the reconstructed South brought two parties but not a two-party system. The opponents of Reconstruction, the Democrats, refused to acknowledge Republicans' right to participate in southern political life. In these southern Democrats' view, the Republican party was the partisan instrument of the northern Congress, and its support was based primarily upon the votes of former slaves. Because Republicans controlled state governments, this denial of legitimacy meant, in effect, a rejection of state authority itself.

From 1870 to 1872 a resurgent Ku Klux Klan fought an ongoing terrorist campaign against Reconstruction governments and local leaders. Although not centrally organized, the Klan was a powerful presence in nearly every southern state. It acted as a kind of guerrilla military force in the service of the Democratic party, the planter class, and all those who sought the restoration of white supremacy. In October 1870, after Republicans carried Laurens County in South Carolina, bands of white people drove 150 African Americans from their homes and committed 13 murders. The victims included both black and white Republican activists. In March 1871 three African Americans were arrested

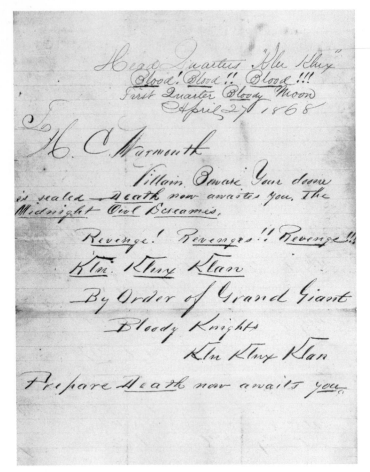

The Ku Klux Klan emerged as a potent political and social force during Reconstruction, terrorizing freepeople and their white allies. An 1868 Klan warning threatens Louisiana governor Henry C. Warmoth with death. Warmoth, an Illinois-born "carpetbagger," was the state's first Republican governor. Two Alabama Klansmen, photographed in 1868, wear white hoods to conceal their identities.

in Meridian, Mississippi, for giving "incendiary" speeches. At their court hearing, Klansmen killed two of the defendants and the Republican judge; thirty more African Americans were murdered in a day of rioting. The single bloodiest episode of Reconstruction era violence took place in Colfax, Louisiana, on Easter Sunday 1873. Nearly 100 African Americans were murdered during a contested election.

Southern Republicans looked to Washington for help. In 1870 and 1871 Congress passed three Enforcement Acts designed to counter racial terrorism. These declared interference with voting a federal offense, provided for federal supervision of voting, and authorized the president to send the army and suspend the writ of habeas corpus in districts declared to be in a state of insurrection. The most sweeping measure was the Ku Klux Klan Act of April 1871, which made the violent infringement of civil and political rights a federal crime punishable by the national government. Attorney General Amos T. Akerman prosecuted hundreds of Klansmen in North Carolina and Mississippi. In October 1871 President Grant sent federal troops to occupy nine South Carolina counties and round up thousands of Klan members. By the election of 1872 the federal government's intervention had helped break the Klan's hold and restored relative law and order.

As wartime idealism faded, however, northern Republicans had too much trouble retaining political control in the North to intervene in the South. In 1874 the Democrats gained a majority in the House of Representatives for the first time since 1856. Key northern states also began to fall to the Democrats. Northern Republicans slowly abandoned the freedmen and their white allies in the South.

Gradually, conservative Democrats "redeemed" one state after another. Virginia led the way in 1869, followed by Alabama and North Carolina in 1870, Georgia in 1871, Texas in 1873, and Arkansas in 1874. In Mississippi white conservatives used violence and intimidation to wrest control in 1875 and "redeemed" the state the following year. Republican infighting in Louisiana in 1873 and 1874 led to a series of contested election results, including bloody clashes between black militia and armed whites, and finally to "redemption" by the Democrats in 1877. Once these states returned to Democratic control, African Americans faced obstacles to voting, more stringent controls on plantation labor, and deep cuts in social services.

Several Supreme Court rulings involving the Fourteenth and Fifteenth Amendments effectively constrained federal protection of African American civil rights. In the so-called Slaughterhouse cases of 1873, the Court issued its first ruling on the Fourteenth Amendment. The cases involved a Louisiana charter that gave a New Orleans meat-packing company a monopoly over the city's butchering business, on the grounds of protecting public health. A rival group of butchers had sued, claiming the law violated the Fourteenth Amendment, which prohibited states from depriving any person of life, liberty, or property without due process of law. The Court held that the Fourteenth Amendment protected only the former slaves, not butchers, and that it protected only *national* citizenship rights, not the regulatory powers of states. The ruling in effect denied the original intent of the Fourteenth Amendment: to protect against state infringement of national citizenship rights as spelled out in the Bill of Rights.

Three other decisions curtailed federal protection of black civil rights. In *U.S.* v. *Reese* (1876) and *U.S.* v. *Cruikshank* (1876) the Court restricted congressional power to enforce the Ku Klux Klan Act by holding that the Fourteenth Amendment extended the federal power to protect civil rights only in cases involving discrimination by states; discrimination by individuals or groups was not covered. The Court also ruled that the Fifteenth Amendment did not guarantee a citizen's right to vote; it only barred certain specific grounds for denying suffrage: "race, color, or previous condition of servi-

tude." This opened the door for southern states to disfranchise African Americans for allegedly nonracial reasons. States back under Democratic control began to limit African American voting by passing laws restricting voter eligibility through poll taxes and property requirements. "Grandfather clauses," which restricted voting to those descended from a grandfather who had voted, became an effective tool for limiting black suffrage, because most African Americans had been slaves before Reconstruction. Finally, in the 1883 *Civil Rights Cases* decision, the Court declared the Civil Rights Act of 1875 unconstitutional, holding that the federal government had no power to protect social, as opposed to political, rights. Together, these Supreme Court decisions marked the end of federal attempts to protect African American rights until well into the next century.

King Cotton and the Crop Lien System

The Republicans' vision of a "New South" remade along the lines of the northern economy failed to materialize. Instead, the South declined into the country's poorest agricultural region. Cotton growing had defined the economic life of the large plantations. In the post–Civil War years King Cotton expanded its realm, as even greater numbers of small white farmers were forced to switch from substance crops to growing cotton for market.

The spread of the crop lien system as the South's main form of agricultural credit forced more and more farmers, both white and black, into cotton growing. A chronic shortage of capital and banking institutions made local merchants and planters the sole source of credit. They advanced loans to sharecroppers and tenant farmers only in exchange for a lien, or claim, on the year's cotton crop, and often charged usurious interest rates on advances, while marking up the prices of the goods they sold in their stores. Thus at the end of the year, sharecroppers and tenants found themselves deep in debt to stores (many owned by northerners) for seed, supplies, and clothing.

The near total dominance of King Cotton inhibited economic growth across the region. Unlike midwestern and western farm towns burgeoning from trade in wheat, corn, and livestock, southern communities found themselves almost entirely dependent on the price of one commodity as more and more farmers turned to cotton growing as the only way to obtain credit. Expanding production depressed prices. Competition from new cotton centers in the world market, such as Egypt and India, furthered the downward spiral. As cotton

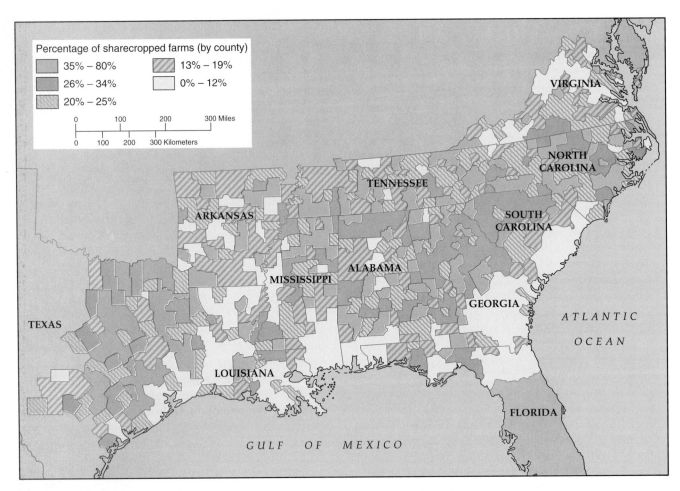

Southern Sharecropping, 1880

The economic depression of the 1870s forced increasing numbers of southern farmers, both white and black, into sharecropping arrangements. Sharecropping was most pervasive in the cotton belt regions of South Carolina, Georgia, Alabama, Mississippi, and east Texas.

prices declined alarmingly, from roughly eleven cents per pound in 1875 to five cents in 1894, per capita wealth in the South fell steadily; by the 1890s it equaled only one-third that of the East, Midwest, or West. Cotton dependency also prevented planters from acquiring the capital to purchase the farm equipment needed to profitably cultivate wheat or corn.

By 1880 about one-third of white farmers and nearly three-quarters of African American farmers in the cotton states were sharecroppers or tenants. Many former slaves and poor white people had tried subsistence farming in the undeveloped backcountry. Yet to obtain precious credit, most found themselves forced to produce cotton for market and thus became enmeshed in the debt-ridden crop lien system. A cotton-dominated commercial agriculture, with landless tenants and sharecroppers as the main work force, had replaced the more diversified subsistence economy of the antebellum era.

Reconstructing the North

Abraham Lincoln liked to cite his own rise as proof of the superiority of the northern system of free labor over slavery. But the triumph of the North in the war brought with it fundamental changes in the economy, labor relations, and politics that called Lincoln's ideal vision into question. The spread of the factory system, the growth of large and powerful corporations, and the rapid expansion of capitalist enterprise all hastened the development of a large unskilled and routinized work force. Rather than becoming independent producers, more and more workers found themselves consigned to a permanent position of wage labor.

The old Republican ideal of a society bound by a harmony of interests had become overshadowed by a grimmer reality of class conflict. A violent national railroad strike in 1877 was broken only with the direct intervention of federal troops. Northern society, like the society of the South, appeared more hierarchical than equal. That same year, the last federal troops withdrew from their southern posts, marking the end of the Reconstruction era. By then, the North had undergone its own reconstruction.

The Age of Capital

In the decade following Appomattox, the North's economy continued the industrial boom begun during the Civil War. By 1873 America's industrial production had grown 75 percent over the 1865 level. By that time, too, the number of nonagricultural workers in the North had surpassed the number of farmers. Between 1860 and 1880 the number of wage earners in manufacturing and construction more than doubled, from 2 million to over 4 million.

The railroad business both symbolized and advanced the new industrial order. Shortly before the Civil War, enthusiasm mounted for a transcontinental line. Private companies took on the huge and expensive job of construction. The federal government funded the project, providing the largest subsidy in American history. An 1864 act bestowed a subsidy of $15,000 per mile of track laid over smooth plains country and varying larger amounts, up to $48,000 per mile, in the foothills and mountains of the Far West. Gangs of Irish American and African American workers were employed to lay track heading west from Omaha, while 10,000 men from China were brought in to handle the difficult

Completion of the transcontinetal railroad, May 10, 1869, as building crews for the Union Pacific and Central Pacific meet at Promontory Point, Utah. The two locomotive engineers exchange champagne toasts, while the chief engineers for the two railroads shake hands. Construction had begun simultaneously from Omaha and Sacramento in 1863, with the help of generous subsidies from the Congress. Work crews, consisting of thousands of ex-soldiers, Irish immigrants, and imported Chinese laborers, laid nearly 1,800 miles of new track.

work in the Sierra Nevada mountain region. On May 10, 1864, the governor of California, Leland Stanford, traveled to Promontory Point, Utah, to hammer a ceremonial golden spike, marking the finish of the first transcontinental line.

Railroad corporations became America's first big businesses. Railroads required huge outlays of investment capital, and their growth increased the economic power of banks and investment houses centered in Wall Street. Bankers often gained seats on boards of directors, and their access to capital sometimes gave them the real control of lines. A new breed of aggressive entrepreneur sought to ease cutthroat competition by absorbing smaller companies and forming "pools" that set rates and divided the market. A small group of railroad executives, including Cornelius Vanderbilt, Jay Gould, Collis P. Huntington, and James J. Hill, amassed unheard-of fortunes. When he died in 1877, Vanderbilt left his son $100 million. By comparison, a decent annual wage for working a six-day week was around $350.

Railroad promoters, lawyers, and lobbyists became ubiquitous figures in Washington and state capitals, wielding enormous influence among lawmakers. Railroads benefited greatly from government subsidies. Between 1862 and 1872 Congress awarded over 100 million acres of public lands to railroad companies and provided over $64 million in loans and tax incentives.

Some of the nation's most prominent politicians routinely accepted railroad largesse. The worst scandal of the Grant administration grew out of corruption involving railroad promotion. As a way of diverting funds for the building of the Union Pacific Railroad, an inner circle of Union Pacific stockholders created the dummy Crédit Mobilier construction company. In return for political favors, a group of prominent Republicans received stock in the company. When the scandal broke in 1872, it ruined Vice President Schuyler Colfax politically and led to the censure of two congressmen.

Other industries also boomed in this period as railroad growth stimulated expansion in the production of coal, iron, stone, and lumber. These industries also received significant government aid. For example, under the National Mineral Act of 1866, mining companies received millions of acres of free public land. Oil refining enjoyed a huge expansion in the 1860s and 1870s. As with railroads, an early period of fierce competition soon gave way to concentration. By the late 1870s John D. Rockefeller's Standard Oil Company controlled almost 90 percent of the nation's oil-refining capacity.

Liberal Republicans and the Election of 1872

With the rapid growth of large-scale, capital-intensive enterprises, Republicans increasingly identified with the interests of business rather than the rights of freedmen or the antebellum ideology of "free labor." The old Civil War–era Radicals had declined in influence. State Republican parties now organized themselves around the spoils of federal patronage rather than grand causes such as preserving the Union or ending slavery. Despite the Crédit Mobilier affair, Republicans had no monopoly on political scandal. In 1871 New York City newspapers reported the shocking story of how Democratic party boss William M. Tweed and his friends had systematically stolen millions of dollars from the city treasury. The Tweed Ring had received enormous bribes and kickbacks from city contractors and businessmen. But to many, the scandal represented only the most extreme case of the routine corruption that now plagued American political life.

By the end of President Grant's first term, a large number of disaffected Republicans sought an alternative. The Liberal Republicans, as they called themselves, emphasized the doctrines of classical economics, stressing the law of supply and demand, free trade, defense of property rights, and individualism. They called for a return to limited government, arguing that bribery, scandal, and high taxes all flowed from excessive state interference in the economy.

Liberal Republicans were also suspicious of expanding democracy. They believed that politics ought to be the province of "the best men"—educated and well-to-do men like themselves, devoted to the "science of government." They proposed civil service reform as the best way to break the hold of party machines on patronage.

Although most Liberal Republicans had enthusiastically supported abolition, the Union cause, and equal rights for freedmen, they now opposed continued federal intervention in the South. The national government had done all it could for the former slaves; they must now take care of themselves. "Root, Hog, or Die" was the harsh advice offered by Horace Greeley, editor of the *New York Tribune*. In the spring of 1872 a diverse collection of Liberal Republicans nominated Greeley to run for president. A longtime foe of the Democratic party, Greeley nonetheless won that party's presidential nomination as well. He made a new policy for the South the center of his campaign against Grant. All Americans, Greeley urged, must put the Civil War behind them and "clasp hands across the bloody chasm."

Grant easily defeated Greeley, carrying every state in the North and winning 56 percent of the popular vote. Most Republicans were not willing to abandon the regular party organization, and waving the bloody shirt was still a potent vote getter. But the 1872 election accelerated the trend toward federal abandonment of African American citizenship rights. The Liberal Republicans quickly faded as an organized political force, but their ideas helped define an increasingly popular conservative agenda in the North. This agenda included retreat from the ideal of racial justice, fear of trade unions, suspicion of working-class and immigrant political power, celebration of competitive individualism, and opposition to government intervention in economic affairs.

The Depression of 1873

In the fall of 1873 the postwar boom came to an abrupt halt as a severe financial panic triggered a deep economic depression. The collapse resulted from commercial overexpansion, especially speculative investing in the nation's railroad system. By 1876 half the nation's railroads had defaulted on their bonds. Over the next two years over 100 banks folded and 18,000 businesses shut their doors. The depression that began in 1873 lasted 65 months—the longest economic contraction in the nation's history.

The human toll of the depression was enormous. As factories closed across the nation, the unemployment rate soared to about 15 percent. In many cities the jobless rate was much higher; roughly one-quarter of New York City workers were unemployed in 1874. Many thousands of men took to the road in search of work, and the "tramp" emerged as a new and menacing figure on the social landscape. The Pennsylvania Bureau of Labor Statistics noted that never before had "so many of the working classes, skilled and unskilled . . . been moving from place to place seeking employment that was not to be had." Farmers were also hard hit by the depression. Agricultural output continued to grow, but prices and land values fell sharply. As prices for their crops fell, farmers had a more difficult time repaying their fixed loan obligations; many sank deeper into debt.

Mass meetings of workers in New York and other cities issued calls to government officials to create jobs through public works. But these appeals were rejected. Indeed, many business leaders and political figures denounced even meager efforts at charity. They saw the depression as a natural, if painful, part of the business cycle, one that would allow only the strongest enterprises (and workers) to survive.

The depression of the 1870s prompted workers and farmers to question the old free-labor ideology that celebrated a harmony of interests in northern society. More people voiced anger at and distrust of large corporations that exercised great economic power from outside their communities.

The Electoral Crisis of 1876

With the economy mired in depression, Democrats looked forward to capturing the White House in 1876. New scandals plaguing the Grant administration had weakened the Republican party. In 1875 there surfaced a conspiracy between distillers and U.S. revenue agents to cheat the government out of millions in tax revenues. The government secured indictments against over 200 members of this "Whiskey Ring," including Orville E. Babcock, Grant's private secretary. Though acquitted thanks to Grant's deposition, Babcock resigned in disgrace. In 1876 Secretary of War William W. Belknap was impeached for receiving bribes for the sale of trading posts in Indian Territory.

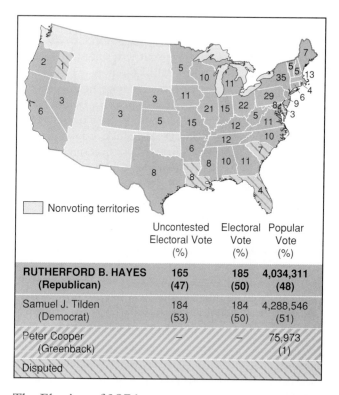

	Uncontested Electoral Vote (%)	Electoral Vote (%)	Popular Vote (%)
RUTHERFORD B. HAYES (Republican)	**165 (47)**	**185 (50)**	**4,034,311 (48)**
Samuel J. Tilden (Democrat)	184 (53)	184 (50)	4,288,546 (51)
Peter Cooper (Greenback)	–	–	75,973 (1)
Disputed			

The Election of 1876

The presidential election of 1876 left the nation without a clear-cut winner.

Democrats nominated Governor Samuel J. Tilden of New York, who brought impeccable reform credentials to his candidacy for president. In 1871 he had helped expose and prosecute the Tweed Ring in New York City. As governor he had toppled the Canal Ring, a graft-ridden scheme involving inflated contracts for repairs on the Erie Canal. In their platform the Democrats linked the issue of corruption to Republican Reconstruction policies that had encouraged "a corrupt centralism."

Republican nominee Rutherford B. Hayes, governor of Ohio, also sought the high ground. As a lawyer in Cincinnati he had defended runaway slaves. Later he had distinguished himself as a general in the Union Army. Hayes promised, if elected, to support an efficient civil service system, to vigorously prosecute officials who betrayed the public trust, and to introduce a system of free universal education.

On an election day marred by widespread vote fraud and violent intimidation, Tilden received 250,000 more popular votes than Hayes. But Republicans refused to concede victory, challenging the vote totals in the electoral college. Tilden garnered 184 uncontested electoral votes, one shy of the majority required to win, while Hayes received 165. The problem centered in 20 disputed votes from Florida, Louisiana, South Carolina, and Oregon. In each of the three southern states, two sets of electoral votes were returned. In Oregon, which Hayes had unquestionably carried, the Democratic governor illegally replaced a Republican elector with a Democrat.

The crisis was unprecedented. In January 1877 Congress moved to settle the deadlock, establishing an Electoral Commission composed of five senators, five representatives, and five Supreme Court justices; eight were Republicans and seven were Democrats. The commission voted along strict partisan lines to award all the contested electoral votes to Hayes. Outraged by this decision, Democratic congressmen threatened a filibuster to block Hayes's inauguration. Violence and stalemate were avoided when Democrats and Republicans struck a compromise in February. In return for Hayes's ascendance to the presidency, the Republicans promised to appropriate more money for southern internal improvements, to appoint a southerner to Hayes's cabinet, and to pursue a policy of noninterference ("home rule") in southern affairs.

Shortly after assuming office, Hayes ordered removal of the remaining federal troops in Louisiana and South Carolina. Without this military presence to sustain them, the Republican governors of those two states quickly lost power to Democrats. "Home rule" meant Republican abandonment of freedpeople, Radicals, carpetbaggers, and scalawags. It also effectively nullified the Fourteenth and Fifteenth Amendments and the Civil Rights Act of 1866. The Compromise of 1877 completed repudiation of the idea, born during the Civil War and pursued during congressional Reconstruction, of a powerful federal government protecting the rights of all American citizens.

Conclusion

Reconstruction succeeded in the limited political sense of reuniting a nation torn apart by civil war. But the freedpeople's political and civil equality proved only temporary. The Radical Republicans' vision of racial justice, equal civil and political rights guaranteed by the Fourteenth and Fifteen Amendments, and a new Southern economy organized around independent small farmers never enjoyed the support of the majority of the party or the northern public. The federal government's failure to pursue land reform left former slaves without the economic independence needed for full emancipation. Yet the newly autonomous black family, along with black-controlled churches, schools, and other social institutions, provided the foundations for the modern African American community.

Even as the federal government retreated from the defense of equal rights for black people, it took a more aggressive stance as the protector of business interests. The Hayes administration responded decisively to one of the worst outbreaks of class violence in American history by dispatching federal troops to several northern cities to break the Great Railroad Strike of 1877. In the aftermath of Reconstruction, the struggle between capital and labor had clearly replaced "the southern question" as the number one political issue of the day.

CHRONOLOGY

1865 Freedman's Bureau established

Abraham Lincoln assassinated

Andrew Johnson begins Presidential Reconstruction

Black Codes begin to be enacted in southern states

Thirteenth Amendment ratified

1866 Civil Rights Act passed

Congress approves Fourteenth Amendment

Ku Klux Klan founded

1867 Reconstruction Acts, passed over President Johnson's veto, begin Congressional Reconstruction

Tenure of Office Act

Southern states call constitutional conventions

1868 President Johnson impeached by the House, but acquitted in Senate trial

Fourteenth Amendment ratified

Most southern states readmitted to Union

Ulysses S. Grant elected president

1869 Congress approves Fifteenth Amendment

Union Pacific and Central Pacific tracks meet at Promontory Point in Utah Territory

Suffragists split into National Woman Suffrage Association and American Woman Suffrage Association

1870 Fifteenth Amendment ratified

1871 Ku Klux Klan Act passed

Tweed Ring in New York City exposed

1872 Liberal Republicans break with Grant and Radicals, nominate Horace Greeley for president

Crédit Mobilier scandal

Grant reelected president

1873 Financial panic and beginning of economic depression

Slaughterhouse cases

1874 Democrats gain control of House for first time since 1856

1875 Civil Rights Act

1876 Disputed election between Samuel Tilden and Rutherford Hayes

1877 Electoral Commission elects Hayes president

Hayes dispatches federal troops to break Great Railroad Strike and withdraw last remaining federal troops from the South

Review Questions

1. How did various visions of a "reconstructed" South differ? How did these visions reflect the old political and social divisions that had led to the Civil War?

2. What key changes did emancipation make in the political and economic status of African Americans? Discuss the expansion of citizenship rights in the post–Civil War years. To what extent did women share in the gains made by African Americans?

3. What role did such institutions as the family, the church, schools, and political parties play in the African American transition to freedom?

4. How did white southerners attempt to limit the freedom of former slaves? How did these efforts succeed, and how did they fail?

5. Evaluate the achievements and failures of Reconstruction governments in the southern states.

6. What were the crucial economic changes occurring in the North and South during the Reconstruction era?

Recommended Reading

MICHAEL W. FITZGERALD, *The Union League Movement in the Deep South* (1989). Uses the Union League as a lens through which to examine race relations and the close connections between politics and economic change in the post–Civil War South.

ERIC FONER, *Reconstruction: America's Unfinished Revolution, 1863–1877* (1988). The most comprehensive and thoroughly researched overview of the Reconstruction era.

WILLIAM GILLETTE, *Retreat from Reconstruction: A Political History, 1867–1878* (1979). Covers the national political scene, with special attention to the abandonment of the ideal of racial equality.

JACQUELINE JONES, *Labor of Love, Labor of Sorrow* (1985). Includes excellent material on the work and family lives of African American women in slavery and freedom.

LEON LITWACK, *Been in the Storm So Long: The Aftermath of Slavery* (1979). A richly detailed analysis of the transition from slavery to freedom; excellent use of African American sources.

MICHAEL PERMAN, *Emancipation and Reconstruction, 1862–1879* (1987). A short but very useful overview of Reconstruction, emphasizing racial issues and the end of slavery.

EDWARD ROYCE, *The Origins of Southern Sharecropping* (1993). A sophisticated, tightly argued work of historical sociology that explains how sharecropping emerged as the dominant form of agricultural labor in the post–Civil War South.

MARK W. SUMMERS, *Railroads, Reconstruction, and the Gospel of Prosperity* (1984). The best study of the economic and political importance of railroad building in this era.

ALLEN W. TRELEASE, *White Terror: The Ku Klux Klan Conspiracy and Southern Reconstruction* (1971). The most complete account of Klan activity and the efforts to suppress it.

APPENDIX

The Declaration of Independence

When in the course of human events it becomes necessary for one people to dissolve the political bands which have connected them with another and to assume, among the powers of the earth, the separate and equal station to which the laws of nature and of nature's God entitle them, a decent respect to the opinions of mankind requires that they should declare the causes which impel them to the separation.

We hold these truths to be self-evident, that all men are created equal; that they are endowed by their Creator with certain unalienable rights; that among these are life, liberty, and the pursuit of happiness. That, to secure these rights, governments are instituted among men, deriving their just powers from the consent of the governed; that, whenever any form of government becomes destructive of these ends, it is the right of the people to alter or to abolish it, and to institute a new government, laying its foundation on such principles, and organizing its powers in such form, as to them shall seem most likely to effect their safety and happiness. Prudence, indeed, will dictate that governments long established should not be changed for light and transient causes; and, accordingly, all experience hath shown that mankind are more disposed to suffer, while evils are sufferable, than to right themselves by abolishing the forms to which they are accustomed. But when a long train of abuses and usurpations, pursuing invariably the same object, evinces a design to reduce them under absolute despotism, it is their right, it is their duty, to throw off such government and to provide new guards for their future security. Such has been the patient sufferance of these colonies, and such is now the necessity which constrains them to alter their former systems of government. The history of the present King of Great Britain is a history of repeated injuries and usurpations, all having, in direct object, the establishment of an absolute tyranny over these States. To prove this, let facts be submitted to a candid world:

He has refused his assent to laws the most wholesome and necessary for the public good.

He has forbidden his governors to pass laws of immediate and pressing importance, unless suspended in their operation till his assent should be obtained; and, when so suspended, he has utterly neglected to attend to them.

He has refused to pass other laws for the accommodation of large districts of people, unless those people would relinquish the right of representation in the legislature; a right inestimable to them and formidable to tyrants only.

He has called together legislative bodies at places unusual, uncomfortable, and distant from the depository of their public records, for the sole purpose of fatiguing them into compliance with his measures.

He has dissolved representative houses, repeatedly for opposing, with manly firmness, his invasions on the rights of the people.

He has refused, for a long time after such dissolutions, to cause others to be elected; whereby the legislative powers, incapable of annihilation, have returned to the people at large for their exercise; the state remaining, in the meantime, exposed to all the danger of invasion from without and convulsions within.

He has endeavored to prevent the population of these States; for that purpose, obstructing the laws for naturalization of foreigners, refusing to pass others to encourage their migration hither, and raising the conditions of new appropriations of lands.

He has obstructed the administration of justice by refusing his assent to laws for establishing judiciary powers.

He has made judges dependent on his will alone for the tenure of their offices and the amount and payment of their salaries.

He has erected a multitude of new offices and sent hither swarms of officers to harass our people and eat out their substance.

He has kept among us, in time of peace, standing armies, without the consent of our legislatures.

He has affected to render the military independent of, and superior to, the civil power.

He has combined with others to subject us to a jurisdiction foreign to our Constitution and unacknowledged by our laws, giving his assent to their acts of pretended legislation—

For quartering large bodies of armed troops among us;

For protecting them by a mock trial from punishment for any murders which they should commit on the inhabitants of these States;

For cutting off our trade with all parts of the world;

For imposing taxes on us without our consent;

For depriving us, in many cases, of the benefit of trial by jury;

For transporting us beyond seas to be tried for pretended offences;

For abolishing the free system of English laws in a neighboring province, establishing therein an arbitrary government, and enlarging its boundaries, so as to render it at once an example and fit instrument for introducing the same absolute rule into these colonies;

For taking away our charters, abolishing our most valuable laws, and altering, fundamentally, the powers of our governments;

For suspending our own legislatures and declaring themselves invested with power to legislate for us in all cases whatsoever.

He has abdicated government here by declaring us out of his protection and waging war against us.

He has plundered our seas, ravaged our coasts, burnt our towns, and destroyed the lives of our people.

He is, at this time, transporting large armies of foreign mercenaries to complete the works of death, desolation, and tyranny already begun with circumstances of cruelty and perfidy scarcely paralleled in the most barbarous ages, and totally unworthy the head of a civilized nation.

He has constrained our fellow citizens, taken captive on the high seas, to bear arms against their country, to become the executioners of their friends and brethren, or to fall themselves by their hands.

He has excited domestic insurrections amongst us and has endeavored to bring on the inhabitants of our frontiers, the merciless Indian savages, whose known rule of warfare is an undistinguished destruction of all ages, sexes, and conditions.

In every stage of these oppressions, we have petitioned for redress in the most humble terms; our repeated petitions have been answered only by repeated injury. A prince whose character is thus marked by every act which may define a tyrant is unfit to be the ruler of a free people.

Nor have we been wanting in attention to our British brethren. We have warned them, from time to time, of attempts made by their legislature to extend an unwarrantable jurisdiction over us. We have reminded them of the circumstances of our emigra-

tion and settlement here. We have appealed to their native justice and magnanimity, and we have conjured them, by the ties of our common kindred, to disavow these usurpations, which would inevitably interrupt our connections and correspondence. They, too, have been deaf to the voice of justice and consanguinity. We must, therefore, acquiesce in the necessity which denounces our separation, and hold them, as we hold the rest of mankind, enemies in war, in peace, friends.

We, therefore, the representatives of the United States of America, in general Congress assembled, appealing to the Supreme Judge of the world for the rectitude of our intentions, do, in the name and by the authority of the good people of these colonies, solemnly publish and declare, that these united colonies are, and of right ought to be, free and independent states: that they are absolved from all allegiance to the British Crown, and that all political connection between them and the state of Great Britain is, and ought to be, totally dissolved; and that, as free and independent states, they have full power to levy war, conclude peace, contract alliances, establish commerce, and to do all other acts and things which independent states may of right do. And, for the support of this declaration, with a firm reliance on the protection of Divine Providence, we mutually pledge to each other our lives, our fortunes, and our sacred honor.

The foregoing Declaration was, by order of Congress, engrossed, and signed by the following members:

John Hancock

New Hampshire
Josiah Bartlett
William Whipple
Matthew Thornton

Connecticut
Roger Sherman
Samuel Huntington
William Williams
Oliver Wolcott

New York
William Floyd
Philip Livingston
Francis Lewis
Lewis Morris

New Jersey
Richard Stockton
John Witherspoon
Francis Hopkinson
John Hart
Abraham Clark

Massachusetts Bay
Samuel Adams
John Adams
Robert Treat Paine
Elbridge Gerry

Pennsylvania
Robert Morris
Benjamin Rush
Benjamin Franklin
John Morton
George Clymer
James Smith
George Taylor
James Wilson
George Ross

Delaware
Caesar Rodney
George Read
Thomas M'Kean

Maryland
Samuel Chase
William Paca
Thomas Stone
Charles Carroll,
  of Carrollton

Rhode Island
Stephen Hopkins
William Ellery

Virginia
George Wythe
Richard Henry Lee
Thomas Jefferson
Benjamin Harrison
Thomas Nelson, Jr.
Francis Lightfoot Lee
Carter Braxton

North Carolina
William Hooper
Joseph Hewes
John Penn

South Carolina
Edward Rutledge
Thomas Heyward, Jr.
Thomas Lynch, Jr.
Arthur Middleton

Georgia
Button Gwinnett
Lyman Hall
George Walton

The Constitution of the United States of America

We the people of the United States, in order to form a more perfect union, establish justice, insure domestic tranquillity, provide for the common defense, promote the general welfare, and secure the blessings of liberty to ourselves and our posterity, do ordain and establish this Constitution for the United States of America.

Article I

Section 1. All legislative powers herein granted shall be vested in a Congress of the United States, which shall consist of a Senate and House of Representatives.

Section 2. 1. The House of Representatives shall be composed of members chosen every second year by the people of the several States, and the electors in each State shall have the qualifications requisite for electors of the most numerous branch of the State legislature.

2. No person shall be a representative who shall not have attained to the age of twenty-five years, and been seven years a citizen of the United States, and who shall not, when elected, be an inhabitant of that State in which he shall be chosen.

3. Representatives and direct taxes[1] shall be apportioned among the several States which may be included within this Union, according to their respective numbers, which shall be determined by adding to the whole number of free persons, including those bound to service for a term of years, and excluding Indians not taxed, three fifths of all other persons.[2] The actual enumeration shall be made within three years after the first meeting of the Congress of the United States, and within every subsequent term of ten years, in such manner as they shall by law direct. The number of representatives shall not exceed one for every thirty thousand, but each State shall have at least one representative; and until such enumeration shall be made, the State of New Hampshire shall be entitled to choose three, Massachusetts eight, Rhode Island and Providence Plantations one, Connecticut five, New York six, New Jersey four, Pennsylvania eight, Delaware one, Maryland six, Virginia ten, North Carolina five, South Carolina five, and Georgia three.

4. When vacancies happen in the representation from any State, the executive authority thereof shall issue writs of election to fill such vacancies.

5. The House of Representatives shall choose their speaker and other officers; and shall have the sole power of impeachment.

Section 3. 1. The Senate of the United States shall be composed of two senators from each State, chosen by the legislature thereof,[3] for six years; and each senator shall have one vote.

2. Immediately after they shall be assembled in consequence of the first election, they shall be divided as equally as may be into three classes. The seats of the senators of the first class shall be vacated at the expiration of the second year, of the second class at the expiration of the fourth year, and of the third class at the expiration of the sixth year, so that one third may be chosen every second year; and if vacancies happen by resignation, or otherwise, during the recess of the legislature of any State, the executive thereof may make temporary appointments until the next meeting of the legislature, which shall then fill such vacancies.[4]

[1]See the Sixteenth Amendment.
[2]See the Fourteenth Amendment.
[3]See the Seventeenth Amendment.
[4]See the Seventeenth Amendment.

3. No person shall be a senator who shall not have attained to the age of thirty years, and been nine years a citizen of the United States, and who shall not, when elected, be an inhabitant of that State for which he shall be chosen.

4. The Vice President of the United States shall be President of the Senate, but shall have no vote, unless they be equally divided.

5. The Senate shall choose their other officers, and also a president pro tempore, in the absence of the Vice President, or when he shall exercise the office of the President of the United States.

6. The Senate shall have the sole power to try all impeachments. When sitting for that purpose, they shall be on oath or affirmation. When the President of the United States is tried, the chief justice shall preside: and no person shall be convicted without the concurrence of two thirds of the members present.

7. Judgment in cases of impeachment shall not extend further than to removal from office, and disqualification to hold and enjoy any office of honor, trust or profit under the United States: but the party convicted shall nevertheless be liable and subject to indictment, trial, judgment and punishment, according to law.

Section 4. 1. The times, places, and manner of holding elections for senators and representatives, shall be prescribed in each State by the legislature thereof; but the Congress may at any time by law make or alter such regulations, except as to the places of choosing senators.

2. The Congress shall assemble at least once in every year, and such meeting shall be on the first Monday in December, unless they shall by law appoint a different day.

Section 5. 1. Each House shall be the judge of the elections, returns and qualifications of its own members, and a majority of each shall constitute a quorum to do business; but a smaller number may adjourn from day to day, and may be authorized to compel the attendance of absent members, in such manner, and under such penalties as each House may provide.

2. Each House may determine the rules of its proceedings, punish its members for disorderly behavior, and, with the concurrence of two thirds, expel a member.

3. Each House shall keep a journal of its proceedings, and from time to time publish the same, excepting such parts as may in their judgment require secrecy; and the yeas and nays of the members of either House on any question shall, at the desire of one fifth of those present, be entered on the journal.

4. Neither House, during the session of Congress, shall, without the consent of the other, adjourn for more than three days, nor to any other place than that in which the two Houses shall be sitting.

Section 6. 1. The senators and representatives shall receive a compensation for their services, to be ascertained by law, and paid out of the Treasury of the United States. They shall in all cases, except treason, felony, and breach of the peace, be privileged from arrest during their attendance at the session of their respective Houses, and in going to and returning from the same; and for any speech or debate in either House, they shall not be questioned in any other place.

2. No senator or representative shall, during the time for which he was elected, be appointed to any civil office under the authority of the United States, which shall have been created, or the emoluments whereof shall have been increased, during such time; and no person holding any office under the United States shall be a member of either House during his continuance in office.

Section 7. 1. All bills for raising revenue shall originate in the House of Representatives; but the Senate may propose or concur with amendments as on other bills.

2. Every bill which shall have passed the House of Representatives and the Senate, shall, before it become a law, be presented to the President of the United States; If he approves he shall sign it, but if not he shall return it, with his objections, to that House in which it shall have originated, who shall enter the objections at large on their journal, and proceed to reconsider it. If after such reconsideration two thirds of that House shall agree to pass the bill, it shall be sent, together with the objections, to the other House, by which it shall likewise be reconsidered, and if approved by two thirds of that House, it shall become a law. But in all such cases the votes of both Houses shall be determined by yeas and nays, and the names of the persons voting for and against the bill shall be entered on the journal of each House respectively. If any bill shall not be returned by the President within ten days (Sundays excepted) after it shall have been presented to him, the same shall be a law, in like manner as if he had signed it, unless the Congress by their adjournment prevent its return, in which case it shall not be a law.

3. Every order, resolution, or vote to which the concurrence of the Senate and the House of Representatives may be necessary (except on a question of adjournment) shall be presented to the President of the United States; and before the same shall take effect, shall be approved by him, or being disapproved by him, shall be repassed by two thirds of the Senate and House of Representatives, according to the rules and limitations prescribed in the case of a bill.

Section 8. The Congress shall have the power

1. To lay and collect taxes, duties, imposts, and excises, to pay the debts and provide for the common defense and general welfare of the United States; but all duties, imposts, and excises shall be uniform throughout the United States;

2. To borrow money on the credit of the United States;

3. To regulate commerce with foreign nations, and among the several States, and with the Indian tribes;

4. To establish a uniform rule of naturalization, and uniform laws on the subject of bankruptcies throughout the United States;

5. To coin money, regulate the value thereof, and of foreign coin, and fix the standard of weights and measures;

6. To provide for the punishment of counterfeiting the securities and current coin of the United States;

7. To establish post offices and post roads;

8. To promote the progress of science and useful arts, by securing for limited times to authors and inventors the exclusive right to their respective writings and discoveries;

9. To constitute tribunals inferior to the Supreme Court;

10. To define and punish piracies and felonies committed on the high seas, and offenses against the law of nations;

11. To declare war, grant letters of marque and reprisal, and make rules concerning captures on land and water;

12. To raise and support armies, but no appropriation of money to that use shall be for a longer term than two years;

13. To provide and maintain a navy;

14. To make rules for the government and regulation of the land and naval forces;

15. To provide for calling forth the militia to execute the laws of the Union, suppress insurrections and repel invasions;

16. To provide for organizing, arming, and disciplining the militia, and for governing such part of them as may be employed in the service of the United States, reserving to the States respectively, the appointment of the officers, and the authority of training the militia according to the discipline prescribed by Congress;

17. To exercise exclusive legislation in all cases whatsoever, over such district (not exceeding ten miles square) as may, by

cession of particular States, and the acceptance of Congress, become the seat of the government of the United States, and to exercise like authority over all places purchased by the consent of the legislature of the State in which the same shall be, for the erection of forts, magazines, arsenals, dockyards, and other needful buildings; and

18. To make all laws which shall be necessary and proper for carrying into execution the foregoing powers, and all other powers vested by this Constitution in the government of the United States, or any department or officer thereof.

Section 9. 1. The migration or importation of such persons as any of the States now existing shall think proper to admit, shall not be prohibited by the Congress prior to the year one thousand eight hundred and eight, but a tax or duty may be imposed on such importation, not exceeding ten dollars for each person.

2. The privilege of the writ of habeas corpus shall not be suspended, unless when in cases of rebellion or invasion the public safety may require it.

3. No bill of attainder or ex post facto law shall be passed.

4. No capitation, or other direct, tax shall be laid, unless in proportion to the census or enumeration herein-before directed to be taken.[5]

5. No tax or duty shall be laid on articles exported from any State.

6. No preference shall be given by any regulation of commerce or revenue to the ports of one State over those of another: nor shall vessels bound to, or from, one State be obliged to enter, clear, or pay duties in another.

7. No money shall be drawn from the treasury, but in consequence of appropriations made by law; and a regular statement and account of the receipts and expenditures of all public money shall be published from time to time.

8. No title of nobility shall be granted by the United States: and no person holding any office of profit or trust under them, shall, without the consent of the Congress, accept of any present, emolument, office, or title, of any kind whatever, from any king, prince, or foreign State.

Section 10. 1. No State shall enter into any treaty, alliance, or confederation; grant letters of marque and reprisal; coin money; emit bills of credit; make any thing but gold and silver coin a tender in payment of debts; pass any bill of attainder, ex post facto law, or law impairing the obligation of contracts, or grant any title of nobility.

2. No State shall, without the consent of the Congress, lay any imposts or duties on imports or exports, except what may be absolutely necessary for executing its inspection laws: and the net produce of all duties and imposts laid by any State on imports or exports, shall be for the use of the treasury of the United States; and all such laws shall be subject to the revision and control of the Congress.

3. No State shall, without the consent of the Congress, lay any duty of tonnage, keep troops, or ships of war in time of peace, enter into any agreement or compact with another State, or with a foreign power, or engage in war, unless actually invaded, or in such imminent danger as will not admit of delay.

Article II

Section 1. 1. The executive power shall be vested in a President of the United States of America. He shall hold his office during the term of four years, and, together with the Vice President, chosen for the same term, be elected, as follows:

2. Each State shall appoint, in such manner as the legislature thereof may direct, a number of electors, equal to the whole number of senators and representatives to which the State may be entitled in the Congress: but no senator or representative, or person holding any office of trust or profit under the United States, shall be appointed an elector.

The electors shall meet in their respective States, and vote by ballot for two persons, of whom one at least shall not be an inhabitant of the same State with themselves. And they shall make a list of all the persons voted for, and of the number of votes for each; which list they shall sign and certify, and transmit sealed to the seat of the government of the United States, directed to the president of the Senate. The president of the Senate shall, in the presence of the Senate and House of Representatives, open all the certificates, and the votes shall then be counted. The person having the greatest number of votes shall be the President, if such number be a majority of the whole number of electors appointed; and if there be more than one who have such majority, and have an equal number of votes, then the House of Representatives shall immediately choose by ballot one of them for President; and if no person have a majority, then from the five highest on the list the said House shall in like manner choose the President. But in choosing the President, the votes shall be taken by States, the representation from each State having one vote; a quorum for this purpose shall consist of a member or members from two thirds of the States, and a majority of all the States shall be necessary to a choice. In every case after the choice of the President, the person having the greatest number of votes of the electors shall be the Vice President. But if there should remain two or more who have equal votes, the Senate shall chose from them by ballot the Vice President.[6]

3. The Congress may determine the time of choosing the electors, and the day on which they shall give their votes; which day shall be the same throughout the United States.

4. No person except a natural born citizen, or a citizen of the United States, at the time of the adoption of this Constitution, shall be eligible to the office of President; neither shall any person be eligible to the office who shall not have attained to the age of thirty-five years, and been fourteen years a resident within the United States.

5. In case of the removal of the President from office, or of his death, resignation, or inability to discharge the powers and duties of the said office, the same shall devolve on the Vice President, and the Congress may by law provide for the case of removal, death, resignation or inability, both of the President and Vice President, declaring what officer shall then act as President, and such officer shall act accordingly until the disability be removed, or a President shall be elected.

6. The President shall, at stated times, receive for his services a compensation which shall neither be increased nor diminished during the period for which he shall have been elected, and he shall not receive within that period any other emolument from the United States, or any of them.

7. Before he enter on the execution of his office, he shall take the following oath or affirmation:—"I do solemnly swear (or affirm) that I will faithfully execute the office of President of the United States, and will to the best of my ability, preserve, protect and defend the Constitution of the United States."

Section 2. 1. The President shall be commander in chief of the army and navy of the United States, and of the militia of the several States, when called into the actual service of the United States; he may require the opinion in writing, of the principal officer

---

[5]See the Sixteenth Amendment.

[6]Superseded by the Twelfth Amendment.

in each of the executive departments, upon any subject relating to the duties of their respective offices, and he shall have power to grant reprieves and pardons for offenses against the United States, except in cases of impeachment.

2. He shall have power, by and with the advice and consent of the Senate, to make treaties, provided two thirds of the senators present concur; and he shall nominate, and by and with the advice and consent of the Senate, shall appoint ambassadors, other public ministers and consuls, judges of the Supreme Court, and all other officers of the United States, whose appointments are not herein otherwise provided for, and which shall be established by law; but the Congress may by law vest the appointment of such inferior officers, as they think proper, in the President alone, in the courts of laws, or in the heads of departments.

3. The President shall have power to fill up all vacancies that may happen during the recess of the Senate, by granting commissions which shall expire at the end of their next session.

Section 3. He shall from time to time give to the Congress information of the state of the Union, and recommend to their consideration such measures as he shall judge necessary and expedient; he may, on extraordinary occasions, convene both Houses, or either of them, and in case of disagreement between them with respect to the time of adjournment, he may adjourn them to such time as he shall think proper; he shall receive ambassadors and other public ministers; he shall take care that the laws be faithfully executed, and shall commission all the officers of the United States.

Section 4. The President, Vice President, and all civil officers of the United States, shall be removed from office on impeachment for, and conviction of, treason, bribery, or other high crimes and misdemeanors.

Article III

Section 1. The judicial power of the United States shall be vested in one Supreme Court, and in such inferior courts as the Congress may from time to time ordain and establish. The judges, both of the Supreme and inferior courts, shall hold their offices during good behavior, and shall, at stated times, receive for their services, a compensation, which shall not be diminished during their continuance in office.

Section 2. 1. The judicial power shall extend to all cases, in law and equity, arising under this Constitution, the laws of the United States, and treaties made, or which shall be made, under their authority;—to all cases affecting ambassadors, other public ministers and consuls;—to all cases of admiralty and maritime jurisdiction;—to controversies to which the United States shall be a party;[7]—to controversies between two or more States;—between a State and citizens of another State;—between citizens of different States;—between citizens of the same State claiming lands under grants of different States, and between a State, or the citizens thereof, and foreign States, citizens or subjects.

2. In all cases affecting ambassadors, other public ministers and consuls, and those in which a State shall be party, the Supreme Court shall have original jurisdiction. In all the other cases before mentioned, the Supreme Court shall have appellate jurisdiction, both as to law and fact, with such exceptions, and under such regulations as the Congress shall make.

3. The trial of all crimes, except in cases of impeachment, shall be by jury; and such trial shall be held in the State where the said crimes shall have been committed; but when not committed within any State, the trial shall be at such place or places as the Congress may by law have directed.

Section 3. 1. Treason against the United States shall consist only in levying war against them, or in adhering to their enemies, giving them aid and comfort. No person shall be convicted of treason unless on the testimony of two witnesses to the same overt act, or on confession in open court.

2. The Congress shall have power to declare the punishment of treason, but no attainder of treason shall work corruption of blood, or forfeiture except during the life of the person attainted.

Article IV

Section 1. Full faith and credit shall be given in each State to the public acts, records, and judicial proceedings of every other State. And the Congress may by general laws prescribe the manner in which such acts, records and proceedings shall be proved, and the effect thereof.

Section 2. 1. The citizens of each State shall be entitled to all privileges and immunities of citizens in the several States.[8]

2. A person charged in any State with treason, felony, or other crime, who shall flee from justice, and be found in another State, shall on demand of the executive authority of the State from which he fled, be delivered up to be removed to the State having jurisdiction of the crime.

3. No person held to service or labor in one State under the laws thereof, escaping into another, shall, in consequence of any law or regulation therein, be discharged from such service or labor, but shall be delivered up on claim of the party to whom such service or labor may be due.[9]

Section 3. 1. New States may be admitted by the Congress into this Union; but no new State shall be formed or erected within the jurisdiction of any other State; nor any State be formed by the junction of two or more States, or parts of States, without the consent of the legislatures of the States concerned as well as of the Congress.

2. The Congress shall have power to dispose of and make all needful rules and regulations respecting the territory or other property belonging to the United States; and nothing in this Constitution shall be so construed as to prejudice any claims of the United States, or of any particular State.

Section 4. The United States shall guarantee to every State in this Union a republican form of government, and shall protect each of them against invasion; and on application of the legislature, or of the executive (when the legislature cannot be convened) against domestic violence.

Article V

The Congress, whenever two thirds of both Houses shall deem it necessary, shall propose amendments to this Constitution, or, on the application of the legislatures of two thirds of the several States, shall call a convention for proposing amendments, which in either case, shall be valid to all intents and purposes, as part of this Constitution, when ratified by the legislatures of three fourths of the several States, or by conventions in three fourths thereof, as the one or the other mode of ratification may be proposed by the Congress; Provided that no amendment which may be made prior to the year one thousand eight hundred and eight shall in any manner affect the first and fourth clauses in

---

[7]See the Eleventh Amendment.

[8]See the Fourteenth Amendment, Sec. 1.
[9]See the Thirteenth Amendment.

the ninth section of the first article; and that no State, without its consent, shall be deprived of its equal suffrage in the Senate.

Article VI

1. *All debts contracted and engagements entered into, before the adoption of this Constitution, shall be as valid against the United States under this Constitution, as under the Confederation.*[10]
2. *This Constitution, and the laws of the United States which shall be made in pursuance thereof; and all treaties made, or which shall be made, under the authority of the United States, shall be the supreme law of the land; and the judges in every State shall be bound thereby, any thing in the Constitution or laws of any State to the contrary notwithstanding.*
3. *The senators and representatives before mentioned, and the members of the several State legislatures, and all executive and judicial officers, both of the United States and of the several States, shall be bound by oath or affirmation to support this Constitution; but no religious test shall ever be required as a qualification to any office or public trust under the United States.*

Article VII

The ratification of the conventions of nine States shall be sufficient for the establishment of this Constitution between the States so ratifying the same.

Done in Convention by the unanimous consent of the States present the seventeenth day of September in the year of our Lord one thousand seven hundred and eighty-seven, and of the independence of the United States of America the twelfth. In witness whereof we have hereunto subscribed our names.

[Names omitted]

* * *

Articles in addition to, and amendment of, the Constitution of the United States of America, proposed by Congress, and ratified by the legislatures of the several States, pursuant to the fifth article of the original Constitution.

Amendment I [First ten amendments ratified December 15, 1791]

Congress shall make no law respecting an establishment of religion, or prohibiting the free exercise thereof; or abridging the freedom of speech, or of the press; or the right of the people peaceably to assemble, and to petition the government for a redress of grievances.

Amendment II

A well regulated militia, being necessary to the security of a free State, the right of the people to keep and bear arms, shall not be infringed.

Amendment III

No soldier shall, in time of peace be quartered in any house, without the consent of the owner, nor in time of war, but in a manner to be prescribed by law.

Amendment IV

The right of the people to be secure in their persons, houses, papers, and effects, against unreasonable searches and seizures, shall not be violated, and no warrants shall issue, but upon probable cause, supported by oath or affirmation, and particularly describing the place to be searched, and the persons or things to be seized.

Amendment V

No person shall be held to answer for a capital or otherwise infamous crime, unless on a presentment or indictment of a grand jury, except in cases arising in the land or naval forces, or in the militia, when in actual service in time of war or public danger; nor shall any person be subject for the same offense to be twice put in jeopardy of life or limb; nor shall be compelled in any criminal case to be a witness against himself, nor be deprived of life, liberty, or property, without due process of law; nor shall private property be taken for public use, without just compensation.

Amendment VI

In all criminal prosecutions, the accused shall enjoy the right to a speedy and public trial, by an impartial jury of the State and district wherein the crime shall have been committed, which district shall have been previously ascertained by law, and to be informed of the nature and cause of the accusation; to be confronted with the witnesses against him; to have compulsory process for obtaining witnesses in his favor, and to have the assistance of counsel for his defense.

Amendment VII

In suits at common law, where the value in controversy shall exceed twenty dollars, the right of trial by jury shall be preserved, and no fact tried by a jury shall be otherwise reexamined in any court of the United States, than according to the rules of the common law.

Amendment VIII

Excessive bail shall not be required, nor excessive fines imposed, nor cruel and unusual punishments inflicted.

Amendment IX

The enumeration in the Constitution of certain rights shall not be construed to deny or disparage others retained by the people.

Amendment X

The powers not delegated to the United States by the Constitution, nor prohibited by it to the States, are reserved to the States respectively, or to the people.

Amendment XI [January 8, 1798]

The judicial power of the United States shall not be construed to extend to any suit in law or equity, commenced or prosecuted against one of the United States by citizens of another State, or by citizens or subjects of any foreign State.

Amendment XII [September 25, 1804]

The electors shall meet in their respective States, and vote by ballot for President and Vice President, one of whom, at least, shall not be

---

[10]See the Fourteenth Amendment, Sec. 4.

an inhabitant of the same State with themselves; they shall name in their ballots the person voted for as President, and in distinct ballots, the person voted for as Vice President, and they shall make distinct lists of all persons voted for as President and of all persons voted for as Vice President, and of the number of votes for each, which lists they shall sign and certify, and transmit sealed to the seat of the government of the United States, directed to the President of the Senate;—The President of the Senate shall, in the presence of the Senate and House of Representatives, open all the certificates and the votes shall then be counted;—The person having the greatest number of votes for President, shall be the President, if such number be a majority of the whole number of electors appointed; and if no person have such majority, then from the persons having the highest numbers not exceeding three on the list of those voted for as President, the House of Representatives shall choose immediately, by ballot, the President. But in choosing the President, the votes shall be taken by States, the representation from each State having one vote; a quorum for this purpose shall consist of a member or members from two thirds of the States, and a majority of all the States shall be necessary to a choice. And if the House of Representatives shall not choose a President whenever the right of choice shall devolve upon them, before the fourth day of March next following, then the Vice President shall act as President, as in the case of the death or other constitutional disability of the President. The person having the greatest number of votes as Vice President shall be the Vice President, if such number be a majority of the whole number of electors appointed, and if no person have a majority, then from the two highest numbers on the list, the Senate shall choose the Vice President; a quorum for the purpose shall consist of two thirds of the whole number of Senators, and a majority of the whole number shall be necessary to a choice. But no person constitutionally ineligible to the office of President shall be eligible to that of Vice President of the United States.

Amendment XIII [December 18, 1865]

Section 1. Neither slavery nor involuntary servitude, except as a punishment for crime whereof the party shall have been duly convicted, shall exist within the United States, or any place subject to their jurisdiction.

Section 2. Congress shall have power to enforce this article by appropriate legislation.

Amendment XIV [July 28, 1868]

Section 1. All persons born or naturalized in the United States, and subject to the jurisdiction thereof, are citizens of the United States and of the State wherein they reside. No State shall make or enforce any law which shall abridge the privileges or immunities of citizens of the United States; nor shall any State deprive any person of life, liberty, or property, without due process of law; nor deny to any person within its jurisdiction the equal protection of the laws.

Section 2. Representatives shall be apportioned among the several States according to their respective numbers, counting the whole number of persons in each State, excluding Indians not taxed. But when the right to vote at any election for the choice of electors for President and Vice President of the United States, representatives in Congress, the executive and judicial officers of a State, or the members of the legislature thereof, is denied to any of the male inhabitants of such State, being twenty-one years of age, and citizens of the United States, or in any way abridged, except for participating in rebellion, or other crime, the basis of representation therein shall be reduced in the proportion which the number of such male citizens shall bear to the whole number of male citizens twenty-one years of age in such State.

Section 3. No person shall be a senator or representative in Congress, or elector of President and Vice President or hold any office, civil or military, under the United States, or under any State, who having previously taken an oath, as a member of Congress, or as an officer of the United States, or as a member of any State legislature, or as an executive or judicial officer of any State, to support the Constitution of the United States, shall have engaged in insurrection or rebellion against the same, or given aid or comfort to the enemies thereof. But Congress may by a vote of two thirds of each House, remove such disability.

Section 4. The validity of the public debt of the United States, authorized by law, including debts incurred for payment of pensions and bounties for services in suppressing insurrection or rebellion; shall not be questioned. But neither the United States nor any State shall assume or pay any debt or obligation incurred in aid of insurrection or rebellion against the United States, or any claim for the loss or emancipation of any slave; but all such debts, obligations, and claims shall be held illegal and void.

Section 5. The Congress shall have the power to enforce, by appropriate legislation, the provisions of this article.

Amendment XV [March 30, 1870]

Section 1. The right of citizens of the United States to vote shall not be denied or abridged by the United States or by any State on account of race, color, or previous condition of servitude.

Section 2. The Congress shall have power to enforce this article by appropriate legislation.

Amendment XVI [February 25, 1913]

The Congress shall have power to lay and collect taxes on incomes, from whatever source derived, without apportionment among the several States, and without regard to any census or enumeration.

Amendment XVII [May 31, 1913]

The Senate of the United States shall be composed of two senators from each State, elected by the people thereof, for six years; and each senator shall have one vote. The electors in each State shall have the qualifications requisite for electors of the most numerous branch of the State legislature.

When vacancies happen in the representation of any State in the Senate, the executive authority of such State shall issue writs of election to fill such vacancies: Provided, That the legislature of any State may empower the executive thereof to make temporary appointments until the people fill the vacancies by election as the legislature may direct.

This amendment shall not be so construed as to affect the election or term of any senator chosen before it becomes valid as part of the Constitution.

Amendment XVIII[11] [January 29, 1919]

After one year from the ratification of this article, the manufacture, sale, or transportation of intoxicating liquors within, the importation thereof into, or the exportation thereof from the United States and all territory subject to the jurisdiction thereof for beverage purposes is thereby prohibited.

---

[11]Repealed by the Twenty-first Amendment.

The Congress and the several States shall have concurrent power to enforce this article by appropriate legislation.

This article shall be inoperative unless it shall have been ratified as an amendment to the Constitution by the legislatures of the several States, as provided in the Constitution, within seven years from the date of the submission hereof to the States by Congress.

Amendment XIX [August 26, 1920]

The right of citizens of the United States to vote shall not be denied or abridged by the United States or by any State on account of sex.

Congress shall have the power to enforce this article by appropriate legislation.

Amendment XX [January 23, 1933]

Section 1. The terms of the President and Vice President shall end at noon on the 20th day of January and the terms of Senators and Representatives at noon on the 3d day of January, of the years in which such terms would have ended if this article had not been ratified; and the terms of their successors shall then begin.

Section 2. The Congress shall assemble at least once in every year, and such meeting shall begin at noon on the 3d day of January, unless they shall by law appoint a different day.

Section 3. If, at the time fixed for the beginning of the term of President, the President-elect shall have died, the Vice President-elect shall become President. If a President shall not have been chosen before the time fixed for the beginning of his term, or if the President-elect shall have failed to qualify, then the Vice President-elect shall act as President until a President shall have qualified; and the Congress may by law provide for the case wherein neither a President-elect nor a Vice President-elect shall have qualified, declaring who shall then act as President, or the manner in which one who is to act shall be selected, and such person shall act accordingly until a President or Vice President shall have qualified.

Section 4. The Congress may by law provide for the case of the death of any of the persons from whom the House of Representatives may choose a President whenever the right of choice shall have devolved upon them, and for the case of the death of any of the persons from whom the Senate may choose a Vice President whenever the right of choice shall have devolved upon them.

Section 5. Sections 1 and 2 shall take effect on the 15th day of October following the ratification of this article.

Section 6. This article shall be inoperative unless it shall have been ratified as an amendment to the Constitution by the legislatures of three-fourths of the several States within seven years from the date of its submission.

Amendment XXI [December 5, 1933]

Section 1. The Eighteenth Article of amendment to the Constitution of the United States is hereby repealed.

Section 2. The transportation or importation into any State, Territory, or possession of the United States for delivery or use therein of intoxicating liquors in violation of the laws thereof, is hereby prohibited.

Section 3. This article shall be inoperative unless it shall have been ratified as an amendment to the Constitution by conventions in the several States, as provided in the Constitution, within seven years from the date of the submission thereof to the States by the Congress.

Amendment XXII [March 1, 1951]

No person shall be elected to the office of the President more than twice, and no person who has held the office of President, or acted as President, for more than two years of a term to which some other person was elected President shall be elected to the office of the President more than once.

But this article shall not apply to any person holding the office of President when this article was proposed by the Congress, and shall not prevent any person who may be holding the office of President, or acting as President, during the term within which this article becomes operative from holding the office of President or acting as President during the remainder of such term.

This article shall be inoperative unless it shall have been ratified as an amendment to the Constitution by the legislatures of three-fourths of the several States within seven years from the date of its submission to the States by the Congress.

Amendment XXIII [March 29, 1961]

Section 1. The District constituting the seat of Government of the United States shall appoint in such manner as the Congress may direct.

A number of electors of President and Vice President equal to the whole number of Senators and Representatives in Congress to which the District would be entitled if it were a State, but in no event more than the least populous State; they shall be in addition to those appointed by the States, but they shall be considered, for the purposes of the election of President and Vice President, to be electors appointed by a State; and they shall meet in the District and perform such duties as provided by the twelfth article of amendment.

Section 2. The Congress shall have power to enforce this article by appropriate legislation.

Amendment XXIV [January 23, 1964]

Section 1. The right of citizens of the United States to vote in any primary or other election for President or Vice President, for electors for President or Vice President, or for Senator or Representative in Congress, shall not be denied or abridged by the United States or any State by reason of failure to pay any poll tax or other tax.

Section 2. The Congress shall have power to enforce this article by appropriate legislation.

Amendment XXV [February 10, 1967]

Section 1. In case of the removal of the President from office or of his death or resignation, the Vice President shall become President.

Section 2. Whenever there is a vacancy in the office of the Vice President, the President shall nominate a Vice President who shall take office upon confirmation by a majority of both Houses of Congress.

Section 3. Whenever the President transmits to the President pro tempore of the Senate and the Speaker of the House of Representatives his written declaration that he is unable to discharge the powers and duties of his office, and until he transmits to them a written declaration to the contrary, such powers and duties shall be discharged by the Vice President as Acting President.

Section 4. Whenever the Vice President and a majority of either the principal officers of the executive departments or of such other body as Congress may by law provide, transmit to the President *pro tempore of the Senate and the Speaker of the House of Representatives their written declaration that the President is unable to discharge the powers and duties of his office, the Vice President shall immediately assume the powers and duties of the office as Acting President.*

Thereafter, when the President transmits to the President pro tempore of the Senate and the Speaker of the House of Representatives his written declaration that no inability exists, he shall resume the powers and duties of his office unless the Vice President and a majority of either the principal officers of the executive departments or of such other body as Congress may by law provide, transmit within four days to the President pro tempore of the Senate and the Speaker of the House of Representatives their written declaration that the President is unable to discharge the powers and duties of his office. Thereupon Congress shall decide the issue, assembling within forty-eight hours for that purpose if not in session. If the Congress, within twenty-one days after receipt of the latter written declaration, or, if Congress is not in session, within twenty-one days after Congress is required to assemble, determines by two-thirds vote of both Houses that the President is unable to discharge the powers and duties of his office, the Vice President shall continue to discharge the same as Acting President; otherwise, the President shall resume the powers and duties of his office.

Amendment XXVI [June 30, 1971]

Section 1. The right of citizens of the United States who are eighteen years of age or older to vote shall not be denied or abridged by the United States or by any State on account of age.

Section 2. The Congress shall have power to enforce this article by appropriate legislation.

PHOTO CREDITS

INDEX